Family Worship Bible Guide

Family Worship Bible Guide

Joel R. Beeke, General Editor
Michael P. V. Barrett, Old Testament Editor
Gerald M. Bilkes, New Testament Editor
Paul M. Smalley, Editorial Assistant

Reformation Heritage Books
Grand Rapids, Michigan

Family Worship Bible Guide

Reformation Heritage Books
2965 Leonard St. NE
Grand Rapids, MI 49525
616-977-0889 / Fax 616-285-3246
orders@heritagebooks.org
www.heritagebooks.org

Printed in the Netherlands by Royal Jongbloed
16 17 18 19 20 21 22/11 10 9 8 7 6 5 4 3 2 1

ISBN 978-1-60178-500-8 (hardcover)
ISBN 978-1-60178-501-5 (epub)
ISBN 978-1-60178-513-8 (bonded leather)

For additional Reformed literature, request a free book list from Reformation Heritage Books at the above regular or e-mail address.

Contents

Introduction ix

Old Testament

Genesis.................................. 3
Exodus 31
Leviticus.................................. 54
Numbers 74
Deuteronomy 105
Joshua.................................. 128
Judges.................................. 150
Ruth.................................. 166
1 Samuel 169
2 Samuel 193
1 Kings.................................. 213
2 Kings.................................. 232
1 Chronicles 254
2 Chronicles 270
Ezra 293
Nehemiah 300
Esther.................................. 309
Job.................................. 317

Psalms 348
Proverbs.................................. 450
Ecclesiastes 471
Song of Solomon 480
Isaiah 486
Jeremiah.................................. 524
Lamentations 556
Ezekiel 560
Daniel.................................... 589
Hosea..................................... 598
Joel 607
Amos 610
Obadiah................................... 617
Jonah 618
Micah..................................... 623
Nahum.................................... 629
Habakkuk 633
Zephaniah................................. 637
Haggai 640
Zechariah 644
Malachi 656

New Testament

Matthew.................................. 663
Mark..................................... 684
Luke 698
John 718
Acts...................................... 732
Romans 752

1 Corinthians 765
2 Corinthians 773
Galatians 781
Ephesians.................................... 786
Philippians.................................... 792
Colossians 795
1 Thessalonians.................................... 798
2 Thessalonians.................................... 801
1 Timothy 804
2 Timothy 810
Titus.................................... 813
Philemon 815
Hebrews.................................... 816
James 824
1 Peter 828
2 Peter 832
1 John.................................... 835
2 John.................................... 839
3 John.................................... 840
Jude.................................... 841
Revelation 843

Introduction

How to Do Family Worship

Family worship has fallen on hard times. Parents often say they are too busy to do it. Or else they don't know how to do it because their parents never did it. This book was written to help you do family worship, and/or to do it better. I pray that you will find it to be a great help.[1]

When my parents commemorated their fiftieth anniversary, all five of us children decided to express thanks to our father and mother for one thing without consulting each other. Remarkably, all five of us thanked our mother for her prayers and all five us thanked our father for his leadership of our special Sunday evening family worship. My brother said, "Dad, the oldest memory I have is of tears streaming down your face as you taught us from *Pilgrim's Progress* on Sunday evenings how the Holy Spirit leads believers. At the age of three God used you in family worship to convict me that Christianity was real. No matter how far I went astray

1. This book extracts the sections of Thoughts for Personal and Family Worship for each Bible chapter from *The Reformation Heritage KJV Study Bible* (Grand Rapids: Reformation Heritage Books, 2014). As far as we know, it is a first book of its kind. You can now use it to accompany your Bible reading regardless of the Bible translation you use.

in later years, I could never seriously question the reality of Christianity, and I want to thank you for that."

Christians have long recognized that God often uses family worship to bring reformation and revival to the church. For example, the 1677 church covenant of the Puritan congregation in Dorchester, Massachusetts, included the commitment "to reform our families, engaging ourselves to a conscientious care to set before us and to maintain the worship of God in them; and to walk in our houses with perfect hearts in a faithful discharge of all domestic duties, educating, instructing, and charging our children and households to keep the ways of the Lord."

Given the importance of family worship as a potent force in winning untold millions to gospel truth throughout the ages, we ought not be surprised that God requires heads of households do all they can to lead their families in worshiping the living God. As Joshua declared, "As for me and my house, we will serve the LORD" (Josh. 24:15). This word *serve* is translated as *worship* many times in Scripture.

Family worship will require some preparation. You should pray for God's blessing upon that worship. Have your Bibles ready and a Scripture passage selected. Catechisms and books of questions and answers for children are very helpful. Sometimes you might read through a book like John Bunyan's *Pilgrim's Progress* or *Holy War* and discuss it together. Choose some psalms and hymns that are easy to sing. Pick a place to gather, such as the supper table or living room. Set the times for family worship, ordinarily at breakfast and supper but as it fits your family's needs. Whatever times you set, carefully guard those times like a precious jewel.

During family worship, aim for brevity. Don't provoke your children. If you worship twice a day, try ten minutes in the morning and twenty-five in the evening. Be consistent. It is better to have twenty minutes of family worship every day than to try for extended periods on fewer days—say forty-five minutes on Monday, then skipping Tuesday.

Don't indulge excuses to avoid family worship. If you are tired, deny yourself out of love for God and your family. Even if you lost your temper a half-hour before family worship time, don't neglect it out of false humility. Instead, begin family worship by confessing your sins to your family and seeking their forgiveness in the presence of God. As A. W. Pink said, "It is not the sins of a Christian, but his *unconfessed* sins, which choke the channel of blessing and cause so many to miss God's best."

Lead family worship with a firm, fatherly hand and a soft, penitent heart. Speak with hopeful solemnity. Talk naturally yet reverently during this time, using the tone you would use when speaking to a deeply respected friend about a serious matter. Expect great things from a great covenant-keeping God.

According to Scripture, God should be served in special acts of worship in families today in the following three ways.

Daily Instruction in the Word of God

God should be worshiped by daily reading and instruction from His Word. Through questions, answers, and instructions, parents and children are to daily interact with each other about sacred truth. As Deuteronomy 6:6–7 says, "And these words, which I command thee this day, shall be in thine heart: and thou shalt teach them diligently unto thy children, and shalt talk of them when thou sittest in thine house, and when thou walkest by the way, and when thou liest down, and when thou risest up."

When those words were first written, most believers did not have access to a precious scroll of Holy Scripture. They had to teach their children from passages of Scripture which they heard and memorized! In this age most believers have the tremendous privilege of having the Bible in their own native language. Let's take full advantage of this privilege by reading the Bible together. When reading and teaching the Bible as a family, consider these suggestions.

1. *Have a reading plan*. Read ten or twenty verses from the Old Testament in the morning and ten to twenty from the New Testament in the evening. Or read a series of parables, miracles, or historical portions. Just be sure to read the entire Bible over a period of time. As J.C. Ryle said, "Fill their minds with Scripture. Let the Word dwell in them richly. Give them the Bible, the whole Bible, even while they are young."

2. *Involve the family*. Every family member who can read should have a Bible to follow along. Set the tone by reading Scripture with expression, as the living, "breathing" book it is. Assign various portions to be read by your wife and your children. Teach your children how to read articulately and with expression. Don't let them mumble or speed ahead. Teach them to read with reverence. Provide a brief word of explanation throughout the reading, according to the needs of the younger children.

3. *Be plain in meaning*. Ask your children if they understand what you are reading. Be plain in applying scriptural texts. The 1647 Church of Scotland Directory for Family

Worship wisely teaches us that if a sin is rebuked in the Word, then call the family to keep watch against it; if a judgment is threatened, warn them of it; if a duty is commanded, press it upon them; if a promise is offered, then urge them to trust it and receive its comfort.

4. *Encourage family dialogue* around God's Word in line with the Hebraic procedure of household question and answer (cf. Ex. 12:26–27; 13:14–15). That's where this *Family Worship Bible Guide* can help you. Read aloud with your family the thoughts for each Bible chapter each day. Dialogue about the thoughts expressed. Answer the questions asked. Especially encourage teenagers to ask questions; draw them out. If you don't know the answers, tell them so, and encourage them to search for answers. Have one or more good commentaries on hand, such as those by John Calvin, Matthew Poole, and Matthew Henry. Remember, if you don't provide answers for your children, they will get them elsewhere—and often those will be wrong answers.

5. *Be pure in doctrine.* Titus 2:7 says, "In all things showing thyself a pattern of good works: in doctrine showing uncorruptness, gravity, sincerity." Don't abandon doctrinal precision when teaching young children; aim for simplicity and soundness.

6. *Be relevant in application.* Don't be afraid to share your experiences when appropriate, but do that simply and concisely. Use concrete illustrations. Ideally, tie together biblical instruction with what you recently heard in sermons.

7. *Be affectionate in manner.* Proverbs continually uses the phrase *my son,* showing the warmth, love, and urgency in the teachings of a God-fearing father. When you must administer the wounds of a friendly father to your children,

do that with heartfelt love. Tell them you must convey the whole counsel of God because you can't bear the thought of spending eternity apart from them. My father often said to us, with tears: "Children, I cannot miss any of you in heaven." Tell your children: "We will allow you every privilege an open Bible will allow us to give you—but if we say no to you, you must know that flows out of our love." As Ryle said, "Love is one grand secret of successful training. Soul love is the soul of all love."

8. *Require attention.* Proverbs 4:1 says, "Hear, ye children, the instruction of a father, and attend to know understanding." Fathers and mothers have important truths to convey. You must demand a hearing for God's truths in your home. That may involve repeated statements at the beginning like these: "Sit up, son, and look at me when I'm talking. We're talking about God's Word, and God deserves to be heard." Don't allow children to leave their seats during family worship.

Daily Prayer before the Throne of God

Does not the command to "pray without ceasing" (1 Thess. 5:17) include when we are with our families? Families eat and drink the daily provision of a gracious God at their tables. To do that in Christian way, a family must follow 1 Timothy 4:4–5, "For every creature of God is good, and nothing to be refused, if it be received with thanksgiving: for it is sanctified by the word of God and prayer."

Again, let me offer some specific guidelines for leading the family in prayer.

1. *Be short.* With few exceptions, don't pray for more than five minutes. Tedious prayers do more harm than good.

Don't teach in your prayer; God doesn't need the instruction. Teach with your eyes open; pray with your eyes shut.

2. *Be simple without being shallow.* Pray for things that your children know something about, but don't allow your prayers to become trivial. Don't reduce your prayers to self-centered, shallow petitions.

3. *Be direct.* Spread your needs before God, plead your case, and ask for mercy. Name your teenagers and children and their needs one by one on a daily basis. That holds tremendous weight with them.

4. *Be natural yet solemn.* Speak clearly and reverently. Don't use an unnatural, high-pitched voice or a monotone. Don't pray too loudly or softly, too fast to be understood or too slow to hold attention.

5. *Be varied.* Don't pray the same thing every day; that becomes tedious. Develop more variety in prayer by remembering and stressing the various ingredients of true prayer, such as calling upon God to hear your prayers, adoring God for His titles and attributes, declaring your humble dependence and need, confessing family sins, asking for family mercies (both material and spiritual), interceding for friends, churches, and the nations, giving thanks for God's blessings, and blessing God for His kingdom, glory, and power. Use a prayer list to remember different persons and organizations on different days. Mix these ingredients with different proportion to get variety in your prayers.

Daily Sing to the Praise of God

Psalm 118:15 says, "The voice of rejoicing and salvation is in the tabernacles [or tents] of the righteous: the right hand of the LORD doeth valiantly." That is a clear reference to singing.

Every Christian family should own a few copies of a good psalter (psalms set to meter and music) and hymnal from which to sing. If one of you can play the piano, all the better. But even recorded music is helpful. Use whatever means you can to assist your family to sing God's praises together.

1. *Sing doctrinally pure songs.* There is no excuse for singing doctrinal error no matter how attractive the tune might be.

2. *Sing Psalms* first and foremost without neglecting sound hymns. Remember that the Psalms, called by Calvin "an anatomy of all parts of the soul," are the richest gold mine of deep, living, experiential, scriptural piety available to us still today.

3. *Sing heartily and with feeling.* As Colossians 3:23 says, "And whatsoever ye do, do it heartily, as to the Lord, and not unto men." Meditate on the words you are singing. On occasion discuss a phrase that is sung.[2]

Conclusion

Believers in Christ follow in the footsteps of Abraham's faith, and we must also follow in the footsteps of Abraham's obedient leadership of his family. "For I know him," God said, "that he will *command* his children and his household after him, and they shall keep the way of the LORD, to do justice and judgment; that the LORD may bring upon Abraham that which he hath spoken of him" (Gen. 18:19).

2. For more detail on how to do family worship, see Joel R. Beeke, *Family Worship* (Grand Rapids: Reformation Heritage Books, 2005). Much of this introduction is a condensed summary of this book.

John Paton served as a missionary over a century ago to a cannibalistic people in the islands of the south Pacific Ocean. Those people killed and ate the missionaries who had preceded Paton within minutes of their arrival. Paton faced enormous difficulties and sorrows. But he persevered in the name of Christ. One earthly means by which God prepared him for his labors was his father in Scotland. In later years John Paton looked back upon his father with great gratitude.

Paton's father worked out of a shop in their house. Their family had a small room in their home which was their prayer closet. John was deeply affected by his father's regular devotion to prayer in that room. He remembered, "Thither daily, and oftentimes a day, generally after each meal, we saw our father retire, and 'shut the door'; and we children got to understand…that prayers were being poured out there for us, as of old by the High Priest within the veil in the Most High Place." The Paton children could sometimes hear their father's voice full of emotion, pleading for them before the throne of grace.

Paton also remembered of his father how, "When, on his knees and all of us kneeling around him in family worship, he poured out his whole soul with tears for the conversion of the heathen world to the service of Jesus, and for every personal and domestic need, we all felt as if in the presence of the living Savior, and learned to know and love Him as our Divine Friend."

When John Paton left his home to go to Glasgow to study theology and do urban evangelism, he had to walk forty miles before coming to a train station. His father walked the first six miles out with him. They spoke about the Lord, and his father gave him counsel. Then for the last half-mile they walked in silence. His father's lips still moved, but now in silent prayer for his son while tears streamed down his face. When they came to the place of their parting, father grasped son by the hand, and said, "God bless you, my son! Your father's God prosper you, and keep you from all evil." Overcome by emotion, he could say no more, but his lips continued to move in silent prayer. John Paton later wrote, while reflecting back on this experience, "I vowed deeply and oft, by the help of God, to live and act so as never to grieve or dishonor such a father and mother as He had given me."

May God bless this *Family Worship Bible Guide* to you so that you and I may increasingly become parents like that!

* * *

I wish to thank Michael Barrett, Jerry Bilkes, and Paul Smalley for assisting me in writing these family worship thoughts for most of the Bible books, and for co-editing with me various parts of this work. Any errors that remain are my responsibility. I also wish to thank the following contributors who have written a first draft of these family worship thoughts for the remainder of the Bible books: Geoff Banister, Charles Barrett, Brian DeVries, Ian Goligher, John Greer, Jerrold Lewis, Alan Macgregor, Andy McIntosh, Pooyan Mehrshahi, Colin Mercer, Gerald Procee, Maurice Roberts, David Silversides, John Thackway, and Malcolm Watts. May God bless all the labor expended on this labor of love.

—Joel R. Beeke

OLD TESTAMENT

Genesis

Chapter 1

1. Consider the power of God in creation. If a computer were observing 10 million stars per second, it would still take 63 million years to count all the stars! Such is the power of the Almighty. Remarkably, the stars are the work of His fingers (Ps. 8:3) but salvation is the work of His right hand (Ps. 98:1). In a wonderful way God's work in making believers new creations in Christ Jesus demonstrates a power greater than commanding the world into existence. Let us be amazed at the wonder of creation; let us be overwhelmed with the wonder of grace. How does saving grace display even greater glory than creation?

2. Stand in awe of the power of God's word. God's word is the agency of creation. God said, "Let there be…." Christ demonstrated this power in the miracles both with people such as raising Lazarus from the dead (John 11) and with the inanimate creation such as calming the storm (Mark 4:35–40). God's word is still powerful today through the Scriptures. It is by the word of His power as well that He bears His created world along according to His purpose of providence (Heb. 1:3). The fact that God created gives Him the right to govern and to use His creation as He sees fit (Pss. 24:1–2; 95:5). Since creation, including man, belongs to God, all of creation, including man, is dependent on Him and accountable to Him. The theological implications of creation are far-reaching.

Chapter 2

1. Keep and cherish the Lord's Day (Isa. 58:13–14). The term "sabbath" means "cessation," thus the Sabbath is a day during which normal activity is to stop. In the New Testament, Christ's resurrection marked the end of His meriting salvation for His people, thus the term "Sabbath" is most appropriate to commemorate that momentous day. So the Sabbath has now moved to Sunday and is still blessed by God as the "market day of the soul." How can we guard this day as a special day of rest and communion with God?

2. Honor marriage as a divine institution and picture of Christ and His church. Our marriages should reflect the different roles that the Lord made for man and woman. The woman was made of the man and for the man. Her calling is to assist and support him in submission to his authority. Man was created first and received the commission and commandment of God. His calling is to lead the family in doing God's will and to love his wife as Christ loved the church—with humble and glad self-sacrifice for her good.

Chapter 3

1. Believe in the historic fall. The fall of man is just as literal as the rest of Genesis. Without a real Adam, a real garden, and a real serpent, there is no reason to believe in a real Christ, a real cross, and a real resurrection. The theology of Romans 5 and 1 Corinthians 15 in this regard is inescapable. These are real historical events. Redemption in Christ is predicated upon a literal fall of man in the garden of Eden.

2. Resist temptation. Like Eve we are tempted to sin by first listening to the lie of Satan, conversing in our minds with

the thought of sin, which is then conceived (James 1:15). We look, we desire, and we take. It is not a matter of eating, but of the heart (Matt. 15:11, 18). So begin the battle there.

3. Consider the horrible effects of the fall. Immediately, there was shame (v. 7), separation from God (v. 8), and guilt (v. 10). Consequently, according to God's sentence on the guilty, man now knows toil and hardship in work and women know suffering in childbearing. Yet, in the very statement of curse, God announces the first gospel message of a coming Seed who will reverse the curse itself. As soon as man needs a word of grace, God gives the word of grace. Only Christ can reverse this for He took the curse for sin. How believers should thank the Lord that He did not banish us as He has banished the angels that sinned! We have a Redeemer!

Chapter 4

1. Grieve at the results of the fall. Chapter 4 reveals the horrible consequences of Adam's sin—his children are infected with the pride, hatred, and deception of the serpent. Yet there is hope, for we also see here the fruit of God's promise (3:15). Satan has his seed among men, but God moves some to trust His promise and worship Him acceptably. Though the godly seed suffers persecution, it will triumph at last.

2. Marvel at God's patience. It is remarkable that God converses patiently with Cain and gives him ample opportunity to repent of his jealousy. Even though his offering was refused, Cain should have heeded the warnings. Murder is always in the human heart. "For out of the heart proceed evil thoughts, murders, adulteries, fornications, thefts, false witness, blasphemies" (Matt. 15:19).

3. Beware of the growth of sin. Once we harbor sin, it leads to worse sin, which affects others. Cain's initial sin leads to worse in his descendants, such as Lamech bragging about his murders. Like the godly line of Seth, we need to call upon the name of the Lord. What sins does this chapter teach us to pray against, and what graces should we seek from the Lord?

Chapter 5

1. By God's grace, strive to imitate Enoch. Enoch walked with God. Surely the secret of our Christian life is to abide in Christ: "Without me ye can do nothing" (John 15:5). Spend time in the Word of God, praying, meditating, repenting of sin, and obeying God's laws. Just as God took Enoch to heaven, so walking with God on earth is the best assurance that we will walk with God in heaven. The children of God must bear their Father's image.

2. The repentance and faith of the godly does not exempt them from death, unless the Lord should come and take them home first (1 Thess. 4:16–17). Every generation from Adam onward has seen death as the bitter fruit of the fall. Though most people try to ignore death, we are not ready to live until we are ready to die. What is the best way to face death?

Chapter 6

1. From Noah we learn patience and faith. Noah took more than a hundred years to build the ark. He patiently worked and witnessed to the people who rejected his message (2 Peter 2:5). We live in similar days (Luke 17:26) and need to preach faithfully despite the mocking of men against the

gospel. The only safe place from the flood was the ark. The only safe place from God's eternal judgment is Christ.

2. Noah found grace in the eyes of the Lord and walked with God. Significantly, Noah found grace before he was described as just and perfect. It is grace that enables faith, and God regarded Noah as just in consequence of that grace that caused him to believe and obey. May the Lord help us to walk with Him. Trust in Christ and obey Him, for then you will abide in His love (John 15:10).

Chapter 7

1. God's judgment upon the world of sinners is fearsome. The thought of millions of people drowning while water swept away all human constructions is horrifying. Yet it is a small thing compared to the burning wrath of God yet to come when the Lord Jesus appears with His holy angels. The flood brought death, but judgment day will bring eternal punishment in hell. Let us give sober consideration to this awesome and inevitable reality. How does the flood teach us to fear the Lord?

2. The Lord calls men, women, and children through the gospel to come into the ark of safety, Jesus Christ the Righteous One (Matt. 11:28; Luke 14:17). Just as the Lord shut Noah and his family into the ark and protected them during the flood, so the Lord will save all who trust in Christ alone from the wrath that is to come. After the flood came, no one was left except those in the ark. In the same way, the living church of Jesus Christ will be the only people to escape God's wrath. Therefore come to Christ now, and place your entire trust in Him.

Chapter 8

1. In the midst of overwhelming sorrows and dangers, we tend to think that God has forgotten us. But when the ark was a tiny speck floating in a vast sea of destruction, God remembered Noah. If we are in covenant with Him, He will certainly remember us too. Do not fear that God has abandoned you. His mercies will never forsake those who belong to Him, for His people are forever united to Christ. Christ is righteous; Christ has offered an all-pleasing sacrifice to satisfy God's justice; Christ will save His own.

2. The appropriate response to deliverance from trouble is worship. Noah might well have said to himself that he could not afford the time or resources to worship God after leaving the ark, but instead he built an altar and offered up sacrifices. From what evils, either physical or spiritual, has God delivered you? How are you worshiping Him for it?

Chapter 9

1. Thank God for the rainbow promise that He will never again flood the world. These are days of grace when God "now commandeth all men every where to repent" (Acts 17:30). The covenant with Noah guards the first gospel promise of the Redeemer coming into the human race (Gen. 3:15). The flood destroyed humanity except for Noah's family, and it seemed like the promise was in jeopardy. But God assured the continuation of the human race. Not even the judgment of sin will frustrate God's redemptive purpose in Christ.

2. Noah's drunkenness is a warning against the dangers and consequences of intoxication. The Bible consistently

identifies drunkenness as sin (Gal. 5:21) and strictly forbids being intoxicated or under the controlling influence of any intoxicating drink (Isa. 28.7; Eph. 5:18). Drunkenness is linked to loss of self-control, immorality, and unseemly behavior (Prov. 23:29-35). Therefore, take diligent heed to the warnings and do not be deceived by wine or strong drink (Prov. 20 1). This principle applies to any narcotic substance used for the same kind of effects.

Chapter 10

1. God sovereignly distributes the human race among the nations (Acts 17:26). All the nations come from the three sons of Noah. No man is an island. We are all part of the family of man. There is really only one race: the human race, various colors and cultures notwithstanding. How then should we view other peoples and nations?

2. The Bible is not the property of one particular nation, but God's Word for all mankind. The Lord is the God of all flesh (Jer. 32:27). Jesus is the Lord of all (Acts 10:36; Rom. 10:12). Therefore we must not arrogantly exclude people of other nations and ethnicities from the church. Nor may we foolishly say that every nation has its own way to God.

Chapter 11

1. God judges pride. How wicked and rebellious is the natural heart of man! It is not long since the flood, and yet man is again rebelling. Our own hearts will always naturally turn from the Lord's love and grace to our own schemes of self-exaltation. Yet such schemes always set us in opposition to God's purposes and lead to frustration and dishonor. How

can we recognize and defeat this satanic impulse of pride in our hearts?

2. We must never assume that large gatherings of people and great accomplishments by human ingenuity are good or pleasing to God. Concentrations of people may simply result in concentrations of evil. Though men seek outward glory, God often chooses to work through an unlikely individual following an apparently foolish call—like Abram. Pray for God to teach you how to live by faith and not by sight.

Chapter 12

1. God's covenant motivates missions. God called Abram to receive His blessing in order to be a blessing to all nations. How much more the new covenant in Christ's blood calls the church to make disciples of all nations. God's covenant people must be willing to give themselves to reach the world for Christ.

2. God blesses only believers. We must walk in the footsteps of Abram by following Christ in faith, obedience, and public worship. Abraham's faith sometimes faltered and he sinned; therefore we should not demand a great faith of ourselves before we can rest assured that Christ has saved us. Let us rather trust Christ to save us even through a weak faith and pray, "Lord, increase our faith."

Chapter 13

1. Abram is a model of peacemaking. Like him, we should respond to conflict by speaking directly and courteously to the other person, offering a reasonable solution to the problem, and deferring largely to his preferences. Such

peacemaking is possible only when we exercise faith in God's promises and regularly look to Him in prayer and worship; then we can let go of earthly gain because we have the Lord.

2. God's promises to multiply Abram's offspring and give them dominion over the land found partial fulfillment in the days of Solomon. But they point further to the kingdom of Jesus Christ. Those who follow in the footsteps of Abram's faith are being multiplied in every nation and will one day inherit the earth. Christians may therefore claim these promises and be optimistic about the church's future. Following Christ may result in worldly losses and suffering injustice, but one day a great multitude that no one can number will reign with Christ in the new heavens and earth.

Chapter 14

1. Faith and love draw believers into combat with evil. Though a Christian may at times fall into cowardice, he is not ruled by a spirit of fear but of power, love, and self-control. He is a soldier in the Lord's army. Therefore, believers, let us act like men and engage in the battle between good and evil with courageous action.

2. The church faces overwhelming odds but overcomes. How? First, our God is the Most High, the Creator and Possessor of all things. His power guarantees our victory. Second, believers have a Priest and King to bless us, Jesus Christ, after the order of Melchizedek. His intercession guarantees that God will bless His people despite their sins and not curse them as they deserve. This makes them more than overcomers in Christ Jesus.

Chapter 15

1. God's promise of salvation comes to us in our hopeless inability to save ourselves. In our own strength, we are as spiritually barren as Abram and Sarai. But, by the Spirit's grace, if we trust in the promise of Christ in the gospel, the righteous Judge will declare us righteous in His sight. You have warrant to trust Christ, for the Lord has established His promise in a covenant. It depends not on your worthiness—not even on how strong your faith is or how deep your repentance is—but on the Lord alone, who shed His own blood to save the church.

2. Theologians have often said that God's gracious covenant is one-sided in its establishment, and two-sided in its outworking. Based on this chapter, how can we confirm that God establishes His covenant with His people out of pure, one-sided grace? Why is the covenant two-sided in its outworking?

Chapter 16

1. Waiting on God requires faith. We will be tempted to take matters into our own hands when by prayer and lawful means we do not obtain what we desire. We must resist this and cling to God's promises. It is especially important for fathers not to be passive like Abram during such trials, but to lead their families in justice and love. Compromising God's laws may bring temporary relief but bears bitter fruit. Let us therefore repent of our sins and face their consequences with faith in God's mercy.

2. God grants His precious mercies to those who have suffered oppression for their social status, gender, or ethnicity.

Christ reaches out to all people of all nations in the gospel. He makes the poor rich in faith and enriches the rest of the world through their experience with God. Abram no doubt learned more about God when Hagar returned bearing news of how God met her in the wilderness. Yet God commands us to repent of rebellion and submit to proper authority. His way is not to overthrow all structures of authority and obedience but to renew His creations of marriage and family.

Chapter 17

1. Through the covenant, the Lord creates a bond of shared life between Himself and His people. He gives Himself to the elect in sovereign love and He moves them to give themselves to Him in submissive love. Let us marvel and be filled with joy at the kindness of God—that He would lower Himself thus!

2. Circumcised bodies meant nothing without circumcised hearts. While we must obey God's laws in the outward forms of worship, we dare not be satisfied with external religion. Ishmael had his father's love, prayers, and circumcision, but proved to be a "wild donkey" of a man. Let us cry out to God for a truly converted heart to love Him and keep His covenant. Is this your daily prayer?

Chapter 18

1. When it is hard to trust God's promises, let us remember who God is. Though your problems overwhelm you, nothing is too hard for Him. He created the universe out of nothing and raised Christ from the dead. If you fear His

judgments of sin, remember that He knows how to save those who trust Him.

2. If God is your God, then you can pray to Him, claiming His attributes by faith, for even His righteousness is your friend. Have you learned to place all your hope in His righteousness, both in terms of your justification and your sanctification?

Chapter 19

1. Lot shows us the bitterness of backsliding. Peter tells us that he was a righteous man, but he took one step after another into worldliness. In the end, he lost his wealth, his wife, the purity of his children, his mental health, and his own dignity—and nearly lost his life. When the world promises to please us with sin, how can we use the history of Lot and his wife to reject the world's pleasures?

2. The Lord is a God of both justice and mercy. He will punish sin with flaming fire that will suddenly fall on the wicked when Christ returns. He disciplines His children when they do not repent of sin. Yet He has mercy upon His children, and hears the prayers of their great intercessor, Jesus Christ. Let us therefore flee from sin and flee to Christ.

Chapter 20

1. God rebukes husbands who do not trust Him enough to cherish their wives. Abimelech showed more concern for honoring Sarah than her own husband did! If Christian men fail to give honor and care to their own families, they act worse than many unbelievers. God may discipline them

with public embarrassment. Let men repent of their cowardice and stand up to protect and provide for their wives and children.

2. The Lord remains faithful despite the weak faith of believers. God could have come in judgment against Abraham's sin and failure to trust God fully, but instead He came in grace. God's promises cannot fail for they do not depend upon man's unstable will but upon God's eternal will. Trust in the Lord; do not let the fear of man rule you.

Chapter 21

1. The Lord is faithful. Keep trusting Him even if waiting stretches from days into decades. Though we may have to wait a lifetime, He will keep His promises. If men often keep the solemn oaths of their covenants, surely the Lord will keep His covenant forever. How can God's covenant faithfulness help us in life's daily callings?

2. Never mock the people of God, no matter how weak they may appear. The everlasting God is with them, and one day they will laugh with joy. Those who are wise will join in covenant with them, taking them as their people and the Lord as their God.

Chapter 22

1. What is your "Isaac"? What earthly relationship or possession do you treasure most? If obedience to God required you to let go of it, do you fear Him enough to make the sacrifice? Pray for grace to show the Lord that this, too, is His.

2. The covenant people of God deserve eternal death in hell. To provide a substitute to take their place, God made the highest sacrifice. He did not spare His own Son, His only begotten Son whom He loves. Christ Himself became the Lamb of God's provision. So trust in His redeeming love; trust that if God gave His Son for us, He will certainly provide us with all that is good for us.

Chapter 23

1. By their union with Christ, God's people are kings and heirs of a great inheritance. Yet in this world they may have little; they must live by faith, not by sight. Pray for the God of hope to fill you with all joy and peace in believing the promises about Christ, so that by the power of the Holy Spirit you may abound in hope.

2. God calls believers to live as strangers and aliens—not entangled among the wicked Sodomites and Hittites in their pursuit of this world, but pilgrims waiting for the city of God. This separation from sin does not excuse isolation or rudeness, but instead demands that we do business in this world with honor and courtesy to all. In what ways can you practice this in the spheres where God has called you to live and work?

Chapter 24

1. Our God is the Lord of heaven and earth, controlling even the little details of a young woman's kindness to a stranger. This chapter bears strong testimony to how we should trust Him completely and show love and faithfulness to

the people around us. Who knows how He will use our acts of kindness?

2. We can especially trust that the sovereign Lord will multiply the covenant seed and win a bride for His Son. Such faith should express itself in courageous work to increase the church, joined to confident prayer and humble praise for His great works of power.

3. Like Rebekah, are you willing to follow Jesus Christ unconditionally as Savior and Lord for your salvation?

Chapter 25

1. We must prepare our estates and prepare our children for the time when we will die. Most of all, we must prepare ourselves for the day when our spirits will be gathered to another place. Will that place be heaven or hell?

2. God elected His people before they were born, apart from their works. In one family, God may select one and pass by another. Such election means that the Holy Spirit will produce a change in the sinner so that he hungers for grace. But if God does not elect and call him, then he hungers for this world and despises God's grace, and thus his condemnation is just. Do you hunger and thirst for God, or do you despise His Word?

Chapter 26

1. The Lord is the same yesterday, today, and forever. He still can be trusted to bless His people with physical provision and the hope of future glory. But the richest blessings that believers presently enjoy are the fruits and gifts of the Holy

Spirit. In the midst of famines and other trials, let us seek these riches diligently in prayer.

2. Christians must be wise in their relationships with the world. We must not flee to worldly powers when trials come but trust God's promises and obey His moral law. Do not be surprised when the world is hostile, but do not let the fear of man lead you into lies and sin. Beware of relationships that entangle you with unbelievers.

Chapter 27

1. The sins of believers can hurt and divide their families. Favoritism, broken lines of communication, lies, the love of the world, nominal religion, and seeking God's blessing through sinful means can tear Christian families apart. While God's purposes of grace cannot fail, He will discipline His people, possibly through broken relationships. Let us therefore repent of our sins, speak openly with each other in love, and seek peace.

2. God is sovereign over sin. He does not command it or cause it, but He decreed each sin as part of His plan to fulfill His good purposes (50:20). He is in control. This gives us a powerful reason to seek His blessing by prayer rather than by manipulating others.

Chapter 28

1. Man attempts to grasp heaven but his efforts fail, whether they are the proud labors of the Tower of Babel or the deceitful manipulations of Jacob. However, God bridges the gap with Jesus Christ. He is the only Mediator, the stairway to

heaven. Let us repent of our pride and deceitful ways, and rest contentedly in Christ alone as the Almighty Savior.

2. The church of Christ is the greatest wonder on earth. It is the assembly of many peoples, diverse nations united by the worship of the one true God. It is the house of God and the gate of heaven. Sadly, though "the Lord is in this place," many would have to confess, "I knew it not." Do you come to church with holy fear, since God dwells with His people?

Chapter 29

1. God disciplines His children, at times with poetic justice, when the sinning Christian must suffer similar sins from others. God's faithfulness to His people should not diminish our fear of displeasing Him. He is a strong and holy Father. Let us tremble at the thought of sinning against such a God and not despise His discipline.

2. Are you relying on your own strength to move obstacles or are you crying out to the Lord? Our God has abundant compassion, power, and faithfulness. He is always at work even through human sin. Take your painful situation to Him in prayer, and give Him the praise when He answers you.

Chapter 30

1. Few matters touch a woman's heart more than her children and her husband's love. Men are often driven to seek success in their work and wealth; let us beware lest these natural desires become idols and lead us into sins such as deception and injustice.

2. Sin has consequences but can never defeat God's purposes. Multiple sexual relationships and dishonest and

selfish business practices create sorrow, envy, and hatred. But the Lord uses sin to fulfill His promises and to multiply His people throughout the world. If you are in a family or business situation marred by sin, wait on the Lord and put your trust in His Word. He will bless you and build His kingdom.

Chapter 31

1. Laban is an example of a bully, oppressor, and tyrant. He robs the righteous, envies their prosperity, breaks his promises, alienates his family, worships idols, accuses others falsely, puts on a show of kindness, uses force to take what deceit will not get him, cheats honest employees, constantly changes his words, sees everything he takes as his right, and uses religion to protect his interests. But God will rebuke and judge him. Believers may face and overcome such people with truth, justice, and faith in the Lord.

2. The Lord stands in stark contrast to the gods of this world. Their little idols are ridiculous and helpless, but tragically the world pursues them and treasures them. The Lord, however, is the fearsome and faithful God. He is with His people, and He alone is worthy of our trust. Are you one of His children and are you presently trusting Him in and for all things?

Chapter 32

1. Like Jacob, we should call upon the covenant God and Father of Jesus Christ, pray His words back to Him, confess that we are unworthy of His grace, thank Him for His mercies, ask for salvation, pour out the fears of our hearts, and strengthen our faith with His promises. This is true prayer.

2. If we have sinned against other people, let us first humble ourselves before God and find peace with Him. Then let us humble ourselves before them, ask for forgiveness, and seek to pay back any losses that we caused them. Most of all, we must cling to God that He would bless us whether or not people will make peace with us.

Chapter 33

1. How beautiful when God reconciles enemies and heals broken relationships! It is a picture of divine grace. Repentance is shown for sins committed, restitution is made for damages done, forgiveness is granted to the guilty, and tenderhearted friendship is renewed. Reconciliation is costly—most of all to our pride—but it is sweet and precious. Insofar as it depends upon us, let us pursue peace with all.

2. The best reconciliation is reconciliation with God and returning home to Him. Jacob had gone on an exile of sorts because of his sins, but the Lord brought him home to the land of promise. Perhaps you have backslidden away from the Lord, and as a result have gone far from Him. God delights to bring the exiles home. Turn back to Him today.

Chapter 34

1. Christians should not entangle themselves with the world. Close relationships with ungodly friends may draw us into or make us the victims of their sins. Is there any such relationship alive in your life?

2. We must neither take revenge nor remain passive and quiet in the face of great crimes. Instead, let each person use the rightful power he has to seek justice for the oppressed.

3. Men often treat women as mere objects to be taken and used for their sexual pleasure. Fathers should teach their girls to avoid being naïve, and train their boys to honor and protect women as God's precious image bearers.

Chapter 35

1. Fathers should lead their families to worship the Lord alone. God calls men to exhort their families to bury their idols and to gather their wives and children together to offer God the sacrifices of praise. Just when His people appear at their worst, the Lord surprises them with blessing. Shall we not worship and praise Him in our homes?

2. God's grace has not yet fully rescued us from the miseries of sin and death. It is striking how God's promises of blessing to Jacob come in the midst of weeping by the graves of three beloved family members, plus grieving over the sin of children. Grace and tears mingle together in this life; do not be surprised when believers suffer and die. Take hope that they have a great reward waiting for them.

Chapter 36

1. The Lord reigns over all nations. We must not treat Him like a tribal god who belongs to one people or place; He is not a white god or a black god, a Jewish god or an American god. He is God over all nations. He gives every people their land and every person his life. Let us therefore give Him glory for every good thing in the entire world.

2. Children often reap many benefits from being raised by Christian parents. God may bless their marriages, children, and finances. He may give them property and positions of

leadership. But for all this, they should never assume that they are in a saving relationship with the Lord and the heirs of His promises. Abraham had Ishmael, and Isaac had Esau. Therefore, children, do not rest on your family privileges and covenant privileges, but seek true conversion through repentance and faith so that you rest in Christ alone.

Chapter 37

1. God promises to exalt His servants, but they must often face great humiliations and sufferings first. This was the case for Joseph, as it would later be for Jesus Christ. These experiences test our faith, but we can look back to those who suffered before us, especially the Son of God, and find hope that God has a plan for us.

2. God made families to be havens of love, righteousness, and safety, but sin can twist them into dens of jealousy, hatred, murder, enslavement, lies, and great grief. If you or a friend come from a family like that, have hope. God can use the horrors of an evil family background to bring great blessing, as the story of Joseph reveals.

Chapter 38

1. Apart from grace, sin and God's wrath would destroy His covenant people, just as He killed Judah's two sons. The visible church is too easily drawn into the world. We need more than godly parents; we need grace to forgive our sins and change our hearts.

2. Let us humble ourselves for our sins and glorify God for His power to bring good out of evil. This is one of the most sordid chapters in the Bible, and yet through these sins the

Lord preserved the line of Judah and made Tamar the ancestor of our Savior.

Chapter 39

1. Doing right may bring great pain. Few things are more painful than false accusations, but that is often how the wicked respond when we refuse to join them in sin. We must learn to fear the Lord more than we fear the slanders of men and women.

2. What does it mean that God is with us? It certainly does not mean that we will escape mistreatment at home and at work. Joseph experienced both, but God was with him. How? God blessed his soul with the fear of the Lord, hatred of sin, diligence in labor, and perseverance under both trial and temptation. He blessed him with wisdom and skill in his work and made him a blessing to those around him, gaining the respect of those who knew him. Though God's people suffer, God is with them in a real and powerful way.

Chapter 40

1. Though false teachers deny that God can know what people will choose to do tomorrow, in reality God knows every day of our lives before we are even born. He is able to declare the end from the beginning. We can trust Him with the future; He has plans to do good for all His redeemed people.

2. Painful circumstances in our lives may drag on for years. Sometimes, we must endure great disappointments when our hopes get raised only to be dashed to the ground. We must wait on the Lord. Nothing is more difficult than waiting, but nothing is more profitable for our souls. By grace,

waiting cultivates faith, prayer, submission, and humility; it prepares us for greater fruitfulness in the future. Above all, it focuses our hope not on earthly things or relationships, but upon the Lord Himself. Have you, too, learned to wait actively, prayerfully, and expectantly on God?

Chapter 41

1. Wisdom comes from the Spirit of God. The Spirit gives gifts and abilities to serve, the Word of God to guide us, and experiences of suffering to sanctify us. Pray that the Spirit would fill you with wisdom, developing your knowledge, character, and skills.

2. God glorifies Himself by exalting His humbled servants. Christ suffered from His people's envy and false accusations. He went down into humiliation, even an accursed death on the cross. But just as Joseph's enslavement and imprisonment prepared him for his service as Pharaoh's vizier, so Christ's suffering for our sins laid the foundation for His exaltation as the living Savior reigning at God's right hand. Let us praise the wisdom of God for the strange yet necessary humiliation of His Son, for without it no one would ever be saved.

Chapter 42

1. The exalted lord of Egypt tested his brothers to convict them of their sins against him. Notice the similarities to the first regal act of the Lord after His ascension: He poured out the Spirit and convicted Israel of their sins against Him. Pray for the Spirit of Christ to convict the lost, so that they may begin to long for salvation and be open to hear the gospel.

2. When God uses the Word, the Spirit, and providence to convict us of sin, let us not avoid Him but seek His grace. We will find no help in punishing ourselves. Behind the Lord's fearsome convictions is a warm heart of mercy for all who repent.

Chapter 43

1. God uses hard times to compel us to seek Him, just as He compelled Joseph's brothers to return to Him again. What afflictions can you use as opportunities to seek God?

2. Whereas chapter 42 focuses on the sins of the sons of Israel, chapter 43 reveals the mercy of God in His power, peace, compassion, grace, and hospitality. Though God uses conviction of sin to awaken sinners to their need for reconciliation with Him, He also wins their hearts with displays of His mercy in Christ. Let us remember this when raising our children, evangelizing our neighbors, or bringing the gospel to the lost.

Chapter 44

1. How precious is Jesus Christ, the Son of Judah, who intercedes for the condemned on the basis of His office as their Surety! He died as a substitute for sins He did not commit so that the guilty may go free. Is Christ your Surety? Have you confessed that God has found out your iniquity? Have you cried out for mercy to the Savior? He is full of mercy.

2. When God converts a sinner, he starts becoming like the Savior. He ceases to live for money and pleasure. He loves other people—beginning with his family. He shows a

willingness to sacrifice himself in order to serve others. Does this describe you?

Chapter 45

1. Christ's humiliation and exaltation served the purpose of saving many people. Praise God's wisdom, for the very sins of mankind against Christ serve for our salvation. Even when His purposes seemed defeated by the murder of His Son, God was performing the plans He made in eternity to rescue wicked sinners.

2. When Joseph's brothers first heard Joseph identify himself, they were afraid, but when he added that he was their brother, they drew near. Today when sinners are converted, Christ's heart overflows with love and joy toward them. How does He bring them near to Him as their elder brother and welcome them with the embraces and kisses of His Spirit? Can you draw more parallels between Joseph's encounters with his brothers and a sinner's encounter with Jesus Christ?

3. In union with Christ, we share in His humiliation and one day will share in His exaltation. The Father will welcome us into His presence and give us His best to enjoy forever. Christians should grow in their hope and anticipation of the glory of God; in the twinkling of an eye, poor and persecuted believers will become kings forever.

Chapter 46

1. The Lord says to His people, "Fear not." Sometimes we must travel to a strange or dangerous place or take some step into the unknown. Fear is a natural response, and it is aggravated by our sinful pride. How then can we overcome fear?

We must meditate on the promise of God, "I will go with thee." If the company of a strong and competent friend gives us peace, how much more will the company of the strong, covenant God give?

2. The prosperity of Israel's family in Egypt rested entirely upon Joseph. His position and intercession with the pharaoh was their key to unlock blessing. So we, too, must realize that our place in the kingdom of heaven rests entirely upon Jesus Christ. We must depend upon Him and approach the Father only through Him and according to His Word. In the Mediator we are welcome; apart from Him we are enemies of the King.

Chapter 47

1. Though we are pilgrims in this evil world, we are to be a blessing to our neighbors. We must show respect to whom respect is due, such as government officials, and we must pray for God's blessing upon those who do not yet know Him. Do you pray regularly for your leaders? Do you pray for the physical and spiritual needs of your neighbors?

2. Christ's sufferings and obedience have obtained a vast treasure of blessings for perishing sinners. Unlike Joseph, He offers them for free to all who come to Him. But like Joseph, Christ makes all whom He saves into servants of God to do His will. Praise God that our brother, the Lord Jesus, is rich in blessings and glorious in majesty. By grace, offer yourself to God through Him as a servant, ready to do His will and eager to give back some of what He gives to you.

Chapter 48

1. How beautiful it is to hear an old saint glorify God for His faithfulness! God's character is a rich feast and solid support for both old and young believers. His power gives us hope that His promises will not fail despite the darkest times. Let us seek grace to walk closely with this God all our days, so that when we are old we may give Him glory.

2. When death breaks our fellowship with parents, siblings, and dear friends, we must look to the God who is always there. Let us make use of times of mourning to seek a deeper communion with our Father through Christ, that His Spirit may fill us with comfort.

Chapter 49

1. Many centuries before Jesus was born, God revealed His purpose that from Judah a king would arise to rule the nations. He decreed before the creation of the world that His Son would have a kingdom. Though God's people had to wait for millennia for the Savior, their salvation was certain. How much more, then, should sinners like us have hope?

2. Do not grow weary in waiting upon the Lord. God's plan will not fail; Christ's kingdom will come. Make Jacob's prayer your own: "I have waited for thy salvation, O LORD."

Chapter 50

1. Joseph is a model of forgiveness. A robust view of God's majesty above us, His providence over evil, and His goodness set us free from bitterness to love the people who have hurt us. Learn to see all things under the banner of "God meant it for good."

2. Genesis begins with an account of how God made all things good, but Satan and sin brought evil to man and his world. Surely it is no accident that Genesis ends by declaring that what sinners planned for evil, God planned for good. Furthermore, the account of Joseph's life gives us an example of how God would save many perishing sinners. The fall of man and the curse of death would lead to the humiliation of God's faithful servant, but His very suffering would become the foundation for His exaltation as the Lord of the kingdom and Savior of the nations. Thus Genesis calls us to hope in God's decree to use evil to bring salvation for His glory. Cling to that hope to your dying day.

Exodus

Chapter 1

1. God will multiply His people (Matt. 16:18), sometimes even through persecution. For example, the persecution of the church in Jerusalem actually spread the gospel so that "the word of God grew and multiplied" (Acts 8:1–4; 12:1, 24). If you face persecution, how can you find the courage to not fear but stand firm with other believers (Phil. 1:27–29)?

2. When bullies and tyrants demand that we sin, we should fear God more than men (Matt. 10:28). God rewards those who fear Him (Pss. 33:18; 34:9–10). Disobedience to civil authority is lawful when necessary to obey God (Acts 4:19; 5:29), but breaking God's laws (such as lying) because of danger is never right.

Chapter 2

1. Moses's parents provide examples of doing what is right in an oppressive culture of death. We must trust in God's providence even when life makes no sense. Let us persevere in doing good by having faith that God overrules this wicked world to save His people. He is not cold to our pain, but has warm compassion for all our sufferings.

2. God's servant must suffer rejection. Christ came to His own people, but they did not receive Him. Nor would we receive Him apart from a new birth (John 1:11–13). By grace, do you manifest the fruits of the new birth in your

daily life? As you follow the rejected and crucified Savior, how might you suffer rejection as well?

Chapter 3

1. God's name, *YHWH* or "the Lord," reveals His eternal being, absolute independence, and freedom from all needs or limitations (Isa. 41:4; 43:10–13; 44:6–8; 48:12–13; John 8:58; Rev. 1:8). His being, will, and works are entirely from Himself. He borrows nothing from us and does not need our help (Acts 17:24–25). Yet we can be loved by Him, for He is the God and Father of our Lord Jesus Christ, the God of electing, covenant love. God desires to be known and worshiped for His lordship and love (Ps. 136:1–3).

2. In God's covenant compassion (Eph. 2:4), He comes to His elect in order to deliver them from the oppressive domain of darkness and transfer them into the kingdom of blessing, that is, the kingdom of His dear Son (Col. 1:13). He does not save people to live as they please, but to serve and worship Him in holiness (Eph. 1:4, 6, 12, 14; Col. 3:12). How does salvation from sin and misery motivate Christians to serve and worship God?

Chapter 4

1. Trust God's all-sufficiency. He is Lord over the natural world and Lord over all human ability and disability. We should never let our weaknesses become an excuse for disobedience. When God's Word calls you to act, trust that God will be with you.

2. Those who would lead God's people must be faithful in their home lives. Moses's failure to circumcise his son nearly

cost him his life. David resolved to walk within his house with integrity of heart (Ps. 101:2), but his adultery tore his family apart. Why is it dangerous when leaders neglect to be faithful in marriage and parenting?

Chapter 5

1. Israel's salvation from Egypt is a type of salvation from sin. When the gospel of redemption comes to a sinner, he may experience the evil of his spiritual bondage even more than before he came under the preaching of the Word. Why? To prepare him to glorify God all the more when salvation comes, for he now knows that only a divine Savior can rescue him. How have you experienced the evil of your sin?

2. Servants of God should not assume that obedience will bring them a life of ease and quick success. The kingdom of darkness never rages so fiercely as when the Word invades the world. God's servants face stiff opposition from the enemy and sometimes from the visible church; they may even find their own hearts rising up against God. But Christ will build His church, and even the rage of Satan will result in His praise.

Chapter 6

1. The Lord revealed Himself through redemption to create a relationship with His covenant people. Thus Exodus foreshadows the work of Christ. The Lord Jesus gave Himself to redeem a people who would know Him, zealously serve Him, and hope in the coming of His glory (Titus 2:13–14). His redemption brings sinners into a relationship as children of the living God (Gal. 4:4–7). Do you know this Lord? Is

He your covenant God, and are you in a relationship with Him as one of His covenant people?

2. Redemption requires a faithful prophet to speak God's words, a righteous priest to sacrifice and intercede, and a powerful king to deliver the enslaved. Moses, Aaron, and their family were inadequate to truly redeem God's people, for they were stained by sin. Though mere men are instruments of God's blessings, Christ is the only Mediator of the covenant of grace—the sufficient Prophet, Priest, and King. Trust Him for salvation, and trust Him alone.

Chapter 7

God alone is Lord. Physical goods are blessings, but men turn them into gods. Even in a secular culture, people worship money and the pleasures it can buy. They depend upon the experts to manipulate the world and give them happiness. But the Lord wages war against these idols to show that He alone is sovereign. His war will climax with the coming of Christ. Before it is too late, let us turn from idols to serve the living God and hope in His Son, the Savior. What idols tempt you? What does it mean to turn from them to the Lord?

Chapter 8

1. When Christ confronts Satan's power, victory is sure. Sometimes God's people suffer great injustice; sometimes they fall into idolatry. But Christ will prevail, and the church of His elect and called will overcome (Rev. 17:14). There is no one like the Lord. How can this encourage believers in their sufferings and temptations?

2. In the darkest places on earth, Christ is still able to judge His enemies and save His people. Therefore, even if we are in the shadow of Satan's throne, let us hold fast to the Lord, not deny the faith, and bear witness even to death (Rev. 2:13). Christ will destroy our enemies, and His redemption will deliver us from His wrath.

Chapter 9

1. God will punish His enemies with pain, conviction of sin, and horror by His wrath. All these will fall upon the wicked on judgment day (Rev. 6:12–17; 20:11–15). Even today, the Lord may visit the wicked with these judgments. However, convictions and confessions are not repentance; at times they are accompanied by hardness of heart. Do not rest in them, but strive after the Lord with earnest prayer until you truly turn from sin to God. What is the difference between mere conviction of sin and repentance unto life?

2. Pharaoh's hardening reminds us that the Lord is free to save or to harden sinners as He wills, for He made us all and has the right to glorify Himself by wrath or mercy (Rom. 9:16–23). Therefore, let us fear the Lord and not tremble before the wicked, no matter how stubborn and arrogant they are. God will get glory through them one way or the other.

Chapter 10

1. Let us bow before God as Lord of all our nation's resources. He gives food and famine as He wills. He can shut down our country's industries and businesses whenever He pleases. It is the height of foolishness to turn away from the Lord and

trust in ourselves or our possessions. God can make us helpless in an instant.

2. The Bible reveals both God's total sovereignty over all things and man's real responsibility for his willful choices. If we accept sovereignty but deny responsibility, we fall into fatalism, mysticism, and sin. If we accept responsibility but deny sovereignty, we fall into legalism, self-reliance, and pride. Even if we do not understand how these fit together, we must believe them both. How do both glorify God?

Chapter 11

1. The word of the Lord proves true. God told Moses what would happen beforehand (3:19–22; 4:21–23; 11:1)—and it did. God's great message to us in the plagues and Pharaoh's responses is, "I am the Lord." Therefore, let every knee bow and every tongue confess that He is Lord. One word from God outweighs all the wisdom of mankind.

2. Nothing on earth is more precious to us than our children. Yet even here the Lord reigns. When Job heard that his children had all died, he said, "The LORD gave, and the LORD hath taken away; blessed be the name of the LORD" (Job 1:21). Let us pray for grace to learn this submission so that if we lose a child, we can worship God like David (2 Sam. 12:20).

Chapter 12

1. Christ's work of salvation upon the cross was also a work of judgment against Satan and this world for the sake of the glory of God (John 12:27–33; Col. 2:15; Heb. 2:14). Christ is the Lamb that bought people from all nations for God,

redeeming them from God's wrath with His blood (John 1:29; Eph. 1:7; Rev. 5:9) and setting them free from sin (1 Peter 1:18–19). He ultimately will save His people by pouring out judgment upon this world (2 Thess. 1:8; Rev. 19:1–3).

2. We must remember His sacrifice by preaching the gospel in public worship, celebrating the Lord's Supper, and catechizing our children. Why is it so important for each generation to train their children in the knowledge of God's saving ways?

Chapter 13

1. If Christ bought us with His blood, then we no longer belong to ourselves but to Him and must live for His glory (1 Cor. 6:19–20). Redeeming love produces personal dedication and holiness, a willing giving of ourselves to the One who saved us (Rom. 12:1; Titus 2:14). Christians, let us live under the banner, "He died for me; I'll live for Him."

2. The Lord is with His people. The cloud of glory was a public revelation to the whole people of God's presence and will, similar to the public revelation of the Scriptures given to the church, in which believers see the glory of Christ (2 Cor. 4:6). Christ assures believers that God is with them, directs them, and fills them with awe at His glory. How can Christians seek a deeper experience of Christ through the Word?

Chapter 14

1. God's ways can seem foolish, but the Lord designs them so that He is glorified in our weakness. God finds us in hopeless situations of spiritual death only to raise us to life by grace

alone for His glory alone (Eph. 2:1–10). Christians continue to experience this as they fight sin, Satan, and the world. We must move forward in obedience to God when all means fail us, waiting upon the Creator and Redeemer (2 Chron. 20:1–30; Pss. 27:14; 130:5; Isa. 30:15). What spiritual challenge or crisis are you facing?

2. Passing through the sea marked a decisive break from Israel's former subjection to Pharaoh, just as baptism is a sign of breaking from sin's mastery and beginning to live for God (Rom. 6:3–4, 11). But fear and faith can be superficial and temporary, especially when based on outward signs (John 2:23–3:3; 1 Cor. 10:1–11). Do not rely on outward signs and seals, but rest your hope upon Christ and a living union with Him.

Chapter 15

1. Sing to the Lord! He is the strength and salvation of His people; He must also be our song. Much worship today revolves around our feelings, but biblical worship revolves around who God is and what He does for His people. The song of Moses teaches Christians to praise Him for His works in Christ, for they reveal His glory.

2. When we go from worship on the Lord's Day to the painful trials of the week, let us be careful not to fall into murmuring. Difficult providences prove our obedience and draw us to depend on the Mediator daily for His sweet grace. How are you being tested? How can you respond in a way that honors God?

Chapter 16

1. The Lord can work miracles. Naturalistic explanations of manna from insects or trees fail to account for how it came with the dew, melted in the sun, quickly decomposed, and sustained a hungry people for forty years. God is teaching us to rely on His power. We exercise such faith by observing the holy Sabbath rest, and by sharing what we have (v. 18; 2 Cor. 8:13–15). How do you need to trust God's provision right now?

2. Christ is the true manna (John 6:32, 35), the daily bread of His people's spiritual lives. By faith in Him, we enjoy a sweet foretaste of our heavenly inheritance in the graces of the Holy Spirit (Eph. 1:13–14; Rom. 8:23). Daily nourishment for our souls comes by meditation on the promises and faith in Christ as a hungry mouth takes food.

Chapter 17

1. When judgment fell from the Lord through the rod of Moses, rivers of water streamed out to give life to sinners. When God's wrath fell upon Christ through the cross, rivers of the Holy Spirit flowed from heaven to give life to sinners (John 7:37–39; Gal. 3:13–14). Let us marvel at God's grace and drink deeply of the streams of life He bought with blood. Why did judgment have to fall on Christ for the Spirit to give life to men?

2. We face a cruel and powerful enemy in Satan, but we can overcome him while our Mediator stretches out His hands in heaven. Trust not in your own strength, or the Devil will prevail. How can looking to Him who was stretched out on

Calvary's hill and who even now intercedes at God's right hand help us overcome evil?

Chapter 18

1. God's saving work aims at His glory among all nations. He must be praised by all; He must become the joy of all the earth. This is why we must declare His glory among the nations and the gospel of His great works in Christ to all peoples. How will you use your abilities and resources to help your church to make disciples of all nations?

2. Leaders need help or they burn out. For this reason, God gives His churches elders and deacons for the ministry of the Word and the ministry of physical needs (Acts 6:1–7). Paul appointed more than one elder in each church (Acts 14:23). Every Christian should serve as a member in the body of Christ as he is able—all are needed (1 Cor. 12:21).

Chapter 19

1. God stands at an infinite distance above fallen mankind in His majesty and holiness. In this day of casual worship and irreverent prayer, let us never forget that He is the holy King. We may draw near to Him only through the blood and righteousness of Christ. How should our worship of God show our reverence for His holiness and majesty?

2. It was marvelous grace that the Lord, who can claim "all the earth is mine," took a small, enslaved people as His treasure. Israel broke the old covenant by disobeying the law (v. 5), but the Lord accomplished His larger purposes in the new covenant, which promises inward grace to produce obedience for both Jews and Gentiles (Jer. 31:31–34). The church drawn

from Jews and Gentiles is now called God's "peculiar" treasure, the kingdom of priests and a holy nation by Christ's blood (Titus 2:14; 1 Peter 2:4–5, 9; Rev. 1:5–6; 5:9–10).

Chapter 20

1. Eight of the Ten Commandments are negative—"Thou shalt not"—implying that God gave the law to convict fallen man of sin (Rom. 3:20; 1 Tim. 1:8–11). Conviction is painful and sinners hate the light of God's truth (John 3:19–20), but conviction of sin is a gift of the Holy Spirit (John 16:8) by which the law drives sinners to Christ (Gal. 3:22, 24). How do you respond when God's Word makes you feel guilty? How should you respond?

2. The church's status as God's treasured possession is not based on its obedience to the law, but on the death of Christ (Titus 2:14). Significantly, God gave the law after the exodus and not before. Law followed grace, defining how the redeemed people were to live before God. You become part of God's people by faith in Christ alone. Yet obedience to God's Word is still a vital part of the covenant relationship (John 14:23; 15:5), for the law continues on as a rule of life for believers to which they respond with gratitude (Jer. 31:33; 32:40; Ezek. 36:27). So pursue holiness, but never try to keep God's covenant by your own strength. Rely on the work of Christ and God's grace will enable you to live in holiness.

Chapter 21

1. While the judicial laws of the old covenant do not bind us today, they contain many moral principles. For instance, punishments should fit the crime; murder is not the same as

accidentally killing someone. Another principle in this chapter is that all human beings, including women, servants, and unborn children, are precious persons, not mere property, and they should be protected from injury and death.

2. God's law held people accountable not only for their acts, but for harm done by their property, whether it is an ox, pit, or some modern equivalent. What do you own that could cause harm to others? What reasonable safeguards have you put in place?

Chapter 22

1. God's law requires justice in relationships and society. Not only is theft a crime, but God requires restitution for possessions stolen or destroyed. The Lord especially hates injustice against those who are weak. Human justice systems may fail, but God's wrath will inevitably strike the unrepentant sinner. In the fear of God, can you honestly say that you have not stolen from others, harmed their property, or oppressed the weak? If you have wronged someone, what must you do to make it right with God and man?

2. The strictly judicial laws like the death penalty for witches were abolished in Christ. He ended the earthly theocracy of Israel, ascending to a heavenly throne and bringing the kingdom of God through the means of the Word and the Spirit (John 18:33–37; Acts 2:33–36). However, these judicial laws point ahead to the coming of His kingdom in glory. We deserve death because of our sins (Rom. 6:23). When Christ returns to judge the world, the wicked, including sorcerers, will be cast into hell (Rev. 21:8).

Chapter 23

1. Sinful men promote their party, but the Lord delights in truth and justice regardless of whether a person is rich or poor, in the majority or the minority. Why is it so easy to side with the majority or your particular group instead of standing for truth and justice?

2. God sent His Son, the Angel of the covenant (Mal. 3:1). The King and Captain of His people (Josh. 5:14) came to fulfill His covenant and destroy their enemies (Gen. 12:3). Drawing near to man in Immanuel, the angel of God's presence (Isa. 63:9), God increases our obligation to pay attention to Him, obey Him, and reject all other gods (Judg. 2:1–2; Heb. 2:1–4). We must give our devotion to Christ alone.

Chapter 24

1. The old covenant came with external ceremonies and the blood of animals, none of which can save (Heb. 10:1, 4). These pointed to Christ's blood of the covenant (1 Cor. 11:25; Heb. 12:24; 13:20), for the promised inheritance came only through the redeeming death of Christ, the Mediator (Heb. 9:15–21). The believing remnant in Israel clung by faith to the promise of the coming Redeemer (Gen. 3:15; 49:10). We, too, must cling by faith to Christ, who has established the new covenant in His blood.

2. Even in covenant mercies, God remains God and we must obey Him. This requires more than a verbal commitment; Israel pledged obedience but had no heart to perform it. We need the Spirit of God to sanctify our hearts by faith so that we experience Christ's blood applied to our guilt and obey

God (1 Peter 1:2). Do you have this living hope that produces holiness? Or are you like most of Israel—all words but no reality?

Chapter 25

1. The ark of the covenant (vv. 10–22) symbolized God's chariot-throne carried by the spirits of heaven (Pss. 18:1; 99:1, 5), a sign that the King of heaven lived with Israel. Yet there was no image for God Himself (20:4–6) for He is holy, more glorious than all idols (15:11). Christ is the heavenly King who lives with His people (Matt. 28:18, 20). He is also our mercy seat, the propitiation of all the sins of believers (Rom. 3:24–25).

2. The table of shewbread (vv. 23–30) represented God's fellowship with His people and pleasure in them (Ps. 149:4; Isa. 62:4–5). The golden lampstand (vv. 31–39), formed in the shape of a flowering tree, was a type of the light and life our Priest gives to His people (Num. 6:24–26; Ps. 36:9; John 1:4; Rev. 1:13; 2:1) through the Holy Spirit (Zech. 4:2, 6). How do God's people experience communion with Christ today?

Chapter 26

1. In the tabernacle, God's glory was both present and hidden. The tent curtains (vv. 1–14) in four layers hid its contents well. Outside it looked quite ordinary; inside were royal colors and sparkling gold. However, even the priests in the holy place faced the veil separating them from the most holy place. God's holiness separates Him from sinners (Isa. 59:2). Only Christ can open the way to God by His death

and intercession (Heb. 9:6–8; 10:19–21). The divine glory comes to us hidden in humble, crucified flesh (John 1:14; 1 Cor. 1:23–24). His glorious presence with His people is seen only by faith and enjoyed by those who are humble and contrite over sin (Isa. 66:2; Phil. 3:3, 8–10).

2. The abundance of gold inside the tabernacle, the lampstand shaped like a tree (v. 35), and cherubim (vv. 1, 31) point back to the garden of Eden (Gen. 2:9, 11–12; 3:24). God's presence with His people is a return to Paradise with all its sweet fruit (Rev. 2:7; 22:1–5). How does God give His children foretastes of the heavenly paradise even now?

Chapter 27

1. The only way to draw near to God is through the altar. There the priests killed a sin offering and took its blood into the tabernacle. The Lord Jesus offered Himself once and for all and then brought His human nature into heaven itself to appear on behalf of His people (Heb. 9:11–14, 24, 28). Christians thus have a greater altar—not a physical object, but Christ Himself who strengthens our hearts with grace (Heb. 13:9–10). Let us pray for grace to be quick to use this altar for all our sins and all our needs.

2. Though outside the tabernacle, the court was still a holy place (Lev. 6:16, 26). Here the worshipers would bring their sacrifices to the priests and sing God's praises (Pss. 96:8; 100:4; Isa. 1:11–12). How much more is the church a holy assembly when it gathers to worship on the Lord's Day? Indeed, through faith in Christ, we enter the most holy place and worship before God with the heavenly assembly of

saints and angels (Heb. 10:19–22; 12:22–24). How could believing this transform our attitude toward church?

Chapter 28

1. How glorious and beautiful is our High Priest in the sight of God (Heb. 7:26)—holy, harmless, undefiled, separate from sinners, and made higher than the heavens! Surely the Father is delighted to hear His intercession. Are you relying upon this perfect Priest? Have you become experientially acquainted with the value of His constant intercessions (Rom. 8:34; Heb. 7:25)?

2. The presence of our High Priest before the Lord is a constant appeal for God to remember His covenant and show mercy to His people despite their sins (2:24; 6:5; 32:13; Lev. 26:44–45). Their names were on His shoulders (v. 12) as a sign that Christ took responsibility for them as their Surety, and upon His heart (v. 29) because He loves them. What does it mean to you that Christ has His people on what Thomas Goodwin called His "beautiful heart"?

Chapter 29

1. How does God make sinners like us into priests? Priests must be washed, clothed, and anointed (vv. 4–7). These three ideas appear in three sacrifices. The bull of sin offering (vv. 10–14) took the sinner's guilt and punishment so that he would be forgiven (Lev. 4). The ram of burnt offering (vv. 15–18), while making propitiation, also presented God with total self-dedication so that God would be pleased with the sinner (Lev. 1). The blood of the ram of consecration (vv. 19–34) was put on the ear, thumb, and toe like the

cleansing of the healed leper (Lev. 14:7, 14, 25), and its meat was eaten like a peace offering as a sign of fellowship with God (Lev. 7:11, 15–21). Therefore, God makes sinners into priests by washing away their guilt, clothing them with imputed righteousness, and anointing them for holy fellowship with Him—all by sacrifice.

2. How do Christians act as priests? By faith in Christ (1 Peter 2:4–6), they offer to God spiritual sacrifices—themselves, their praise and thanksgiving, and their financial gifts and intercessory prayers (Rom. 12:1; Heb. 13:15–16). How can you offer spiritual sacrifices to God?

Chapter 30

1. The burning of fragrant spices on the golden altar of incense (vv. 1–10) was a symbol of prayer (Ps. 141:2; Luke 1:10; Rev. 5:8; 8:3–4). Christ's priestly intercession is based on His sacrificial blood (v. 10), and He intercedes morning and evening (vv. 7–8) to shield sinners from God's wrath (Lev. 16:12–13; Num. 16:46–48; Rom. 8:34). How can Christ's priestly intercession encourage us in our prayers to God?

2. The fragrances of the incense were a sign of God's delightful presence meeting with His people (25:22; 29:42–43; 30:6, 36). Limiting this fragrance to the holy things showed that one can enjoy God's presence only through a mediator and the means He appointed. To unbelievers, the gospel is only the stench of death in its revelations of divine justice, but to believers it is the fragrance of life in Jesus Christ (2 Cor. 2:15–16).

Chapter 31

1. The Spirit of God created the whole world, including us (Gen. 1:2; Job 33:4). All life comes from Him (Ps. 104:30), as does all skill and wisdom. What abilities has He given you? Are you grateful for these gifts and do you rely on His help to use them for His glory?

2. The Sabbath was a sign of the covenant (vv. 13, 16), just as the rainbow was for Noah and circumcision for Abraham (Gen. 9:12–13; 17:11). However, the Sabbath was not just a sign of the old covenant with Israel, but a sign of God's created order (Ex. 20:11; 31:17). Therefore, while Christians are not under the ceremonial and judicial system of Israel, they still have an obligation to keep the Sabbath as a day set apart to worship God. It is good to remember that "sabbath" does not mean "seventh" but "rest" or "cessation." It is a day that is to be different from all other days; thus, it legitimately designates the first day of the week. How is keeping the Sabbath a sign of a covenant relationship with Christ and a foretaste of resting with Christ in the heavenly paradise?

Chapter 32

1. Israel's idolatry shows us the corruption of the human heart. They had God's prophet, miracles, and laws; they stood at the foot of Mt. Sinai with God's glory visibly shining over them. Yet they quickly turned aside to idols. Their sin was engraved on their hearts as with a diamond-tipped pen of iron (Jer. 17:1). Unless God gives grace in the heart, there is no hope for fallen man (Titus 3:3–5). What then should we ask for in prayer?

2. Moses here again is a type of Christ. The Lord Jesus is the Prophet preaching against idols, the King bringing the sword of discipline, and the Priest offering Himself as the substitute for His people and interceding for them. But where Moses could only bring truth and temporal deliverance, Christ can save from blindness, guilt, and sin.

Chapter 33

1. The coming of the covenant God did not stop Israel from sinning. On the contrary, they plunged into sin before the face of God. The law does not conquer sin, but only expresses it to show that it abounds within us, for we are no better than Pharaoh. Therefore, let us humble ourselves and grieve over our sins. Our sin spits in the face of God's glory and reacts to His law with more rebellion. God would be right to abandon us forever, sentencing every one of us to "depart from me, ye cursed, into everlasting fire" (Matt. 25:41).

2. Where sin abounded, grace abounded all the more (Rom. 5:20). God used Israel's idolatry as an opportunity to display His goodness. He is sovereign and free to be gracious when He wills, which means we must bow before His sovereign right to damn sinners or to save them. But it also means we can hope in His sovereign love. No matter how bad our sins are, God is still sovereign and free to save. Yet He always saves through the Mediator because God delights in Him. What strong reasons do we have to hope in Christ and Him alone?

Chapter 34

1. The Psalms are full of praise to God for the divine attributes outlined above (vv. 6–7). Moses is a model of how to

respond to God's attributes with humble adoration (v. 8). Let us therefore fill our mouths with praises and focus our minds in worship not upon ourselves and our experiences, but upon who God is. What are some of your favorite psalms, hymns, and spiritual songs? How do they declare the attributes of God?

2. God does not punish anyone for the sins of his parents (Deut. 24:16; Ezek. 18:20; John 9:1–3), except for the sins of our covenant head, Adam (Rom. 5:12, 18). However, children imitate their parents, and those who hate God often raise children who hate God and fall under the same punishment (Ex. 20:5; 34:7). We need not fear our past if we are in Christ. The blood of Christ redeems us from the futile ways of wicked ancestors (1 Peter 1:18–19), blessing our offspring to thousands of generations (Deut. 7:9). Does this strongly motivate you to follow Christ for the sake of future generations?

Chapter 35

1. The resources to build God's dwelling place came from redemption. Slaves do not usually own much gold, but when God redeemed Israel out of slavery, He caused the Egyptians to give them silver and gold (11:2; 12:35–36). Redemption made them rich and provided the resources to build God's tabernacle. Likewise, Christ's redemption won the riches of grace that we need to build the body of Christ (Eph. 4:7–16). Therefore, the only way to build the church is by faith in Christ, obtaining from Him everything His church needs.

2. The motivation to build God's dwelling place comes from a willing heart (v. 29). The church is built through cheerful

giving and voluntary service. The best of pastors can do little without a people willing to serve the Lord (Rom. 12:11). How are you using your abilities to serve in the church? What motivates you and how motivated are you?

Chapter 36

The people's generosity is commendable in itself, for they gave more than enough (v. 5). It is a model to us of cheerful giving. However, their faith in the Lord and obedience to His moral laws were sadly lacking (chs. 14–16; 32; Num. 11; 14). We dare not rest our confidence in external duties such as giving money to church or attending public worship, for these can be done for hypocritical reasons (Matt. 6:1; 23:23; Acts 5:1–11). It is easier to give money than to do justice, love mercy, and walk humbly with God (Mic. 6:8). How can we be zealous in outward things but also avoid hypocrisy?

Chapter 37

The word "gold" appears no less than twenty times in this chapter. Bronze was used in outside furniture, but gold in the holy places as a sign of God's holiness—not merely His moral purity, but His excellence above all other beings in every way (see note at 15:11). The enormous amount of pure gold used in the holy furniture (38:24) displayed the beauty and precious value of His holiness (28:36; 39:30). This King's wealth reflects Himself. Let us treasure Him above all and cast away everything in order to gain Him (Matt. 13:44; Phil. 3:7–8). Do you view God as your supreme treasure? How do true Christians show they view God as their supreme treasure?

Chapter 38

Those consecrated to serve the Lord by the blood of sacrifices still needed regular washing at the laver (30:18–20; 38:8). Jesus taught us the same lesson when He washed the disciples' feet (John 13:1–11). As Christians, we must regularly confess our sins to the Lord so that our consciences can be freshly washed by the blood of Christ (1 John 1:7–10; Heb. 10:22). Confession costs us something. Just as the women gave up their mirrors to make the laver for washing (Ex. 38:8), so must we give up our pride and self-righteousness to find cleansing. Are you able to boldly draw near to God with a cleansed conscience? Why or why not?

Chapter 39

God's church must be built "as the Lord commanded." Whether we are considering the officers who govern the church, the church's worship, its evangelism, or any other aspect of church life, we must order the church according to the will of its King, Jesus Christ. Scripture warns against "will worship," forms of religion and spirituality invented by men according to their wisdom, but powerless to please God or conquer sin (Col. 2:20–23). The Bible is sufficient in every way to guide God's ministers to order the house of God (1 Tim. 3:15; 2 Tim. 3:16–17). What sad consequences result from adding to or subtracting from God's will for His church?

Chapter 40

God's purpose is to fill His people and the new creation with His glory (Eph. 3:19–21; 4:10; Rev. 21:3). Christ has purchased our enjoyment of the fullness of God by His obedience, and is building God's dwelling now of godly people. The church should be filled with the Holy Spirit (Eph. 5:18), but the riches of spiritual experiences are a mere foretaste of glory (Rom. 8:23). One day Christians will enjoy the glory of God in a way that would kill us now. Our hope is to see His glory and be filled with Him (John 17:24; Rom. 5:2; Col. 1:27). How can we cultivate that hope in our hearts so that it controls our lives?

Leviticus

Chapter 1

1. The burnt offering, along with all the other types of sacrifice, was a clear yet imperfect picture of the once-for-all sacrifice of Jesus Christ, the Lamb slain from the foundation of the world (Rev. 13:8). Animal sacrifices could never and were never intended to take away sin (Heb. 10:1–4). Only the sacrifice of Christ could do that (Heb. 10:12). But they were graphic sermons of the necessity of a perfect substitute, of death as sin's penalty, of blood shedding as the means of forgiveness, of reconciliation and consecration. Although it would be a sin against Christ to repeat the animal sacrifices, what aspects of their message preach about Him?

2. The peculiarity of the burnt offering was that the entire animal was placed on the altar. It pictures full and complete consecration; everything is given to the Lord with nothing being held back. It testifies of both the total dedication of Christ who gave Himself as a sweet savor (Eph. 5:2) and the consecration of the believer to the Lord of his life in view of gospel grace (Rom. 12:1–2). The burning of all on the altar would not have been a pleasant aroma to us, but it pleased the Lord. So putting ourselves on the altar of consecration may at times be unpleasant to us, but it is pleasing unto the Lord. In view of Christ's sacrifice, how are you offering yourself as a living sacrifice to God?

Chapter 2

1. The meat or grain offering was an expression of the worshiper's confession that his daily bread was from above. With that recognition, the worshiper offered a token in consecration and dedication to the Lord. Similarly, we are to be thankful for outward and temporal benefits! The offering also points to the Lord Jesus who perfectly and completely lived in dedication to His Father. How can you express your dependence on God and your thankfulness for the daily bread He supplies?

2. Significantly, this sacrifice without blood was never offered independently; it was always in connection with one of the bloody sacrifices. To offer the work of our hands to the Lord apart from the blood of Christ is to repeat the sin of Cain who assumed his works would be acceptable on their own merit. It is only through the blood of Christ's sacrifice that anything we offer to the Lord, even in thanksgiving, will be acceptable. How can we keep in mind that all our worship can only be offered with His blood?

Chapter 3

1. The peace offering was a shared meal in which the offerer celebrated the benefits of a peaceful relationship with God, a reconciliation accomplished by the shed blood. In this meal, God, the priest, and the offerer all received a portion, symbolizing that all the parties were satisfied with the atonement. The features of the peace offering draw a straight line to the blessings and benefits Christians know and enjoy in the new covenant. Our peace with God flows from Christ's atonement. God is satisfied with Christ's sacrifice; Christ is

satisfied with those He purchased; and we are satisfied with peace with God through Him. How does the gospel bring satisfaction to the soul?

2. There are significant parallels between the peace offering and the communal meal that believers can experience at the Lord's Table. The table is not a sacrifice but it declares the fact of the sacrifice Christ offered that removed every barrier, obstacle, and impediment to our fellowship with God as believers; it declares that we have peace with God through our Lord Jesus Christ. Rejoice in the One who accomplished this on your behalf!

Chapter 4

1. Sin is the transgression of the law, and ignorance of the law is no excuse. God is so holy and His law is so inflexible that as fallen mankind we cannot help but offend God. The heart is "deceitful" and "desperately wicked" (Jer. 17:9). Sin is instinctive, and we can commit it carelessly, thoughtlessly, or unintentionally. We can be guilty of such sins more than we know, imagining all is well. But God has devised the means to deal with sin; there is a sacrifice for sins of ignorance. And when we realize and confess them, they are covered by the atonement of Christ. Let us pray with David, "Cleanse thou me from secret faults" (Ps. 19:12). How can you develop a habit of keeping short accounts with God?

2. The chapter ends with a glorious statement that links atonement with forgiveness (v. 35). Since the sacrifice appeases God's wrath and satisfies His justice for the sinner, forgiveness is the wonderful result. All those who truly trust Christ alone for salvation are covered by His precious blood

and exempt from any personal experience of God's wrath. Christ took the wrath in our place, and God is, therefore, "faithful and just to forgive us our sins" (1 John 1:9). How would you counsel a person who sincerely trusts in the Lord Jesus Christ, but still feels guilty and afraid of God's wrath?

Chapter 5

1. How wonderful is God's grace! If people could not afford to offer the lamb or kid, just some flour would be acceptable. This is important evidence that there was nothing in the animal blood that had the power to deal with sin. God is always more concerned about the condition of the heart than conformity to ritual. Faith could see beyond whatever the sacrifice was to the reality casting the shadow—Jesus Christ. When our Lord fulfilled all these offerings, our forgiveness cost Him everything and cost us nothing (Rom. 6:23). What is the condition of your heart in light of Christ's sacrifice?

2. The trespass offering sees sin as debt to God: compensation must be paid to Him. Thus Christ taught us to pray, "forgive us our debts" (Matt. 6:12). What we owed, Jesus paid. He satisfied God's justice. His passive obedience paid the law's penalty; His active obedience paid the debt to the law's precepts. These comprise His justifying righteousness. With our debts paid, what should be our focus? (See John 14:23–24.)

Chapter 6

1. Wrong done to others is wrong done to God. Verse 2 says, "a trespass against the LORD, and lie unto his neighbour." Sin breaks both tables of the law (James 2:10). Psalm 51 is a classic example of this principle. David's sin was against

several people; yet he confessed that he had sinned only against God (Ps. 51:4). Why does God see our sins against others as being foremost against Him?

2. Scooping up ashes and removing them from the camp is humble, yet sacred service for priests. So with us who are priests (1 Peter 2:5, 9). Not only worship but also practical service can be done as unto the Lord (Col. 3:17, 22–23). Nothing is mundane or secular for us. What little things are you able to do for the Lord that cause divine rejoicing? (See Zech. 4:10.)

3. The perpetual fire in part symbolizes the Holy Spirit (Isa. 4:4; Acts 2:3). His influences are enlightening, warming, comforting, and corrective. He also consumes our sin and purifies our hearts. Just as the priests ensured the continuous burning, how can we be sure to not quench the Spirit (1 Thess. 5:19)?

Chapter 7

Eating together was a symbol of fellowship and friendship. That the priests shared in some of the offerings and even the people in the peace offering was a beautiful picture of the reconciliation between God and the sinner. Even when the meal was limited to the priests, it points to what Christians enjoy, for we are kings and priests (Rev. 1:6). Rejoice in the fellowship we have with Christ in His love and strength, for He carries us in His bosom (Isa. 40:11; cf. John 13:25) and strengthens us (Phil. 4:13).

Chapter 8

1. God swears no oath when consecrating the Levitical priests because they were to be only temporary pictures of the perfect Priest to come. However, God consecrates His Son as Priest with an oath to an everlasting priesthood after the order of Melchizedek, a more complete type of Christ (Ps. 110:4; Heb. 7:20–21). The most outstanding fact demonstrating Aaron's necessary obsolescence as a priest was his own sin that had to be addressed before he could serve others. Christ was perfect and undefiled with no sins of His own to limit the power of His service and sacrifice. How does Christ's sinless perfection help us to trust Him to satisfy God for our sins?

2. Oil upon Aaron is a symbol of the Holy Spirit equipping him for service. Israel's kings were anointed (1 Sam. 10:1) as were their prophets (Ps. 105:15; Isa. 61:1). Our Lord, by His anointing (Ps. 45:7), is the Prophet, Priest, and King of His elect people. He lovingly teaches them, saves them, and governs them. Pray that God would help you hear Him, rely on His mediation, and obey His gracious will. In Psalm 133:2 the anointing flows down to Christ's members, His church. Believers are all anointed ones, "Christians" (1 John 2:20). How does Christ's anointing upon all believers affect your life choices?

Chapter 9

1. The outstanding moment of Aaron's first day of work was the fire of blessing that came out from the Lord (v. 24). The fire that consumed the sacrifice symbolized God's acceptance and pleasure. Three things stand out as points to ponder.

First, the fire was preceded by obedience. Throughout the chapter, Aaron did as the Lord commanded (v. 6). Second, the fire revealed the divine glory. Third, the fire was received with reverence as the people enthusiastically shouted for joy and fell in worship. This is a genuine encounter with God. The whole narrative depicts the grace of the gospel. How does the church encounter God and experience His acceptance today?

2. After Aaron offered the sacrifice to the Lord, he lifted up his hand toward the people, and blessed them (v. 22). We are reminded of when our Lord "came out" from death and the grave having finished His work. As He ascended to heaven, "he lifted up his hands, and blessed them" (Luke 24:50). How is the blessing of Christ better than that of Aaron?

Chapter 10

1. Nadab and Abihu's sin concerned God's worship. Serious consequences followed because they departed from God's Word. There must be no "will worship" (Col. 2:23) such as worshiping as man wants and not as God commands. Divine worship is not a secondary issue. God is jealous for pure worship because it belongs to His glory. The contrast between the fire of blessing in chapter 9 and the fire of wrath here is instructive. Blessing was preceded by obedience; wrath was preceded by disobedience. Both revealed God's glory, and both were received with reverent fear. What principles must direct the church's worship if it is to obey God and honor His holiness?

2. Aaron's silence at the loss of his sons is impressive. Are you able to acknowledge the Lord in His chastisements (Heb.

12:5–6)? When we submit to God, we accept His discipline, then He sanctifies it to our good and His glory.

3. Fleshly and intoxicating worship is an abomination to God. This is why strong drink was forbidden to the priests (1 Tim. 3:8). Today, fleshly excesses mark worship styles in many churches. Use of worldly music and bodily movement appeal to the flesh instead of the understanding (Ps. 47:7), violate Scripture (Isa. 66:2; John 4:24), and resemble the worship of the heathen (Ex. 32:6–8). How can we ensure that we worship God in a reverent and glorifying way as He fills our praises (Ps. 22:3)?

Chapter 11

1. The laws of cleanness and uncleanness were designed to teach the meaning of the holiness required if man were to fellowship with God. Unclean things are to be avoided—a stigma is upon them. They are typical of sin, which is spiritual and moral uncleanness (Isa. 6:5). Nothing is literally unclean now under the gospel (Acts 10:13–15), but the principle applies that sin must be branded, repented of, and avoided (Prov. 4:14–15; 2 Cor. 6:17; 7:1). Significantly, the ultimate reason for keeping the laws was redemption. "For I am the LORD that bringeth you up out of the land of Egypt, to be your God: ye shall therefore be holy, for I am holy" (Lev. 11:45). What can we as the redeemed do to be more conformed to the image of our Redeemer (1 Peter 1:13–17)?

2. Some of the restrictions are very specific, naming the things to avoid; some are general, simply identifying characteristics such as fins and scales for water creatures. Even though a catfish is not specifically named, the absence of scales meant

it was unclean. God expected His people to think. This parallels the call to walk in holiness in the world. The Bible does not identify every conceivable sin, but the principles of God's Word are clear enough to inform us what sin looks like. God expects us to think as well. Why is it necessary to cultivate discernment and careful thinking in order to be holy?

Chapter 12

1. The ceremonial uncleanness associated with childbirth is a vivid picture sermon of the inherent depravity of mankind from the inception of life. Circumcision, while it is a sign of the covenant, also declares by the removing of the flesh from the infant that sin is a problem from the beginning of life before any conscious transgression occurs. Here is the transmission of sin. The mother is classed as ceremonially unclean because she bears another sinner in Adam—a humbling reminder that "in sin did my mother conceive me" (Ps. 51:5). We need to guard against what is outside us and inside us. What are evidences that sin is in our hearts from our youth?

2. Although childbearing rendered mothers unclean because the children were born sinners, there were sacrifices in place to deal with sin and restore the mother to the place of fellowship. How wonderfully this anticipates the birth of One who would be without sin and would offer Himself as the sacrifice to restore sinners to an offended God. Rejoice that Christ came made of a woman and under the Law so that He could save sinners like us from our sin—actual and original.

Chapter 13

1. Many of the details of this chapter are obscure and difficult to understand. Yet the message is remarkably sobering and clear. These leprous skin conditions depict sin and its effect on the whole man. They vividly depict sin as defiling, ugly, loathsome, and disfiguring. The skin sores also show that God is concerned for purity. He cannot have fellowship with iniquity (Hab. 1:13). The leper must dwell alone, outside the camp. Nothing spoils fellowship with God like sin (Isa. 59:2). Ironically and beautifully, lepers also point to Jesus Christ who alone could touch the leper without becoming defiled and who could so graciously provide healing. What more can we do to avoid sin? When we defile ourselves, what should we immediately do to receive the cleansing provided for us in Christ (1 John 1:7, 9)?

2. The priests had the responsibility to discern the status of the potential leper, taking time and precautions to make their judgments. They had to patiently examine, wait, and come to conclusions based on evidence. This is a good rule for us when seeing faults in others. "Charity…thinketh no evil" (1 Cor. 13:4–7; cf. Zech. 7:10)—always think the best of a person until you are compelled to think otherwise. Why is it important for the church, especially its elders, to discern evil and exclude unrepentant sin from the church?

Chapter 14

1. The bleakness of chapter 13 gives way to the hope and rejoicing of chapter 14. The healed sufferer can return to the camp. Leprosy could be cured (Num. 12). Regardless of how terrible the sin and its consequences, there is an appropriate

sacrifice to provide its remedy. All of this points wonderfully to the Lord Jesus both in His willingness and ability to heal lepers of His day, but also in His provision of the only sacrifice sufficient to deal with the root cause which is sin. Spend time in worship of Him!

2. All the sacrifices depict some aspect of Christ's atoning work, but the two birds together illustrate the two essential components of the gospel message. The slain bird along with its blood typifies the atoning death of Jesus; the living one that is let loose points to His resurrection (cf. Rom. 4:25; 1 Cor. 15:3–4). At the same time, the pair illustrates something of the nature of the atonement itself that involves both propitiation (the satisfaction of God's wrath) and expiation (the removal of sin and guilt, Ps. 103:12). What blessings are you reminded of as you imagine that bird flying away?

Chapter 15

1. The bodily emissions addressed are part of the normal course of life and are not statements of the individual's personal relationship or standing with God. Inwardly one could be right with God and still be outwardly ceremonially unclean, thus prohibited from the public rituals of worship. These were graphic object lessons of spiritual truth. Discharge from the organs of procreation reminds us of our fall in our first parents and the transmission of sin to us and to our descendants. Sin is internal and oozes from within us, from our nature (Ps. 51:5). It is often secret (Pss. 19:12; 90:8). But what does God deem as essential (Matt. 5:8)?

2. This chapter provides an outstanding lesson regarding the contaminating power of the unclean thing. Everything and

anyone that had contact with the unclean became unclean. Sin is an impurity that not only defiles us but others (1 Cor. 15:33). It is a warning for every believer to walk through this world circumspectly to avoid anything that would rob us of our fellowship with God. What are some things around you that could contaminate you? How can you avoid their defilement?

Chapter 16

1. One of the most striking events of the Day of Atonement concerned the two goats, which together depict the effects of the one sacrifice for sin offered by Christ. The slain goat depicts the godward effect of the atonement to propitiate or satisfy God's wrath against sin. The sprinkling of the blood on the mercy seat that covered the righteous demands of the law satisfied the broken law. The scapegoat bearing the sins of the people away depicts expiation, the necessary consequence of propitiation. The guilt of sin was removed never again to appear; the goat did not wander back into camp. All the sins of the people were upon it and away into the wilderness it went forever (Ps. 103:12). The two are inseparably linked: if there is propitiation there must be expiation. Christ did not die in vain. How does this double sacrifice illustrate the assurance of the believer that God is pleased with him?

2. Aaron's role on the Day of Atonement dramatically portrayed the work of the ideal High Priest to come. When Aaron stripped himself of the royal garments of his priestly office to do the work in the Most Holy Place, it depicted Christ's work of humiliation whereby He became obedient unto death. When Aaron entered behind the veil, it depicted

the death of Christ whereby He presented the evidence of His sacrifice to the Father. But when Aaron exited the veil and put on his royal robes again, it depicted the resurrection of Christ and His earned exaltation. He entered with the blood of sacrifice; he exited as evidence of the accepted sacrifice. As dramatic as the events were, Aaron's sacrifice for himself was a clear indication that One greater than Aaron was necessary and was certain to come. Pray for grace to rejoice in the Savior, the fulfillment of these shadows!

Chapter 17

1. We must have no do-it-yourself worship. Only what God has prescribed is acceptable and glorifying to Him. To worship otherwise is to serve the Devil (v. 7; 1 Cor. 10:20–21). How are modern Christians tempted to worship God in ways outside His commandments and thus unacceptable to Him?

2. The definition of the blood puts the atonement in view. Blood stands for life. Blood is a vital liquid circulating in our bodies conveying nutrients and oxygen. When blood is shed, life is taken. Sin's penalty is death. "The soul that sinneth, it shall die" (Ezek. 18:4). "The wages of sin is death" (Rom. 6:23). Our Lord shed His blood. This culminated in John 19:34 when one of the soldiers pierced His side with a spear, and blood and water came out. The One who is the Prince of life was sacrificed to the justice of a sin-hating God, which appeased His anger. On the cross Christ poured out His life. Take time to glory in the cross, the heart of the gospel.

Chapter 18

1. Incest, voyeurism, adultery, homosexuality, and bestiality characterize a degenerate society. They show the unrenewed

and unrestrained heart (Jer. 17:9). These perversions were rife in ancient Egypt and throughout Canaan. So perverse was the pagan society that even some Hittite laws identified what kinds of animals were permitted for bestiality. Under God's judgment, those civilizations decayed and were destroyed. It is a solemn warning to Western nations with their liberal and relativistic outlook. Have God's standards of holiness changed (see James 1:17)?

2. God takes sexual sin very seriously. In verse 22 "abomination" means "disgusting," "hated," "abhorrent." For such perverted behavior the Canaanites were ejected from their land (vv. 25, 28) as Israel was from that same land afterward (Ps. 106:40). Because sin is an outbreak, it needs the bounds and reins of God's laws to keep it in check. Pray to be kept from such sins. How can God's Word help you (Ps. 119:9–10)?

Chapter 19

1. Many of these laws apply to inward feelings and are based on the fact that the Lord is our God. If there were no other reasons for obedience than to acknowledge the Lord and the relationship we have with Him, that would be enough. This is where obedience must begin (Ps. 51:6; Eph. 6:6). According to Romans 8:13 and Colossians 3:5, why must sin be put to death?

2. Leaving some of the corn and grape harvest behind for the poor shows that God is kind, and we also should be kind to those less favored. Even though we may not have fields or vineyards, it is still possible to keep the spirit of the law. However it is manifested, we are to love our neighbors as we

love ourselves. It may look different for us than for historic Israel, but what might it look like for you?

3. God prohibited Israel from cutting or permanently marking their bodies as the pagans did (v. 28). Christians should not mar their bodies, for they are God's temple (1 Cor. 6:19–20). They also should not participate in customs that identify them with paganism. What does this imply about tattoos and body piercing?

Chapter 20

1. A beautiful contrast to horrendous Molech is our Lord Jesus. He took infants in His arms and blessed them! Thank God for revealed religion: we are not left in heathen darkness and barbarity. How can we stand for the children today, both born and unborn, against those who would sacrifice them to the gods of pleasure, money, and selfish ambition?

2. The Lord who calls for holiness also works it in His people. Verses 7–8 say, "Sanctify yourselves.... I am the LORD which sanctify you" (cf. v. 26). His will is that we be holy, and His power will make believers holy (1 Thess. 4:3; 5:23–24). This does not excuse laziness, but on the contrary it encourages and empowers our utmost effort, knowing all our efforts to become holy are from Him and through Him (Phil. 2:12–13). How does it encourage you knowing that God makes His children holy?

3. Some of the sexual sins prohibited defy imagination, but they were common practices in the world in which God's people were going to live. Some ancient cultures even had laws to regulate the circumstances in which some of these

horrendous acts were permissible. They testify to the depravity that is in man's heart. These perversions were also rife in Paul's day (Rom. 1:24–28) and are becoming so in our day (2 Tim. 3:1–3). We cannot be the friend of this corrupt world (James 4:4). True religion, based on God's law, lifts society's morals; when our true religion declines, so does our society. Remember to pray for those in authority and those who make our laws, so many of which, like Canaan of old, regulate rather than prohibit sin.

Chapter 21

1. The priests were man's representatives before God, and each one foreshadowed the coming of the ideal and perfect Priest, the Lord Jesus Christ. Christ alone was free from blemish without any spot of imperfection, so all of these personal restrictions on the imperfect Old Testament priesthood were means of showing the absolute necessity of the Priest to come. Worship the perfect High Priest (Heb. 3:1–6)!

2. Although they were imperfect, the priests had to guard themselves so as not to distort any more the One they served and represented. So modern-day ministers, elders, and deacons must live beyond reproach so as not to obscure the One they serve and represent (1 Tim. 3). The example of God's servants is important. As chief men among His people (Lev. 21:4), people will look to them. How can you better reflect the image of Christ to those around you?

Chapter 22

1. All believers are priests in Christ (1 Peter 2:5, 9). They owe it to their God to be clean and abstain from all appearance

of evil (1 Thess. 5:22). Those that belong to the Lord in this special relationship have a responsibility to behave differently and separately from the norms of the world. They must only offer their best to God—their wholehearted devotion. How should the knowledge that he or she is a priest shape a Christian's life?

2. That the Old Testament priests had to be free from outward blemish (v. 21) points to and anticipates the ideal Priest, our Lord Jesus, who alone is free from any inner or moral defect, and whose sacrifice, being perfect, perfects us (Heb. 10:14). When you see your spiritual blemishes, how can you look to Him who is the righteousness of God for sinners?

Chapter 23

1. Whereas the weekly Sabbath belongs to the moral law and is thus timelessly relevant, the feasts are part of the ceremonial law and thus are temporary pictures or object lessons of some aspect of gospel truth, all of which are things to think about when keeping the weekly Sabbath. Notice "in all your dwellings" in verse 3—we must observe the Sabbath at home as well as in the assembly. How do we keep it as "the sabbath of rest"? How do we keep it as "the sabbath of the Lord"?

2. Worship the Lord as you consider the ways He fulfilled the feasts. The Passover is fulfilled in the Lord's Supper (1 Cor. 5:7), that we might not forget the grace that redeemed us, by an infinitely greater Lamb without blemish (1 Cor. 11:24–25). The first fruits of the harvest were for God, then the rest for His people. It's a picture of resurrection—Christ first, and afterward we all shall follow (1 Cor. 15:20). That this occurred the day following the Sabbath points to the

day of Christ's resurrection. The Feast of Weeks is the New Testament day of Pentecost. Similarly, fifty days from the day after the Sabbath means Pentecost lands on the first day of the week—the new day for the Sabbath (Matt. 28:1–6). Thus, the day of Pentecost in Acts 2 fell on the Lord's Day. What more appropriate day for the giving of the Spirit (Acts 2:33; Rev. 1:10)? The blowing of trumpets is a type of gospel preaching which is always music to the convicted sinner's ears (Ps. 89:15). It calls us to rest in Christ (Matt. 11:28–30) and assemble with His people (Gen. 49:10; Acts 2:41–42).

Chapter 24

1. Two features of the tabernacle suggest aspects of worship. The candlestick represents Christ, who is our Light (Luke 2:32). It also represents His churches in a dark world (Phil. 2:15; Rev. 1:13, 20). Some friends asked Robert Murray M'Cheyne about preparing sermons. He said, "Beaten oil—beaten oil for the lamps of the sanctuary" (cf. Ex. 27:20; Lev. 24:2). Diligent and thorough preparation, under God, will produce enlightening sermons. The loaves symbolized the Lord's presence with His people, and His provision for them. He is our "staff of life" who always satisfies our needs. Worship our Lord as the Light of the World and the Bread of Life.

2. The fact that the half-Israelite was subject to the Ten Commandments indicates their application to *all* men. The moral law summarized in the Ten Commandments is universal, timeless, and inflexible. The particular penalties for breaking the law were part of the civil laws given as specific applications of the moral law suited for that society. Whereas the moral law that defines God's unchanging standards retains

its relevance, the applications vary. God has ordained governments for the administration of His justice (Rom. 13). Pray for those in authority over you (1 Tim. 2:1–3).

Chapter 25

1. The land lying fallow each seventh year helps it to replenish and produce more the following year. The Lord's commands are wise and beneficial (Rom. 12:2). Also, if God gives the land a sabbath, He owns it, not the Israelites. All we have is entrusted to us as stewards. How should it change our attitude and use of our possessions when we know that God is the Owner, and we are just servants managing His property?

2. The year of Jubilee foreshadows the blessings of the gospel. Its trumpet was sounded immediately after the Day of Atonement. When sin is put away, God's favor makes joyful blessings abound toward us (Ps. 103:1–5; Isa. 61:1–3). How should we respond (Isa. 61:3)?

3. Throughout the chapter, the responsibility of the near kinsman to act on behalf of his needy relative is in focus. In the most sublime sense, the Lord Jesus is our kinsman-redeemer, who does for us what needs to be done for our welfare. He has the relational right, for through the covenant and incarnation he calls us brothers (Heb. 2:11–14). He has the resources and the love to release us and make us His own (Eph. 3:8; 5:25). According to these same verses, what responsibilities do we have as His redeemed?

Chapter 26

1. The blessings and curses of the law remind us that God is a righteous Judge who rewards obedience and punishes

disobedience. The law threatens sinners with horrifying divine wrath, so that they might flee to the gospel of Christ crucified. Christ won the blessing by His perfect obedience and carried the curse in His death in the place of sinners (Gal. 3:13–14). If you have turned from your sin and trusted in Christ, rejoice that God's blessings are on you and that He will never curse you in His wrath because of what Christ has done (Isa. 54:9–10).

2. The warnings of God's law and the afflictions of His providence should motivate us to repentance, turning us away from sin and back to the Lord. If you are not converted, God is using these things to call you to repent and be saved. If you are converted, then God may still discipline you as a Father lovingly disciplines His erring child to bring him back to Himself. This chapter highlights key elements in true repentance: (1) grieving over sin (v. 39); (2) confession of sin (v. 40); (3) humiliation for it (v. 41); (4) acceptance of God's chastening (v. 41); and (5) divine mercy (v. 42). Do you know the reality of this repentance in your experience?

Chapter 27

Beware of rashness in God's service. These people meant well when they vowed but they changed their minds and wanted to redeem their pledges. Much better to consider beforehand, and then follow through with whatever we promise to God (Eccl. 5:2, 4). It is easy to act on impulse under pressure. Vows are not a means of bargaining with God. These penalties deter us from doing this. God wants us to be wise as well as zealous. The key point is that God takes vows seriously.

Numbers

Chapter 1

1. The numbering of the tribes of Israel reminds us that the Lord "knoweth them that are his" (2 Tim. 2:19). By this count an exact figure was revealed (Num. 1:46). Likewise, as God gathers a people from all nations, He knows their number, and He will keep each one. How does this truth bring comfort to your soul?

2. God revealed through Moses that every man numbered had to give "a ransom for his soul" (Ex. 30:12). God's numbered people are a ransomed people. No one can be in their ranks except on the basis of a price paid, and that price is the precious blood of Christ. Sinner, have you sought a place in the company of the saints through faith in Jesus's blood and righteousness?

3. Those numbered were to be "able to go forth to war." God's people are by nature and calling soldiers of the cross, for they are in warfare with sin, Satan, the flesh, and the world. Many would desire to be counted among the ranks of the redeemed, but they are not prepared to engage in the spiritual conflict that comes to the believer. We must enter the kingdom of heaven through much tribulation. In what ways is the church of Jesus Christ like an army at war? How is this spiritual warfare different from earthly wars?

Chapter 2

1. In the human heart there is the tendency to do that which is right in one's own eyes. But the arrangement of the tribes reminds us that God is the God of order, not confusion (1 Cor. 14:33). Every tribe had to be in its own place contributing to a smoother passage through the wilderness. Our steps must be ordered according to His Word so that our walk to the heavenly Canaan will be less complicated with self-imposed difficulties. In the arrangement of the tribes the command was, "every man shall pitch by his own standard." In this way the entire company kept rank, providing for the unity and cohesion of the congregation. God's people need to know where they belong in the spiritual life of Christ's church and seek to remain there faithfully. How can this strengthen the whole life of Christ's church?

2. The tribes were all ranged around the tabernacle, on which the cloud of glory descended, the assurance of God's presence in the wilderness sojourning. Psalm 46 reminds us that "God is in the midst of her." The center is the Lord's place alone and must be guarded against all usurpers. To have Him in the midst is a comforting truth. In the midst, He goes with us, secures us from all danger, and will bring us safely to our haven of eternal rest. How does the church know and experience that God is in its midst?

Chapter 3

1. The Levites were given to Aaron to keep his charge as well as that of the whole congregation. They remind us of the ministers of Christ and the charge given them, which is to keep the holy things that belong to the great High Priest,

things centered on His sacrifice for sin. They are also to be faithful to the souls charged to them, being instant in season and out of season too (2 Tim. 4:2). Negligence is forbidden. How often do you pray for your pastors, that they would be faithful?

2. "The Levites shall be mine; because all the firstborn are mine" (vv. 12–13). The Lord laid claim to the Levites on the ground of redemption. The Levites stood in the place of the firstborn of the Israelites, and the firstborn child was redeemed (Ex. 13:13). God's claim to His people is based on Christ's redemptive work by which they are rescued from the stroke of death and become the Lord's. To be regarded as the firstborn is to enjoy privilege and honor. How can we more consciously claim this wonderful allotment as believers and the ownership of our Redeemer over us?

Chapter 4

1. In their enlistment for service the Levites were said "to perform the service," or "war the warfare" (v. 23). Serving the Lord brings the believer into a spiritual battle, for the enemy is opposed to the things of Christ. From this conflict there is no escape. He who is a servant of Christ is a soldier of Christ too. Read Ephesians 6:10–18 and consider how to prepare for our battle.

2. The Levites did not commence their actual service until the age of thirty, after they had passed through a probationary period of five years (8:24). The principle is clear—the servants of Christ must not be novices. Tried and proven men are needed to serve the Lord and then He will be well served. Who can help to mentor you as you prepare?

3. "So shall they serve"—these words spoken of the Gershonites' service are striking. Their sentiment was true for all the Levites: their service was to be rendered according to the revealed will of God. Scripture directs the believer to serve within the framework of the divine will. Not all have the same abilities and gifts, and some are more in the public eye than others. But God distributes His gifts according to His sovereign purpose, and as each member of the body functions according to its place and purpose all goes well. There is harmony when each part functions with a view to the whole, and there is discord when any one part becomes too concerned with self. Pray that God would help you to be satisfied with the calling He has given you and to serve Him with all your heart.

Chapter 5

1. The expulsion of people from Israel's camp for ceremonial uncleanness reminds us that "the ungodly shall not stand in the judgment, nor sinners in the congregation of the righteous" (Ps. 1:5). What a solemn matter! Have you been to Jesus for the cleansing from sin found only in His blood? If we are in Christ then we know that we have been made fit to approach the Lord and we can enjoy fellowship with Him.

2. As odd as the trial of jealousy seems to us, it teaches vital spiritual lessons. Sins hidden will eventually be revealed. Sometimes the discovery of the concealed iniquity will be made in this life, like it would have been for the adulterous woman. But, if not, it most certainly will be at the coming of the Lord. "Some men's sins are open beforehand, going before to judgment; and some men they follow after" (1 Tim.

5:24). Then Christ, the Judge of all, "will bring to light the hidden things of darkness" (1 Cor. 4:5). Do not cover your sins; you will not prosper. Confess and forsake them and God will have mercy.

Chapter 6

1. Christ was not a Nazarite, yet in Him there converged all that the Nazarite vow signified. As the God-man He is the personification of all purity. He who could not sin was holy, harmless, undefiled, and separate from sinners. Spend time worshiping Christ as the Savior of sinners, who offered Himself without spot to God to procure redemption for men and to save them from their sins.

2. To mark the close of the time of his vow the Nazarite brought an offering to the Lord. Though he had been specially set apart to the Lord he was not without sin. Even among the holiest of the saints, none is pure before a holy God. Thankfully, we are accepted in the Beloved (Eph. 1:6). Because God is pleased with Christ, He is pleased with those in Him. It is union with Christ and the power of His cleansing blood that makes any of our service to the Lord acceptable. For the remaining sin that taints the very best of our service, flee to Christ's merits and atonement.

3. Aaron pronounced blessing on Israel. Likewise, Christ our High Priest was sent into the world to bless sinners by turning them from their sins (Acts 3:26). At His ascension, Christ's final act was to bless His disciples with His uplifted hands (Luke 24:50–51). On those hands were the marks of His suffering—suffering that bought all spiritual blessings for us. The Aaronic blessing should be wonderfully directed

to the living church through Christ's merits. Do you believe that, in Christ, God's face is shining upon you with grace and peace? Why or why not?

Chapter 7

1. The twelve-fold repetition of the gifts offered to the Lord appears redundant, but it teaches a wonderful lesson. We should remember that what is offered to the Lord is not to enrich Him but to praise Him. The principle is that God does not tire of the sincere offerings of His people even when they are all the same. Some Christians get discouraged because they think they have no special talents and cannot really do anything special for the Lord. The Lord knows the heart and that is what He desires more than "stuff." Take to heart that the Lord "is not unrighteous to forget your work and labour of love, which ye have shewed toward his name" (Heb. 6:10). How can this encourage the Lord's people?

2. The offerings of the princes were for the dedicating of the altar, where the offerings for sin were made. Such liberal giving in relation to this altar of sacrifice underlines that the preaching of the cross must be richly supported (1 Cor. 9:13–14; Phil. 4:14–19). The message of Christ and His crucifixion deserves the willing, liberal, and cheerful giving of God's people. How are you giving to this great cause?

3. To the sons of Kohath no wagons or oxen were given, for in their service they were to "bear upon their shoulders." They carried the most sacred things that especially pointed to Christ, a great privilege but one that brought a weighty burden. They needed to be strong men, just as gospel ministers

must be to lift up Christ in this world. Pray that such men will be strengthened in the inward man by the Spirit of God.

Chapter 8

1. The Levites were set apart to serve by the laying on of hands, signifying their presentation to the Lord as a sacrifice (vv. 10–11). In that manner they were truly "living sacrifice[s]" just as the believer is to be (Rom. 12:1–2). The Christian is the New Testament Levite (Jer. 33:19–22). In light of Christ's atonement and the benefits enjoyed because of it, serving the Lord is our reasonable service. Let us be careful that everything about us in body and soul is the Lord's and is spent in unceasing labor for Him, His glory, and His kingdom. If you are a Christian, what does it mean, practically speaking, for you to offer yourself to God as a living sacrifice today?

2. When the Levites officially retired from their set period of service, they did not cease from all work for the Lord (vv. 23–26). By ministering "with their brethren in the tabernacle," they brought their years of experience to good profit. Long after the earlier and more active years have passed, the child of God has much to contribute to Christ's cause, still bringing forth fruit in old age (Ps. 92:13–14). There is a wonderful sense in which servants of the Lord never retire. How can we honor this principle today?

Chapter 9

1. The purpose of the Passover was much like the purpose of the Lord's Supper: an occasion for remembering God's gracious redemption through the sacrificed Lamb. Just as Moses

reminded Israel of certain regulations about the Passover, so Paul reiterates to the Christian church the Lord's will concerning the communion feast (1 Cor. 11). God's people are forgetful. Often our minds grow so dull that it becomes essential to be taught again "the first principles of the oracles of God" (Heb. 5:12). But, knowing our infirmities, the Lord graciously repeats His truth in both the written and visible Word. Do not resent it when a preacher repeats truth you already know, but pray for grace to hear and see with profit.

2. That the Lord made provision for those who were providentially hindered from keeping the Passover at the designated time reminds us that God is more concerned about the heart than mere external performances of religion. Though unavoidably defiled by a dead body the Israelite was not permitted to keep the Passover. It is good when the Lord's people are so anxious for fellowship that they mourn when unable to partake of the means of grace. We need more of the spirit of the psalmist when, in his exile, he was jealous of the sparrow and the swallow enjoying their access to God's house (Ps. 84:3). But at the same time, it warns us that some can go through the motions of religion without any real heart of worship for the Lord. In our sin, we can turn the very best of religious means into empty acts that mean nothing to God. How can we, as Paul admonished, "keep the feast…with the unleavened bread of sincerity and truth" (1 Cor. 5:8)?

3. The cloud and the fiery pillar, representing the presence of God, made it clear to Israel that wherever they were they were in God's presence. It was not for them to speculate or wonder where they might be next, but just to enjoy where they were and to serve the Lord in the place He had put

them. The equivalent for Christians today is the Word of God illuminated by the Spirit of God. Too often we tend to fixate on where the Lord will lead us next rather than serving Him to our fullest in the place He has put us now. How can we balance contentment with where we are, experiencing God's presence in the Spirit, and, at the same time, sensitivity to obey the commands of God's Word, following His directions promptly and eagerly?

Chapter 10

1. The preaching of God's Word is symbolized by the blowing of the trumpet. The silver trumpets were blown for various purposes but obviously in such a manner that all were sure of the meaning of the sounds heard. How can we ensure that the Lord's message goes out with a clear sound that men will know the mind of the Lord (1 Cor. 14:8)?

2. The Levites remind us of the need to labor together in harmony. The Gershonites and the Merarites went first in the marching order to set up the tabernacle to receive the sacred furniture carried by the Kohathites. God has set each member of Christ's church to function in a certain way for the good of the whole body. Are you a member of a church? What is your place in the body? How has God equipped and called you to serve? Are you serving there in harmony with the other church members?

3. Just as Moses pled with Hobab to go with Israel to Canaan, so the child of God longs to take every family member to glory. Loved ones are all we can take to heaven. All earthly things will be left behind, for they are temporal. But the souls of family and friends are eternal and will live forever in

heaven or hell. What more can you do to plead with them, to win them, and to bring them to the better country?

Chapter 11

1. Complaining is a prevalent sin among those who profess to be the Lord's. It is easy to become discontent with whatever the situation of life may be. The first instance of murmuring in this chapter gives no reason, and that in itself is instructive. Complaining is never justified. It seems clear, too, that this complaining was in secret. Moses appears to have known nothing of it, but the Lord heard it. How foolish to conclude that complaining can be concealed from an omniscient God. Why is complaining such a great sin and offense to God?

2. It was "the mixt multitude" who "fell a lusting" (v. 4). These rabble-rousers had no heart for the Lord, but instead yearned for Egypt. Their complaining spread like wildfire throughout the entire camp. They had a leavening influence and the lusting spread among the Lord's people, quickly developing into contempt for the manna, that wonderful reminder of God's provision. The church should guard from impurity and purge the leaven whenever it is known. The protection of the body as a whole sometimes requires the discipline and expulsion of the few. Pray for your church, that it would be spared division, but that it would be preserved in faithfulness if some members desire to return to worldliness.

Chapter 12

1. The meekness of Moses was unparalleled in the Old Testament. He did not retaliate when Aaron and Miriam spoke

against him. The natural response against criticism is to respond in kind, to answer fire with fire. Meekness, or godly humility, stops us from leaping to our own defense and is content to leave all injustices with the Lord, believing that He will defend and vindicate us as He sees fit. In this way, Moses is a good example for us all—and an image of Christ (1 Peter 2:21–23). How do you respond to criticism? How can you grow more like Christ in this?

2. How Moses responded to Aaron's request to him on behalf of Miriam is also a good pattern. Immediately, Moses interceded on her behalf to the Lord. It would have been so easy to rejoice in her affliction. But that kind of bitterness is never right, and Moses held no bitterness against Miriam though she led the rebellion against him. Nor did he find pleasure in her chastisement. Instead he prayed for her healing. Here also is a likeness to Christ who prayed for His crucifiers (who acted out of ignorance) to be forgiven (Luke 23:34). It is good to follow the example of Moses, but far better to follow the example of Christ, whom Moses had in view from the beginning (Heb. 11:26). For whom should you be praying, instead of stewing in bitterness?

Chapter 13

The nation had reached the southern frontier of Canaan, the Promised Land. They were right on the border of blessing, but faced another crisis of faith. The spies returned from the land with vivid proof that the land was all God promised it would be. The evidence of blessing was unmistakable, but ten spies also reported a serious risk in claiming the promises. The grapes testified to incomparable blessing, but the giants threatened immense opposition, particularly when they saw themselves as grasshoppers in comparison. They were not adequate to face the risk. So they admired the blessing but failed to possess it. Many professing Christians tend to live on the border of blessing as well. It is one thing to consider all that we have in Christ, to theorize about it from every theological angle. We know it is good and we want it but for whatever reason we stay on the fringes and do not lay claim by faith to all the promises we have in Christ which are yea and amen. God is greater than all the giants and can enable the grasshoppers to conquer. Caleb understood that and so should we. How can we overcome fear and unbelief in our hearts?

Chapter 14

1. In the midst of all the unbelief and doubt, Joshua and Caleb sought to counter the report of their colleagues by drawing attention away from the greatness of the dangers to the greatness of God. They highlighted the invincible power of God, who could remove every defense of the enemy (v. 9); the immutable purpose of God, who, based on His sovereign good pleasure, would give them the land (v. 8); and the immediate presence of God, who would dispel every reason for being afraid (v. 9). The truths about God that should have encouraged ancient Israel to trust the Lord should encourage us today. The God of then is the God of now. How can these truths help you to follow the Lord fully, just as Caleb and Joshua did?

2. Apart from Jesus Christ, none was a more fervent intercessor than Moses. His intercessory prayer in this chapter is a

great example not only of what prayer should look like but of his noble character. God had offered to make him the father of a nation, a prospect that most would have taken. Instead, he put thoughts of his glory aside and argued for God's reputation. His burden was that if the Lord destroyed Israel, then the enemy would mock the Lord and allege that He was not able to bring His people into the land as He had sworn to do. Prayer that is jealous for the Lord's name and glory will prevail. Moses prayed that God would pardon and He did. As remarkable as Moses's prayers are, they should point us to the One at God's right hand who ever lives to make intercession for us—One whose prayers are always answered. What encouragement do you find in that today?

Chapter 15

1. "Sin is the transgression of the law" (1 John 3:4). God's moral law is inflexible, timeless, universal, and unchangeable. Any violation of it constitutes sin and is subject to penalty, even those violations that are unintentional or accidental. Ignorance of the law is no excuse. God in His mercy and grace has made provision by which sins may be forgiven, and we should make use of that cleansing in Jesus Christ. But it is a reminder that we should also walk carefully lest even by carelessness we offend the Lord. In what ways might you be tempted to live carelessly?

2. The tassels on the hems of the garments were visible reminders to the people of the special relationship they had with the Lord. Every step they took reminded them of a relationship with the Lord their God that was based on His grace and redemption. The tassels also declared to others

that they belonged to the Lord, and must live as God's holy people. We no longer wear tassels but the Lord has given us something to look at to remind us of redemption and our obligation as the redeemed to be marked as different from the world. The Lord's Supper is a visible Word to declare these truths. How can observing the Lord's Supper help us to remember what Christ has done and who we are in Him?

3. God's sacrificial ordinances had a place for the Gentile. Those foreigners who embraced Israel's God on the grounds of the shed blood were as fully accepted as those of Israel. The Lord testified, "as ye are, so shall the stranger be before the Lord" (v. 15)—both the believing Jew and Gentile are children of God by faith in Christ Jesus (Gal. 3:28–29). Rejoice in the Lord's lack of favoritism!

4. The man gathering sticks on the Sabbath day was stoned to death. The ungodly object to the severity of the penalty, yet in this manner the Lord teaches that "the soul that sinneth, it shall die" (Ezek. 18:4). God's law demands perfect obedience; disobedience will bring the wrath of God. Thank God for the perfect obedience of Christ for therein lies our shelter from the terrible stroke of judgment.

Chapter 16

1. Korah's rebellion teaches the necessity of the divinely chosen Mediator. Trying to get to God otherwise is fatal. The rebellion of Korah, Dathan, and Abiram was an attempt to usurp the divinely appointed priesthood. Consequently, the attempt was answered with holy wrath. Aaron's priesthood typified Christ's. The lessons are clear. Man cannot approach God on his own because his sin is too great and God's

holiness is too glorious. The punishment for standing alone before God is eternally severe. Korah's death was unusual and inescapable, teaching us to fear the Lord. According to Matthew 10:28, what other reasons are we given for fearing God?

2. The plague that occurred after Korah's destruction teaches the effectiveness of the divinely chosen Mediator. After the drama of the burial and charred remains of the rebels, many accused God of not being fair because they had a faulty understanding of how holy God is and how sinful man is. So God's glory again was revealed in judgment. But Moses rushed to grace and instructed Aaron to stand between the living and the dead. The plague could not get past the priest. Here is the gospel lesson. God's wrath against sin is just, but God in grace sent His Son, the Mediator, to make atonement. Christ and the power of His sacrifice stands between the sinner and God's justice, and God's wrath cannot get past our great High Priest. Christ's sacrifice was successful. So this is our only hope: to have Christ stand between us and God. Are you trusting arrogantly in yourself or trusting dependently on the Mediator?

Chapter 17

1. Aaron's rod that budded teaches the uniqueness of the divinely chosen Mediator. It confirmed God's choice of Aaron and his line to be the priestly line in the old covenant, and it was to be kept as a reminder of that uniqueness. This all points to Christ, the eternal Priest (Ps. 110:4; Heb. 5). It underscores the vital truth that Christ is the only Mediator between God and men (1 Tim. 2:5), the only way by which man can be saved (John 14:6). Praise Him for His provision!

2. The rod was kept inside the ark (Heb. 9:4), where only God could see, for it declares that the covenant Mediator is always before Him. The central work of the High Priest is toward God, appearing in His presence for the sake of the people (Heb. 9:24). God sees His Son and the glorified scars of His atonement and remembers the covenant. What assurance does this give to those of us who are united with God's Son about our relationship with the Father?

3. For the sake of review put chapters 16–17 together for important lessons regarding the mediation of Christ. From the pit, we learn the necessity of the Mediator. From the plague, we learn the effectiveness of the Mediator. From the budding rod, we learn the uniqueness of the Mediator. Looking at John 14:6, how do these all come together in the person of Christ?

Chapter 18

1. His office having been vindicated, Aaron, along with his sons and the Levites, is now solemnly charged with preserving the sanctity of the tabernacle. Those whom God honors with office in His church He solemnly charges to preserve the holiness of His cause. Those who fail will "bear the iniquity of the sanctuary." They will be held accountable if they do not strive against sin. The ministry is a sacred task with extreme responsibility and accountability (James 3:1). Pray for your ministers that they may remain faithful to the charge to which God has called them.

2. The Levitical family was allowed a portion of the offerings of the people. Paul alludes to this provision and applies it to the support of God's servants in the New Testament church

(1 Cor. 9:13–14). Let none who are taught in the Word fail to provide for those who teach (Gal. 6:6). What can you do to show gratitude for the blessing of having a faithful minister?

Chapter 19

Death is the ultimate evidence of the curse of sin, and its effects are pervasive. But the beauty of the gospel is that God has devised the means to reverse the curse. The ashes of the red heifer and the water to be used for the ceremonial cleansings were shadows pointing to the real curse-reverser, the Lord Jesus. The red heifer was only a type, and the water of purification could only provide a symbolic cleansing. "The ashes of an heifer sprinkling the unclean, sanctifieth to the purifying of the flesh," but "the blood of Christ" can "purge your conscience from dead works to serve the living God" (Heb. 9:13–14). The red heifer was slain outside the camp, the place of the curse. This is a picture of Christ who "suffered without the gate" (Heb. 13:12). He was made a curse for us to give us a place in the camp of God. How can we find cleansing in Jesus Christ? How should a Christian wash his conscience daily?

Chapter 20

1. Because of his disobedience, Moses would not enter the Promised Land. God ordered him clearly to speak to the rock, yet Moses struck the rock twice instead (which symbolized Christ, 1 Cor. 10:4). The essence of Moses's sin was not how he handled the rod but how he spoke to the people (Num. 20:10; Ps. 106:32), driven by a heart that failed to

trust and honor God. The penalty seemed harsh, but his position of leadership increased his accountability. It is a reminder to us all how important it is to obey God completely so that all glory is His. Though the water was given when Moses smote the rock, yet it would have been a greater miracle and more glorifying to the Lord had the water been obtained as a result of simply speaking. Let us seek to do His will without fail for then the Lord will make known that He is the glorious and holy God. What are some ways that you have a responsibility to obey God exactly as He commands?

2. One of the great tragedies in this episode is that it was the new generation that grumbled and complained against Moses. The wilderness wanderings were about to end; the old generation was out and the new was in. This generation had seen over and over again the complaining of their parents and how God had disciplined them. But they had failed to learn the lessons. Proverbs 19:25 says, "Smite a scorner, and the simple will beware." The simple refer to those who should be easily influenced and taught. How have you learned from the sins and punishments of others?

Chapter 21

1. Meditating on Christ's comparison of Himself to the bronze serpent (John 3:15) teaches important lessons about sin (Num. 21:5). The people accused God of being evil, not good, in His ways toward them. They refused to be content with God's good provision of food and turned from it in disgust and ingratitude. The penalty was severe; the fiery serpents brought death. This is essentially what happened in the fall of man when he was tempted by another serpent:

he rejected God's goodness and provision in the garden and so broke His law (Gen. 3:1–6). We, the fallen children of Adam, validate this hatred of God every time we turn discontentedly from God's will and choose to sin. According to Revelation 21:8, what penalty do we face if we do not look to Christ for salvation?

2. Christ's analogy also teaches us lessons about salvation. Provision for dying sinners was made in the bronze serpent on the pole. The symbolic curse-reverser took the shape of the curse. So God sent His Son in the likeness of sinful flesh to deal with sin (Rom. 8:3). He had to be lifted up on the cross becoming the curse (Gal. 3:13). Appropriation of salvation happened by gazing at the serpent. Simply having the serpent on the pole was not enough; there had to be the look of faith. How does this help you understand your need for trust and faith in Christ alone for eternal life (John 3:15–16)?

Chapter 22

1. All of these events were happening behind Israel's back. They had no knowledge of the conspiracy that was being schemed against them. But what was unknown to Israel was openly known to God. It is a wonderful blessing to know that God is with us when we are in the midst of difficulties and dangers. Here we learn that God's protection extends to unknown dangers as well. The extent to which God has kept us from danger is something we may never know (Ps. 139:5–6). Take time to rejoice and be thankful for these truths.

2. God is not fickle; unlike a sorcerer-for-hire, He cannot be paid off to change His ways. God's blessing is irreversible. No one can curse what God has blessed (v. 12). The

unchanging and constant truth for everyone united to Christ is "if God be for us, who can be against us?" (Rom. 8:31). How can these truths help us when it seems that everything is against us and when the enemy gloats over our failures and desires our demise?

Chapter 23

1. Balaam's efforts to curse Israel highlight some amazing realities about God's blessings on His covenant people. (1) God's people are special: they dwell alone (v. 9). All the earth is the Lord's but His people are unique; there is no people like God's people. (2) God's people are saved, redeemed from bondage by power, by blood, and by grace (v. 22). (3) God's people are strong (v. 24), like a strong beast, powerful and relentless in the pursuit of prey. Grace has made the believer capable of doing all things through Christ, more than conquerors through Him. (4) God's people are serene (v. 10). There is a peace for believers in death that the wicked can only envy. (5) God's people are secure (vv. 21, 23). Those whom God has blessed cannot be cursed now; they will be free from the curse forever (Rom. 8:31–39). Balaam confessed "he hath blessed; and I cannot reverse it" (Num. 23:20). This was really Satan's admission of defeat. Believer, how can you keep the knowledge of the irreversible blessing that you have in Christ before you every day?

2. The exclamation "What hath God wrought!" (v. 23) stands over the whole chapter. It was because God is who He is that Israel was protected from Balaam's efforts to curse. The whole episode highlights three truths about God worthy of meditation. (1) He is sovereign, a king in the midst

(v. 21). His sovereignty is evident in His choice of Israel (no inherent worth), His use of Balaam (contrary to his will and efforts), His use of a donkey (contrary to nature), and His dominion over nations then and nations to come. (2) He is immutable (v. 19). It is because He does not change that Jacob is not consumed (Mal. 3:6). (3) He is active (Num. 23:23). God is not a spectator rooting for His people; He is actively engaged on their behalf. His activity covers the past (v. 22), the present (v. 21), and the future (24:8). Rejoice that Israel's God is our God and He neither slumbers nor sleeps (Ps. 121:3–4).

Chapter 24

Balaam tried his best to curse Israel, but God used him to utter grand prophecies concerning His unfailing promise of Christ (vv. 17–19). Under the forced influence of God's Spirit, Balaam declared that all the promises of God are yea and amen in Christ. The welfare of Israel by covenant was linked to Christ, and so it is for every true believer. He declared two particular truths about the coming Messiah. The "Star" title declares the glory of Christ. All the radiant glory of God is in the face of Jesus Christ. The "Scepter" declares the might of Christ, His royal authority. This is a fuller development of Jacob's prophecy of the scepter or kingship being in Judah (Gen. 49:10). He will crush every enemy from then until the distant future. This victory is not just by the coming judgment, but is evidenced every time a sinner surrenders to King Jesus, being conquered by His grace. In a sense every conversion marks a fulfillment of Balaam's prophecy. Christ links Jacob's and Balaam's prophecies when He says, "I am the root and the offspring of David, and the bright and morning star" (Rev. 22:16). Is Christ shining in your heart? Is He ruling as your King?

Chapter 25

1. The fornication committed by Israel with the daughters of Moab was followed by idolatry. One sin leads to another. When the visible church gives way to the fleshly allurements of a corrupt world, it will not be long until she entertains and joins with its false religion. Purity of life and purity in worship go hand in hand. How are you guarding the purity of yourself, your family, and your church?

3. Phinehas was not deterred by the failure of others. The judge of this tribe of Simeon failed to carry out the command, thus Phinehas acted. What a dreadful day when there is no man to stand in the gap to deal with sin (Ezek. 22:30–31)! But the Lord had His Phinehas. Pray for Christlike men to stand and deal with sin and turn away the judgments of God.

3. Phinehas's zeal was like his God's, for literally the Lord said he was "zealous with my zeal" (v. 11). He had imbibed the nature of his God, who is a jealous God. Indeed this is one of His names (Ex. 34:14). He is jealous for His own holiness, and Phinehas had the same holy jealousy in his soul. What does God's holy jealousy desire for the people of God today? (See 2 Cor. 11:2.)

Chapter 26

1. Those who died in the rebellion incited by Korah "became a sign" (v. 10). They were monuments of justice and served as an example both then and now (see comments in the

Worship Sections for chs. 16–17). That the children of Korah did not die in the overthrow (26:11) stands out as a monument of divine mercy. Obviously they had not partaken of their father's sin and so did not die as God's law stipulated (Deut. 24:16). Every man will be judged for his own sin. Neither the sins of your parents nor their godliness will determine your eternal destiny. What will determine whether or not you escape the wrath that swallows up the ungodly and disobedient? (See Titus 3.)

2. In this second numbering there was not one of those adult men who had been numbered at Sinai, except for Caleb and Joshua. God had sworn that they would surely die and so it came to pass (vv. 64–65). The divine Word that threatens judgment for sin will certainly be executed. Do not cling to the empty notion that you will escape the due reward of your evil deeds if you do not repent. It took almost forty years for the completion of the divine sentence, but it was completed. Judgment delayed is not judgment denied. Why must unrepentant sinners certainly be punished?

Chapter 27

1. Zelophehad's daughters wanted a place for their father's name to continue in the Promised Land. He was a sinner, but had not forfeited his familial inheritance. However, they needed a mediator to bring their case to the Lord. So Moses brought their cause before the Lord, and they received their portion. This illustrates the need of sinners who on their own have no inheritance in heaven with the saints. They, too, need a mediator, and the only Mediator is the Lord Jesus Christ. According to 2 Corinthians 5:20, what part can you

play in bringing others to understand the work of Christ on their behalf?

2. Moses was a most selfless man. When the Lord reminded him that he was not permitted to enter Canaan, his only concern was that there would be a man to bring Israel into their possession. He did not want the Lord's people to be "as sheep which have no shepherd" (v. 17). This is the compassionate spirit of Christ (Matt. 9:36–38). The Lord indicated to Moses that Joshua was the man qualified to lead Israel. But the only quality He underlined was that Joshua had the Spirit in him (Num. 27:18). When a man has the Spirit of God filling him he will have everything required to minister. Spirit-filled men are always the need of the hour (Acts 6:3). Are you prepared to serve?

Chapter 28

1. The constant repetition of the sacrifices in the old dispensation was evidence of their inherent ineffectiveness to address the sin problem and pointed to the need for the once-and-for-all sacrifice of Jesus Christ (Heb. 10:1–4). This is a key argument in the book of Hebrews to show the superiority of Christ and His sacrifice over the priests and sacrifices in the old order. Yet they were graphic pictures of the necessity of blood shedding if man were to be accepted before the Lord (Heb. 9:22). From the old we can learn the necessity of atonement by the death of a substitute. Rejoice that Christ, the spotless Lamb of God, has offered Himself as the only atonement that directly and finally satisfies God for sins.

2. On the "day of the firstfruits" (v. 26) a new meat offering was brought to the Lord, an offering of thankfulness. The

feast in view is the Feast of Pentecost when the Holy Spirit was poured out and a great harvest of sinners was gathered to the Lord by the apostles. Those converted were the first fruits of a great harvest still to come, a harvest that continues to be gathered and is presented to Christ continually. Read Ephesians 1:15–16 and then offer your own offering of thanks for those in your life who have been converted.

Chapter 29

1. The blowing of the trumpets that called the congregation together suggests a couple of important principles of worship. First, corporate worship is important. When the trumpets sounded the people gathered together. Likewise, we are not to forsake the assembling together (Heb. 10:25). Mutual exhortation and edification is important. Second, worship requires a frame of mind that is free from the distractions of life. Hence, they were to refrain from their normal occupations to have the time and mindset to worship. Thus observing the Sabbath is a key component of worship. How can you free yourself from the normal routines of life so that you are able to think about spiritual matters with undivided attention in your weekly worship services?

2. The repetition of the details for the various offerings and particularly the eight days of the Feast of Tabernacles teach the vital lesson that we must worship the Lord according to His revealed will. The fallen, fleshly mind cannot be trusted, so the Lord leaves no room for figuring out on our own how to worship Him. We are too susceptible to deception and to deviation from the Lord's mind. While we can thank God that new covenant worship does not have such complicated

ceremonies to follow, we should also thank God that still today the church has clear instructions in the Scriptures about how God commands us to worship. How are we tempted to add to them or subtract from them?

Chapter 30

1. The solemn comment about the one who made a vow was, "He shall not break his word" (v. 2). A believer's word should be his oath. A Christian essentially is one who claims to have bound himself to the Lord, so he must be careful not to violate that claim. "He shall do according to all that proceedeth out of his mouth" (v. 2) is a striking reminder of the Lord, who keeps His word and will never alter it (Ps. 89:34). Let us be conformed to His image in everything (Rom. 8:29), including the words of our mouths. In what ways are you tempted to fail to live consistently with what you have said?

2. In the making of vows, daughters were under the jurisdiction of fathers, and wives under husbands. In this manner it was shown that the man is to be the head of his house and is to guide prudently and properly (1 Cor. 11:3; Eph. 5:23). It is not a position of dictatorship, but it is a position of authority that demands spiritual perception and maturity. The responsibility to lead others on the proper path is daunting and one that requires dependence on the Lord. Pray that God will help you to fulfill your role in a way that honors Him.

Chapter 31

1. God gave the command for Israel to take just vengeance on the Midianites because vengeance belongs to Him (Deut. 32:35). By the deceptions of the Midianite women the men

of Israel had been seduced into immorality and idol worship. Now the divine dictate came for divine vengeance. Sinner, remember that "God is not mocked: for whatsoever a man soweth, that shall he also reap" (Gal. 6:7). How have you seen this principle at work in your own life or the lives of those around you?

2. This battle also marked God's vengeance against Balaam. He expressed his desire earlier that he would die the death of the righteous (23:10). But tragically, what a sad end he met! He had sold himself to do evil. Even when God frustrated him from pronouncing a curse on Israel, he schemed against them. He forsook the right way and went astray (2 Peter 2:15), and eventually his sin found him out. Hypocrisy can only have one of two ends: true repentance or total destruction. How do hypocrites fool themselves into thinking they will escape judgment? Why are they fools to think so?

3. Of all those who went to war against Midian, not one was lost (v. 49). Consequently, the officers of Israel's army brought an offering of thanks to the Lord for their preservation in the battle. They were fighting the Lord's battle, and the Lord preserved them. Engagement in warfare for the Lord does not necessarily guarantee exemption from casualties, but it does ensure victory for all those enlisted in the Lord's army. How can this serve to encourage you as you fight the good fight?

Chapter 32

1. Moses put a very relevant question to Reuben, Gad, and the half tribe of Manasseh who had gained their inheritance easily on the east of Jordan: "Shall your brethren go to war,

and shall ye sit here?" (v. 6). Christ's body is one, thus none can be at ease when other members are facing conflict. We are to bear one another's burdens and remember those in bonds as though we are bound with them. There is a unity in the body of Christ that cannot be overlooked and should be cherished. How are you fighting alongside other Christians to support them in their spiritual battles?

2. "Be sure your sin will find you out" (v. 23) is a classic text with a sobering message. The consequences of sin will catch up to the sinner eventually. Some men's sins are openly found out in this life. But the sins of all who die impenitent will be found out at the great day of judgment. Then the Lord will bring to light the hidden things of darkness and will judge the secrets of men by Jesus Christ. Cover your sins and you will not prosper. Read Psalm 51, then spend some time confessing and forsaking your sins and resting in God's great mercy.

Chapter 33

1. The Lord commanded the record of the journeys of Israel from Egypt to Canaan. God's people are to keep in mind all the ways in which the Lord leads them, both as individuals and especially through the history of His people. God led them out of Egypt through every turn and circle through the wilderness. There were times when Israel thought that they were lost; where they were did not make any sense. But Moses makes it clear that God led them all the way. Even though the trek goes through the wilderness of trouble, looking back makes it clear that goodness and mercy followed

them all the days of their lives. How does this encourage you as you move ahead?

2. Once they entered the land, Israel was to drive out the inhabitants of Canaan and destroy the relics of their idolatry. Toleration of their enemies would place God's people in jeopardy. Likewise, sin must be put to death in the lives of the saints. If not it will vex the soul and rob of the Lord's blessing. Every true Christian has crucified the flesh with its affections and lusts and labors to progressively kill remaining sin in his life. What sins and inward idols do you regularly confront that you must destroy?

Chapter 34

1. The Lord set Israel's borders. He appoints the bounds of our earthly existence in space, time, and influence (Job 14:5; Ps. 31:15; Dan. 4:25, 35; Acts 17:26). There is a border to life in this world that cannot be passed for "it is appointed unto men once to die" (Heb. 9:27). As you recognize the limits within which God has placed you, are you able to live with contentment within them and know that all is well with your soul?

2. The delineation of Israel's border began and ended at "the salt sea" (the Dead Sea, vv. 3, 12). The salt sea was an enduring monument of the destruction of Sodom and Gomorrah (Gen. 19; Deut. 29:23). In this manner Israel had at their border a reminder not to cross the boundaries of God's law, a warning of the destruction that sin brings. How has God given you reminders of the consequences of sin? How can you use them like boundaries that hold you from evil?

3. The land of Canaan was comparatively small, nothing like the great empires that rose and fell in the Ancient Near East. Its smallness reminds the saints that, though they may possess little in this world, they are to be content. How can they do that? They must stay focused on the "better country, that is, an heavenly" inheritance, just as the patriarchs did (Heb. 11:16). Great lands and wealth will slip from the rich man's fingers at death, but the Christian will receive, "an inheritance incorruptible, and undefiled, and that fadeth not away, reserved in heaven" (1 Peter 1:4). How should this help you live in contentment?

Chapter 35

1. Israel was commanded to provide cities as dwelling places for the Levites, the ministers of God. Thus, God clearly reveals that His servants are to be supported by His people. They who preach the gospel should live by the gospel—this the Lord has ordained (1 Cor. 9:13–14). How well does your church provide for its pastor?

2. Christ is the sinner's city of refuge. Every sinner desperately needs to flee for refuge to lay hold on the hope set before men in Jesus Christ, the great High Priest (Heb. 6:18–20). His death releases sinners from the danger of divine vengeance so that they may return from their exile back to God. Even if you have not physically murdered anyone, your heart contains the inner murder of hatred and sinful anger (Matt. 5:21–22; 1 John 3:15). Go to Christ at once and find refuge for your soul.

3. The city of refuge was not only for the Israelite but for the stranger and sojourner (v. 15), revealing the glorious

truth that the gospel is for the Gentile as well as the Jew. Irrespective of the differences that exist among men, all who enter into Christ are one and enjoy the same privileges. In Christ there is no difference. How should that affect the way Christians evangelize and welcome people of other nations and ethnicities?

Chapter 36

1. If the daughters of Zelophehad married into other tribes, that part of the inheritance of Manasseh would have been lost. The leaders of God's work should be watchful lest any part of what the Lord has given His people should be forfeited. Our spiritual inheritance has been dearly won. Let us seek by wisdom and prudence to retain and enjoy it. This issue pertaining to Zelophehad's daughters resulted in an injunction for every Israelite. Each man was to cleave or cling intensely and faithfully to "the inheritance of the tribe of his fathers" (v. 7). How can we cleave to the Lord's inheritance and preserve God's work as a whole?

2. The daughters of Zelophehad were to marry within their own tribe, as the Lord commanded. Personal choices must be governed by more than personal desires; we must take into consideration the needs of others, especially our families and churches. This is especially true of whom we marry. This principle illustrates the point that God's people are to marry only those who are their people in the spiritual sense. They are to marry in the Lord and not be yoked together with unbelievers (1 Cor. 7:39; 2 Cor. 6:14). Disobedience in this matter will usually bring sorrow to the entire family.

Deuteronomy

Chapter 1

1. God led Israel "as a man doth bear [carry] his son" (v. 31). This picture of God's loving care should inspire love and trust for Him. "He shall feed his flock like a shepherd: he shall gather the lambs with his arm, and carry them in his bosom, and shall gently lead those that are with young" (Isa. 40:11). Our Good Shepherd seeks the lost sheep, "and when he hath found it, he layeth it on his shoulders, rejoicing" (Luke 15:4–6).

2. God set the land before Israel and instructed her to take it (1:21), but Israel hesitated, yielded to human wisdom (v. 22), then succumbed to human fear (vv. 26–27) and unbelief (v. 32), resulting in loss of blessing (vv. 34–39), rebellion (vv. 26, 40–43), defeat (v. 44), and alienation from God (v. 45). God's people must take Him at His Word (Prov. 3:5). Caleb "wholly followed the LORD" (Deut. 1:36). He and Joshua, a tiny minority, entered Canaan. Obedience may be a lonely, bumpy road, but its travelers always reach their destination. Why is it necessary to trust in God's wisdom if we will obey Him over the long term?

Chapter 2

1. Moses told Israel that God "knoweth thy walking through this great wilderness" (v. 7). God knew their experience, for He was with them in the cloud and fire (Ex. 40:34–38). It is comforting to know that "the Word was made flesh, and

dwelt among us" (John 1:14); that Christ was made like His people (Rom. 8:3; Heb. 2:17) to experience the believer's plight in this sin-cursed wilderness. "For in that he himself hath suffered being tempted, he is able to succour them that are tempted" (Heb. 2:18). Christian, how can this comfort you, to know that the Lord understands your experience and has suffered Himself?

2. "For indeed the hand of the LORD was against them, to destroy them from among the host, until they were consumed" (v. 15). Disobedience wreaks horrible consequences. Even among God's people, those who rebelled made themselves God's enemies. They became the focus of God's progressive elimination, until all were gone.

Chapter 3

1. God gave to Israel "all Bashan, which was called the land of giants" (v. 13). God would have His people remember the magnitude of His power to save. They went against giants and prevailed. Though God may lead His people into circumstances that appear insurmountable, they can be overcome when undertaken with God's help (Eph. 6:12–17).

2. For forty years Moses led Israel through desolate wilderness, bringing them to the edge of Canaan. But one reason Moses himself could not enter was because the people had rebelled in unbelief at Kadesh-barnea (v. 26). Although Moses speaks to the children of those who rebelled, he reminds them of the price he is paying for their parents' sin. He speaks as if they and their parents are one, stressing again the unity of Israel. It is important to remember that

our unbelief and rebellion affect others (1:37; 4:21). How have your sins hurt others?

Chapter 4

1. God's love is inseparable from His omnipotence. It is therefore effective in all of His purposes. His love for Abraham, Isaac, and Jacob (Mal. 1:1–4; Rom. 9:10–13) brought Israel into Canaan (Deut. 4:37) and will bring all of His elect to glorification. Believers are sons of God because the Father bestowed His love upon them (1 John 3:1–2). He has loved believers with an everlasting love (Jer. 31:3). Why are both God's love and His power necessary for the hope of believers to be secure?

2. If a stranger who never saw your father purported to draw a picture of him, you might be offended. Should not this be our response when imagination produces drawings of unseen persons of the godhead? Such misrepresentation of God was one reason graven images were prohibited. Revelation, not imagination, is the only legitimate portrait of God. Ultimately, the only legitimate image or manifestation of God is Jesus Christ, the eternal Son of God (Heb. 1:3).

Chapter 5

1. At Mt. Sinai the people could not bear the terrifying manifestation of God. They needed a mediator. God provided in Moses a foreshadowing of Christ, who was given to be the one Mediator between God and men (1 Tim. 2:5). He is our only access unto God (John 14:6), by whom we come to God with confidence (Heb. 4:14–16).

2. Israel was awestruck in God's presence. So are the seraphim and inspired prophets (Isa. 6:1–5). Worship should manifest this sense of wonder and awe. It is not a venue for entertainment or novelties, but a time when the realization of our inadequacy compels us to desire the one Mediator, Jesus Christ, and to offer Him humble adoration.

3. God's law is given to aid, not to burden. Man's religion lays burdens upon people, but God's laws, given by grace, are given "that it may be well with you" (v. 33). What are some ways that keeping the Ten Commandments brings blessing to a person's life?

Chapter 6

1. We need continual God-consciousness. Israel was commanded to talk of God's laws, to bind them to their hands and to write them upon their houses (Ex. 13:9, 16; Deut. 6:7–10; 11:18–21). In Christ's day this was observed, yet without conscience toward God (Matt. 23:1–5). Righteous people meditate on God's law day and night (Pss. 1:2; 119:97–99). They "pray without ceasing" (1 Thess. 5:17). Their lives are a growing exercise in God-consciousness.

2. God's law is never a burden but a delight for those who love God (Pss. 1:2; 119:70; 1 John 5:3). This was Christ's testimony through the psalmist (Ps. 40:8; Heb. 10:5–7) when He was made "under the law" (Gal. 4:4–5) and did only those things that pleased the Father (John 8:29). He came to fulfill it (Matt. 5:17) because it was delightful to Him. How can God's people cultivate their delight in the written Word and communion with the living Word, Jesus Christ?

3. This chapter is a great summary of the theme of total devotion to God. The imperative of devotion is to love God completely (v. 5). The logic of devotion is based on who God is (the one true God, v. 4) and what God has done in redeeming His people (vv. 12, 20–23). The performance of devotion includes fearing God (vv. 2, 13, 24), serving Him (v. 13), obeying Him (vv. 6, 17, 25), and remembering Him (vv. 7–9, 12).

Chapter 7

1. God's zeal for holiness compels us to forsake the ways of wicked people. We are not to be fascinated by their gods. Israel was to destroy images, not to keep gold or silver parts of an idol. These would have been valuable in Israel's economy, but their association with idols was repugnant to God, so they were to be destroyed. We must recognize God's abhorrence of things that seduce man's devotion, and hate the things God hates.

2. God's delivering over the Canaanites and Israel's smiting the Canaanites (v. 2; 9:3) illustrate what happens in sanctification. God assured the victory, but Israel had to fight. Similarly, on the one hand, sin has been thoroughly defeated by Christ, who crushed the serpent's head. By faith we live in the reality of Christ's victory by not allowing sin to have dominion over us (Rom. 6:1–14). What sins do you need to conquer? How must you look to Christ for victory? How must you fight?

3. God's sovereign dominion extends to every creature. Even insects serve His kingdom. It is edifying to contemplate those instances where He utilized animals for His purposes

(Ex. 8; 10; Num. 21:5–9; 22:21–31; 1 Sam. 6:7–14; 1 Kings 17:2–7; Dan. 6:16–24; Jonah 1–2; Luke 5:1–11; John 21:5–11).

Chapter 8

1. "They that will be rich fall into temptation and a snare, and into many foolish and hurtful lusts" (1 Tim. 6:9). God's goodness to Israel included abundance (Deut. 8:7–10). But blessings can be perverted in curses by forgetting that they are God-given (v. 17). Thus, the church of Laodicea said, "I am rich," ignorant that it was "wretched, and miserable, and poor, and blind, and naked" (Rev. 3:17). How can you guard your heart from this?

2. God does not always take His people on an easy path. He led Israel through the wilderness. Serpents and scorpions assaulted; drought and hunger oppressed. But trials were for their good, to humble them and to expose what was in their hearts. God purposes all things to conform His people to the image of His Son (Rom. 8:28–29). Christ Himself faced the most severe trials of all, and overcame them (Matt. 4:1–11; Heb. 5:7–9).

Chapter 9

1. Israel "turned aside quickly out of the way" (v. 16). How quickly we are ensnared in sin! Our lusts war against our souls (1 Peter 2:11), and we remain one thought away from yielding. Satan is swift like a lion, so we must be sober and vigilant (1 Peter 5:8). "Wherefore let him that thinketh he standeth take heed lest he fall" (1 Cor. 10:12). How can we strive to be humble and watchful against sin?

2. Great men will be great in prayer. When God offered to make Moses the father of a greater nation, replacing Israel, he prayed for Israel's preservation. His prayers were self-denying. He prayed persistently (forty days with fasting), and powerfully: "the LORD hearkened unto me" (v. 19). The intercessory prayer of Moses points to the even greater intercession of Christ on behalf of His people. In a sense, Israel owed their existence to the intercession of Moses. Believers owe all to Christ, who ever lives to make intercession for us.

Chapter 10

1. "Fear the LORD thy God" (vv. 12, 20). Reverent awe of our Creator will result in obedience, love, and service for God. The fear of the Lord is the beginning of wisdom and knowledge (Ps. 111:10; Prov. 1:7; 9:10). It hates evil (Prov. 8:13), prolongs life (Prov. 10:27), and brings prosperity (Prov. 14:26–27; 16:6; 19:23; 22:4). The Spirit of Christ is the Spirit of the fear of the Lord (Isa. 11:2). Why is the fear of God right for those in Christ?

2. "What doth the LORD thy God require of thee?" (v. 12). This question must penetrate the conscience. Nothing else matters. God is worthy of wholehearted devotion, "with all thy heart and with all thy soul" (v. 12). Significantly, right in the middle of the five things God requires is to love Him, the greatest of all the commandments. "Thou shalt love the Lord thy God with all thy heart, and with all thy soul, and with all thy mind, and with all thy strength: this is the first commandment" (Mark 12:30).

Chapter 11

1. That God gives rain in recognition of Israel's obedience demonstrates His sovereign power and authority. God is the author of both biblical law and natural law. Thus, they harmonize, and obedience to the former will usually be in sync with the latter, producing blessing. Psalm 1 illustrates the principle: attention to God's Word results in divine blessing, here symbolized by the appropriate and timely rain.

2. Although possessing Canaan would involve military conflict, Israel's preparation to enter Canaan did not involve basic training in combat, but was rather to focus on spiritual readiness. God would deliver Canaan to Israel, and they were simply to follow Him to victory. He must therefore be their highest priority, demonstrated by obedience to His commandments. Israel's strength was in that obedience (v. 8). The strength of Christ's church is not in human schemes and methods, but by wholehearted adherence to God's Word.

Chapter 12

1. Israel was not to ask, "How did these nations serve their gods?" (v. 30). God's people must never pattern their worship after unregenerate men. True worship is done according to the directives of God's law—the Scriptures. Worship is defined and designed by God, not by man (v. 32). When seeking a church in which to worship, many look for one that pleases them. But we should ask, "Does it please God? Does it worship by the Word?"

2. Israel was to destroy every place where idolatry was practiced, to leave nothing of ungodly religious activity. So we must "have no fellowship with the unfruitful works of

darkness, but rather reprove them" (Eph. 5:11). We must separate ourselves from the idolatry and uncleanness of this world (2 Cor. 6:16–17). What idols does your nation worship? How must you separate yourself from this idolatry?

Chapter 13

1. Satan will employ our dearest friends to distract us from God: "thy brother…or thy son, or thy daughter, or the wife of thy bosom, or thy friend, which is as thine own soul" (v. 6). Judas was one of Christ's disciples. Jesus warned, "If any man come to me, and hate not his father, and mother, and wife, and children, and brethren, and sisters, yea, and his own life also, he cannot be my disciple" (Luke 14:26). Nadab and Abihu, Aaron's sons, were destroyed for their godless action, and God forbade Aaron to mourn (Lev. 10:1–6). Allegiance to Christ must supersede all other relationships (Luke 9:59–62). How can you prepare your heart now to follow Christ above all others when temptation comes?

2. False teachers do not announce that they are deceivers. Rather, they come with an "improvement" to the gospel message, with a "truth" everyone else has missed. Jesus said, "Beware of false prophets, which come to you in sheep's clothing, but inwardly they are ravening wolves" (Matt. 7:15). Like Paul, Christians must recognize and reject false teachers, for they are under the curse of God (Gal. 1:8; 2:1–5).

Chapter 14

1. God's people must be separated unto Him. This was prescribed in Israel's customs of mourning (v. 1), their diet (vv. 2–21), and their tithes (vv. 22–29). We are not to be

poured into the world's mold: "be not conformed to this world: but be ye transformed by the renewing of your mind" (Rom. 12:2). We are not to love this world or its traditions and fads, which consist of "the lust of the flesh, and the lust of the eyes, and the pride of life" (1 John 2:16). As Israel was a holy people unto the Lord, chosen to be a peculiar people (Deut. 14:2), God's people in every age are "an holy nation, a peculiar people; that ye should shew forth the praises of him who hath called you out of darkness into his marvelous light" (1 Peter 2:9). Christians must be different, as pilgrims in this world.

2. God's goodness is evident in His care for the needy (Matt. 6:25–34). He designated that every third year the tithe be used for widows, orphans, and aliens who had no land on which to cultivate food (Deut. 14:28–29). He instructed that grain in the corners of fields be left for the needy to glean (Lev. 19:9–10; 23:22). Believers should honor this principle. They must "remember the poor" (Gal. 2:10), and "visit the fatherless and widows in their affliction" (James 1:27). Whereas this is not the gospel, it is an important part of Christian living. How are you caring for the poor and needy?

Chapter 15

1. Christ came "not to be ministered unto, but to minister, and to give his life a ransom for many" (Matt. 20:28). This spirit should thrive within God's people. The law required creditors to forgive debtors (Deut. 15:1–2), avoid greed (vv. 7–11), show compassion toward the poor, release bond slaves, and supply them with life's necessities (vv. 12–14). From their herds and flocks they gave their first and best

unto God. All of these requirements were fulfilled to the fullest by Christ. Therefore, strive to be conformed to the image of God's Son (Rom. 8:29).

2. When servants were released, the master shared his bounty with them: "wherewith the LORD thy God hath blessed thee thou shalt give unto him" (v. 14). This demonstrated that possessions come from God, that "the earth is the LORD's, and the fulness thereof" (Ps. 24:1), and that man is but a steward of God's possessions. We are to treat everything within our sphere of influence as the Lord's, not our own. How will this change the way we use our money and possessions?

Chapter 16

1. God instructed men of Israel to assemble three times annually for feasts: Passover, Weeks, and Tabernacles (v. 16; Ex. 34:23–24). One reason for this was to maintain national and spiritual unity among Israel. It is important for God's people to assemble, and He commands this. Attendance at public worship should be a priority with every believer, just as it is with God. How is our public worship like a feast?

2. God also established the feasts to memorialize His works for Israel. God desires that we remember His works. "Bless the LORD, O my soul, and forget not all his benefits" (Ps. 103:2). "I meditate on all thy works" (Ps. 143:5). Remembering God's works reminded Israel to remember His law (Deut. 8:11). God would have us remember His great work when Christ fulfilled the law through His sacrifice at Calvary. God has given us two (and only two) visible means of remembering Christ's work: baptism and the Lord's Supper.

Chapter 17

1. God's instruction to kings pertained to personal discipline and obeying God's law, not to skill in governing. "When the righteous are in authority, the people rejoice: but when the wicked beareth rule, the people mourn" (Prov. 29:2; cf. 2 Sam. 23:3). The ideal of a perfectly righteous king points to King Jesus, who alone fulfilled all the requirements of God's expectation. What does Deuteronomy 17:16–20 teach us about the kingdom of Christ?

2. Two or more accusers were necessary to convict a man of a crime. This protected the innocent who might be accused and also restrained the schemer who might bear false witness out of jealousy or hatred. It also shows the high value God places upon truth. He is truth. God and truth are inseparable, thus truth will always stand.

Chapter 18

1. False prophets "presume to speak a word in my name" (v. 20). Christ warned that there will be many of these (Matt. 7:22–23). The test of their legitimacy is whether they do "the will of my Father which is in heaven" (Matt. 7:21). The will of God is revealed in Scripture; thus, teachers must be measured by its truth. It is imperative that we know what God says in His Word in order to guard against the false teaching that is more and more rampant as time progresses (1 Tim. 4:1; 1 John 4:1–2).

2. Priests and Levites were sustained by the offerings brought to God. This should have been a guard against greed, of which ministers are warned (1 Tim. 6:6–11). However, the Old Testament records violations of the principle (1 Sam.

2:12–17). Although the mechanics of application are different today, this remains the pattern of sustaining ministers (Matt. 10:9–10; Gal. 6:6; 1 Thess. 5:13; 1 Tim. 5:17–18). Will the Lord commend your church on judgment day for how it paid its pastor? Why or why not?

Chapter 19

1. God authored Israel's judicial plan and specified who its judges should be (16:18). God also prescribed the penalty for one who defended a false claim before those judges (19:16–19). To appear before the judges was to appear in God's court. An intentional misrepresentation there exhibited unbelief and contempt toward God Himself. Ultimately, deceit assaults God, the author of justice. God is truth, and every lie is against Him. Are you lying about something? What will repentance involve?

2. Without uttering a word, you can tell a lie: removing an established landmark (v. 14) misrepresented property boundaries. As long as that misrepresentation stood, the perpetrator lived a lie without speaking a word. Often people have misrepresented truth by various means of fraud and deception. But ultimately, the Lord is a God of truth (32:4), so the truth will prevail.

Chapter 20

1. God ordered utter destruction of Canaanite peoples, "that they teach you not to do after all their abominations" (v. 18). Idolatry was Israel's greatest threat and had to be eliminated, whether idol, shrine, or idolater. God is zealous for His undivided honor and for the purity of His people. That zeal

instructs us, "Love not the world, neither the things that are in the world. If any man love the world, the love of the Father is not in him" (1 John 2:15). The church does not kill sinners by the sword, but it must kill its sin by the Word.

2. The end of all war will come from the Prince of Peace, and Israel was the conduit through which He would come to mankind. Israel's advantage of having divine counsel in war ensured that end. It secured Christ's coming by annihilating peoples who would annihilate Israel via war or idolatry. Therefore foreign threats were subjugated (vv. 10–11), enemies rendered powerless (vv. 12–15), and idolatrous occupants of Canaan destroyed (vv. 16–18).

Chapter 21

1. The regulations for treating a captive or hated wife demonstrate the importance of kindness and equity to all. These women were in circumstances beyond their control and for which they were not responsible. To add to their misery, unfair and cruel acts violated the second greatest commandment to love your neighbor as yourself. God is concerned with protecting innocent victims of injustice, and we should follow His example. How are women mistreated today? What would God have us do?

2. Disobeying parents equates to disobeying God: "Honour thy father and thy mother: that thy days may be long upon the land" (Ex. 20:12). When respect for parents is gone, the root of respect in society has perished, jeopardizing all. Consequently, in Israel's theocracy, the rebellious son was a menace to civilization and was to be put to death by the society he threatened. Disruption in the family is no longer

a capital offense, but it remains a serious threat to the welfare of society. Family structure and harmony should be a high priority in every Christian home.

Chapter 22

1. We have a community responsibility for others' possessions (vv. 1–4). God instructed Israel to be attentive to the welfare of straying livestock or overly burdened beasts. Cain's question, "Am I my brother's keeper" (Gen. 4:9), is hereby answered. It was disobedience to ignore the straying beast. If care must be taken for an animal, how much more is it to be taken for a human (Luke 14:1–6)? Why is sharing responsibility to care for each others' lives and property foundational for society?

2. Sexual purity is very important. Violators suffered severe penalties, and lies against an innocent person were punished. The matter of immorality was serious. Nations surrounding Israel were grossly immoral, and their idolatrous practices often included perverse actions as worship. The value God places upon sexual purity cannot be overstated, and the warnings of the law are reiterated in the New Testament (1 Cor. 6:9–10, 15–18). Marriage is a holy union of man and woman, and only within that union are sexual relations sanctified.

Chapter 23

1. God is concerned for the purity of His congregation (vv. 1–6, 17–18). Consequently, groups of people were excluded from the congregation of Israel. A church must not purpose to have a large congregation so much as a pure one. Purity must be of highest concern for all of God's people. Since a little leaven leavens the whole lump, the church

must discipline and ultimately expel the unrepentant sinner (1 Cor. 5:6).

2. God warns against stinginess and opportunism (vv. 24–25). Crops could be eaten by one passing by, helping travelers and widows, but only for immediate necessity; no supply could be taken. This implies that we are to be charitable in giving, but not selfish with others' charity. This illustrates the second greatest commandment to love our neighbor as ourselves. How are you sharing a portion of what God gives you with those in need?

Chapter 24

1. Powerless people are often abused, but God condemns the abuser. We are to help the powerless in their distress, never adding to their burden. Throughout Christ's ministry He helped and healed beggars and the afflicted, people who were at the bottom of the economic hierarchy. Deacons were appointed to address these needs (Acts 6), and the apostles were mindful of this duty (Gal. 2:10; James 2:1–9; 5:1–5). How does your church meet these needs today?

2. Farmers were to leave crops in the field for the poor to glean (vv. 19–22). This concept reappears in Scripture as an admonition to compassion and a warning against greed (Lev. 19:9–10; Ps. 41:1; Prov. 19:17; Luke 12:16–21). This principle is not limited to farmers. How we demonstrate concern for others will vary, but it is imperative that we show kindness to others, especially in light of what God has done for us.

Chapter 25

1. Esau's animosity toward his younger brother, Jacob, was kept alive by his descendant Amalek (vv. 17–19). This is one example of a pattern traceable throughout Scripture, in which an older sibling is unwilling to accept God's blessing upon a younger. Consider Cain and Abel (Gen. 4); Ishmael and Isaac (Gen. 21:9); Esau and Jacob (Gen. 24:41); Joseph and his brothers (Gen. 37:18–27); Miriam, Aaron, and Moses (Num. 12:1–2); Eliab and David (1 Sam. 17:28); and the elder brother and the prodigal (Luke 15:15–29). In blessed contrast, Christ, the elder brother of all the elect, "is not ashamed to call them brethren" (Heb. 2:11). Are you envious of those with greater privileges, or are you Christlike toward them?

2. Israel's practice of taking a brother's widow as wife (vv. 5–10) ensured the continuation of family lineage, clans, tribes, and the nation. This proved to be critical in the fulfillment of God's purpose to send Christ our Savior. Although the details differ, Boaz's marriage to Ruth approximates the principle and was a means of continuing the messianic line (Ruth 4:1–11, 17–22; Matt. 1:1–17; 22:24).

Chapter 26

1. Israel was to remember that Canaan was given to them by God by tithing the harvest. No less than Israel, all people should recognize that the land they inhabit is God's. The crops they harvest and consume are produced by His power and goodness. We are all indebted to Him for our very lives. All that we are, own, and enjoy is the Lord's (Ps. 24:1).

2. God's people are "his peculiar people" (v. 18). God sets them apart to Himself and regards them as special. They

must remember and reflect this in obedience to His commandments, resisting the evil passions of this present world (1 John 2:15). They are "a chosen generation, a royal priesthood, an holy nation, a peculiar people; that ye should shew forth the praises of him who hath called you" (1 Peter 2:9). Which commandments especially make obedient Christians different from other people in your culture? Why?

Chapter 27

1. Moses instructed Israel to "obey the voice of the LORD thy God, and to do his commandments and his statutes" (v. 10), because they were "the people of the LORD thy God" (v. 9). God's grace establishes one's relationship as a member of God's people, and obedience to His Word evidences that grace. Some confuse church membership or theological persuasion with citizenship among God's elect. But the primary mark that God observes and demands is obedience to His Word (1 John 2:3–5).

2. The ceremony at Ebal and Gerizim included all Israel affirming the curses proclaimed by saying "Amen" which means "may it be so." God expected the entire congregation of Israel to affirm His Word. In some congregations "Amen" is said audibly within the assembly. However, all Christians should affirm the Word in their hearts. The essence of faith is saying "Amen" to God's promises in Christ Jesus (2 Cor. 1:20).

Chapter 28

1. "Among these nations shalt thou find no ease…but the LORD shall give thee there a trembling heart" (v. 65). Fear

is a result of sin (Gen. 3:10); thus Israel's sin would beget fear. "The wicked flee when no man pursueth: but the righteous are bold as a lion" (Prov. 28:1). The godly have nothing to fear, for they rest in the sovereign rule of God, which is good. The ungodly have every reason to fear. "The wicked are like the troubled sea, when it cannot rest, those waters cast up mire and dirt. There is no peace, saith my God, to the wicked" (Isa. 57:20–21).

2. God warned Israel that He would judge her sin by sending her into idolatry (v. 64). Sin becomes its own punishment. Divine wrath delivers the disobedient unto uncleanness, vile affections, and reprobate minds (Rom. 1:18–32), giving rebels over unto greater sin, corruption, and contamination. They sin without conscience. This counsels everyone to immediate repentance before they become past feeling toward sin in the blindness of the heart (Eph. 4:18–19). Of what sins do you need to repent right now?

Chapter 29

1. Warning against departure from God's law, Moses equated cursed actions with one who says, "I walk in the imagination of mine heart" (v. 19). Thereby he identifies the root of sin: the hardness of the heart. The heart is deceitful above all things, and desperately wicked: who can know it and its secrets (Ps. 19:12; Jer. 17:9)? Those who follow their own hearts ignore God's law, resulting in sin (Prov. 3:1–8, Mark 7:15–23, Rom. 1:20–21). The heart departs from the Lord (Jer. 17:5). How can we overcome our own hearts?

2. Scripture provides information to satisfy faith, but not curiosity. God reveals and God conceals, thus "the secret

things belong unto the LORD our God" (v. 29). Prophets did not understand all of the things they wrote (1 Peter 1:10–12), and Paul confessed "now we know in part" (1 Cor. 13:12). This should promote diligence in searching out what God has revealed and humility in our limited understanding. Even the God-inspired, inerrant writers possessed partial knowledge. God has not chosen to reveal everything concerning Himself, and it is not wise to speculate beyond what the Bible reveals.

Chapter 30

1. God foreknew that despite His mercies Israel would rebel against Him and suffer the curses of the law. However, He had already planned long beforehand that He would restore His exiled people. Even more, He planned to restore them to repentance and supreme love for Him by the inward work of His grace. God is not trying to catch up with our sins and figure out how to patch up the mess we have made. God planned it all, and His sovereign grace will transform His elect at the time He has decreed in Christ.

2. The Lord has linked together love for Him, obedience to His commands, and experiencing His blessings (v. 16). We should see these three as inseparably one. Let us never divide what God has joined. Love and law are not opposites, but one. To love the Lord is to obey His laws. To walk in His ways is to be blessed by Him. It is not merely the way to happiness, but it is our happiness to love Him and do His will. How would seeing love, obedience, and joy as one change the way people think about religion?

Chapter 31

1. Chapter 31 is a study in divine mercy. God knew that Israel would depart from Him. Yet He loved Israel and remained faithful. He provided the song of chapter 32 to remind and to reprimand Israel when they turned away. Anticipating our sinfulness, God calls us to repentance and promises grace before we even know we need it, grace to forgive and grace to change the heart, both through Jesus Christ (Acts 5:30–31).

2. One might imagine Joshua's burden as he contemplated leading Israel to claim the Canaanite homeland. This anxiety was addressed by Moses: "Be strong and of good courage, fear not…nor forsake thee" (31:6, 23). God assured Joshua, "Thou shalt bring the children of Israel into the land," and promised, "I will be with thee" (v. 23). God ensures the completion of His call and purpose. What God has instructed us to do, He enables us to do.

Chapter 32

1. "Bless the LORD, O my soul, and forget not all his benefits" (Ps. 103:2). Moses's song reviews God's blessings and warnings. Israel would thus review God's goodness and cautions whenever the song was sung. God's works should be remembered by frequent recitation, and His words should be quoted as the key to understanding life's events.

2. We see in this chapter a sobering contrast between the Lord and humanity. God is the "Rock," righteous and true, powerful and unchangeable. However, despite all that the Lord did in choosing, redeeming, and caring for Israel, the people despised Him and provoked His holy vengeance. Centuries later, those returning from exile would remember

their national history and confess to the Lord, "thou hast done right, but we have done wickedly" (Neh. 9:33). Therefore, let us humble ourselves, for we are no better than they, and let us worship the Lord, for He is the Rock of salvation.

Chapter 33

1. A leader's proper role is to selflessly bless his followers. Moses chose "to suffer affliction with the people of God" and esteemed "the reproach of Christ greater riches than the treasures in Egypt" (Heb. 11:25–26), so that he might bring Israel into the blessings promised to them centuries earlier. Fathers and leaders are to be "used up" for the good of those placed under their authority. Jesus Christ is the premier example of this.

2. "Happy art thou, O Israel: who is like unto thee, O people saved by the LORD" (v. 29). No other nation has experienced such blessing as Israel. This signified that God had set Israel apart unto Himself. What national Israel experienced is ultimately true of the church. Christ's people are set apart unto Him and blessed. There are no peoples comparable to Christ's true church. "Behold, what manner of love the Father hath bestowed upon us, that we should be called the sons of God" (1 John 3:1). It is good to ponder this truth and then to offer praise to God for all the benefits of His saving grace.

Chapter 34

1. Moses led the nation out of Egypt and through the wilderness, but the privilege of leading Israel into Canaan was reserved for Joshua. Piece by piece, portions of God's work are done by servants of His choosing. Each should recognize

that he is a small piece of a larger work that God is doing. We work earnestly in the progress of God's kingdom, yet it may be God's wisdom to allow others to take the prize we sought. In God's plan, there is always a Joshua to replace a Moses, and in the end all is of the Lord.

2. Moses, whom the Lord knew "face to face" (v. 10), experienced divine intimacy unknown to any other leader except Christ (18:18; John 1:17–18; Acts 3:20–23; Heb. 3:4–6). Yet the Son of God reveals the Father to whomever He pleases (Matt. 11:27). He enables us to know the true God, and such knowledge gives eternal life (John 17:3, 6; 1 John 5:20). One day, believers in Christ will also know God face to face (1 Cor. 13:12; Rev. 22:4), and intimacy with Him will be their eternal joy. How does that give us hope?

Joshua

Chapter 1

1. Moses was dead, but the work of God was continuing without him because it was the work of God and not of Moses (1:1–2). Notwithstanding how great Moses was and how many extraordinary things he did, he was not indispensable. Joshua was there with the same promises God had given Moses to carry on the work. There was a work for Joshua to do that Moses could not do. This transition from Moses to Joshua stands as a warning to not put hope in man. Too often today Christian men try to build empires around themselves, and their work ultimately falls because it was centered in a personality. On the other hand, church history is full of outstandingly great men who served the Lord in their generation only to be replaced by others who served the same Lord in another generation. Thank God that He gives these leaders as His gifts for the good of the church (Eph. 4:11–13).

2. The book of Joshua illustrates how God uses men as His ordained ministers or servants to lead His people. The recurring pattern is that God speaks to the leader who in turn speaks to the people (vv. 9–10). It is imperative, then, that ministers know God's Word so that they can effectively communicate that Word to the people. However, the instructions for Joshua to meditate on and obey God's Word constantly as the means for successful living is a paradigm that should

be followed by all of God's people. How can you follow Joshua's example in his attitude toward God's Word?

Chapter 2

1. Rahab is a wonderful example of the power and sovereignty of grace. She appears to be an unlikely candidate for grace, but that is the point. She is a vivid picture of all who are dead in sin and who are made alive by the greater Joshua, the Lord Jesus Christ. The depths of her sin magnify the beauty of grace. From every appearance Rahab was without hope, a citizen of a doomed city, alienated from the commonwealth of Israel, a stranger to the covenant promise. But God sovereignly directed the spies to her house. Indeed, God had put the "scarlet cord" there in eternity long before the spies arrived. Although Joshua sent the men to spy the land, they had a commission from God to preach to Rahab. Significantly, James refers to them not as spies but as messengers (James 2:25). They had a word for Rahab. Faith comes by hearing the Word of God and that hearing comes through preachers (Rom. 10:13–14). How has God's sovereign hand reached out to you?

2. Grace both finds and awakens the sinner. Rahab believed (Heb. 11:31), and she made a confession of her faith. She acknowledged God's mighty and fear-producing power that had saved Israel (Josh. 2:9–10). She knew that it would be a fearful thing to fall into the hands of such a God (Heb. 10:31). She expressed the sure conviction that Jehovah was the one true and living God in heaven and earth (Josh. 2:11). According to Paul, no one can make such a genuine heart confession except by the Holy Spirit (1 Cor. 12:3). By

pleading for mercy (Josh. 2:12–13), she recognized that God was her only hope, her only place of refuge. Reflect on these components of her confession since the object and nature of saving faith is the same now as it was then.

Chapter 3

1. The statement "for ye have not passed this way heretofore" (v. 4) certainly describes the new venture that Israel was about to experience. But, in reality, it is the headline over every day of life for all of us. Every day brings new experiences, situations, and so many uncertainties. It had to be an encouraging comfort and source of confidence for Israel to know that the ark, the visible token of God's presence, was leading them. As believers today, we do not have a visible object to assure us of God's presence, but we have His word that He will not leave nor forsake us. We have the abiding presence of the indwelling Holy Spirit as our comforter and guide. Spend time praising God that even though every step of life is new, we can confidently walk through even the darkest shadows knowing that He is with us (Ps. 23:4).

2. Joshua 3:10 is a wonderful reminder that even though ministers change, God's Word remains constant. The word that Joshua gives to the people on the eve of their crossing the Jordan is the same that Moses had given them earlier (Deut. 7:1–2). Nothing had changed except the mouthpiece. God's Word is forever settled in heaven (Ps. 119:89), and the authority is in the Word and not in the spokesman. How have you seen this to be true in your own life?

Chapter 4

1. Raising the monument to commemorate the crossing of the Jordan illustrates the responsibility one generation has to the next to teach about the Lord and His mighty acts. The memorial became the occasion for children to ask fathers, "What mean these stones?" (v. 21). It provided fathers the opportunity to direct their children to the knowledge of God. So Christian parents must erect the "family altar of witness" in the home as a means of fostering a spiritual curiosity among their children and of teaching them to fear God and obey Him, which ultimately and primarily involves obeying the gospel in repenting of their sins and believing in Jesus Christ. God has set the home as a principal place of religious training, both by precept and example. What can you do to pass on your faith stories?

2. Joshua 4:24 suggests that the memorial witness to God's covenant faithfulness and mighty power would serve as a means of evangelism to the world as well as to the family. For the world to see the effects of gospel grace in the lives of His people gives effective witness to the power of grace. Living in the fear of God is then a private matter, speaking to the family, and a public matter, speaking to strangers. Fearing God affects all of life. How are you able to make God's work of grace in your life public to unbelievers around you?

Chapter 5

1. Gilgal was Israel's first claim in the Promised Land; it anticipated future blessings and served as a reminder to future generations of past blessings. It is where the strategy for the conquest was set in place and suggests a strategy for

all believers as they seek to advance in their spiritual lives. First, circumcision shows the importance of dealing with the flesh. Circumcision is important on many levels, but certainly the removal of the flesh pictures the cleansing from sin and the necessity of separation from the old life (Egypt). Every Christian must experience what it means for old things to pass away and all things to become new. How have you experienced this in your life?

2. Second, the Passover celebration shows the importance of remembering the redemption we have through the sacrifice of Christ in our behalf. The Passover teaches lessons about grace, the power of God, the necessity of blood atonement, the objectivity of faith, and spiritual sustenance as we feast on the Lamb. How have you been able to celebrate Christ's sacrifice lately?

3. Third, the Christophany underscores the importance of meeting with Christ Himself. The sacraments serve as helpful, visible signs of spiritual truths, but there is no substitute for experiencing and enjoying a personal relationship with Jesus Christ, worshiping Him and listening to His Word. "What saith my lord unto his servant" (v. 14) ought to be the sincere question of every believer every time he opens the Scripture. The bottom line is that we all need a place we call Gilgal. What can you do to help develop a daily habit of meeting with your Lord?

Chapter 6

1. Jericho is a real example of Bunyan's City of Destruction. Its destruction puts in bold the severity of divine justice. Three thoughts particularly are in focus. First, divine justice

is patient. Jericho was one of the world's oldest cities. Archaeological evidence indicates a level of occupation predating Abraham by hundreds of years. We know that the sins of the Canaanites were not yet full in his day (Gen. 15:16), but now they were. The city had been given years of time and opportunity to repent but it did not. Now the day of judgment had arrived. We should not presume on God's longsuffering but repent without delay. Second, divine justice is irresistible. The city was securely shut, and the inhabitants trusted the security of walls that appeared to be impenetrable. But, without a hand, God took away their security. Jericho prefigures a judgment ahead in which more than walls will fall (Heb. 12:26). Sinners will not be able to stand in that day (Nah. 1:6). Third, divine justice is not capricious. Both the Old Testament and secular historic records show the extent of the wickedness of Canaan: Jericho got what it deserved. That none were spared shows that justice is without discrimination: all souls belong to the Lord and the soul that sins will die (Ezek. 18:4). Jericho is a lesson in how God deals with sin. Spend time praising God for His patience, His justice, and His mercy.

2. Jericho is also a pattern for sanctification. As Jericho stood in the way of Israel's possession of the land, so sin looms large as the obstacle every believer must encounter. God promised that Jericho would fall, and so He has promised us that sin will no longer have dominion over us (Rom. 6:14). The power to overcome Jericho was the Lord's. Note how the divine plan to defeat Jericho focused on the ark, the symbol of God's presence, and the atonement (Josh. 6:4, 6–9, 11–13). This points directly to Christ, His atonement, and

our union with Him as the ultimate power for victory (Col. 2:14–15; Heb. 2:14–15). Although the victory was God's, Israel had to march and stick close to the ark. According to Heb. 11:30 they did so in faith. So in sanctification by faith we know what we have in Christ, we reckon it to be personally true, and we behave accordingly (see logic of Rom. 6). Ask God to give you victory through grace and the will to live by faithful obedience.

Chapter 7

1. There is always an Ai to follow Jericho. Jericho was an amazing victory and remarkable start to the conquest of Canaan. But the rest of the Canaanites did not automatically surrender; they were going to defend their territory. The battles were going to continue, and Israel could not rest in past victory. The parallels to the Christian life with its struggles against sin and striving for holiness are noteworthy. Because of the ultimate victory Christ won on the cross, sin no longer has dominion over the believer. But just like the Canaanites, sin is going to defend its territory in the heart and not surrender easily. We must fight against sin and temptation and experience the victory by faith and obedience. It is imperative to remember that getting the victory over one temptation does not prevent the next one from coming. Sanctification is a lifelong process. What can you do to keep this important perspective in mind?

2. The connection between Achan's sin and Israel's defeat at Ai teaches important and sobering lessons. The disobedience of one culprit caused defeat for the entire nation and ended with the punishment of his entire family. Although he

sinned in secret, his sin was detected and the consequences were public. In a very real sense, there is no such thing as a private sin. Either by results (the loss of thirty-six lives in battle) or by imitation (apparently the case with his family who became privy to his crime), sin affects others. The narrative also underscores the fact that secret sins are openly known by God, and in His time all sin will be detected and dealt with. Paul said, "Some men's sins are open beforehand, going before to judgment; and some men they follow after" (1 Tim. 5:24). Eventually all sin is exposed and its penalty executed. How can knowing this help you in your own battle for sanctification?

Chapter 8

1. Achan's sin and the nation's presumption (7:3) resulted in tragic loss at the first encounter with Ai. But defeat was not the end of the story. After they dealt with the sin and renewed their dependence on the Lord's Word, victory was assured. This is a wonderful message of hope for every believer who has failed the Lord. Defeated believers often convince themselves that there is no hope of ever enjoying spiritual victory again. But Israel's second encounter with Ai suggests otherwise. If we confess our sins, He will forgive (1 John 1:9), and if we hear and obey His instructions, the way to victory over sin is set before us. That Ai is a heap and desolation to this day (Josh. 8:28) testifies to how God gives His people yet another chance to experience victory and to enjoy the inheritance He has given. How have you witnessed the place of defeat become the place of victory in your own life or the life of another believer?

2. The reading of the Law (at that time the totality of inspired Scripture) to all the population is a reminder of the importance of the Bible for the life and welfare of every believer. As the leader of the people, Joshua was to devote himself to the Word of God (1:8). But it was just as important for the people to listen firsthand to what God had to say. Similarly, it is not just the obligation of the minister to read and obey the Scripture, but that of every believer. How can you give God's Word a more prominent place in your life?

Chapter 9

1. Notwithstanding the intrigue and deception employed by the Gibeonites, their pursuit of peace with Joshua illustrates gospel truths. They recognized that unless they entered into covenant with Joshua they would be doomed. Only identification with Israel would save them. The way they sought mercy was flawed and far from perfect but the fact of the matter is they recognized their need for mercy. Similarly, there has never been a sinner who has come to Christ with perfect faith or repentance, but the gospel promise is that Christ will not cast out those who come to Him (John 6:37). It is only as sinners sue for peace with the greater Joshua through the blood of His cross that they can be delivered from death. The key difference between the lesser and the greater Joshua is that the lesser was duped into showing mercy whereas the greater knows every sinner who comes to Him for what he really is and receives him nonetheless. His grace is greater than our sin. Praise Jesus for His grace and mercy!

2. Verse 25 expresses the proper sentiment of all who have been delivered from the sentence and bondage of death:

surrendering to the will and good pleasure of the new master. The Gibeonites gladly became servants to those who by covenant oath had spared them. So Christians, who by a greater covenant and oath have been delivered, ought gladly to surrender themselves to the service of Jesus, the new Lord and Master. In the light of grace, how can you find joy in serving Jesus?

Chapter 10

1. God's providence is often mysterious but is always wise and always leads to His glory and His people's good. At first glance, the Canaanite coalition would be a fearful thing: multiple enemies ganging up against a people inexperienced in warfare. They had only engaged in two battles, the first of which (Jericho) did not even put them in harm's way. But God was fighting for them, and this alliance was a means of bringing the enemies out from the fortifications into the open so that they could be defeated all at once. What would normally have required years to achieve was accomplished in essentially one battle. It involved a supernatural occurrence (the "long day"), which provided obvious evidence of the battle being the Lord's. In the moment, we sometimes question why God's providence does what it does—seeing only the moment can be deceiving. God knows the end from the beginning, and His wise providence employs the best means to accomplish His intended purpose. So it is important to trust Him, walking by faith and not sight. Even if the immediate circumstance appears to be against us, it cannot be, because if God is for us none can successfully be against us. How have you seen God work in overwhelming circumstances to bring about His glory and your good?

2. Joshua, coming to Gibeon's defense, illustrates a beautiful gospel truth. They were being threatened because of their covenant relationship with Joshua. The enemy could not get to Joshua, so they came against those who had made peace with him. Because of the covenant, Joshua was obligated to their protection. Undoubtedly, the world hates Christ but because it cannot get to Him it takes out its hatred against those with whom Christ has a relationship, His church. We are not to marvel if the world hates us (1 John 3:13) because it hated Him first. Pray for God to give you confidence to live boldly, knowing that Christ is our guaranteed Protector and in union with Him we are secure (Rom. 8:31–39). "If God be for us, who can be against us?" (v. 31).

Chapter 11

1. God's good providence is often contrary to expectation. The gathering of a huge army against Israel would have been a terrifying scene. It would have given the appearance of the enemy getting the upper hand; defeat would have seemed certain in light of all the chariots and horses. Humanly speaking, Israel was out-armed. Yet appearance and reality were far different. God had Himself mustered the army as a means of bringing them out into the open and away from their fortified cities to hasten their utter destruction. It did not look like victory at first, but God was working all out for the good of His people. So often it is only as we look back on the events of providence that we recognize the good. Have you learned to walk by faith and not by sight even when what you see contradicts what you think to be good? How have you seen that God's ways are always best?

2. Over and again, the chapter declares that what Joshua accomplished is what the Lord had commanded Moses ("he left nothing undone of all that the LORD commanded Moses" [v. 15]). It provides a wonderful reminder of God's faithfulness in keeping His promises. Recall other ways that God has kept His promises.

Chapter 12

The detailed summary of the conquest, and particularly the list of the conquered kings by name one by one, provides an important lesson for praise and thanksgiving. It is an example of naming our blessings one by one in conscious recognition of what God has done in fulfilling His promises and keeping His word. Too often our thanksgiving to God is expressed in sweeping statements. Be specific in giving thanks for each and every benefit that He has provided for you.

Chapter 13

1. The distribution of the land among the tribes gives material substance to God's promise and testifies to His faithfulness to fulfill His promises. As far back as Abraham God had promised that His covenant people would possess this land. That promise was repeated by Moses and claimed by Joshua as he led the nation into conquest. And now as the tribes received their "titles" of possession, they experienced the tangible evidence of God's fidelity. This provides a wonderful example for all believers that regardless of how far off God's promises may appear to be, He is faithful to fulfill His Word. It is never a vain thing to wait upon the Lord, for those who wait will never be disappointed. Let us take every token of

blessing as tangible evidence that all the promises of God are yea and amen in our greater Joshua, Jesus Christ (2 Cor. 1:20). How have you seen God's faithfulness to those who wait upon Him?

2. The contradiction between Joshua 11:23 and 13:1–2 is only apparent and reflects a significant truth that every Christian knows in experience: the tension between the "already" and the "not yet." Every believer is complete in Christ (Col. 2:10) and is blessed with "all spiritual blessings in heavenly places in Christ" (Eph. 1:3). The wonder of this is beyond comprehension. Yet as amazing as this is, we now have the Holy Spirit who promises even more, for He is "the earnest of our inheritance until the redemption of the purchased possession" (Eph. 1:14). Already it is good, but the best is yet to be (1 John 3:2).

Chapter 14

1. Caleb and Joshua were the only two of the twelve spies that recommended to Israel that they should enter and possess Canaan (Num. 13–14). Consequently, they were the only ones preserved through the wilderness and allowed to enter the land of promise. Although Caleb was just as faithful as Joshua, the Lord had commissioned Joshua as the successor to Moses, and Caleb was in the background. Nonetheless, he remained loyal to the Lord even though Joshua was in the spotlight. What attitudes can we foster that will not allow any place for competition or envy in the work of the Lord?

2. Only Caleb and Joshua (19:50) were allowed to choose the place of their inheritance in the Promised Land. Although Caleb was advanced in years, he claimed that his strength

had not abated. He could have chosen wherever he wanted, but he laid claim to what potentially was the most difficult and dangerous to possess. He chose the place where the Anakims were. Ironically, it was the sight of the Anakims, the giants, that caused the fear and convinced the nation that they could not possess the land. Not only had Caleb's strength not abated, neither had his faith. Before the wilderness, he believed God would deliver the giants into the hands of His people, and nothing had changed. Believers often hesitate to ask of God the big things. Caleb is a wonderful example of asking God for big things because nothing is impossible for Him. What big things should you be asking and trusting God for?

Chapter 15

1. It is astonishing at times how God uses His people to do great exploits for His glory in fulfilling His own promises when they trust solely in Him. Israel was condemned to wander in the wilderness for forty years because the nation as a whole refused to embrace God's promises, fearing that they could not defeat the giants of Canaan, particularly the sons of Anak (Num. 13:28, 33). After forty years, Caleb, who followed God fully all those years, goes into Canaan and, with his sons, singlehandedly "drives thence" those giants. In what areas of your life are you holding back from acting by faith out of fear that God will not fulfil His promises?

2. Caleb is much more than an exemplar of faith. The story of Caleb is ultimately about the historical progress of God's redemption. For those who truly trust in Christ alone for salvation, this history will find its ultimate fulfillment in the

inheritance of salvation in Christ (Matt. 25:34; Col. 3:24; Heb. 9:15). What comfort should believers draw from this for their daily lives?

Chapter 16

The details in chapters 16–19 are significant. Together they show how minutely God fulfills His promises. For years He had promised that the covenant people would inherit this land so often described as flowing with milk and honey. It seemed to be a broad and general promise of good things to come. But as the promise comes to fact, the point-by-point distribution of districts, towns, and villages to every tribe shows how specifically, definitely, and tangibly God keeps His Word. Every part of the nation received its portion; none was left out. Often Christians regard God's promise of a glorious future in eternity in happy but general terms that things will someday be better. But the day will come when every promise will be experienced as fact in real and tangible ways that we cannot imagine. And so it will be that every one of God's chosen people will receive his inheritance; none will be left out. How does it encourage you to know that we will never tire of enjoying all the details of God's blessings?

Chapter 17

God had commanded Israel to destroy the Canaanites completely. These nations that represented the world and sin were not to coexist with God's people. The failure to drive them out completely was incomplete obedience, and the attempt to subdue them to compulsory labor was folly (vv. 12–13). This illustrates an important lesson that we must learn regarding sin. When they felt strong, they thought they could use the Canaanites to their advantage as their servants. But it was not long before they lost control, as the book of Judges records. We cannot control sin in our own strength. It will not be long before the sin we think we can manage overcomes us. It is only as we rest by faith in the victory over sin won by Christ that we can be freed from sin's dominion (Rom. 6). Willpower by itself is never powerful enough. According to Rom. 6, how can we live out this truth in our daily lives?

Chapter 18

Israel's taking possession of the land of Canaan was an act of faith. Not to take possession of that land, therefore, or to be slow to do it, as was the case of the seven tribes (vv. 2–3), was an act of unbelief. Accordingly, Joshua admonishes the people in these tribes for their slackness (v. 3). It is fascinating that he does not just admonish them, however; he also provides them with a plan of action (vv. 4–7), which God blesses to stir the men up to act (v. 8). What can we learn from Joshua's leadership, counsel, and call to action in this chapter that can assist us in guiding those who struggle with unbelief and indecisiveness?

Chapter 19

It is fascinating that at the end of this long, detailed list of how Israel's tribes received their allotted territory in Canaan, Joshua also received an allotment (v. 49). Thus, both of Israel's heroes of faith, Joshua and Caleb, received an inheritance—Caleb at the beginning of the allotment chapters (14:6–15) and Joshua at the end. In this way, the book of Joshua, which is "the book of the land," continues to teach us that both the history of progressive redemption and our ultimate journey to the heavenly Canaan must always be placed in the framework of faith. Joshua and Caleb, who had risked their lives to live by faith and had remained steadfast for forty years in the midst of murmuring Israelites while in the wilderness, are now rewarded. We again learn that faith will always be more than amply rewarded by God's grace. What additional lessons does this history teach us about the importance of living and persevering consistently by saving faith?

Chapter 20

1. The cities of refuge indicate that the spirituality of the law that Jesus underscored in His Sermon on the Mount (Matt. 5) was true in the Old Testament as well. Christ made it clear that those who hated were guilty of murder even if they did not actually take a life. The cities of refuge show the other side by revealing that those who inadvertently took a life without malice or forethought are not held guilty of murder and thus not liable to its consequence. The heart is the key. It does not remove the tragedy of the loss of human life but it does focus on the spiritual significance of God's law. The fact that those guilty of intentional murder receive no asylum teaches the same. Take this opportunity to apply this principle to all the Ten Commandments and remember that the heart, although unseen to man, is known by God. Motives matter.

2. The avenger is the kinsman-redeemer whose responsibility it was to help his family in whatever way was necessary. Sometimes it involved purchasing property to keep it within

the family like Boaz the near kinsman did for Ruth. Here in this context the act involved the execution of justice. The main point is that the kinsman does whatever must be done for the welfare of family. Significantly, the term is used of God (Ps. 19:14). The wonderful truth is that because of His covenant relationship with His people, the Lord will do for them whatever needs to be done for their welfare. Ultimately, it points to Christ who as our kinsman-redeemer has delivered us from death and has provided for us an inheritance of spiritual blessing. We can count on Him to act on our behalf in whatever way is needful for us. Spend some time exalting Christ as our kinsman-redeemer!

Chapter 21

1. The tribe of Levi was divinely chosen to be the special servants of the Lord for the ministry of the tabernacle. Not all were priests, but all in some capacity enjoyed the unique privilege of being employed in sacred service. The Lord Himself was their ultimate inheritance, and so they did not inherit land as the other tribes. But as the servants of God, He had a place for them to serve for the welfare and advantage of the entire nation. He scattered them in such a way that their influence and ministry could be experienced throughout the nation. They were God's gift to the nation. Similarly, God has called men to sacred ministry and given them to local and specific congregations for the edification and spiritual welfare of believers (Eph. 4:11–12). How can you show honor and appreciation for these men?

2. Verses 21:43–45 declares the fulfillment of God's promise of land in absolute terms, yet Judges reveals that not all the

land was actually conquered, and another rest was to come in the time of David (2 Sam. 7:1, 11). The focus of the promise included something beyond just a geographical component. Ultimately, this rest involved the enjoyment of God's presence and was the experience of faith. Under Joshua, this generation had conquered the enemies before them and entered into their inheritance. The fact that there was more to come did not distract from the fullness of their enjoyment of what God had promised. This illustrates once again the "already/not yet" principle that characterizes the Christian experience. How does it encourage you today to know that, in Christ, we are blessed with all the spiritual blessings in the heavenly places, but the best is yet to be (Eph. 1)?

Chapter 22

1. This episode illustrates the unity of God's people and the pervasive consequences of sin that can affect the whole body. The nation remembered the terrible consequences of the sin of many at Baal Peor and the sin of one (Achan) at Jericho that caused the shameful defeat at Ai. They learned the lesson and did not want to repeat it. So if the eastern tribes were guilty of violating God's commandment, they were ready to deal with it immediately lest the whole nation suffer. They knew that a little leaven leavens the whole lump and therefore they had to purge out the old (1 Cor. 5:6–7). We must remember how powerful sin is, and that by either example or consequence the most private of sins has the potential to affect others. For the sake of the body, it is imperative for the church to exercise discipline when aware of sin in others. How can we, for the sake of ourselves and of the body, strive for victory over every sin?

2. The manner in which the western tribes handled the issue with their eastern brothers is exemplary. There was no rush to judgment. Inquiry was made before action was taken, and they gave them the benefit of the doubt. Too often, some Christians think the worst and condemn fellow believers on the basis of suspicion rather than fact. Here is an Old Testament example of the procedure Christ outlines in Matthew 18 for dealing with offending brothers. When they talked together and the facts were known, the result was peace and not war. Since it is good to preserve the unity of the brothers rather than incite unnecessary division, what wise practices should you establish?

Chapter 23

1. Israel's possession of the Promised Land was rooted in God's fulfillment of His promise and experienced in terms of their faithful obedience. God promised victory and fought for them, but they had to love and obey Him in order to experience the blessing. This spiritually parallels the procedure for our sanctification. Christ has conquered our spiritual enemies so that sin no longer has dominion over us. In the light of that victory and promise, we must die to sin and live to righteousness. Our sanctification is progressive and involves cooperation between what God has done in Christ and what we must do in Christ to experience victory. Ponder or discuss Paul's logic in Romans 6.

2. Loving God and loving the world are mutually exclusive. As evidence of their obedience and love for God, Israel was to have no alliance with the worldly and pagan inhabitants of the land. Those nations were cut off by God and destined

to destruction. So we as Christians, who love God, are not to love the things of this world, which are opposed to God and destined to pass away (1 John 2:15–17). How can we keep our hearts from the love of the world?

Chapter 24

1. Joshua's final charge outlines a formula for keeping and enjoying God's blessing. First, remember that sovereign grace is the cause of blessing. Abraham was as guilty of idolatry as anyone else in Ur, but God graciously entered into covenant with him. Israel was as guilty as the Egyptians that held them in bondage but God graciously redeemed them with His power and the blood of the sacrifice. So it is that we are not saved by any self-merit or effort but purely by grace which is so undeserved. Spend time praising God for His gifts of grace.

2. Second, remember that divine faithfulness is the guarantee of blessing. Joshua's review of history cited instance after instance of God's faithfulness in keeping His word, defeating every enemy they confronted. They inherited the land because God's promise was certain. And so we should remember that all of God's promises are yea and amen in Jesus Christ. God was faithful to every covenant promise to send His Son to be the Redeemer of His people, and Christ faithfully fulfilled His commission to redeem them. What future promises can we then cling to with great hope?

3. Third, acknowledge that personal commitment is the condition for blessing. In the light of God's grace and faithfulness, Israel was to fear Him and serve Him in sincerity and truth. Joshua flatly said they could not do this on their

own. That commitment was the evidence of grace received. This parallels what Christ expects of His disciples. In Luke 14, the greater Joshua said three times that one cannot be His disciple unless he regards Christ above others (v. 26), above self (vv. 26–27), and above everything (v. 33). Pray for God's continued gift of grace that makes this kind of commitment possible.

Judges

Chapter 1

1. Living under the threat of the ungodly we must pray for God's help to remain separate unto Him and the gospel. We constantly need spiritual victory to drive the spirit of the world out of our hearts. What are some specific forms of worldliness calling you and your friends to compromise?

2. What Judah and Simeon accomplished together with the Lord's help is a model for us. We need fellowship for our spiritual growth, we need the prayers of God's people, and we need the means of grace ordained by the Lord through the ministry of His church. No one can live the Christian life alone.

3. As Achsah realized the importance of a water supply in the dry southern land, we should recognize the need of God's grace for our souls in this barren world. God has promised the supply of His Spirit to meet the needs of our fainting hearts (Phil. 1:19).

Chapter 2

1. Godly leaders are God's instruments for blessing. Each judge raised up by the Lord was used to lead the people away from sin and unto godliness. Hence, it is important to pray for the leaders that God raises up that they might be instruments of peace (1 Tim. 2:2). In addition, every godly man or woman will be God's instrument to influence others for good.

Particularly parents are to direct their families in the paths of blessing. Ask the Lord to use your example to bless others.

2. When God allows oppressors against us, He is drawing us to seek His plan of mercy. Adversity often increases our sense of dependence on God (Eccl. 7:14). By this means God will work true repentance in our hearts for sin and true faith toward our Savior. Why do we often need to suffer in order to seek God?

3. Generation degeneration set in as "there arose another generation after them, which knew not the LORD" (2:10). The spirituality of the next generation is always a pressing concern for the church. Parents must fulfill their God-given responsibility to train up their children in the way they should go (Prov. 22:6). Every family needs a daily devotional time with solid Bible teaching.

Chapter 3

1. The Spirit's coming upon Othniel sets a pattern for the book of Judges and provides a good lesson for believers regarding the Spirit's ministry. The Spirit empowered the judge, enabling him to accomplish the work of the Lord. The Spirit's empowerment is usually for service in the work of God's kingdom. Whereas in the Old Testament era that kind of empowering was often limited to Israel's leadership, at Pentecost the Spirit came down upon all flesh (Joel 2:28) enabling every believer to serve the Lord with that special divine energy and power. Judges will illustrate over and again what man can do when God gives the power. That same power is available for every Christian. How can we seek it and take hold of it?

2. God's indignation was rightly directed against those who paraded their sins "in the sight of the LORD" (v. 7). Every sin is an affront against God and committed directly in His face. God's wrath and punishment against sin, evidenced when he sold them into the hands of Chushan-rishathaim, is well justified. Israel's bad example should be a warning to live in the reality of God's presence and avoid offending Him. As well, we should remember that the rod of chastisement is God's way of bringing His erring people to a renewed repentance and happy service under His loving hand (Heb. 12:6–7).

Chapter 4

1. "Hath not the LORD God of Israel commanded" (4:6)? Knowing that God has spoken and revealed His will generates confidence and assurance for doing His will. Even though militarily the odds were against Israel, God's word assured the victory. Often times doing God's will seems to go against what appears to be the logical course of action, but when we have the Lord's Word to direct us in God's service we must rise up in faith to obey His commands and plead His power. It is imperative to trust His Word and then to go.

2. It is God's pattern to choose "weak things of the world to confound the things which are mighty" (1 Cor. 1:27). No one is too weak to be used by the Lord. Deborah was a woman, but God used her. Jael was a woman with only a nail, but God used her. Barak had no weapons equal to Sisera's iron chariots, but God used him. As Christians, we should be encouraged that God demonstrates His strength through our weakness (2 Cor. 12:9). How do you feel weak when facing your spiritual enemies? How does this principle encourage you?

Chapter 5

1. The Song of Deborah provides a pattern for worship with its focus on praise. Much of our time in public and private worship should be in the attitude of praise unto the Lord as the giver of every blessing (James 1:17). Singing is a key means by which we can render our praise unto the Lord. A well-used hymnal in the home will glorify the Lord. A Spirit-filled people who know the victory of Christ in their lives will feel compelled to sing. When are you singing His praise?

2. Tragically, there were some in Deborah's day who refused to join in the Lord's battle, and, sadly, the case is the same today. Let our names be among the worthies who rise up for the cause of Christ. When the battle for Christ is on let there be no sitting on the fence as Reuben, standing on the sidelines as Dan, or remaining careless as Asher.

Chapter 6

1. The tension between faith and experience is common among believers. We cannot determine God's blessing by circumstances alone. God stated categorically, "The LORD is with thee" (v. 12), but Gideon felt compelled to ask, "If the LORD be with us, why then is all this befallen us?" (6:13). It was hard to see what was happening as evidence of God's presence and blessing. We need to read our circumstances in the light of God's revealed Word. His promise, "I will never leave thee, nor forsake thee" (Heb. 13:5), is every bit as true during the Christian's worst day on earth as on his best day. Faith must interpret sight in the light of God's Word. What promise do you need to cling to by faith today?

2. When determining God's will, first impressions are to be checked by earnest prayer but always with our wills submitted to His. God will call us in His time and in His way. God finds His man when busy at his common work (v. 11), confirms His will through His Word (v. 16), and equips him by His Spirit (v. 34). But Gideon's reaction to second guess God's word and look for more confirmation is a common experience. God takes our frailty into account and may give further confirmations, but the time must come when we submit to and rest in His Word without doubt or fear.

Chapter 7

1. The reduction of the army illustrates that God's work is not accomplished by might or power but by His Spirit (Zech. 4:6). God works in ways to show His own glory. While praying, preaching, or evangelizing we are all too quick to take honor to ourselves. We need to humble ourselves in submission to the cross of Christ. The cross is God's instrument to slay our fleshly pride. When we boast in Christ's cross we give our Lord Jesus all the glory for the victory He won for His people (Gal. 6:14).

2. On the other hand, God does use human means to do His work. The army was small, but it was an army. It should be our desire and prayer to be used as God's instrument to carry out His purposes. God does not use angels to preach the gospel, but He does use redeemed sinners. To be useful to God we need to obey His call and the commands of His Word. What are some ways God is using obedient people in your family or church to accomplish His work?

Chapter 8

1. The men of Succoth and the men of Penuel were deficient in faith and thereby lacking in courage. They were opportunists without principles, fearful of taking the right stand just in case things did not turn out. They failed in the day of opportunity to help those whom God raised up to help them. Let this be a check to us. It is better to be fellow helpers to the truth (3 John 8) than to waste God-given opportunities. Living by the principles of God's Word rather than by sight of circumstances is the essence of walking by faith. What opportunities do you have to stand?

2. Gideon's fall into idolatry did great harm. Even the best of men have the potential of failure and disappointment. Gideon's failure increases the anticipation for the One who will neither fail nor disappoint. Flaws in the best of men must not keep us from following our Lord Jesus who was perfect in all His ways. He alone is worthy of our worship and our praises. He will never disappoint us, nor lead us in a wrong path. Therefore, let us keep "looking unto Jesus the author and finisher of our faith" (Heb. 12:2).

Chapter 9

1. From Jotham's parable we learn that good men are reluctant to promote themselves while useless men tend to consider themselves suited to any task. Great harm can come when the wrong man is in leadership. The best person for God's work will be the one found busy in his own sphere of service. Let us beware of the man who promotes himself over his fellow men, for such men as Abimelech who offer their services at will may have nothing of worth to offer.

2. The whole chapter illustrates principles of divine judgment. God's use of the evil spirit shows His absolute authority over every realm. He may well bring judgment upon His enemies by allowing Satan to work his wicked will in evil hearts. The spirit of treachery is self-destructive, and part of divine judgment is to abandon the wicked to their own devices. The principle of poetic justice ("eye for eye," Ex. 21:24) is also evident. There is nothing more fearful than to get from God's justice what is deserved. God's justice is on the side of those who obey His Word and do right, but they who do evil shall be judged according to their works. How does this teach us to fear the Lord and turn from evil?

Chapter 10

1. God will not be manipulated, and certainly not by superficial prayers. God is not an instrument to be used just to rescue from trouble (v. 13). If we understand the holiness of God, we cannot make a game out of our Christianity and still expect God's blessing. We must not develop a cheap "bunker theology," thinking that we can sow to the flesh and still have God by our side in any time of crisis. God wants our first love and full loyalty, not sham cries from unrepentant hearts. What is the difference between using God and crying out to Him in true faith?

2. If we are true believers, our God is a true Father to pity us in our sufferings (v. 16). Isaiah wrote of God's tenderness toward His suffering people, "In all their affliction he was afflicted, and the angel of his presence saved them: in his love and in his pity he redeemed them; and he bare them, and carried them all the days of old" (Isa. 63:9). God takes no

delight in our self-destruction, but is moved by divine pity at our cries for mercy. When overwhelmed by life's struggles be sure to cry to your heavenly Father for deliverance. God knows the difference between sincere cries of repentance and superficial cries for temporal relief.

Chapter 11

1. Though Jephthah was of questionable heritage and rejected and despised by his fellows, God took him up to deliver Israel. In this way, his ministry draws a straight line to Christ. The Lord Jesus was also despised of men (Isa. 53:3; John 1:11) but He was the instrument of God's mighty power to redeem His people from the bondage of sin. This is a reminder as we read Judges that every deliverer God raised up anticipates and points to the ultimate and only Redeemer, the Lord Jesus Christ, who in no way fails His mission or disappoints His people.

2. Regarding vows, we must take Jephthah's position, "I cannot go back" (v. 35). There is wisdom for us in Ecclesiastes 5:5: "Better is it that thou shouldest not vow, than that thou shouldest vow and not pay." Vows are not to be put off, but to be paid immediately. However, a rash vow that proves to be unlawful to God should be repented of and not carried out. If the vow was wrong in the first place it would be wrong to fulfill it when we know better. Though vows should never be made casually or lightly, they are permissible when they are based in truth and intended for greater dedication to God's service. What vows have you taken over the course of your life? What does fulfilling them mean now?

Chapter 12

1. The Gileadites were a small, insignificant component of Joseph's descendants who had settled east of Jordan. They were despised and ridiculed by Ephraim, their more significant "cousins." Ephraim's pride got the best of them when they saw the accomplishments of little Gilead. Pride is a tinderbox that only needs the match of envy to start fires of conflict. Pride is at the root of wars and world conflicts, strife in local politics, misery in homes, and trouble in the Lord's church. Pride must be rooted out of our hearts by much prayer. It can be broken by the power of Christ's cross. How has pride shown itself in your life? How are you fighting it?

2. While God raises up key men for mighty acts in His service there is a lot of ordinary work to be done. Not every servant of God will leave a legacy of memorable accomplishments. But every servant must serve the Lord in the venue and with the influence He orders. History knows nothing of the accomplishments of Ibzan, Elon, or Abdon, but God raised them to serve their generation. We may never be famous but it is important that we be found faithful in our sphere of service.

Chapter 13

1. God planned to deliver His people from the Philistines before they cried out for help. When we are believers, this parallels also the order in our salvation. Before we were born or ever knew our need to be saved God had prepared the way for His Son to suffer and die for us. From all eternity Christ's redeeming work was laid out. Let us lift up our praises to the

Lord in the same thankful submission as the apostle John, "We love him, because he first loved us" (1 John 4:19).

2. The Lord is not only omnipotent to deliver us from our enemies, He is also immanent to be with us in our struggles of life. At a moment of crisis, the pre-incarnate Christ appeared to give a message of hope and encouragement. Can we doubt our Emmanuel when He took on our very nature to dwell among us? The Lord will not fail us for He has promised, "I will not leave you comfortless: I will come to you" (John 14:18). The angel of the Lord who announced the birth of Samson is our Lord Jesus Christ, "the same yesterday, and to day, and for ever" (Heb. 13:8).

Chapter 14

1. God's purpose cannot be frustrated regardless of the enemy's opposition or even the folly of His servants. The Philistines were among Israel's most powerful enemies, but they would not ultimately prevail against God's kingdom. Although Samson violated God's law and was not a clean vessel to be used, God nonetheless used him and manipulated circumstances in such a way that Samson would begin a deliverance from the Philistines that ultimately climaxed with David. We can rest knowing that God brings good out of evil and even though there appears to be no deliverer, everything is on track for David's greater Son to achieve the ultimate and final victory.

2. Whereas Samson was the strongest of men physically, in the face of temptation he was the weakest of men. No matter how strong we think we are, we must all beware lest we fall through the lust of the flesh. Entrust the care of your soul

to the Lord only, for the arm of flesh will fail you. In what areas of your life do you especially need to watch and pray against temptation?

Chapter 15

1. Israel binding Samson and handing him over to the Philistines parallels the betrayal of the Lord Jesus by the Jews when they handed Him over to the Romans. God sent His Son to be their Savior but they cried out, "Away with him, crucify him" (John 19:15). Sin is so severe that man cannot recognize the Savior without divine aid. We learn that God, not man, is the author of salvation. He first loved us and sent His Son to save us. Only when we are brought to behold the glory and saving power of Christ are we made to comprehend the love of God for our souls (Rom. 5:8). Do you believe that apart from God's grace you would hand over Christ to death? Why?

2. Samson, the weakest of men in temptation, became the strongest of men when "the Spirit of the LORD came mightily upon him" (v. 14). Being a God-appointed judge or deliverer of Israel, he was given the power to fulfill his work. Every servant of God needs the Spirit of the Lord for power in God's service. Remember to pray for the power of God to fall on your minister to do his work. Remember those on the mission field who are facing the forces of evil and the enemies of the Lord every day. Pray for God's power to come upon them.

Chapter 16

1. Contrary to expectation, Hebrews names Samson among those "who through faith subdued kingdoms" (Heb.

11:32–33). There was apparently more to Samson's ministry than is recorded in the book of Judges. He judged Israel for twenty years (Judg. 16:31); yet the narrative isolates just a few incidents in his career, none of which were high-water marks of spirituality or which covered significant periods of time. In those low points, he achieved great things for the cause of God's kingdom in the power of God's Spirit but without much faithfulness. But the Holy Spirit records that he subdued kingdoms through faith. None of God's servants are perfect, and all are prone to failure. But Hebrews would suggest that between those low points Samson was not always doing that which was right in his own eyes. Judges does not put him in a great light, but the last word about him marks his faith. Better is the end of a matter.

2. Certainly not by virtue of his person but by virtue of his office, Samson (like all the judges) pointed to Christ, the ultimate Savior. There are lines in Samson's life that parallel the life of Christ. Like our Lord, Samson was a specially announced son; and like our Lord, he was despised by his own people as a deliverer in Israel. As Samson brought down the house of Dagon, destroying Israel's enemies, so our Lord Jesus conquered all His and our enemies at the cross. While we see a mixture of failure and hope in Samson's life we see only perfection in our Lord Jesus. Let us go to Him with confidence that He is an all-sufficient Savior.

Chapter 17

1. The second commandment is absolute: "Thou shalt not make unto thee any graven image, or any likeness of any thing that is in heaven above, or that is in the earth beneath,

or that is in the water under the earth. Thou shalt not bow down thyself to them, nor serve them" (Ex. 20:4–5). Breaking this commandment leads to the greatest of perversions. Any sort of idolatry is an abomination to the Lord. Our God is a jealous God who will not share His glory with another. What are the popular forms of idolatry in your culture?

2. The Levite was a religious mercenary who abandoned the God-given ministry that was his heritage to serve man-made gods for personal gain. Micah was so blinded by his idolatry that he presumed that his hireling was evidence of God's favor. Herein is a danger. Too many charlatan preachers have controlled and convinced people that adhering to them and their teaching will bring them divine blessing. It is imperative to worship God in spirit and truth and to test the legitimacy of any minister in the clear light of God's Word. Everything in this chapter is a violation of God's law.

Chapter 18

1. The Levite again shows himself to be a religious mercenary for hire to the highest bidder. He had no convictions or concerns apart from himself. It will be terror on judgment day for false prophets who enrich themselves on religion. True worship and true Christian service demand loyalty to God and His Word. We must be willing to pay the price of faithful discipleship that we may receive the "well done, good and faithful servant" (Matt. 25:23).

2. Micah thought the presence of his idols in his shrine would be his safety (17:13). But there is no security in apostate religion, and his gods were easily stolen by others. The Lord alone is the protector of His people. The Christian

who trusts in the Lord Jesus as Savior has found a true refuge. "For this God is our God for ever and ever: he will be our guide even unto death" (Ps. 48:14). In what ways do you tend to trust in idols instead of the Lord?

Chapter 19

1. This chapter describes the tragedy of how far sin will go when there is no thought of God. Although there was no king in Israel (v. 1), there was a God in heaven who observed all the perverse behavior and would in due course punish accordingly. The chapter's closing admonition to consider and make plans to avoid the same tragedy remains valid. We should tremble for any people who are given over to practice vile sins. Judgment is not far away from those who stoop to these practices and we must remember that on the eternal day there awaits "the lake which burneth with fire and brimstone" (Rev. 21:8) for the unbelieving and the abominable in God's sight. These are warnings for us to flee from all forms of sin.

2. The master-secondary wife relationship between the Levite and his concubine is contrary to God's design for marriage. The whole episode betrays an unscriptural union and portrays a denigrating view of women. We should be thankful for the Christian gospel that has lifted societies out of such depths. Christianity has restored a nobility to manhood and womanhood, for in the power of the gospel "there is neither male nor female: for ye are all one in Christ Jesus" (Gal. 3:28). Let us thank the Lord for the new minds, new hearts, and new lives the gospel has given to us and let us pray for gospel power to evangelize the nations that are headed for terrible judgment.

Chapter 20

1. By sending a piece of his wife's body to each of the tribes of Israel, the Levite created a remarkable unity of purpose to punish the tribe of Benjamin. If only Israel had been so united in the cause of the Lord in past times they would have known many victories. When Christians stand together, pray together, and show forth the love of Christ with one accord, evil and wickedness can be put to flight. Solomon's maxim holds true, "A threefold cord is not quickly broken" (Eccl. 4:12).

2. The consequences of Gibeah's sins were certain and severe. "Be sure your sin will find you out" (Num. 32:23). God's righteous character demands that sin be punished in full. The just punishment leveled against Gibeah points to just execution of God's wrath against Christ. The whole gospel stands upon God's demand to judge sin fully. As believers, we confess that on that awful day at Calvary the full weight of divine justice fell on our Lord Jesus when He suffered in our place as our substitute. The gospel is not a covering up of sin, for in Christ's redeeming work justice was fully and legally settled. Justice being settled, it now stands guard for our salvation, for "Payment God cannot twice demand— / First at my bleeding Surety's hand, / And then again at mine," as hymnwriter Augustus Toplady expressed it. Because of Christ's sacrifice at Calvary there is a sure hope for every soul who trusts in Him for salvation. How does it stir your soul to consider that God's wrath fell on Christ instead of sinners?

Chapter 21

1. This caveat at the close of the book (v. 25) is a reminder that these were days of deep apostasy. The dark and distressing days of the judges provide warnings that man's heart is evil and that without restraint that evil progresses to unimaginable depths. Should we try to follow our own imaginations we will depart from God and stoop to heathen practices; we are not exempt. Grace and God's law must rule our hearts.

2. The book of Judges serves redemptive history by intensifying the desire and expectation for the perfect and final deliverer to come. Let us rejoice in the wonderful Savior God has given to deliver us from our sin. As the Savior of sinners our Lord Jesus is the great Judge. He is given by the Father to declare us righteous according to the law and to empower us to live godly in fellowship with Him. When we are born from above, we will seek those things which are above. When we are raised up with Christ by His resurrection power, we will reign with Him as sons of God. Heaven, the city of the great King, will be all the brighter when compared with the darkness of this rebellious world, where there is no king, no law, and no shame.

Ruth

Chapter 1

1. God's people can experience times of great darkness. Their nations may fall away from true religion into idolatry and immoral living; their families may face devastating consequences of poor decisions. In such times, all can seem like bitterness and emptiness, but it is essential that we cling to each other with faithful, committed love. To have a true companion like Ruth means the world to someone in pain. Be a true friend.

2. God converts pagan outsiders into believers who love the church. In His free grace, He may do so even when the church flounders in sin and misery. Like Ruth, true converts embrace the Lord and His people and hold on with holy stubbornness. The promises of the covenant of grace are written on their hearts and confessed by their mouths—God is their God. Are you experientially acquainted with Ruth's remarkable confession in verses 16–17?

Chapter 2

1. Ruth served her family, honored her mother-in-law, and demonstrated humility, respect, and gratitude. Boaz led his household to worship God in everyday life, protected and provided for the needy, spoke blessing on the faithful, and loved the foreigner and outsider. They are models worthy of our imitation.

2. The fatherly love of Boaz points us to Christ. Christ is full of strength and compassion as our mighty God and everlasting Father (Isa. 9:6). He protects and provides for all who hide under His wings. He reaches out to all nations. How beautiful is Christ, our Boaz! Love Him, adore Him, and trust in His mercy.

Chapter 3

1. Faith energizes love, submission, and self-denial. Naomi's renewed hope led her to take positive steps for the future of her family. Ruth's faith in the Lord made her a woman of excellence, who honored her mother and sought a godly husband. What fine examples they are of the impact godly women can have on their families!

2. The Lord has given His pledge to His waiting bride, the church. God gives His oath to anchor our covenant hope in Christ (Heb. 6:17–18), for He cannot lie, and He gives His Spirit as the seal of our assurance and down payment on our inheritance in Christ (Eph. 1:13–14). Let us therefore have hope, for Christ will come for poor sinners who cast all their hope on Him.

Chapter 4

1. Christ redeemed His people; He paid their ransom price at His own expense. He took the outsider as His bride. He made a public and binding commitment. He did it all so that poor outsiders might rejoice in His love and give glory to God. If you are a believer, never lose sight of the wonder of your redemption. It should always put a song in your heart. If you have not been brought into spiritual union with Christ

Jesus, consider seriously that you are lacking the greatest joy in life. Do not rest until you, too, can say that by God's amazing grace, Christ is your perfect Bridegroom.

2. God uses ordinary people to build the reputation and kingdom of His Son; this is the great aim of providence. Jonathan Edwards wrote, "God hath had it much on his heart, from all eternity, to glorify his dear and only-begotten Son." This kingdom is built of faithful love—the love of God and the love of believers being blessed by God. Therefore, do not grow weary in doing good, especially to the family of God. If you are faithful to serve where God puts you, it will impact generations to come.

1 Samuel

Chapter 1

1. This chapter teaches us so much about effectual, fervent prayer. Hannah is in complete submission to the will of the Lord, confessing that she is His "handmaid" (v. 11). She is dependent upon God; therefore she prays with real purpose and desires that her request will be to the glory of God. Her prayer is earnest; she "wept sore" (v. 10), and like the widow in the parable of the unjust judge (Luke 18:1–8) she persevered until her request was answered. How can we pray like Hannah?

2. Hannah's taking Samuel to the tabernacle and dedicating him to the service of the Lord demonstrates the importance of keeping vows made to the Lord. Humanly speaking, this had to have been an emotional trauma, but Hannah was not deterred from keeping her promise. Her vow was not rash. Vows are not "bargaining chips" to be used in prayer to get God to answer us according to our own will or desires. God takes vows seriously and expects us to keep our word (Eccl. 5:2–7).

Chapter 2

1. Hannah sets a wonderful example. When God answered her heartfelt prayer she was quick to acknowledge His goodness and to rejoice in Him. If we desire the Lord to answer our prayers, let us be sure to give Him our thanks and praise for those petitions already granted. "It is a good thing to give

thanks unto the LORD, and to sing praises unto thy name, O Most High" (Ps. 92:1). We should always rejoice in the Lord for His saving us through the work of His anointed, Jesus Christ. How have God's acts in your life revealed His glorious attributes in Jesus Christ? How are you praising Him for this?

2. There is a stark contrast between the wickedness of Eli's sons and the righteousness of Samuel. Both had the advantage of having godly parents; yet how differently they turned out. Despite the immense privilege of being born into a family of high spiritual standing, Hophni and Phinehas turned their backs upon the Lord and spurned His ways, seeking rather to exploit the people for personal gain. By way of contrast, Samuel was growing "in favour both with the LORD, and also with men" (v. 26). You who are the parents of young children, pray not only that the Lord would have mercy and save your offspring, but also seek by God's grace to correct any wayward behavior in them. Do not wait too long, as Eli did. Let us remember that the Lord says, "them that honour me I will honour" (v. 30).

Chapter 3

When the Lord called young Samuel, Samuel imagined it was Eli who spoke; yet his response provides a model of how we should perform our duties. No doubt Samuel's training for the Lord's service was demanding, with many chores. He probably looked forward to a good night's rest. Having "laid down to sleep" (v. 3), Samuel heard a voice calling him. He did not lie in bed or pretend to be asleep; he did not get up begrudging this interruption to his rest; instead he "ran unto Eli" (v. 5). There was a willingness to serve. Three times he got up and went to Eli without complaint or bitterness. It was only after this that he came to understand that it was the Lord who was calling him. Could there be times when we miss what the Lord is saying to us through His Word because we are overwhelmed by circumstances of life? Let us be sensitive to God's Word and not miss the blessings by failing to answer the Lord's calling us. What does it mean to pray "Speak, LORD; for thy servant heareth" (v. 9)?

Chapter 4

1. The defeat of Israel (v. 2) clearly revealed that the Lord was not among them. This defeat should have humbled them to seek the Lord, as Joshua did after Israel's defeat at Ai (Josh. 7:6–13). However, neither Hophni and Phinehas nor the people humbled themselves and prayed. Instead, they foolishly thought they could force God's hand to defend them by unlawfully bringing the ark onto the battlefield. They imagined that God would never allow the ark to fall into enemy hands. After all, the ark had been central in so many miracles and victories in the past (e.g., crossing the Jordan, Josh. 3, and the fall of Jericho, Josh. 6) that they viewed this sacred item as a mere good luck charm. The result was catastrophic for Israel. Religion is not a means of manipulating God for personal advantage. God will not be used. If we want to enjoy the blessings of His presence, we must obey His commands (Josh. 1:8–9). God hides His face from the wicked (Deut. 31:17). What religious objects or rituals do people trust in today?

2. The name "Ichabod" represents a tragedy for the Lord's people. The glory of the Lord departed from Israel because

of their sins, and likewise we find it gone in many churches today. Some churches may appear to be lively and well attended. Some individuals may put on an outward, public show of humility and faith. But appearance may not equate to reality. Christ's accusation is this: "I know thy works, that thou hast a name that thou livest, and art dead" (Rev. 3:1). What about you? What does the Lord Jesus say of you? Oh how we need, by God's grace, to hide His Word in our hearts that we do not sin against Him (cf. Ps. 119:11). Whenever we do sin let us ensure that we make all haste to truly repent and wait upon the Lord.

Chapter 5

1. Although the ark was not the reality of God's person, it was symbolic of His presence, and the Philistines were aware of its significance. For the sake of His own glory, God would not allow the heathens, who in their ignorance equated the box with Jehovah, to elevate their idol above Himself. Without human aid, He demonstrated that Dagon was nothing, a figment of their imagination without life or power. We learn an important lesson here: while God is often pleased to use human instrumentality in His service, He needs no one to rescue Him or help Him. Therefore we must always ensure that our work for Him is carried out in reverent humility, for the Lord is not dependent upon anyone. His power and might are beyond human comprehension.

2. The Philistines acted ignorantly but were nonetheless held accountable for their blasphemy and violation of the first commandment. God's law is absolute, and ignorance of it is no excuse. What are the implications of this for missions?

Chapter 6

1. That the Philistines kept the ark for seven months (v. 1) testifies to the nature of spiritual deadness and insensitivity. Notwithstanding the irrefutable evidence of God's power and the excruciating pain of the plague, they refused to acknowledge God and the consequences of their sin. Why did they wait so long before returning the ark? This is reminiscent of Pharaoh's putting off Moses's offer to rid the land of frogs (Ex. 8:10). But it is the nature of sin to make us blind to sin's solution. It ought to be our desire to remain sensitive to sin and to be quick in dealing with it before the Lord.

2. "Who is able to stand before this holy LORD God?" (v. 20) is an important question. The Philistines could not, nor could the men of Beth-shemesh. Whether by the heathen or religious, trying to access God in a way that He has not prescribed is fatal. The question points to the ultimate answer that the only way man can stand before the Lord and live is through the only Mediator, the Lord Jesus (Heb. 10:19–22).

Chapter 7

1. Samuel served as a prophet, a judge, and a priest. This chapter illustrates two connected functions of the priest, both of which point to work of the ideal Priest, the Lord Jesus: he offered sacrifices and then interceded for the people (vv. 8–9). Likewise, our Savior's intercession for His people is on the grounds of His supreme sacrifice for sin, which is pleasing unto the Father (1 John 2:1–2). The Lord heard and answered Samuel (Ps. 99:6), and we can have even more confidence and assurance of faith that God will never turn

away from the intercessions of His Son. Israel owed deliverance from the Philistines to Samuel's intercession; we owe everything to Christ's intercession for us. How does this encourage you to call upon Jesus Christ in prayer for your spiritual needs?

2. It is a blessed and comforting thought to know that God is faithful in all of His dealings with His people. He has promised to always be with those who are called by His grace. Surely every true child of God can say with Samuel, "Hitherto hath the LORD helped us" (v. 12). He has walked with us in our trials. He has comforted us in our grief. He has protected us from our foes and been to us an ever-present help in trouble. Christ says, "I am with you alway, even unto the end of the world" (Matt. 28:20). Let us therefore raise our Ebenezer of praise and rejoice in the Lord's goodness.

Chapter 8

1. Dissatisfaction with government is common, regardless of what form it takes. Israel was discontent with judges and assumed that a monarchy would solve their problems. Samuel rightly predicted that the day would come when monarchy would disappoint as well (v. 18). It is imperative to remember that all government is ordained by God (Rom. 13), and it should be our prayer that God would favor us with a government that is wise and righteous (2 Sam. 23:3; Prov. 8:12–16; 1 Tim. 2:1–2). But let us never forget that government cannot be our God, for it consists of fallen human beings. How can we honor civil leaders and honor God above all?

2. Kingship in Israel was part of God's purpose for His people and had notable messianic significance (Gen. 49:10).

Israel's request for a king was a great disappointment to Samuel because it was motivated by selfish interests (1 Sam. 8:20) rather than concern for God's glory and the progression of His redemptive purpose. He also took it personally, as a rejection of his ministry. But at this critical point, Samuel provides the pattern of how we should respond to displeasing news: "Samuel prayed unto the LORD" (v. 6). Our very first thought should be to take it to the Lord. Praying for God's will to be done and for His kingdom to come focuses the heart where it needs to be.

Chapter 9

1. The circumstances leading to Samuel's meeting with Saul illustrate the remarkable providence of God that directs all the affairs of life, including human choices and seemingly random events, to accomplish His ultimate purpose (Gen. 50:20; Prov. 16:33). The search for lost donkeys appeared to be an exercise in futility and failure, but it was the means of bringing Saul to a critical moment that defined his life from that day forward. Little did he know when leaving home on the donkey hunt that he would return as the "king elect" of the nation. This is a reminder that we do not know what a day will bring forth and that it is good to know that our times are in the hands of God.

2. The occurrence of the titles "man of God," "Prophet," and "Seer" in this chapter reminds us both of the necessary character and of the authority of the one God called to declare His word to others. The prophet's character is to be godly, and his message is never self-generated. The prophet is to speak only what has been spoken to him, and the seer is to

reveal only what has been revealed to him. The principle applies to modern ministry as well, as preachers are to be examples of godliness and have the authority to preach only God's Word (2 Tim. 4:1–2).

Chapter 10

Opinions differ on exactly what Saul's "another heart" means. Regardless, the narrative of Saul's anointing illustrates a vital truth: God is able to transform people. Notwithstanding Saul's physical stature, he lacked self-confidence and evidenced no particular skills of leadership. But God equipped him for his ordained office, and his transformation was evident to those who knew him before and after his anointing. The Holy Spirit is able to equip people with spiritual gifts (v. 6; 1 Cor. 12:4–7). Only by His power can we serve God's kingdom effectively. However, the greatest gift is the transformation of the new birth. Let us never rest in gifts and abilities, but earnestly seek assurance that we are true children born of God (John 1:12–13).

Chapter 11

1. When Israel gained victory, Saul reminded the people that their triumph did not come because they had an earthly king but because "the LORD hath wrought salvation in Israel" (v. 13). This is a principle that we also must remember: whenever we obtain a victory, it is solely the result of God's power. As Christ reminds us, "without me ye can do nothing" (John 15:5).

2. It is significant that when Samuel confirmed Saul as king, he did so by calling the people to gather at Gilgal (v. 14).

This was the place where Israel first set up camp when entering the Promised Land (Josh. 4:19). It was the place where Joshua instructed Israel to take twelve stones from the midst of the Jordan "for a memorial unto the children of Israel for ever" (Josh. 4:7). In coming to this place, the people were surely reminded of the Lord's past help. When looking to the future, it is a good thing for us to consider the past. Such reminders of His goodness will be of great benefit to our souls, especially when the future looks uncertain.

Chapter 12

1. Samuel declares to the people that he would not hold their sin against them, he would not cease to pray for them, and he would teach them the good way (vv. 20, 23). In considering this, do we not see a far greater One than Samuel who intercedes on our behalf? What a blessing it is to know that though we have sinned against Christ, He never ceases to remember us in mercy, He pleads with the Father on our behalf, and He teaches us the good way through His Word and by His Spirit. How are you consciously exercising faith in Christ in all of these?

2. It is a sad failing in many of us that there are times when we are prone to dwell upon the disappointments and miseries of life rather than upon the many blessings that we receive from the Lord's merciful hand. Samuel could have wallowed in self-pity at the passing of his judgeship and the failure of his sons, but instead he said, "Consider how great things [the Lord] hath done for you" (v. 24). The greatest thing is that Christ suffered and died that we might be redeemed through the shedding of His precious blood. Let us consider this

and give Him all the glory, that our hearts may rejoice even in tribulation.

Chapter 13

Waiting is often one of the most difficult tests of faith. Impatience can result in rash acts that dishonor the Lord. From impatience came the golden calf (Ex. 32:1). Here it was Saul's impatience in waiting for Samuel that led to his infringing on the priestly office, a most serious offense for kings (2 Chron. 26:16–21). In Christ these functions would merge. Saul's impatience warranted severe consequences: only two years into his reign and the prospect of a dynasty was gone. Waiting time is never wasted time, as it increases our sense of dependence on the Lord. Those who wait on the Lord will never be disappointed with the Lord and His timing (Ps. 37:7–11; Isa. 40:31). Let us learn from Israel's and Saul's impatience that God's timing is best and that we can trust Him completely.

Chapter 14

1. The situation looked hopeless for Israel, but Jonathan looked beyond the circumstances to the Lord. Like Caleb, his confidence was in God (Num. 13:30; 14:6–9). He knew the Lord could "save by many or by few" (1 Sam. 14:6). What an encouragement Jonathan ought to be to us in our service to the Lord. His faith and love raised him above any anxious cares. His first concern was for the honor of the Lord. By God's grace, let us strive to uphold this same principle, by "looking unto Jesus the author and finisher of our faith" (Heb. 12:2). How can we grow in such a faith?

2. Saul issued a very foolish command that his army should not eat until the Philistines were defeated. It was a command that God had not required, and it nearly cost Jonathan his life because he was unaware of the oath (v. 27). It is of vital importance that Christians never seek to impose upon the Lord's people those things that God has not insisted upon. Too many in the professing church seek to turn their own ideas into biblical commands. Let us never make a personal preference into a precept.

Chapter 15

1. God's dealing with the Amalekites illustrates how slow God is to express His anger, and yet how certain it is that His judgment will fall on the wicked (Nah. 1:3). God had announced in Exodus 17:14 that He would destroy the Amalekites because of their wicked attack upon Israel as they traveled through the wilderness. Many years had passed, evidencing the patience of God. But God had not forgotten, and the sin of Amalek had now come to full fruition; their judgment was impending. Sinners often interpret the delay of justice as evidence of God's inability to judge (Ps. 94:5–11; Ezek. 12:21–25; 2 Peter 3:4–7). Rather, the patient goodness of God is designed to lead to repentance (Rom. 2:3–4). How has God been patient with you? How should you repent thoroughly of your sins?

2. The mere outward expression of worship without the engaging of the heart means nothing to God. Saul had disobeyed the Lord and had tried to appease Him through the sacrifice. The Lord requires and delights in the submission of the human will to His Word: "Behold, to obey is better than

sacrifice" (v. 22). Obedience demonstrates our love for God (Ex. 20:6; John 14:21). Through His obedience our Lord Jesus Christ saved sinners and brought them to eternal joy in God (Ps. 40:6–8; Matt. 26:42; John 4:34; 6:38–40; 17:4; Rom. 5:19; Phil. 2:8). Therefore, love obedience, delight in obedience, treasure obedience, and pursue full obedience by the grace of Christ.

Chapter 16

1. Man looks on the outside, but God looks on the inside (v. 7). This should produce sobriety and the fear of the Lord (Prov. 15:11; 16:2; Heb. 4:13). It ought to be our constant desire and prayer that as the Lord looks at us He will see nothing that displeases Him (Pss. 17:3; 139:23–24). But man's looking on the outside ought to be a motive for proper living as well, since trees are known by their fruit (Matt. 7:16–20). As Christians we should strive to live before men bearing fruit in such a way that evidences that we are united to Christ, the vine (John 15:5).

2. That Saul's troubled soul could be soothed by David's harp suggests something about the inherent power of music to affect the person even apart from its words. Music is often the instrument of Satan to arouse passions and behaviors that are destructive to self and society. On the other hand, music is a means of praising and worshiping God and can direct our hearts heavenward. Let us be careful therefore not to listen to music that incites the works of the flesh, like sensuality and anger, but instead to listen to music that helps us to think, feel, and act for the glory of God.

Chapter 17

1. The conflict between David and Goliath is a microcosm of the conflict between the seed of the woman, Christ, and the seed of the serpent (Gen. 3:15). Since David was in the line of Christ, his death at this time would have put the messianic promise in jeopardy. But against all odds, for Goliath had every natural advantage, God gave David the victory and advanced the promise leading to the fullness of time when Christ came. The hostility continues, and it often seems as though the advantage belongs to the serpent. But God's redemptive purpose in Christ is certain, and Christ's church and kingdom will advance regardless of the opposition. The King greater than David will keep on slaying the enemies greater than Goliath until every enemy is placed under His feet (Ps. 110:1–2). How do you need to look to Christ for victory over sin and Satan today?

2. Reflecting on past victories from the Lord fuels faith for the next battle, which will certainly come. God enabled David to slay the lion and the bear, and he believed that God would likewise enable him to slay the giant. The God of the past is the God of the present. How much easier our own trials would be if we would remember this principle! Were there not many times in the past when God delivered you from situations that would otherwise have defeated you and brought you down? Then why would He not do the same in your present difficulties? Christian, remember and take hold of this thought: "The LORD is my light and my salvation; whom shall I fear? The LORD is the strength of my life; of whom shall I be afraid?" (Ps. 27:1).

Chapter 18

1. David and Jonathan exemplify the beauty of friendship (Prov. 17:17; 18:24). They enjoyed a bond of love and loyalty that transcended even blood relation. This was evidenced throughout their lives and by David even after Jonathan's death (2 Sam. 9:1). The bond subdued envy and endured even at personal risk. Today the idea of friendship has been reduced to refer to mere acquaintances who share little in common. Christians should seek out good friends for mutual accountability and edification. We should, likewise, rejoice that in the ideal sense we have the Friend who by virtue of His covenant is closer to us than anyone else could be.

2. Desire for self-glory rather than God's glory is always disastrous. Saul and David fought a common enemy in the Philistines; they were both engaged in advancing the kingdom. But because David received accolades for slaying more than he did (v. 7), Saul became envious, bitter, and obsessive against David. All too often in the work of God there is the temptation to look at what others are doing in the church and become envious of their ministries. Those in "small ministries" may turn their attacks against those in "larger ministries" rather than battling the common enemy. As Paul said, some plant and some water, but the increase is God's (1 Cor. 3:6–9). We should learn to be faithful in the service God has given us and rejoice at every advance of the kingdom, even when God places someone besides ourselves in the spotlight.

Chapter 19

1. That "there was war again" (v. 8) sums up much of the Christian life. No matter how many times David killed some Philistines, they kept showing up as a renewed threat. David could rejoice in past victories, but he could not rest in them. So it is in the battle against self, sin, and Satan. The enemy of holiness is relentless, and we must be on constant guard. We can rejoice that God has given victory over temptations in the past, but we cannot assume that past victory guarantees the next. Such is the nature of sin and our weakness that the same temptations show up over and over. But new victories are possible every time as we rely upon the provision we have in Christ.

2. Although various people came to David's rescue, God was the ultimate deliverer (vv. 20–24). The Spirit of God intervened, turning every threat—even Saul himself—into an instrument of praise. The power of God's Spirit is irresistible (Zech. 4:6–7). So as we fight against sin's dominion, we should do so through the Holy Spirit (Rom. 8:13).

Chapter 20

1. David's difficulties teach us that God's love and favor do not shield us from the trials and bitter experiences of life. Indeed, God's blessings often promote hostility from the world and enmity from those who are mere professors of Christianity. David's trials were particularly hard to bear because he had been Saul's faithful servant. Yet he could say "weeping may endure for a night, but joy cometh in the morning" (Ps. 30:5). It is at these very times of trial that we need to rest upon the promises of God. How can trusting

that trials are ordained for our good (Rom. 8:28) enable you to rejoice even now in the sorrows you are facing?

2. David's lament "there is but a step between me and death" (v. 3) had pointed bearing on the issues David was facing. Yet it is a statement with universal and timeless relevance. The preacher said, "For man also knoweth not his time…when it falleth suddenly upon them" (Eccl. 9:12). The time of death is uncertain, but the fact of it is unavoidable (Heb. 9:27). We are not to morbidly wonder about the day of death, but we are to live in its certainty, knowing that it is only during life that we can get ready for eternity. Awareness of being only a step away, indeed a heartbeat away, from death should generate urgency in every heart that today is the day of salvation (2 Cor. 6:2).

Chapter 21

1. The Lord Jesus appeals to the episode with the priests' bread to refute and rebuke the Pharisees for their legalism regarding the Sabbath. Christ taught that works of necessity, such as eating, do not violate the spiritual precept of the law (Mark 2:25). David's eating the consecrated bread was out of the norm but necessary. The Lord reminds us that God looks on the heart, which is more important than rigid and heartless conformity to form. It is possible to do things right on the outside, like the Pharisees, without a heart toward the Lord. How can we avoid this?

2. Proverbs 29:25 says that fearing man brings a snare. This episode in David's career illustrates this truth; he feared Saul and Achish (1 Sam. 21:10, 12). That fear led to foolish and sinful behavior, including a lie to the priest and trying to find

safety with the enemy. Given the circumstances, David's fear was understandable, for his life was indeed under threat, but his actions were inexcusable. Proverbs 29:25 also says that the one who trusts the Lord will be safe. There were times and there would be times in the future when David's trust and fear of the Lord, instead of his circumstances, overwhelmed him (Pss. 31:13–16; 112:7). David learned his lesson even in this particular situation (see Ps. 34:4 and its superscription). We all should follow his counsel and "fear the LORD…for there is no want to them that fear him" (Ps. 34: 9).

Chapter 22

1. Some things are hard to understand, especially when evil runs rampant and innocent blood is shed. Yet even in this God is working out His purposes; even the "wrath of man" will praise the Lord (Ps. 76:10). The slaughter of the priests was a fulfillment of God's word of judgment against them (1 Sam. 2:31–33).

2. The death of the priests also puts in bold the truth that sin has consequences that go beyond the sinner himself. David's lie to Ahimelech may have seemed trivial. At the time, he may well have justified it as a "harmless" sin to help him escape from Saul, yet what terrible consequences resulted. There is actually no such thing as a private sin. Either by consequence or example sin affects others. How have you justified "little" sins in your life? What is the right way to deal with them?

Chapter 23

1. David's dealings with Keilah show the importance of discerning and doing the Lord's will in making decisions. David

inquired of the Lord through prayer and through the priest who apparently employed the Urim and Thummim, the means God had ordained for discovering His will. He used the means of grace. How important it is to commit matters to the Lord before embarking on any venture, even when we think we know what we should do (Josh. 9:14). The Christian is not an independent agent but rather the servant of Christ. There should be no place for rash action or even calculated reasoning apart from the Lord (Prov. 3:5–6). We should take everything to the Lord, seeking Him in prayer and searching His Word for direction.

2. How wonderful the providences of God are! David and his men were completely surrounded by Saul's forces. He was between the rock and the hard place, with seemingly no way of escape. But at the critical moment the Philistines invaded the land, diverting Saul from his pursuit of David. Ironically, the Philistines David defeated at the beginning of the chapter unknowingly come to his rescue at the end. This intervention gave David the opportunity to escape. Let us therefore take heart when things seem hopeless: "For with God nothing shall be impossible" (Luke 1:37). What situations seem impossible to you now? Take them to the Lord in prayer.

Chapter 24

1. David's sparing Saul illustrates two important principles: respect for office and reliance on divine justice. Saul had abused the office and on the personal level deserved no respect or honor. But David recognized that Saul was the Lord's anointed. Heads of government often fail to govern justly, but God's command is that we are to fear Him and

honor the king (1 Peter 2:17). David also shows a willingness to wait upon the Lord rather than take action himself to improve his status or remove the threat to his own life. Vengeance belongs to the Lord (Heb. 10:30), and He will execute justice (Rom. 12:19). The temptation when justice is delayed is to take matters into our own hands, but those who fear God know that ultimately justice prevails (Eccl. 8:11–13). How can you apply this lesson to your life?

2. Saul's reaction to David's sparing his life is emotional and seemingly sincere, but only temporary. Saul's tears were no doubt real. His conscience was sufficiently moved to feel some remorse for his vindictive behavior toward David, yet his sorrow is not that of one who is truly penitent. There is more to true repentance than just being sorry for a particular deed. There must be turning from sin to God.

Chapter 25

1. It is significant to note the emphasis that Nabal places on his possessions: he says "*my* bread, and *my* water, and *my* flesh that I have killed" (v. 11, emphasis added). This proud boast of his possessions is similar to the parable Jesus tells where the farmer says "*my* barns...*my* fruits and *my* goods" (Luke 12:18, emphasis added). In response to this boasting, we read, "But God said unto him, Thou fool, this night thy soul shall be required of thee: then whose shall those things be, which thou hast provided?" (v. 20). Let us never boast of the possessions that God has given us or selfishly keep all for ourselves, but rather let us use such gifts in the Lord's service, as He directs. Nabal was a fool by name and a fool by nature,

and the Lord smote him (1 Sam. 25:38). How can we avoid such foolishness in our own lives?

2. In stark contrast to Nabal, what wonderful spiritual qualities we see in Abigail. She typifies the virtuous woman whose "price is far above rubies" (Prov. 31:10), and she uses her God-given gifts to turn David's heart from revenge against her husband and all in his household. She displays wisdom and grace. David came to understand that the hand of God was upon Abigail, and he said, "Blessed be the LORD God of Israel, which sent thee this day to meet me" (1 Sam. 25:32). Let us pray that such spiritual qualities might be seen in us, and let us be quick to rejoice when we find them in others.

Chapter 26

1. Once again Saul is delivered into David's hands, yet once again David is convicted by the Spirit of God not to take Saul's life. Scripture repeats the lesson of 24:1–22 that we might learn from David's example. We must never take matters into our own hands; instead we must wait upon the Lord to vindicate us. Those who wait on the Lord will never be ashamed, for they follow in the footsteps of Christ, who patiently endured suffering while entrusting Himself to a faithful and just Judge (1 Peter 2:19–23; 4:12–19). In what ways are you tempted to take revenge? How can you resist this urge?

2. Toward the end of his life, Saul makes a very sad confession: "I have played the fool, and have erred exceedingly" (v. 21). Tragically, there are many like Saul who, looking back on their lives, must also confess to having played the fool. What a multitude of missed opportunities and failures there

can be for such people! What a blessing therefore at the end of our lives if we can say with the Saul of the New Testament (Paul), "I have fought a good fight, I have finished my course, I have kept the faith" (2 Tim. 4:7). May God help us to be like Paul and make an exclamation of triumph rather than a confession of tragedy as King Saul was forced to utter.

Chapter 27

1. Failures of faith often come immediately after victories of faith. David's refusal to take personal vengeance on Saul was a high-water mark of faith (26:1–25); his consulting with himself and fleeing to Achish was a low point. Notwithstanding the number of times God had preserved him, David convinced himself that sooner or later Saul would succeed. He thought about negative possibilities rather than the certain promises of God. We must never let down our guard and must remember that we are often most susceptible to falling immediately after times of blessing and spiritual victories.

2. In the spiritual realm, appearance and reality are seldom the same. David made a carnal decision, and it appeared from circumstances to be the right move. Saul no longer pursued him, and he was able to engage in kingdom work by fighting against the enemies of God's people. But these ends did not justify the means. Just because something seems to work does not mean it is God's will. It must always be God's Word, rather than circumstances, that governs. We are to walk by faith, not sight.

Chapter 28

This chapter illustrates the tragic consequences of sin. Saul's public sin started with incomplete obedience to God's command (v. 18) and ended with his blatant violations of God's command. Sin indeed is a slippery slope that leads to a very deep bottom. Saul was pressed down from the outside in and felt desperation because God had departed from him. He could get no word from the Lord. What a warning this is to listen to God's Word and to keep our accounts with the Lord short so that we can have access to His Word. Child of God, is it not the most wonderful blessing that you were made to hear His voice? How you ought to praise the Lord that He has not left you! Ironically, the chapter begins with David in a most compromising situation. Will David descend the slippery slope? Will you?

Chapter 29

1. Fearing the threats of Saul and failing to fully trust the Lord, David and his men sought shelter with the Philistines, Israel's enemy. This led to a very difficult situation. They found themselves united with Achish, who would do harm to the Lord's people. Mercifully, providence intervened, and God used the ungodly as His agents to keep David from further sin. They said, "What do these Hebrews here?" (v. 3). A similar question might be asked of those professing Christians who side with the world. Are we not commanded, "Be ye not unequally yoked together with unbelievers" (2 Cor. 6:14)? Christian, where are you standing at present? Let us ensure that we are always on the Lord's side, and with the Lord's people.

2. This chapter wonderfully illustrates the principle set out in 1 Corinthians 10:13: "There hath no temptation taken you but such as is common to man: but God is faithful, who will not suffer you to be tempted above that ye are able; but will with the temptation also make a way to escape, that ye may be able to bear it." Perhaps to David's eyes there was no way to extricate himself from the mess he had gotten himself into, but God delivered him. Let us take comfort in this when we find ourselves in wrong situations of our own making, and let us confidently call on the Lord to deliver us.

Chapter 30

1. It is very often in times of distress and adversity that we acknowledge our dependence on God the most. So it was with David. At Ziklag, God brought him to the end of himself; he lost everything. However, it is here that David shows himself a true man of God: "David encouraged himself in the LORD his God" (v. 6). What an example David is to us here. When terrible catastrophes come upon us, how easy it is to become overwhelmed with sorrow and grief. Yet if we would know true deliverance and desire spiritual benefit, there can be no better way than to look to the Lord and encourage ourselves in Him. He has promised "I am with you alway, even unto the end of the world" (Matt. 28:20), and has assured us of "an inheritance incorruptible, and undefiled, and that fadeth not away" (1 Peter 1:4). Let us, then, look to these promises and encourage ourselves in the Lord; then we shall grow in grace and be better fitted for the Master's service.

2. The two words "recover all" (vv. 8, 18–19) constitute a statement of hope. Everything that David lost because of

his sin and God's chastening hand was recovered when he strengthened himself in the Lord and sought to do God's will. There is hope for the backslider that God will restore him to fellowship and usefulness upon returning to Him. David's recovering all parallels the equally encouraging promise that God later gives through Joel after the devastation of the locust plague: "and I will restore to you the years that the locust hath eaten" (Joel 2:25). Let us never fail to seek the Lord because He will draw near to those who draw near to Him (James 4:8).

Chapter 31

1. The narrative of Saul ends tragically with a shameful death in defeat. His life seemed so promising and full of potential but took a disastrous turn with his disobedience. From that moment on it was filled with misery and envy, and his death came in excruciating agony. People debate whether Saul was an unbelieving hypocrite or a backslidden believer, but it is clear that he descended into great depths of spiritual darkness. His life is a sober warning that sin leads to great sorrow, and repentance can never come too soon.

2. On the same day Saul died and in the same battle, Jonathan also died. His righteous behavior and loyalty to David as God's anointed did not spare him. Thus, the book ends with a sober reminder that it is appointed unto all men to die and after that the judgment (Heb. 9:27). Death comes to the wise and foolish alike (Ps. 49:10). It is imperative and urgent in the life that remains to be ready for the judgment to come. If you knew you would soon die, what would you do differently? Why not seek God's grace to change today?

2 Samuel

Chapter 1

1. The Amalekite lied, assuming the deception would earn him a reward. Almost every lie is motivated by self-preservation or self-advancement. Very often lies are discovered and consequences must be faced. Here the Amalekite's lie is not discovered, but he suffers the consequence of being believed. The bottom line is that one way or another and sooner or later our words will betray us. We can be sure that our sins will find us out. There is no covering ourselves or escaping the One who sees all, no matter how well we plan or how detailed our lies. In this life or the next, sin will be punished unless Christ has borne the penalty. Why must we be totally honest to the Lord when confessing our sins?

2. David's anguish over Jonathan is intense. How tender the son of Jesse's love is for his friend! But as close-knit as the friendship of David and Jonathan was, it pales in comparison to Christ's friendship with His people. "I have called you friends," He says to His disciples, who were at the point of either denying or abandoning Him (John 15:15). We see here why David is the prophetic image of Christ, who, "having loved his own which were in the world, he loved them unto the end" (John 13:1).

Chapter 2

1. Although David had been promised the kingdom years earlier (1 Sam. 16), he did not try to establish it on his own.

He refused to kill Saul even though he had multiple chances, and now he is still patient. He was willing to be guided by the Lord's will as to both time and manner of his promotion. This reminds us that "He that believeth shall not make haste" (Isa. 28:16). By David's example we are reminded that in all of life's dealings, hopes, and fears, we must seek the will of God by faith and prayer. "In all thy ways acknowledge him, and he shall direct thy paths" (Prov. 3:6). David's example also reminds us not to give up on God's promises. Delay of promise is not denial of promise. We must learn to wait on the Lord with the confidence that He will accomplish His word in His way and in His time. How does waiting on God increase your faith and dependence on Him?

2. Resorting to violence to resolve differences, even at the national level, should be the last resort. It was God's will that David rule in Saul's place (1 Sam. 13:13–14; 15:28). Had Israel sought the Lord, David's kingdom could have been established without bloodshed. Discerning God's will ought to always be a priority for God's people. But instead, the narrative records the brutality of the battle. If we love our neighbors as ourselves, let us use the best means possible to advance the principle of peace with all men and look to that perfect day when "they shall beat their swords into plowshares, and their spears into pruninghooks" (Isa. 2:4).

Chapter 3

1. It was God's purpose for David to reign over Israel. Divine providence assured that the divine will would happen. As God is able to turn the hearts of kings (Prov. 21:1), so He turned the heart of Abner, the chief leader in Saul's house, to

become a principal agent in uniting the nation under David. Regardless of Abner's motives, selfish or otherwise, God used him to accomplish the divine will. We can be confident that God's power to control circumstances and people has never diminished. Thus, as we pray for God's will to be done and for His kingdom to come, we can be sure that nothing can ultimately prevent either from occurring.

2. Vengeance belongs to the Lord (Heb. 10:30). To presume to take upon oneself a work that belongs to God is always going to have serious consequences. Joab's treacherous murder of Abner is a tragic illustration. Abner had indeed killed Joab's brother, but it was in battle and not a surprising casualty of war. Joab's murder was calculated, hateful, and under the guise of peace. David recognized the cold-blooded nature of the crime and pronounced a curse on Joab and his family. In all likelihood there are going to be times when we will be wronged by others, and our natural impulse will be to get even. We should learn to leave with the Lord what belongs to Him and not take matters into our own hands. Indeed, Christ teaches us that when we suffer personal wrong we are to turn the other cheek (Matt. 5:39).

Chapter 4

Ish-bosheth was sleeping when he should have been vigilant and on guard. While he slumbered, the enemy came in, and he was slain in his sleep. It is only common sense to stay awake and watchful in the face of danger. But this is an important strategy for spiritual life as well. First Peter 5:8 says, "Be sober, be vigilant; because your adversary the devil, as a roaring lion, walketh about, seeking whom he may devour." Christ's words to His sleepy disciples are also to the point: "Watch and pray, that ye enter not into temptation: the spirit indeed is willing, but the flesh is weak" (Matt. 26:41). How can Christians stay vigilant in the spiritual battle?

Chapter 5

1. One of the most important statements in this chapter is in verse 19: "And David enquired of the LORD." He was the king of a great realm, but David felt that even on a throne he needed the Lord's counsel. David was not satisfied without something higher and greater than himself. There is no status in life beyond the necessity of prayer. The day will come when prayer gives way to only praise. But in this world no one can rise above their circumstances. No one can escape the many needs to be filled, sins to be forgiven, and tears to be wiped away. We need to inquire of the Lord. There is nothing so small that He does not know, care for, and control. Do you inquire of the Lord as you should? How can you grow in your prayer life?

2. God leads His people in different ways, and we must learn to be sensitive and open to Him. It was just the sound of rustling leaves that was David's sign to move against the enemy—something very ordinary and very subtle. Yet having prayed for God to lead, he was paying attention to the divine instruction. Too often in seeking God's will we try to set the terms or devise scenarios in which we challenge the Lord to act in the most obvious of ways (fleece after fleece). Sometimes He does. But more often it is just the "whisper" of His Spirit through His Word that gives the answer we need. The key is to fear Him so that He gives us His counsel (Ps. 25:14).

Chapter 6

1. David's desire for the ark expressed his desire for the manifest presence of God. This man after God's own heart purposed to put the ark of the Lord in the place of preeminence it deserved. He had nothing but the glory of the Lord in mind. But tragically, he was taken away with the fervency of his zeal. His desire was good and his motives pure, but he displeased the Lord he sought to honor. It is not sufficient to claim a worthy purpose without conforming as well to the clear mandates of God's Word. He adopted the practice of the pagans in transporting the ark (1 Sam. 6) in violation of the precise method that God had prescribed. Methods of worship do matter, and we must avoid adopting or adapting the practices of the world for use in sacred worship. There are many Christians who desire the right things but are lax in the mode of practice. Not only is God the sole object of worship, but He has revealed the acceptable way of worshiping.

2. The ark was the ultimate symbol in the Old Testament for God's presence. This narrative highlights four important lessons about experiencing God's presence. First, it is something to be understood. The ark declares God's sovereignty, holiness, righteousness, grace, and mercy, all of which are realized in Christ (see notes at Ex. 25:10–22). Second, it is something to be desired. David's desire was intensified by the ark's long absence (1 Sam. 7:1–2). The absence of God's presence should be intolerable to us. Third, it is something to be feared. This was learned the hard way in the death of Uzzah. Not even the godliest dare become familiar with holy things by treating them as common. Fourth, it is something to be enjoyed. The house of Obed-edom experienced real

and obvious blessing, which motivated David to desire the blessing for himself. Enjoying God is worth doing things the right way. When David brought up the ark according to God's way, he was overwhelmed with joy and humble worship. How should these principles shape the way that we approach God in worship?

Chapter 7

1. Although God's covenant promise to David narrowed the identity of the Messiah to the family of David, David realized that the significance of the promise went far beyond the concerns of his family and little kingdom. He made a profound statement reflecting his faith and insight into worldwide significance: "this is the revelation for humanity." David saw that his Seed was going to be a source of blessing for the world, just as in the promise to Abraham hundreds of years earlier (Gen. 12:3; 22:18). How does the gospel make the covenant with David good news for us today?

2. David's prayer following the promise provides a wonderful pattern for us as we pray. As you work through the prayer, note the recognition of God's free grace (v. 21), greatness (v. 22), goodness (v. 23), and gracious covenant (v. 24). Our prayers likewise should be full of praises for these things. Note also the desire for God's glory (v. 26) and the plea for God's revealed will to be done (vv. 28–29). In the same way we should seek God's honor in all our prayers and turn God's promises into petitions that He would do what He has said.

Chapter 8

1. David's subduing one enemy after another is a wonderful picture pointing to the One greater than David, the Lord Jesus. He is the messianic and mediatorial King of His people who conquers all of His and our enemies. He conquers His people by grace, making them willing in the day of His power (Ps. 110:3). He conquers His enemies with the rod of His strength (110:2). But whether by grace or by rod, He conquers. Those of us who are willing subjects should be careful to pledge to Him our allegiance and to praise Him for His benefits to us. Those who remain rebels should obey the call of the Spirit to honor the Son before it is too late (2:12).

2. David's just rule of his people is another pointer to the ideal King. God's decree regarding Messiah's kingdom was "to order it, and to establish it with judgment and with justice" forever (Isa. 9:7). Similarly, Ps. 72 details Messiah's execution of righteous judgments; His rule is ideal (45:6–7; Isa. 11:1–5). None other than Jesus satisfies the inspired job description of kings: "He that ruleth over men must be just, ruling in the fear of God" (2 Sam. 23:3). This should be great comfort to believers. So often it appears that wickedness reigns supreme and that life is filled with inequities. But the King and Judge of all the earth does only right, and justice will prevail (Eccl. 8:12–13). How can this truth strengthen Christians?

Chapter 9

1. This narrative is rich in parallels to the gospel that deserve meditation. We are reminded of the love of Jesus, who seeks out, saves, loves, and dwells with poor, ruined, worthless sinners and lays on them great and lasting mercy. David is a

picture of the Savior who graciously and mercifully seeks those whom He will save. Mephibosheth is a picture of the sinner. His being lame and his living in Lo-debar (no pasture) illustrate the sinner who has no power or resources of his own to remedy his dreadful state of misery. The bountiful provisions depict salvation itself. Being regarded and treated as the king's son and feasting at the royal banquets point to the believer's adoption into God's family and the enjoyment of all the benefits of grace as He brings poor, vile sinners into His house of wine (Song 2:4).

2. The episode also teaches very practical lessons. As David remembered his promise to Jonathan, so the child of God should always keep his word to others. Let it never be said that the men of this world keep their word better than the believer. The example of David here is worthy of imitation. The kindness that David showed to Mephibosheth also teaches us to show kindness to those who are in need. All true kindness shown by a child of God is Christlike. "Let us do good unto all men, especially unto them who are of the household of faith" (Gal. 6:10).

Chapter 10

1. Hanun's rejection of David's kindness is analogous to the way sinners reject the mercy of God in the gospel. So many benefits were offered, but he was blinded to them by his own mind and by those who advised him. In this regard, he is much like the cursed man described in Jeremiah 17 who listens to his own deceitful heart leading him to depart from God (vv. 5, 9), and is like the desert shrub that is insensitive to the good (v. 6). It is the deadness of the heart and

the blindness of the eyes caused by sin that keeps man from seeing the beauty and wonder of the gospel. Hanun's repudiation of David's mercy was foolish and resulted in devastating consequences. But even more foolish and more severe are the consequences of rejecting the gospel.

2. Although Hanun rejected David, he showed his rejection by humiliating David's servants. Hanun could not get to David, so he took things out on those who represented him. This parallels the treatment believers often receive in this world, which is so hostile to God and grace. It is impossible for the world to get to God, so it demonstrates hatred of God by persecuting the church. But this should not be surprising. We should not marvel if the world hates us (1 John 3:13) because Christ said, "if the world hate you, ye know that it hated me before it hated you" (John 15:18). In the end, the Son of David will repay the humiliation heaped on His people from the impenitent, unbelieving, and disobedient world. "Vengeance is mine; I will repay, saith the Lord" (Rom. 12:19). How have you suffered humiliation for Christ?

Chapter 11

1. Here we see sin in its progression from lust to act. In this case it arose from a casual glance at a beautiful woman. This shows how Eye-Gate, as John Bunyan calls it, is an entrance for sin into Man-Soul. We have a great need to do what Job did, to make a covenant with our eyes (Job 31:1). The eyes are not only a window to the soul but the inlet of many sins. Here we also see sin in its growth. A look led to lusting, lusting to adultery, adultery to lying, and lying to the murder of a valiant soldier. A conscience that is hardening to sin is

a dangerous thing. The lusts of the flesh are powerful and deceitful. When we are out of God's plan we cannot expect His protection. If our eyes wander from Him, our hearts and feet will soon follow. Check your armor. Hold tight the sword of the Spirit, waging war against your own flesh. Never stop praying, "And lead us not into temptation, but deliver us from evil" (Matt. 6:13).

2. David created this temptation by neglecting his duty as the Lord's king. As is true of so many other occasions in life, David should have been leading the battle, not relaxing at home. Thomas Watson said, "An idle person is the devil's tennis ball, which he bandies up and down with temptation till at last the ball goes out of play." In many ways the whole Christian life is the time for battle, and there is no discharge in this conflict. The enemy of the soul is constantly on the prowl, looking for places to attack. It is imperative that we do not neglect our duty to be on guard, to be equipped with the armor and arsenal God has provided, and to fight the good fight.

Chapter 12

1. David had persisted in unconfessed sin for some time, though as far as anyone else could tell all was well. But according to Psalms 32 and 51 a battle was raging within David: his sin was ever before him, as two armies lining up for war (51:3; also the turmoil described in 32:3–5). David was miserable in his sin, yet he made no confession to the Lord. God graciously sent the prophet with a word, not to remind David of his sin but to bring David to his spiritual senses to appeal to God for mercy. Although God is plenteous in

mercy and ready to pardon (Neh. 9:17), believers are often slow to confess and enjoy restoration to the place of fellowship with God. It is wise to keep our accounts short before the Lord, confessing our sins immediately, lest the sense of guilt rob us of all spiritual joy. First John 1:9 should be the Nathan-like word for sinning Christians: "If we confess our sins, he is faithful and just to forgive us our sins."

2. The death of the child indicates that consequences for sin are necessary parts of God's discipline (Ps. 94:12; Prov. 3:11–12; Heb. 12:5–11; Rev. 3:19). Even sorrow over sin and the resolution to turn from it do not exempt us from all its consequences. Sometimes erring children assume that simply telling their parents they are sorry for bad behavior will excuse them from any disciplinary action. But learning that sin has consequences and then experiencing those consequences is itself a sanctifying process (Prov. 20:30). The best way to avoid sin's consequences is to avoid sin. Why is it a mercy that God disciplines His people?

Chapter 13

1. The friendship between Amnon and Jonadab is a warning about having the right kind of friends. Godly friends can be effective in providing accountability and preventing behavior that is displeasing to God. But Jonadab was just the opposite. Instead of trying to quench the lusts that burned in the heart of Amnon, he advised him how he might satisfy his lust. Christian parents should always keep before their children the directive of Proverbs 1:10: "My son, if sinners entice thee, consent thou not." We all should avoid the kind of friendships that corrupt and foster those that aid godliness.

2. Amnon was a fornicator before he forced Tamar (Matt. 5:28). Similarly, Absalom was a murderer long before he plotted Amnon's death, for he hated him (2 Sam. 13:22; see Matt. 5:22; 1 John 3:15). Both testify to what happens when lust is not subdued. Sin begins in the head and heart before it shows itself in action. This is why it is so vital to think proper and godly thoughts. Had the minds of Amnon and Absalom been filled with the thoughts expressed in Philippians 4:8, the tragedy of this narrative could have been avoided. Let us learn from their tragedy to keep our minds and hearts fixed on spiritual matters. Right thinking produces right living.

Chapter 14

1. In her story to David, the woman of Tekoa makes a remarkable statement deserving of pause and meditation (v. 14). The first part reminds us of the certainty of death: "we must needs die" (cf. Pss. 49:7–12, 17, 20; 89:47–48; Heb. 9:27). Acknowledging the certainty of death is not to generate morbid thoughts, but it should be a motive to take full advantage of the time that God allots us to be ready for eternity by trusting in Christ and serving Him wholeheartedly, since death marks the end of earthly opportunity (like water that is spilled, 2 Sam. 14:14).

2. The second part of verse 14 draws a straight and bold line to the gospel: God devises "means, that his banished be not expelled from him." In Adam, all humanity was banished from Paradise (Gen. 3:24). But God in His grace devised a plan whereby sinners, outcasts from His presence, might be reconciled to Him. The promised Seed of the Woman, the

Seed of Abraham and David, would come in the fullness of time to redeem those who were under the curse. Because of the work of Jesus Christ, the way of access has been opened to the very presence of God for all those who trust in Him as the only way, truth, and life. The first Adam lost the earthly Paradise; the second Adam regains the heavenly paradise for His people.

Chapter 15

1. In many ways, David's family trouble is his reaping what he has sown. On the one hand David is reaping the sad consequences of the complex home situation of having multiple wives with competing children. Marriage outside God's revealed standard is always an open door to trouble. But most to the point is that this rebellion by Absalom is the consequence of David's sin with Bathsheba: "the sword shall never depart from thine house" (12:10). His sin was forgiven, and even some good things followed from this union, including the coming Christ (Matt. 1:6). Nonetheless, there are unavoidable consequences of sin; hence the warning of Galatians 6:7: what you sow you will reap.

2. Although Absalom's rebellion was a component in David's predicted family trouble, Absalom was not exempt from personal responsibility and guilt for his actions. He was deceitful, treacherous, and disloyal to his father, whom he should have honored (see the fifth commandment). His charisma and bold promises appealed to the temporal needs of those he seduced from David's kingdom. He had ambition, but ambition in fools is a dangerous thing. He thought more highly of himself than he ought and sought a position for

himself that was not ordained by God. His folly stands as a warning against all selfish ambition. We must remember that God makes men what they are, and the child of God should always be submissive to the place to which he is called (1 Cor. 7:20). Are you envious of others or content to serve the Lord where He has placed you?

Chapter 16

1. Proverbs 18:17 says, "He that is first in his own cause seemeth just." This is why it is always wise to hear both sides of a matter before rushing to judgment. The interchange between Ziba and David is a case in point. Ziba sought to gain favor with David by misrepresenting Mephibosheth, and David took Ziba at his word without consulting Mephibosheth to get his side of the story, which later exposed Ziba's deception (2 Sam. 19:24–30). Ziba's actions were contemptible, and David's were rash and unfounded. Too often we rush to judgment without knowing all the facts and do harm to our fellow believers. Before believing every accusation or rumor, let us learn all the facts and give priority to meeting directly with the other person (Matt. 18:15).

2. David once again expresses his confidence in God's justice. Rather than taking personal vengeance on Shimei (which he had the opportunity to do), he left the matter with the Lord (v. 12). This relative of Saul (v. 5) experienced the same mercy from David that Saul himself had experienced when David passed up opportunities to take revenge. It is always easiest to fight fire with fire, but allowing oneself to be abused and then showing mercy is often a more powerful weapon (Prov. 25:21–22).

Chapter 17

Verse 14 is the key thought in the chapter. The scene is filled with intrigue, political maneuvering, daring courage, and humanitarian relief, but behind the scene is the throne of God. The Lord decreed and orchestrated every detail to bring down Absalom in order to preserve David and his throne (Ps. 33:9–11). As events unfolded, there were moments when it seemed that Absalom would prevail, but God ordained his failure, and David's safety was never in real jeopardy. This should be a comforting thought for all of God's people. It is easy to become distracted and discouraged by the things we see happening, but we should always remember that God is in heaven and that He does what pleases Him (Ps. 135:5–6). No power in hell or on earth can stop Christ (Rom. 8:38–39). How do you need to rely upon Him today?

Chapter 18

1. Absalom has been justly denounced as "the first of traitors and the worst of sons." We see in this chapter that the end of the rebellious is destruction. Absalom aspired to the crown and found a grave instead. Ironically, he had set up a monument to his own name and was buried beneath a heap of stones. He had hoped to make his name famous, similar to Shebna, who made a conspicuous grave for himself, only to be cast out in shame (Isa. 22:15–19). Pride comes before destruction. We should all learn that there is a watchful eye of justice for rebellion and disobedience against authority.

2. We see the pain of heart in a good father. The sins of children are always a grief to Christian parents, and tragically so

when rebellious children persist in their sins to the end without repentance. David was overwhelmed with grief when he heard of his son's tragic end, for he knew that his son had died without hope in the world. Like Paul, who wished himself accursed from Christ if it meant the salvation of his kinsmen (Rom. 9:3–4), David wished that he could have died if it had meant sparing his son from condemnation. Children should always remember how much their salvation means to their believing parents and follow their parental instruction to submit to the Lord.

Chapter 19

David's treatment of Shimei illustrates how to deal with those who have wronged us and points to the even greater mercy shown by Christ, David's greater son. David never looked more Christlike than when he pardoned Shimei. Shimei's sins were great, making David's forgiveness that much greater. This reminds us of the great work of Christ, that "God commendeth his love toward us, in that, while we were yet sinners, Christ died for us" (Rom. 5:8). As Matthew Henry says, "They that are forgiven, must forgive."

Chapter 20

1. Joab's treacherous murder of Amasa shows the depths to which envy and selfish ambition can plunge. Because of Amasa's promotion, Joab no longer enjoyed the rank and privilege that had once been his, and he was willing to and capable of doing anything to regain it, including murder. Discontent with one's position and envy over another's may not lead to the same horrific crime, but those attitudes are always

violations of the tenth commandment not to covet what belongs to another. It is a noble Christian virtue to be able to rejoice with others (Rom. 12:15) without yielding to the temptation to envy. Sadly, the church of Christ is not immune to this creeping sin. The Lord's own disciples were guilty of it. We must pray against the spirit that asks, "Who is the greatest in the kingdom of heaven?" (Matt. 18:1). The only remedy is to be like Christ, who humbled himself (Phil. 2:5).

2. The wise woman of Abel mirrors the poor wise man who by his wisdom delivered a city (Eccl. 8:14–15). Without her actions, a whole city of innocent people would have been destroyed because of the rebellion of one man. Should not the believer follow her example and strive, even if the task is hard, to calm the storm of contending parties? "Blessed are the peacemakers" (Matt. 5:9). Do you know people in conflict? How might you speak a word of peace?

Chapter 21

1. Covenant promises are binding, and breaking them has serious consequences. Joshua made a covenant with the Gibeonites to let them live (Josh. 9:15). Years later, Saul broke that covenant by slaying the Gibeonites (2 Sam. 21:1). Years after that Israel suffered a famine, and it is not until David seeks the reason from the Lord that he learns that it is because of Saul's covenant transgression. Saul did not make the covenant, but he was liable to it. David had not violated the covenant, but he was liable for it. Could it be that troubles and trials that seem to come without reason can be traced to vows made long ago that have been forgotten? We

may forget, but God does not. Vows, if made, must be kept (Eccl. 5:4–6). God takes them seriously.

2. That the nation suffered because of Saul's sin is a vivid reminder of the powerful influence of sin. In one sense, there is no such thing as private sin. Either by example or by consequence, sin affects others. This is magnified when leaders sin because the sphere of their influence is so great. It is particularly important for those in authority, whether civil, religious, or in the home, to live in such a way as to influence positively those under their authority. It is important to pray for those in authority that they might rule well for our own benefit (1 Tim. 2:2).

Chapter 22

This song of David testifies to his recognition that he owes everything to the Lord's mercy, covenant faithfulness, and timely providences. He is careful to give the Lord the thanks and praise He deserves. Similarly, we should be conscious of and sensitive to all that God does for us in preserving, protecting, and providentially meeting our every need. Like David, we should lift our hearts and voices in praise and thanksgiving. God does not grow weary of the praise of His people, even when they are praising Him for the same things over and again. That David's song in this chapter is virtually the same as Psalm 18 directs us to never forget the Lord's benefits to us and to never cease praising Him for them. It is quite acceptable to repeat; God is not looking for originality so much as He desires genuineness and sincerity.

Chapter 23

1. David's description of the ideal ruler (vv. 3–4) points directly to the one and only King who meets the requirements, the Lord Jesus. David rejoiced at the prospect of the coming of Messiah, the ultimate fulfillment of the covenant promise. He acknowledged Christ as his salvation and the totality of his desire. David looked to Christ's coming; we rejoice in the fact that He has come and indeed is coming again. Christ is the salvation of His people. Let it be true that He is all our hearts' desire as well.

2. The exploits of David's mighty men are noteworthy. Each of these men was completely devoted and loyal to David to the extent that they risked their own lives for the welfare of their king. They were courageous and determined in serving their king. If they were willing to expend themselves in such ways in the service of an earthly king, how much more should the servants of Christ, the heavenly King, give themselves in total devotion and selfless service to Him and the advancing of His kingdom? He has given us the equipment we need to fight our battles (Eph. 6:10–18), so let us abandon ourselves to His service. In your particular calling and place in life, how can you strive to be a mighty man or woman for the Lord?

Chapter 24

1. Nebuchadnezzar boasted, "Is not this great Babylon, that I have built…?" (Dan. 4:30). In many ways that boast is an echo of David at the close of his reign. David's numbering the people expressed his pride and sense of self-achievement. Throughout David's career, the evidence was unmistakable

that it was God who built David's house, his kingdom (2 Sam. 7:8–16). During his reign, David himself confessed that even though some trusted in chariots and horses, he would acknowledge God (Ps. 20:7). Sadly, at the end his focus, at least momentarily, is on self. What appeared to be an innocent act had tragic consequences, touching the object of his pride. Let us be warned and let us walk humbly before God in all things to His glory, not our own.

2. That David confessed immediately when his heart struck him (v. 10) is one of the most encouraging statements in the narrative. The Spirit dwelling in the believer reveals sin to the conscience and leads him to repentance. David did not delay; as soon as his conscience smote him he appealed to the Lord for mercy. That is the pattern to follow: deal with sin immediately. Sacrifices (v. 25) point to Christ's sacrifice that keeps on cleansing from sin (1 John 1:7). Significantly, David offers the burnt offering, which in part depicts complete consecration (everything on the altar), and the peace offering, which depicts the fellowship between God and the repentant sinner. When we receive forgiveness from God (1 John 1:9) we ought to dedicate ourselves anew to Him in thanksgiving (that's our reasonable service, Rom. 12:1). That the burnt offering particularly depicts consecration of self explains why David refused to offer to the Lord something that cost him nothing (2 Sam. 24:24). Christ's sacrifice cost Him everything upon the cross. While you cannot pay for your sins, following Christ will be costly. What has it cost you to be a Christian? Is there any area of repentance that you are avoiding because of the cost?

1 Kings

Chapter 1

1. Adonijah shared with Absalom, his elder half-brother, not only good looks but also a selfish, unharnessed ambition for power. Proverbs teaches that the judgment that falls on the mocker should be a warning to others not to follow the same course (Prov. 19:25; 21:11). Unfortunately, Adonijah failed to learn from Absalom's rebellion and demise that elevating self above and against God's will is foolishness with devastating consequences. Adonijah knew that Solomon had been designated as the successor to the royal throne, and yet he opposed this. Opposing God's will always leads to misery. Man needs to be on guard for pride and rash presumption that will motivate self-promotion. To defer to another with regard to some promotion when we think we possess all the necessary qualifications is an unnatural response that requires the kind of humility exemplified by the Savior. This was Paul's directive against the strife in the church: to have the mind of Christ (Phil. 2:1–5). What can you do when you are tempted to be like Adonijah?

2. Although Adonijah's motives are suspect, his taking hold of the horns of the altar suggests a beautiful gospel picture. The altar was the place of sacrifice, reconciliation, and deliverance. Solomon, the peace giver, spared Adonijah even though he deserved death. This is a symbol of a sinner taking hold of Christ Jesus, who is greater than both Solomon and the temple with all of its furniture and rituals. It is only

when the sinner lays hold of Christ that he is delivered from death to life.

Chapter 2

1. God often delays the execution of His justice, but He never sets it aside. Joab had sinned greatly, seemingly with impunity. But "though a sinner do evil an hundred times, and his days be prolonged…it shall not be well with the wicked… because he feareth not before God" (Eccl. 8:12–13). The goodness and longsuffering of God should lead to repentance (Rom. 2:4), but the impenitent persist in wickedness, eventually getting from God what they deserve. Joab had shed man's blood, and by man his blood would be shed. In the same way, sinners today should not interpret "life as usual" to be evidence of God's inactivity or His ignoring of justice. God will repay the sinner for the evil he has done. The Lord remembers the evil deeds of the wicked, and sooner or later He will execute His punishments upon them. The only remedy for us is to flee to the Lord Jesus Christ and be washed from all our sins in His blood by true, saving faith alone.

2. Joab's vainly hanging on to the horns of the altar provides a sobering lesson in the ineffectiveness of trusting in religious routines, rituals, or traditions for salvation. Religion without Christ and a saving dependence on Him is worthless. Yet so many convince themselves that just going to church or performing some other religious acts will be good enough. Going to the tabernacle was not enough to save Joab, and simply going to church is not enough to save anyone. What must we do in order to be forgiven of our sins?

Chapter 3

1. The Lord granted Solomon's unselfish request for wisdom, as well as gave him things he did not ask for (vv. 12–13). This testifies to God's amazing goodness and grace; in Paul's inspired words, he "is able to do exceeding abundantly above all that we ask or think" (Eph. 3:20). We should learn from this that prayer is not just a list of wants in order to enrich ourselves but a means of seeking the Lord for His will to be done. We need to pray that God will grant us the wisdom or skill to fulfill whatever calling and tasks He has for us. What wisdom do you need from the Lord today?

2. Christ the King has received the Spirit in His fullness to reign in perfect wisdom and justice. His Word and Spirit are the source of all the church's wisdom (Eph. 1:17; Col. 3:16). It is not enough to pray for wisdom and then to consult this world for guidance. We must look to Christ in faith and depend upon the Holy Scriptures as the Word of our King. Then we show Christ the reverence He deserves (1 Kings 3:28).

Chapter 4

1. The glories and expanse of Solomon's kingdom serve as a beautiful picture or type of Christ and His kingdom. As great as Solomon was, he pales before Christ, who is greater (Matt. 12:42). Solomon received wisdom from God, but Christ is Himself the Wisdom of God (Prov. 8:12–35; 1 Cor. 1:30). The borders of Israel were expansive under Solomon's administration, but the kingdom of Christ is without borders, including subjects from every nation and people on the planet (Ps. 2:8). Solomon had to build up a military, but

Christ rules with an irresistible rod of iron against all His enemies and has people who are irresistibly made willing in the day of His power (110:2–3). Solomon ruled over a kingdom at peace in which all his subjects had what was necessary for a contented life (1 Kings 4:20). How much more do those citizens in Christ's kingdom enjoy a peace that surpasses all understanding!

2. Solomon displayed profound wisdom, not only in human affairs and in politics but also regarding the matters of nature and biology. All of creation testifies to God's glory and reveals something of His great person and work. Christian faith encourages learning. Many universities were started at the initiative of godly men who desired an institution of sanctified learning. True godliness promotes scholarship, and true science is in strict adherence to the Word of God. "The fear of the LORD is the beginning of wisdom" (Ps. 111:10). How can researchers and scientists glorify God?

Chapter 5

1. When Christ ascended into heaven, His earthly warfare had come to an end and He entered His rest. However, Solomon's kingdom reminds us that our own day is not a time of inactivity for our King but the era during which He is using His wisdom to enlist people from the nations to build His living temple, the church. One day the whole church will enter its rest; then the glory of God will dwell with man so that no temple will be needed.

2. One lesson from this chapter is the importance of preparing for the tasks before you. Wise Solomon put it this way: "If the iron be blunt, and he do not whet the edge, then must

he put to more strength: but wisdom is profitable to direct" (Eccl. 10:10). Getting the tools ready before using them only makes sense. Solomon demonstrated his wisdom by making due preparations for the construction of the temple. This was a matter of common sense, but a lack of common sense can dishonor the Lord, as with a half-built construction project by a church. Christ applied this principle to spiritual life (Luke 14:25–33). Following the Lord Jesus incurs a cost—hardships and even suffering. To follow Him to the end you must look ahead, count the cost, and prepare yourself.

Chapter 6

1. We read that there was "neither hammer nor axe nor any tool of iron heard in the house, while it was in building" (v. 7). The temple was built in relative silence. Since the New Testament identifies believers, both individually and corporately, as the temple of God, this is suggestive or characteristic of the manner in which the Lord builds His church. Without much public show or loud proclamation the Lord converts sinners and expands His church. He performs His work in the private lives of people and causes them to be His witnesses in this world, but without ostentatious display or fanfare.

2. The temple, like the tabernacle before it, symbolized God's dwelling with His people. The temple was beautiful and ornate, a most special place filled with pointers to the One coming who was greater than the temple (Matt. 12:6). In the person of Christ, God came to dwell directly with man and revealed His glory, full of grace and truth (John 1:14). Solomon's temple was glorious, but nowhere does the glory of God shine more brightly than in the face of Jesus

Christ (2 Cor. 4:6). An even greater wonder is that Christ dwells now in a most special and intimate way in the hearts of His people (Col. 1:27). However, God's dwelling with Christians does not depend upon the obedience of a fallen, sinful man like Solomon but upon the perfect righteousness of the God-man (Heb. 7:26). Therefore, believers in Christ will enjoy God's presence forever.

Chapter 7

1. Solomon's priority in finishing the temple before finishing his own palace (6:38; 7:1) stands in stark contrast to the rebuilding of the temple after the Babylonian exile. Haggai lamented that those who returned to the land were comfortable in their finished houses while the temple was still in ruins (Hag. 1:4). They put their own interests ahead of God, and the work of God suffered. Solomon's example charts the proper course. Putting God and His kingdom work first puts everything else in its proper place. Significantly, Solomon's personal interests did not suffer, and the construction projects in his kingdom were magnificent. God is no man's debtor; He will take care of His people. He will honor those who honor Him.

2. Every component of the temple has significance in what it reveals about God and how to worship Him. Special attention in this chapter is given to the molten sea (v. 23), the washbasin in the outer court just beyond the altar of sacrifice. The whole tripartite design of the tabernacle/temple, with its corresponding furniture, teaches how to approach God. The altar is first because approaching God cannot begin apart from the blood sacrifice. Then, before entering the holy

place, the priests had to wash at the laver, illustrating Psalm 24:3–4, "Who shall stand in his holy place? He that hath clean hands, and a pure heart." What the priests depicted remains the requirement for Christians today. Fellowship with God requires pardon and purity, both walking in the light and being cleansed with Christ's blood (1 John 1:7).

Chapter 8

1. As beautiful and glorious as the temple was, it was nothing but a building until the Lord filled it with His glorious presence (vv. 10–11). It is the Lord's presence that makes a house to be God's house. How much more is that true today, when God has no holy buildings, but His temple is the people of the church (1 Cor. 3:16)? Beautiful architecture and impressive gatherings of people are no substitute for the presence of the living God. Let us beware of the error of Laodicea, thinking that our church is rich while Christ is outside knocking to enter (Rev. 3:17, 20). Praying for God's special presence ought to be a regular routine in our preparations for worship.

2. We can learn to pray from the prayers recorded for us in Scripture. Solomon's prayer offers a pattern to follow. His prayer involves praise and worship, confession, intercessions, and supplications. He often appeals to God's words and promises. It would be a good spiritual exercise to work through the prayer, praying with Solomon and addressing your own personal needs and issues. Prayer is always evidence of our sense of dependence upon God. The more conscious we are of needing the Lord, the more often and effectively we will pray.

Chapter 9

1. The Lord appeared to King Solomon to reiterate the covenant promise given to David and to warn him against forsaking the covenant obligations (vv. 1–9). As king of Israel, he represented the nation before God in the covenant. His obedience would establish God's kingdom and presence among them, whereas his disobedience would lead the nation into apostasy and judgment. How precious then is the promise of a King of perfect righteousness, even divine righteousness (Jer. 23:5–6)! Christ's perfect obedience has secured God's kingdom and presence forever for those united to Him. In Christ they are counted righteous before God, and by Christ's Spirit they too walk in sincere obedience.

2. The Lord explains what the cost would be if Israel were to forsake His commandments and embrace false gods (v. 9). The Lord would forsake His temple and give up the people of Israel to discipline and misery. Enjoying fellowship with God required purity of life and the forsaking of sin (2 Cor. 6:17–18; 1 John 1:5–10). Today there are many temptations alluring churches away from the truth of God's Word. The stakes for such apostasy are high: the Lord withdraws Himself. When Christians start backsliding, let them be quick to confess their sins and seek forgiveness and restoration by the blood of Christ.

Chapter 10

1. The glorious reign of King Solomon is a reflection of the glorious kingdom of Christ, the One greater than Solomon. The wisdom, prosperity, abundance, wealth, and glory are but a weak resemblance of the eternal glory of the reign of

Christ, whose kingdom shall endure forever in blessing and peace (Ps. 72; Eph. 1:3). The Queen of Sheba saw all the glory of Solomon and declared that the half of Solomon's glory had not been revealed to her. When God's people enter heaven and see the glories of His kingdom and the blessedness of His people, they will also be, so to speak, breathless, and each one of them will have to say that the half of the glories of Christ had not been told to them. Just as King Solomon gave regal gifts to the Queen of Sheba, so Christ shares with His people from the abundance of His riches the very fullness of God (1 Kings 10:16–19).

2. Solomon's gathering of many horses (vv. 26–29) casts a shadow across his kingdom, for this defied the Lord's command and suggests a worldly glorying in earthly strength. The temptations of affliction are hard, but the temptations of prosperity may be much worse. The king was ever to be a servant of the Lord. Let us all beware of glorying in our strengths and resources and always live as humble servants, even if God blesses us with success.

Chapter 11

1. When Solomon was old his wives turned his heart away from God (v. 4). Solomon's downfall was gradual. At the beginning of his reign he married Pharaoh's daughter (3:1). Although that violated God's stipulation not to intermarry with pagans, apparently Solomon was able to hold in check its consequences, as the first part of his reign was marked by his service to the Lord. But this led Solomon to more sin. Let us be warned that apart from repentance, sin will only grow and take us further from the Lord. It is imperative that we

address sin immediately, confessing it and seeking the Lord's forgiveness and help to resist temptation.

2. Solomon's downfall is a reminder of what he himself summarized: "Better is the end of a thing than the beginning thereof" (Eccl. 7:8). Solomon had an exemplary beginning as he acknowledged his utter dependence on the Lord by seeking wisdom and dedicating himself whole-heartedly to the work of the temple. But, sadly, Solomon is often remembered as much for his folly as for his wisdom. Church history, ancient and modern, is filled with tragic examples of those who started well but ruined their testimonies by some sin after years of God-honoring service. We should devote ourselves to constant prayer and vigilance that we will remain faithful until the end.

Chapter 12

1. Rehoboam is a classic example of the folly of bowing to peer pressure. From the divine perspective, all this was orchestrated to accomplish the divine purpose. Yet from the human perspective, had he listened to the counsel of his elders, with their wisdom and experience, he could have avoided the calamity of losing the majority of his kingdom. This should be a warning to all, and particularly to young people. Listen to what Solomon, in all likelihood, told Rehoboam directly, as well as us: "My son, if sinners entice thee, consent thou not" (Prov. 1:10), and, "My son, hear the instruction of thy father, and forsake not the law of thy mother" (v. 8). Why is it hard at times to listen to our elders?

2. Rehoboam listened to foolish friends, but Jeroboam listened to himself, which is even more dangerous. He devised

a course of action in his own heart (v. 33) that put the newly formed kingdom on the downward slope from its inauguration. The heart is deceitful above all things, leading us to depart from the Lord (Jer. 17:5, 9). The plan he devised was logical in its policy and apparently successful in its effect, but it was neither right nor wise. God had given him the condition for establishing the kingdom: obedience (1 Kings 11:38). Following God's ways may seem to jeopardize our future, but it actually secures it.

Chapter 13

1. The unnamed prophet is a lesson in contrast. On the one hand he is to be imitated. The Lord commissioned him with a dangerous task, but without hesitation he obeyed God, entering hostile territory with a fearless message to the hostile king. In the same way we all should have the courage to witness for God and Christ in the midst of a hostile world.

2. On the other hand, the prophet stands as a stark warning against disobeying God. He trusted an older prophet who appeared to have more experience but who contradicted God's Word rather than trusting in the clear, unmistakable commands that God had given. He paid the consequence for his disobedience, and justly so. We should always be careful to discern the spirits. We are not to obey our own reasoning, nor are we to follow the words of others, but to abide with the clear directions of God's Word.

3. The prophecy about Josiah (v. 2) illustrates the amazing accuracy of God's prophetic word (2 Kings 23:14–17). The events of fulfillment occurred more than 300 years later and yet were accurate to every detail of the prediction. God

knows and has decreed the end from the beginning, so predicting the future is not difficult for Him; it is evidence of His deity (Isa. 46:9–10). Seeing how accurately prophecy has been fulfilled should encourage us that what God has predicted is as certain as though it has already happened.

Chapter 14

1. God remembers mercy in His wrath (Hab. 3:2). God pronounced His just wrath and punishment on Jeroboam because of his sin. The fatal illness of his son Abijah was a component of that wrath, but it is here that God shows His mercy. This child would be spared the disgraceful death to be suffered by all his male relatives, as God mercifully brought him to death through natural causes. We know virtually nothing about this child, neither his age nor anything regarding his behavior, but God saw in Abijah something that pleased Him. The Lord takes no pleasure in the death of the wicked (Ezek. 18:32), yet the death of the saints is precious to Him (Ps. 116:15).

2. Jeroboam owns the most dreadful legacy in the entire history of the Northern Kingdom: the one who made Israel sin. Any and every sin is a terrible offense against God, but the Lord Jesus said that leading others into sin deserves special punishment (Mark 9:42). What a tragedy it would be to be remembered for sin rather than for piety. "A good name is better than precious ointment" (Eccl. 7:1). Having a good reputation and godly testimony should be a concern for every believer. None of us will be remembered for very long (Eccl. 1:11), but as short-lived as our legacy may be, let it be

that we feared God and influenced others for righteousness (Dan. 12:3).

Chapter 15

"Asa did that which was right in the eyes of the LORD" (v. 11), and his "heart was perfect with the LORD all his days" (v. 14). Yet notwithstanding his overall devotion and uncompromising loyalty to the Lord, he did things that evidenced a lack of faith, a fearing of man more than God. Asa used temple money to bribe Benhadad to deliver him from Baasha. Instead of trusting a heathen king, he should have sought deliverance from the Lord. The Lord was not pleased and sent a prophet to rebuke Asa for his folly (2 Chron. 16). The danger was real, but he allowed the fear of what he saw to cloud his faith. Walking by sight instead of by faith is always easier, but we are to fear God above all and to trust Him to direct our paths in every circumstance of life (Prov. 3:6).

Chapter 16

Comparing the biblical assessment of Omri with that of the secular historian illustrates how differently God sees things and what is truly significant. In terms of statesmanship, this king accomplished much. He conquered the Moabites and forged trade treaties with the Phoenicians, marrying his son Ahab to one of their princesses. He founded a dynasty of kings in Israel and built a brand new capital city, controlling the trade routes and securing income for his kingdom. Yet none of his accomplishments is even mentioned in Scripture. What is recorded is that he did not fear the Lord but did more wickedly than all who had reigned before him. This shows us that the important matter in life is not what we accomplish in terms of prestige or income but whether we fear and love the Lord. That will bring eternal blessings, but all the accomplishments in this life will soon wither and come to nothing. Of your life's efforts, which will last for eternity?

Chapter 17

1. The ministry of Elijah introduces a period of miracles. Christians rightly see God's providence in all events, but miracles in the strictest sense are extraordinary works of God's supernatural power that occurred at crucial moments in redemptive history to testify to His unique glory. For example, the Bible speaks of the miracles done through Moses to glorify the Lord above the gods of Egypt, those done through Elijah and Elisha to declare God's supremacy against Baal worship, and those done in the days of the Lord Jesus and His apostles to bear witness to Christ's coming and accomplishment of redemption. Though such miracles are rare, they teach us that God's power has no limits. Therefore, just as Elijah called down the covenant curses of the law upon Israel through His prayers, so we can pray God's promises with great faith (James 5:16–18), since He is able to do more than we can ask or think (Eph. 3:20).

2. The miracles performed by Elijah (and later Elisha) stand by themselves as testimonies to God's power, but it is clear from the ancient literature that virtually every miracle was directed at some pagan belief about Baal. Point by point the prophets proved that the powers associated with Baal in truth belonged to Jehovah alone. It seems as though they knew what the worshipers of Baal believed. This is a good

lesson in apologetics, the discipline of defending the Scriptures against those who attack them. The aim of apologetics is to display the emptiness and futility of the idolatrous beliefs of this world and to demonstrate that power, wisdom, and goodness belong to the Lord alone.

Chapter 18

1. The Lord works to make Himself known as the only true God. Idols always challenge His sovereignty over some area of life. Christ's death on the cross, like Elijah's sacrifice at Carmel, decisively defeated the powers of this world (Col. 2:15). Now, through the proclamation of the cross and the power of the risen Savior, the Lord is causing all peoples to know that He is the Lord God, and that there is no other (1 Kings 8:60; Deut. 4:35). This is a key component of our witness: telling people that the Lord alone is God (Isa. 43:10–13) and calling all peoples to turn to Him as the only Savior (45:21–22).

2. James says that Elijah was "a man subject to like passions as we are, and he prayed earnestly" (James 5:17–18). When we consider the boldness of Elijah in confronting Ahab and the prophets of Baal, or the power of Elijah in performing so many miracles, it is hard to see any similarities at all between him and ourselves. Yet he provides for us an example, particularly in the practice of prayer. He prayed *humbly*, with his face to the ground; *specifically*, for the need of the people; *persistently*, despite six prayers without an answer; and *effectively*. Elijah was able to do what he did because he knew God's Word and trusted God to accomplish it. How does Elijah's example challenge you to grow in prayer?

Chapter 19

1. All too often low points in our spiritual lives immediately follow the high points. On the top of Mt. Carmel Elijah performed bold exploits for God and prayed exemplary prayers. Yet immediately after the extraordinary victories, he became overcome with fear, fled for his life, and thought irrationally. Elijah was "subject to like passions as we are" (James 5:17)—and we can relate to him. Most likely he was physically exhausted, which contributed to his depression. There is a connection between the physical and the spiritual that cannot be ignored. Significantly, before the Lord said anything to him, He allowed Elijah to sleep and then provided necessary nourishment. The Lord knows the frailty of His people, and He gave no rebuke to Elijah. But this should be a warning to us to be on special guard after spiritual victories and to give attention to our physical as well as spiritual needs.

2. Elisha's response to his commission to be a prophet is exemplary for all who would be followers of Christ. He left his oxen behind, unlike those who refused to follow Christ because of their new oxen (Luke 14:19). But as the disciples left their nets and followed the Lord Jesus (Mark 1:18), so Elisha left his life of farming to do the will of God. Christ said, "whosoever he be of you that forsaketh not all that he hath, he cannot be my disciple" (Luke 14:33). The Lord calls for total commitment to Himself. He first gave Himself on the cross, and now He calls us to take up our cross (v. 27). Whatever the cost to follow Christ, it is worth it. What will it mean for you to take up your cross?

Chapter 20

As wicked and undeserving as Ahab was, God gave him an opportunity to come to his spiritual senses. Although he was vastly outnumbered by the enemy and was willing to surrender, God sent a prophet promising victory so that Ahab would "know that I am the LORD" (vv. 13, 28). Ahab received God's word and saw firsthand its truth, yet he did not repent of his sins and turn to the Lord with saving knowledge. It is easy to see Ahab among the fools who hated knowledge and did not choose the fear of God (Prov. 1:22–33). This is a warning to those who sit regularly under the teaching of God's Word and have opportunity after opportunity to submit in faith and repentance. Remember that the same message that can bring life can harden those who hear and reject. This is an opportunity to press this truth upon the children in every Christian home.

Chapter 21

1. Ahab's behavior in response to Naboth's refusal to turn over his vineyard was like that of a selfish child who does not get his own way. He got mad and pouted (v. 4). Rather than being grateful for the many things he did have, he wanted what belonged to another. His breaking of the tenth commandment led to the breaking of commandments six and nine as well. Children should learn early to be content with what the Lord has given them, not to envy what belongs to another and not to pout when they don't get their own way. That is a lesson for all to learn, regardless of age.

2. Tragically, earthly tribunals do not always serve justice (Eccl. 3:16; 5:8). Jezebel's mock court appeared to follow the proper

legal procedures. The law required two or three witnesses to condemn in the case of a capital offense (Deut. 17:6), and she arranged for the two witnesses to make the accusation. The just one was condemned, but God, who is higher than any earthly court, knows, and in the end justice prevails. The greatest miscarriage of justice the world has ever known was in the trials of the Lord Jesus, where He was falsely accused by the Jews, recognized as innocent by Pilate, but nonetheless condemned. Even though we stand aghast at the debacle that transpired at Christ's trial before wicked men, we must rejoice that His death sentence that led to Calvary was the execution of God's will for our salvation (Acts 2:23). God rules despite human injustice. How can that comfort us when we face the injustice around us today?

Chapter 22

1. "And a certain man drew a bow at a venture" (v. 34). This is a simple yet profound illustration of the unfailing providence of God. Ahab was sentenced to death in the battle, and he did his best to hide from that judgment by disguising himself. An unnamed soldier shot his arrow, apparently aiming at nothing in particular, but God guided the flight of that arrow to the precise point it needed to go. We can learn from this that there is no escape from judgment by disguise, flight, or hiding (Amos 5:19). Instead of hiding ourselves and trying to escape, it is eternally better to surrender to Him whose eyes are a flame of fire (Rev. 1:14). Christ is the sovereign King over all mankind, even over kings (Matt. 28:18; Rev. 1:5). In what specific ways are you to honor Him with the power or authority He has given you?

2. "Jehoshaphat made peace with the king of Israel" (v. 44). This was an unlikely alliance between the worst of Israel's kings and a king of Judah who received the epitaph that he did "right in the eyes of the LORD" (v. 43), except for failing to remove the high places and for making peace with Ahab. God mercifully spared him from being killed in battle (vv. 32–33), but his own foolishness put him in danger. Second Chronicles 20:35–37 also records God's rebuke to Jehoshaphat for entering a commercial relationship with Ahab's son, who acted wickedly. Paul warns that believers are not to be unequally yoked with unbelievers because light has nothing in common with darkness (2 Cor. 6:14–15).

2 Kings

Chapter 1

1. Calling down fire from heaven was an unmistakable sign of divine power. But even beyond the immediate consequence, it was another demonstration of Jehovah's superiority over Baal. We know from Canaanite literature that fire, and particularly lightning, was considered to be Baal's domain. One common image of Baal depicts him holding a bolt of lightning as his scepter. Ironically, those going to seek Baal met the real God, who controlled every force of nature as the Creator. They were seeking help in the wrong place. It is only in the one true and living God that we can find help, regardless of the need. We should never follow the ways of the world and its perceived notions. Our dependence should be on the Lord.

2. The Lord will punish with fire those who seek to destroy His servants. This is not a justification for taking personal vengeance, nor a promise of immediate judgment on the wicked—now is the time of enduring affliction for the sake of the gospel (Luke 9:54–56). However, the time will come when the fire will fall, and those who have conspired to destroy the church will face the wrath of Christ (Rev. 20:9). How can this give hope to persecuted believers?

Chapter 2

1. Elijah's ascent to heaven without dying was a final act of humiliating Baal and glorifying *Jehovah,* since Baal was the

rider of clouds who supposedly had power over death. This is one of the principal passages in the Old Testament dealing with life after death, showing that the Old Testament saints had essentially the same hope as the New Testament saints. Absence from the body is presence with the Lord (2 Cor. 5:8). God will take all who are His into His very presence.

2. The ascension of Elijah foreshadowed the ascension of Jesus Christ, who also physically went up into heaven attended by angels (Acts 1:9–11). His mantle of spiritual power has fallen upon the church, filled with the Spirit of Christ to continue His mission (2:1–47). Christ will return, calling His people up to meet Him in the sky so that they will be with the Lord forever (1 Thess. 4:13–18).

3. In all likelihood the young people who mocked the prophet echoed what they had learned at home. Bethel had earned the name Beth-aven, as God had been replaced with wickedness. Exposing children to vicious criticism of God's servants can have devastating effects. Christian parents should raise their children in the fear of the Lord, teaching them to honor God and those who preach the Word.

Chapter 3

1. Though Jehoshaphat's alliance with Israel was questionable, it was his presence that caused the prophet to seek the Lord on behalf of the coalition. God's children should be a blessing for those around them. There is a principle that the presence of the remnant is a preserving influence. Isaiah said that were it not for the remnant the nation would have been like Sodom (Isa. 1:9). The Lord Jesus expressed this in terms of being salt (Luke 14:34). Salt is a preserving agent, but it is also a source

for irritation and aggravation to a sore spot. We are in the world but cannot be of the world or like the world. We should strive to be the kind of influence in society that reflects well on the Lord. Before Jehoshaphat sought the Lord, he shared in confusion; blessing came when he asked for God's guidance through the Word of the Lord. So it is with us.

2. The Lord's instruction to "make this valley full of ditches" (v. 16) is suggestive. God was going to do the miraculous in defeating the Moabites, but He wanted the people to prepare for the blessing of deliverance. Digging the ditches beforehand was an expression of their confidence that God would work. The spiritual application is significant: we should make due preparation of our hearts in anticipation of the Lord's blessing. There is a sense in which before every Sabbath worship we should "dig some ditches" in preparation for and anticipation of being filled with all that the Lord has in store for us. God says, "Open thy mouth wide, and I will fill it" (Ps. 81:10).

Chapter 4

1. In His providence God takes His people through hard times, but always ultimately for their good. The widow suffered bereavement, debt, and potential bondage, but the Lord had not forsaken her. He had brought her to this low position to make her like the empty vessels in her home so that He could fill her with His grace. Similarly, the Lord uses trials to empty His children of their self-sufficiency so that He can lovingly fill them with His Spirit. How has God been doing this for you through your afflictions?

2. God is no man's debtor. The Lord Jesus said, "But seek ye first the kingdom of God, and his righteousness; and

all these things shall be added unto you" (Matt. 6:33). The widow had been the wife of a preacher, and after his death God was more than a husband to her, meeting all her financial needs. For her part, the Shunammite went out of her way to provide for the prophet, and God repaid her kindness with a son. The prophets were servants of the Lord, and He provided their food even during the famine. In one way or another God takes care of His own.

3. Elisha's strange method of raising the boy from the dead is a wonderful picture of the saving work of Jesus Christ. Christ embraced His people when they were spiritual corpses, taking the uncleanness of their sins upon Himself and so closely uniting them to Himself that when He rose they, too, rose from the dead. Look to Christ, and He will be your life, your sight, and your strength each day.

Chapter 5

1. Leprosy is a picture of sin and the uncleanness that prevents any relationship with God. When Naaman first learned the prescribed manner of cleansing, he rejected it as being too demeaning and too simple. He was ready to do anything and pay any price (v. 13), but to humble himself by doing nothing other than obeying the prophet's word to wash in the Jordan repulsed him. That is so often the sinner's reaction to the gospel message. Sinners think they have to add something on their own. Indeed, they want to merit something. It is humbling to acknowledge that there is nothing one can add or contribute to salvation, which comes only from taking God at His word. But until a sinner so humbles himself

he remains unchanged. Salvation is by grace, through faith, without works (Eph. 2:8–9).

2. Gehazi is a portrait of a hypocrite. Like Judas at the feet of Jesus, so Gehazi at the feet of Elisha did not take into his heart the benefits of the grace that surrounded him. Hypocrites are not what they appear to be. Gehazi lived in a good environment, knew the language of Zion, and had the respect of men. He fooled Naaman with his lies. However, a hypocrite cannot fool God. The eyes of the Lord see the evil and the good. God will judge hypocrites. In a great reversal, the outsider was healed, but the servant of the prophet was struck with leprosy. Remember that God knows us for what we really are; that ought to drive us to Christ as our only hope. There is hope for the hypocrite who repents and seeks the Lord with all his heart.

Chapter 6

1. Elisha's ministry was marked by miracles. Some were big; others were small and personal. But all demonstrated the absolute ability of God and His supremacy over all His creation. The floating of the iron axe head was personal yet instructive, apart from the surface warning it provides against borrowing (Prov. 22:7). The prophets were engaged in the work of the kingdom. Then something happened that stopped progress: they lost the axe head. Today that seems to be such a small problem, as a new axe could be attained quite easily. But that was not the case then. They were doing their best, and now a situation had occurred that was beyond their ability to remedy; there seemed to be no hope for going forward. Something extraordinary had to happen. The lesson is

that God is not hindered by obstacles—sinking iron was no problem for Him. He caused the iron to float, and the work continued. There may be times when the church today seems to have lost its axe, the power and means to do its work. The answer is prayer. How should you be praying that God will "float the axe" for your church?

2. Elisha's prayer for God to open the eyes of his servant to see the angelic army surrounding the enemy that was surrounding them should encourage all of God's people. The servant's eyes being opened did not bring the angelic army but rather revealed what was already there. Before his eyes were opened he saw only the danger. Physical sight sees only what appears; spiritual sight (faith) sees what really is. The angel of the Lord encamps around those that fear Him (Ps. 34:7). Our inability to see him with the physical eye does not negate the fact that he is there. We are to walk by faith and not by sight. This is the way to peace and joy.

Chapter 7

1. This episode detailing the prophetic prediction, followed immediately by the details of the fulfillment, is instructive as to how we ought to understand those parts of God's Word that have yet to be fulfilled. A key purpose of predictive prophecy is to demonstrate the sovereignty of God over all time and circumstance. Declaring the end from the beginning is evidence of deity (Isa. 41:21–29). There can be no doubt from this chapter that every detail of the prophecy was specifically fulfilled. Yet Elisha did not reveal all the specific details in the prophecy as to how the fulfillment would take place. He made no reference to the Syrian retreat, the

lepers' role, or the mocker's inability to control the crowd that led to his seeing the supply of cheap food without experiencing it. Enough details are given to affirm the certainty, but not so much as to replace faith by sight. Prophecy is not to produce fatalism but faith. So as we consider the great things about the future that God has revealed in His Word, we should have the confident assurance that everything God says will happen is going to happen. Even if we can't sort out all of the details of prophecy, let us learn to trust God now.

2. The initial behavior of the lepers was tragic in their selfish thoughtlessness for others. They gorged themselves with food and stashed away as much spoil as they could gather. Thankfully, they came to their senses. Even more tragic is how their behavior mirrors that of many Christians who enjoy the benefits and blessings of salvation but never share the good news of the gospel with those who are starving for truth all around them. May the Lord bring every believer to recognize the obligation to share the gospel with a lost and dying world. For whose salvation are you praying? With whom are you seeking to share the gospel?

Chapter 8

1. Jeremiah declared that the "heart is...desperately wicked" beyond comprehension (Jer. 17:9). It is rare that sinners recognize the depths of their sin nature and what they are capable of doing. When Elisha told Hazael the heinous things he was going to do, he immediately protested that he was incapable of such atrocities (2 Kings 8:12–13). Yet the very next day he committed coldblooded murder (v. 15). We must understand the wickedness of the human heart

and admit that apart from the grace of God every man has within him the ability to commit the darkest of sins. Those who profess to have experienced God's grace must live daily in dependence on that grace, praying that the Lord will preserve them from evil.

2. Jehoshaphat in many ways was a good king, but his alliance with Ahab put in motion circumstances that threatened the continuation of the Davidic line. His son and grandson were so wicked that their careers were compared to that of Ahab, the worst of Israel's kings. Much of their sin is traced to the influence of Athaliah, the daughter of Ahab and Jezebel, the wife of Jehoram, and the mother of Ahaziah. This was a marriage fostered by Jehoshaphat's compromise with Ahab. Let us be warned, and let us be cautious regarding the unforeseen effects of sins. The best way to avoid the future consequences of sin is to resist the temptation to sin now.

Chapter 9

1. Justice delayed is not justice denied. Perhaps as many as twenty years passed between the treachery of Ahab and Jezebel against Naboth and the execution of the judgment that Elijah had pronounced against them at that time. But God's justice is certain, and His timing is perfect, as Jehu is set apart to be the agent of God's wrath. Ruthlessly and relentlessly he executes the judgments of the Lord, precisely as Elijah had declared. From a purely human perspective, his actions seem to be harsh and without mercy, but to every detail the punishment fit the crime. So also the final judgment will come upon the world according to God's will and in His timing. That judgment will be terrifying, and yet

heaven will ring in songs of praise because God is just and righteous in His judgments (Rev. 19:1–2). In view of that far greater judgment in which sinners will get what they deserve, there is a great urgency to be reconciled to God by the blood of Christ, the only way to escape judgment. Jezebel tried to escape Jehu by exhibiting her self-perceived beauty; it is the beauty of Christ's righteousness that will rescue His people.

2. Jezebel's horrific end is a vivid illustration of Psalm 49, which teaches that death is the great equalizer. She had used her wealth and power to get everything she had wanted during her life, but when it came to dying none of that availed. All she had possessed remained behind for others. The psalmist said concerning the rich and powerful that "when he dieth he shall carry nothing away: his glory shall not descend after him" (Ps. 49:17). So horrific was Jezebel's death that she did not even leave a body to take to the grave. Her life of luxury paled in comparison to the ignominy of her death and the terror of her eternal fate. Death indeed will come to all. Are you prepared for eternity? How can you live in such a way that you are prepared to die?

Chapter 10

The Lord commended Jehu for doing right in His eyes, according to all that was in His heart (v. 30). Jehu was the effective instrument in the Lord's hand to execute justice against the house of Ahab, precisely fulfilling Elijah's prophecy. However, he did not follow the law of the Lord with all his heart, for he retained the worship of Jeroboam's golden calves (v. 31). Even if keeping the official state religion was politically motivated to prevent any possible reunion with the south and not an expression of his own religious convictions, his actions were still offensive to God and contrary to His Word. Jehu was indeed "a double minded man" (James 1:8) who acted according to pragmatism rather than principle. How long would his dynasty have lasted had he devoted himself wholeheartedly to the Lord? Be sure to guard your own heart and keep your focus singularly on seeking to please the Lord in all that you do. In so doing, you follow Christ, who always rules His kingdom with righteousness (Isa. 9:7; Jer. 23:5).

Chapter 11

1. Athaliah's renegade rule over Judah after slaying all but one of the royal line of David underscores two significant lessons. First, it warns against the far-reaching and unpredictable consequences of sin. She was in a position to execute her dastardly deeds because of the unwise compromise of Jehoshaphat with Ahab that had brought her into Judah's royal family. Her godless influence affected her husband, infected her son, and brought Baal worship openly into Judah, just as Jezebel, her mother, had done in Israel. Her godless heart caused innocent blood to be shed as she usurped the very throne of David. We should never take sin lightly or dismiss it as simply being a private matter. As devastating as the effects of sin are to the guilty sinner, the potential of its poison spreading in one way or another should serve as an additional deterrent. Let us pray that God will stop us short of sin, and let us think of the implications of our behavior beyond ourselves.

2. A second lesson from Athaliah's rule is that it encourages us to have confidence in God's unfailing purposes. Although

Athaliah's treachery was experienced by the royal seed, it was directed ultimately against God and Christ. Had she succeeded in destroying the royal family, God's promise to David would have become null and void. There had to be a line of David through which the Christ would come. Athaliah was just one more expression of the hostility of the serpent's seed (Gen. 3:15) that is always doomed to failure. God's Word is certain. Christ came. We can be certain that every other component of God's purpose and plan are just as sure, both in terms of the big picture and of our individual lives, for our times are in His hand. This should give us great courage to serve Him in the face of terrible danger, as did Jehosheba, Jehoiada, and Joash's nurse.

Chapter 12

The career of Joash illustrates the truth of Ecclesiastes 7:8 that "better is the end of a thing than the beginning thereof." His first days as the boy-king of only seven years old were his best. Without doubt, it was the godly influence of Jehoida that directed his behavior and determined his policy. But being instructed in the ways of the Lord is not enough. Such instruction needs to be appropriated by God's Spirit in the heart, and that apparently did not take place. When the external pressure to do right was gone, there was no internal impulse to holiness. Second Chronicles 24 gives greater detail regarding how quickly and dramatically things deteriorated. Ironically, at the beginning of Joash's life he was spared from the hands of a wicked assassin, but his life ended at the hands of assassins who were avenging his wicked acts. This tragic story should be a warning to every young person under godly influence and direction in a Christian home. It is not enough just to hear and externally follow. There must be a personal appropriation by the Holy Spirit of all that is taught from the Scriptures. To rebel after a good beginning is tragic.

Chapter 13

1. Do not assume that you are in a right relationship with God just because He has answered some of your prayers. God is merciful, but His mercies are not tokens by which we can presume to belong to Him. Jehoahaz appealed to the Lord when he was in trouble (v. 4), but he continued in the sins of Jeroboam and even some Baal worship as well (v. 6). He did not display a heart of true repentance, yet the Lord mercifully helped him and Israel to break free from their oppressors. Perhaps you have experienced an answer to your prayers for temporal help. Thank God for it. However, do not make that an excuse for remaining in half-hearted religion. How should God's kindnesses move us to serve Him with all our hearts?

2. God's mercies to Israel even as they worshiped idols and false gods vividly illustrate the truth that God answers prayer because of His grace alone. He is full of mercy and compassion, and He remembers His covenant (vv. 4, 23). Therefore, let us not think like Jehoahaz that we can manipulate God into hearing us. Even our most sincere prayers God does not answer for our sakes or because of our merit. Let us turn to him in humility, confessing our transgressions and asking Him for His undeserved mercy. Any mercy received is mercy undeserved.

Chapter 14

1. "Pride goeth before destruction, and an haughty spirit before a fall" (Prov. 16:18). This describes Amaziah. His victory over Edom led to his bravado to Israel, which led to his fall before one stronger than himself. He was warned about the certain outcome, but thinking more highly of himself than he ought, he rushed to the battle and to defeat. We must assess ourselves realistically (Rom. 12:3). Humility should mark every Christian, for it is Christlike (Phil. 2:5).

2. The mercy and loving kindness of the Lord are beyond understanding. He delivered Israel from their oppressors even though the nation was deserving of immediate judgment. The Lord's patience was very great during the administration of Jeroboam II. Read the prophets Hosea and Amos to see how entrenched the nation was in sin while they enjoyed significant economic and political prosperity. In due course the judgment came, but not before God had extended His patient calling for their repentance over and again. Even when we are least deserving of receiving mercy from the Lord, let us not despair of His goodness. The Lord receives sinners who repent. He is willing to grant deliverance and grace to us.

Chapter 15

No less than four times are the careers of Israel's final kings compared to that of Jeroboam I, who provoked Israel to sin (vv. 9, 18, 24, 28). What started as a single step on a slippery slope snowballed into an avalanche of wickedness that ended in disaster. The only northern king who escaped this evaluation was Shallum, and that was only because his reign was cut so short (one month, v. 13). After the relative stability of Jehu's dynasty, the kingdom was in chaos, resulting ultimately in captivity under the Assyrians as God used this wicked people as the instrument of His judgment (Isa. 10:5). The history of the Northern Kingdom illustrates the uncontrollable power of unchecked sin and its certain and terrible consequences. The kings of Israel all committed evil in the sight of the Lord. Sooner or later judgment comes. Do not think you will escape it just because it has not come yet. The only way to escape punishment from evil is to bow to the Lord Jesus Christ, believing in the gospel.

Chapter 16

1. "Like father, like son" is not always true. Sometimes that is a bad thing and sometimes good. Ahaz was the son of Jotham, one of Judah's kings who "did that which was right in the sight of the LORD" (15:34). But Ahaz was nothing like his father, and he became the most wicked king in Judah's history up to this point. He was so wicked that his career is evaluated in terms of Israel's kings and his religious practices in terms of the heathen (16:3). He refused to trust the Lord for help (Isa. 7:1–25). He erected a pagan altar to replace what God had designed and desecrated the temple. However, his son Hezekiah thankfully was nothing like him. Ironically, Judah's worst king gave birth to one of Judah's best. Such is the grace of God. This is a reminder that environment is not what makes a sinner or a saint. Ahaz was in a good home with all of its blessing and benefits, but he rejected his father's God. Hezekiah likewise rejected his father's gods and came to genuine faith in the one true and living God. This should be a warning to everyone raised in a Christian home that you

must individually come to a personal knowledge of the Lord, believing and obeying the Word of the Lord.

2. Ahaz's replacing God's altar with a pagan altar illustrates a fundamental error of all false religion: the assumption that God can be approached in a way other than what He has commanded. The brazen altar was the place for all of the sacrifices that represented the sacrifice of Christ, the Lamb slain from the foundation of the world. Replacing God's ordained worship with man-made worship ("will worship") ultimately leads to rejecting the gospel of Jesus Christ (Col. 2:19, 23).

Chapter 17

1. Had there been newspapers or news blogs back when Israel fell to the Assyrians (722 BC), the reports would have been much the same as news reports today about the affairs of the state. There would have been headlines regarding Assyria's ruthless military machine and commentaries on their newly devised scheme of deportation and reassignment of populations in order to maintain control over their annexed territories. Although there were indeed military and political explanations for what happened to Israel, those were not the real story. The Scripture makes it clear that all of this happened because of Israel's sin and that godless and fierce Assyria was the weapon God used to accomplish His purpose of judgment (Isa. 8:7). God is still on His throne, governing all the events of this world with a view to His unfailing purpose. Let us place our trust in the Lord and not in men or governments.

2. The worship of the Samaritans resembles far too much of modern worship. They had a problem (lions), so they

learned how to give to God what they thought He wanted in order to alleviate the trouble. Worship was not about God but about making life better. So today, many think that Jesus is a quick fix to their problems, whether financial, physical, relational, or otherwise. Going to church or praying is just a means of giving to God what they think He wants in order to gain what they want. We must learn that God will not be manipulated or used as a means to an end.

Chapter 18

1. God's people, even those who live exemplary lives, are not exempt from trouble. Hezekiah was a man who depended completely on the Lord. He trusted God, clung to Him, opposed false worship, and obeyed His commands (vv. 4–6). He demonstrated his dependence on the Lord by his boldness against enemies (vv. 7–8). Yet after fourteen years of consistently doing what was right, trouble came in the person of Sennacherib. A proper relationship with God does not eliminate threats and troubles. In fact, the closer to God one is, the greater the potential for hostility from the world, for it hates Christ (John 15:18; 1 John 3:13). So trouble is not necessarily God's chastening; it can be a means of testing and strengthening faith and dependence. Submit to God's tests, that they may do their good work.

2. Rab-shakeh represents the tactics Satan often uses to intimidate God's people, and we are not to be ignorant of his devices (2 Cor. 2:11). First, he accused Hezekiah of narrow-mindedness (2 Kings 18:22), deception (v. 29), and misguidance (v. 30), all attempts to get the people to turn against their king. Second, he tried to make surrendering to

the enemy attractive, with the prospect of a stronger army (v. 23) and prosperity (vv. 31–32). Third, he cast doubt on God's goodness (v. 25) and power (vv. 32–35), a tactic that dates back to the garden of Eden (Gen. 3:1–6). Similarly, Satan attempts to turn us against King Jesus, to woo our hearts with the supposed joys of sin, and to weaken our faith in God. How can Christians resist each one of these temptations?

Chapter 19

1. Hezekiah provides a wonderful example of how we are to bring all our needs before the Lord. Hezekiah was a man of prayer, and both his prayer and his preparations for prayer set a pattern to follow. Consider first his preparations. *He recognized his need* (v. 3). He was in deep distress, without any ability or power to find remedy without divine intervention. Prayer is always a mark of our sense of dependence upon God. *He was contrite* (v. 1). With humility and reverence and without presumption he entered the Lord's house. His attire spoke of his confession and repentance. *He depended on the Word of God* (v. 2). His calling for Isaiah was not just to gain a prayer partner but to get a fresh word from the Lord to take to prayer to plead before the Lord. *He received the word of promise* (vv. 6–7). Linking prayer to God's Word is a principle found throughout Scripture (Dan. 9:1–27). We should learn to go to the Lord with our Bibles open as we pray for His will to be done.

2. Consider the prayer itself (vv. 14–19). Spreading the letter symbolized what it is for us to cast all our cares and concerns before the throne of grace. First, note the *Person*

addressed (v. 15). He appeals to *Jehovah,* the covenant-making and covenant-keeping God, who has entered into a living relationship with His people. Second, note the *praise.* He focuses on God's unique position as sovereign and His unique work as Creator. All power and authority are His. Third, note the *petitions.* He uses five imperatives, pleading with God to take note of his problem and be moved to act on his behalf. Prayer should be specific. Fourth, note the *purpose* of the prayer. Ultimately nothing matters but the glory of God (v. 19). He argues that God's name is at stake (v. 16). We can be certain that whatever God does to glorify Himself will benefit His people.

Chapter 20

1. Hezekiah's sickness unto death became a most personal test of his faith. His first response was not panic but prayer. When the nation was confronted with certain defeat, he took the matter to the Lord. He did the same when the problem was uniquely his. He is an example of consistency. The fact that he had already demonstrated himself to be a man of prayer gives more credence to his behavior now. This was not desperation; it was normal procedure. We see God's mercy and goodness shining forth in the fact that He heard Hezekiah's cries. Let this be a major encouragement for us to pour out all our needs and cares before the Lord and to do so consistently. God loves to hear and answer prayer.

2. Even the best of men are only men and thus are subject to flaws. Hezekiah had demonstrated a humble spirit before God when seeking Him for deliverance. But it appears that some pride rose up within him after receiving that divine

help. This is evidenced in the private tour he gave to the emissaries from Babylon, showing off "*his* precious things," "*his* armour," "*his* treasures," "*his* house," and "*his* dominion" (v. 13, emphasis added). In reality, all these things had come from God's goodness and grace to him. It is tragic when tokens of grace become objects of pride and boasting. It is good to remember that we have nothing apart from what God has given to us; we own nothing but owe Him all our thanks and praise. Being the recipients of God's goodness is never reason for arrogance.

Chapter 21

After the godly reign of Hezekiah, Manasseh departed from the ways of the Lord. The heart of man is inclined to all wickedness. Godliness is not automatically inherited. Every man must receive heart-renewing grace. This is a personal matter. Every generation must discover the blessing of fearing the Lord. By nature, we all have a wicked heart. Therefore the Lord Jesus teaches us that we must be born again (John 3:3). Let us emphasize this necessity and pray for this grace, that our eyes may be opened, our hearts circumcised, and our lives renewed. Children, do not think that just because your parents are Christians you are a Christian. Conversion is personal.

Chapter 22

As soon as Josiah heard the law of God, he became a doer of the Word and not just a hearer (James 1:22). During his days the inspired Scriptures were still in the process of being revealed, and actual copies of Scripture were rare. It was a wonderful providence of God that led to the discovery of a portion of Scripture that had been hidden somewhere in the temple. Josiah heard it read only once, and it immediately changed him. Most of us have multiple copies of the whole Bible that we can access so easily. Tragically, many homes have Bibles that are hidden in plain sight, never being read. Some people read the Bible on a regular basis without being affected by its message. We should acknowledge the wonderful privilege that is ours in having ready access to the Scriptures and remember that increased privilege increases responsibility. How can we train ourselves to consciously approach the reading or preaching of the Bible with an eye on immediate obedience?

Chapter 23

1. Civil authority is a blessing when it has the courage and convictions to address moral issues with wisdom from God (Prov. 8:12–16; Rom. 13:1–5). We should pray that our leaders will use their authority such that the godly may live in peace and the gospel may be freely proclaimed (1 Tim. 2:1–2) and not give legal sanction to immorality and injustice (Dan. 4:27). Righteousness brings honor to a nation, but sin brings disgrace to a society (Prov. 14:34). Do you regularly pray for the leaders in your national and local governments?

2. Josiah's life also demonstrated the inherent powerlessness of legislation to change the hearts of people. He was able to force outward conformity but unable to effect inward obedience. As soon as he died all of the pent-up wickedness had free reign once again. It is certainly better to legislate morality than immorality, but we must never lose sight of the real

issue: the need for a new heart (Deut. 30:6; Ezek. 36:26). The principle is the same in our homes. We set and enforce rules for our children, but we cannot assume that outward obedience equates to inward conversion. As parents we must always press upon our children the necessity of a personal and inward relationship with Christ that will demonstrate itself in outward behavior as well. God desires "truth in the inward parts" (Ps. 51:6).

Chapter 24

The sins of Judah had finally ripened, and the judgment began. God had warned of this day as far back as Moses (Deut. 28:1–68), and He had sent prophet after prophet to them, encouraging repentance so that this day could have been averted. But they persisted in their sins, rejected the prophets' preaching, and now had crossed the line. The exile was inevitable and inescapable. The nation's history testifies to both God's patience and His inflexible justice. But Judah's judgment pales before the final judgment to come. Throughout Scripture God has warned of its coming and has through His Word and servants offered hope and deliverance for all those who will repent and believe the gospel. The fact that judgment finally came on Judah testifies that delay of judgment does not alter its certainty. It appears that, while life goes on with generations going and coming, the end remains certain. Interpret the delay as evidence of God's patience, and flee to Him through Christ, the only way to escape the otherwise inescapable.

Chapter 25

The book of 2 Kings seems to end in dismal darkness and gloom. But in His wrath God remembers mercy (Hab. 3:2). Where sin abounds, grace super-abounds. The last verses point to the beginning of a new future. Although the royal throne of David had been cast down, God's promise that David would always have one of his sons on the throne remained true (2 Sam. 7:16). God used the pagan king to ensure the continuation of His promise. Jehoiachin received royal treatment and bore sons (1 Chron. 3:17). One of these sons was Salathiel, who in turn bore Zerubbabel, who became governor of Judah when the exile ended. Although he did not sit on the throne, he was of the royal line and designated as God's signet, guaranteeing the Messiah to come (Hag. 2:23). Christ is the true and ideal son of David, and His kingdom shall never end (Luke 1:33). He is now enthroned at the right hand of God in glory (Acts 2:34), and unto Him is given all power in heaven and on earth (Matt. 28:18). The Lord still continues His plans, even if everything seems to fall apart. God's Word endures and will certainly be fulfilled.

1 Chronicles

Chapter 1

We have all descended from one man: Adam. The existence of Adam was as much history as the existence of David. In Adam, we were all made in God's image and likeness. God's purpose for His people therefore remains to fill the earth with His living image. In Adam, we all sinned and have fallen into spiritual corruption and enduring misery. We all share the same fallen nature as the Canaanites. We all die and face judgment, and human life is so transient that from God's perspective all the generations from Adam to Israel fit on a single page of history. God's people consequently must be redeemed by the Lord's grace if they will ever achieve their high calling and eternal life. Mankind needs a new Adam. How has God met that need in Christ?

Chapter 2

The history of God's people is full of examples of sin, such as sexual lust and selfishness (Judah, Onan, and Tamar, vv. 3–4), and greed and disobedience (Achan, v. 7). The Old Testament warns us not to follow in their footsteps, lest we suffer God's judgment. However, it also teaches us to trust in God's grace, for from such sinful families God brought the Savior. How do the examples of such people lead us to faith and repentance?

Chapter 3

God's plan for a new Adam to undo the effects of the fall and restore man to His divine purpose focuses upon Israel (ch. 1), zooms in from all Israel to Judah (ch. 2), and comes to rest on David (ch. 3). David plays a very central role in the book of Chronicles. In a sense, all of Old Testament history leads up to David, and then follows upon David. The Savior declared to Adam (Gen. 3:15) would be a king of the line of David. Christ was born from the seed of David (Matt. 1:1; Rom. 1:3) and He is the promised Savior-King (Luke 1:31–33, 69; 2:11). In turn, Christ has made all His people "kings," spiritually speaking (Rev. 1:6). They will sit with Him on His throne (Rev. 3:21). How can you know if you are part of His kingdom?

Chapter 4

Jabez's prayer (vv. 9–10) should not simply be taken as a request for earthly or temporal blessings. He prayed by faith to the God of the covenant to prosper him in the promised inheritance. God's people today should plead God's promises, looking past their painful circumstances to the riches of Jesus Christ (Eph. 1:3). Presently this means praying for a deeper experience of the work of the Holy Spirit, who is the down payment of our inheritance (Eph. 1:13–14). Ultimately this is a prayer driven by hope in Christ's coming with glory (Eph. 1:17–18). How does Jabez's example encourage you to pray today?

Chapter 5

As Reuben's adultery with his father's concubine cost him the right of the firstborn (vv. 1–2), so Israel's spiritual adultery with idols cost them their inheritance in the land (vv. 25–26). God is a jealous God. He rules as the Sovereign over all people and all events (v. 26). He demands our complete allegiance, and will bless those who seek Him as their only Lord, but will punish those who cherish idols in their hearts or worship them with their lives. What idols are popular in your nation? What idols tempt your own heart?

Chapter 6

The prominence of the Levites in the genealogies reminds us that God's purpose required not just a king but also a priest. The primary function of the priesthood was to "make an atonement for Israel" (v. 49). Only by the forgiveness of sins could God dwell among His people as He once dwelt with Adam without violating His holiness. The sons of Aaron could only cleanse the flesh with outward rituals, but Christ alone cleanses the conscience with forgiveness (Heb. 9:13–14), for He "put away sin by the sacrifice of himself" (v. 26). It was a great consolation to Israel that they had the high priest appointed by God living among them. To whom do you look to make atonement for your sins? Anyone besides Christ who claims to be a priest and offers you absolution for your sins is a pretender and an offense to God, for He said to His Son, "Thou art a priest for ever" (Ps. 110:4; Heb. 5:5–6).

Chapter 7

This chapter contains a lot of disparate information. However, a common thread through it all is the bravery and strength of military men (vv. 2, 4–5, 7, 9, 40). It also speaks of those who died violently at the hands of enemies to the grief of their surviving family (vv. 21–23). It is very fitting that the most famous person in this chapter is Joshua, who led Israel to successful war in order to receive its inheritance in the land (v. 27). Far from being ashamed of military service, the Bible teaches us that God's people are a spiritual army (Eph. 6:10–18), and Jesus, our greater Joshua, is the Captain of our salvation (Heb. 2:10). How do we fight for Him?

Chapter 8

Though Benjamin was the youngest of the sons of Jacob, his tribe was by no means the least significant. Jacob had prophesied that Benjamin would be like a wolf: "In the morning he shall devour the prey, and at night he shall divide the spoil" (Gen. 49:27). From Benjamin would come the important judge Ehud (1 Chron. 8:6), a clan of skillful archers (v. 40), and the first king of Israel, Saul (v. 33). The apostle Paul, known for his zealous work for the gospel, hailed from the tribe of Benjamin (Rom. 11:1; Phil. 3:5). This reminds us that God's purposes for His people are not reserved for the greatest leaders or those from the most prominent families. However, the reference to King Saul also reminds us that the crucial factor in a person's service to God is obedience (1 Chron. 10:13–14; 1 Sam. 15:13–23). Why is obedience to God so much more important than skill or family pedigree?

Chapter 9

Rather than just a boring list of names, Chronicles has thus far outlined the story of the whole Bible. These genealogies begin in the garden of Eden (1:1) and end with people worshiping God in His city, Jerusalem, after the exile (9:33–34). In between there is much sin and sorrow, but also God's grace in the raising up of kings and priests. Chronicles taught the returning exiles that they should hope in the Lord because, although man's sin abounds, God's grace will abound much more through His chosen and coming King. The gospel of Jesus Christ reveals this King, who is both Priest and sacrifice for His people, so that they will worship God in the new Jerusalem coming down from heaven (Rev. 21:2). How can this vision give us hope?

Chapter 10

Saul's tragic rebellion and death stands as a solemn reminder that Israel's hope did not merely rest in restoring a king to its throne. The returned exiles must learn from history that kings are curses if they do not obey the Lord and give Him their undivided allegiance. Too often the kings reigning in Jerusalem had failed at precisely this point, and thus came the exile. In the same way, we all deserve eternal punishment from God because we have broken God's laws and given our hearts to false gods. The need of Israel and of all mankind is not just a king, but a king who is the obedient servant of the Lord. How does Jesus Christ perfectly meet this need?

Chapter 11

1. Israel submitted to David's reign because they recognized their close bond with him ("thy bone and thy flesh") and his loving leadership of them like a shepherd (v. 1). How much more then should the church submit to Jesus Christ (Eph. 5:23)! He has taken on our flesh (John 1:14; Heb. 2:14). He loved the church supremely as its Shepherd by laying down His life for His sheep (John 10:14–15; Eph. 5:25). He has united us to Himself as His own body, His flesh and bone (Eph. 5:30). What would it look like for you to humbly give your allegiance and submission to King Jesus?

2. David's mighty men had developed their strength and skills to a high degree, and performed remarkable feats out of love for their king. Yet every victory was from the Lord (v. 14). This teaches us to give all our heart and all our strength to perform our callings with excellence, and simultaneously to do all things in dependent prayer and give all the glory to the Lord. How can Christians strive to be mighty men and women for the Lord, and yet remain humble before Him?

Chapter 12

If the Spirit moved Amasai to declare Israel's allegiance to David and God's peace upon him (v. 18), then how much more does the Holy Spirit move people to declare the son of David, Jesus Christ, as Lord (1 Cor. 12:3)? The Lord's presence with David attracted many people from all walks of life to serve David, and in the same way the Spirit's anointing of Christ draws many different kinds of people to serve Him (Luke 15:1; 1 Cor. 1:27). Have you felt that spiritual attraction to Christ? Has the Spirit drawn you to serve Him as your King?

Chapter 13

1. Uzzah may have thought he had good motives in grasping the ark. However, he refused to recognize the holiness of God and his own sinfulness. He assumed his hand was cleaner than the dirt on which the ark would have fallen, if God did not sovereignly prevent it. The root of inventing our own worship instead of following God's Word is a disregard for God's holiness (Lev. 10:1–3; 1 Sam. 6:19–20). We should not presume to be able to approach or worship God according to our own imagination. How can we worship in the fear of the Lord and bow under the revelation of His will for worship?

2. We know that it was a great disappointment to David that the ark did not arrive in Jerusalem after this first attempt. We see how deeply David desired communion with God. "How shall I bring the ark of God home to me?" (v. 12). Do you desire communion with God? Do disappointments strengthen your desire for that communion?

Chapter 14

Though God established a human king over His people, that king was not to reign by human power or wisdom. The Lord confirmed the kingdom (v. 2). The king sought and found his wisdom in God (vv. 10, 14). God broke out to destroy the enemies of the king (v. 11). God's invisible armies fought for him (v. 15). The king obeyed God's Word (v. 16). The Lord caused the nations to fear the king (v. 17). In these ways David foreshadows Christ and His kingdom.

Jesus was truly human, but He did not build His kingdom on human strength. His kingdom comes in the Holy Spirit. He sought His Father regularly in prayer. The angels gave Christ strength in His darkest moments. He obeyed God to the death, even death on the cross. And now, risen from the dead, Christ has received authority from the Father to make disciples among all nations. If this is true of Christ, who is both God and man, how much more is it true of Christians? What lessons can we learn from this chapter about how we should seek the kingdom of God?

Chapter 15

1. When King David took care that the people follow God's commands in worship (vv. 13–15), God assisted their worship with His grace (v. 26) and the people worshiped with great humility and joy (vv. 27–28). In the same way, the Lord Jesus, the King of the church, has directed the church in the right way of worship. Why is it crucial that the church worship God according to the Word of Christ? What does this mean, practically speaking?

2. Ironically, precisely when King David worshiped God in obedience to His Word, his wife Michal despised him for rejoicing in great humility (v. 29). How should we respond when worldly people likewise despise Christ and us if we are following Him in biblical worship?

Chapter 16

1. At the heart of worship is seeking God (vv. 10–11). By nature, we have lost God and have turned our backs to Him. Nevertheless, it is only in His presence that there is light

and life. It is only through Jesus Christ that we can have fellowship with Him and taste of His goodness and grace. Through Christ, we can have access to the Father in the Holy Spirit. This was David's one passion: to seek God and enjoy His glory (Ps. 27:4, 8). How can you kindle the same passion in your own heart?

2. Thanksgiving (v. 34) is the overflow in the heart of what God has done in His grace for undeserving sinners. It is the response of human love to the love of the Lord. It shows itself in our thoughts, words, and actions. David was overwhelmed that God would draw so near to him and his nation. He spent a lot of time and energy praising Him. How thankful are we? Why do we lack a thankful attitude many times?

Chapter 17

1. God promised that through David He would provide a king to rule His people in His presence forever. The good news of the New Testament is that this king has come, the very Son of God who has risen from the dead (Rom. 1:1–4). Jesus Christ presently reigns from heaven by His Spirit. If God kept His promise to David by bringing His Son to earth, how much more now that Christ has come can we trust God to keep His promise that His Son will return? How is the kingdom of Christ (both present and future) the hope and joy of His people?

2. David was overwhelmed by God's tender mercies not only in the present but also regarding the future. He was deeply humbled and exclaimed in amazement and wonder, "Who am I, O LORD God, and what is mine house, that thou hast brought me hitherto?" (v. 16). Whenever God manifests His

grace, He brings an abiding sense of wonder, for we could never fathom any reason from our perspective that God would deal with us in such grace. Spend some time praising God for His mercy and grace.

Chapter 18

1. God prospered David so that the surrounding nations were either conquered by David or they came to serve him with gifts. Concerning Christ, the great son of David, the Bible says, "Be wise now therefore, O ye kings: be instructed, ye judges of the earth. Serve the LORD with fear, and rejoice with trembling. Kiss the Son, lest he be angry, and ye perish from the way" (Ps. 2:10–12). To kiss the Son is to give Him your sincere submission. How do you show your respect to our King?

2. David understood the need for structure and order in his administration, appointing qualified men to specific offices. Christ, the great son of David, has established a spiritual order for His kingdom with church officers with specified qualifications (1 Tim. 3). All the gatherings of the church should be well ordered, since God is not a God of confusion, but of peace (1 Cor. 14:33). Why are order and officers important for justice and righteousness?

Chapter 19

1. Like the servants of King David, the servants of Jesus Christ may experience times of humiliation (v. 4) and face overwhelming forces of opposition (vv. 6–7). Yet they should take heart, be courageous, and fight for the people of God, trusting that the Lord will do what is good (v. 13). In what

ways do you need courage today? How can you find it in the Lord?

2. Just as the Ammonites distrusted David's heart of mercy and thus insulted him and his servants, so the wicked view Christ with unbelieving, suspicious eyes and greatly dishonor Him. How foolish it is to distrust and dishonor the Lord of love and kindness, especially in His gospel invitations. They greatly provoke His wrath. It was wise for the servants of Hadarezer to make peace with David when they saw his victory (v. 19); it is even wiser for sinners to find peace with God through repentance and faith in the gospel, for Jesus is Lord. Which group do you belong to? Who can you pray for?

Chapter 20

David's victory over Goliath by faith in the Lord (1 Sam. 17) evidently inspired his servants to take on similarly gigantic enemies and defeat them. The bravery and victory of one's king can strongly motivate his servants to attempt great feats as well. In the same way, Christ's victory over sin and Satan makes believers strong and courageous to fight their own personal spiritual battles and anticipate victory by faith in Him (John 16:33; Eph. 6:10; Col. 2:15; 1 John 5:4–5). What spiritual enemies seem gigantic to you right now? How can you look to Christ's victory?

Chapter 21

1. Even godly David fell into sin, a warning to us that the best of men is but a man. His sin brought deadly consequences upon the people because he was their king. The plague that

came from David's sin is a small reminder of the death that has consumed billions of people because of Adam's sin (Rom. 5:12). How does God view sin so that it causes Him to pronounce such terrible judgments?

2. David took full, personal responsibility for this calamity, offering to bear the punishment himself (v. 17) and insisting on paying the price for atonement at his own expense (vv. 24–25). As a result, he obtained a lasting place for the temple where the people would find forgiveness of their sins (2 Chron. 6:21–39). Here we have a beautiful picture of Jesus Christ. Although He never sinned, He took full responsibility for the sins of His people, personally paying the price for atonement by His own obedience and death, so that they may enjoy God's forgiveness forever. What does this teach us about the character of God?

Chapter 22

1. David was a type of Christ, who also went through a bloody conflict, but not in the killing of others. Christ's kingdom was not of this world (John 18:36), and He conquered not by killing but by submitting to a violent death (Rev. 5:5, 9). Yet by His death on the cross He conquered the powers of hell (Col. 2:15). Solomon also was a type of Christ, reigning in the peace He won by His blood (Eph. 2:14–17). Christ is building a new temple, not of stones and gold (Eph. 2:18–22). Of what is His new temple being built and with what and whom will it be filled?

2. David challenged Solomon not to take his privileges for granted. Faith, courage, and obedience must propel him to his work (vv. 11–13). He needed to be busy and active

fulfilling the calling with which he had been charged, using the resources prepared by his father (vv. 14–16). What resources and calling has God entrusted to you? How are you busily serving the Lord?

Chapter 23

David said, "The LORD God of Israel hath given rest unto his people, that they may dwell in Jerusalem for ever" (v. 25). Thus the Levites ceased to carry the tabernacle in its travels, but instead served God in the permanent home for His presence. In this way, the earthly Jerusalem foreshadowed the heavenly Jerusalem which was to come. The heavenly Jerusalem will usher in the eternal rest for God's redeemed people forever. Presently, we travel as on a pilgrimage, and God assigns every Christian duties necessary for our pilgrim state. However, when Christ returns with His kingdom of glory and peace we will enter into our eternal worship and the permanent enjoyment of His glory. All God's people will serve as priests and reign as kings in His presence (Rev. 5:10; 22:4–5). How does that promise comfort you?

Chapter 24

The service of God's worship requires plans, organization, and structure. Many people may be involved, and they need to have a clear knowledge of their responsibilities. It is often helpful to set up schedules of rotating duties among those qualified to perform them. Just as King David determined the distribution of the offices of the Levites (v. 3), so King Jesus determines the structure and officers of the church by the directions of His Word and gifts of His Spirit (1 Cor. 12:4–7;

Eph. 4:7–8, 11). However, some practical details about the church and its worship are not specified by the Scriptures, and therefore must be determined by other means. Why is it so important that the church have well-organized structures and plans governed by the Word and Spirit of Christ?

Chapter 25

David separated the musicians for the service of the temple and these men were to "prophesy with harps, with psalteries, and with cymbals" (v. 1). It is no accident that David was known as the sweet psalmist of Israel (2 Sam. 23:1). He loved music and loved singing to the Lord (Pss. 89:1; 101:1). He knew the power of music as it relates to shaping one's worldview. Above all, David realized that God inhabits the praises of His people (Ps. 22:3). Why is song so important and helpful for worship? Why must church music be made in submission to Christ and the officers He appoints in the church?

Chapter 26

God gives people different callings. We should not envy what God has asked others to do in His kingdom. In order for God's kingdom to function, we need people, all in their own stations of life, to do what God has called and gifted them to do. Hence, the Bible says: "Ye are the body of Christ, and members in particular" (1 Cor. 12:27). How precious it is to have people of ability and wisdom (1 Chron. 26:6–9, 14, 30–32)! Each member should realistically evaluate his abilities, strive to develop them, and seek to serve in the church accordingly (Rom. 12:3–8). What are some things that by

God's grace you can do well? How are you using them in the church?

Chapter 27

1. By having a rotating force from the twelve tribes, David not only made the tribes share the burden of Israel's defense, but he trained the men so that they could be leaders in their own areas of labor. God's people have to stand ready for spiritual battle at any time (Eph. 6:10–18). If we are skilled in this battle this will help us greatly to be strong wherever God has placed us. How can we train for the battles we face?

2. Instead of constantly counting people and their resources to assess our strength, believers should be counting the promises of God (v. 23). Why is it a trap for churches to measure themselves by attendance or finances? How can we cultivate gospel optimism by learning to focus on the promises of the riches of glory in Christ?

Chapter 28

David's words at the close of his life reveal that the building of the temple was more than constructing an attractive building for worship. It was the culmination of God's purposes in old covenant history, and a type of Christ's work. Through God's chosen and Spirit-led King, the Lord is establishing His presence with His people. God will live among them as their King as He promised in His covenant. He will receive their obedient worship while they enjoy the peace He gives them. How does it affect your view of public worship to see it as drawing near to the King? How does it affect your view of heaven to see it as dwelling in God's presence?

Chapter 29

1. In all our giving to build the church, whether with our abilities, time, or money, we must recognize that God does not need us. He is all-sufficient in Himself to accomplish all His will. In fact, our ability to give, willingness to give, and actual giving are the gifts of His grace to us (2 Cor. 8:1–5; Phil. 2:12–13). The sovereignty of God's grace releases us to be cheerful givers, rejoicing in the infinite depths of God's indescribable grace even as we pour out our resources for Him (2 Cor. 9:7–8, 15). Who can ever out-give a God like this?

2. Solomon's reign opened with unprecedented splendor and universal obedience among the people. Yet by its end it had fallen into the darkness of pride and idolatry. The kingdom of Solomon was but a small and passing shadow of Christ's eternal kingdom. Truly, Christ sits on the throne of the Lord, for He is the all-sufficient Lord. He has a perfect heart toward His Father. All of His redeemed people willingly submit to Him and serve Him. How should it affect our lives knowing that the son of David reigns now on the throne of heaven?

2 Chronicles

Chapter 1

Solomon's famous prayer for wisdom is a model for our prayers. He acknowledged God's faithful love and sovereignty over his life (v. 8). He took hold of God's promises and turned them into petitions, asking God to do what He had said (v. 9). He prayed for the ability and gifts to do what God had called him to do (v. 10). He did not pray out of worldly lusts for riches, honor, or revenge (v. 11). God answered his prayer by doing more than he asked (v. 12). Think of some concern weighing upon your heart. How does Solomon's example guide you in how to lift that concern up to the Lord in prayer?

Chapter 2

The temple was "an house for the name of the LORD" (v. 1). God designed it so that people would know His glorious attributes. Yet it could not contain His glory, for God is infinite. Indeed, God's purposes could not be contained by Israel, for His temple would bring Him glory among the nations as the only true God. In the new covenant the Lord no longer links His presence to a special building, but Christ and His people are God's house (1 Peter 2:4–5). Yet God's nature and purposes remain the same. What then does this teach us about the church?

Chapter 3

The gold and precious stones in God's holy house communicated the precious value of His holiness. The emblems of palm trees and pomegranates and the names of the pillars invited Israel to find abundant life and strength in God's presence, but the cherubim stood as a warning that man was still excluded from paradise for his sins. How can sinners be brought back to God and find life in Him? It was no accident that the temple was built on the very spot where a millennium earlier Isaac's life was spared through the sacrifice of the substitute ram (Gen. 22:13). Abraham prophesied that on that mountain the Lord would provide a lamb for sacrifice in the future (Gen. 22:8; cf. 22:14). The type of that sacrifice appeared in the sacrifices of the priests at Solomon's temple, and the reality appeared when the Lamb of God took away the sin of the world by dying upon the cross just outside the city. How can a sinner draw near to God through the blood of Christ?

Chapter 4

The temple had many of the things that we would have in our homes: wash basins, lights, tables, and so on, communicating that God really dwelt with His people. The brazen altar at the entrance was a visible message that blood needed to be shed for there to be communion between the holy God and unholy sinners. Notice that, unlike our homes, there were no chairs in the temple. The priests who labored in the temple never sat down. They only stood as servants ministering before their Master. The closest thing was a footstool, the ark (5:7). God alone could sit down, so to speak, between the cherubim (Ps. 80:1), as on His throne. Christ now sits on the throne of heaven (Heb. 1:3). How should it affect us to know that God really dwells with His people through Christ, our Prophet, Priest, and King?

Chapter 5

1. The event of the ark coming to rest in this splendid sanctuary is given a good amount of space, showing its importance (vv. 1–10). The stability of rest that God had promised to give the Israelites when they departed from Egypt was finally realized (Ex. 15:17). With this event, God visibly took up His residence with His people in the temple, showing His permanence in the land and His abiding peace with His people. Today God dwells in His people by the Holy Spirit. How can you celebrate this important blessing God has given us today?

2. After the dedication of the temple and the praises of the people, the temple was filled with God's glory (v. 13). In Jewish history this would later be known as the Shekinah glory, based on the Hebrew word "dwell" (*shakan*, 6:1). In the fullness of time, God's glory would dwell among His people through His Son Jesus Christ, of whom John writes that He "dwelt among us, (and we beheld his glory…)" (John 1:14). Through the Word and the Spirit of Christ, the glory of God shines in the heart of every believer (2 Cor. 3:17–18; 4:6). Why is it better for us to have the glory of God dwelling in us by the Spirit than to have it outside us in a visible cloud?

Chapter 6

1. God's purposes for the temple revolved around five things highlighted here: humility in the presence of the infinite

God, repentance of sin, prayer for forgiveness and restoration, confidence in God's faithfulness to keep His promises, and drawing the nations to seek God. In the new covenant there is no particular nation in covenant with God, and Christ has sent His people out to make disciples of all the nations. However, these remain His purposes for the church. Consider each of these five purposes. How does your church seek to fulfill them?

2. Solomon envisioned the temple as a place where sinners would come repenting and praying for grace. How do you come into God's presence? Does your church encourage turning from sin to God and praying for His forgiveness and restoration? Why or why not?

Chapter 7

1. Three great themes should direct our worship: adoration of God's glory, praise of God's faithful love, and repentance of our wicked ways (vv. 1–3, 6, 10, 14). We should always come to worship with a sense that God is so glorious that we belong on our faces before Him. We should never approach the Lord without an inward brokenness and hatred of our sin against Him. Yet humility and contrition of sin should never take away our sense of joy in His goodness in Jesus Christ, the son of David (v. 10). Our constant refrain should be, "He is good; for his mercy endureth for ever" (v. 3). How can we cultivate in our worship a rich experience of God's love?

2. Israel's enjoyment of the temple and the land depended upon the obedience of their king, upon whom the Lord had focused the demands of His holy law. As the rest of Chronicles makes plain, no mere man could bear this burden; all

sinned and sinned greatly. However, long after the covenant curses fell upon Israel, another Son of David came to the remnant. God sent His Son, born of a woman, born under the law, who fulfilled all righteousness. If we are in union with Him by a Spirit-worked faith, then we will enjoy God's presence forever in a better land than Canaan. Praise God for His faithfulness, that He has done it all in His Son.

Chapter 8

1. Solomon's kingdom extended far to the north and south. Christ's kingdom is, however, all over this world. Since a sovereign's authority is limited to his borders, Christ's authority is absolute and universal. His kingdom has no borders. This gives Christians the right to preach the gospel and make disciples of Christ in all nations, regardless of whether the governments of those lands approve, for Christ is King of kings. How can you become involved in God's mission?

2. From the Bible we know that Moses, David, and Solomon, all mentioned in this chapter, were preoccupied with the worship of God. Our lives will only be worthwhile to the extent that we are properly and biblically focused on the glory of God in all we say, do, and think. Let us not assume that we are living for God's glory, but search the Scriptures and worship by the Word. How can we bring more glory to God in our worship and in our lives?

Chapter 9

The queen of Sheba marveled at the wisdom and wealth Solomon had from God. His wisdom attracted the attention of the world. Yet Solomon's kingdom pales in comparison to the kingdom of Christ, and it quickly faded after his death. How much more then should we marvel at the wisdom of Jesus Christ (Matt. 12:42; 13:54), who is anointed with the Spirit of wisdom (Isa. 11:2)? In Christ are all the treasures of wisdom, and He is our wisdom if God has united us to Him (1 Cor. 1:30–31; Col. 2:3). Therefore, let us boast in Christ alone. The beauty of His wisdom will attract all nations to seek Him, so let us walk in His light, and make it shine to all the world (Isa. 2:1–5). Why is Christ's wisdom one of the greatest treasures of His kingdom? How can we showcase His wisdom in our families and churches to win lost sinners?

Chapter 10

1. It is remarkable that Rehoboam, the son of Solomon, threw away his father's wisdom: "A soft answer turneth away wrath: but grievous words stir up anger" (Prov. 15:1). We often confuse meekness with weakness. Moses was a great leader, but the meekest man on earth (Num. 12:3). It is far wiser for leaders to exercise their authority with love and humility, listening to legitimate complaints from people, than to try to rule by sheer force. On the other hand, the people took Rehoboam's pride as an occasion to throw away their inheritance in Christ. Beware of a spirit of rebellion against authority, for it often hides wicked unbelief toward God. Can you think of examples of both kinds of leadership in the people around you?

2. The Bible teaches us to view history and contemporary events through a double perspective. On the one hand, we see the human causes and acknowledge the responsibility of each person for his own attitude and actions. On the other

hand, the believer sees the divine cause ruling over all, using even sin to accomplish His righteous purposes. How does this teach us both to fear the Lord and to hope in His mercy?

Chapter 11

Shortly after renouncing the house of David, the northern tribes turned to false worship and idolatry from which they never recovered. The path of apostasy is a dreadful slide to hell. Faithfulness to Christ as the king of the church is inseparable from faithfulness in worship to God. If we begin to replace the authority of the Word of Christ with human ideas, then we will soon replace God-glorifying worship with idols. Why is this so? How can we guard against it?

Chapter 12

God blesses those who humble themselves and repent of their sins, confessing that God is right in all the hardships He sent upon them. Whatever your sins may be, repentance is the only path of escape from God's wrath. Do not cling to your pride. When Rehoboam proudly turned away from serving the Lord, he found himself serving the wicked king of Egypt. We all serve someone, and rebellion against God only puts us under a far worse master. Do not trade your gold for bronze. The service of the Lord is the best service we could ever be in, for Christ's yoke is easy and his burden is light (Matt. 11:30). How does this chapter encourage you to repent?

Chapter 13

1. If we would count ourselves God's people and look for His help, we must hold to God's appointed king, the son

of David, and cling to God's commanded form of worship through His appointed priest. The true church is defined by its submission to Jesus Christ as its head and by its worship of the true God through His righteousness (Eph. 5:23–24; Phil. 3:3; Heb. 13:15). Spend some time giving your "sacrifice of praise to God."

2. The key to experiencing God's salvation is relying upon the Lord (v. 18) through heartfelt prayer (v. 14). When we rely on God, no matter how weak we are, we are strong (2 Cor. 12:10). Therefore, the greatest danger we face is our own pride, for it leads to self-sufficiency. How can we develop a heart of humble reliance upon the Lord?

Chapter 14

1. Asa's religion was not just positive in the sense that he sought the Lord and encouraged others to seek the Lord. He also tore down institutions of false worship. This would have made some unhappy, but Asa had a comprehensive and thoroughgoing view of what God demands of us. Faithful service to the Lord requires us to oppose what is evil. How can we be this proactive in our culture? What obstacles do we face?

2. What seemed to be a terrifying threat turned into a remarkable blessing through the Lord's delivering hand. Powerless in himself, Asa entrusted himself to the powerful God. When our troubles stir anxiety in our hearts, let us bring our concerns to God with believing, thankful prayer, and His peace will guard us (Phil. 4:6–7). What concerns can you bring before the Lord today?

Chapter 15

1. This chapter gives us a vivid picture of a major theme in Chronicles: seeking God. All people pursue something, and ours is meant to be the pursuit of God in Christ (Phil. 3:12–14). What does it mean to seek God? Asa's example shows that we seek God by finding strength and courage in God's promises, by removing idols from our lives and circles of influence, and by worshiping God with all our hearts in the ways He commands in His covenant. What would it mean in your life to seek the Lord with all your soul?

2. Asa showed remarkable consistency, removing his own mother from her royal position because she promoted idolatry (v. 16). Reformation must begin in the home before it can take root in the church or nation. This can be extremely costly, but Christ taught us that His disciples must hate their parents and families in comparison to their love for Him (Luke 14:26).

Chapter 16

1. Asa was not constant in his faithfulness. The backsliding of a godly man into inconsistency is perplexing to all who know him. Pride and unrepentance can turn a good leader into a stubborn oppressor. The end of a matter is more important than the beginning. We need God's grace to finish well. In particular, Asa's sins sprang from weakness of faith in God's promises, and resting his hope in man. How can we stay alert against such misplaced trust?

2. We have here a magnificent promise: "For the eyes of the LORD run to and fro throughout the whole earth, to shew himself strong in the behalf of them whose heart is perfect

toward him" (v. 9). God engages His knowledge of all things and His infinite power to strongly support every man, woman, or child who trusts in Him alone. How does this promise show the foolishness and wickedness of trusting in man? How does it encourage us to look to the Lord?

Chapter 17

1. Chronicles draws parallels between Jehoshaphat and David. Both sought the Lord in wholehearted devotion. Both kept God's commandments. Both enlisted the services of mighty men. Through these comparisons, Chronicles fostered hope in the people after the exile that God would raise up a new king, of whom David was only a shadow. How does this foster hope for us?

2. Jehoshaphat's reformation of the people of God had two sides: he destroyed the idols of Judah, and he sent out teachers to instruct Judah in God's Word. The reformation of the church always requires both. We saw this in the sixteenth century, when God used the Reformers to root out idolatry from the church's worship and to train men to teach the Bible to the people. Why does reformation require opposing idolatry? Why does it involve teaching the Word?

Chapter 18

1. Beware of binding yourself in agreements with the wicked as Jehoshaphat did with Ahab. Perhaps Jehoshaphat cherished hopes that Judah and Israel and Ahab would enter a new phase of cooperation; however, he barely escaped alive. While we are to love all people, we must separate ourselves from sin and therefore not yoke ourselves with unbelievers

(2 Cor. 6:14). Do not say, "I am as thou art, and my people as thy people" (2 Chron. 18:3), unless you are one in Christ. Where do you see unhealthy alliances happening in our day?

2. Treasure the Word of God in the fear of God. One man speaking God's truth is worth more than 400 men telling us what we want to hear. Thank God for faithful ministers who refuse to speak anything except God's Word. The Word of the Lord proves true because it is backed by the providence of God. When God threatens death on an unrepentant sinner, be sure it will come, even if by a random shot by an archer. How then should we respond when God's Word says hard things against us and our sin?

Chapter 19

1. While we should love the wicked in the sense of having mercy on them even when they harm us (Matt. 5:45; Acts 7:60), we must not love them in the sense of joining ourselves to them or sharing in their wicked deeds (Eph. 5:7–14). Though we must live in the world, we must be wise not to compromise ourselves with the world. What can we do to pursue this wisdom that begins with the fear of the Lord in the heart, hates sin, and turns from it in disgust?

2. Spiritual reformation is not confined to the worship services of the church any more than God's sovereignty is limited to the church building. Repentance must reach the people in their day-to-day lives (v. 4). The dread of God's judgment must penetrate into the halls of power and courts of justice (vv. 5–7). The fear of God must control the decisions of church elders (vv. 8–11). Just as King Jehoshaphat labored to bring reformation to every part of society, so the greater

son of David works to save and sanctify all kinds of people, including kings (1 Tim. 2:1–7). Why does the fear of the Lord transform everything and not just part of human life?

Chapter 20

God gave Jehoshaphat another opportunity to either trust in man's strength or God's infinite power, and this time the king sought the Lord (vv. 3–4). This time Jehoshaphat relied on divine omnipotence and sought the favor of the Lord. It must have been intensely difficult to wait upon God in such frightening circumstances, but the battle belongs to the Lord (v. 15). We need to trust in the Lord at all times, pouring out the concerns of our hearts in prayer (Ps. 62:8). With God is everlasting strength (Isa. 26:4), and if we will wait quietly upon Him then in His time the Lord alone will be exalted (Ps. 46:10). Then, like Jehoshaphat and Judah, we can bow down and worship the Lord (2 Chron. 20:18). It is good, however, to begin praising Him before His salvation comes (v. 21), so that by faith we may find strength (v. 20). How is your faith being tested even now?

Chapter 21

A godly father can still leave a bitter legacy if he does not separate himself from the wicked world, for his children may very well fully embrace the world. A horrible example of this principle appears in Lot's daughters (Gen. 19), and we see it again with Jehoram, son of Jehoshaphat. Not only did he sin in dreadful ways, but he forced others to sin and died under God's judgment. Sin is like a cancer that spreads unless it is mortified by God's grace of repentance. Do not play with sin or with alliances with the world. If you continue in sin, you do so having been warned of the dreadful consequences. Heb. 12:1 says that sin can "easily beset us." What example did Christ leave us for resisting sin in our lives?

Chapter 22

1. Jehoshaphat's foolish alliance with the house of Ahab (18:1) reaped such a bitter harvest that it nearly destroyed the line of David. The promise of God's covenant seemed to hang by a thread (1 Chron. 17:11–12). Satan certainly would have been happy with Athaliah's design to kill "all the seed royal of the house of Judah" (2 Chron. 22:10). He has been set against the seed of the woman from the first promise of God (Gen. 3:15). Sometimes Satan works by drawing the church into compromise and entanglement with the world. Sometimes Satan uses violence, as when he killed all the children of Bethlehem. Whether he entices us to sin or threatens us with persecution, how can we be prepared to stand against him?

2. The bravery of two women saved the line of Christ from extinction. One was a daughter of a king, but the other an ordinary (and unnamed) servant. They risked their lives to preserve the house of David, and proved to be instruments in God's hand to fulfill His covenant. Never underestimate the significance of ordinary men and women who trust the Lord and do His will. God's sovereignty often works through human means, and the godly are His servants. How does the courage of both Jehoshabeath and the nurse motivate you to serve God courageously?

Chapter 23

1. Just as the courage of Jehoshabeath saved the line of David from total destruction (22:11), so the patient and careful planning of her husband, Jehoiada, restored the son of David to the throne of Judah. The house of David appeared to be in ruin for more than seven years, a terrible test for those who believed God's promise but knew nothing of Joash's preservation. However, by faith in that promise (23:3), the priest and Levites took their lives into their hands to crown the boy-king Joash. God had not abandoned His people. The gates of hell cannot prevail against His church. God will ever preserve His kingdom in this world through the living faith of His people. How is your faith producing patience in seemingly hopeless days, as well as wise and bold actions?

2. The monarchy was lost because they abandoned God's covenant (22:4), and so the restoration of the kingdom must engage the people to keep covenant with the Lord as faithful worshipers. We cannot cry out to God, "Thy kingdom come" (Matt. 6:10), with true hearts unless we also turn from our disobedience and idolatry and renew our commitment to obedience and faithful worship. How then should we pray for revival in the church?

Chapter 24

1. Joash was faithful as long as Jehoiada was alive (v. 2). The prayers, counsel, and presence of godly people make an incalculable difference for good. This is what Christ means when He speaks about His people as the salt of the earth and the light of the world (Matt. 5:13–14). When faithful Christians are gone, much often goes with them. Thank God for

spiritual fathers and mothers who have influenced you. Yet ask yourself, if they were to die, would you continue to walk with God as faithfully as you do while they are here?

2. Zechariah was faithful unto death. Empowered by the Holy Spirit, he courageously stood against the king, princes, and people. He rebuked them of their sin and warned them of God's anger, but they would not hear God's message and killed the messenger. As Zechariah died, broken by the stones of the wicked, he entrusted his case to the righteous Judge. Pray for God to give to the church preachers like Zechariah, filled with the Spirit's boldness and humility.

Chapter 25

It is extremely dangerous to remain in a condition of half-hearted religion (v. 2). Though we may do some good things, like Amaziah we may also waste our resources pursuing the favor of the world (v. 6), make ourselves vulnerable to the wicked by our alliances with them (v. 13), be attracted to imitate the world in its corrupt forms of worship (v. 14), proudly take on projects beyond our means to our defeat and disgrace (v. 19), and alienate those around us (v. 27). It is far wiser to humble ourselves before the Lord, give Him our total devotion, and submit to all that His Word counsels us to do. What are the benefits of wholehearted religion?

Chapter 26

1. The Lord prospered Uzziah for much of the five decades that he reigned. Prosperity, however, is dangerous when we do not guard our hearts. We read, "But when he was strong, his heart was lifted up to his destruction" (v. 16). It is sad

but far too common that when the Lord prospers us, we seize His gifts as an occasion for pride. How has the Lord blessed you? How can you make that an occasion for humility instead of pride?

2. Uzziah's pride particularly showed itself when he presumed to intrude into the worship God had reserved for the priests. He made himself spiritually unclean, and so God made him physically unclean with leprosy. Pride is often at the root of presumption in worship, whereas humility leads us to worship God in exactly the way He has commanded it. Christ alone is the Mediator between God and man, our great High Priest. Do you trust in yourself or anyone or anything else to gain access to God?

Chapter 27

Jotham reigned successfully and admirably because "he prepared his ways before the LORD his God" (v. 6). This is a summary of true religion. First, it means that a godly person lives in the presence of God. He does not limit his religion to sacred places or times, but constantly walks with a sense that God is here to keep His promises. Second, it means that a godly person directs his life according to God's covenant. His authority is not mere tradition, for he knows that his fathers erred in some things. His guide is not popularity, for the majority can be wicked. He does not simply follow his impulses. He orders his ways before his covenant Lord according to His Word. What would that look like in your own life?

Chapter 28

1. In a way that seems insane, Ahaz threw himself and his nation into the worship of idols, even at the cost of sacrificing some of his children. When the Lord gave him over to the forces of Damascus as punishment, Ahaz added the idols of Damascus to his worship instead of turning back to the Lord. His mind was so ruled by idolatry that he assumed he was defeated by the power of a superior idol. People today run from idol to idol in their trials, but apart from God's grace, they will not turn to the Lord. How do you see this around you today?

2. After so many years of apostasy in the northern kingdom, it seemed like a hopeless case for the prophet Oded to call Israel to show mercy on the captives of Judah. However, when he faithfully preached God's Word, some leaders in Israel responded with a touching display of kindness to their defeated brothers. Let us never assume that it is worthless to speak God's Word to a group of sinners, no matter what their reputation. They may put us to shame with how they respond. When are you tempted to think that it is not worth sharing God's Word?

Chapter 29

1. Reformation centers upon worship, and nothing is more urgent than to begin to restore biblical worship after it has been corrupted or lost. Central to this work is the calling of the ministers who lead worship back to their holy duties. They must lead the church to cleanse away all that offends the Lord and to sanctify God's temple, which in Christ is the people themselves. They must take both the structure and

content of worship from the Word of God. How can you pray for your leaders? And how can you use God's Word in your own private worship?

2. The only way that leaders can bring the people to willingly and gladly embrace reformation, especially in worship, is if God prepares the people. Apart from divine grace, people will resist godly leadership and reject godly example (27:2). However, when the Lord works in their hearts, they embrace reformation willingly and eagerly to the joy of all involved (29:36). How should this motivate us to pray?

Chapter 30

1. Just as King Hezekiah sent messengers throughout all Israel to call people to turn back to God, so the Lord Jesus, King of heaven and earth, sent messengers into all nations to call people to repent and become His disciples (Matt. 28:18–20; Luke 24:44–49). Hezekiah called them to celebrate the Passover, but Christ is our Passover, the Lamb of God whose blood saves sinners from the wrath to come (John 1:29; 1 Cor. 5:7). Missions and evangelism are matters of obedience to our King. Let us therefore not be lacking in this great effort, nor let us be discouraged because many mock and scorn the message. Who can you be in fervent prayer for, that the hand of the Lord would be with him or her, and that by His grace many will turn to the Lord?

2. Just as Hezekiah asked God to overlook the ceremonial uncleanness of some of the people eating the Passover, so Christ intercedes for His people that God will pardon the sins that mar their sincere worship. Breaking the ceremonial law required God's forgiveness (v. 18), so how much more

do we need His forgiveness for our violations of the moral law? However, the Lord is pleased to forgive such faults by the intercession of His Son if our hearts sincerely seek Him. How does this encourage the repentant sinner? How does it warn the hypocrite?

Chapter 31

1. The renewal of worship that God worked through Hezekiah was not just one big event, but a transformation that overthrew idolatry in the ordinary lives of the people and made them zealous to support true worship, to the joy of their leaders. Real revival is not just a big meeting with a lot of excitement, but a Spirit-worked transformation that touches the home life and finances. Pray for such revival in your nation and in every nation.

2. Hezekiah gave much attention to making sure the ministers of the temple were provided for and organized. Christ also has given instructions for the ministers of His church so that they can be freed from the necessity of providing for their families to focus their time and energy on the work of the ministry. Why is it important for churches to care for the physical and financial needs of their pastors?

Chapter 32

1. The people "rested" upon the words of Hezekiah (v. 8). They leaned the weight of their fears and futures in the promises of God. What strength God's promises prove to be to those who lean the weight of their lives on them! Apart from His grace, we will quickly slip into pride and destruction (vv. 25, 31). We must therefore earnestly seek His grace

for everything and give Him thanks for every good gift, because apart from Christ we can do nothing, but in Him we can do many good things (John 15:5).

2. Sennacherib sent his servants to Judah to mock the God of Judah, but God will not be mocked (Gal. 6:7). God struck the king down by the hand of his own sons in the house of his own idol (2 Chron. 32:21), showing His sovereignty over everyone everywhere. How is this a warning to all who mock God and trust in the resources and idols of man?

Chapter 33

Manasseh gives us a model of a sinner's repentance. Affliction often serves God's providence to bring down the proud (v. 11). The proper response to outward humiliation is inward humiliation with earnest prayer to God based upon His covenant promises (v. 12). God is amazingly patient and kind and willingly saves sinners who turn to Him in repentance, so that they know by experience that He is the Lord (v. 13). True repentance results in putting old patterns of sin to death (v. 15) and establishing new habits of obedience (v. 16), especially with regard to what one worships and serves. Reflect upon this model. How has God used affliction to bring you to an end of yourself? How have you responded to affliction and conviction of sin? Have you experienced the salvation and lordship of God? How has your lifestyle changed as a result?

Chapter 34

1. Josiah did these things when he was very young (vv. 1, 3, 8). God does not care whether you are young or old; the Lord

looks at the heart. Josiah's heart was soft to God's Word, so that he grieved deeply and humbled himself over his sins and the sins of his people (v. 27). His heart was also fully engaged to pursue the Lord and keep His commandments (v. 31). Do you have a heart like Josiah? You may not be a king, but if you follow God with your whole heart, who can tell how God will use you for His glory?

2. Josiah had a burden that the whole nation would hear God's Word and walk in God's ways. It is a mark of God's work in our hearts when we want others to know God's truth and experience the grace He has shown to us. How big is your heart for others? How are you using the calling and influence God has given to you to engage other people for the kingdom of God?

Chapter 35

1. Josiah led Judah to celebrate the Passover in a grand manner. It was a glorious remembrance of how God redeemed Israel through the blood of the lamb. Josiah directed them to keep it in accordance with the law of Moses (vv. 6, 11) and the writings of David, Solomon, and the prophets (vv. 4, 15). In a similar though far greater way, the Lord Jesus leads His people to remember His body and blood by which He redeemed them and to worship God according to the commands of the new covenant. Worshiping God and celebrating the Lord's Supper according to the principles of Scripture is obedience to our King. Why does Christ, as the king of His church, care so much about its worship?

2. Josiah came to a very untimely end. The godly among Judah were crushed to see this good king slain at an early age

(vv. 24–25). After his death, the kingdom rapidly declined (ch. 36). How could this happen? On the divine level, God had ordained his death. However, on a human level, he died because he thrust himself into a battle that did not belong to him. Scripture warns that meddling in strife that does not belong to us can have tragic results (Prov. 26:17). How did Josiah make this mistake? How can we avoid it?

Chapter 36

1. The words, "they burnt the house of God" (v. 19) must have been like a flaming brand pressed into the hearts of God's people. It must have felt like God's promise to David was revoked forever (1 Chron. 17:12). However, God was keeping His Word, for He had told Solomon that if the king and the people turned away from the Lord to other gods, He would make His people into exiles and His house into a horror (2 Chron. 7:19–22). God's judgments prove His faithfulness and call us to hope in His promises of restoration, which He will fulfill in His timing by His sovereignty over all nations (36:21–23). Do you wholeheartedly believe in both God's promises of grace and His threats of wrath? How can you order your life accordingly?

2. The end of the monarchy must have raised questions in the minds of believers. How would God fulfill His covenant with David? Chronicles encourages us to hope in a righteous son of David. How could God keep His promises if the people were so guilty and hardened in sin? The Lord must provide satisfaction for sin and a transformed heart. How would the kingdom come if Israel lived under foreign domination? It must come first as a spiritual kingdom, not like the kingdoms

of this world but composed of true worshipers. All these questions and answers point to Jesus Christ and His life, death, resurrection, ascension, and pouring out of the Spirit. Worship our Lord for His faithfulness to His promises!

3. The last verse of Chronicles must have greatly encouraged Israel after it returned from exile: "Who is there among you of all his people? The LORD his God be with him, and let him go up" (v. 23). God's people are not to brood passively over the sorrows of the past, but to press on in the building of God's temple for His glory. This is a call that rings down through the ages. God's judgments fall upon the nations, but the church continues its mission to build a living temple where God dwells by the Spirit, and Christ is with us to the end of the age. How can this encourage you as you seek to build the kingdom today? (See Phil. 3:13–14.)

Ezra

Chapter 1

1. God never forgets His Word to fulfill it. This is true of what He threatens as well as promises. Though we forget God's Word, He does not; He is faithful to it. Bring His own Word back to Him in prayer and plead that He would fulfill it in your life.

2. God is sovereign. He works on the level of nations and the heads of nations (v. 1). However, He also stirs up individual people to walk in His ways and seek His promised inheritance (v. 5). How does this encourage you to pray for nations? For individuals?

3. Cyrus had a unique role in God's plan and purpose (Isa. 44:28; 45:1). God used him to set His people free. Christ, however, would set His people free in ways that Cyrus never could. He would enter into death and pay the penalty they deserved. Praise God for delivering us from the kingdom of darkness and translating us into the kingdom of light (Col. 1:13).

Chapter 2

1. Though Zerubbabel was not a king, he descended from the kingly line and was in the genealogy of the Lord Jesus (Matt. 1:12–13, "Zorobabel"). The exile would not prevent the coming of the Christ. The Lord saw to it that priests, prophets (5:1), and the line of David resettled the land. Christ would combine the three offices in Himself as the

Prophet, Priest, and King of His people. In that office, He draws people from darkness to light and makes them citizens in His kingdom (Eph. 2:19). Despite the sins of man, encourage one another that Christ's kingdom will be established and prevail.

2. The Urim and Thummim (v. 63) refer to stones kept in the breastplate of judgment worn on Aaron's heart (Ex. 28:30). We know very little about how the Urim and Thummim functioned, but as they appear in Israel's history, we learn that they were used in discerning the will of God (Num. 27:21; Deut. 33:8; 1 Sam. 23:6–12; 28:6). Regardless of how they functioned, we know that they communicated to the Israelite community what God's will was for them. What has God given to His people today to lead us in the ways of truth (John 16:13)?

3. What a disappointment it must have been to those who could not show their proper credentials to work in the temple service (v. 59)! Do you have assurance to rejoice that your name is written in heaven (Luke 10:20)?

4. Note how the people gave to the work of the Lord. We are told that they "gave after their ability unto the treasure of the work" (v. 69). How beautiful it is to see many giving cheerfully to the work of the Lord (2 Cor. 9:7)! How are you offering yourself and your money to His work?

Chapter 3

1. The people quickly worked to reinstitute the sacrifices. It is a good sign when we sense that we need to have our sins blotted out and we need to know God's favor through

His appointed sacrifice, Christ Jesus, to whom all the sacrifices pointed (Heb. 7:27). How eager is your heart to run to Christ's sacrifice for forgiveness? How long do you linger in guilt before confessing your sin? Why?

2. The joy of those who witnessed the foundation rising was mixed with weeping. Is it not true that often the Christian's joy is mixed with weeping? As long as believers dwell in flesh, we carry this tension of rejoicing and weeping with us (2 Cor. 6:10), until the day when every tear shall be wiped from our eyes (Rev. 21:4). Then joy will be unmixed but, incidentally, there will be no temple (Rev. 21:22). Why is that? What do we know about that day?

Chapter 4

1. We might be tempted to shrink back from what seems to be a harsh response of Zerubbabel and Joshua and the other leaders (v. 3). But this is not just an Old Testament emphasis as can be seen from Heb. 13:10: "We have an altar, whereof they have no right to eat which serve the tabernacle." Spiritual fellowship and partnership can only be had with those who share the same Spirit, worship the same God, and glory only in Christ (Phil. 3:3). Pray for discernment, so as not to compromise.

2. Christ told His disciples that they should expect persecution (John 16:33). Some victories are not achieved within one generation, as the fight continues beyond it. We need to arm ourselves for a drawn-out battle against those who take aim at the cause of Christ (Eph. 6:10–13). What battles face the church today? How can the church prepare itself to fight these with endurance over the long term?

Chapter 5

1. God uses His Word to give life to His people. After twenty years, the preaching of Haggai and Zechariah was the catalyst for encouraging the Jews to finish building the temple. God used His Word to move His people to action. Therefore, let us strongly support the preaching of God's Word. How can we be doers of the Word, and not hearers only (James 1:22–27)?

2. This section is proof of the following truth: "The king's heart is in the hand of the LORD, as the rivers of water: he turneth it whithersoever he will" (Prov. 21:1). Behind the actions of princes and rulers, the hand of divine providence brings about His purposes for His people. How can this encourage Christians when government leaders seem to frustrate God's purposes?

3. Why did Judah face so much opposition? Could God not have made things much easier for them? Through trials, God strengthens His people. He teaches them patience. God is not just working around His people, but within them (Phil. 2:13).

Chapter 6

1. The books of Moses continued to be the guide for these people (v. 18). Whenever there is a heaven-sent awakening or revival, people will go back to the Word of God (Neh. 8:1). There may be great emotional excitement, large crowds of people, or impressive acts of religious devotion, but if they are not driven by faith and love toward the Holy Scriptures, they are not of the Spirit of the Lord. Do you need to renew your commitment to God's Word?

2. Our chapter commemorates and celebrates a milestone. When God's people go through difficult or disciplinary times they must always remember that the end is better than the beginning (Eccl. 7:8) and that all things work together for their good (Rom. 8:28). Have you experienced seasons of celebration after times of great trials?

3. The Lord alone can work true joy in His people's hearts (v. 22). As the psalmist sings, "His anger endureth but a moment; in his favour is life: weeping may endure for a night, but joy cometh in the morning" (Ps. 30:5). If you are in a season of weeping, how can you find the strength to endure with hope?

Chapter 7

1. Every Christian can learn from Ezra. He prepared his heart to study God's Word, practice its teaching, and pass its teaching on to others (v. 10). This is the duty of everyone charged to teach the Word, whether heads of household in the family or pastors and teachers in the church. Even if we do not have official responsibilities to teach, we can still share the Word of God with others. Pray for parents, teachers, leaders in your church, and yourself that all would have the heart of Ezra.

2. Artaxerxes helped Ezra and thus also the cause of God. We can be thankful for how God used him. Nevertheless, Artaxerxes never had a heartfelt attachment to the Lord. Is it enough to simply advance the cause of God? Or, like Ezra, have you learned to love God and His commandments more than gold (Ps. 119:127; Matt. 6:24; 22:37)?

3. Ezra recognized God's hand of mercy in his circumstances (v. 28). If we are the Lord's, our lives are filled with tokens of God's mercy. Like Ezra, do you trace them and thank the Lord for them? How has God's hand of mercy appeared in your life recently?

Chapter 8

1. God's will was Ezra's chief concern (v. 21). Even to a man like Ezra who relied on God, discerning God's will was not always easy. He went to great lengths to discern God's will, fasting and seeking the Lord. We, too, must invest time and energy into seeking God and His will when we face significant decisions. The very process honors Him. What major decisions do you face as an individual, family, church, or society? How are you seeking the Lord?

2. Ezra knew the power of seeking God. He also knew that those who forsake God are under His wrath (v. 22). Paul writes something similar: "Behold therefore the goodness and severity of God: on them which fell, severity; but toward thee, goodness, if thou continue in his goodness: otherwise thou also shalt be cut off" (Rom. 11:22).

Chapter 9

1. The inhabitants of Judah were at risk of being swallowed up by the nations around them and their idolatries. Still today, we are called to a life of separation from worldliness. Paul challenged the Corinthians, "For what fellowship hath righteousness with unrighteousness? and what communion hath light with darkness?" (2 Cor. 6:14). Why might a

romantic relationship with an unbeliever attract a Christian? How can he or she resist this temptation?

2. Ezra readily confessed sin as sin. He knew that God had punished the nation far less than it had deserved (v. 13). If we know anything of our wicked hearts, we will find it difficult to complain that our circumstances are unfair. When we are tempted to question God's goodness, let us give consideration to our sinfulness and to what we deserve.

3. We can only fight sin by the grace of God. Ezra shows the right way by running to the Lord in prayer. How does God say He will help us in the midst of temptation (1 Cor. 10:13)?

Chapter 10

1. If leaders in church, state, and family could, like Ezra, lead in repentance, who can tell what would happen? Of what major sins does your nation need to repent? Are there ways that your church or denomination needs to repent? Begin praying for God to give hearty repentance through Jesus Christ, beginning with the leadership—and with you.

2. Though true repentance begins with the mind, its essence is a change of heart that produces action, as we see with the people in this chapter. Paul gives us a picture of such repentance in 2 Corinthians 7:10–11. Of what sins have you repented recently? How does your repentance match up with these biblical models? Where do you need to implement a more thorough repentance?

Nehemiah

Chapter 1

1. This affluent servant of the king was touched with the suffering and anguish of his fellow Jews. Far greater is Christ's love for His people. Though He dwelt in the greatest places of honor and glory (John 17:5), He came down to die for them (Matt. 1:20–21; 20:28), and, being raised for their justification (Rom. 4:25), He now intercedes in heaven for them (Rom. 8:34). Just as it was a great comfort to the Jews that they had a Nehemiah, so it is an infinite comfort to Christians that we have a sympathetic Savior at God's right hand. Praise God for His love and intercession on our behalf!

2. As is clear from his prayer, Nehemiah knew and believed the truth of Scripture. How does knowing and believing God's Word help in prayer? Using Nehemiah as an example, how can we use God's attributes (v. 5) in prayer? How can we use His laws (v. 7)? His promises (vv. 8–9)? His great works of salvation (v. 10)?

Chapter 2

1. Nehemiah was a man of prayer. Again and again we read of him praying before he does something (vv. 4, 20; 1:11; etc.). Some prayers were long times of devotion; others very short but heartfelt cries to heaven. A man who realizes his dependence on God will be frequently directing prayer heavenward. How would you describe your prayer life?

2. Nehemiah did not rush into a plan without surveying the rubble firsthand. Once he was intimately acquainted with what was needed, he called others to rise up and build with him. He is a model of wisdom, especially wise leadership. Why is it important to carefully investigate and understand a situation before proposing action? (See Prov. 18:17; 29:20; Luke 14:28–30.)

3. The cause of God will be opposed by the world, yet the gates of hell cannot prevail against it (Matt. 16:18). God's servants should expect opposition and victory, suffering and success if they seek God's kingdom and righteousness. Reading through Hebrews 11–12, what should be our sources of encouragement, endurance, and optimism?

Chapter 3

1. It is sad to see some who have no heart for the work of the Lord (v. 5). What a blessing they missed through failing to put their shoulders under the work! God has made sure their stubborn and selfish spirits were recorded for succeeding generations. Let this be a warning to us. How do you want to be remembered by generations to come?

2. It is stirring to see people both small and great doing their part to help protect the city of God. Though each built only a portion, God noticed the labors of everyone and honored them in Scripture. The church is a body and none can say he or she does not need another member (1 Cor. 12:21). Every Christian has a part to play in building the church. Let us not be lazy, nor envy the gifts and position of another, but let each of us work hard to serve according to his gifts and calling. God will reward us. How are you helping to build the city of God?

Chapter 4

1. The adversaries of the Jews looked at their work and mocked it as feeble (v. 3). Often when the world looks at the church, it sees the imperfection, the faults, the sins, and its "rubble," but fails to see and understand that it is a work in progress (Phil. 1:6). One day, however, the church will be a pure and spotless bride to our heavenly Bridegroom (Eph. 5:25–27; Jude 24–25). How can this hope help you be diligent with the work at hand?

2. Nehemiah prayed and worked. Prayer should not be a substitute for exercising our responsibility. It is true that builders build in vain without the Lord's blessing (Ps. 127:1); however, having His blessing does not mean we do not have to build. God's servants must mix intense labor with devotion to prayer as they seek the kingdom of God. How might someone use prayer as an excuse not to work? How might he use work as an excuse not to pray? How do we exercise both prayer and work together?

Chapter 5

1. As the Jewish community faced problems from without as well as within, so believers face a war with multiple fronts. Never be surprised when the church must face sin in its midst, but be prepared to deal with it with love and justice (Gal. 6:1–2). Our own hearts are our worst enemy in the spiritual battle, so beware first of the log in your own eye before criticizing another (Matt. 7:3). How can we stand for justice among Christians without becoming cynical or bitter?

2. Nehemiah led both by what he said and what he did. Leaders in home, church, and society have much to learn

from Nehemiah. Even so, Nehemiah was imperfect, like we all are. Only Christ led in a stainless way. Take time to pray for those in leadership in your life.

Chapter 6

1. Though the Lord had called Nehemiah, He did not keep him from challenges or make everything easy for him. Often difficulties come to the situations and people that God is using for great good. We should not be discouraged when difficulty arises, but trust in God's providence and press on with great courage. Courage may be found by faith and prayer (v. 9). Pray that God would help you to continue steadfast through temptation and intimidation, to cry to God, rely on Him, and view your situation and challenges with much spiritual discernment (v. 12).

2. "This work was wrought of our God" (v. 16). God's cause is not in doubt. He is never without resources. He says, "My counsel shall stand, and I will do all my pleasure" (Isa. 46:10). He will keep His covenant (Neh. 1:5). This is the foundation of our courage and the bedrock of our prayers. How can you build on this foundation and shore up your walls of defense?

Chapter 7

1. The fear of God is a necessary element of any good leader (v. 2). For that matter, it is a basic mark of true believers (Jer. 32:40). They fear God more than they fear people. To fear God means to reverence His majesty, love His glory, obey His will as revealed in the Bible, be afraid to sin, and seek His grace and mercy. It directs both worship and behavior.

What are signs in a person's life that he does or does not fear the Lord? Why is the fear of God so important in leadership?

2. "And my God put into mine heart" (v. 5). Nehemiah traced his good ideas and godly actions back to God (Phil. 2:13). Apart from God's grace, our good intentions, attitudes, and inventions will mean nothing. We need to be led by the Spirit of God (Rom. 8:14). How quick are you to give glory to God for any good in you, both with your lips and your heart? Do you secretly boast in yourself?

Chapter 8

1. Just like the walls of Jerusalem provided physical protection (chs. 1–6), so the precepts of God provide spiritual safety (Ps. 119:165). Rebuilding the walls without returning to the Word of God would be foolish. Why would this be foolish and how would it provoke the Lord to jealousy?

2. Ezra did not merely read the law in the presence of the people, but the Levites were assigned to teach and instruct the people in the will of God. Give thanks for godly ministers from the past as well as the present whom God has sent to explain and apply the truth of God in your life.

3. Has God's truth ever broken your heart so that you wept like these people here in verse 9? When God's Word takes hold of us, we can weep over our sins, which God's Word unmasks. We can weep because we long for (more) communion with God.

4. There is a time for mourning, but the other side of godly emotions should not be forgotten. Here, the Levites direct the people so that their sadness is turned to gladness

(v. 10). Indeed, the joy of the Lord is a great defense, or shield, against undue sadness. How can the Christian learn to rejoice in the Lord always?

Chapter 9

1. For centuries, it was quite customary for governments and churches to call for days of fasting, humiliation, and prayer, especially during times of calamity, trouble, war, and so on. We ought to read God's providence with an eye to God's righteousness. Times of humbling ourselves, whether in a personal or public way, are important to any close walk with God. How could you incorporate these habits into your walk with the Lord?

2. The memories of most of us are poor. For this reason, it is necessary that we continually hold before our mind's eye the great acts of redemption and salvation that God has wrought. Our children, grandchildren, and all around us need to hear of the great ways that God has worked in and for us (Pss. 78:4; 96:3). Share with someone close to you how God has worked and is working in your life.

3. Reviewing the history of Israel from Abraham to the exile, one can sum up its lesson in these words: God is righteous and keeps His promises, but man is wicked and breaks God's laws. How then should we live? We must humble ourselves very low, recognizing that we and our families would have rebelled against God's laws as badly or worse than the Israelites, and resting our hope in the grace of God alone. Cry out for the grace of Jesus Christ even as we have seen in this chapter.

Chapter 10

1. These people are not reenacting what God had done through Moses at Sinai in making a covenant with Israel. That had happened and was still binding. These people are expressing the vow to keep these things God had ordered with an emphasis on specific things that thus far had slipped. It is very important for all believers, especially leaders, to discern in what areas our spiritual boundaries are under attack and vulnerable. Pray for wisdom to know what sins God is convicting you of by His Holy Spirit.

2. This agreement does not only emphasize negatives, but also positives, such as an offering to God and support for the Levites. Obedience to God is not only forsaking what is sinful, but doing that which is good. Read James 4:17. What "good" have you been neglecting?

3. Note the strong resolution at the close of this chapter, "We will not forsake the house of our God" (v. 39). Christ preeminently had a zeal for the house of the Lord (John 2:17). Can you put your amen to this? Are you zealous for the church of Christ and the worship of God? How are you showing your support and zeal?

Chapter 11

1. Here one-tenth of the people of God lived in Jerusalem. This was a special "tithe," consecrated to the Lord to sustain His holy city. Through Zechariah, God envisioned a time when every place, not just one city, would be called holy (Zech. 14:20–21). This is true in Christ. There is no longer one city where God has His presence in a particular way (John 4:21–24). The "city of God" touches believers

throughout this world, and is found in its glory in heaven (Heb. 12:22–24). Praise God for the hope we have of His glory to be revealed one day!

2. What a note of joy there is in this verse: "And the residue of Israel, of the priests, and the Levites, were in all the cities of Judah, every one in his inheritance" (v. 20). After a long time of exile, these prodigals were back, each in its own inheritance. Have you returned to the Lord and the heritage of Abraham, Isaac, and Jacob? This is a lifelong process, but it begins with turning to God and forsaking the world.

Chapter 12

1. The priests descended from Levi foreshadowed the greater Priest. Christ did not come from the line of Levi, but the line of Judah. Thus He could be a king. However, He is also a priest, but after a different order, the order of Melchizedek (Ps. 110:4; Heb. 7:14–16). The work of this greater Priest would be to forever rebuild and reestablish the spiritual house of God. Read Hebrews 7:23–25 and then spend time worshiping our great Priest!

2. Chapter 12 includes one of the climactic moments in the books of Ezra and Nehemiah. After such a long time the walls and city of Jerusalem were dedicated (v. 27). When God does a work of revival like this, the refrain is: "God had made them rejoice with great joy" (v. 43). Revival brings life to bear on what was otherwise dull and dead. Joy is the only fitting response, so do not be ashamed to rejoice and celebrate over God's works. What inhibits joy in worship?

3. The Bible everywhere is concerned about purity of worship. This same concern appears here: they worshiped "according to the commandment of David" (vv. 24, 45). Revival is not a time of innovation in doctrine or worship, but a time of returning to the old paths of God's Word. It is a pressing need today to see the worship of God regulated by the commandments of God. In what ways do you think your worship could follow more closely the purity found in God's Word?

Chapter 13

1. There will always be forces for evil. The history of Balaam and Balak reminds us that people will try to work against the people of God and the purposes of God. However, God is such that He will turn "the curse into a blessing" (v. 2). How can we be on our guard that we do not fall on the side of the curse, but experience God's work unto blessing through Christ?

2. How is it possible that an arch-enemy of Israel got a great chamber in the house of our God? In many churches and seminaries in our day, enemies of the gospel have a lot of sway. We should pray and labor that this not happen on our watch.

3. Many have felt that Nehemiah's actions were too harsh (v. 25). Let us remember, however, the time when Christ made a whip to drive out the money changers from the temple (John 2:15–16). Certainly no one can say that Nehemiah was without sin, but Christ was. And Nehemiah was a man who desired fervently and acted decisively for the honor of his God. We may not have the authority to use physical force, but how are we using the authority and influence we do have for the glory of God?

Esther

Chapter 1

1. The world's ideas regarding marriage are warped. Still today, the marriages of famous people rarely speak well of the institution of marriage, but instead they reflect the sinful hearts of men and women by nature. Christ's glorious marriage to the church is the great model for marriage (Eph. 5:22–33). How can we as Christian husbands and wives follow Christ's model and display marriages that are nobler than kings' marriages?

2. We often wonder how God is working through our world and its leaders—corrupt, vain, and petty as they often are. Yet God's hand is in control, whether we recognize it or not. As Esther unfolds, we will see that God is working straight through the whims and follies of Ahasuerus and his officials. Pray that God will help you to trust that His hand is at work in our times as well.

3. God's law sets the rules for how men and women, parents and children, and superiors and subjects ought to relate. It is pitiful to see a king who lacks all fear of God try to gain by civil law the respect that he did not earn by his actions and personal dignity (v. 20). How can God's values help you to gain respect?

Chapter 2

1. The world prizes the outward appearance of people. Sadly, it also has no regard for the beauty of Christ (Isa. 53:2). The

Bible prizes inward, moral, and spiritual beauty, particularly the beauty of a submissive spirit toward authority (1 Peter 3:3–6). This was a key character quality of Esther, who sought wise counsel and obeyed Mordecai (vv. 15, 20). How can you exercise and develop such humility? Do you follow the world's standards of beauty or God's?

2. Christ desires the beauty of His bride, as you can read in the messianic song, "So shall the king greatly desire thy beauty: for he is thy Lord; and worship thou him" (Ps. 45:11). Are you part of Christ's bride? Paul identified the bride of Christ by her submission to the Lord as her head (Eph. 5:23–24). Is your heart submitted to Jesus as Lord? How does that show in your actions?

Chapter 3

1. We do not know exactly what Mordecai's reason was for not bowing to Haman. However, we do know that the world wants us to submit to its schemes and often demands a public sign of submission (Dan. 3). When we fail to fall in line, we face the consequences, which may include social isolation, insult, and incarceration—or worse. The great question is this: will you bow to God alone with all your mind, heart, and strength?

2. The way in which Haman schemed and bargained for the destruction of the Jews reminds us that the world hates God's people and delights in their destruction (John 15:18; Rev. 11:7–10; 20:7–9). Certainly the world showed its true colors when it tortured and murdered the Son of God on the cross. When you face persecutors and rulers like Ahasuerus and Pontius Pilate, who permit such gross injustice,

pray that as a Christian you will not respond in hatred but remember that you, too, were once full of hatred. Labor to be respectful and gentle to all men, hoping and praying that God will regenerate them by the Holy Spirit (Titus 3:1–8).

Chapter 4

1. Though God's name does not appear in the book of Esther, Mordecai's conviction that deliverance will come to the Jews (v. 14) clearly suggests he has confidence in the fact that God would not forsake His people and promise. His confidence in God's providence did not make him passive, however, but energized him to call Esther to act decisively for her people. Believing that God is in control never excuses us from using our positions and abilities for the good of His people. Instead, it gives us hope that God has put us here for that very purpose, and will therefore give success to our efforts to serve His cause. How do God's promises energize you?

2. Esther listened to the counsel of Mordecai, evidently believed the promises of God about His people, and resolved to take action. And yet she needed discernment about her course of action and called for fasting (v. 16) and presumably prayer as well. Likewise with us, knowing the will of God requires listening to wise people whom God places in our lives (especially parents and pastors), knowing and believing His Word, resolving to obey Him at any cost, and praying for His wisdom while asking other Christians to pray too. What significant decisions are you facing or will you face soon? How can you use these same means to discern God's will?

Chapter 5

1. What a difference there is between Ahasuerus's throne and the Lord's throne! Because of Christ, heaven's throne is called a throne of grace, which is always open for needy sinners to come to "obtain mercy, and find grace to help in time of need" (Heb. 4:16). As believers, praise God that we can come before the Lord's throne with boldness (Heb. 10:19–22).

2. When Esther fasted and sought God with God's people (4:16), it resulted in remarkable courage and wisdom. She risked her life to speak with the king in order to save Israel. Yet she did not rashly rush to him demanding help, but thoughtfully and with apparent calmness invited him to a feast. This is the power of God's grace obtained through fervent prayer. While this was brought about through a crisis, it was also the result of habits of humility developed over years (2:15, 20). How can you grow in wisdom and peace like Esther so that you can respond well to crises?

3. Haman's arrogance, we might say, was 75 feet high. The perceived insult of a single man outweighed all the honor and wealth he had received. As a result, he was provoked to murder a faithful servant in the king's administration. Which weighs most heavily upon your heart: gratitude for the honors and blessings you have undeservedly received or an insult? Beware, lest your pride drive you to hatred and perhaps even the harm of others.

Chapter 6

1. God's providence not only appears in mighty miracles, but in mundane events like a king who cannot sleep and

so reads some boring government records. Billions of such events take place every day and we scarcely notice them, but the Lord directs every one of them according to His decree (Eph. 1:11). His timing is perfect, reminding the king of Mordecai's faithfulness just as Haman comes to have him hanged. How can this give Christians hope to know that this God of providence is our Father?

2. Haman was a high official in the mighty Persian Empire, yet he could not destroy a conquered and dispersed people, for they were the people of the living God. On the contrary, his empty boasting and foolish pride only led him into shame and defeat. Let us not fear those who persecute the church, but rather pity them and pray for them.

Chapter 7

1. Esther here is a picture of Christ. Just as Esther publicly identified herself with the Jewish nation so that the king would not destroy them, so Christ publicly identified with His people of all nations so that His Father would not destroy them. Esther risked her life by identifying with the Jews; Christ gave His life as the substitute and surety of His people, bearing the punishment for their sins. Esther pled for her nation, and Christ intercedes for each of His children from heaven. How does this picture help you appreciate the work of Christ on your behalf?

2. Haman's devices were all brought to light and punished. Many today walk in pride and seem to have everything going for them. God's Word reminds us that the day is coming when everything that has been done in secret will be brought

into full light (1 Cor. 4:5). How does Haman's story motivate you to be humble and live in the fear of the Lord?

3. Haman's death illustrates the work of Christ, yet with great irony. Haman was destroyed by the gallows he constructed for Mordecai. Like Haman, Satan plotted Christ's destruction through the cross, only to have his power shattered by Christ's death (John 12:31–33; 13:2; 14:30; 16:11). However, though Haman was hung upon the gallows (Hebrew, "tree"), it was not Satan but Jesus Christ who was hung upon the cross ("tree," Acts 5:30; 10:39; 13:29) to pacify God's righteous wrath by bearing the curse of God against lawbreakers (Gal. 3:13). Oh, the wonder of His love! Worship Christ in light of this strange victory: death for Him and salvation for sinners!

Chapter 8

1. Just as Ahasuerus gave Mordecai his signet ring and glorified him as a great prince in the Persian Empire in order to save the Jews from destruction, so God the Father has given Jesus Christ all authority in heaven and earth as our exalted Priest and King in order to save His people from eternal destruction (Matt. 28:18; John 17:2; Heb. 8:1). He is glorified at the Father's right hand with unspeakable beauty, joy, and riches. If we belong to Christ, what things are ours (1 Cor. 3:21–23) and how is God working on our behalf (Rom. 8:28, 32)?

2. Note the great joy of the Jews as the king grants Esther's petition to respond in kind to their enemies (vv. 15–17). The Jews had essentially been brought back from a sentence of death. If the Jews' redemption from physical death caused

such joy and elation, how much more should this be so of us, if we have been redeemed from a far greater death than physical death? Why then do Christians sometimes have so little joy? Look in Philippians 4:4 for the key. Just as the Jews rejoiced in the glory of Mordecai, so believers must focus their minds and engage their hearts to rejoice in the glory of Jesus Christ, our heavenly King.

Chapter 9

1. In an amazing reversal, the destruction of the Jews was turned into their victory over their enemies. The seed of Israel went from the bottom to the top. Our God is a God of great reversals (1 Sam. 2:4–8; Luke 1:52–53), the greatest of which is the resurrection of Christ, who died the accursed death on the cross, and His exaltation to God's right hand. Christian, even if you are the lowest of the low in this world, take heart. Humble yourself right now before the Lord, and He will lift you up, even into the glory of Jesus Christ.

2. God's works deserve to be commemorated. Though all the shadows of the Old Testament, including the feasts, are fulfilled in Christ (Col. 2:16–17), Christians are called to lives of sacrifice to God for the redemption He has performed. We are also called weekly to commemorate the final victory of Christ over death in His resurrection (1 Cor. 16:1–2; Heb. 10:25). Christians should ever be characterized by giving thanks to God for His mercies to oneself, one's family, one's people, and the church throughout the world.

Chapter 10

This book concludes with a lovely image of Mordecai reigning as the king's right-hand man for the peace of the covenant seed. Christ is our peace through His blood, and the gospel is His proclamation of peace to those near and far, Jew and Gentile (Eph. 2:14–17). He reigns forever over heaven and earth and is enjoying the fulfillment of God's promise that He will see His spiritual seed and be satisfied with the fruit of His sorrows (Isa. 53:10). He is a far better king than any Persian emperor, for rather than using up His subjects' money and labor, He gives them all good gifts (Eph. 4:7–8). Are you part of Christ's spiritual family? Has He spoken peace to your soul through the gospel of His death for sinners? Does He reign over you as your Lord? Is He your hope for glory? If so, rejoice. If not, pray for grace to surrender to Christ today.

Job

Chapter 1

1. Job loved his family and understood his responsibility to pray for his children (v. 5). His offering finds its application today in parents pleading the substitutionary atonement of Christ for the salvation and sanctification of their children. Perhaps the most impressive aspect of Job's devotion is that it was demonstrated before his trial began. How often times of prosperity become times of spiritual carelessness. How can you imitate Job's example of family devotion?

2. The first chapter in Job lays the foundation for the rest of the book by taking the reader behind the scenes, enabling him to see that Job had the blessing of God's commendation. The test to the Christian's faith comes when circumstances around him are shouting at him that God must have condemned him. When friends and even loved ones lend their voices to such a chorus, it becomes a daunting challenge for faith to continue to affirm the favor of God. The key is for the Christian to see that the burnt offering points to Christ and that so long as God is pleased with Christ, God will be pleased with the Christian that is joined to Christ, circumstances notwithstanding.

Chapter 2

1. Job's submission to God's will was remarkable. He lost his wealth, his children, his wife's favor, and his own health, and yet he honored God humbly. He was no superman, and we

will see his struggle with doubt and questions. However, he fundamentally honored God (42:7). Why does bitterness so quickly rise up in our hearts when suffering comes? How can we become more like Job?

2. Because of the ineffective way Job's friends ministered to him it is easy to overlook the fact that they were acting as true friends by setting out to comfort him. We, too, must bear each other's burdens and so fulfill the law of Christ (Gal. 6:2). Real love means laying down our lives for others and grieving with them (Rom. 12:15; 1 John 3:16). Job's friends were at their best through their ministry of silent empathy (Prov. 10:19). Often the best comfort that we can give to those who suffer is just to be present with them.

Chapter 3

1. The contrast between Job in chapter 3 against chapters 1 and 2 is great. The only difference in the settings is time ("after this," v. 1). Suffering and sorrow become overwhelming when they persist without an end in sight. Even a righteous man who fears God and turns from evil (2:3) still possesses sin. He is capable of misunderstanding and of questioning what God is doing. The tension between faith and experience is real. One of the purposes that trials serve is to make the believer face the reality of his inherent weakness and the truth that he must walk by faith, regardless of the perceptions of his sight. Without painful trials the believer is vulnerable to pride. Trials help the believer bridge the gap between belief and experience by a deeper trust in God.

2. We find Job in this chapter sinking to the depths of despair, and the question that naturally arises is, "Why?" The

answer is not as mysterious as a believer might think when he remembers Christ. Christians tend to think of conformity to Christ in terms of the radiant splendor that was displayed by Christ on the Mount of Transfiguration (Matt. 17:1–2). However, as Paul makes plain to the Philippians, conformity to Christ also means conformity to his death (Phil. 3:10). The suffering Christian is not only learning through his trials to die more and more to sin and live more and more to righteousness, but he is learning to identify more closely with the One who loved him and gave Himself for him.

Chapter 4

1. We should not be impatient with believers when great suffering throws them into doubts and confusion. Just because someone like Job possesses much wisdom (v. 3) does not mean that he is above questioning God when tragedy strikes. This is not necessarily a sign of hypocrisy, but of the weakness of our humanity. How might Eliphaz have responded better to Job's lamentation?

2. The most important question in all the world for a man to consider is, how can a man be right with God (v. 17)? This is a question with eternal ramifications because the answer impacts the destiny of a man's soul in heaven or hell forever. The book of Job, as well as the entire Bible, is devoted to answering the question of a man's standing before God. Time spent in God's Word, therefore, becomes an investment in eternity.

Chapter 5

"Happy is the man whom God correcteth" (v. 17). No experience of correction or discipline is pleasant, but it brings great benefits. It purifies believers from sin and strengthens them in faith. Rather than a sign of God's anger against His children, chastening is evidence of His love. We should be sensitive to God's Word that exposes our sin and dependent upon the Holy Spirit to lead us by that Word to behavior that is pleasing to our heavenly Father. We should not rebel under God's chastening hand but quickly submit to it. The believer desires correction because he has been given a new heart that loves the law of God (Ps. 119:97). He who hates correction is a fool. How can we learn to love correction, and even discipline, from God?

Chapter 6

1. We should show faithful love to suffering friends (v. 14). As well intentioned as Job's friends were, they actually made his situation worse (v. 27). Parents can fail in the same way if they fail to take into account the weight with which matters may be pressing their children. It is easy to dismiss the burdens of our children as being insignificant or due entirely to their sin. Beware of the danger of digging pits for your children. How can you respond more compassionately to the burdens of other people, whether children or adults?

2. There comes a time in every Christian's life when he will be called upon to encourage a friend whose trial may run deeper and be more prolonged than anything he himself has ever experienced. In such circumstances that Christian does well not to pretend he understands something he does not

but instead to point his friend to someone who does. Christ was "in all points tempted like as we are, yet without sin" (Heb. 4:15). In all of Job's sufferings he would never suffer more than his Savior would eventually suffer. The Christian's ability to minister encouragement, therefore, does not depend on similar experiences so much as it does on his ability to point a tried and afflicted friend to Christ.

Chapter 7

1. Life is short (vv. 6, 16). The Bible is filled with symbols that emphasize that truth: "a tale that is told" (Ps. 90:9) and "a vapour, that appeareth for a little time, and then vanisheth away" (James 4:14). Job's afflictions taught him the brevity of life not just in theory but experientially. During times of prosperity, the brevity of life becomes easy to forget. Like the foolish rich man (Luke 12:18), it is easy to grow comfortable, thinking that life will go on indefinitely. Afflictions preach to us that we should use our time wisely in light of death and eternity (Ps. 90:12).

2. Job demonstrates the believer's freedom to go to God even with his complaints (Pss. 73; 77; 88). The Christian should ever keep in mind that God invites him to come boldly before the throne of grace (Heb. 4:16). Job laid his heart bare before the Lord and expressed his concerns forthrightly. Too often even though God knows the thoughts of our heart, we are reluctant to speak to Him candidly and honestly. This does not mean that the Christian approaches God irreverently, but it does mean that he is free to bring to God the burdens of his heart even when those burdens pertain to how

we perceive God's dealings with us. What burdens do you need to honestly take to Him today?

Chapter 8

1. Though Bildad's argument was misapplied, he did nevertheless recognize that God will do justice (v. 3); His relationship with the Christian stands upon His righteousness. Moses said, "He is the Rock, his work is perfect: for all his ways are judgment: a God of truth and without iniquity, just and right is he" (Deut. 32:4). Justice is not compromised in salvation but rather is satisfied in Christ's atoning death. To enjoy God's peace we must understand not only God's mercy and grace in salvation but God's righteousness also (Rom. 3:21–26). Only when we realize that God does not set aside justice but fulfills it in Christ can we trust Him. Why is it dangerous when we focus so much on God's love that we neglect His justice and righteousness?

2. Bildad's appeal to the teachings of the "fathers" (v. 8) reminds us to be careful when citing tradition to support our point of view. To be sure, much biblical truth is contained in the traditions of the church, but the teachings of the fathers lack divine authority in themselves and often err and contradict each other. They may also fail to reflect biblical balance by so emphasizing one truth that they virtually contradict another.

Chapter 9

1. God is "wise in heart, and mighty in strength" (v. 4). He is beyond man's comprehension (vv. 5–11). The world in its wisdom cannot know God (1 Cor. 1:21). Despite all

our technological achievements, man cannot discover God. If we arrogantly insist that we cannot believe in what we cannot understand, then we logically exclude believing in a God who is so much greater than ourselves. The only way to know Him is to humble ourselves and quietly listen to His Word. The greatest wonders of the Bible, such as God's creation of the world in six days, are completely believable if we start from the premise, expressed as a rhetorical question, "Is anything too hard for the Lord?" The Christian must ever keep this in mind in a world of arrogant skepticism and foolish unbelief. He must especially remember that he cannot comprehend God when God's ways with us are hard. Let us remember that it was precisely when Christ's disciples could not trace God's purpose that He was accomplishing our salvation by the crucifixion of His Son. Much of life is beyond our understanding, but nothing is without purpose.

2. Job saw himself in the court of the almighty Judge (vv. 3, 15–16; cf. 10:2, 14, 17), unable to speak for himself yet in need of vindication before the Lord. No one on earth could be the mediator to lay a hand on both God and man and to plead for men (v. 33). However, his longing was perfectly fulfilled by the One who would come to earth, Jesus Christ. Do you see yourself as one who stands in the courtroom of God, the glorious Judge? How will you be counted righteous before Him? There is no other way than by the heavenly Mediator, the righteous Son of God (1 John 2:1).

Chapter 10

God's sovereignty implies that He is intimately involved in our lives. He forms us in the womb (vv. 10–11), knows us completely and perfectly (vv. 4–7), and sustains our lives (v. 12). When one is convinced of God's love and grace, these truths are a great comfort (Ps. 139). However, the sovereignty of God can become an offense when someone feels trapped in a living hell of bitterness and weariness under a sense of God's condemnation (Job 10:1–2). When we meet a godly Christian in such a sad condition, it may not help him simply to tell him that God is in control. This book reminds such a sufferer that he is not alone or unique but stands in solidarity with people like Job, and especially with the Lord Jesus Christ, who cried out on the cross, "My God, my God, why hast thou forsaken me?" (Mark 15:34). Christ alone could say to God, "Thou knowest that I am not wicked" (Job 10:7). He suffered for sinners. On the basis of His agony, whatever taste of hell the believer may endure on earth will never become the eternal hell. What a Savior!

Chapter 11

1. Zophar exemplifies something every Christian should want, as well as something he should avoid. He demonstrates a jealousy for the honor of God. This jealousy is something that is too rare in times when ungodliness permeates the world. Blasphemy and the profaning of God's name become so commonplace that the Christian too often accepts them and becomes desensitized to them. To the degree that Zophar was jealous for God's honor, he is commendable. Unfortunately, Zophar lacked proper humility. It never crossed his mind that he could be wrong, and so with unrelenting dogmatism he condemned Job as though speaking for God. His theology was sound, but his spirit and applications were wrong. May the Lord grant a proper jealousy

for His honor, accompanied by the proper humility. There is hardly a worse manifestation of pride than the assurance of always being right.

2. This chapter presents one of the most sublime statements about the transcendence of God (vv. 7–9). The Christian need never fear overestimating the greatness of God. There is a constant danger, on the other hand, of underestimating His greatness. Beware of limiting the Holy One of Israel (Ps. 78:41). Meditate frequently on how small you are compared to Him, both in mind and in strength. What are some ways you have recently been reminded that God is far beyond your understanding?

Chapter 12

1. Job said, "I am not inferior to you" (v. 3, cf. 13:2). One of the Devil's tactics for keeping a Christian in despair is to make him feel inferior to his critics. Job's antidote to inferiority, however, was not self-esteem but the knowledge of his God (Jer. 9:23–24). Understanding God's sovereignty both shielded him from their false arguments and made all men look very small and insignificant. When you are despised because of your suffering or weakness by those at ease, do not respond with hatred and vengeance but by looking to the greatness of your God. He will be your wisdom and your strength. If the Christian can lay hold of the most basic of all truths, that God rules over all, he will not be crushed to despair by what he perceives to be his shortcomings, sins, or failures. He does not need to be a god, for he has God.

2. "Who knoweth not in all these that the hand of the LORD hath wrought this?" (v. 9). Nothing escapes the sovereign rule

of God. Not even a sparrow can fall to the ground apart from God's rule. The Christian may not understand why God is dealing the way He does. Job did not understand. Yet all the Christian's seasons of adversity are known to God and, in a mysterious way, directed by God. The affirmation of the simple and sublime truth of God's sovereign dominion over every realm of life will instill in the Christian hope that his trial will not only pass but will have a sanctifying effect on his life, preparing him for service here and for future service in the glories to come. How has God's sovereignty comforted you in your trials?

Chapter 13

1. "Though he slay me, yet will I trust in him" (v. 15). At times Job's faith seemed to waiver, but he never gave up trusting God. Trials test the quality of the Christian's faith. There is such a thing as temporary faith (Matt. 13:20–21) or vain faith (1 Cor. 15:2), but saving faith perseveres when life seems dark and God's dealings do not seem right. God is pleased to subject Christians to trials so that they may perceive the quality of their own faith (1 Peter 1:6–7). For Job to affirm that he would continue to trust God even if God were to slay him means that Job saw beyond this present life (1 Cor. 15:19). Does your faith see beyond this world?

2. "But I will maintain mine own ways before him" (v. 15). It's amazing that such a statement could follow Job's strong affirmation of faith. The first part of the verse brings Job's faith into view. But the second part brings the corruption of Job's flesh into view. Trials work to strengthen faith by highlighting and exposing the weakness of our faith and the reality

of our sin. Apart from such fiery trials, it becomes easy to become self-righteous or self-sufficient.

Chapter 14

1. "Who can bring a clean thing out of an unclean? not one" (v. 4). Man must be born again (John 3:3), as he is helpless to wash away his defilement (Jer. 2:22). However, what is impossible for man is possible for God (Matt. 19:26). God cleansed sinners by sending His Son to shed His blood for their sins (1 John 1:7). Today it can be said of the Christian that he is completely clean in his position before God (John 13:10). The Christian also needs practical cleansing each day by confessing his sins and calling upon Christ (1 John 1:9).

2. "All the days of my appointed time will I wait, till my change come" (v. 14). Job demonstrates in this saying the kind of groaning that characterizes every true child of God (Rom. 8:23). As long as the Christian lives in a world that is marked by sin, he will experience dissatisfaction. But like Job he can anticipate a coming change: we "look for new heavens and a new earth, wherein dwelleth righteousness" (2 Peter 3:13). What a change will be marked by the second coming of Christ! That change will also come to the Christian himself: "when he shall appear, we shall be like him; for we shall see him as he is" (1 John 3:2). How can this hope give a Christian patience in suffering?

Chapter 15

1. Eliphaz was under the mistaken impression that Job was treating God lightly so that He would not be feared (v. 4). If this were true, as a result sin would not be hated, for "the

fear of the LORD is to hate evil" (Prov. 8:13). Though falsely applied to Job, this was a very serious charge. We should be careful, whether in suffering or in prosperity, never to say or do anything that would diminish the awe and respect people have toward God or to encourage a light view of sin.

2. Sin is not only engaging in bad behavior or making poor choices but is an inward love for what is bad that deeply motivates mankind to pursue evil (v. 16). The heart itself is corrupt, and this corrupts everything in human life (Gen. 6:5; Prov. 4:23; Mark 7:21–23; Rom. 3:9–18). Our problem is who we are and what we love (1 John 2:15–16). How should this truth affect how we view ourselves? How should it affect our sense of need for Christ?

Chapter 16

1. "Miserable comforters are ye all" (v. 2). Counsel that is void of Christ is also void of comfort. There is a place for the Christian to come under a sense of sin, but if all a counselor manages to do is to keep his focus on sin, real or imagined, then his counsel will accomplish no more than that of Job's friends. Job recognized that true encouragement will strengthen the weak and relieve the grieving (v. 5). Whether it is a pastor speaking to a church member, a parent dealing with a child, or a person coming alongside a suffering friend, let us seek by God's grace not to degenerate into "miserable comforters" who only dwell on sin and fail to make much of Christ.

2. Job desired a sympathetic high priest (v. 21). The function of the priest was to plead for the people he represented. And in order to plead effectively, that priest had to have some idea of the struggles that were being experienced by the people

he represented. Christ is such a High Priest for his people (Heb. 2:17–18; 4:14–16). As He is a man, Christ can sympathize with men. As One without sin He can offer a perfect plea for the men He represents. When your friends fail you, Jesus Christ is a friend who can both comfort you and obtain grace and mercy for you from God.

Chapter 17

The striking of hands was the customary form for entering into a contract (v. 3). Just as Job had expressed his hope in a mediator, he now expressed his desire for an advocate or guarantor (surety). We are at once reminded that Christ serves both functions as the Priest of His people. He is their advocate (Heb. 7:25; 1 John 2:1) and their surety by the oath of the Lord (Heb. 7:21–22). Outward circumstances may seem to convey a different message, but when the Christian sees Christ as his advocate and surety, he can affirm like Paul that nothing can separate him from the love of God (Rom. 8:38–39). Yet he may also feel like a sheep destined for slaughter and have little expectation of deliverance in this life (Rom. 8:36). How can a believer simultaneously have such a strong hope and yet experience such darkness?

Chapter 18

1. Bildad's description of death as the "king of terrors" (v. 14) is a reminder of the power of the gospel that can "deliver them who through fear of death were all their lifetime subject to bondage" (Heb. 2:15). The fear of death can be alleviated for the Christian because Christ has removed its sting (1 Cor. 15:55) by His victorious resurrection, and

God delivers all His people from the power of death and the grave (Ps. 49:15). Life after death is certain, and even entering into the valley of death's shadow God's people have no reason to fear because the Lord, our Shepherd, has promised His presence (Ps. 23:4).

2. The wicked do not know God (v. 21)—the most profound ignorance possible. God's purpose in creating man was that he might know God. It was man's highest privilege before the fall to enjoy the presence of God, to walk with Him and talk with Him (Gen. 2:15–25; 3:8). When Adam plunged the human race into sin, this privilege was lost. But through the gospel, knowledge lost is knowledge restored so that the Christian can know God anew (Col. 3:10). The Christian should ever keep in mind the difference between knowing God and knowing about God, striving to know Him better whom to know is life eternal (John 17:3).

Chapter 19

1. Job exclaimed, "Oh that my words were now written! oh that they were printed in a book!" (v. 23). God answered Job's desire in the very book we now read. God had a purpose in Job's sufferings that would benefit future generations of Christians throughout the history of redemption. Who of us has not found comfort for his own sufferings by seeing a purpose of grace behind Job's sufferings? Christians should consider during their seasons of suffering that the purpose in their affliction is not just for their good and God's glory but also for the good of others (2 Cor. 1:6), including generations to come. How might that help those who are suffering?

2. "I know that my redeemer liveth" (v. 25). This statement shows the indestructible nature of true, saving faith. In the midst of circumstances that Job did not understand, he nevertheless fell back on the most basic truth of the gospel—his Redeemer lives! When the storms of life are intense and there does not seem to be any end in sight, the Christian must affirm that Christ is his Redeemer. Redemption brings to mind the glorious truth that the Christian is owned by God, purchased with His own blood (Acts 20:28; 1 Cor. 6:20; Eph. 1:14). And he must make such an affirmation on a personal level. Can you say, "I know that my Redeemer lives"? Is He yours?

Chapter 20

1. "The triumphing of the wicked is short" (v. 5). Although his assessment of Job was wrong, Zophar's theology was right on this point. The Christian is tempted at times to believe that the triumphing of the wicked is long-lasting. It seems that wicked men rule in high places and that men who make dishonest gains are the ones who get ahead, while the Lord's people are plagued and chastened. So bothered was the psalmist by this phenomenon that he concluded it was vain to serve the Lord (Ps. 73:13–14). When the Christian's heart becomes so overwhelmed by the inequalities of the world, he needs to put things in proper perspective (Ps. 73:16–17). Eternity is the best interpreter of time.

2. Zophar described the portion of the wicked man that awaits him in eternity: "he shall perish for ever" (v. 7); "God shall cast the fury of his wrath upon him" (v. 23); "the heaven shall reveal his iniquity" (v. 27). This life is the best it will

ever be for the wicked, unless they repent. Here is cause for Christians to thank God, for apart from Christ the portion of the wicked would also be their portion.

Chapter 21

1. Job's friends had come to comfort and console him in his sufferings. They proved, however, that good intentions do not always lead to good results. Far from meeting Job in the depth of his need, their counsel became a mockery (v. 3). In order to enter into the ministry of encouragement, we must be able to meet a person in his need or be honest enough to confess that our friend's distress is beyond our comprehension. Either way, we must point the sufferer to the Lord's compassion. How much more is this our duty after the Lord has taken on our own flesh and suffered with us? There is no depth to our distress that Christ does not know.

2. We must face the reality that sometimes the wicked enjoy long and prosperous lives. They may boast in their self-sufficiency and mock God without immediate consequences. At the same time believers may be suffering horribly, even at the hands of these boasters. However, Christians can endure by embracing three principles. First, we are to reject "the counsel of the wicked," to refuse to see life through their twisted perspective (v. 16). Second, we are to rest in the judgment to come on the sinner, for "he shall drink of the wrath of the Almighty" (v. 20). Third, we are to remember that our minds cannot fully comprehend God's ways, much less correct Him: "Shall any teach God knowledge?" (v. 22).

Chapter 22

1. God owes men nothing (v. 3). God is not indebted to men, but men are indebted to God. The Christian's understanding of this truth will enable him to magnify God's grace all the more, for in the covenant of grace God obligated Himself to accomplish and apply salvation to the elect. He did so not because He needed them or they deserved it, but because He is love. Be sure to magnify God's grace today!

2. Eliphaz gave good advice to those who have strayed from God: "Acquaint now thyself with him, and be at peace... lay up his words in thine heart...Return to the Almighty" (vv. 21–23). The Christian life may be described as a life of constantly returning to God. So long as sin remains in his heart, the Christian will always have a propensity to drift from God, but on account of Christ's atoning death the way is always open for him to return to the God who loves him. Have you drifted from God? How? Your peace can be restored to you by returning to Him through Christ.

Chapter 23

1. There are times in the Christian's life when God seems far from him and his prayers (v. 3). The psalmists complained of feeling forsaken by God (Pss. 13:1; 77:7–9; 89:46). This was Job's worst affliction, more terrible than losing his possessions, worse even than losing his health and his family. This was also the crowning affliction of Christ as He died under the punishment for man's sins (Matt. 27:46). God designs times of divine withdrawal to increase the Christian's sense of dependence upon God, to whet his appetite for closer

fellowship, and to focus his hope on the vindication of judgment day. Do you groan in the hope of the glory of God?

2. "He knoweth the way that I take: when he hath tried me, I shall come forth as gold" (v. 10). When Christians experience painful seasons or when God seems far away, God knows precisely where we are and the way that we take (v. 10). He has not abandoned us. Even though the trial may be long and hard, there is a gracious purpose behind it that will lead to our coming forth as gold. Thank God today that the trial of your faith will lead to praise and honor and glory at the appearing of Christ.

Chapter 24

1. Those who know God do not always see His judgment upon the wicked (v. 1). Yet justice will be executed. Regardless of how long the wicked seem to get away with their wickedness, death comes (v. 24) and after that the judgment (21:20; Heb. 9:27). The Christian should not judge before that time but look ahead to the time when Christ will return to set things right. Does the wickedness of the day cause you to groan for Christ's return? Be encouraged. His cause will prevail in the end.

2. The heinousness of sin is magnified all the more when those engaged in sin know better (v. 13). Sinning in the light increases responsibility and accountability. To those who receive much, from them much will be required. When a nation has received much truth from God, its sins are all the more offensive to God, whether that nation is Israel or a modern land that has received the gospel of Jesus Christ. What does this imply about your nation? How should you respond?

Chapter 25

"How then can man be justified with God?" (v. 4) The placement of this question in Bildad's argument sets in bold the tension that can only be resolved in the gospel. He begins with a lofty description of God's sovereignty, power, and authority and ends with a vivid, if disgusting, image of the depths of man's condition (maggots and grubs). The distance between the two is infinite, and there is nothing a worm can do to elevate itself from the dirt. So the question is raised, and the answer, though not given here, is man's only hope. The infinite God in the second person of the holy Trinity became man, indeed a worm (Ps. 22:6). The God-man did everything necessary in His living to earn life for His people and everything necessary in His dying to pay the penalty for His people's sins. Because of Christ God remains just but can also be the justifier of those who believe (Rom. 3:26). The gospel answers Bildad's question. Have you experienced that answer by finding peace with God through our Lord Jesus Christ?

Chapter 26

1. Orthodox theology is important, and it must be guarded, but orthodoxy in the head without its proper application in the heart does little good (v. 1). Job in no way disputed Bildad's theology, and he indeed even expanded on it. God is infinitely great. Yet Bildad failed to apply the truth to Job in a way that helped him. We must learn to receive and apply biblical truth with faithful love and grace so that we might find and share true spiritual comfort (6:14; 19:21).

2. True knowledge of God must also be held with a profound awareness that we know only a small portion of God's

greatness: "but the thunder of his power who can understand?" (v. 14). While we should trust all that Scripture tells us about God, we are at best stammering children in the things of God. Why is this so important to remember when we stand up for the truths of the Bible?

Chapter 27

1. Job's integrity (v. 5) was the focal point of his spiritual warfare (2:3). A Christian's integrity consists of a loving life, heartfelt pursuit of purity, good conscience, and sincere faith (Ps. 26:1–5; 1 Tim. 1:5; 2 Tim. 2:22). Had Job yielded to the arguments of his friends, he would have denied his integrity. If the Devil cannot lead us into unrepentant sin, he will attempt to destroy our assurance, unjustly inflame our conscience, and cripple our faith with hard thoughts of God. How can the Christian resist the Devil and hold on to his integrity?

2. The mystery surrounding the suffering of the righteous should never hinder us from clearly seeing that God will punish the wicked (vv. 13–23). Job believed this even in the midst of his questions about God's justice (v. 2). Do not be deceived by temporary circumstances or the lies of Satan. Sinners will face the wrath of God (Eph. 5:6). Therefore, do not envy them, but repent.

Chapter 28

1. The Hebrew word for "wisdom" has the basic idea of skill or ability (Ex. 31:3–6). With respect to God, it refers to His infinite skill to accomplish all His purposes in the best possible ways. With respect to believers, it refers to the skill to

live well in God's world. This is why the starting place and the essence of wisdom is the fear of God (v. 28). Only as the reality of God in all His perfection governs the conscience and consciousness will we be rightly motivated to worship God as He is and to avoid doing things that displease Him. Likewise, fearing God means trusting His wisdom that all the circumstances He brings into our lives are according to a perfect plan He is executing in the best possible way. That is the lesson Job had to learn in the throes of his troubles, and indeed the lesson he would learn.

2. Christ is our wisdom (1 Cor. 1:30). Wisdom is the ability to please God—something we can never achieve by ourselves. It cannot be found by man's technological skill (vv. 1–14) or procured with gold because its value exceeds that of all gold (vv. 15–17). Christ is for His people what they cannot be for themselves. The pursuit of wisdom, therefore, is nothing short of the pursuit of Christ (Col. 2:2–3; 3:16). How can we pursue wisdom in Jesus Christ?

Chapter 29

1. We learn much about Job in this chapter through his personal testimony. He walked in the light of God (v. 3), fellowshipped with God as with a friend (v. 4), and knew the presence of God (v. 5). Job's self-assessment agreed with God's testimony about him (1:1; 2:3). This is the mark of a true Christian. He had been born again and through the new birth had tasted the goodness of God (Ps. 34:8), not just God's blessings but God Himself. How does your own testimony compare with Job's? Have you experienced God's spiritual grace?

2. Job had a reputation for compassion (vv. 12–17). We cannot know the love of Christ without being moved to demonstrate that love to others. Christ says that everything hangs on two great commandments: to love God completely and to love one's neighbor as oneself (Matt. 22:37–39). James describes pure and undefiled religion as visiting the fatherless and widows in their affliction and keeping one's self unspotted by the world (James 1:27). By God's definition, Job's religion was pure religion. Can it be said of you that you are generous, compassionate, and separated from the contamination of the world? Why or why not?

Chapter 30

1. Job laments that he had become a reproach to his neighbors (vv. 9–10). Suffering contempt or insults from our neighbors is not unusual for Christians. To this we are called, for Christ suffered as an example that we should follow in His steps (1 Peter 2:21–23). The challenge Christians face when it comes to bearing reproach is to make sure the reproach is not on account of their sins but on account of Christ (1 Peter 2:20).

2. Comparing chapter 29 with chapter 30, the reader can perceive how Job had gone from the mountaintops of spiritual bliss to the deepest valleys of humiliation. The providence of God leads Christians through both the mountaintop of blessing and the valley of humiliation as parts of His work of making them holy. When Paul wrote that "all things work together for good to them that love God" (Rom. 8:28), he was not limiting "all things" to the mountaintop experiences of God. How have you seen God's wisdom and goodness in

both the peaks and valleys of your life or those of others? How can that give you patience today?

Chapter 31

1. In this climactic finish to his speech, Job forcefully declared his righteousness. Since God commended Job as a model of righteousness, we should carefully observe and follow his example. Job made a covenant with his eyes (v. 1). He was careful about his conduct (v. 5). He resisted sins within his heart (v. 9). He showed consideration toward those who were under his authority (v. 13). He had compassion for the poor (v. 16). He was careful not to put his hope in the riches of this world (v. 24). While not a complete picture of righteousness, this chapter is a beautiful example of the obedience produced by a living faith in the Lord. When you reach the end of your life, will you be able to say such things? How can you prepare now?

2. Job recognized the essential equality of men as God's creations, as well as the implications of this reality for how to treat one another (v. 15). People under his authority and below his social rank still shared with him a common humanity. In this statement Job set forth the foundation for compassion and justice that ought to characterize every Christian. In what ways do people in your circles commonly treat others as less important or less valuable than themselves? How should you be different?

Chapter 32

1. On the one hand, Elihu showed some humility, so he is a good example to all, and particularly to youth. Despite his

desire to enter the conversation, he respected his elders and allowed them to speak until they were finished. This conforms to the principle of the fifth commandment to honor one's parents, including all others of higher rank. Failure to honor others contributes to the breakdown of society and introduces all manner of sin and misery. So young people should learn to respect their elders, even those who are not their parents.

2. On the other hand, Elihu demonstrated that youthful zeal can be quick to recognize problems without offering any real solutions. His claim to have the answer was idealistic and expressed with a degree of pride. Christ said, "Wisdom is justified of her children" (Matt. 11:19). In other words, wisdom is vindicated by what it produces. Before we start talking about our wisdom, we should invest time in practicing wisdom so that it bears good fruit in our lives (James 3:13–18).

Chapter 33

1. God is absolutely independent and not accountable to any creature (v. 13). What He does, He does according to His pleasure (Ps. 115:3). We are not to presume to know why God acts as He does. The lesson is plain, therefore, that when the Christian does not understand God's dealings he must realize that God's thoughts and ways are beyond him, but also that God is righteous and always does the right thing (Gen. 18:25). It is the Christian's duty, therefore, to submit to God rather than expect God to submit to him. The cross of Christ is sufficient to demonstrate that every dealing of God with His people has a purpose of grace behind it (Rom. 8:32).

2. Elihu's statement points directly to the Lord Jesus Christ (vv. 23–28). Christ is the messenger of the covenant, the divine ambassador who spoke the final Word from God (Heb. 1:1–2). He is truly one of a kind, the only Mediator between God and man (1 Tim. 2:5). When He humbly laid down His life, He presented Himself to God as the ransom, as the substitute for many sinners (Mark 10:45). His death redeems His people from the hellish curse of God's law and wrath (Rom. 3:19–26; Gal. 3:13), and His resurrection will restore them to immortality (1 Cor. 15:20–23, 53). Whenever the Holy Spirit works prayerful faith and sorrowful repentance for sin, the saving power of Christ has taken hold of a lost soul. Has He taken hold of you? How do you know?

Chapter 34

God will never do wrong (v. 10). Elihu, as every character in the book, knew some good theology. It is an absolute truth that "the righteous LORD loveth righteousness" (Ps. 11:7). This statement provides a basic and necessary principle for the Christian when it comes to interpreting the difficulties of life. Whatever the Christian does or doesn't understand about God's dealings with him, and whether he agrees or disagrees with those dealings, he can mark this as being absolutely certain: God is righteous in all his dealings and does not commit iniquity. God is so pure and unchanging that He cannot even be tempted to sin (James 1:13, 17). How might a person be tempted to accuse God of doing wrong? How might you counsel him?

Chapter 35

The independence of God is an important truth with practical implications. God is not reactionary, constantly plotting His next move on the basis of our actions. The sinful behavior of men does not diminish or detract from His righteousness, nor does the righteous behavior of men add anything to Him (vv. 6–7). On the other hand, God is our strength and song for He has created mankind, exalting us above the animals (vv. 10–11). All men are accountable to God, but God is accountable to no one. God owes no man anything. That He is righteous means He is always in conformity with who He is. For Job or Jeremiah (Jer. 12), Asaph (Ps. 73), or us to think we deserve better because we seek to serve the Lord betrays an improper motive. We serve Him for who He is. Therefore, Elihu's admonition to trust Him regardless of what we see is good counsel (v. 14). How does a view of God's glory and independence help us to trust Him?

Chapter 36

1. Verse 26 declares an essential truth about God that magnifies both His infinite being and His amazing grace. God is incomprehensible because He is infinite in all His perfections, whereas we are finite. There is no limit to God's greatness, but there is serious limitation to our ability to understand. Our knowledge of anything can go only so far. Although we can never understand all that is true about God, He has chosen to reveal Himself to us in ways that allow us to understand some things. The very fact that God reveals Himself magnifies His grace. To know God as He has revealed Himself is to fear Him.

2. The most significant way in which God has revealed Himself is in the incarnation of the second person of the Trinity (John 1:1, 14, 18). Jesus Christ is the express image or manifestation of God, and the glory of God is found in the face of Jesus. Hence, Christ says that seeing Him is seeing the Father. Wesley's hymn of the incarnation, "Hark, the Herald Angels Sing," has a line that says it well: "Veiled in flesh the Godhead see—Hail the incarnate Deity." So as we contemplate how infinitely great God is, let us stand in wonder and awe at His marvelous grace by which He makes Himself known to us.

Chapter 37

Elihu's focus on God's sovereignty over the affairs of nature, and especially the weather, links directly to what we should acknowledge regarding His sovereignty over the affairs of our lives. Few things are less predictable than the weather, and certainly nothing is less controllable, even when forecasts prove to be accurate. Nothing can stop the wind from blowing or the rain and snow from falling. But this all happens according to the will of God. We should learn from looking at the weather that God is in control of all His creation, including all of the circumstances of our lives. It should encourage and comfort us to know that God has a purpose for everything (v. 13) and that nothing happens apart from His providence. What can we learn about God by looking at the weather?

Chapter 38

1. The fact that the Lord answered Job "out of the whirlwind" (v. 1) indicates that this manifestation of God was a

fearful event not altogether different from the Lord's appearance on Mt. Sinai, where there were thunder and lighting, an exceedingly loud trumpet, and a quaking mountain (Ex. 19:16–19). And yet this appearance of God to Job was also a gracious event, as it was when God revealed Himself to Ezekiel, assuring him of the divine presence (Ezek. 1:4). We should not be surprised that when God visits His people in grace He still inspires fear (Gen. 28:15–17; Luke 5:8). Even in mercy, He remains God.

2. The Lord "answered" Job (v. 1). In speaking to Job, God never addressed the problem of suffering, though He gave him the answer he needed. Job and the other men had been trying to answer the question *Why?* But this was the wrong question, which accounts for all their wrong answers. The right question was not *Why?* but *Who?* Once Job understood who he was (v. 2; 42:3) and who God is (vv. 5–6; etc.), all was well. The ultimate answer to all our questions about evil and suffering is not information but a person: the Lord Himself. The heart cry of believers is always to see the glory of their God and Savior; one day that cry will be answered forever (John 17:24; Titus 2:13).

Chapter 39

Since ancient times people have studied the animal world and been fascinated by its biology and behaviors. From the wild donkey to the ostrich to the thundering horse to the soaring eagle, the beauty and mystery of these creatures capture man's imagination. By challenging Job with this series of questions, God drove into his mind the recognition that mankind does not fully understand and cannot completely control the birds and beasts. This remains true even thousands of years after Job. God, however, created them all, and He determines the strengths and weaknesses of each. Our awe and wonder at the natural world should remind us that if we cannot master God's creatures, how much less can we judge God? What are some of your favorite animals? How do they remind you of the glory of God?

Chapter 40

At the conclusion of God's first speech, Job had learned his lesson. Throughout the book Job had desired to be in God's presence to have the opportunity to question Him regarding his troubles. Now that he is in God's presence and given the opportunity to speak, he has nothing to say. Being overwhelmed with the greatness of God has caused him to stop thinking about himself. He has learned that God controls everything in the universe, including himself. That is the key lesson. The more we can be overwhelmed with God, the less we will be consumed with ourselves. Seeing God's greatness fosters faith in Him, regardless of circumstances. When we are tempted to judge God, we should consider how unqualified we are to sit upon His throne and rule the world for Him.

Chapter 41

1. After God had taught lessons to Job through various animals (38:1–39:30), He focused on two enormous creatures, behemoth and leviathan (40:1–41:34). These beasts terrify men, but God made them and controls them. In this way they illustrate the point God had made just before speaking of them, namely, that we do not have the right to judge God

because man completely lacks the qualifications to rule the universe (40:8–14). If Job could not master the king of the proud beasts (v. 34), how much less could he sit on God's throne to judge proud and wicked men (40:12)? Therefore, what right did he have to judge Him who does sit on that throne?

2. Through these real (though difficult to identify) creatures, God also illustrated a great spiritual reality. Leviathan is used in Scripture as a symbol of the powers of evil, specifically the Devil. Like leviathan, this monstrous evil spirit terrifies men but is under God's control. This takes us back to the first two chapters of the book, where Satan attacked Job with terrific power but acted only at the sovereign initiative and will of God. Just as Job's inability to master leviathan called him to humbly submit to the Creator, so also Job's inability to master evil and suffering called him to humbly entrust himself to the Lord, who reigns over Satan.

Chapter 42

1. Having heard the Lord, Job had nothing to say except to confess and submit (vv. 1–6). He made this confession while still in the throes of suffering and loss; the Lord had not even hinted that restoration and vindication were coming. What had bothered him for so long was no longer a concern once he saw the Lord. As far as the Bible informs us, Job never learned the reason for his sufferings, and that was fine once he became overwhelmed with God and His greatness. He affirmed God's sovereignty throughout the book, but at the end he gained an experiential knowledge of the glory of God. Like Job, God's people are called to humbly confess

God's sovereignty in the midst of the furnace of suffering while they wait for Christ to appear in glory and restore them to honor and happiness. In light of the book of Job, consider these questions: Do you have a big enough view of God's glory to accept the mystery of suffering without an explanation? Has your knowledge of God entered into the experience of your heart to make you humble and submissive to His ways? What does the way you presently respond to suffering say about your relationship with God?

2. When God vindicates His people, He often restores to them more than they lost when in the thick of their trials. He does "exceeding abundantly above all that we ask or think" (Eph. 3:20). This will be exponentially true on judgment day. Does this thought make you long for Christ's second coming?

The Psalms

Chapter 1

1. Believers should be the happiest of people, for we know God and His wonderful love, covenant promises, abundant pardon, strong comfort, and abiding presence. We have sorrows, but no reason to be miserable. Although tempted to enjoy the company and pleasures of worldly people, God's grace makes believers different from them and allows us to derive our enjoyment from Scripture and the Holy Spirit, which promote holiness in us. On judgment day we will escape the wrath of God and discover how He has watched over us in love all our days. How does this encourage you to follow Christ?

2. Christ is supremely the man who is blessed (72:17). He is the ideal king who is separated from sinners (Ps. 1:1; Heb. 7:26) and engaged to keep God's law (Pss. 1:2; 40:7–8). Accordingly, He becomes like a fruitful and flourishing tree, nurtured by the Holy Spirit (Isa. 11:1–2) and full of good works (Isa. 4:2; Acts 10:38). In union with Him by a Spirit-worked faith, we, too, can become fruitful out of His fullness. What does this teach you about true prosperity?

Chapter 2

1. The world is full of opposition to Christ. Hence there is need for powerful and efficacious grace to convict, enlighten, and persuade. Churches should therefore concentrate on gospel preaching and prayer for the work of the Holy Spirit.

Whatever the opposition, no human power can ever nullify or undo the divine purpose. Are you allowing pessimism to affect you, or are you hanging on to the hope that Christ's kingdom will prevail in every nation?

2. God commands all nations to submit to His Son. Let us begin with ourselves. Have we "kissed the Son"? Have we obeyed His command to repent and believe? One day, maybe very soon, Christ will return as Judge. Will He find us still holding out against Him, or will He find us serving Him? Eternal destiny is linked to the Son. How can a person know that the Son has taken him as His inheritance?

Chapter 3

1. There will be times when troubles come from every side; but God proves to be our shield, very strong, always ready at hand, and surrounding us in His protecting love. We must never sink into despair. Prayer is absolutely vital. In His sovereignty, God is prepared to respond to prayer and work on our behalf. Committing everything into God's hands, we may rest assured that He will grant both help and peace. Remembering former deliverances, we will find courage to face the unknown future. He is the same as ever He was. We go forward, feeling there is much we do not know, but one thing is sure: "thy blessing is upon thy people" (v. 8). How has God proven to be your help and peace?

2. David's troubles foreshadowed the sufferings of Christ. Many people turned against Christ and questioned that God was with Him (vv. 1–2; Matt. 27), but He knew that His Father would keep and deliver Him, and therefore He prayed (Ps. 3:3–4; Matt. 26:39). Answering His prayers, God gave

Him victory by raising Him from the dead (Ps. 3:7; Heb. 5:7; 8:1). Salvation *for Him* and, through Him, *for us* is of the Lord (Ps. 3:8). When troubles surround you, how can you rest by faith in Christ who went ahead of you through distress, and how will He help you endure to the end?

Chapter 4

1. In times of difficulty and distress, we should always quickly go to God in prayer. His past deliverances are so many pledges of future deliverances. Since He has proved to be our faithful heavenly Father, let us always hope in God. Remembering the past provides fuel for faith. We must understand that God, in His grace, has made us for Himself. We are meant to be His: bound in covenant to Him, desiring a closer walk with Him, and serving Him in life and death with a single eye to His glory. What comfort will this provide us as we look ahead to our future in heaven with Him?

2. This psalm is indirectly messianic, for Christ, too, experienced profound distress, even unto death, and was set free (Acts 2:24). On earth men denied His glory and falsely accused Him, but He knew God had set Him apart and would hear His prayers. Through the gospel, He calls upon sinners to fear the Lord, quiet their hearts in submission, and trust in the Lord—offering them peace that passes understanding. Have you heard Christ's gospel call? To what degree do you enjoy His peace?

Chapter 5

1. Never let us be content with saying our prayers. What God requires of us is not formality but personally drawing

near to His presence at the throne of grace. True religion is finding, knowing, and enjoying God—do not be satisfied with anything less. True believers have much to be joyful about: God is our portion, we are precious in His sight, and our sins are all forgiven. In addition to all this, God sees our tears, hears our sighs, and is able and willing to answer our prayers. How is it then that we are so often cast down? How can loving God's name lead us into more joy?

2. Jesus Christ, though God Himself, was also a man and the Mediator for men, and so was much in prayer (Matt. 26:39; Mark 1:35; 6:41, 46; Luke 5:16; John 11:41; 17:1). He called God, "my God," as One in covenant with Him (Matt. 27:46; John 20:17). Through prayer, Christ found strength to overcome His wicked enemies despite their lies and violence. How can we, in union with Christ, find the strength we need as well?

Chapter 6

1. God will not allow sin in His children to go unchecked. When troubles come our way, we do well to examine ourselves to find out if God is correcting us for some sin in conduct or heart. Whatever the case, we must take it to God in prayer and not give up. If we are truly His by faith in the covenant, God has graciously bound Himself to hear when we call on Him. Though the trial drags on and you feel exhausted, cling by faith in Jesus Christ to God's faithful love. How can this psalm help depressed Christians?

2. Amazingly, the sinless Lord Jesus experienced God's punishment for sin, for the sins of Christ's people were counted toward Him (Isa. 53:4–5; 2 Cor. 5:21; 1 Peter 2:24).

Eternity was compressed into time as Christ bore the curse to redeem sinners from everlasting fire. He felt abandoned by His Father's loving presence, and clung to Him as His faithful, covenant God (Matt. 27:46). However, God did not leave Him in the tomb, but raised Him up to the glory of the Father forever. One day, Christ will return to judge all His enemies who have not repented, and they will "be ashamed and sore vexed" just as Christ was "sore vexed" by sinners (Ps. 6:10, 3). Will you be counted among Christ's people? Worship Him for the salvation He procured on our behalf.

Chapter 7

1. Believers can be misrepresented and even slandered in this world. Thankfully, we can always turn to God, who knows everything and never does anyone wrong. In times of trouble, our prayers need to be, as here, not formal and heartless, but serious, fervent, and insistent. This should be followed through with persuasive arguments and earnest appeals, as Abraham, Jacob, Moses, and others did in former times, striving with God and ultimately prevailing. What relief might we experience as we pour out our hearts to Him, telling Him all that has been said and just how we presently feel?

2. The Lord Jesus Christ patiently endured the slander and abuse of the wicked because he "committed himself to him that judgeth righteously" (1 Peter 2:23). He leaned His human soul upon the righteous character of His God and trusted that the Father would make all things right. Through the Spirit, Christ imparts to His suffering people the patient and prayerful character He forged in the fires of persecution.

How can we "put on Christ" when we are in the fire or even before it comes?

Chapter 8

1. Human theories about the origins of the world and mankind lead to depravity, degradation, and despair. However, the truth is that God gave man high privileges and dignity in His creation. It glorifies the Lord for man to rule the world. Honoring God does not drag men and women down, except from their self-made thrones of arrogance. Though God's people are weak and lowly like children, they have a nobility about them, for they are children of the King, destined to reign with Him. What is one way that you could be mindful to treat every man, woman, and child as a person of dignity?

2. This psalm about man finds its fulfillment in the man Jesus Christ. The New Testament applies this psalm to Christ, the last Adam, four times (Matt. 21:15–16; 1 Cor. 15:22–27; Eph. 1:20–22; Heb. 2:6–9). He is the glorious Creator, who with His Father fashioned all the universe (John 1:1–3; Heb. 1:2–3). He has regarded our helpless estate and has taken our nature to Himself, so that through His humiliation and exaltation the Father would be glorified forever (Phil. 2:6–11). How does seeing Christ in this psalm give us hope that God's noble purpose for man will be completely fulfilled?

Chapter 9

1. It is important to remember that God holds our eternal destiny in His hands. He will judge all mankind in righteousness. Even before judgment day, death snatches people away from this world. If we know the Lord and seek Him,

He will never forsake us. However, if we put God behind our backs and forget Him, then He will cast us into hell. Thomas Manton said, "As they cast God out of their mind and affections, so God will cast them out of his presence." Are you prepared for death? Why or why not?

2. Christ echoed the thoughts of this psalm when He said, "And fear not them which kill the body, but are not able to kill the soul: but rather fear him which is able to destroy both soul and body in hell" (Matt. 10:28). The greatest people on earth are but men. Christ's life was an embodiment of this principle, as He faced powerful and violent enemies with boldness and determination born out of a childlike fear of the Lord. As we wait for Christ to return, how can we follow Him in this path?

Chapter 10

In a time of trouble we sometimes feel God is standing at a distance from us, so that we no longer have the comfortable sense of His presence. It is then that we must concentrate on prayer. With a holy boldness, we need to lay hold of Him. Although we should never complain *of* Him, we are permitted to complain *to* Him. One of the chief complaints of the godly is the success of the wicked. Sadly, the world in which we live is one where the fear of God is often conspicuous by its absence. Atheism, humanism, and secularism have usurped the place of true religion, producing bitter fruits in society. The church's prayer and hope is that God will arise on behalf of His people. He will bring His kingdom by His Word and Spirit, by His providence, and ultimately by the second coming of His Son. How does this psalm teach us to pray for persecuted believers as we wait for His coming?

Chapter 11

1. Sometimes the powers of evil seem to have swept the field, and the best the godly can hope for is to hide in desperation. The thought may come to us to desert our post and forsake the work to which God has called us, but this is rarely the right thing to do. We must remember that if we are Christians, our foundation is not set upon anything that man can destroy, but upon God's character and His Word. No matter what happens, God is the righteous Judge and He is on the throne. How can faith in who God is give us courage to stand firm against impossible odds?

2. Christ faced death threats (Luke 13:31) and schemes to murder Him (Luke 22:2), and yet He set His face to do His Father's will. He knew that not one of the arrows of the wicked could kill Him until the Father's appointed time, and then His death would glorify God. He trusted that the righteous Lord would glorify Him, but "fire and brimstone" would fall upon the wicked (Luke 17:29–30). Does your heart ever tell you to fly like a bird to the mountains? Pray to find strength in the Lord Jesus and stand firm when those times come.

Chapter 12

Even in times when the church seems to disappear and the lies of the wicked threaten to drown us, believers can cling to the perfect trustworthiness of the Bible. God's Word is as precious as pure silver. It contains no error in anything it teaches. If we have a right estimate of its worth, we shall surely treasure it in our hearts, follow its pure precepts, and trust its pure promises. Thank God for His infallible truth, especially in this time of mass falling away and confusion. It is confidence in Holy Scripture that will enable you to pray with hope, "Help, Lord!" How can the trustworthiness of God's Word strengthen you in times of spiritual darkness?

Chapter 13

1. The Lord's people sometimes experience spiritual desertion when they feel abandoned in their afflictions without His presence, yet that desertion is never total or final. Jehovah is always there for believers. And so although their troubles may last long, they will not last forever. It is always best to cast our burdens on the Lord rather than mulling them over in our hearts trying to find solutions on our own. God's delays in answering us are not His rejection. When heaven seems silent to our prayers, how can we continue to cling to God's faithful love?

2. Christ also cried out, "How long?" as He endured the faithlessness and perversity of the human race in its slavery to the Devil (Matt. 17:17–18). It wearied His human soul to endure the constant presence of evil in our fallen world. Yet Christ did not despair, but persevered in His mission to bring justice to the world (Isa. 42:4). The greater His sorrow, the more He cast Himself upon the Father in prayer. Now, exalted to the right hand of God, He is able to fully sympathize with His weary people and to give them exactly the grace they need to endure (Heb. 2:18; 4:15–16).

Chapter 14

1. Atheism is no mere intellectual problem: it is a manifestation of sin in the naturally deceptive heart. It stands contrary to the light of nature that so evidently reveals the existence and glory of God, not to speak of the clear revelation of God in His Word. In fact, the conscious decision to deny God leads invariably to a lifestyle that is corrupt. Sadly, there are many who may not profess to be doctrinal atheists but nonetheless live as though God does not exist—a practical atheism. Even some professing Christians approach that kind of atheism. How can we seek to have God in all our thoughts?

2. During His ministry, our Lord Jesus spoke of "the fool" who for all practical purposes denied the reality of God (Luke 11:40; 12:20). As the great prophet of the church, Christ revealed not only the goodness of God but also the evils of man, rooted in the corruption of our hearts (Matt. 7:17; 12:33–34; 15:19; 19:17; John 7:7). He taught that men were unable and unwilling to understand and to seek God (Matt. 13:15; John 6:44; 8:43). If we would count ourselves Christians, we must receive Christ's teaching about the corruption of mankind. How should this truth affect us?

Chapter 15

1. While the *ground* of our salvation is the finished work of Jesus Christ, the *evidence* of our faith in Him is a life of godliness and holiness. It is right and good that we subject ourselves to self-examination, so that as we discern marks of grace, we may attain to a good measure of assurance that we will inherit eternal life. Examine your life for these evidences of a true faith: a life of integrity, obedience to God's laws,

honesty and sincerity of heart, not seeking to harm others with your words or actions, despising the wicked and honoring those who fear God, and not cheating or exploiting people. What does self-examination reveal about your status in God's kingdom?

2. The man described in this psalm is preeminently the Son of God. He lived in pure and sincere righteousness, enduring much slander but always speaking the truth in love (1 Peter 1:19; 2:23). Rather than exploiting others, He became poor in order that they might be made rich forever (2 Cor. 8:9). He reigns in God's heavenly Zion (Ps. 2:6) as the Father expresses His unending pleasure in His Son's obedient life and death (Phil. 2:8–9). Those who are united with Christ by faith are justified by His righteousness and sanctified by the Spirit to become like Him. How should believers' union with this righteous Lord give them hope that they too will share in His kingdom?

Chapter 16

1. This psalm is directly messianic. David wrote it as a prophet of the Lord, knowing that God would raise Christ from the dead to reign forever in fulfillment of God's covenant with David (1 Chron. 17:11–12; Acts 2:30). It is not about David, who died, was buried, and his body returned to dust (Acts 2:29; 13:36). Thus the Scriptures revealed the resurrection of Christ centuries before He was born. How does this help you to have absolute confidence that the Bible is true, and Jesus is the Christ?

2. This psalm sheds light upon the hope that strengthened Christ to endure and "the joy that was set before him" by

which He despised the shame of the cross (Heb. 12:2). The incarnate Lord Jesus lived in daily dependence upon God. He believed God's promise to raise Him from the dead and to bring Him and His people into an eternal fullness of life and joy in the manifest glory of God. The Son loves the Father and counts Him to be His eternal portion and delight. How does this encourage your own faith in God?

3. The Lord Jesus taught us by His example that in trouble and sorrow we must turn to God and count Him and His people to be all our joy. He is to believers far more than we could ever need, and in His hands are our spiritual and eternal happiness. It is good for Christians to keep in mind what we have in our God, lest we be tempted by the possessions and pleasures of the world. In Him we have a suitable, sufficient, soul-satisfying, secure, and everlasting portion. Compared to Him, the world offers us nothing and cannot harm our true source of happiness. How should that affect the way we view death? How should that affect the way we view this world?

Chapter 17

1. While we can never lay claim in this life to sinless perfection, it is greatly to our comfort if before men we have the testimony of a good conscience, especially at times when we are wrongly criticized. We should not be overly troubled by the censures of men. God knows us for what we really are. How can this help us to maintain our constant desire to please Him and wait for His vindication?

2. Christ well understands what it was like to be surrounded by wicked men, and to wait quietly upon God's justice as they

attacked Him like lions. If ever there was a person with the right to cry out for justice, it was the innocent Son of God. Yet He received insult and injury so very meekly. How does this psalm show us the way to follow in Christ's footsteps?

Chapter 18

1. All believers, like David, should confess love for the Lord their God, because they have experienced how He hears and answers their prayers. Our troubles and conflicts become opportunities to experience the many ways the Lord is our strength. When God hears our prayers and rescues us, let us give public testimony for His glory. How has God answered your prayers? How have you glorified Him for it?

2. God's works of salvation center upon the salvation of His anointed king (v. 50). David's song in this way foreshadows Christ's salvation. Though caught in the ropes of death (vv. 4–5; Acts 2:24), the Lord delivered Him because God delights in His righteousness (Ps. 18:19–24). With a great earthquake (v. 7), He was drawn out of the depths of death (v. 16). Therefore, Christ rules over all the nations (vv. 43–44) and is leading them to praise, exalt, and give thanks to the living God (vv. 46, 49). How does this psalm help you to see the glory of Christ? How can that move us to love God?

3. David described God's intervention to save him from Saul in terms of an earthquake, fire, cosmic disruption, flying angels, and a violent hailstorm. Such figurative language points forward to the day of the Lord (Ezek. 38:19–23; Matt. 24:27–31). Christ will return as both God and the anointed Son of David to save His people and destroy His

enemies. How does God's faithfulness to His covenant in the past assure us of His guarantee to honor it in the future?

Chapter 19

1. God graciously reveals Himself. This is grace to us, for our knowledge of Him is completely dependent on what He chooses to reveal. God constantly reveals to all mankind His being and basic attributes through the natural revelation of what He created. No one has any excuse for not worshiping the Lord. Yet nature conveys no saving message: it justly condemns man for refusing to glorify God but it does not point to the remedy. God's special revelation of His Word is the means of grace that reveals the wonderful remedy to condemnation. The Scripture is more precious than gold and sweeter than honey. Nowhere else do we learn of the Lord as the Redeemer of sinners—God in Christ reconciling the world to Himself (2 Cor. 5:19). Praise God for His creation and the Bible which are both means of revelation. Are you taking time each day to read what God has caused to be written?

2. Significantly, David communes with God in response to God's communication. There is always a link between God's Word and prayer. It is a link that we should use daily. While creation should fill us with awe toward God, only the Bible can teach us how to draw near to God as a forgiven and transformed people in acceptable worship. How can we use each benefit of Scripture (vv. 7–11) as a means of guiding our prayers?

Chapter 20

1. Warfare is part of the Christian life, and believers are called to fight the battles of the Lord (Eph. 6:10–18). It is important that the weapons of our warfare are not carnal but spiritual (2 Cor. 10:4). We often use human means, but they will do nothing apart from the power of God's Spirit and the victory of Jesus Christ. How can we make better use of the greatest means of victory in our spiritual battles—prayer and faith in God's Word?

2. The troubles and victories of Israel's kings foreshadowed the great crisis and victory of Christ. Christ knew His day of trouble, especially toward the end of His life. He prayed to His Father to grant Him strength. He offered His righteous life and sacrificial death to God for sinners—and God fulfilled all of Christ's holy desires. His people rejoice in His victory, for they do not trust in themselves, but in the character of their Lord. How does this psalm help explain what it means for us to pray, "Thy kingdom come"?

Chapter 21

The royal psalms point to Christ, the ideal King. Supported by the strength of God, Christ rejoices in the salvation given to Him and His people from their enemies. He obtains these blessings by prayer and intercession, and now reigns with great honor and joy upon His heavenly throne. One day He will return to judge the wicked with devouring fire so that all their schemes against His kingdom will fail. The ultimate purpose of His reign is the exaltation of the Lord in the praises of His people. Christ's victories are the victories of all who belong to Him by faith. How does this psalm encourage you and give you hope?

Chapter 22

1. The first part of this psalm concerns the suffering Savior (vv. 1–21). This is holy ground, allowing us to enter in a small way into the experience of Christ. Here is the man who has faithfully kept covenant with God since His birth (vv. 9–10). And yet He cries out in anguish, "Why hast thou forsaken me?" (v. 1). The answer to this question addresses the very heart of the atonement. God does not forsake the faithful, but the wicked that break His covenant (9:10; 37:28; 94:14; Deut. 31:16–17). Why then did Christ suffer? Christ died for sinners. God withdrew all sense of His gracious presence from His faithful Son and placed upon Him all the guilt and punishment due to the sins of His people (Isa. 53:5–6, 8). On this basis, Christ can save sinners from all the penalty of their sins. How does this psalm humble us? How does it call us to place all our trust in Christ?

2. The second part of this psalm concerns the successful Savior (vv. 22–31). God answered the prayers of His afflicted Son and delivered Him from evil (v. 24). Therefore, the Son proclaims God's glory to the world and calls people to praise the Lord. The testimony of His salvation will effectively turn people from every nation to repent and seek God in humble faith and worship (vv. 26–27). This worldwide mission will continue for generations (v. 31). How is Christ doing this today?

Chapter 23

1. The title of Shepherd belongs to Christ as the God-man, the Lord, and the Son of David (Isa. 40:11; Ezek. 34:12–16, 23, 31; Zech. 13:7; John 10:1–16, 27–30). He fulfills this role with very special care for His people's souls (Luke 15:3–7; 1 Peter 2:25). It is no small comfort, especially in difficult and sad times, to realize that the Lord Jesus is looking after us as our wise and gentle leader, provider, and protector. How can the promises of this psalm give comfort and peace to believers in Christ?

2. Without distracting from Christ's loving work as the Shepherd of His people, it is also possible to see Jesus experiencing in His humanity the blessings of knowing God as *His* shepherd. Christ followed the will of God meekly like a lamb, even to the death (Isa. 53:7). He looked to the Father to protect Him and provide for His needs. Even in the presence of enemies, the Father granted Him the satisfaction of doing His will by the anointing of the Spirit. Now the Lord Jesus dwells in His Father's house forever. How would Christ's experience as a sheep help Him to care for us as our Shepherd?

Chapter 24

1. This psalm found glorious fulfillment in the ascension of Christ to heaven. Truly the Lord Jesus had fought a bitter war against sin at the cost of His own blood. But He proved Himself mighty in battle and went up into heaven as the risen King of glory. What must it have been like for the angels and saints to greet Him on that day? How does it comfort believers on earth to know that the Crucified One is now the Lord of glory?

2. Like Psalm 15, this psalm reminds us that only those purified by grace will enter into God's holy presence. Justification by faith alone gives us our title to heaven, but the sanctification of our lives gives us a fitness to enter and enjoy it, for heaven is a holy place. Those who desire to dwell with the King of glory must begin submitting themselves to His reign even now. How do verses 3–4 teach us what that means in practical terms?

Chapter 25

This psalm sets a pattern for praying to know God's will. Since He is good, delighting in our well-being, He will give directions if we humbly seek Him with a teachable spirit. A key element in discerning God's will is to submit to it even before we know it (John 7:17). We shall find that He will fulfill His promise according to His rich mercy and unchanging truth. If we fear Him, He will lead us. To fear God is to factor Him into every thought and situation, to live in the reality of God. It is not a terror that keeps us distant from God, but a friendship that brings us under His intimate guidance. God's Son lived in daily dependence and reverence for His Father, seeking to do His will because it was His will (Isa. 50:4–5). If we seek to trust in Christ, His Spirit will enable us to do the same. How does this psalm illuminate what it means to live as God's *child*?

Chapter 26

1. The person who professes to trust in the Lord must live a consistently godly life. But being aware of the deceitfulness of our hearts even when we have a clear conscience, we

should be willing not only to examine ourselves but to allow the great searcher of hearts to examine us. We may pray for God to judge us, not to be condemned, but that we might repent of sins and walk in the good way that pleases God. How often do you pray for God to show you your sins? How often should you?

2. David's resolve to walk with integrity is a mirror of Christ's absolute determination to avoid all sin (101:2–4; John 8:46; 14:30; 2 Cor. 5:21). Though the Lord Jesus loved sinners, He kept Himself separate and unstained from the world's corruption (Heb. 7:26). This is the basis of our salvation, for believers are in union with Him. How and why do we pursue holiness in our own lives?

Chapter 27

The Lord is our light in the sense that He reveals to us our sin through the law and our Savior through the gospel. Then in our experience He becomes our salvation. He then proves to be our strength, enabling us to persevere. The Lord Jesus found His own strength in God's presence with Him (Isa. 50:6–9), and His strength becomes ours through the Spirit (Phil. 1:18–19). Christ is thus everything to the believer, and the believer's great desire is to be with Him and see His beauty. He taught us to make Him our "one thing" above all earthly treasures and activities (v. 4; Luke 10:42; 18:22). The apostle Paul likewise made Christ the "one thing" he pursued (Phil. 3:8, 13). Let us seek Him in all that we do, and view all His good gifts as valuable only insofar as they help us to glorify and enjoy Him. What practical difference would it make in your life if you began to pursue Christ with this single-minded focus?

Chapter 28

1. In the troubles of this life, men react in different ways, but the godly man will turn to the living and true God who, like a massive rock, is a shelter in the storm and a shade in the heat. This God is everything we need. Yet we must not approach Him as hypocrites, who may say fine prayers to God and nice words to people while their lives cry out for punishment from God's justice. Rather, we must draw near to God as those coming under His shepherding care, submitting to His sovereign authority. Why do we often turn to other sources for the help and strength we need?

2. The salvation of God's people is inseparably bound up with God's power in His anointed king (vv. 7–8). God's power for believers is precisely the power by which He raised Christ and exalted Him to the highest place (Eph. 1:19–21). Our strength to fight Satan is to be strong in the Lord Jesus (Eph. 6:10–12). This has two great implications. First, we must have a real union with Christ by faith, or we will never be saved. Second, we must enjoy regular communion with Christ by daily exercising our faith in Him, or our experience of salvation will be crippled. How does David's example (Ps. 28:1) teach us to cling to Christ with holy desperation?

Chapter 29

1. Nature can be very impressive but, when confronted with its power and might, we should raise our thoughts to the God behind it who is the cause of its great wonders. How

great He is! We should bow in fear before Him, ever showing profound reverence. If a mighty thunderstorm raging over the ocean can inspire fear and awe, how much more should the Lord who controls it by His mere word (Matt. 8:26–27)? What things in nature produce awe in you? What do they show you about God?

2. The voice of natural revelation can produce fear, but true worship only arises among the people who have God's Word (v. 9). The wonders of the natural world need not terrify them, for the God of the storm is also the Lord who speaks peace to His people (v. 11). They view God's power with joyful awe and reverent comfort, for He is their God in Christ. How should faith in Christ affect the way we face the frightening power of storms and other potentially dangerous things?

Chapter 30

1. David had grown self-confident, interpreting all that God had done for him as evidence of invincibility. His power had gone to his head, and he looked to the power of man instead of the Lord. God sent judgment to awaken David to his spiritual senses, bringing him back to reality. David's experience warns us not to rest in the blessings of God rather than in the God who blesses. Take time to express your gratitude to God for His discipline of us, for the dependence it instills in us, and for the humility we gain—our pathway to joy.

2. Christ never rested His confidence in His human ability, but constantly looked to God for His present and future success (John 14:10). Yet Christ did experience God's anger as He received the curse for the sins of His people (Gal. 3:13), and then entered into the eternal glory and joy for which He

was destined (Matt. 25:21; Luke 24:26; Heb. 12:2). How can Christ's experience of sorrow leading to eternal joy give courage and hope to those who follow Him?

Chapter 31

1. If our trust is in God through Christ, we shall never be disappointed; instead, we may have strong confidence to face whatever is before us. We should not only believe in the sovereignty of God, but also apply it when in any trouble. Our times of sorrow and of joy are all in His hands. Though men may attack us with lies, God will hide us in His presence, and He has prepared rich goodness for our future with Him. How does it help you today to know that the best is yet to come for believers in Christ?

2. Even when Christ was broken on the cross and insulted by His enemies, He took up the prayer of this psalm and offered it to His Father, "Into thine hand I commit my spirit" (v. 5; Luke 23:46). His whole life was a model of submission to God's sovereign will (Ps. 31:14–15). How does His example stir us to entrust ourselves to God?

Chapter 32

1. The gospel of forgiveness is the basis of the repentant sinner's happiness. It is most wonderful to know that our sin is covered and forgiven. Though sin is offensive to God, He is ready to pardon and faithful to forgive sins as soon as we turn back to Him in honest confession. It is a foolish thing to go without confessing, for delay only causes misery of heart to the true Christian, and endangers the unbeliever with unending sorrows. It is pointless to try to cover our sins

before the all-knowing God. However, when we stop making excuses and openly confess our guilt before God, we discover the blessedness of His forgiveness. Why is it so sweet to a sinner to know that he is completely forgiven by God?

2. The forgiveness of sinners is possible because of the death of Christ, represented to Old Testament Israel in promises of a suffering Savior (22:1; Gen. 3:15) and the types of sacrifices (Lev. 4:20). Sin is not counted to believers because it was imputed to Christ (2 Cor. 5:21). The Lord Jesus bore the guilt of sin so that His people would be released from its consequences and its hold upon their consciences (Isa. 53:5–6; Heb. 9:14). God hears our prayers of confession because of Christ's prayers of intercession. How can you better incorporate prayers of confession into your daily habits?

Chapter 33

1. Joyful, reverent, and fervent praise springs from knowing God in His power. The denial of the doctrine of creation directly undermines the worship of God, as does the denial of His sovereign control over all things, including the hearts of men. Our God reigns over the whole world and no one can defeat His will. It is no small comfort to the church that His saving plan shall be fulfilled, no matter what mankind may do to thwart it. Faith in God's sovereignty produces both the fear of the Lord and hope in His faithful love. Why is it crucial for us to worship this aspect of Him?

2. Christ rejoiced in the sovereignty of God. He taught the doctrine of creation, arguing on that basis that the Creator has the authority to determine the meaning of marriage (Matt. 19:4–6). He revealed the Father's control over the

smallest details of His creation (Matt. 6:26, 30; 10:29–30). The Son of God also worshiped His Father for determining whom He would save through the gospel (Matt. 11:25–27). Furthermore, in His divine nature, Christ is the sovereign Creator (Heb. 1:2, 10), the Son who with the Father and Spirit made all things and rules them for the salvation of God's elect (John 1:1–3; 17:2). Use this psalm as a song of worship for Christ, in whom we trust.

Chapter 34

1. The title links this psalm to David's retreat to the Philistines in order to escape from Saul. In trying to flee from one enemy he ran to another, only to learn that salvation comes by fearing and trusting the Lord. Now through inspired song he would teach others to turn from sin and to humbly look to the Lord. The key to safety is repenting of sin and praying to God. In moments of crisis do you immediately seek help from the Lord or do you tend to depend on your own schemes? Why?

2. The statement, "Many are the afflictions of the righteous" (v. 19), applies to no one more than Jesus Christ. He experienced horrible pain and cried out to God in agony of soul (Heb. 5:7). Considering His sufferings, one may question this psalm's promises of protection for the faithful. How can they be true of anyone if not of God's Son? However, this psalm finds a surprising fulfillment in the crucified Lord, for even on the cross, not one of His bones was broken (Ps. 34:20; John 19:31–36). God was still with Christ, guaranteeing to the smallest detail that His mission as the Lamb of God would take place as promised (Ex. 12:46; Num. 9:12). In the same

way, God does not promise to shield His faithful ones from all suffering, but He orders our sufferings so that nothing will defeat His good purposes for our lives (Rom. 8:28, 35–39). How does this change the way we view the trials we face?

Chapter 35

1. One of the most perplexing experiences of the righteous is facing false accusations from those whom we have loved. Such charges can break our hearts, mar our good reputations, and bring down unjust legal and social consequences. In life's troubles and conflicts, we must always remember that God is ready to stand for our defense. If we belong to Jesus Christ, then He is our Judge and Advocate. A desire for vindication is not necessarily selfish or vengeful, for God is glorified in the good of His servants (v. 27). How then should we pray in such circumstances?

2. Christ wept over sinners in His compassion (Luke 19:41), but the wicked hated Him without cause (John 15:25). They accused the Innocent One of blasphemy against God and rebellion against the state, producing many false witnesses in their scrambling attempts to condemn Him to death (Matt. 26:59; Mark 14:57). Though He loved them, He also proclaimed the judgment of God against them for murdering the Son of God (Matt. 21:33–44; Luke 19:27, 42–44). God raised Him from the dead and is now greatly glorified in the display of His pleasure in His Son. How can Christ's experiences give us comfort and hope when we suffer unjustly for His sake?

Chapter 36

1. This psalm reveals the horrible corruption of the human heart. Though created by God and living in His world, man does not honor the Lord with true reverence. Instead of glorifying God, he flatters himself. His heart is a constant fountain of lies and evil. Despite all his pride, his destiny is to be cast down, never to rise again. This diagnosis reveals the desperate need of humanity for Jesus Christ. They need Christ to give them a new heart by His Spirit so that they will repent and receive forgiveness for their sins so that God will not punish them. See in this psalm a description of yourself as you are by nature. How does it affect you?

2. In amazing contrast to the wickedness of man, the perfect character of God shines like a thousand diamonds in this text. God's love, faithfulness, righteousness, and justice tower over mankind like an awesome range of mountains, and elude our full comprehension like the depths of the ocean. Yet God does not stand aloof from fallen man, but He draws sinners to Him through faith in Christ so that His goodness becomes their eternal satisfaction. The gospel call is an invitation to a feast, and Christ is both the host and the food for sinners. Are you hungry? Are you eating?

Chapter 37

1. The success of the wicked tests the faith of the righteous. The apparent contradiction between the promises of prosperity to the godly (1:3) and our experiences in a fallen world can provoke us to confusion, anxiety, and bitterness. This psalm encourages believers to look to the Lord in faith and look forward to the future with hope. Resting in the Lord

and seeking happiness in Him provides contentment regardless of life's circumstances. By faith in God's promises, we see the end of all things and know that the wicked, though prospering in this life, have no future, but the righteous will receive a glorious inheritance. How do you need to put these two principles into practice?

2. The Lord Jesus used the wisdom of this psalm in the Sermon on the Mount (Matt. 5:5, 7, 16; 6:8, 25, 30, 33; 7:23). He also exemplified the life recommended here through His trust in His Father, delight in Him, good works, patient endurance of the wicked, meekness and self-restraint, and hope in a future inheritance. Thus His mouth spoke wisdom because the law of God filled His heart (Ps. 37:30–31). This gives Him all the more moral authority to call us to embrace Psalm 37 as well. How does this show us the importance of having a teacher of God's Word who also lives out God's Word in his own life?

Chapter 38

1. Without the realization of our sinfulness, we will not feel any need for the Savior. The Holy Spirit applies the law of God to the conscience to produce a piercing conviction of sin, a sense of God's wrath, and a cry for salvation (John 16:8; Acts 2:37; 16:27, 30; Rom. 3:20; 4:15). The mark of a believer is turning back to God with hatred of sin and prayers for mercy. Even if our friends turn away from us in our distress, we can rest assured that the Father of our Lord Jesus Christ is full of mercy to repentant sinners (Luke 15:17–24). Is the Lord convicting you of sin? How are you responding?

2. If conviction of sin horrifies sinners, what must it have been like for Christ to experience the guilt of countless sinners placed upon His sinless person (Isa. 53:6)? This troubled Him deeply (John 12:27). In the garden of Gethsemane, Jesus staggered under a fearful apprehension of divine wrath (Mark 14:33). His situation was aggravated further when He was surrounded by those who hated Him without cause (John 15:25). His best friends abandoned Him (Matt. 26:31). Yet as He agonized on the cross, bearing our sins, He entrusted Himself to God (1 Peter 2:23–24). When we come under conviction of sin, we can find relief by faith in Him because He was crushed for sinners. How should this both humble and release us?

Chapter 39

1. Emotional outbursts do not honor God. The believer needs to keep a careful watch of his tongue, for it can be the instrument of many sins. Particularly when under pressure, we must do everything to ensure that what we say is ordered by grace, pleasing to God, and edifying to others. Controlling our mouths also helps us to engage our minds to think about life's uncertainty, brevity, frailty, vanity, futility, anxiety, and stupidity (if we live for this world). As foreigners in this world, how can we, as Christians, discipline ourselves to fix our hope on God?

2. Christ was resolved not to sin, not even in His speech when wicked men taunted Him (1 Peter 2:21–23). This was particularly evident at the end of His life when, arraigned before the Jewish and Gentile rulers of the nation, He maintained a dignified silence (Isa. 53:7; Matt. 26:63; Luke

23:9–10; John 19:8–9). However, Christ was human, and we must not forget the holy power He had to exercise in order to control Himself in this way. That same power comes to believers in Christ through the Holy Spirit. How can we draw from Christ's self-control to grow in holy quietness?

Chapter 40

1. Even in the Old Testament, the righteous understood that animal sacrifices could not please God, who desires sincere and perfect obedience from people (vv. 6–8). However, God had instituted the sacrifices to give people a picture of atonement by substitution. These two great themes of Scripture come together in Christ's work of complete atonement by perfect obedience (Heb. 10:5–10). Christ took up the words of this psalm when He came to do the will of His Father who sent Him to save the world (John 4:34; 5:30; 6:38–40). God's will required His descent into the horrible pit of death under God's curse for sins more numerable than the hairs of His head (John 10:17–18; Gal. 1:4; 3:10, 13). The incarnate God willingly humbled Himself and obeyed all the way to the cross (Phil. 2:6–8). Because of Christ's obedience His Father exalted Him to the highest place (Phil. 2:9–11). Take time to extol Him in worship.

2. Perfect delight in obeying God's will characterizes Christ alone among all who have walked upon this earth. Yet He shares His heart of obedience by His Spirit with the people in union with Him (119:32; Deut. 30:6, 8; 2 Chron. 30:12; Jer. 31:33; Rom. 7:22; 2 Cor. 3:3; Heb. 8:10; 10:7, 16). True believers can never be satisfied with merely going through the motions of outward worship. What is the evidence that

by grace a person delights to do God's will and that God's law is within his heart?

Chapter 41

When misunderstood and misrepresented, we should remember that this has always been the experience of God's people (and was the experience of the Lord Himself). This happens to believers because they have grace, which is no small comfort. In all life's conflicts, they must look up and realize that God, in love, is looking down. The Lord Jesus fully understands the pain of treachery and betrayal, for He experienced it from one of His own apostles. He looks upon Christians with great sympathy as their hearts are broken through unfaithful friends. Through the love of our God, they shall persevere and endure; and one day, set before His face, they shall know that it has been worth it all to behold Him in His glory. In the meantime, how can giving ourselves to serving people in need strengthen our assurance in God's faithfulness?

Chapter 42

1. There is a natural thirst common to everyone who seeks goodness and happiness (4:6), but there is also a spiritual thirst produced within them when by the Holy Spirit they taste God's goodness and desire to be fully satisfied with Him (36:8–9; 1 Peter 2:2–3). True believers can only be satisfied by the presence, grace, and comfort of God. Experiencing God's presence should be like a desperate thirst that must be quenched. If depressed, we need to preach to ourselves, even to argue with ourselves, to hope in the Lord and keep seeking

Him. In times of spiritual exhaustion, to what lengths are you willing to go to find your satisfaction in the Lord?

2. Christ experienced horrible physical thirst on the cross (John 19:28), but far worse was His thirst for the departed presence of God (Matt. 27:46). He suffered the deprivation of good that is the doom of sinners (Isa. 65:13; Luke 16:24). Taking the curse for us, He won for us the blessing. As a result, Christ can now satisfy the deepest thirsts of mankind through the Holy Spirit (John 4:14; 7:37–39; Rev. 21:6; 22:17). The question is, do you thirst for God? How do you know?

Chapter 43

Believers may experience inward anxiety and despondency, but they need not settle into despair. They know that God is their festival of joy. Even if they are not feeling joy now, they should stir themselves to hope in God and persevere in prayer for growth in grace and truth. No one experienced deeper darkness than Christ, and no one has entered into richer joy. The Lord Jesus is able to shepherd His people through their times of sorrow. The key for believers is keeping their focus upon God and giving glory to Him. How does this psalm direct the despondent believer to pray?

Chapter 44

1. The God of then is the God of now. Reflecting on the great works of God in the past, whether in biblical times or in church history, should increase our desires and prayers for God to do great things in our day. When we recognize that God is not with us as He has been with His servants in some periods of history, we should pray relentlessly that

God would arise for our help. This is not to demand that the extraordinary be experienced every day, but to request more grace while you persevere in faithfulness today.

2. That we should suffer as a consequence of our sins should not surprise us, but it may perplex us when we glorify God and find ourselves as sheep appointed for the slaughter (vv. 11, 22). Yet Paul cited this truth as the common experience of God's children (Rom. 8:36). He did so in the context of explaining the consequences of their union with Christ by the Spirit: God's children suffer with God's Son so that we can be glorified with Him (Rom. 8:17). This same union with Christ, however, guarantees that nothing can separate us from God's love (Rom. 8:37–39). Though God may seem to sleep and neglect His children (Ps. 44:23), He remains the King who fights for His people (vv. 4, 26), and in Him we are more than conquerors. Why is it so hard to live in the tension of this paradox? How can Christians exercise their faith in such trials?

Chapter 45

1. The expressions of this psalm can hardly refer to anyone else but the incarnate Lord Jesus, both God and the human Son of David, as the New Testament confirms (Heb. 1:8–9). Neither Solomon nor any king in Israel's monarchy could be rightly addressed as "God" without further qualification (Ps. 45:6), nor receive the eternal praise of the people (v. 17). Even in the Old Testament, believers looked for a coming king who would be God and man (Isa. 9:6). What light does this psalm shed on your understanding of Christ and the church?

2. Meditate on Christ as the king-husband and His church as the queen-bride. The King is beautiful beyond words. With His might He protects and defends His bride. His Father delights in His righteousness and anoints Him to reign with joy by the Holy Spirit. The King shares His royal glory with His bride and delights in her. She submits to Him in total adoration. How do the words of this psalm move you to love the Lord Jesus? How do they call us to treat His church?

Chapter 46

1. The great reformer Martin Luther claimed this to be his psalm. It provided the inspiration of his well-known hymn, "A Mighty Fortress Is Our God," often called the battle hymn of the Reformation. It expresses a kind of confident security in the Lord that ought to be the experience of every believer when facing or anticipating the crises of life. God is the comfort and salvation of His people in their troubles, even when disasters shake their world.

2. The principle of "Immanuel" (God with us) pervades the Old Testament and reaches its climax in the incarnation. The Son of God became our living tabernacle and sanctuary when He took on human flesh (John 1:14). Though ascended into heaven, His Spirit remains with the church as a constant stream of living water (John 7:37–39). Thus Christ is with us in His authority over all things, even to the end of the age (Matt. 28:18–20). If He is with us, who can be against us (Rom. 8:31)? How does this psalm teach us to handle our fears?

Chapter 47

1. There is hardly a more practical truth for daily living than the absolute sovereignty of God. He is the supreme King over all, and mere human kings are under His dominion. The wicked attempt to escape from His authority but in the end will face it with terror. The godly find in God's sovereignty a joyous cause for praise and confidence. There should be no place for pessimism, only glorious optimism. The kingdoms of this world will become the kingdom of God and Christ. How would you describe biblical optimism? How should it affect believers in their daily lives?

2. The gospel of Jesus Christ is the good news of God's kingdom (Isa. 52:7; Mark 1:14–15). Thus the gospel announces that Christ is Lord over all and calls all who hear it to enter by faith into covenant relationship with the God of Abraham. How should an optimistic view of God's kingdom affect how Christians approach missions and evangelism? How can faith that God is King strengthen the church when its efforts to reach the lost are frustrated or provoke persecution?

Chapter 48

The church has its enemies; it has often suffered oppression and persecution, sometimes with physical violence (as in many nations today), sometimes with insults and verbal attacks (as from false religions and atheism). We may tremble for the church but we should remember that God has decreed its establishment and therefore we should take heart. We should be concerned to tell the rising generation that God has always been faithful to His people, that their hope is in Him and their confidence should be unshaken.

The key to resting in the Lord is thinking deeply about His faithful covenant love (vv. 9, 14). How has God proven Himself faithful and loving through Jesus Christ? How can that move us to trust and praise Him when threatened?

Chapter 49

1. There are so many who think that wealth is all-important, but death will test people and their beliefs. Such men will then bitterly regret placing confidence in the things of this world. Only the living and true God can save in that dread hour. Many rich men now suffer in hell for their sins, without a single one of the comforts they enjoyed on earth (Luke 16:19–26). Unlike the unbelieving, believers possess the hope and expectation that, when they die, they shall see light—the light of God and the light of all the glories and beauties of the heavenly kingdom. Rest assured that those now in God's everlasting kingdom have no regrets at all over the fact that, through grace, they once came to know God in Christ as their Redeemer and King. How can we strive to keep wealth in its proper perspective?

2. Christ speaks as the great prophet and the voice of all true prophets, having authority to declare wisdom and truth to all people of this world (vv. 1–3). His teaching alone can enable us to view life and death, riches and poverty, in the right way. Christ said, "What shall it profit a man, if he shall gain the whole world, and lose his own soul?" (Mark 8:36). Are you listening to Christ? One test is whether you view the rich with awe and admiration (Ps. 49:16–17), or set your hope upon the Lord and His redemption (v. 15). You cannot serve both God and money, and you cannot seek both earthly

treasure and heavenly treasure (Matt. 6:19–24). What does this test show about your heart?

Chapter 50

1. One of our chief faults in life is to think that God is like us (v. 21). People tend to be satisfied with religious rites, so they assume God will be satisfied as well. But ritual by itself, even those rituals commanded by God, mean nothing apart from a genuine heart of praise and obedience. To think of God as He has revealed Himself is to view Him as the God of power, authority, glory, wrath, righteousness, and faithfulness (vv. 1–6). Such thoughts of God will lead us to worship Him in spirit and truth. What habits will encourage this kind of humble attentiveness to His Word and sincere repentance of sin?

2. In Christ, God has spoken to men (Heb. 1:2), calling them everywhere to the gospel that is preached in the world. His glory shines in the gospel (2 Cor. 4:3–6). Christ shall one day come again with fire (2 Thess. 1:8). He will gather His saints (Matt. 24:31; 2 Thess. 2:1) and punish the wicked, including religious hypocrites (Matt. 7:21–23). Does this frighten you or comfort you? Why?

Chapter 51

1. Nathan's word of rebuke brought David to confession, but it was not required to remind David of his sin. A battle was raging inside that no one else could see. David saw his sin as a criminal offense, a ruinous stain, and ceremonial uncleanness. He was guilty, worthless, and unfit for worship. Although others were impacted by his sin, David acknowledged that

he had primarily offended God and thus appealed to Him for mercy. His prayer is a model for believers seeking forgiveness and restoration through God's mercy in Christ (1 John 1:5–10). What motivations does this psalm give to Christians to confess their sins? How does it teach us about how to confess our sins? Though it was written by a believer, how might it guide an unbeliever to seek salvation from his sins?

2. The mention of "hyssop" beautifully connects repentance with faith in the cleansing power of the blood of a sacrifice for sins (v. 7). The stalk of this plant was used to apply the sacrifice directly to the unclean person. Hyssop was also used to put the blood of the Passover lamb upon the doorposts, so that death would not enter the home (Ex. 12:21–22). Faith seeks the particular application of Christ's blood to our sins, so that we may escape God's wrath and draw near to His holy presence to worship Him. Has Christ's blood been applied to your soul?

Chapter 52

1. The perversity of man is astonishing. The wicked do much harm with their lies, sometimes resulting in the death of many righteous people while the wicked grow in their power and wealth. Fallen mankind takes a horrible delight in its sins, actually choosing evil instead of good. The corruption of our race showed itself in the persecutions of David, and even more in the sufferings of Christ. Jesus felt the full force of unjust human hatred, and His cross should humble us with its declaration of how evil mankind has become, that we would do such a thing when God came to us. How can we learn to hate wickedness like God does?

2. Though the wicked may seem to succeed and prosper, the Lord will rip them out of His world like noxious weeds. However, the righteous will flourish in the presence of their God. His judgments of the wicked will move the righteous to worship. How does knowing that God will punish the wicked encourage us to trust His goodness now?

Chapter 53

The teaching of Psalm 14 is repeated in Psalm 53, and appears again in Romans 3:10–12. This implies that we need to pay careful attention to the doctrine of sin. Apart from a piercing sense of our sinfulness, we will not care much about the gospel of Christ. This psalm reveals that by nature fallen human beings are practical atheists. They are corrupt. Though they may do some good in society, not one of them does true spiritual good. They might be religious, but they do not desire God or seek after Him. They do not know Him in their hearts. As a result, they do not really pray to the Lord, and they persecute God's people. Despite all their boasting, they feel guilty and afraid, sometimes for no apparent reason, and God will punish them severely. What does this show you about your need for Jesus Christ? What specifically do you need Him to do for you in order to rescue you from this dreadful condition?

Chapter 54

David knew what it was to be betrayed by his kinsmen. Trouble is bad enough when it comes from expected sources, but it always feels worse when it comes from those with whom we have some relationship. How painful it must have been for the Lord Jesus for His fellow Israelites to hand Him over to the Gentiles to be crucified! Although we may be hurt or even betrayed by those close to us, there is one who has promised never to forsake us in adversity. We can wholly rely on Him, and He will not fail us. Since we are safe in God's keeping, let us not give way to unrestrained anxiety. Rather, let us praise the Lord that He is with us and that soon we shall be both free and triumphant.

Chapter 55

A believer can experience heart-wrenching trouble that overwhelms him with fear and horror. The Lord Jesus Himself felt this way (John 12:27; Mark 14:33–35). When the believer is in trouble, it is always possible for him to flee to God, in whose presence he will find a place of quiet rest far away from the reach of those who have given him grief. Sometimes in life it is a best friend, even an apparently godly friend, who lets us down badly, causing us a great deal of pain. We do well to rely upon the Lord Jesus, "a friend that sticketh closer than a brother" (Prov. 18:24). In prayer, we should roll the burden of suffering or sorrow upon the Lord, and although He may not remove it altogether, He will uphold us and strengthen us to bear it. As a sympathetic friend and High Priest, He knows exactly how to sustain His servants in their greatest trials.

Chapter 56

1. We must understand that this world is no friend to God or the people of God. However the world treats us, the trial will be used for our sanctification if it drives us to the Lord

in prayer. In all our troubles, God's Word provides comfort, strength, peace, and hope. Long indeed may be the time of sorrow, but even if we are tempted to think that God is unmindful of our sufferings, the truth is that He knows all about them and is moved with compassion. Have you witnessed God's provision in your own life or the life of another? How has this impacted you?

2. Since the Lord became incarnate as a real human, the One who has put "my tears into thy bottle" (v. 8) has Himself wept tears (Luke 19:41; John 11:35; Heb. 5:7). Fear, grief, and the opposition of malicious liars were quite familiar to Him. Christ is able to show us sympathy, yet in a way that does not leave us in a self-centered pity party. He will lead us instead in the pathway of this psalm: enduring evil by faith in His Word, resulting in the praise of His glorious grace. Why do we need to know that Jesus Christ can empathize with us?

Chapter 57

1. Calamities tend to come and go. David being delivered from one trouble soon finds himself praying his way out of another. In the middle of trouble, it is always best to draw near to God and find that place of quiet rest near to His heart. This requires us to fix our hearts' desires and hopes upon His love and His glory. There we shall find the shelter of divine mercy. Recall a difficult time when your comfort was found in the assurance of God's love.

2. In all of Christ's troubles, the cry of His heart was, "Be thou exalted, O God" (vv. 5, 11; see John 12:27–28). The aim of Christ's humiliation and exaltation was the glory of God the Father (Phil. 2:6–11). Christ taught His disciples

to seek the glory of God's holy name first and foremost in their prayers (Matt. 6:9). How can the Lord Jesus enable us to fix our hearts more firmly upon the glory of the Lord?

Chapter 58

1. People have become sinful and wretched creatures by the fall in Adam. One of the worst manifestations of this is hatred against truth, so that we are quick to lie. It is tragic when sin reigns in us to the point that we refuse to listen to powerful warnings and sweet arguments. Why do children tell lies? What does this teach us about our fallen human nature?

2. Mankind's propensity to sin and lie moves us to resist the gospel of salvation. The Lord Jesus taught that sinners *cannot* listen to His Word because they do not belong to God but to the Devil, the father of lies (John 8:43–47). Though people may hear the Word of God from the mouth of Jesus Christ Himself, they are not willing to come to Christ in faith (John 5:38–40). Only the sheep of the Lord will listen to His voice (John 10:26–27), not because they are inherently better than others, but because God draws them to Christ by the inner teaching of the Holy Spirit (John 6:37, 44, 63, 65). How should these truths affect the way we seek salvation for ourselves? For others?

Chapter 59

The world is not neutral to believers but constantly opposes righteousness and sometimes actively conspires to destroy them. Some of the world's most powerful weapons are evil words. Christians may find themselves in the frightening position of being under attack by a group of wicked and violent people. In such times, this psalm teaches us to cling to God. He is the "strength" of the believer, giving him power to keep hoping and obeying. He is his "defense," a high cliff where the believer may hide himself and find peace. His "mercy" or faithful love assures the ultimate salvation of His people and the punishment of their wicked enemies. This confidence gives the people of Jesus Christ the ability to say that even if they are being slaughtered, they are more than overcomers, for nothing can separate them from the love of God in Christ (Rom. 8:31–39). How can we build up our confidence in our God?

Chapter 60

1. God's people, because of their sins, may incur His fatherly displeasure and be brought to a sad condition. Yet they are never reduced to hopelessness because God is still true to His promise in Christ. However formidable the task and however great the difficulty, we are still by prayer within reach of God. When He hears us, He will confirm and fulfill to us the promises He has made. The Lord is sovereign over all the world, and therefore we may always hope in Him.

2. God's promises should particularly give us confidence to make disciples of all nations, for Christ has received authority over heaven and earth and will be with us (Matt. 28:18–20). His gospel is like a banner of His love over us. Although we are to expect God to work for us, we are not to sit down and do nothing. "Through God we shall do valiantly" (Ps. 60:12). How should we get up and get busy doing His will by His grace?

Chapter 61

David's prayer looked ahead to the day when Jesus Christ would rise from the dead to live forever as the king of Israel (v. 6). Christ sought refuge in God during His many trials, and now the risen Christ is the solid rock and strong tower of His people. God's loyal love and faithfulness belong to all who are in union with Christ by a living faith. Believers do well to remember that whatever their outward situation or inward condition, they are always able to turn to God in prayer. Although we may feel totally inadequate, God is stronger than we are, and bigger than any problem we may face. Christ's kingdom cannot fail, and even now His Spirit covers and shelters us with joy and peace. How can knowing that Christ will live forever, and that believers are joined to Him, give comfort and peace to the Christian when he cries out to God in prayer?

Chapter 62

1. The psalm's theme of exclusive trust is vital and far-reaching. The value of faith is determined by its object; and faith is worthless unless it rests upon the Lord alone. Trusting in mankind and human resources is foolish, for the greatest and the least of men are all lighter than a feather in the balances of God. Instead, we must trust in the Lord at all times, building our lives upon His power, reliability, love, and justice. How do we see these divine attributes in Jesus Christ?

2. Such faith in the Lord alone will express itself. First, it will move a person to pour out his heart to God in prayer. Second, it will cause a person to think lightly of men and their wealth. Third, it will create a heart that is open and eager to

listen to God's Word. Such a person can truly say that his soul hopes in God alone for salvation. Is this true of you? What evidence is there of it in your life?

Chapter 63

1. David's desire for the presence of God in the wilderness sets a pattern for responding properly to trials and troubles. First, no trial should distract us from contemplating and desiring God's presence (vv. 1–5). God's glory is not limited to any location or circumstance. Second, no trial should keep us from remembering God's faithfulness that we have experienced so many times in the past (vv. 6–8). Third, no trial should cause us to forget God's justice as sooner or later those who would seek our hurt will receive from God what they deserve (vv. 9–11). So if we seek the Lord with all our hearts, regardless of where we are or what we are going through, we will find Him. True religion is found where we are satisfied in God and pour forth God's praise. How can a believer cultivate such God-centered joy every day?

2. "The king shall rejoice in God" (v. 11). No man or angel has more joy than the Lord Jesus Christ, exalted to God's right hand and given the fullness of the Holy Spirit (16:11; 45:7; 110:1). Amazingly, Christ desires to share His joy with His followers, so that their joy will be full (Matt. 25:21; John 15:11). How can we taste His joy even in this world as we wait for His kingdom to come?

Chapter 64

Let us not be naïve; the wicked hate the righteous and implement careful plans to destroy them. On the other hand, let the righteous not live in fear. God is their ally, ready to enter the field for their cause (9:4; 35:23; 140:12). The wicked may aim their bows at people of integrity, but God has a bow too. They have lies, slander, and false accusations, but the godly have a Witness to the truth. In fact, the Lord uses the very schemes of the wicked to destroy them. If you doubt this, consider Satan's attack upon Christ, for through His crucifixion Jesus conquered the Devil (Col. 2:15; Heb. 2:14). Christ's victory belongs to all who believe in Him, and all that sinners say and do against them will ultimately harm only the sinner. How should this change the way we view the hard words and violence that the church must endure from the world?

Chapter 65

The mighty power of the Creator and the goodness of God's providence in watering the earth and producing crops teach us that the best gift of all is closeness to God. The Giver is greater than the gifts. Therefore, the greatest benefits in the universe belong to the person whom God chooses, draws near to Him by the Holy Spirit, forgives his sins by the blood of Christ, and satisfies with His goodness and holiness. There is nothing sweeter than the sovereign grace of Jesus Christ. Sadly, nothing is more common than for people to enjoy the gifts of creation and providence but have no desire for Christ. In our gratitude, we must look beyond earthly blessings to the deepest blessing, seeking the presence of God through Christ. We must seek Him in quiet reverence and believing prayer. Why is nearness to God the greatest blessing?

Chapter 66

1. God's works of power for Israel at the Red Sea and the Jordan River called all nations to praise Him. Even the wicked were compelled to give Him some honor. Much more do God's works of redemption in Jesus Christ call all nations to worship Him. The death of God's Son for sinners declares God's love, wisdom, mercy, justice, and wrath against sin like no other event in history. His resurrection and exaltation to supreme glory reveal God's unspeakable power and faithfulness. Now, through the gospel, Christ calls the world to come and see (John 1:39), for He has made known God's name (John 17:6). When Christ returns, even His enemies will be forced to bow before Him and confess that He is Lord (Phil. 2:10–11). Have you become a true worshiper of God through faith in Christ? If so, how are you working with the church to declare the gospel to everyone on earth?

2. God despises hypocrisy. He is very tender and forgiving toward those who fear Him and hope in His love, despite their many faults. However, hypocrites say prayers with their lips while in their hearts they look to sin as their great delight. How can we be careful to pray with our thoughts and desires fixed upon God, acknowledging His faithful love but despising our own sin?

Chapter 67

Through this psalm, godly Jews prayed for centuries that God would so bless His covenant people that through them the Gentile nations of the world would come gladly under the Lord's reign and give Him the praise He deserves. It may be that they did so as they celebrated God's provision of another harvest at the Feast of Pentecost. With the coming of the Messiah of Israel, the psalm took on an even richer significance. Jesus the great High Priest now blesses believers, for He has fulfilled the law and brought the covenant blessing by His death on the cross. Christ the risen King rules His people by the Spirit so that they rejoice in obeying Him. At Pentecost He poured out that Spirit so that a harvest of souls was gathered from all nations. The church now prays and labors so that all people will join in the worship of God, as Christ the Prophet preaches God's salvation through the gospel that the church proclaims. Christians must pray toward this today, longing for the full harvest to come in from every nation. As a largely Gentile church, we can rejoice in the blessing promised to Abraham, pray for missions, and specifically pray also for the salvation of the Jewish people through whom this blessing came.

Chapter 68

1. This psalm speaks of the victory of Christ. The apostle Paul quoted it with reference to the ascension of Christ to bless His people (v. 18; Eph. 4:8–10). Christ is exalted and, as Captain of the Lord's hosts, He leads His people to victory over all His enemies, which is a cause for great rejoicing in His church (Josh. 5:13–15; Isa. 55:4; Rev. 6:2). Christ has ascended to the heavenly Zion, and He has sent down His many blessings in the Holy Spirit (Acts 2:33; 5:30–32). Give thanks to the Lord for today's daily load of blessings (Ps. 68:19)!

2. Our greatest need today is for the Lord, in answer to our prayers, to arise and display His power, reviving His church, promoting His cause, and overcoming His many enemies.

Lest we lose heart, we should remember in discouraging days that Christ rules on high over heaven and earth. As the God of salvation, He is able to do wonderful things for His church. There can be no room for pessimism. The victory of the Lord belongs to His people. How can we take hold of the strength that Christ has for us?

Chapter 69

1. This is one of the psalms most frequently quoted in the New Testament. Though it resonates in some ways with the experience of believers, it especially embodies Christ's love for the glory of God and His unjust sufferings at the hands of His own countrymen who were hardened in their unbelief. We often suffer as a consequence of our own sins, but Christ suffered because He took the guilt of other people's sins, making payment for a debt He did not personally incur (2 Cor. 5:21; Col. 2:14; 1 Peter 2:24). As a result, the deep waters of divine wrath flooded his life, overwhelming Him (Matt. 26:38; Luke 12:50) until the Lord answered His humble cry (Heb. 5:7). Reading this psalm should profoundly humble believers as they consider what their sin did to the Son of God. How can it also bring deep comfort to those who experience unjust persecution?

2. Unbelievers should see in these words a warning against the incredible evil of sin, that it would move men to do such things to the innocent and loving Lord. They should fear lest they also be hardened in unbelief and quickly run to Christ to save them from the wrath of God. What promises does this psalm give to sinners who seek the Lord?

Chapter 70

David prayed this prayer more than once because his troubles kept returning. In this world, surrounded by dangers, we are totally dependent upon God and we need to constantly turn to Him in prayer. We cannot live safely and happily without prayer. Therefore prayer must not be neglected. Our prayers do not always need to be long; sometimes the most effective prayer is a desperate cry for help. Our God can come to us in any and every time of crisis. God does not tire of hearing our prayers for His help even if we repeat the petitions, just as long as we seek Him sincerely and not out of thoughtless routine. Christ understands what it means to be poor and needy (v. 5), for He embraced poverty that He might make us rich (2 Cor. 8:9). Now, out of His riches, He is glad to bless those who call upon the name of the Lord (Rom. 10:12–13). How does that encourage you to pray more often and with more hope?

Chapter 71

When in serious trouble, we feel the need of God as never before, and in such a time, it is no small comfort to realize that He is there for us, ready to hear our prayers. This truth delivers us from reaching the point of desperation and hopelessness. What is most encouraging is the thought of God's continuing and unchanging faithfulness throughout every season of life. It is a fact of life that we transition from youth to old age, but Jesus Christ is the same yesterday, today, and forever (Heb. 13:8). He has been raised from the dead, ever lives to intercede for His people, and is the forerunner who has gone ahead of them into eternal glory (Heb. 6:19–20; 7:25). Spend time praising Him for His presence in your life.

Chapter 72

1. No royal descendant of David, other than the ultimate Son of David, ever ruled over an eternal kingdom without borders with universal subjects. This psalm celebrates the reign of Jesus Christ. We should always remember that Christ is on His throne. Though the church may be attacked or in a state of decline, He is well able to restore it and cause it to thrive and prosper once again. In these sad days, too many think in terms only of survival, whereas they should be thinking of reformation, recovery, and revival. Believers do well to have a vision for the success and advance of Christ's kingdom. The gospel calls for optimism, for it announces, "Jesus reigns!" How does this encourage you as one of God's ambassadors (see 2 Cor. 5:20)?

2. Gospel optimism leads to kingdom prayer. This psalm should move us to pray—and to pray with great hope and expectation—that the kingdom of Christ will prevail against the powers of evil and that all His elect will be brought in and made holy. As we are instructed, let's pray for Christ's kingdom to come and for His will to be done (v. 15; Matt. 6:9–13).

Chapter 73

The tension between faith and experience is common in Christian life. We believe that the faithful man is blessed (1:1–3), but sometimes it appears that the opposite is true. Asaph, like many before and after him, wrestled with the problem and found the answer in the sanctuary. There the priestly work of sacrifice reminded him of the holiness of God, the doom to fall on sinners, and the grace of God to believers. There he was reminded that the life of the wicked will end in grief and their prosperity will vanish like the dream of a waking man. What will follow is divine retribution. God will show them neither love nor pity. It will be so different for believers. They enjoy the life of grace, knowing God's presence, support, and guidance, and one day they will be introduced to the life of glory to enjoy God forever. How can we use an eternal perspective to overcome doubts and questions about the goodness of God?

Chapter 74

At times God gives His people over to their enemies, and the church is shattered. It seems that God has rejected them. In such times of desolation, we may still cry out to the good shepherd who laid down His life for the sheep (John 10:14–15). We can gather courage and faith by remembering God's past acts of salvation for His people, just as Israel turned back to their salvation from Egypt when Babylon destroyed them (Ps. 74:12–15). The greatest of these acts are the death and resurrection of Christ. We can find refuge in His infinite power as the Creator (vv. 16–17). We can appeal to God's love for His glory (vv. 18, 21), His tenderness for His people ("thy turtledove," v. 19), and His commitment to keep His covenant (v. 20). How can leaning on such supports enable Christians to pray with faith? How can these truths give us the strength to wait with enduring hope for the Lord to intervene on our behalf?

Chapter 75

1. This psalm celebrates the hope that at His own appointed time God, who now sustains the earth and all that is in it,

will come in all the fury of His righteous wrath to judge the wicked. In that day there will be no escape, and no defense will be possible. Sinners will drink the cup of wrath down to its last drop. The Judge will take away their strength ("horns") so that they can do no more harm, and He will lift up the righteous with power and glory. While this is good news for the godly, it is a dire warning to the wicked. It admonishes them to be arrogant no longer. What will it be like for unrepentant sinners on judgment day?

2. One amazing link between this psalm and the New Testament is Christ's prayers in the garden of Gethsemane, "O my Father, if it be possible, let this cup pass from me: nevertheless not as I will, but as thou wilt.... O my Father, if this cup may not pass away from me, except I drink it, thy will be done" (Matt. 26:39, 42). The Lord Jesus took the cup of God's wrath against sinners and, in submission to His Father's will, drained it dry so that His people would never have to taste it. How does this affect your view of God's love for sinners? How does it affect your view of Christ's cross?

Chapter 76

The church is at times under serious attack, but in vain do Satan and evil men seek its destruction. Greater is He who is in us than he who is in the world. God Himself is its indwelling Sovereign and Protector. In due time, He will take up its cause and arise for its help. Whatever evil may be allowed to overtake the church, it shall all be overruled to God's greater praise, and any further evil will be harnessed and rendered ineffective. Thus, in His keeping, the Lord's people are both safe and well. How does this enable believers to remain humble, quiet, and meek in affliction?

Chapter 77

1. When stress robs us of sleep, our difficulty is doubled by physical and emotional fatigue. Yet in that situation, we may devote ourselves to prayer and meditation. It is striking that precisely when the disciples were dozing off from grief and exhaustion, Christ was fervently seeking God in prayer though His soul was burdened far worse than theirs (Mark 14:33–40). Let us follow the Master in this too: turn sleepless nights into opportunities for earnest prayer, meditation on Scripture, and intercession. What tends to rob you of sleep? How can you make spiritual use of this opportunity?

2. When it seems like God has forgotten us, it is time for us to remember His works. Biblical history is full of marvelous displays of God's power and faithfulness to redeem His people. If you are a believer, your personal history is also a rich resource for meditating on the kindnesses of God's providence and saving grace. How can a Christian make use of these things to find strength and comfort?

Chapter 78

1. Biblical history teaches reliable facts about real people and events, and yet its purpose is to communicate spiritual truth and to call for a spiritual response. It is good to teach the Bible's stories to children and adults, but if we do not draw doctrine out of the story and apply it to the heart then we have not been faithful to God. He calls each generation to train future generations to hope in God and obey His

commands. What implications does this have for family worship and church classes?

2. The history of Israel teaches us that God is faithful to His covenant and works powerfully to save His people. However, humanity is not faithful to God, but rebellious at heart, even when this rebellion is cloaked in the religious flattery of hypocrisy. As a result, God's wrath burns against them. God's loving solution to man's problem centers upon the household of David, giving Israel a king to shepherd them in kindness and righteousness. Yet even David's line failed, resulting in the exile among the Gentiles. This psalm thus implies that Israel's hope lies in a coming Son of David who will keep covenant with the Lord so as to gain His blessing on the people. This King must also have the ability by God's grace to change the hearts of sinners so that they repent of sin and trust in God's promises. The salvation that this King brings will be like Israel's exodus from Egypt, only it must be a spiritual exodus. How are the expectations of this psalm fulfilled in Jesus Christ and His Spirit?

Chapter 79

Great damage, disgrace, and distress can come upon God's church (Rev. 13:15; 17:6). Sometimes God gives the wicked victory over the professing church because of its sins. In such times of disaster, we must give ourselves to prayer for His compassion and forgiveness. Even when the Lord is disciplining His people, we may appeal to His justice to punish the wicked oppressors if they will not repent (Rev. 6:9–11). Christ is ever the shepherd of His sheep (Ps. 79:13), and He will never abandon them. When God rescues His church from troubles, or if we do not live in a time of severe persecution, we should give public thanks and praise to the Lord for the peace we enjoy. How do the church's present circumstances call it to prayer and praise?

Chapter 80

When the tears of God's people flow, they can remind themselves that Christ is the divine shepherd of His chosen flock, present with them as an enthroned king by the Holy Spirit. He is the Lord God of hosts, the all-powerful Commander of all creation. His face shines upon believers, indeed shines within their hearts, through the gospel (2 Cor. 4:6). They are God's vineyard, and Christ Himself is the vine whose sap gives life to all branches that abide in Him (John 15:1–8), for He has joined Himself to us by taking our human nature as the Son of Man so that we might be joined to Him by His Spirit. Therefore, when the church suffers defeat, believers should call upon Christ to revive them so that they may bear the fruit God desires. How often are you praying for the revival of Christ's church? How can this psalm help you to pray?

Chapter 81

Through the Psalms the Lord Jesus Christ teaches us to worship God according to His will. God's people must worship Him by singing with energy and joy (v. 1), exercising faith in His power and faithful love (v. 1), offering God psalms with music (vv. 2–3), following the instructions of Scripture (v. 4), remembering God's great works of salvation in Jesus Christ (vv. 5–7), listening to the preaching of the Word (v. 8), renouncing the gods of this world (v. 9), drawing near to God with expectant desire for Him to satisfy us with Christ (vv. 10, 16), and repenting of our sins (vv. 11–15). How are you following each of these directions in your public worship? How do you need to change?

Chapter 82

God has given men great authority in the world to rule as His representatives (Gen. 1:26–28), but with this authority comes accountability. People, especially people with power, tend to confuse themselves with God. Instead of defending the weak against the wicked, they show favoritism and overthrow the fundamental principles undergirding society. The injustice of human courts reached its pinnacle of perversity when the Jewish council condemned Christ to death, and the Gentile ruler authorized Christ's crucifixion even after finding Him innocent. Nevertheless, when justice miscarries, we may look to the Judge of all the earth to do right. The Lord reminds rulers that they are mere men, fallen and mortal in Adam. If the rulers of this earth do not follow God's principles of justice, then God will judge the judges, for He is the Owner of all nations. How does this psalm teach the officials of civil government to walk in the fear of God?

Chapter 83

God's enemies often attack His people, and they should not be surprised if they find themselves surrounded by the wicked seeking their ruin. The comfort of the church is that God will arise to help in answer to prayer. Christians can rest assured of the final victory, because God has shown His power and will to save repeatedly through history. The wicked, however, should fear, because the Lord will fill His enemies with shame and torment them with fire. While God's judgments may seem harsh, in reality they are good and necessary, for they demonstrate to the world that the Lord alone is the sovereign King over all the earth. Judgment serves God's glory. How does this encourage believers to pray for justice? How does it admonish unbelievers to repent?

Chapter 84

1. In the new covenant, the house of God is not a building, but the congregation of people united in Christ by the Holy Spirit (1 Cor. 3:16; Eph. 2:22; 1 Peter 2:5). There is great blessing in going up to worship in the house of God. God's Word calls us to that holy gathering (Ps. 99:9) and the Holy Spirit draws us (Ezra 1:5). There believers see God's beauty and are satisfied in Him (63:1–2). Love for God's church and its worship of God is a sign of God's saving blessing upon a person. How much do we value the meetings of the church? How frequently do we attend them? What do we seek when we go—God or something from man?

2. No one is more zealous for God's house than Jesus Christ (John 2:17). Even as a twelve-year-old child He loved to be there (Luke 2:46–49). As an adult He was often in the temple teaching (Luke 22:53; John 10:23). He especially delights in being with His believing people, who are God's spiritual house. To them He has promised His special presence (Matt. 18:20; 28:20). The risen Lord is our great temple, and He shines like the sun with the beauty of the triune God (John 2:19–22; Rev. 21:22–23). Better is one day with the church in the presence of Christ than a thousand elsewhere.

What often hinders our own attitudes from being Christlike in this matter?

Chapter 85

Thinking about the past ways God has dealt with us is a good way to increase our desire for God to continue to show His grace. As you meditate through this psalm, follow the logic. First, we remember the past, thinking about God's mercies, restoration, forgiveness, and peace (vv. 1–3). Then, we pray for the future that God might revive us and show His mercy or covenant loyalty (vv. 4–6). Finally, we express faith for the present by resolving to listen to the Lord's Word, hoping in His salvation and glory, and admonishing ourselves and each other to not return to the old ways of folly but to follow in the way of peace provided (vv. 7–13). How would you apply this pattern specifically to your own situation or that of your church?

Chapter 86

Biblical prayer is driven by meditation upon God. God's covenant in Christ attracts us to approach Him with humility and trust (vv. 1–2). God's goodness and forgiveness draw us to seek Him in prayer regularly despite our sinfulness (v. 5). God's greatness turns us from all other gods to seek Him alone in our need (vv. 8–10). God's love, compassion, grace, and faithfulness give us hope to call upon Him even when proud sinners work to destroy us (vv. 13–15). God's mercies to us in the past encourage us to boldly ask Him to give us signs of His goodness in the present (v. 17). What concerns do you have to take to the Lord in prayer? Which of God's attributes seen in God's covenant through Christ allow us to pray with confidence?

Chapter 87

In the new covenant, the church is God's spiritual Zion, the heavenly Jerusalem, and His living temple among people (Gal. 4:26; Heb. 12:22; 1 Peter 2:5–6; Rev. 3:12; 21:2, 10). God's promises to Israel are being fulfilled in the church through faith in His Son, whose person and work is the foundation of God's dwelling with sinners (1 Cor. 3:11; 1 Peter 2:6–7). The church of Jesus Christ is more beautiful, precious, and holy than any other institution on earth (Isa. 60–62). Its citizens are of a heavenly birth by the Holy Spirit (John 3:1–8; Gal. 4:29–31). The Lord knows each of them by name (2 Tim. 2:19). God has promised His special presence to its gatherings in a way that surpasses even private communion with God (Matt. 18:20; 28:20; Eph. 2:18–22). How precious is the meeting of the church! How does this psalm give us reasons to love the church and its public worship? What changes do you need to make in your attitudes and habits to reflect the importance of the church in God's sight?

Chapter 88

1. The Lord may bring a crushing sense of His wrath upon the soul of a sinner, causing the conscience to pierce and the affections to burn with fear. If so, then the right response is to cry out to God for salvation from sin (v. 1; Acts 2:37; 16:29–30). Everyone who calls upon the name of the Lord, trusting in the risen Christ, will be saved (Rom. 10:9–13).

Have you ever sensed the wrath of God against your sin? Do you trust Christ alone to save you?

2. God may withdraw a comforting sense of His fatherly love from the believer, and the Christian enters into a time of darkness and horror from the guilt of his sins. Though objectively the believer remains justified in God's sight, subjectively he may lose his sense of assurance and peace of conscience, feeling that God is against him (38:1–8). Such seasons may be compounded by physical illness and isolation from friends. They call the Christian to patient endurance and continual prayer (88:1–2, 9, 13).

3. Though the spiritual desolation of Christians may disturb us, we should be most moved by the sufferings of the sinless Son of God, in whom this psalm is fulfilled. He experienced divine abandonment in the highest degree, though faithful to God from His youngest days (22:1, 9–10). He suffered for the sins of others and was crushed for their guilt (Isa. 53:5–6, 10). He propitiated God's wrath for sinners by bearing the curse Himself (Rom. 3:25; Gal. 3:13). As a result, though we may feel abandoned by God, the Lord will never truly forsake the believer. How can meditating on Christ's time of horrible darkness help believers to endure times of darkness themselves?

Chapter 89

1. This psalm is a commentary on the Davidic covenant (2 Sam. 7), which marked a significant advance in God's revelation of redemption. The Lord told David that through his royal offspring, God's presence and kingdom would be established on earth forever. David's sons, beginning with

Solomon, failed in one way or another. Their sins seemed to put the promise in jeopardy, bringing down God's judgment and finally destroying the kingdom of Judah. Believers in that time lived in the tension of the promise of a kingdom and the reality of desolation and foreign domination. How does this psalm teach us to pray when life's reality seems to contradict God's promises? How does it encourage both faith and honesty?

2. Though God had threatened discipline upon the line of David if they broke His law, he also guaranteed that His faithful love and reliable covenant could not be nullified. This called Israel to hope that God would raise up a righteous Son of David whose obedience to God's laws would bring the everlasting kingdom. The failure of Israel's kings reflected the fall of man in the first Adam from his blessed and royal position on earth. Therefore God's promise held out the hope of the last Adam, God's Son. All the hope of believers rests upon Him. Already His kingdom has begun in Christ's coming, death, resurrection, ascension, and pouring out of the Holy Spirit to begin worldwide missions. Yet the church still waits for His coming to reign in glory and lives under the cross of persecution. How can this psalm help us to seek His kingdom in prayer as we live in the "already but not yet"?

Chapter 90

1. Death is not a natural event to which we should resign ourselves, but a sign of God's anger upon mankind for our sins. Though we would rather not think about it, we gain much wisdom by meditating on the brevity of life, the certainty of death, and the eternity of the God who rules both

life and death. The reality of death strips away our pretenses of pride and independence and reminds us of God's absolute power over us and wrath against sin. How should these truths humble us?

2. The reality of death also moves us to find a dwelling place in God that will outlast this life. This world loses its charm when we see it as a temporary home, but God is eternal. This is the great wisdom given to us by the gospel, to trust in the Lord Jesus Christ for eternal life (2 Tim. 3:15). Pray that God would have mercy upon you for your sins, give you eternal joy and satisfaction in His love, and work in you so that your works will have lasting value.

Chapter 91

1. God's people have long cherished this psalm as a promise of God's protective presence. It should not be interpreted to say that no harm can come to believers (v. 10), but rather that God will work all things to the good of those who love Him, making them more than conquerors over Satan and this evil world (Rom. 8:28, 37). God's ordinary way is to answer the prayers of Christians by sustaining them in the trouble, then rescuing them from the trouble, and ultimately giving them glory and eternal life (Ps. 91:15–16). What do the images of the first part of the psalm (vv. 1–4) teach us about trusting the Lord?

2. Satan abused this Scripture in his temptation of Christ in an attempt to get Jesus to test God in an extraordinary way by leaping from the temple so that angels could carry Him down (vv. 11–12; Luke 4:9–11). The Devil omitted the words "in all thy ways," perhaps because they imply trusting

in God's ordinary providence over all our life, not forcing His hand to some extraordinary show. Christ refused to test the promised angelic protection, and then angels came and cared for the ordinary needs of His weary humanity (Matt. 4:11). What lessons can we learn from Christ about how we should and should not use God's promises of protection?

Chapter 92

As the title of this psalm implies, it teaches us about how to keep the Lord's Day holy. The Sabbath is a day devoted to praising God for who He is and what He has done in the public worship of God's house. We should sing His praise morning and evening—as much as possible. Life can be brutal as we are surrounded by the wicked, but the Lord's Day offers a unique opportunity to renew our perspective by faith in the promises of God's sovereignty, judgment of the wicked, and blessing on believers. Thus the preaching of the Word is central to the day. By worshiping in God's presence, God's people flourish and grow like trees. Even into their old age they are renewed in strength and declare God's righteousness for others to hear. Truly, the Sabbath is a blessed day! How does this psalm call you to change the way you spend your Sabbaths?

Chapter 93

Unwelcome, unexpected, and unexplained things happen in our experience. There is hardly a more comforting truth for God's people than that God is the absolute Sovereign ruling His kingdom unfailingly for purposes of His glory and His people's good. The Lord God only is King, ruling in power, justice, and wisdom over the entire world (Isa. 46:10–11; Eph. 1:11). The triune God reigns through the Mediator, Jesus Christ (Pss. 2:6, 110:1–2; Matt. 28:18). As absolute monarch, God guides everything by His Son to His predetermined goal (Prov. 16:4; Rom. 11:36; Heb. 1:3). What does this teach us about how to respond to the threats of powerful people (Ps. 93:3–4)? How should this affect the way we approach His Word and worship (v. 5)?

Chapter 94

1. This is a psalm for the persecuted church. Whenever believers suffer unjustly, they can appeal to the God who occupies the seat of supreme power and jurisdiction. He is able to intervene, righting apparent wrongs, and bringing relief to His troubled people. It is solemn to reflect on the truth that God takes account of everything that happens in this world. Even now, all things are clearly seen by the eyes of the Judge before whom all will stand. This gave Christ the strength to patiently endure injustice and malicious persecution, and Christians are called to walk in His footsteps (1 Peter 2:19–23). What injustices trouble you now? How can this truth help you?

2. As God's people wait for the Lord to rescue them from their oppressors, they can find comfort in knowing that God has a purpose in this for them. First, He is blessing them through the teaching of His chastening and discipline (v. 12). Even persecutors are God's instruments to make believers holy. Second, He is bringing them into deeper communion with Himself. The sorrows of persecution drive us to drink more deeply of the secret comforts of God's Spirit

(vv. 18–19). Do you know the soul-delighting comforts of Christ? If not, why not? If so, how can you grow in them?

Chapter 95

1. Worship engages people to sing God's praise as the trustworthy Savior, supreme King, and only Creator of the entire universe. We hear God's voice in the reading and preaching of the Word. What do verses 1–7 teach us about our response to God's Word in true worship?

2. In the worship service, there really are only two options: either we gladly glorify God through Jesus Christ, or we harden our hearts and put Him to the test. If we refuse to believe God's Word, then even seeing miracles will not help us—Israel saw many miracles, but most of the congregation in the wilderness rebelled against God. The tragic reality is that many come to worship services only to fall under God's wrath. The only way to enter the blessing of God's rest is by faith in Christ. Therefore, do not deceive yourself, thinking you can remain neutral. Which of the two options do you find your heart taking? Flee from the wrath of God, place yourself under the care of the Good Shepherd who laid down His life for the sheep, and engage your heart to worship God.

Chapter 96

1. This psalm teaches that praise and worship is God-centered, with every component of praise, whether in song, speech, conduct, or appearance, directed to His glory. Worship responds to His holiness, that is, the radiant majesty, glory, and beauty that display Him as the only true God. Therefore, worship revolves around the preaching of God's

glory from the Word. How can we keep our worship centered on God?

2. Worship must be missional, that is, calling all people regardless of ethnic or cultural background to join in knowing and adoring this one God. Biblical evangelism is a call to worship God. Authentic worship fuels a longing for all nations to glorify this great God and Savior. How can we reach out to the nations through our worship?

3. Worship must be in the beauty of holiness, that is, by people clothed in Christ's perfect obedience and sanctified by the influences of the Holy Spirit to obey God's commands. In our public worship services, our resolve must be to promote His glory and to please Him, not to entertain ourselves and others. Cheapening the holiness of God and His worship does not assist evangelism, but robs it of its core attraction: God Himself. How can we strive toward a worship that is beautiful in holiness?

Chapter 97

1. God is enthroned. His people should rejoice, for the world is not governed by random chance or fate. There is Someone in sovereign control; right and righteousness will prevail. Life does have purpose. Wicked men cannot overcome the Lord, evil will be judged at last, and the future lies entirely with God. If you are in the midst of adversities, remember that all things are being directed from on high, by Someone too wise to err and too good to cause needless grief. Pray for others you know who may be facing struggles at this time as well.

2. God reigns in His Son, who is the Lord (2:6–8; 110:1–3). This psalm's graphic imagery will ultimately find fulfilment in the return of Jesus Christ in the skies to judge the world, disrupting this creation to bring in a new creation and bringing believers into everlasting joy. How could this psalm motivate Christians to turn from sin with wholehearted hatred and love the Lord with all their hearts? Why should it move unbelievers to turn from their idols to serve the Lord alone?

Chapter 98

1. Consider the marvelous things done by God. In creation, He made, by a mere word and out of nothing, the substance of the entire universe (Rom. 4:17; Heb. 11:3). In providence, He preserves, governs, and directs everything according to His will (Neh. 9:6; Isa. 46:10; Eph. 1:11). In redemption, His greatest work, He delivers at great cost to Himself those imprisoned in sin and misery (Ex. 6:6–7; Deut. 7:7–8). How do each of these great works give us reasons to praise the Lord?

2. God's great works of salvation are not meant to be celebrated by a few, but to be broadcast among all nations so that all creation will be filled with His praise. What reasons does this psalm give us for evangelism and missions?

Chapter 99

1. When approaching God in worship, men should tremble in awe of His infinite majesty and holiness. There is no place for casual familiarity or flippancy, for God is above us in every way. He is God and not mere man. Although He is so infinitely different from the creature, He nonetheless

is approachable, to which Moses, Aaron, and Samuel bear witness. So let us rely on His forgiveness and worship with fear and also joy. Why is it no contradiction to worship God with fear and joy?

2. God gave people limited access to Him through the pillar of cloud, the priests, and the temple on "his holy hill" in Zion, yet these were but types of how the King would dwell with His people in Jesus Christ. How does God's holiness shine in His Son?

Chapter 100

1. Worship is a duty required of all mankind. God's works of creation all around us summon us to it (Rom. 1:19–21). God's gospel message calls the nations to glorify Him (Rev. 14:6–7). Nor is it enough for people to go through the outward acts of worship, but we must serve Him with joy and energetic praise (Ps. 100:1–2), springing from the knowledge of who He is (v. 3), and expressed in the public gathering of His church (v. 4). Why is joyless worship an insult to God? Why is ignorance a barrier to worship? Why must we worship God in the public assembly of the church instead of merely praising Him at home or on a private walk?

2. The worship of God is fueled by the knowledge of Him as the covenant Lord of His people (v. 3), the God who is eternally and faithfully good in His covenant love and loyalty (v. 5). How does the person and work of Jesus Christ reveal these things about God? How does the gospel of Christ fuel the kind of worship this psalm commands?

Chapter 101

1. When we reflect upon God's perfections, we can only be profoundly grateful that He is the God He is, worthy of our sacred songs and worthy of our sanctified lives. To that end it is good for us to have resolution and purpose of heart to behave in a way that is above and beyond reproach, testifying to the power of His grace. How can we live in such a way that we avoid temptations as much as possible, avoid association with those who would lead us astray, and use whatever authority we have to oppose sin?

2. This has been called "the householder's psalm" for its resolutions to live with integrity in the home and to exercise authority righteously. As such it has application to every head of household. However, it applies yet more directly to the resolution of the king of Israel to live a righteous life and govern a righteous kingdom. It is fulfilled in the perfect purity of Jesus Christ, His kingdom, and the coming judgment. How can Christ's absolute resolve to be the righteous king of His people give believers hope and comfort? How is it a dire warning to those who continue unrepentant in sin?

Chapter 102

Trouble drives many onto the rocks of unbelief but it drives true believers into the harbor of God's presence. In the worst of times it is best to draw near to Him in prayer. Whatever happens to us in life, there should be no place for despair. In our hearts there should spring up the grace of hope, which assures us that beyond the gloomy present is a bright and glorious future. God's kingdom will fill the world and all nations will join God's worshipers. How can we know this with certainty? The hope of the Christian rests upon God's unchanging nature. He is always the same God, and therefore we know that He will do what He promised to do in Jesus Christ. Christ is the unchanging Lord, and so believers can know that He will never abandon them (Heb. 13:5, 8). How can we find contentment in Christ even as we groan?

Chapter 103

1. How richly and abundantly God has blessed His people. We are prone to forget the good things He has lavished upon us and therefore we need to reflect and recall the wonderful blessings He has given. We need to engage in holy argument with ourselves to stir up our hearts to praise the Lord. What does this psalm teach us about the reasons why we should praise God?

2. The wonder and infinite glory of God's love and forgiveness shine brightly in the death of His Son. Nothing could communicate the heights of God's love for sinners more than the words, "For God so loved the world, that he gave his only begotten Son" (John 3:16). Nothing could make God's forgiveness more secure or complete than the fact that God placed all the sins of His people upon His Son and punished those sins there (Isa. 53:5–6).

Chapter 104

This psalm describes the divine works of creation and providence. In fact, it is like a poetic version of Genesis 1. A true, biblical understanding of creation moves us to admire and adore God's attributes of power, wisdom, and love. Failure to maintain the doctrine of creation diminishes God's glory.

In our thoughts, we should rise from creation to the Creator and meditate often upon Him. We shall find our meditation to be a sweet antidote to all the trouble and cares of life. We should also rejoice in the daily demonstrations of God's providential care for what He has created. Yet as great as God's creations are, the Lord is far greater. Spend time even now worshiping the triune God alone, honoring the Father, the Son, and the Holy Spirit far above even the angels.

Chapter 105

1. Thinking about God's mighty works in the past is a good way to fuel faith and generate praise. Biblical history is not just a list of facts and dates, but a testimony to God's faithfulness, to His covenant, and to His power to keep His promises. Knowing that His Word cannot fail is a great comfort to believers in life and death and gives them ample reason to praise the Lord. How can the history of God's people encourage us to seek the Lord, His strength, and His presence?

2. God still keeps His covenant with Abraham today, for Jesus Christ is the blessed seed of Abraham (Matt. 1:1; Gal. 3:16). Those who are joined to Christ by a living faith, the spiritual offspring of Abraham, are also heirs of the promise (Rom. 4:16; Gal. 3:29). The Lord's mighty acts in judging Egypt, bringing out His people, and preserving them in the wilderness prepared the way for Christ's coming in the flesh and foreshadowed the power by which King Jesus saves His people through the gospel and ultimately in His glorious coming. How is Old Testament history a book of comfort for Christians?

Chapter 106

1. This psalm teaches again how important it is to remember the past as a guide for the present. The history of Israel's sins against the Lord is not an occasion to despise the Jews, but to consider the corruption within us all, to go beyond external religion to real union with Christ, to recognize how easily we can fall, and to flee from lust and idolatry (1 Cor. 10:1–14). Miracles, great acts of salvation from earthly troubles, the presence of godly prophets to declare God's Word, and painful defeats from God's hand of discipline should have turned Israel back to God, but the wickedness of fallen mankind is too deep for external means to root it out. Our only hope for salvation is God's love and faithfulness to His covenant. Seeing our sinfulness reflected in the history of Israel should move us to pray, "Save us, O LORD our God" (Ps. 106:47). Then His salvation will move us to praise Him forever for His goodness and mercy. How could you use this psalm to prove that people cannot save themselves?

2. What do we need from God to avoid repeating Israel's history in our own lives? God must provide a spiritual salvation beginning with the gift of faith (v. 24), not a superficial belief that passes away (vv. 12–13), but an enduring trust that produces a lifelong practice of justice and righteousness (v. 3). Rather than forgetting God (vv. 13, 21), sinners need God to give them an experiential knowledge of Him. Furthermore, to atone for their sins God must provide them with an eternal righteousness through an intercessor greater than Moses (v. 23) or Phinehas (vv. 30–31). Jesus Christ turned aside God's wrath by receiving God's judgment upon Himself (Gal. 3:13). The Spirit of Jesus Christ works faith (1 Cor.

12:3). The only hope for the human race is Christ, the one Mediator of the triune God. Have you known God's gifts of salvation and intercession as your own? If so, you can "come boldly unto the throne of grace" (Heb. 4:16).

Chapter 107

1. If we are redeemed, we should be willing and eager to say so, telling others about the Savior. Whenever God acts for our deliverance and displays His covenant love, it is that we might praise His name. We must therefore learn to never neglect this, for it is our duty and delight. Whenever God answers our prayers or saves us from the consequences of our sins, let us give Him public thanks for His amazing grace and power. However, it requires wisdom and watchfulness to observe God's goodness at work, or we will take it for granted in our self-righteousness and pass it by without a word. How can we develop an attitude of watchfulness for mercies and a quickness to praise the Lord?

2. Mercy and goodness flow to sinners through Jesus Christ. He is the only Mediator between God and sinners. He is the Redeemer who has delivered men from their fearful bondage to sin and its horrifying consequences in the wrath of God. Therefore, give thanks and praise to God *for* Christ and *through* Christ.

Chapter 108

1. Having a heart that is fixed and steadfast is important, for "a double minded man is unstable in all his ways" (James 1:8). Having our hearts focused on the Lord and being sensitive to all His faithfulness are the means of having such a

fixed mind. Follow David's pattern by being quick to praise God for His goodness and to pray for His renewed help daily. What makes it hard to fix your heart on God? How can you overcome these distractions?

2. The salvation of God's beloved leads to His praises among the nations and the demonstration of His sovereignty over all peoples. This took place supremely when God conquered Satan through the death and resurrection of Jesus Christ, exalted Christ to the highest place, and initiated the mission of evangelizing the world. The success of this mission depends upon the past victory of God's Son, and the present assistance of the Holy Spirit. "Through God we shall do valiantly" (v. 13). How can the Holy Spirit's work in your life lead to God being glorified and praised?

Chapter 109

1. This is one of the outstanding imprecatory psalms where the psalmist prays for God's direct judgment on the enemy who is hostile to the operations of God's purposes and kingdom. It is not a prayer for personal vengeance but for the advancing of God's cause through His judgment upon those who refuse to repent of sin. Pray for God to turn your enemies from their sins (Matt. 5:44), but then also pray for God to punish those who persecute the church and refuse to repent (Rev. 6:10).

2. The righteousness of this kind of prayer is confirmed by its direct application to Judas who betrayed Christ (Acts 1:20). Christ was surrounded by enemies who hated Him without cause (Matt. 26:60; John 15:18, 25). Judas's betrayal of Christ into their hands was decreed by God and foretold

in Scripture (John 17:12; cf. 41:9; 55:12–14, 21; 69:4), but Christ still held him responsible and pronounced God's "woe" upon him (Matt. 26:24). God inflicted severe punishment on Judas, who died in suicidal despair and utter humiliation (Matt. 27:3–5). It should be a warning to all enemies of God's kingdom and Christ's church that God will hear the cries of His people and will judge their enemies. How can this hope release Christians from taking revenge?

Chapter 110

1. Our Savior reigns. Jesus is Lord of all. He wields the scepter of His Word across the world and we are either made His subjects or we remain His enemies. Those who claim to be Christ's should be distinguished by true holiness. The power of Christ's Spirit causes His true people to willingly offer themselves to Him as living sacrifices. Those who persist in rebellion against Him will be smashed when He returns to destroy the kingdom of Satan. Are you in submission to King Jesus? Do you obey Him from the heart?

2. Not only should we yield to Christ's sovereignty, but we should submit to His priesthood. We do this by trusting in the sacrifice that He offered and by relying on His intercession that He conducts in His session at God's right hand. We have all sinned against this great King, and therefore need His priestly forgiveness and grace. Do you trust in Christ alone to save you from the guilt and punishment of your sins against God?

Chapter 111

1. In worship, it is of paramount importance that our hearts be engaged, right, and true. It is also most essential that we take our places in congregations of faithful people who embrace sound doctrine. Corporate worship is God's design for His church. The Sabbath is especially well suited for us to meditate on the divine works, both of creation and of redemption. There is so much to discover in them that will fill our souls with wonder and joy. The fear of God is a grace that today is conspicuous by its absence in so much of modern worship. In church, we should not tolerate anything worldly, casual, or flippant. How can we encourage an awe of our God?

2. The themes of this psalm point to the Son of God: His glory, righteousness, mighty works, faithfulness to His covenant, and redemption of sinners. God intends for His people to think much about the work of Jesus Christ. Those who love the works of our Lord will delight to meditate on them. Therefore, Christian worship revolves around engaging our thoughts and feelings with the doctrines of the gospel. How are you privately meditating on Christ's work so as to grow in your understanding, faith, love, joy, and peace? How are you doing this in public worship?

Chapter 112

1. Note the contrast between "feareth the LORD" (v. 1) and "shall not be afraid" (v. 7). Everyone fears something. What we fear is what we are most conscious of and allow to dictate our attitudes and actions—whatever is biggest in our hearts and dominates our lives. The fear of God and the fear of man or things are mutually exclusive. If the consciousness

of God is our predominant mindset and we factor Him into all the situations that surround us, we will know blessedness indeed. In essence this is what it is to walk by faith and not sight. How can we learn to live as those convinced that the One we cannot see with the physical eye is more real than what we see around us?

2. This psalm gives us a beautiful picture of Jesus Christ. In His human nature, the Son of God fears the Lord (Isa. 11:2; Heb. 5:7) and delights in His commandments (40:8; John 4:34). He is gracious, compassionate, and righteous (Isa. 53:11; Luke 7:13; John 1:14). He is glad to dispense His riches to poor sinners (Rom. 10:12; 2 Cor. 8:9). Therefore, Jesus is the most blessed of men (Ps. 21:6) and exalted to the right hand of God (110:1). His blessings overflow to His spiritual family (22:30; Isa. 53:10; Gal. 3:29), and though the wicked rage they shall perish under His wrath (Ps. 2:1, 12).

Chapter 113

Exalted in majesty, God has to stoop to consider the angels and the sun, moon, and stars, yet He actually reaches down to lowly men and women to deliver them from their fallen state and place them among the princes of His people. The Son of God is infinitely glorious, equal to the Father in His deity, and yet He lowered Himself by taking on a human nature so that He could lift up poor sinners into glory and bring outsiders into the family of God. Now this is grace: love to the loveless, the unlovely, and the unlovable, to give to them inconceivable privilege and dignity. If you have experienced His grace, then you have cause to say "Hallelujah" every day. For what mercies should you bless the Lord today?

Chapter 114

1. God has power to turn obstacles into blessings for His people, even in the most unexpected ways. Egypt was the most powerful nation on earth, but it was nothing before God. Man exerts massive efforts to control the least part of the seas, rivers, and mountains, but the Creator so easily manipulates them. Rocks are dry and lifeless but God can transform them into life-giving fountains. God can turn obstacles into stepping-stones. How can this encourage us to rely upon God the next time we find ourselves in a seemingly hopeless situation?

2. The redemption of Israel from Egypt was a shadow of Christ's spiritual redemption of His chosen people of all nations from sin, Satan, and hell (Luke 1:68, 73–74; 1 Cor. 5:7). The greatest obstacles to our happiness—sin, death, and divine judgment—became the means of our salvation when sinners killed Christ and He died under the curse of God for our sins. What can we learn from this when our own spiritual condition seems hopeless? How have you turned to the Lord in trust? How have you experienced His grace that is greater than any obstacle?

Chapter 115

1. Ironically, just as genuine believers are to be conformed to the image of the Lord, the unregenerate resemble the gods of their own making and imagination (v. 8). Sinners may look impressive outwardly (v. 4), but they have no spiritual mouths to cry out for His grace or confess His praises (vv. 5, 7), no spiritual senses to experience the beauty of God in Christ (vv. 5–6), no spiritual hands to offer Him worship

(v. 7), and no spiritual feet to walk with Him in faith and obedience (v. 7). They are as spiritually dead as the wood or stone they worship (Eph. 2:1), utterly incapable of pleasing God (Ps. 14:1–3; Rom. 8:6–8; 2 Cor. 4:4). Ultimately God will also remove all their natural abilities as well, leaving them powerless and hollow as vessels for everlasting fire. Therefore flee idolatry and fervently pray for Christ to save you from its soul-killing influences.

2. The hinge upon which true worship turns is faith. Idolaters are like their idols because they trust in them (v. 8). Salvation is by faith in the Lord (vv. 9–11). This also suggests that if we trust in the Lord alone for salvation, we will become like Him (112:4). Why would exercising trust in Christ make you more like God?

Chapter 116

1. Such is the blessing of salvation, in this life and in the next, that our praises and thanksgivings should never ever cease. True believers feel that it is just impossible to tell the Lord how much they appreciate His lovingkindness and tender mercies. They will need eternity to tell Him what they feel and how much they love Him. However, the greatest way they express their gratitude is by drinking deeply of the joys of His salvation and praying for yet more grace (vv. 12–13). God is glorified not by receiving (as if we could give Him anything) but by giving all (1 Chron. 29:10–16). How does that encourage us to pray great prayers?

2. No one loves the Father more than the Son (John 14:31), and no one has had a more earnest and effective prayer life than Christ (John 11:41–42; Heb. 5:7). He entered fully

into the sorrows of death, but was raised up and entered His heavenly rest. Today He drinks from the cup of salvation and intercedes for all His redeemed to enter into His glory. He will never fail to keep His commitments to the Father, whose will is for Christ to bring everyone given to Him by the Father to resurrection glory (John 6:37–40). How does this psalm show us the joys that belong to Jesus Christ?

Chapter 117

God is not the God of the Jews only but also of the Gentiles. His love extends to the world, His covenant provides for all nations, and His redemption is effective for sinners everywhere. Christ came to draw people of all nations to worship God for His saving grace. The church must therefore be committed to world missions. Our meditations on Christ and praises to the Savior should be mingled with fervent prayers for the success of the gospel in all nations. How are you regularly praying for missions in your private or family devotions? How can you do so more?

Chapter 118

1. One of our greatest comforts is knowing that the Lord is on our side and taking part with those who help us. There is no reason to fear anyone or anything because, with the Lord at our sides, we shall be kept both strong and safe. Paul summed it well: "If God be for us, who can be against us?" (Rom. 8:31). How can a person know that God is on his side? How can that knowledge give him hope and boldness?

2. Long before Jesus came to Jerusalem on His last Passover, God had revealed that the Christ would be rejected by the

leaders of His people, but would be exalted by God in an amazing way to become the foundation for the church. This calls for two responses. First, we must pray, "Hosanna," not just with our lips like the crowds on Palm Sunday, but with hearts crying out for the Lord to save us from our sins. Second, we must rejoice in Christ's coming to be the sacrifice for sins (v. 27), and His resurrection and ascension to heaven (v. 22). God's faithful love will last forever for those in union with Jesus Christ. How can you incorporate these practices and heart attitudes into your life?

Chapter 119

1. This psalm, as an Alphabetical Psalm, was evidently meant to be laid up in the memory and heart. God's Word is a great treasure and it is good not only to meditate on, but also to commit to memory (v. 11), so that, in a time of need, it can be readily recalled. Since in nearly every verse God is addressed, we are reminded that along with reading the Bible we need to pray. Our prayer should be that God, by His Holy Spirit, will reveal wonderful things to us, so that we derive from Scripture great and lasting profit. Although believers pass through many changes in this life, it is important to realize that God's written Word is settled and remains forever the same. To our great comfort, it is truth unchanged and unchanging. What is one verse in this psalm that especially comforts or challenges you? How can you make it a prayer?

2. The psalmist wrote of himself more than a dozen times here as "thy servant." The great Servant of the Lord is His Son (Isa. 42:1). The Lord Jesus loved God's Word (Ps. 40:6–8; Isa. 50:5; Matt. 5:17–18; John 10:35; 17:8, 17), for

He is God's eternal Word (John 1:1). Just as the fullness of this psalm reflects the fullness and completeness of the Holy Scriptures, so Christ is the fullness of God in bodily form, and in Him we are complete (Col. 2:9–10). Always read the Bible with this desire and prayer: "Father, open my eyes by Thy Spirit that I might see the glories of Thy Son."

3. In all but a few of the 176 verses of this psalm, reference is made to words like law, testimonies, ways, precepts, statutes, commandments, judgments, and word. Most of these words refer directly or indirectly to God's law. Why does the psalmist have such deep respect and love for God's law? Should we have that same love for God's law today? Why or why not? How should a Christian use God's law today?

Chapter 120

1. There is a sense in which all Christians live in Meshech and Kedar as the world is no friend to grace or to God. It is easy to feel out of place in a world where values are the opposite of truth. God, the gift of salvation, the hope of eternal life, and our obedience to God's laws receive mockery. But we should expect this because although we are in the world we are not of it (John 17:14). What example can we follow (Ps. 120:1–2) when we find ourselves opposed?

2. Christ came unto His own, but they did not receive Him (John 1:11). Exposed to malice and cruelty, our Lord felt isolated and rejected even among those who should have welcomed Him (Matt. 12:39; Luke 17:25; John 8:23; 15:23–25). He spoke a gospel of peace purchased by His blood (Luke 7:50; 10:5; John 14:27; 20:19–21, 26). Nevertheless, His words brought division and conflict with sinners

(Matt. 10:34–38). What does this teach us to expect if we follow Him?

Chapter 121

One of our greatest comforts is to know that God always acts as the guardian of believers, so that even in the greatest trouble they have no reason to fear. Faith assures the Christian that all will be well. God is always there for us, never asleep, always vigilant, and without fatigue. He will never fail and therefore we shall never fall. If believers in ancient times could cling to this promise, how much more should we who trust in the incarnate Lord Jesus? If God did not spare His Son but gave Him up for all His elect, then surely He is totally for them and will work all things to their good and ultimate glory in Christ (Rom. 8:28–32). When do you feel most in need of this assurance? How can you use this psalm to find peace in those times?

Chapter 122

1. Going to God's house is an occasion for joy. As that was true in the Old Testament economy, so should it be true today. Corporate worship in the visible and local church should be the delight of every Christian. To experience fellowship with those of like precious faith and to join in praise and worship of the Lord should be the highlight of the week as the church gathers on the Lord's Day. Love for the church should also motivate prayer for it (v. 6). Do you prepare for the Lord's Day with prayer, delight, and expectation? How can you make a habit of doing this?

2. The joy of public worship revolves around the presence of God. For Israel this was the temple and throne of David and his sons. For Christians, this is the Lord Jesus Christ, reigning through His Word and Spirit. Our joy in worship comes from exercising faith in the gospel of Jesus Christ by the power of the Holy Spirit (Rom. 15:8–13). When you engage in worship with the church, are you drawing near to the Father by faith in Christ in the power of the Spirit? How can you tell?

Chapter 123

One of the most difficult trials in the world is to face disrespect and contempt for following Christ. We inherently sense that doing right should bring honor, yet this corrupt world turns things upside down. The unfairness of it grinds against our consciences, especially when our mockers are at ease in their pride and success. The scorn of the world is one of Satan's great weapons to turn people back from godliness and to weary and embitter the faithful. What are we to do? This psalm teaches us that we must take the posture of servants before our Lord, fixing our eyes upon His sovereign grace, expecting His provision and vindication, and yet submissively waiting on His timing because He is the Master. Christ carried the cross before He entered His glory, and we must follow Him. What practical steps can we take to fix our eyes upon Jesus (Heb. 12:2) when we experience trials?

Chapter 124

Apart from divine support, the church of Christ would quickly fall before its raging enemies. They would devour believers like ravenous lions, wipe them out like a tsunami wave, and catch them like a professional trapper in the woods. The only reason the people of God continue in this world is the almighty power of their Savior. His strength is more than sufficient. Believers can revel in the promise of Christ, "I will build my church; and the gates of hell shall not prevail against it" (Matt. 16:18), for all authority in heaven and earth belong to Him (Matt. 28:18). How does the world threaten to destroy the church today? How does it comfort you to say, "Our help is in the name of the LORD, who made heaven and earth" (Ps. 124:8)?

Chapter 125

Whether we need protection against an evil that we fear, or provision of some good that we desire, the Lord is sufficient for all our needs. His power and righteousness surround His people like impassable mountains. He will give peace to those whose hearts trust in Him and do good. However, those who live in sin will be led away to destruction. How can this psalm help Christians when their lives are shaken by difficulties? How can it help people who are tempted to run to sin or worldly security when trouble threatens?

Chapter 126

Many are the tears of God's children, but God promises them that their mouths will be filled with laughter. This is gospel optimism, for Christ has taken the curse of sin and won the promised blessing (Gal. 3:13–14). Whenever the Lord has done great things for us, we should praise Him for the glory of His grace. One day all our sowing will come back in the harvest, and we will shout for joy. How can we cultivate an optimistic view of life that is based upon God and the gospel?

Chapter 127

1. This psalm calls for a balance between hard work and trusting God. Both are essential. Work without trust is self-sufficiency; trust without work is presumption. As Christians, we must recognize that nothing in life can succeed, whether business or family, without the Lord. Trusting God does not make the believer passive or inactive. On the contrary it should make him faithful, diligent, and hopeful in his calling, believing that the will to work as well as our abilities, opportunities, and successes are gifts of God. In which direction are you tempted to become unbalanced? What can you do to help keep the balance in focus?

2. If manual labor and physical procreation cannot succeed without the Lord, how much more do we need His grace to build the living house of the Lord, construct the city of God, and multiply the family of God! Apart from Christ we can do nothing (John 15:5). What reasons can you give why Christian service requires both prayer and work?

Chapter 128

Strange as it is to this unbelieving world, those who fear God are genuinely happy people. This fear of God will lead us in the right and best way, and it will bring upon us the favor and great goodness of God. In many ways, the home is where the sincerity and reality of true religion should be the most evident. In fact, the home becomes an index to how real our fear of the Lord is. Yet this psalm is not limited to domestic families. Christ never married or had physical children, yet He experienced God's blessing in the deepest way. In union with Christ, single people, childless people, and all kinds of people can enjoy deep happiness and fruitfulness in the family of God. Why does the fear of God bring blessing and make us a blessing to others?

Chapter 129

Suffering is the believer's lot in this world. Sometimes it cuts us deeply. Yet in the most grievous times, know that the Lord is righteous. He will release believers from the power of the wicked and cause sinners to wither and forfeit their blessings. Christ knows this: the Roman soldiers truly plowed His back with horrible wounds (Isa. 50:6; 53:5; Matt. 27:26; John 19:1). Yet in it all God was righteous, carrying out His plan for the salvation of His church, the exaltation of His Son, and the destruction of His enemies. Therefore we can trust the Lord in many afflictions. What afflictions are you or your loved ones enduring? How can this psalm help?

Chapter 130

1. Affliction and guilt can bring men very low indeed, but in the worst of depths sinners must not abandon themselves to despair. They should pray with great earnestness to the One who alone can rescue them. They must acknowledge that they cannot stand before God on their own merits. They must look to God as the God who forgives sin through Christ. They must rest their hope entirely in Him. What about you? Do you think you can stand before God on your own? He knows all your sins. Do you fear your sins are too

great? God's salvation is abundant. Do you think your sins are too many or you have sinned too long? God will save His people from all their guilt.

2. The great means by which God saves the guilty sinner is the redemption in Christ Jesus. Christ paid the ransom to satisfy God's justice. Sinners need not suffer for their sins because Christ suffered and died in the place of sinners (1 Cor. 15:3). Faith focuses its hope and desire upon Jesus Christ. He is the only Mediator between God and men, for He gave Himself as "a ransom for all" (1 Tim. 2:5–6). Do you trust in Christ alone for salvation from sin? If so, then how has your faith evidenced itself in a childlike fear of the Lord?

Chapter 131

Pride causes great trouble, but humility brings right thinking, speaking, and living. It is a grace most pleasing to God. True humility expresses itself in confident reliance on the Lord. It releases a person from the strife of arrogance and personal ambition. It quiets the heart with contentment to live near to God. It makes us like Christ, who did not use His equality with the Father for selfish pursuits, but became a humble and crucified servant to obey His Father (Phil. 2:5–8). Yet He counted it His food to do His Father's will (John 4:34), living in joyful hope (Heb. 12:2). Why is humility so essential to peace and hope?

Chapter 132

David's resolution to establish a place for God's holy presence (vv. 4–5) reminds us that one great purpose of God's king is to build God's temple. Nothing is more important to the kingdom of God than worshiping the Lord. His presence with His people is their joy and His glory. Jesus Christ is the anointed Son of David and the fulfillment of these promises (Acts 2:29–30). He was born in Bethlehem Ephratah (Mic. 5:2). He declared, "I will build my church" (Matt. 16:18). Christ is Lord of heaven and earth, and in Him the presence of God is coming to all nations (Matt. 28:18–20). God's worshipers no longer gather around a physical location, but worship God through Christ in the Holy Spirit regardless of where they meet for public worship, for they are the temple of the living God (John 4:21–24; Eph. 2:18–22). How does God's covenant with David encourage us to pray, "Thy kingdom come"? How does it help us understand what we are asking for in those words?

Chapter 133

1. Unity, based on truth, is most desirable. It is to God's glory and His people's good, and therefore we must never do anything to produce discord or division. Since the Holy Spirit is the source of love and peace, we must constantly pray to be filled with the Spirit, and the whole church needs to pray for further outpourings of the Spirit. Is this a petition in your daily prayers? Is it a petition regularly heard in your prayer meetings?

2. Just as the unity of Israel was compared to the anointing oil that flowed from Aaron's head down to his garments, so the spiritual unity of the church consists of the Holy Spirit who anointed Christ and now overflows to every member of His body (1 Cor. 12:12–13). Our unity is found not by ignoring doctrine, but in knowing and trusting Jesus Christ (Eph.

4:13). He is our great High Priest, and our worship revolves around drawing near to God through Him and confessing our hope in Him (Heb. 10:19–22). How does making Christ the center of our worship promote unity in the church?

Chapter 134

1. Very special attention should be given to public worship since man's chief end is to glorify and enjoy God. Just how much do we love God's house and how devoted are we to Sabbath worship? Tiredness can sometimes hinder us in worship, but it should never be an excuse to leave it off altogether. Godly priests saw it as their duty to worship even at night, and we do well to be as zealous and keen as they were.

2. Just as the priests led Israel's praise and declared God's blessing upon the people (Lev. 9:22; Num. 6:22–27), so the Lord Christ, our great High Priest, leads the spiritual Israel to praise God and receive His blessings (Luke 24:50; Rom. 15:8–13; Heb. 2:11–13). As the King reigning in the heavenly Zion, Christ applies God's blessing to His people. In practical terms, how can Christians bless God *through Christ* and receive God's blessing *through Christ* when they meet for worship?

Chapter 135

1. God is good and the source of all the good we enjoy. He is also great and able to do anything and everything for His people. Therefore He is most worthy of our praise. The psalmist praises God for His election, redemption, and preservation. Praise must go forth from the church to the world that men might come to know and fear the Lord, turning

from their idols to the true God. It is solemn to reflect on the fact that the matter and manner of our praise are means of instructing unbelievers. Does our worship impress men with God's greatness, sovereignty, and holiness, or is it mere entertainment to soothe the worshipers?

2. The promise that God will judge His people (v. 14) is a fearful warning to those who profess faith in Jesus Christ but later turn away from Him forever (Heb. 10:29–31). They have known the true God but have chosen worthless idols, provoking God's eternal wrath. What reasons does this psalm give for why it is foolish to reject the Lord?

Chapter 136

1. This psalm provides a pattern for praising God's faithful love. It begins by reflecting on who God is both in His goodness and greatness (vv. 1–3). The psalmist enumerates His amazing works (v. 4) of creation (vv. 5–9), redemption (vv. 10–15), and leading His people to their inheritance (vv. 16–22). It concludes by considering the gracious and compassionate nature of His love to the lowly, and the breadth of His blessings (vv. 23–25). Why is it good to praise God with songs that recount His great works in history and highlight His attributes?

2. The refrain repeated in every verse implies that all God does throughout the world is soaked in His faithful love. Yet the focus of the psalm is upon the salvation of Israel, which is a type of salvation through Christ. In Him the love of God comes to its grandest expression and accomplishes its eternal purpose toward His elect people. What reasons from

God's work in your own life motivate you to say to God, "Thy mercy endureth forever"?

Chapter 137

1. Sin brings inevitable consequences. Vengeance is the Lord's. Though the enemies of God's people may mock their sufferings, one day the Lord will bring back on the wicked what they have done. Even as believers may weep over the persecuted church, they can also rejoice that Christ is coming and will make all things right. How can this hope enable us to wait patiently and not take personal revenge?
2. When God finally deals with sinners on judgment day, it will mean far worse than anything written here, for the Lord will banish them from all enjoyment of His goodness into the everlasting fires of hell. The Lord does not take lightly the persecution of His children. If you have harmed or mocked believers in Jesus Christ, repent quickly before it is too late. Pray for others who have fallen into this sin.

Chapter 138

1. Christians must not fear to confess Christ before the world and give praise to God in the presence of great men and women (Matt. 10:18, 26, 32–33). Though the rich, powerful, and celebrities of the world may be regarded as gods, they will die like all other men (Ps. 82:6–7). They need to hear of the glories of the only true God, so that they can be saved and give Him the praise that He deserves. Is there anyone whom you find it very hard to speak to about the Lord? Why is this? How can you overcome that fear?

2. God has chosen to invest His glory in His Word, not to make the Bible into God, but so that people will honor the Lord in the way they honor His Word. A mark of true conversion is receiving the Holy Scriptures not as the word of men, but as the powerful and authoritative Word of God (1 Thess. 2:13). How should this affect our attitude when we hear the preaching of God's Word? How should this affect the way that preachers study and proclaim the Word?

Chapter 139

1. This psalm is a wonderful example of the connection between theology and life. Doctrine should impact our hearts and affect the way that we live. Believing that God sees and knows everything comforts us because He therefore knows our needs and can supply them. However, this same truth challenges us, for nothing escapes His glance, not even our secret sins. Therefore we should be careful, walking in the fear of God. Here is the sum. Since God is omniscient, He knows me personally and is with me constantly. Since God is the Creator, He owns me completely. Since God is righteous, He demands my loyalty. Learn to factor God into all of life. Pick one of God's attributes mentioned in this psalm. What difference should it make in your life today?

2. Before Christ left to ascend into heaven, He sent His church to make disciples of all nations, and He promised, "I am with you alway, even unto the end of the world" (Matt. 28:20). Knowing that Christ is with us, indeed that His special presence is promised to every gathering of the true church (Matt. 18:20), is a great comfort as we do His work in the world. How could that encourage people to move to

other locations, even to other nations, in order to advance the kingdom of God there?

Chapter 140

1. Given that we live in a world where Satan is very active, we should at all times be vigilant. Believers cannot do without God for a single day, for only He can keep us in the evil day when we feel particularly under attack. He alone is a sovereign Protector. It is the greatest of comforts to have God on our side, maintaining our cause. Since He does not change, nor ever will, we have confidence for the future, even for the eternal future. Instead of being cast down, we should abound in hope. Spiritual alertness and optimistic hope are key motives to a life of continual prayer. If we rarely pray for God to defend us against evil, what does that say about us?

2. The words of fallen man are full of secret poison (v. 3; Rom. 3:13). One of the earliest signs of human depravity is sinful speech (Ps. 58:3). Though many would deny it, Christ taught that our speech reveals our hearts, and God will judge our spiritual conditions in part by the patterns of our talk (Matt. 12:34–37). Examine how you talk to people, praying that God will reveal to you any pride, sexual lust, greed, sinful anger, hatred, and lying. How does the way we talk to each other show that we need Jesus Christ to save us from sin?

Chapter 141

1. Prayer is vital and must never be neglected, particularly in difficult times. The storms of life should always drive us into the harbor of God's presence. Notice what David asked God to give him: salvation from sin, accountability from godly

friends, rescue from the traps of the world, and judgment upon the wicked. How often do you pray for such things?

2. Comparing prayer to incense is most instructive and encouraging. The smoke arising from the altar would waft over the veil entering the inner sanctuary that represented the immediate presence of God. So it is that prayer is the earthly means whereby we may enter into God's presence. Prayer takes us as close to God as we can get this side of the veil in this life. The comparison of prayer to incense also reminds us that all our prayers depend upon the intercession of the High Priest, Jesus Christ. His intercessions fill the prayers of a believer with a delightful fragrance to God, for Christ obeyed God perfectly and paid for our sins completely. True prayer must always be offered to God by faith in Him. What confidence does it give you to know that Christ is interceding for you (Rom. 8:31–39)?

Chapter 142

In the worst of life's troubles, God is only a prayer away from us and, if we turn to Him, He will make known to us His power and comfort. Remember, God is a present help in times of trouble. It is a relief to realize that God knows our path and feels concern and sympathy for us in this state. Furthermore, knowing exactly where and how we are, He will draw near to help. Friends may let us down, but God will never fail those who trust in Him. Christ understands exactly how it feels to be alone (Matt. 26:31, 56), and in His sympathy He helps all who come to God through Him (Heb. 4:15–16). How will hoping in God's faithfulness to His covenant promises affect the attitude of our prayers?

Chapter 143

We pray with hands stretched out to heaven (v. 6) and souls lifted up to God (v. 8) because we are like beggars seeking everything from Him. As human beings who fell into sin with our first father, Adam, all our prayers are ultimately prayers for Christ, to whom the Father joins sinners when He calls them to faith in Him (1 Cor. 1:23–24, 30). We need wisdom from God, and so we must set our minds upon God's Word (Ps. 143:5) with prayers for Christ to be our *wisdom*. We need justification in God's sight and cannot obtain a righteous status by our own merit (v. 2), so we must pray for Christ to be our *righteousness*. We need to become obedient to God's will, so we must pray that Christ would be our *sanctification* through the Holy Spirit (v. 10). We pray for deliverance from enemies, persecutors, and death (vv. 3, 7, 9, 12), and Christ is our *redemption*. Of which of these do you most feel in need right now? How can you seek for what you need in Christ?

Chapter 144

1. Trust in the Lord goes hand in hand with a sense of how small and insignificant we are (vv. 2–4). When our hearts and mouths are full of boasts about ourselves, it is hard to sing God's praises with much interest. However, when we see ourselves as sinners quickly passing from this earth to face judgment, then we will count ourselves blessed only if the Lord is our God and we are in covenant relationship with Him through faith in Jesus Christ. How can meditating on the vanity of man (v. 4) help you to trust in the Lord and give all the glory to Him?

2. David, the divinely empowered warrior (v. 1), was a shadow and type of Christ. In an amazing act of condescension, the Son of God became a mortal man (v. 4). He placed Himself in a position of complete dependence upon the Father (v. 2), who amply supplied Him with the Spirit to overcome the Devil. Christ is the Servant of the Lord (v. 10). The Lord Jesus perfectly obeyed the law of God, winning the riches of glory promised to covenant keepers as Israel never could (vv. 12–15). Now His spiritual offspring inherit the blessings He deserves. Christ will tear open the skies and come down with fire and glory to destroy His enemies, save believers from their persecutors, and bring them into His blessing. Can you say with the church of Jesus Christ, "Happy is that people, whose God is the LORD" (v. 15)?

Chapter 145

1. Meditation upon God is vital to spiritual life, for as we comprehend more of God, the knowledge of Him will provide matter for more excellent praise. This psalm offers a lyrical catalog of God's attributes. In what verses do you find reference to the following attributes: greatness, incomprehensibility, power, majesty, fearsomeness, goodness, righteousness, grace, compassion, patience, faithful love, glory, kingdom, eternality, presence, and holiness? Focus on one of these. What does it mean? How has God displayed it through His works in Jesus Christ?

2. Singing praise is a means of instruction and edification. It is good for this generation to sing God's praise to the next; and therefore we should encourage little children to be present in the congregation. Let them know how His love for

us draws forth our love for Him and how we have learned to look to Him for all our needs. Then shall the prayer of the ages—"Hallowed be thy name"—be answered. What opportunities do you have to pass on the joy of worship to the next generation?

Chapter 146

Only believers know true happiness. The world thinks our religion is gloomy and miserable, but they could not be more mistaken. We are the happiest people. God is our God. He is the all-powerful Lord of all His creation. He is faithful to all His promises. He acts with justice and compassion for the oppressed. He loves those who walk in faith and obedience. His kingdom will never end. In every way, the Lord is the hope and joy of believers. For all His qualities belong to them and serve their good if they are joined to Jesus Christ by a living faith. As a result, their happiness is far deeper, more stable, and more satisfying than that of those who trust in man. One of the best ways for believers to enjoy their happiness and demonstrate it to the watching world is by praising the Lord. Do you have a habit of praising God? Why or why not? How can you develop a habit of praising Him as long as you live?

Chapter 147

1. If the Lord has blessed us, praise is the most suitable response; and the more blessed we feel, the more our hearts will well up with gratitude and the more we will want to find vent in greater praise. The Lord is looking after the whole world and since His people are more precious to Him than

everything else, we can be assured that He will take special care of us. Since His compassions are new every morning, what do you need to stop worrying about, and for what should you start trusting God?

2. The greatest gift from God is His Word. Even today many millions of peoples do not have access to the Scriptures in a language they can understand. Yet how precious is His Word. It is powerful, for it is the Word of He who rules all things. It is full of wisdom, for it is the Word of He who is infinite in understanding. It is a message of hope and salvation, for it is the Word of the compassionate and merciful God. If you have a Bible that you can read in your own language, then thank God for it, read it daily, attend the worship service of a church where it is faithfully preached, and pray that God would use you to help others to receive this invaluable gift of God's Word.

Chapter 148

1. All creation praises God and testifies to His glory, from the mightiest angel to the smallest bird. How much more should mankind, the apex of creation, praise Him! Even more so, His redeemed people ought to praise His name. Let us seek to excel in this most excellent work. Praise should be integral to both private and public worship. When in private prayer, begin with praise and not with a list of your needs and requests. In the worship of God's house, make a joyful noise. We should never be at a loss in the praise of His name. Are you eager to praise the Lord?

2. A fundamental belief of Christianity is the absolute distinction between the Creator and His creation. There are great differences among what God has created, whether

angels, stars, sea monsters, mountains, cattle, kings, or infants. However, they all fall into one category: those which were made by God and therefore should praise Him (v. 5). Worship belongs to God alone, for "his name alone is excellent; his glory is above the earth and heaven" (v. 13). On the one hand, this should impress us with a humbling realization that we exist for His glory. On the other hand, it shows us that Christ our Savior is God, for He is to be worshiped (Heb. 1:6; Rev. 5:8–14). How are we tempted to worship part of God's creation rather than the Creator?

Chapter 149

1. We find delight in people who already appear beautiful or honorable. It is a notable mark of God's grace that He delights to take the poor, humiliated, and ugly who trust in Him and make them lovely and glorious (v. 4). He is a King who does not take riches from His people, but joyfully gives to them. How does Christ beautify His people with the graces of justification, sanctification, and glorification? How should this motivate us to praise Him?

2. Zeal for God's praise motivates God's people to fight against all powers that oppose His kingdom (vv. 6–9). In the old covenant, this required physical violence to preserve the nation of Israel and bring God's judgments on the wicked (18:34–44; 101:5, 8; 144:1). Since Christ abolished Israel's earthly theocracy (Matt. 21:43) and established a heavenly and spiritual kingdom (John 18:36–37), this zeal expresses itself not in physical force but in sacrificial efforts to bring the Word of God to all nations (2 Cor. 10:3–6; Eph. 6:10–18; Heb. 4:12), until Christ returns to destroy His enemies (Rev. 19:15–21).

How does your praise of God translate into zealous action to spread His Word throughout the world? If you are not a preacher, how are you using your vocation for His glory and working with the church to fulfill the gospel mission?

Chapter 150

1. Song is an integral component of worship and should be offered to God with joy and reverence. The command that God be praised with an orchestra of instruments (vv. 3–5) reflects the old covenant economy of temple worship instituted by David, who appointed the Levites to serve as musicians (1 Chron. 15:16, 24). No such requirement is made in the new covenant, where God's sanctuary is not a building where a nation meets, but a people gathered in local congregations (1 Cor. 3:16; Eph. 2:21–22). The New Testament directs its instructions for worship at the hearts and voices of the people as they are moved by God's Spirit (Eph. 5:18–20). Just as the Levites played a variety of instruments in harmony, so God's people are diverse but worship in one Spirit through Christ (Eph. 2:18). How is your church like a spiritual orchestra, with each believer an instrument played by the Holy Spirit to praise the Father through the Son?

2. Our worship of God must revolve around His personal glory and amazing works (v. 2). This should shape the content of our songs, which should primarily focus upon the triune God and not our works or feelings. It should also direct the feeling with which we sing, for the glory of God should impress us with reverent fear and awe even as we rejoice in Him. There is no place for superficial lyrics, mindless repetition, or casual attitudes in the worship of God.

Pray for a heart to praise Him and for such a filling of the Holy Spirit that this sacred work will be performed in a way that truly glorifies God.

3. It is fitting that the Psalter ends with a climactic call to praise God (v. 6). The Psalms take us through the full range of human experiences, but they center upon the glory of the Lord. They recount the history of God's people from creation through the second coming of Christ in a way that constantly reminds us that all God does in Christ He does to the praise of His glory (Eph. 1:6, 12, 14). This is God's ultimate purpose for His creation. Have you embraced God's glory and praise as your ultimate purpose in life? If not, then your first act of worship must be to repent of your self-centeredness and idols, turn back to the living God, and trust in the Lord Jesus Christ to save you from your sins. If by grace God's glory has become your great aim, then devote yourself with all your might to living for His praise.

Proverbs

Chapter 1

1. God's inspired oracles are designed to give solid and precious instruction about things that relate to time and eternity. Therefore, they are to be studied and carefully observed by all groups of people, both mature adults and, even more so, young people. In youth, the physical and mental faculties are more quick and retentive, and the direction of one's life is being shaped. Hence, for those who want true wisdom, it is necessary to cultivate deep regard for God and for parental counsel, especially the teaching of godly, Christian parents. Do you seek the wisdom of more mature believers in your life?

2. One's relationship to Christ is a matter of eternal life and death because He is the Wisdom of God. This is a good opportunity to press home the gospel call to repent before it is too late. There is a point when judgment comes and repentance is no longer possible. The gospel call is urgent. If this message is missed, nothing else in Proverbs will matter. Why would it be a tragic mistake to try to live by the Proverbs without first receiving Christ to be your wisdom, righteousness, sanctification, and redemption from God?

Chapter 2

Your heart is where your treasure is (Matt. 6:21, 33). It is natural to expend effort and energy in the pursuit and enjoyment of what we treasure. That is how we ought to estimate the wisdom of fearing and knowing God. It is like digging for hidden treasure. One does not normally just stumble over treasure as he shuffles along. It requires diligent and sometime difficult digging, but finding the treasure is worth it (Job 28:1–11). So our reading and studying in God's Word should not be casual, but serious. The Lord is ready to bless those who sincerely and diligently seek His revealed will with great success, satisfaction, and protection. God's Word must rule our hearts as an antidote against the multitude of corrupt principles and lustful temptations. What practical actions will you take to seek God's wisdom like silver?

Chapter 3

1. How we keep the commandment to love our neighbors is an index to how we keep the greatest commandment to love the Lord. Therefore, we should prayerfully plan how to help those in need. In so doing, we are serving the cause of God. Let us use the finances and gifts that God has given to us for His glory. Be consistent and regular in this service. Trust in God's provision for your life and give, knowing you can never outgive God. To whom should you give assistance now?

2. Think about how you should respond to afflictions. Ask: "What can I learn from this chastening of the Lord?" The Hebrew word "chasten" is also translated "instruction" (8:33), "correction" (22:15), and "rebuke" (Hos. 5:2). Although the experience is not pleasant, it is for good and is evidence of God's love. As God so deals with His children, so should parents, in patiently instructing their children, tenderly reproving them, and at the last resort using the rod of punishment. What can parents learn from God's example of discipline?

Chapter 4

This chapter puts much emphasis on the heart, the place of feeling, thinking, and choosing what to do or not to do. We are to guard the heart above all else for it is the index to what we really are and the source of all our attitudes and actions. The best way to keep the heart is by seeking from the Lord Jesus that living water, the sanctifying Spirit from whom comes everlasting life. It is by His strength and wisdom that we are given help to put away rebellious words and attitudes, to keep our eyes from looking at vanity. In everything always look to the Lord and do not be sidetracked. What steps can you take to get wisdom and guard your heart?

Chapter 5

1. The chapter contains warnings about the dangers of temptation. So often when temptation comes there is no time to seek advice, but response must be immediate. It is important to remember what has been taught from God's Word to be able to use it when needed. The eyes and ears must be guarded to not allow lustful and tempting words to enter the mind and to stir the sexual passions for wrong things. Avoid the people and media that use sensual words and sexual provocations. Fill the mind rather with things that are virtuous (Phil. 4:8), and remember the great disgrace and pain that comes with giving yourself away to immorality. What are some lies commonly believed about immorality today? What is God's contrasting truth?

2. God's definition and purpose of marriage is radically different from worldly notions and norms. Marriage is the God-ordained means by which one man is to be united to

one woman. Marriage is itself a safeguard against sinful vices. Those united together, who honor the Lord and His Word, can truly enjoy one another. Husbands and wives should enjoy a mutual admiration and be intoxicated with each other's love. Do not merely strive against temptation. Labor and pray for your sexual desires to focus entirely on your spouse.

Chapter 6

1. The ant is a positive example to follow. Industry, entrepreneurship, and hard work are every person's wisdom and duty. As believers we should redeem our time and work effectively so that we will not be a burden to others and will be able to promote and use our income for the kingdom of God, which will not perish. In what areas of life are you called to diligence?

2. Proverbs again warns against sexual sin. The frequent warnings need to be heeded particularly in our day when temptations abound on every hand. Immorality and its many promoters and snares are seen all around us. It is a multi-million-dollar industry that grows by enticing both men and women. The entertainment industry is the greatest promoter of it in the world. Christians should use great caution as they use the world's media and should beware of relationships with people who flatter and attract them. Which temptations do you most need to guard against?

Chapter 7

This chapter gives good direction to avoid impurity. Keep the mind pure from any kind of media that generates fantasies or desires. Stay away from places where temptations are likely. Limit or break off relationships with flattering and enticing people. Avoid flattering and enticing others to win their affection and learn contentment in your calling. Focus on the future rather than on momentary experiences. The daily, careful intake of the Word of God, by searching its teachings, will be a key component for resisting temptation. View and discern the world and your life through the spectacle of the Scriptures. Occupy your time with righteous and good things. How can you use this chapter to guide you in your prayers for yourself and others that God would save you from sexual sin?

Chapter 8

1. In this chapter we have a remarkable revelation of the Son of God as Wisdom. Wisdom is God's eternal offspring, not just His attribute of wisdom but a divine person who is the living expression of divine wisdom, power, and righteousness. Wisdom exists in a relationship with God of mutual love and joyful cooperation in His greatest works, including the creation of the universe. Wisdom especially delighted in the creation of mankind. How does this beautiful picture we have here of God's only begotten Son help you to know and worship Him?

2. Though humanity rebelled against the Lord, this same Wisdom still communicates with fallen man, publicly proclaiming the fear of the Lord and calling people to a treasure more valuable than gold—the gift of life. In Jesus Christ, the person of Wisdom has come to us in the flesh. In order to be saved from eternal death, you must submit to Him and receive Him as the Wisdom of God. How should knowing

that Christ is God's living Wisdom affect how we listen to His teachings in the Bible?

Chapter 9

1. Wisdom's call to the banquet parallels Christ's parable in Luke 14:15–24. Many are invited, and many have excuses why they cannot attend. Ultimately, nothing is more important than being part of the feast prepared by Christ, the provision He has made for His people. No excuse is legitimate and the consequences for refusing to come are eternally severe. At which banquet are you dining, that of Wisdom or Folly? How do you know?

2. No one likes to be corrected or rebuked, but how one responds to legitimate criticism says a lot about his or her character. The contrasts in verses 8–9 are instructive. We should be open to criticism, receiving it for our welfare rather than responding in anger or in such a way as to turn the criticism to others. That is the way of wisdom. How do you respond to correction and criticism? How can you learn to respond better?

Chapter 10

1. Loving one another is a Christian grace that seeks to promote peace rather than strife (v. 12; 1 Cor. 13:6; 1 Peter 4:8). We must learn to bear with others in patience and seek to stir up love and harmony with those in the family, church, and society. Expressing that love requires control of the tongue. As Christians we should learn to use our speech to promote and foster life and help for others rather than stirring up contention or spreading slander. How do you use

your tongue? Does your speech give wisdom? Is it true? Does it do good to men?

2. It is part of godly wisdom to redeem our time and to use it appropriately. To slumber during the harvest time is foolish (v. 5). There is only so much time in life to accomplish the tasks that God has given us. Let us be productive, taking advantage of every opportunity the Lord has given to us to serve Him. How can you use your time better for the Lord?

Chapter 11

1. As God is just and fair in His dealings with us, the life of a true child of God should be marked by honesty, fairness, and faithfulness in business and relationships (v. 1). Be aware of the uncertain riches of this world, and do not be dazzled by their golden baits. In the hour of death, riches will not be the source of our comfort. Make it your daily resolution that by God's grace you will seek first the kingdom of God and His righteousness! How can keeping your eyes on the Lord protect you against dishonesty and injustice?

2. Whatever your status or position, live with integrity before God and man; then you will not be ashamed if your life is laid open before the world. When faced with critical decisions, call upon godly, serious, experienced people to give you counsel and advice (v. 14). Give to those in need and to the Lord's cause cheerfully and generously, as the Lord prospers you (vv. 24–26). Remember how the Father gave His Son, and His Son gave His life, and the Holy Spirit gives of Himself to His people's everlasting happiness, grace, mercy, pardon, and peace. How can you imitate God (Matt. 5:44–48)?

Chapter 12

1. We love what we value; our hearts are with our treasure (Matt. 6:21). The person who desires wisdom and abundant life values the Word and ordinances of God; he is thankful for any corrections and is patient and diligent in applying their truths. A wise man loves God's instruction and the knowledge that is gained from it. Knowing God is the most precious treasure we can have. What does the way *you* listen and speak reveal about *your* heart?

2. Beware of self-sufficiency and self-confidence, as they are the attitudes of the foolish. Those who are to make a difference and leave a good inheritance for the future are those who exercise diligence, modesty, prudence, constancy, and integrity, which are fueled by a saving relationship and love for God and His glory. The wise Christian does not make a show of his knowledge. How can your conduct lift up those who are dejected and give hope to those who wait upon the Lord?

Chapter 13

1. Disciplining children is never pleasant, neither for the parent nor the child, but it is an important part of raising children in the nurture and admonition of the Lord (Eph. 6:4). It shows the parent's genuine love for the child (Prov. 13:24). It teaches the vital truth that sin has consequences. It is an opportunity to point children to the gospel as the only means of avoiding sin's ultimate punishment. Discipline should not be administered with impatient anger but always lovingly and in self-control with a view to instructing children in behavior that pleases the Lord. Why is it an act of hatred *not* to discipline your children?

2. Remember that many contentions among people in families, churches, and nations are the result of pride in one or both of the parties (v. 10). Esteeming others more highly than we esteem ourselves (Phil. 2:3) will prevent a lot of quarreling and will imitate the humble spirit of the Lord Jesus (Phil. 2:5). Are you involved in a conflict? How should you humble yourself and fight against your pride?

Chapter 14

1. Whatever position you hold in your home (v. 11), seek to build others up in godliness. Do not seek worldly joys, which are neither solid nor lasting, but seek the joys of the Spirit, which are unmixed and everlasting. Backsliding from the Lord begins in the heart (v. 14); therefore, guard your heart through deep meditation and prayer, as well as sincere obedience. How are your heart attitudes toward the Lord demonstrated?

2. Be thankful for godly and righteous laws in your nation and those godly men and women who serve in the public sphere (vv. 34–35). Aim to support and encourage them. In what ways does your society honor justice and godliness, and in what ways do the laws and practices of your people offend God?

Chapter 15

1. A sanctified tongue is an important component of Christlikeness—conformity to Christ, the goal of predestination. Our communication can honor God or harm others. Ironically, words communicated in private often have greater power than those in public. Controlling and guarding the

tongue and using it well are no small matters in the cultivation of godliness. Weigh all things carefully and from God's viewpoint before you respond. Make sure that your responses are loving, being given gently for the benefit and building up of the hearers. It is a wicked and condemning thing to use our God-given tongues to cause damage or to speak idle words. How can you cultivate a habit of wise and self-controlled speech?

2. God is omniscient (vv. 3, 11), knowing everything, searching all our hearts, and seeing all our ways. We should aim to bring Him worship with a heart that is humble and right in His sight. God is also sovereign in His creating, sustaining, and planning all that goes on in the world. This knowledge should fill our hearts with worship and encourage us, since nothing is overlooked in our lives. To the unconverted, this truth should be humbling and produce dread, as they cannot hide from Him. Has this truth driven you to trust Him with a repentant heart? How can it be a source of encouragement in your daily life?

Chapter 16

1. The chapter begins and ends with God's sovereignty (vv. 1, 33). He is pleased to order the affairs of men; therefore, we must always live in full trust of His wisdom in ordering our ways and be comforted that even the mundane things of life are ordered by the Lord. Yet resting in God's sovereignty should not breed passivity. Seek the Lord and labor in all you do with the purpose of glorifying God, who will show you the way forward. There is nothing better or more satisfying than knowing what we want is what God wants for us. Have

you committed your plans and actions unto the Lord (v. 3) allowing Him to conform your will to His?

2. In contrast to so much of modern thought which glamorizes youth and modern efforts to delay the aging process, the Bible places a premium on the gray head of old age. Reaching old age should be regarded as evidence of God's favor and should be venerated by the young who, if the Lord so grants, will one day be old themselves. Godly elderly people have much to offer in way of warnings and advice. What ways have you found to honor the elderly and listen to their wisdom?

Chapter 17

1. Knowing that God searches our hearts ought to be a powerful motive for right thinking and behaving (v. 3; see Ps. 139). All things are naked and open before His eyes (Heb. 4:12–13) and each of us will give an account before Him. Can you stand before God with the confidence of David when God examines you knowing that you have purposed not to transgress (Ps. 17:3; 2 Cor. 5:21)?

2. God's law is a unity, and to refuse to love our neighbors is to reject God (v. 5). An offense against one commandment results in guilt for all of them (James 2:10). How we treat others is an index to how we really view God. Professing to love Him while at the same time mistreating others is evidence that our love for God is not in keeping with His demand. If we love Him as we ought, we will love and treat others as we should. Consider your relationships with people who are less powerful and prosperous than you are. How does the way you treat them reflect what you think about the Lord?

Chapter 18

1. There is a striking contrast between trusting in the Lord and trusting in wealth (vv. 10–11). Where one finds spiritual security and safety has eternal consequences. To trust the Lord is a certain and inviolable place of safety forever; to trust one's own resources is nothing more than a delusion (Ps. 49; Matt. 6:19–24). The object of faith always determines the value of faith, and the only infinitely valuable object is the Lord. What does it mean to run to the Lord as your strong tower instead of seeking security in wealth?

2. The advice given in verses 13, 15, and 17 is crucial and should be followed in all matters of dispute and controversy. It is common sense, but far too often ignored. Do not make any judgments until all the facts are known; factor in both sides of the story before taking sides. Jumping to conclusions is not only unwise, but it has the potential of doing great harm. Ask many questions before giving any answers. How are these manifestations of humility?

Chapter 19

1. We are to be tenderhearted and fair toward those who do not have the privileges and blessings that we enjoy (v. 17). Too often treatment of others is motivated by selfish concerns of what might be received in return. That kind of partiality does not reflect the kind of gospel love that God requires of His people (1 John 3:16–18). Our love for others should mirror our love for God and how God loves us. He treats us graciously in spite of our unworthiness. God is not a respecter of persons and neither should we be. Whom do

you know in financial difficulty? How can you show them love and respect?

2. There must be respect for all earthly authorities, as they are ordained of God and can do us much harm or good (v. 12; Rom. 13:1–5). However, we should not forget that ultimately Jesus Christ is the King of kings. We are to have the greatest respect, faith, and love for Him, and remember that the One who is called love is also the Judge of all the earth. He displays His wrath upon all His enemies like a roaring lion (Ps. 2:12; Amos 1:2; Rev. 5:5; 10:3). If we were to fear and honor Christ knowing that we are accountable to Him, then we and the society around us would live more soberly and godly under God's blessing.

Chapter 20

1. Our society is increasingly poisoning itself by excess, and one of the destructive and enticing excesses is the abuse of alcoholic beverages and other mind-altering drugs. We must take to heart the many warnings associated with wine and alcoholic drink, which can affect the emotions and can control our judgment in ways that lead to sin. Be aware of the entanglements of addiction that come with such intoxicating drinks. How might you be tempted to sin with regard to alcohol or drugs? How can you resist?

2. To know that our daily experiences are of the Lord must encourage our continual trust of Him and submission to His mysterious ways (v. 24). He will provide for all His people who follow Him. Think of your past and how you have been guided and carried through to this point in your life. Praise the One who has richly sustained you. Look to the future

glory that will follow those who have trusted and continue to live "looking unto Jesus the author and finisher of our faith" (Heb. 12:2). Walking by faith rather than by sight is the theme of much of Scripture and Christian experience. Though we may not fully understand the meaning of our lives, how can we build up our faith and trust in the God who rules over us?

Chapter 21

It is a source of great comfort to know that all the governments of earth are subject to God, who rules and manipulates them according to His purpose and pleasure (v. 1). Reasoning from the greater to lesser leads to the conclusion that the Lord governs everything else as well. Nothing can stand against His will (v. 30). Take comfort from this truth that all hearts and all the ways of men flow according to divine direction. This drives us to ask for greater and childlike faith in His dealings with us, and that we may not sin against Him by hardening ourselves against His providences. Trusting the Lord is always the wise thing to do. How can you grow in humility and fear before this sovereign Lord?

Chapter 22

1. Guard your character and name by a godly life (v. 1). Christians must be concerned for their reputations because their lives should mirror that of Christ. We should live in such a way that no reproach is brought to the name of Christ because of our sinful behavior. Just a little folly has the power to destroy a whole life of good (Eccl. 10:1). How does a person develop and protect a good reputation?

2. When rearing children in the nurture and admonition of the Lord, parents must be sensitive to a child's God-given traits and abilities (v. 6). They should dedicate their children to the kind of training that will do them good for life. At the core of all training must be the religious and spiritual education that will teach children the gospel and way of life that is pleasing to the Lord (1:7–9). It is that kind of life that will do them good both in this life and the life to come. Why is it important to craft child training to the individual and yet to teach all our children the common calling of fearing the Lord?

Chapter 23

1. In a society that increases in wealth and luxury, it is essential to cultivate godly contentment, to be thankful and satisfied with all that God has provided, and not to be lured by anyone or anything that seems to offer us greater advantages. Let us not "envy sinners" (v. 17), but live conscientiously in the fear of God all the day long, and wait "for the mercy of our Lord Jesus Christ unto eternal life" (Jude 21). Remember that when the end of your life comes, your expectation in God will fully be answered; you will find that true "godliness with contentment is great gain" (1 Tim. 6:6). How can we develop more self-control and contentment regarding our physical desires and possessions?

2. Listen to the warnings of Scripture against drunkenness and addiction, which destroy the body, harden the heart to spiritual things, and bring condemnation upon the soul. Instead of being filled with things that will take control of your life and lead to sin, fill your life with God's Word and Spirit so that you may joyfully give yourself to praise,

thanksgiving, submission to authority, and wise living (Eph. 5:15–21). How does your society attempt to make drunkenness or drug abuse acceptable and desirable? How does this chapter help us to see the truth?

Chapter 24

1. We should not desire the destruction of people, nor should we rejoice when our enemies fall (v. 17). Regardless of how we might have been treated by someone, we must not allow any emotion of revenge to rise and embitter us, for our Lord will see it and will be displeased by it. He is not pleased when His people have a malignant spirit. Christian love never rejoices at another's sin or calamity, but delights in mercy. What is the difference between desiring personal vengeance and desiring divine justice?

2. The overgrown and ruined state of the field of the slothful is a testimony to the foolishness of laziness (vv. 30–34). What is true in the physical realm applies as well to the spiritual. Far too often people neglect the care and cultivation of their hearts and spiritual lives. For many, all their faculties are thrown open to the delusions of the world and suggestions of the Devil, and they are slothful about their sinful souls. How can you be more diligent to watch and pray, and daily trust in Christ and His finished work on your behalf?

Chapter 25

1. To call attention to self and to seek attention from others is foolish (v. 27) and potentially embarrassing (vv. 6–7). Humility is a godly virtue, and true honor comes to those who wait on the Lord. It is better to assume the lowly place

without expecting or desiring the praise of man. Wait on the Lord to honor you as He sees fit. How can you pursue His glory with your life and not your own?

2. Fighting fire with fire or answering in kind is not the best way to treat those who mistreat us. Soft words and gestures of kindness are more effective than force (vv. 21–22). When we see our enemy in need or in trouble, we should be proactive in showing kindness to him by doing what we can to help and relieve him. This may melt him to be kind in the future or even to turn to the Lord for forgiveness and salvation. How have the loving responses of other people helped you to turn from sin and anger?

Chapter 26

1. The old saying that "sticks and stones may break my bones but words will never hurt me" is far from true. At least bone-breaking sticks and stones are direct; so often hurtful words are behind the back and capable of hurting deeply (v. 22). Gossipers delight in spreading their "news" like a wildfire to as many as will listen. The best way to stop a fire is to remove the fuel (v. 21); the best way to silence the backbiter is to not listen. When are you tempted to gossip? How can you keep yourself silent in those times?

2. Minding one's own business is wise. To interfere in the disputes of others without knowing all the facts or taking sides is asking for trouble, like yanking on a dog's ears (v. 17). It is best to wait for the parties to request input or arbitration before barging in. This is common sense, but also divinely revealed wisdom. When you are tempted to interfere, what can you do to pursue wisdom?

Chapter 27

1. Good friends can sometimes be closer than family. A good friend will tell you the truth even when it hurts (v. 6) and will be a means of making you a better person (v. 17). It is important, therefore, to cultivate friendships that will be mutually beneficial and edifying. Rather than waiting for someone to be a good friend to you, make an effort to be a good friend to those whom God has put in your life who are open to His wisdom. How can you sharpen one another?

2. Foolishness is so stubbornly rooted in fallen human nature that the worst suffering cannot break it loose from us (v. 22). This implies that when external means such as parental correction (22:15) or a friend's rebuke (v. 5) prove effective, it is only because of the powerful grace of God acting through them as divine discipline (3:11–12). Some people go through great sorrows but only come out more bitter, proud, and evil. Therefore, pray for yourself or people you know who are going through trials that God's grace would soften the heart, that foolishness would be rejected, and that Christ's wisdom would be embraced.

Chapter 28

1. God is never satisfied with external religion that is not the expression of a true heart of faith and devotion (v. 9). Even praying, a most spiritual endeavor, can be idolatrous (the word for abomination commonly applies to idolatry and false worship). Turning from God's law or instruction reveals the true condition of the heart and renders prayer as something detestable before God. How we view God's Word is an index to how we view the Lord Himself. Give genuine

attention and obedience to His Word so that He will hear your prayers. Spend time confessing your sins to God, knowing that He shows compassion and forgiveness to those who confess and forsake sin (v. 13; 1 John 1:9).

2. How we treat those less fortunate than ourselves is the essence of pure, undefiled religion and the fulfillment of the royal law (vv. 21, 27). James was echoing Proverbs when he taught us not to show favoritism to people and that helping others is a source of blessing (James 1:27; 2:8). On the other hand, being stingy and greedy is selfishness and ultimately self-defeating (Prov. 28:8, 20, 22). How we love others says much about how we love God since the two great commandments of loving God totally and loving one's neighbor as one's self are inseparably linked. Whom do you know in need? How should you be compassionately and wisely involved to help?

Chapter 29

1. One of the severest judgments of God upon a rebellious and hardened nation is to give them unjust rulers who will do injustice in order to retain power or increase in it (vv. 2, 4). This should cause the child of God to cling to and follow the King of Zion, the Lord Jesus Christ, whose throne is established forever in righteousness (Ps. 45:6; Heb. 1:8). How can the believer's hope in Christ give him comfort and strength to do right in a corrupt society?

2. Without divine revelation, man has no hope (v. 18). Faith comes by hearing and hearing by the Word of God. It is God's grace that He has revealed truth to us. It should be our desire to be under the faithful preaching of God's Word that exalts Christ in all things. We should receive it in meekness

and faith. Pray as well that the Lord of the harvest would send forth faithful ministers and Christian workers throughout the world, because without the Word of God, men will perish. How are you assisting in this great work?

Chapter 30

Agur was a wise man who did not think too highly of himself or his wisdom. His wisdom lay in the fact that he placed all his trust in God and His revealed wisdom rather than in his own learning. He sought to lift the reader's thoughts heavenward to the infinite glory of God and His Son, the Creator of the vast universe. He gives great credence to the Bible being the inspired, pure Word of God, always and in all places the most relevant truth. In this he is a model of humility for us before God, complete dependence upon God's Son and His Word for true wisdom, and absolute confidence in the Scriptures as the infallible truth of God. Why does humility before God lead to dependence on the Bible? Why does pride entangle people in foolish speculations and in adding human ideas to Scripture?

Chapter 31

1. Lemuel's mother is a model for parenting. The concern and wisdom of a godly mother causes her to admonish and give wise counsel to her son concerning the temptations and responsibilities of his calling in life. The love that parents have toward God and toward their children encourages them to do likewise. It is the responsibility of parents to judge their children rightly and not to turn a blind eye to their sin. Parents should, with loving admonition, help the child understand

the law of God and give due warnings to practical and spiritual dangers. To be warned of the dangers is to be prepared, and a wise man will hear wise counsel. What wisdom that you received from your parents do you especially treasure? What wisdom does each of your children need?

2. Proverbs says much about the kinds of women to avoid, so it is significant that it ends with a most noble example. The description of the virtuous woman is a paradigm for every Christian woman. Her virtue is evident both in character and action. What is striking is the selflessness of this wife and mother. Everything she does, whether within the home or without, is for the good of her family. And even more striking is the spiritual motive behind all she does. She fears the Lord, living in awareness of Him and serving Him in what may otherwise seem to be just mundane affairs. For the Christian everything in life must be directed by this great aim: to please the God who has saved us. Whether you are a man or woman, adult or child, married or single, what are some specific qualities about the virtuous woman portrayed here that you should imitate? How does her example teach you what it means to fear the Lord?

Ecclesiastes

Chapter 1

1. The opening poem about the endless and monotonous cycles of life and nature reminds us of our insignificance in the whole scheme of creation. That generations come and go without remembrance by the next is a sober reminder that life will go on without us and that none of us is the center of the universe. Yet notwithstanding our insignificance in comparison to all creation, God has given us His special attention and cares for us graciously (Ps. 8). Our contentment in this life will never come from the things in this world but only from the Lord Himself.

2. No one in his day had more God-given wisdom and more material resources than Solomon, and yet he was not able to find the answers to all the questions of life no matter how diligently he sought for those answers. That there are things about life that we will never understand is a fact. The inability to understand everything about the present is reason for us to find the ultimate reason for everything in God, who knows the why of everything because He has ordained all things.

Chapter 2

1. The Preacher's counsel against the folly of seeking pleasure and possessions is most relevant for this day that is so consumed with momentary experiences and materialism. So many today pursue happiness by living for the moment and by trying to get as many things as possible. Such is an

imaginary happiness that really does not exist. Pleasure and things can never ultimately satisfy because they are unsubstantial and temporary. It is an endless cycle that only breeds frustration and disappointment.

2. The refrain in verse 24 occurs again in 3:12–13, 22; 5:18–19; 8:15; and 9:7–9. In each instance, the sense is the same. It is the Preacher's way of instructing us to recognize that the provisions we have for life are God's gift that He has intended for our enjoyment. That enjoyment entails being content and satisfied with what God has given and to use these gifts to their fullest potential. In many ways, this refrain parallels Paul's testimony that he was content in whatever state God put him (Phil. 4:11).

Chapter 3

1. Recognizing that all the times and circumstances of life are ordained by a good, wise, and sovereign God should encourage us to use correctly the times that God has purposed. For instance, God brings times of both weeping and laughing into life. He expects us, therefore, to weep in weeping times. As believers, we do not sorrow like the world which has no hope, but we do sorrow in times of grief. It is not distrust but rather a contented belief in God's sovereignty that allows us to experience all His appropriate times for our ultimate good.

2. Verse 11 is the key verse that explains why all the temporary things of life under the sun cannot bring ultimate satisfaction. Since God has put eternity in our hearts, only the eternal God can satisfy. Living now with a view to eternity is the essence of a Christian worldview. The Preacher's references to death are not intended to be pessimistic but

realistic. Certain death makes life temporary. We are not to be morbid, but we are to live under the sun with a view of life "beyond the sun."

Chapter 4

1. Diligence in labor is a virtue; laziness is self-destructive (v. 5). God has given us the ability to labor both for its inherent enjoyment and for its provisions for life. However, laboring just to get ahead of someone else (v. 4) or in order to hoard what is earned (v. 8) is an abuse of what God has given for good. Although work is good, to be motivated to work out of envy or greed violates God's law (the tenth commandment). Christians should work hard but not with the tension and pressure of trying to keep up with someone else. Moderation and contentment with what one has is attainable, but always striving for more is chasing after the wind.

2. God has made us to be social creatures (vv. 9–12), and there is blessing and advantage attached with companionship, including marriage, family, and friends. We should be thankful for those God has brought into our lives and let family and friends know of our gratitude. Thinking of family and friends should also direct our hearts to Christ who is our husband, our elder brother, and our friend that sticks closer than any brother could.

Chapter 5

1. A proper view of God's greatness will govern how we approach Him in worship. That He is in heaven and that we are on earth means that we should be cautious and reverent as we enter into His holy presence. That we can approach

Him is itself a wonderful privilege that must not be abused with triteness or triviality. Self-restraint, submission, sincerity, and spiritual sacrifice (heart-generated praise) should characterize the place and practice of worship.

2. The instructions regarding vows are important reminders of how seriously God regards the promises we make. Some carelessly try to make bargains with God, promising to do something for Him if He does the special something they desire from Him. Then they forget all about it. In every situation, but most certainly before God, our yeas should be yeas and our nays, nays. This is not a prohibition of vows, for there are legitimate vows, such as swearing truth before tribunals or pledging faithfulness to marriage bonds. It is a solemn reminder that God does and therefore we ought to take vows seriously and to make them thoughtfully.

Chapter 6

1. Too often it is easy to look at someone who seems to have everything and to become envious. Even apart from such envy being a transgression of the tenth commandment, the Preacher shows the folly by highlighting the difference between appearance and reality. Although a lot of money, a big family, and a long life may appear to be ideal, the reality is that having those things is no guarantee that all is well. In fact, many who appear to have it all are in reality most miserable. It is best to trust the wisdom of God who has determined our times and circumstances and learn to be content.

2. The Preacher's reminder that life is but a shadow reinforces the frequent and important theme of life's brevity. A shadow is unsubstantial and fleeting. It is particularly vivid

given the hypothetical example of one who may live for two thousand years (v. 6). Even for him, life comes to an end and most likely before he expected. In the light of eternity, the longest of lives is just a passing moment. The vital issue in this life, therefore, is to be ready for eternity. Being ready for eternity requires looking to God and the provision for eternal life He has given in His Son.

Chapter 7

1. Coffins are powerful sermons (v. 2). Mourning the loss of life is one of the times God has ordained (3:4), but through and beyond the tears are important life lessons. As we experience life under the sun, death is always something that happens to someone else. But the Preacher reminds us of the sobering reality that sooner or later we will be the "someone else" that will be preaching the message of the brevity of life to others by our own deaths. The place of mourning, therefore, ought to be an occasion to face reality and to be sure that we are ready for eternity. The only way to be ready is by trusting Christ.

2. It is not a hard thing to be joyful in the day of prosperity (v. 14). But all too often there is a tendency to forget God when everything is going well. Moses warned Israel about the potential of forgetting God when they would enter the Promised Land and enjoy all its bounty (Deut. 8). It was going to be so different from the wilderness wanderings when they were forced to depend on God for daily bread (the manna). Although the days of adversity are not as enjoyable, they serve to teach a vital spiritual lesson. It often takes the trials and troubles of life to remind us of how much we need

the Lord. Trouble does not mean that God no longer cares about us; on the contrary, it shows His concern for us by bringing us again to the realization of how much we depend on Him for everything

Chapter 8

1. The Preacher's counsel to obey the king parallels the New Testament's teaching regarding the Christian's submission to civil authority (Rom. 13:1–7; 1 Peter 2:13–17). This is a component of the fifth commandment, which defines the duties and responsibilities between inferiors and superiors. How much we agree with the state is not an issue. Unless the state legislates contrary to the law and government of God, good citizenship is the Christian's duty (Acts 4:19).

2. Fearing God defines the essence of Christian living, encompassing both our attitude of reverence toward God and our behavior before God. Verses 12 and 13 make it clear that fearing or not fearing God will be a crucial factor in the day of judgment. The true fear of God is the essence of true religion and includes, therefore, saving faith in Christ.

Chapter 9

1. That God holds the lives of His people in His hand (v. 1) is a most comforting truth given all the events and circumstances of life that appear to be so random and contrary to expectation. Without this assurance we would be subject to frustrations and disappointments when the unexpected happens (like the events described in vv. 11–12). Not knowing the future is not a problem when we know the One who holds the future in His hand. We must trust Him that in

His infinite wisdom all things happen according to His plan for His glory and our good.

2. That a living dog is better than a dead lion (v. 4) is a vivid way of saying there is hope so long as there is life. This truth has evangelistic application regarding the urgency of the gospel call. If conversion occurs, it must occur during life for there are no chances after death. Today is the day of salvation.

Chapter 10

1. The opening verse is a powerful reminder of how careful we must be to guard and preserve our reputations and testimonies. Regardless of the fact that most of the vat was filled with the pleasant perfume, those floating, dead flies ruined the whole batch. So a reputation that has been earned through a lifetime can be easily destroyed by a single sin. We should, therefore, be diligent to walk circumspectly, relying on the Holy Spirit to guide us through the Word of God to a life of consistent holiness. A good testimony is something that takes time to earn but can be so easily lost in a moment.

2. The closing verse illustrates the spiritual and internal aspect of God's moral law. Obedience is more than external behavior. The proper relationship and attitude regarding civil authorities is a component of the fifth commandment that deals with relationships between superiors and inferiors. It may be possible to pledge allegiance and to perform all the duties the state requires while at the same time disrespecting and dishonoring the authorities in our hearts. This too is a violation of God's holy law, and He knows it even if no one else does.

Chapter 11

1. That the opening verses address very mundane issues of how to handle money and go about daily tasks illustrates the inclusiveness of God's Word that speaks to every area of life. Psalm 19:7 says the law is complete having an effect on every part of man's being. If God regards the unplowed fields of the wicked to be sin (Prov. 21:4), it would seem to follow that He will be pleased with the mundane activities of His people. As Christians, we should realize that there is no part of our lives exempt from God's grace and concern for us. We should live wisely in every sphere of life, being conscious that all our times and circumstances are in His hands.

2. The closing verses provide pointed application to youth. Godly living is not something that can be put off until old age. Youth is gone before we know it, and the time of youth should not be wasted with carelessness and godlessness. There are experiences that only youth can fully enjoy, and they should be experienced with contentment to their fullest, but always with God and eternity in view. The best way to enjoy youth is to live consciously before the Lord.

Chapter 12

1. The imagery of the words of the wise being as goads and fastened nails describes important functions of Scripture. God's Word is often like a goad to prod us and to direct us to the proper course of behavior. It sometimes hurts the flesh but it is always designed to adjust our actions in such a way as to cause us to follow the paths of righteousness. The Word is also like a nail that is fixed in a sure and solid place upon which we can hang our hope. It is for us to walk

according to all of God's commandments and to rest confidently in His certain promises.

2. Fearing God involves both an attitude of awe that generates worship and actions that reflect the kind of behavior pleasing to God. For instance, Job feared God and turned away from evil (Job 1:1); that is always the pattern. Fearing the Lord is the consequence of knowing Him as He reveals Himself in His Word where He prescribes the kind of life that is pleasing to Him. To fear God is to factor Him into every situation and circumstance of life. To live in that awareness of God is a powerful motivator to proper living. According to Jesus, loving God is the same motivation to obedience as fearing Him (John 14:15). In many ways, fearing God and loving Him are exactly the same. This is the kind of life that God demands of us, and if, by God's grace, we can fulfill this duty on earth we will be fit for the judgment then. Only in and through the Lord Jesus is such a life possible.

Song of Solomon

Chapter 1

1. The relationship between Christ and His people is not merely one of faith or service, important as these aspects are. Believers are loved by Christ, and they in turn love their Lord. The gospel reveals God's love, and the greatest commandment is to love the Lord. Why is it important to make divine love the center of our religion?

2. The expressions used in this wonderful book of the Bible speak of physical love and describe gestures and attitudes that are familiar to us in our human understanding of marital love. God has seen fit to represent His love for His people in the institution of Christian marriage (Eph. 5:22–33). Yet the love of God in Christ transcends all earthly relationships, for His love is infinite, eternal, and unchangeable in His being, wisdom, power, holiness, justice, goodness, and truth. Why does that make this the Song of all songs?

Chapter 2

1. None but a true Christian knows the inward experiences of delight that may be enjoyed in fellowship with the blessed Jesus (vv. 4–6). These are elsewhere in Scripture called "the love of Christ, which passeth knowledge" (Eph. 3:19); "the peace of God, which passeth all understanding" (Phil. 4:7); "joy unspeakable and full of glory" (1 Peter 1:8); and similar expressions. Have you tasted the supernatural happiness in Christ? Has it awakened you to long for more?

2. The believer needs to be careful not to do anything that might offend or grieve his Lord (v. 7). This means that we need to attend to our lives so as to do nothing that might disturb or displease Him. To displease Jesus might mean to lose some of His sweet presence and blessing. We must therefore keep watch against sin, resist temptation, and quickly confess and repent of sin, seeking renewal of fellowship with Christ.

3. The believer's comfort in this sad world is that one day he or she will be beyond all sorrow and all care. Hence Christians, while in this life, look forward to the happy day when they will be with Christ in glory. This is expressed beautifully here: "Until the day break, and the shadows flee away" (v. 17).

Chapter 3

1. Those who have the grace of God in their hearts value communion with Christ above all earthly experiences. They are ready to do all in their power to enjoy again their fellowship with Christ when they lose a sense of it (vv. 1–5). Believers should organize their time and their lives so as to seek after the felt enjoyment of Christ's love. What does it mean to seek Him, and when finding Him not to let Him go?

2. Christ is most glorious and powerful. A sight of Him will change you. The unbelievers in Jerusalem wondered at the changed lives of the apostles: "They took knowledge of them, that they had been with Jesus" (Acts 4:13). This alteration will be perfect at last in glory, when believers will "shine forth as the sun in the kingdom of their Father" (Matt. 13:43). The happiness of heaven will very much consist of gazing upon Christ and appreciating His love and His divine beauty. The Day is coming when all His people, being spiritually espoused

to Him, will rejoice with joy unspeakable at the sight of His glorious majesty as He comes upon the clouds to marry His church to Himself forever. How can this give you hope?

Chapter 4

1. It is a very great strength to the Christian to know how greatly Christ loves him. The Devil would have believers despair at the thought of our sinfulness and failure in so many ways. But Christ, though so well aware of believers' failings, does not hesitate to tell them plainly that He has this immense love for all who believe in Him. He tells His church, "Thou hast ravished my heart" (v. 9). How can believers use this text to defend themselves when Satan comes to accuse them?

2. The church prays for the wind to blow. This is a reference to the Holy Spirit. God's people need the Holy Spirit to blow on them. He blows like the chilling north wind so as to convict us in our carelessness (John 16:8). He touches our hearts as a warm south wind to cause our lives to bring forth the fruits of the Spirit (Gal. 5:22–24). All the graces of the Christian are the gifts of Christ by His Spirit. Are you part of the garden of God? How often are you praying for the Spirit to cause you to grow for Christ's pleasure?

Chapter 5

1. Christians have experiences from which they may benefit all their lives. Here the church recounts an experience she has of failing her Lord (vv. 1–4). We must expect to pay a price when we are too slow to rise to meet Christ when He calls. The bride longs for the felt presence of Christ but fails for a time to experience it. Her laziness has taught her an important lesson. Christ never forsakes His people completely in

this life (Matt. 28:20; Heb. 13:5, 8). However, Christ may teach us a needed lesson if we do not seek Him as we should. He may hide His face from us for a time. Let us never rest in such a condition but earnestly seek Him through the public means of grace, the help of godly friends, and especially meditation and praise regarding His beauties. How are you seeking Christ's presence by your regular habits?

2. God frequently brings good out of our evil. This is no reason for us to do what is foolish. But it comforts us when we make mistakes and go astray, as we too often do. So here, the bride's failure to open to her Beloved is a means whereby she is roused to confess her heartfelt love for her Lord: "Yea, he is altogether lovely" (v. 16). Believers, we must never despair. No matter how wrongly we may have behaved, we must not give up hope of finding again the love of Christ. Even when we fall badly we are to return to Christ with tears of repentance and expect to find Him ready to bless us still.

Chapter 6

1. Christ greatly values His people's devotion to Him (v. 5). Some believers suffer the contempt of men for His sake, some financial loss, and some martyrdom. Our Lord well knows the motive of love in the hearts of His own dear people. No sacrifice that we can make could ever be too great for Him who died for us. Christ is looking for fruit (v. 11). He will reward every faithful act of His people in the Great Day. What comfort it will then be to hear Him say, "Well done, thou good and faithful servant" (Matt. 25:21)!

2. Christ describes His church in words that indicate her excellence in His eyes: "Fair as the moon, clear as the sun, and

terrible as an army with banners" (v. 10). There is excellency in Christ's church that is not to be found elsewhere in this world. She shines as a light in the darkness of this world's sin and superstition. She is ever rising higher in the sky as God's providence unfolds, just as the sun soars higher and higher till it reaches its zenith. She is a powerful force for good, ever conquering in the name of Christ till at last all nations shall be blessed in her and call her blessed. How can this encourage believers to serve God zealously even in sorrow?

Chapter 7

1. Christ takes note of the way in which believers walk. "How beautiful are thy feet with shoes, O prince's daughter" (v. 1). This is a lesson to us of great practical importance. We are called upon to walk in the light of God's Word, the Holy Scriptures. This includes walking by faith in the gospel and in obedience to the Ten Commandments. The believer should take every care to walk in the light of God's Word and to honor Him in thought, word, and deed.

2. The word "come" is often on the lips of Christ and of His church (e.g., v. 11). The gospel invites sinners often with this word (e.g., Matt. 11:28). Christ welcomes all sinners who hear His gospel to come to Him and be saved. Those who have already walked with Christ for a long time are still invited with that same call. Has this word become necessary, suitable, and precious to you?

Chapter 8

1. We know that Christ's love for His bride went so deep that He was willing to go to death and the grave for her

(v. 6). There is no doubt but that Christ has His church on His heart and has her engraved on the palms of His hands (Isa. 49:16). He cannot leave her or abandon her. Therefore, the greatest source of peace and joy a person can have is to know that he is sealed by the Spirit and belongs to Christ's eternal love. If you have that assurance, cherish it and pursue a deeper communion with Christ. If you do not have it, seek it through faith in the gospel, prayer, and the use of the means of grace.

2. The church prays for elect persons who have not yet been called to salvation but who will be called in the course of God's providence (v. 8). Believers should always have a deep desire to be of help to those who are not yet saved. The Lord commands the church to be diligent in prayer and in witness (v. 13). We should particularly long for the salvation of the Jews, just as believing Jews longed for Christ to save the Gentiles (Luke 2:25–32). We should long for God to transform ethnic Israel into spiritual Israel again (Rom. 11:23). How are you praying for the salvation of unconverted people, both Jews and Gentiles?

3. "Make haste, my beloved" (v. 14). With these words of hope and expectation the Lord's people look forward to the coming of their blessed Savior. The practical import of these words is that we should seek to be a people given to watching and praying. We do not know the hour when our Lord will return. As our Savior Himself tells us, "Behold, I come quickly; and my reward is with me, to give every man according as his work shall be" (Rev. 22:12). How should this give believers an incentive to serve Christ faithfully?

Isaiah

Chapter 1

1. In our folly we often view sin lightly, but God hates it. We need to impress this thought upon our own hearts and confess with David, "My wounds stink and are corrupt because of my foolishness" (Ps. 38:5). How foolish we can be in failing to consider the effect sin has upon us! We can so easily be influenced by worldly opinions that we forget that God is dishonored when our outward profession is not matched with heartfelt love for His Word and His ways. What do verses 2–4 teach us about how God views sin?

2. The wickedness of Israel was so great that they deserved to be punished as Sodom and Gomorrah had been. Yet in spite of their heinous sins, they were going to the temple and offering all the appropriate sacrifices as though all were well between them and God. They had a form of religion but knew nothing of its power or reality. They were satisfied with themselves, but God regarded their religion as idolatry. It is tragically possible to frequent church and to go through all the motions of worship without sincerity and truth. What does this teach us about worship that pleases God?

Chapter 2

1. Judah had become extremely prosperous during the reign of Uzziah, and this turned their hearts away from God. We, too, live in a very materialistic society, where wealth and riches have become the idols of many. By God's grace

we need to guard ourselves against the love of riches. The antidote to such excesses is surely found in verse 5: "Come ye, and let us walk in the light of the LORD." The apostle John reminds us, "If we walk in the light, as he is in the light, we have fellowship one with another, and the blood of Jesus Christ his Son cleanseth us from all sin" (1 John 1:7).

2. An important exhortation is given in verse 22, "Cease ye from man." In other words, do not put your trust in man, not even the greatest of men, for man is an unreliable and often false guide. Those who would rather trust in man show contempt toward God; therefore the believer is warned against such folly, which in the end leads only to great disappointment, sorrow, and shame. How does believing in the coming day of the Lord (vv. 10–21) help us to stop relying on mere men?

Chapter 3

The materialism with its outward display that characterized Isaiah's day is the trademark of much of society today. Part of God's judgment on that pretentious people was His removal of all their trinkets and His sentencing them to a government of weak and ineffective leadership. If society today is guilty of the same sins, it is liable to the same punishments. In many ways reading this chapter is like reading the newspaper and then looking in the mirror. In government, there is a display of foolish and irresponsible action in the overturning of God's laws and their replacement with the whims of godless and immature politicians whose unholy statutes can only drag our societies down further into sin and spiritual poverty. How can this chapter guide Christians in their prayers for our nations?

Chapter 4

This short chapter, though beginning with judgment, quickly moves to the wondrous subject of salvation. It speaks of Christ and of the great comfort that stems from Him. He is the Branch who is at once the Son of God and the Son of David. He is the One in whom all our hopes lie. It is a great blessing to know that one's name is written in the Book of Life, to be cleansed and purified from the filth of sin, and to bear luscious fruit by union with Jesus Christ. Believers in Christ can know the God of all comfort in times of trial and adversity, for He is our refuge from the heat and the storm.

Chapter 5

1. The song of the vineyard illustrates Christ's teaching that "unto whomsoever much is given, of him shall be much required" (Luke 12:48). The song describes the great privileges of care, attention, and cultivation that the Lord provided. But notwithstanding the fact that every advantage was supplied, the vine produced wild and sour grapes. As a consequence, the Lord left them vulnerable. In particular, this is a warning to all who grow up in a Christian environment and take spiritual benefits for granted. What kind of fruit are you producing: justice and righteousness or sin and oppression?

2. It would be profitable and sobering to compare the six woes in this chapter to the situation that exists in society today. Selfishness, hedonism, self-sufficiency, perverted thinking, arrogance, and a perverted legal system are as

prevalent now as then. It is the sad fact that nearly all sense of right and wrong has been turned upside down as man has rejected God's law and authority (vv. 20, 24). Yet the believer must never be discouraged. Our God reigns, and He will glorify His holiness and justice by humbling proud sinners. Though many admire proud rebels against God, this chapter teaches us to pity them and pray for their conversion.

Chapter 6

Nothing is more necessary in times of crisis than a fresh experience of the Lord. Uzziah had ruled for more than fifty years, and now he was dead. The future was uncertain, and God had a special word for Isaiah that directed his ministry from that day forward. What God showed Isaiah is good for us to see as well. As you meditate through his vision, note the directions Isaiah received and the lessons he learned. First, he looked up to see that God is absolutely holy, sovereignly ruling from His glorious throne. Worshiping and serving Him are essential, as exemplified by the seraphim. Second, he looked inside himself to see his own uncleanness and unworthiness. Third, he looked to God's altar to see the greatness of God's grace that provided the cleansing and atonement for his sin. Finally, he looked outside to the world into which the Lord had sent him to preach. Though most people would reject Him, this, too, was God's will, but some would be saved as God's holy seed. How does each aspect of this vision apply to the church of Christ today?

Chapter 7

What a blessed promise is conveyed in verse 14, and it is all the more wonderful to us who view it from the perspective of the New Testament. The promise has been gloriously fulfilled: Immanuel, "God with us," has come, and we who are the recipients of His grace have the joy of Christ within us. What confidence this ought to bring to our souls; what consolation during times of troubles and trials! Our God is with us every step of the way and will lead us safely to our eternal rest. Let us therefore adore Him and praise Him. How can knowing that God's Son took on our own flesh and blood assure believers that He will never leave nor forsake us?

Chapter 8

1. As believers, when the Lord appears to hide His face from us in difficult times, we must say with Isaiah, "I will wait upon the LORD" (v. 17). Let us remember that He is with us. This is not resignation to whatever will be but a vibrant and expectant faith. Rather than fear what the plans and conspiracies of men may be, let us fear the Lord alone. Let us call upon Him in prayer and plead with Him, for if we wait with patience He will surely come to us and guide us every step of the way.

2. "To the law and to the testimony" should be our regular practice (v. 20). Christians believe that the Bible is our only divine rule for what we are to believe and do. The Bible must be the touchstone for everything. It is our lamp enabling us to see and our guide to follow. God's Word will teach us how to discern; its counsel may go contrary to popular opinions and practices, but it is the absolute truth. In a world caught

up in all kinds of false spirituality, how can we walk in the light of the Bible every day?

Chapter 9

1. The heart of Isaiah's Immanuel trilogy (v. 6) details the amazing difference Christ's presence makes in the world. When Isaiah issued this prophecy, the nation was in the darkness of Assyrian domination and oppression. With prophetic insight he saw a time when those in darkness would see a great light. The presence of Christ changes everything; He always shines light into darkness. What was true for Galilee during Christ's earthly ministry is true in every individual to whom the light of the glorious gospel shines. Christ makes a difference. Is He shining in your heart?

2. Jesus is the wise counselor to the foolish and ignorant, bringing them the very wisdom of God. He is the powerful defender of the weak and oppressed, rescuing them from their enemies. He is the loving father of the orphans and isolated, caring for them forever. He is the peaceful ruler over those who have known only conflict with God, others, and themselves. Which of the four titles for Christ (v. 6) is most helpful to you now? How can you take hold of it and use it to walk by faith in Him?

Chapter 10

There are many things happening in the world that are a great discouragement to the Lord's people, and these things become all the more difficult when they affect us personally. It is at such times that we must remember that our lives are in God's hands and that "all things work together for good to them that love God" (Rom. 8:28). The Lord reigns over even the most wicked men. They can only do His will, though they do not intend it, and in the end He will punish them for their sins. Let us take great comfort in this when trials and tribulations come upon us. The Lord chastens us only for our good. We may face the rod, which may be in the form of an enemy, just as Israel faced the Assyrian army, but let us remember that the rod is in the Lord's hand. He is ultimately in control. The heaviness of our trials is but for "a season" (1 Peter 1:6).

Chapter 11

This is the third part of Isaiah's Immanuel trilogy and provides another opportunity to worship Christ for His person and work. Think of Christ along these lines. First, consider the *mystery* of the God-man. The focus is principally on the humiliation of the incarnation. For God to be with us (Immanuel) meant that God in the Person of the Son condescended very low (v. 1). What a mystery is His mercy! Second, consider the *power* of the God-man. The Father has fully equipped Him for all His mediatorial duties by the Holy Spirit (v. 2). Third, consider the *work* of the God-man. He saves His people, destroys sinners, and judges infallibly (vv. 3–5). Our destiny is directly linked to our response to Him. Surely we can trust this Savior completely. What reasons does this chapter give us to trust the Lord Jesus with all our hearts?

Chapter 12

How wonderful it is for the believer to know that God's anger is turned away because Christ has stood in the sinner's place! He has done for us what we could never have done for ourselves. He has delivered and "hath triumphed gloriously" (Ex. 15:1). What a comfort it ought to be to our souls that we can declare with Isaiah, "Behold, God is my salvation; I will trust, and not be afraid" (Isa. 12:2) When the Word of God speaks to our hearts it should thrill us. We ought to be like those two disciples on the road to Emmaus who declared, "Did not our heart burn within us, while he [Jesus] talked with us by the way, and while he opened to us the scriptures?" (Luke 24:32). Do you have a desire to praise God and declare His great works to others? Why or why not? What motives does this chapter give believers to stir such a desire?

Chapter 13

Here is a warning against the arrogance and pride of those who seek to ignore God and challenge His rule. Babylon represents the height of worldly hostility toward the Lord. Yet we see how easily such a haughty spirit is crushed by the might of the Lord. None can stand against Him. The enemies of the gospel may be powerful and threatening, but Christians need not fear. We have One who is mightier. The wicked have but an allotted time, and when it is over they are taken from the scene of this life. As the psalmist reminds us, "Surely thou didst set them in slippery places: thou castedst them down into destruction. How are they brought into desolation, as in a moment! They are utterly consumed with terrors" (Ps. 73:18–19). How should unbelievers respond to the news of the coming day of the Lord? How should believers respond?

Chapter 14

It is a tragic thought that multitudes of religious men and women now reside in the terrible place of torment because they never leaned wholly upon Christ. Oh, how this question from the place of torment ought to stir us up to truly examine ourselves: "Art thou become like unto us?" (v. 10)? If we would avoid hearing these words from the pit, we must ask ourselves questions now: Are we in Christ? Is our house built upon the solid rock that is the Lord Jesus, or have we built our religion upon the shifting sands of pride and foolishness? Let us pray with the psalmist, "Search me, O God, and know my heart: try me, and know my thoughts: and see if there be any wicked way in me, and lead me in the way everlasting" (Ps. 139:23–24).

Chapter 15

Moab was a nation that overindulged itself. The Moabites had lived in peace and prosperity for many years and were overconfident that things would continue to go well for them. They were blinded by the foolish philosophy that says there will be no judgment to come. They carried on in their own selfish lifestyles, till all of a sudden they were caught unawares. Let us never envy those who prosper in this world through ungodly ways, for their end is destruction. Rather, let Christians thank God that He has worked a miracle of grace within their hearts so that they are born again (1 Peter 1:3–4). Let us also pray for God to awaken sinners to their need before destruction comes.

Chapter 16

Pride is such a destructive sin because it fails to listen to sound advice. The proud think they have all the answers. They will not be told by others. Hence, we read in Prov. 16:18, "Pride goeth before destruction, and an haughty spirit before a fall." What a blessing it is to have a teachable spirit, especially concerning the things of God! Moab was offered refuge, but their pride would not allow them to accept the gracious offer from the Lord of submission to a good and righteous King. There are many like Moab today, whose pride ruins them because they refuse to submit to the Son of David, King Jesus. Why is our pride such a bitter enemy of the kingdom of Christ?

Chapter 17

The enemy of our souls is always subtle in his approaches, seeking to convince men and women that the Lord's demands are unjust. The people of Ephraim listened to such a lie and turned their backs upon their covenant God, associating themselves with a pagan people. The Lord caused them to prosper, but in their prosperity they listened to the voice of evil. Imagining they would do much better without God, they turned away from Him. Do we not see the same foolishness in society today? Lust for self-interest has brought misery and heartache to countless multitudes who have been stripped of all that is good and left vulnerable—all because they have forgotten the Lord. Blessed are they who set their minds on Him as their true rock and salvation. How can we develop an attitude of always remembering God as our only hope?

Chapter 18

God's purposes for the Ethiopian people were judgment and salvation. Isaiah's prophecy intertwines these two in all of God's dealings. On the one hand, we must fear the Lord because of the woes He sends upon the wicked nations. On the other hand, we must hope in the Lord because He is gathering worshipers to Himself from all nations. Judgment and salvation will come upon all the world for the glory of God. This is the driving motive for missions and evangelism. Whenever you hear of the nations in the news, or meet people from other countries, view them through the twin lenses of judgment and salvation. How should this change the way you live?

Chapter 19

This chapter reveals the wonderful grace of God toward the Gentiles. In Christ, we who were once strangers and foreigners and at enmity with Him are brought into sweet communion. In Him we speak the holy language of Scripture; for the new heart within us, given by our gracious God, has changed our speech. We no longer ought to have interest in the worldly and the vile, for our thoughts are now toward the Lord who has redeemed us and healed us of our iniquities. What a privilege to be blessed by God, to be the work of His hands, and to have our inheritance in Him. How amazing is the grace of the gospel that transforms former enemies into a fellowship of saints! How have you experienced the way God unites very different people through a shared love and worship for Him?

Chapter 20

We learn from this short chapter the folly of trusting in human resources and power. Such things will always let us down and cause us to be ashamed. You have a responsibility to "trust in the LORD with all thine heart" (Prov. 3:5). If you lean on your own understanding, you will not succeed. Resting your hope in man will lead to disappointment and ultimately to a divine curse (Jer. 17:5–6). Trust the Savior, Jesus Christ; lean on Him with all your weight. "For the scripture saith, Whosoever believeth on him shall not be ashamed" (Rom. 10:11). The Egypts of this world will always fail, but the Lord cannot fail. What are some ways in which you are tempted to trust in man's help? How can you place your confidence fully in the Lord?

Chapter 21

Although God's people sometimes suffer severe persecution, even akin to being threshed and winnowed, they may still wait with confident hope in the God of Israel. The sovereign Lord will overthrow the empires of this world, and one day His people will cry "Babylon is fallen!" while Christ's glory fills the skies. God has decreed it, and therefore it will certainly come to be. Christians, therefore, may suffer with expectation that God's justice will prevail. How can this hope protect us from being attracted to this world's ways and intimidated by its threats?

Chapter 22

Shebna is an illustration of foolish pride. He enjoyed a position of honor and it went to his head. He lost his vision of mission to the king and desired his own legacy. His concern was how he could be remembered in this world (v. 16), and so he devoted his efforts toward creating a memorial for himself. But God had different plans and showed how dispensable Shebna was by replacing him with Eliakim. God's work is more important than any one man, and it will go on. Let us learn from Shebna that God looks to him who is contrite in spirit (66:2) and He knows the proud only from afar (Ps. 138:6). How might you be tempted to be like Shebna? How can you live entirely for the kingdom of Christ?

Chapter 23

This chapter brings a severe warning to all who would make money and possessions their main goals in life. Such things are easily taken away by the Lord, and they must be ultimately given up and left behind when death comes. The Savior declares, "For what shall it profit a man, if he shall gain the whole world, and lose his own soul?" (Mark 8:36). Let us, therefore, get our priorities in order. Rather than setting our hearts on material possessions, we must seek God's kingdom first by obeying His will and trust that He will care for our needs (Matt. 6:31–33). How can we avoid being seduced by the allure of money and what it can buy?

Chapter 24

There is a day coming when the Lord will bring this present world to an end. The Christian should always be ready for this by watching and waiting in prayer. We need to diligently observe the days we are living in. The wickedness upon the earth is becoming ripe for harvest. All too suddenly the Lord will send His angels as reapers into the world, and none shall escape who live unrepentant lives. Let us ensure that we are walking in the ways of the Lord and that we are bearing fruit that is pleasing in His sight. For then that day will be filled with joy, and we shall join the heavenly host in praising our blessed Redeemer who loves us and washed us from our sins with His blood (Rev. 1:5). However, if we are not saved by Christ's blood, His coming will cause us to wail in terror (Rev. 1:7). If Christ were to come today, how would you greet Him, with praise or in horror?

Chapter 25

1. There is much in this chapter to encourage the believer. When the enemies of the gospel seem to have the upper hand, we must look with expectancy beyond the present to that glorious and certain event when the Lord will be seen to reign in Zion. On that great day we shall surely declare with Isaiah, "O Lord, thou art my God; I will exalt thee, I will praise thy name; for thou hast done wonderful things; thy counsels of old are faithfulness and truth" (v. 1).

2. In this tragic and sinful world, death and weeping are the inevitable consequences of the fall. Yet how blessed will that day be when death is swallowed up in victory, God will wipe away all tears, and believers will feast with Christ (vv. 6–8)! The thought of this should spur us on to live for Christ now with steady perseverance in good works (1 Cor. 15:58). If the anticipation of the destruction of this world can help us to reject worldly lusts and fears (ch. 24), how can the hope of the resurrection help us to set our affections on Christ and His kingdom?

Chapter 26

1. The Lord Jehovah is the Rock of ages (v. 4). In Him we need not fear. In Him is all our hope. Therefore, we must trust Him in every situation. The trials of life often bring doubts to our minds, but these we must cast off. It is only when our minds and thoughts are propped up upon the Lord, thinking of Him, that we will experience peace regardless of circumstances. What anxieties trouble you? How can you lean upon the Lord?

2. The resurrection of the dead is a strange doctrine to this world, but it is the center of the Christian hope. Christ's resurrection raises His elect spiritually to a living hope and will raise them one day to physical glory and immortality. What practical difference should the doctrine of the resurrection make in our lives?

Chapter 27

The Lord gives His people a double grace in Christ. First, He pacifies His righteous anger against their sins and establishes a relationship of peace with them (vv. 4–5). Second, He purifies their souls of sin and idolatry so that they bear the fruit of good works for His pleasure and the good of the world (vv. 2, 6). Justification and sanctification are distinct but inseparable, and we need both to be saved. Through both of these graces the Lord gives His people victory over their ancient enemy, Satan, their tempter and accuser (v. 1). One day grace will become glory when the trumpet calls Christians to the side of their King (v. 13). However, these great blessings belong only to those who receive God's offer of peace by taking hold of Christ (v. 5). Faith is the hand that receives Him. Do you trust in Christ alone for these blessings?

Chapter 28

1. It is important to have a teachable spirit and to willingly be taught from the Word of God. We should never think so highly of ourselves as to regard the instruction of God as childish and beneath us. In reality, we are far beneath Him, for God's wisdom is infinitely beyond our understanding (v. 29). Therefore, we should gladly submit to being taught like children. There is great benefit in the sincere milk of the Word (1 Peter 2:2), and our faith is built "precept upon precept; line upon line" (vv. 10, 13). How can we approach the Word with true humility and openness?

2. The believer has a "sure foundation" in Jesus Christ (v. 16). He alone is our hope and stay. If we build on anything else, our structure will fall. Meditate upon each aspect of the description of Christ as the stone upon which our faith must stand. How is Christ proven and reliable? Extremely valuable? Fundamental and necessary? Solid and stable?

Chapter 29

The Lord's indictment against hypocritical and manmade worship (v. 13) is a sobering reminder of the importance of worshiping the Lord in spirit and in truth (John 4:24). It is all too possible to be in a religious environment and to go through all the routines of worship and yet have a heart that is far from God and a form of worship never commanded by God. God rejects both heartless worship and humanly invented worship, for true worshipers worship God as the Holy Spirit engages their hearts with the truth of His Word. Those raised in the church must ask themselves two questions. First, are you giving God mere lip-service or worshiping Him with love and fear in your heart? Second, are the forms of worship you use in your services commanded by God's Word or based merely on human ideas?

Chapter 30

1. There is "a time to keep silence" (Eccl. 3:7). Great comfort is found in the words, "In quietness and in confidence shall be your strength" (Isa. 30:15). When we are in quiet trust before the Lord, we are better placed to hear Him speaking through His Word and to submit to His will for us. We receive confidence through the promises of God. They strengthen us in times of trial. Faith is always the best way, but too often the Lord must say "and ye would not" (v. 15).

2. We are often impatient and find waiting hard. Why do our prayers seem to go unanswered for so long? Verse 18 gives us some of the answer: we are waiting because God Himself is waiting for the right time to give us the blessing He desires for us. We must trust that He is faithful and just to bless those who humbly hope in Him. We must also learn to desire that He will be glorified in the way He shows us mercy more than we desire to have the mercy exactly when and how we want it. How does this help you understand what it means to find strength in quietness and confidence (v. 15)?

Chapter 31

The destructive nature of sin is such that it drives men and women to foolish, would-be remedies. Judah's sin kept them away from the only One who could help. They preferred to seek help from the nation that had once enslaved them and vainly opted for the support of Egypt's horses and chariots rather than submitting to the will of the Lord and trusting in Him. Oh, that God would save us from such foolishness and hardness of heart! He alone can deliver us. Let us therefore always look unto Him. Why is it foolish to trust in men and their resources instead of in God?

Chapter 32

1. Christ's reign in the world is wonderful, and believers ought to rejoice that Christ reigns in their hearts by the Holy Spirit. Child of God, there was once a time when you could not see spiritual things, but now your eyes are opened to see the truth. Your ears were once deaf to the gospel, but now they hear. Your heart was once rash and foolish, but now the Lord has given knowledge so that you can speak plainly of what God has done through Christ. Take time now to praise and thank Him for His grace!

2. Peace is illusive to the world. It is impossible to find true peace from this passing world because sin ruins any possibility of doing so. Yet how blessed is the Christian, for the promise of God is, "My people shall dwell in... quiet resting places" (32:18). The child of God rests in the peace the Savior brings to the soul. He says, "Peace I leave with you, my peace I give unto you: not as the world giveth, give I unto you. Let not your heart be troubled, neither let it be afraid" (John 14:27). In what ways do you need peace today? How can you seek it from God through Christ?

Chapter 33

1. Let us never doubt the Lord's ability to provide for our needs. He promises to be our hiding place and to provide all we need (v. 16). If God cares for the sparrow that falls to the ground, will He not also care for His children? Sometimes trials are brought upon us to shake us from our complacency in order that we might flee to the Lord, depend solely on Him, renew our commitment to fear Him (v. 6), and obey His laws as the highest priority of our lives (v. 15). Rather than fretting over earthly concerns, let us seek above all to escape the fires of hell (v. 14) and praise the Savior.

2. We easily fix our eyes upon this passing world. We need to remind ourselves of this promise: "Thine eyes shall see the king in his beauty" (v. 17). This is the blessed hope of every Christian. Surely Christ should be the center of our thoughts. The most joyful heart is the one that delights to meditate upon the Savior, and the more we meditate on Him the more of His beauty we shall see. How can you work to set your mind upon things above, where Christ is seated?

Chapter 34

1. God is remarkably patient, having waited thousands of years already to gather in His elect. However, the day of the Lord will come and completely destroy the heavens and the earth. All that worldly men have labored to accumulate and build as their treasures will be gone. The masses of wicked people that fill the earth will be exterminated. God will summon all mankind before His judgment throne and cast the wicked into the fire of His wrath, where they will suffer burning pain forever and ever. Therefore, do not presume upon

God's kindness. Repent of your sins now, and live for the kingdom of Christ that will endure forever. Receive Christ as your King and look to Him for the forgiveness of your sins.

2. The Lord's judgment will come true, both in time and in eternity, exactly as He has promised in the Bible (v. 17). God's almighty Spirit will see to it that this happens. So devote yourself to reading the Bible, studying it, and seeking the Lord in it.

Chapter 35

This chapter paints a wonderful picture of what it is to be redeemed. Our sin and separation from the Lord caused us to become dry and parched like a barren desert, but the grace of God has been poured into His people. His Spirit satiates the soul, causing the good seed that He has planted to spring up and blossom. What a transformation God brings to the hearts of His people, yet He does much more: He prepares a highway of holiness to walk on, where His people are kept safe. When we stay on that highway, no harm can come to us. The path is so clearly marked that it is impossible to go astray except by deliberate detour. Let us be careful to follow the path with joy for what God has done for us. What in this chapter is most attractive or delightful to you? How does it encourage you to a life of hope and holiness?

Chapter 36

The proud and overconfident Rab-shakeh instructed the men on Jerusalem's walls to ask Hezekiah in whom he trusted (v. 5). This is a question to which each of us needs to give a clear and unequivocal answer, and this is especially so when we are in the midst of severe trials. The world may challenge our faith in the Lord and mock Him as weak and worthless (v. 20). Or it may claim that He is against us, an evil and fickle God (v. 10). The mockery of the wicked is all the harder to bear when they are more powerful or successful than we are. Our King teaches us to bear it quietly and patiently, as He did when He went to the cross for our sins (v. 21; 1 Peter 2:19–25). Let us trust in the Lord, persevere in doing good, turn away from anger, and wait for Him (Ps. 37:1–11). The Lord will save us and glorify His holy name. Whom do you hear mocking the Lord and His people? How do you need to respond?

Chapter 37

1. Hezekiah provides a pattern to follow in dealing with our problems. First, he recognized the seriousness of his need (vv. 1, 3). Second, he sought a word from the Lord (v. 2). He had Isaiah; we have the complete Bible. Third, he spread the matter before the Lord in prayer (v. 14). Note that his prayer begins with worship (v. 16), proceeds to petition (v. 17), and argues for God's glory (v. 20). Fourth, he receives the answer (v. 21), assuring him of deliverance even though he would have to wait twenty years for the full outworking. How can you follow this pattern in dealing with your problems?

2. Though the great men and women of the earth mock the Lord, the Lord will have the last word. He is the supreme King and the only God. Other gods are worthless and cannot save, but the Lord both saves and destroys. Therefore our greatest ambition should be that "all the kingdoms of the

earth may know that thou art the LORD, even thou only" (v. 20). Make this your guiding principle and constant prayer.

Chapter 38

Hezekiah was going to die, and he was told to set his house in order. This was fearful news to him, and he pleaded with the Lord that it would not be so. God heard his cry and granted him another fifteen years. Hezekiah therefore voiced this testimony: "The LORD was ready to save me" (v. 20). Surely this is the testimony of every true child of God. The Lord has saved His people, and He will continue to keep us unto the end, saving us from all that would destroy us. Are there not many times that we can look back to in our lives when He saved us from harm and delivered us from all our fears? Cannot we be sure that He will save us to the end since He has already cast all our sins behind His back? Therefore, like Hezekiah we should give the Lord praise and thanksgiving, even in writing if we have the skill. Believer, how do you glorify God for answering your prayers, especially your prayers for salvation?

Chapter 39

This chapter provides a somber lesson to us all. Hezekiah, one of the godliest kings to ever sit on the throne in Jerusalem, in a moment of weakness became puffed up in his pride, revealing to the Babylonians all of his treasures. How easily the human heart behaves unwisely! No wonder the exhortation comes, "Wherefore let him that thinketh he standeth take heed lest he fall" (1 Cor. 10:12). We need to be on our guard, watching and praying vigilantly against pride, especially after experiencing great success. How can we recognize the first motions of pride in our hearts? How can we put them to death by the blood and Spirit of Christ?

Chapter 40

1. In this ever-changing world it is good to know that "the word of our God shall stand for ever" (v. 8). That Word is reliable in every circumstance of life. When we are facing trials and affliction, it is good for us to rest upon the certain promises of God. When we fall into sin, what a comfort it is to know the way to confession and forgiveness. The immutable Word of God stands firm for every situation. The Lord will never change His mind or go back on a promise. How is that a solid ground for comfort?

2. It is good to reflect on the absolute greatness of God, who is infinite in all His perfections and beyond our highest thoughts of Him. In an uncertain world we have confidence in the God who made the world and all that is in it and governs even the things that may cause us to fear for His own glory. This infinite Lord has come to us in human flesh in the person of Jesus Christ. Though no man-made image suffices to honor Him, the fullness of His deity now dwells in a man who is His living image. Thus we have a divine and sympathetic Shepherd. If Christ is all this to us, it makes sense to wait on the Lord with the full anticipation and confident expectation that He will supply our needs, enabling us to soar as the eagle. What does it mean, practically, to wait upon the Lord by faith in Christ?

Chapter 41

Christians may fear when they fail to appreciate the wonderful relationship they have with the Lord. Child of God, there are many precious promises in the Word that we need to appropriate to ourselves; how wonderful is the promise that the One who is incomparably great is always with His people (v. 10). The nations of this world are "as a drop of a bucket" (40:15), so what have we to fear when the Lord says, "I will uphold thee" (v. 10)? Not only is the Lord's presence with His people, but so is His strength. He says, "I will strengthen thee" (v. 10.) Fearlessness is appropriated by faith in these promises. If you are a believer, how do you need to apply these promises today? How does this show to unbelievers how good it is to be a Christian?

Chapter 42

1. Here we have a rich mine full of the sparkling gems of Christ's glory. Let us meditate on just two precious truths. First, God sent Christ to produce justice ("judgment") in the world (vv. 1, 3–4). This means that He came to change the way we relate to each other so that our relationships conform to His laws (Ex. 21:1; Lev. 19:37). If we would claim Christ as our King and His Spirit as our lives, we must demonstrate the reality of Christ's saving work in our lives by walking in obedience to His commands. Christians bear the mark of the Servant of the Lord. What evidence do you see in your life of being a servant of God like Christ?

2. Second, Christ will not break the bruised reed or quench the smoking wick (v. 3). He is tender and compassionate with those broken by suffering, especially those contrite

under sorrows over their sins (57:15; 66:2). He will not snuff out the faith of weak Christians but will work in them that their faith and love may burn brightly. How can this promise encourage believers going through times of spiritual darkness?

Chapter 43

1. It is both a blessing and a challenge that God says to His people, "Ye are my witnesses" (v. 12). It is a blessing that the Lord's people have tasted of His goodness and have experienced His saving power. It is a blessing to speak of His goodness and faithfulness. However, it is also a great challenge, for we have a responsibility to tell the lost and perishing that there is hope in Christ. How do we measure up to this challenge? How can this chapter help us to be His witnesses?

2. God says to His people, "I...will not remember thy sins" (v. 25). We may look back on our own lives with shame that we could ever have done the wicked things we did. We may find it difficult to get such shameful thoughts out of our minds and find ourselves confessing the same sins over and over again. Our hearts may condemn us, but God is greater than our hearts. How can believers rest their consciences in the truth that our forgiveness is complete?

Chapter 44

1. God's Spirit is poured down from heaven through the ascended Mediator, Jesus Christ. He comes like a heavenly river to give life to dead souls. He satisfies all the thirsts of God's elect and causes them to prosper in the inner man, and one day in visible glory. There is nothing more important

than having the Spirit of God dwell in you, for if anyone does not have the Spirit of Christ, he does not belong to Him (Rom. 8:9). A defining mark of the people renewed by the Spirit is their public and personal confession, "I am the Lord's." They belong to the Lord and identify with His church. What practical effects does this produce in your life?

2. Isaiah's diatribe against idolatry (vv. 9–20) shows the incredible stupidity and blindness of giving our adoration to objects (v. 18). This applies not just to images and statues of divine beings but also to sinful lusts after riches and pleasures. Why is it foolish and degrading to give your heart to any mere object instead of to God?

Chapter 45

A wonderful promise is found in verse 22: "Look unto me, and be ye saved, all the ends of the earth: for I am God, and there is none else." Faith is a look of utter dependence and need, and this is the only way to be healed of our sins and their just punishment (Num. 21:8; John 3:14–15). God's gospel call goes out to all nations, for there is no other name under heaven by which we must be saved besides that of Jesus Christ (Acts 4:12). God will be glorified. We may either turn to Him now and be saved or His glory will compel us to honor Him even when He punishes us for our sins. How should this motivate us to repent and believe now? How should it motivate us to work together to bring the gospel to all nations?

Chapter 46

1. God will glorify Himself against all the idols of man. The things the nations worship are burdens for them to carry, but God is not so. He is the Lord of all events, carrying out His eternal plans without fail. Even pagan kings serve Him without realizing it. Certainly then we can be confident that He will bring complete salvation and glory to His people. Why do people tend to trust in idols? Why should they trust in the Lord?

2. There are many times when discouragement springs from our many failings and weaknesses and the difficulty of our way. The Lord promises His people, "And even to your old age I am he; and even to hoar hairs will I carry you: I have made, and I will bear; even I will carry, and will deliver you" (v. 4). Believers can persevere because the Lord will persevere with them.

Chapter 47

Babylon had become used to the good life (v. 8) and lived as though it would last forever, feeling safe and secure. Nebuchadnezzar expressed such pride before God humbled him (Dan. 4), and Belshazzar hosted a party on the very night of destruction (Dan. 5). It is easy to grow comfortable with the things of life and assume that nothing will ever interrupt the flow of pleasure and contentment. Such is the presumption of horrendous pride. Babylon did not bring to heart or mind the latter end (v. 7) and suffered extreme consequences. Let us all be warned that security is not in the things of this life but only in God. Thinking about our latter end should lead us to trust the Lord, for the things of this world will surely pass away.

Chapter 48

1. The great motive and highest aim of all God's actions is to make people know and praise His glory (vv. 9–11). He does not seek this out of any need, for He is all-sufficient in Himself. However, it is right for Him to glorify Himself, it is His delight, and it is the most loving gift He can give to His people.

2. Afflictions should bring us nearer to the Lord, for they are His furnace to refine believers like precious metal (v. 10). We should not fear the fire, for He will be with us (43:2). His purpose is to make us pure and holy, so that our peace may be like a river and God's children may multiply and fill the earth (48:18–19). When we face the furnace of affliction, we do not walk alone any more than Daniel's three friends were alone in the fire (Dan. 3:1–30). How can viewing suffering as refining help believers to endure it?

Chapter 49

Christ was fully qualified and powerfully gifted to do His Father's will, but His glory was hidden and His ministry strangely wrapped in weakness, frustration, and rejection. Nevertheless, God not only saved His elect among the Jewish nation through Him but also redeemed people from all over the world. Under Christ as their shepherd, the international church experiences deliverance from its former imprisonment and is beginning to enjoy the satisfaction of His kingdom. If believers ever question Christ's love for them, they should remember that He is more closely united to them than a mother is to her nursing child. Just as surely as His wounds pierced His hands for their sins, so they themselves are engraved upon His loving heart forever.

Therefore, let us never despair, even if our lives are strangely wrapped in suffering and rejection. Let each Christian learn to say, "Christ loved me and died for me, and nothing can separate me from His love" (cf. Rom. 8:35, 39; Gal. 2:20).

Chapter 50

1. Christ is the Mediator of God's truth and a model of patient suffering and persistent witness. He willingly gave His human body to the torments of His enemies, and yet did so with an unflinching determination to declare the Word of God and an unwavering hope that His Father would vindicate Him in the end. How does Christ's suffering assure us that His message is true? How does He set an example for believers?

2. The closing verses teach important lessons about faith. The object of faith determines its value. Saving faith puts all its trust and confidence in Christ, leaning on Him for support and safety. Trusting in Christ never fails. So many spend their efforts trying to kindle their own light that would give the appearance of safety and calm. But all those who trust their own efforts are doomed, regardless of the sincerity or fervency with which they have worked up their own religion. To walk in the true light is salvation and fellowship with God. To walk in one's own light leads to eternal darkness. Make sure that you trust the only sure Savior.

Chapter 51

1. It ought to be a great source of encouragement to every believer that the Lord says, "On mine arm shall they trust" (v. 5). There is no mightier arm than the Lord's. His strength can never fail or diminish. When we lean upon Him we shall

never fall; hence Jude writes, "Now unto him that is able to keep you from falling" (Jude 24). What a folly it is, then, when we seek to walk in our own strength or depend upon those in the world rather than leaning wholly upon the Lord. Remember that He commands us to depend and lean upon Him.

2. It is surely a sad affair when Christians suffer and yet fail to go to the One who has said, "I…am he that comforteth you" (v. 12). Why suffer and mourn alone? Why seek the help of those who cannot alleviate your sorrows, when there is One who bids you come and be comforted? Remember this: "He that spared not his own Son, but delivered him up for us all, how shall he not with him also freely give us all things?" (Rom. 8:32). Does this not bring comfort to your soul?

Chapter 52

1. The gospel announces that God rescues sinners from the slavery and oppression into which the guilt of their sins has plunged them and brings them into peace with Himself. Just as the Lord promised to save Israel from its exile in Babylon, so He promises today to save believers in Christ out of this present, wicked world. The preachers of this gospel are precious gifts from God. How are you supporting and encouraging them in their labors?

2. Though Christ humbled Himself as God's servant, His very sufferings won Him the ability to cleanse unclean sinners from every nation. God the Father has exalted Him to the highest place, declaring that Jesus is our Lord and God. The kingdom of God is invading this dark world with the good news that our God reigns! Has Christ washed you

with His blood? Are you trusting in Him and confessing Him as Lord?

Chapter 53

This chapter presents one of the most wonderful declarations of the gospel in all the Bible. It should affect us deeply and eternally. We should be amazed that the holy, pure, and loving Lord was despised and rejected by men. How blind we are to the things that really matter! We should tremble that the horrors of Christ's cross reflect God's hatred of our sins, and that Christ willingly carried them at His Father's command. Truly this is a love beyond all human comprehension. We should rejoice that Christ's perfect obedience is counted to believers as their righteousness before God and that they are welcomed into His spiritual family to enjoy the riches of His glory forever. Most importantly, we should trust in Christ alone to save us from our sins and misery. If He has done all this in order to save sinners, will we dare to ignore Him? Far be it from us to insult Him in such a way. Let us instead rest our entire hope and confidence in Christ, the righteous Servant of the Lord. How does this chapter help you to trust Him more now than ever before?

Chapter 54

1. Israel's sins and covenant-breaking could not stop the purpose of God's covenant love to multiply a people for Himself. He would fill the world with the children born of His spiritual union with the church, and they would inherit righteousness and glory. How does this chapter look back to the finished work of Christ described in chapter 53? How does it look forward to a glorious hope?

2. Believers are in a blessed state, for they are the bride of Christ (v. 5) and the heirs of beauty and riches (vv. 11–12). Their future is secure beyond the reach of any enemy or accuser (v. 17) because God's covenant of grace is unconditional and everlasting (vv. 9–10). God Himself will teach the hearts of His elect to believe and obey (v. 13). How should these promises motivate the church to sing (v. 1)?

Chapter 55

This whole chapter is full of encouragement to come to the Lord. Man cannot earn God's grace but must turn back to the Lord in humble faith and repentance in order to receive life and forgiveness without cost. At the heart of the gospel is the Son of David, who has paid the price for salvation and now serves as the great Prophet and King, calling the nations to Himself. He promises nothing less to believers than a return to paradise. His very words are powerful to give life, though we are barren and fruitless. Why not come to Him now? If you are not yet a Christian, what holds you back? How does this chapter answer that with its call?

Chapter 56

Leaders, both religious and civil, have significant responsibility and are liable for their failures. Isaiah indicts those who are blind, dumb, and sleeping. They are not watching for signs of danger. Sadly, there are many in the ministry today who are like this, and they must bear a large measure of responsibility for the weakness and ineffectiveness of much of the professing church today. We need to pray that the Lord would deal with those in leadership, that either He would awaken them and give them a holy zeal for the gospel or remove them from office. If the Lord has blessed you with a faithful pastor, pray for him continually.

Chapter 57

This is a chapter of great contrast between the depths of man's sin and the greatness of God's grace. Were it not for God's grace, sinners would have no hope. The statement in verse 18 highlights the wonder of grace as God says, "I have seen his ways, and will heal him." What God sees is sin and depravity, nothing worthy of His love and goodness. But in spite of what He sees, He is willing to save and make peace. That is what makes grace what it is: God's favor that He gives to those who are so undeserving of it. It is not by works of righteousness that any are saved but only because of His grace. How does God's grace motivate believers to praise Him?

Chapter 58

It may seem strange that the Lord should rebuke His people for seeking daily to know His ways and delight in Him (v. 2). However, this seeking was not done from right motives but in proud hypocrisy. They were not taking care of the poor who lacked food and clothing. They were oppressing those in servitude (Ex. 21:2; Deut. 15:12). We learn here that outward devotion without a true change of heart is worthless in the sight of the Lord. Let us ensure that our worship is real and born out of a heart of gratitude to God for His grace and mercy to us. To that end, learn how keeping the Sabbath is a safeguard to spiritual worship. If we observe the Sabbath as the day of rest and spiritual delight that God has designed for our good, our worship will be spiritual and not perfunctory show. What does it mean to call the Sabbath a delight?

Chapter 59

Sin separates us from God because He can have nothing to do with iniquity. Do not think that God will bless you if you continue unrepentant in sin. Sadly, mankind is conquered by sin. No one seeks justice and truth, but the entire race is quick to sin, meditating on iniquity, and in constant strife with God and each other. No one in the entire human race is qualified to save himself or another person from sin. The Lord saw this, and He took on the full responsibility to come and work salvation and judgment as the divine warrior. Christ, the Son of God, is the only Redeemer of God's elect. If you trust in yourself or in another person to save you from evil and bring you happiness, you are like one leaning on a spider's web to keep you out of hell. How does this chapter call us to trust in Christ alone for salvation?

Chapter 60

What glorious prospects there are for every child of God! How wonderful that day will be when we truly walk in the full Light of the Lord, where no shadow of sin can fall upon us and where no darkness of any kind can hinder us. On that great day all sorrowing and mourning shall cease. How this thought ought to lift us up out of any present sorrows and fill us with the hope of that which is to come. Such thoughts of future bliss should therefore encourage us now to be faithful to the Lord and not hide the light He has given us under a bushel (Matt. 5:15). Whatever light we have let us by God's grace display for all to see. How has the light of God's glory already come to the church? How does it draw the nations to the Lord?

Chapter 61

In considering the wonder of salvation, Isaiah breaks forth with rejoicing (v. 10), and we should as well. Christ's blood has cleansed us and clothed us in the garments of salvation. We have been covered with the robe of righteousness, which is Christ Himself. So when God the Father looks upon us, wretched, unworthy sinners as we are, He remembers our sins no more and instead sees the absolute perfection of Christ covering us. Beloved in Christ, how blessed we are! Believers ought to praise God with joyful adoration. We should draw near to the Lord with boldness, for Christians are priests in Christ. How can you use this chapter as fuel for heartfelt praise?

Chapter 62

1. One of the most beautiful pictures given to us of Christ's relationship with His people is that of a marriage of mutual love and delight (vv. 4–5). Salvation is not just a matter of legal verdicts and rescue from danger but of bringing people to the Lord so that He may love them forever. One of the fruits of the Spirit is joy in the Lord. How should the Christian life reflect this spiritual marriage?

2. In their prayers to God Christians should "give him no rest" until He builds up His kingdom and church throughout the earth (v. 7). Before we even ask for our daily needs, we should pray "Thy kingdom come" (Luke 11:2). God welcomes such bold prayers for revival and missions; indeed,

He commands them. Why is this the duty of every believer? Why is it especially the duty of those whom He calls to be the "watchmen" of His people (v. 6), their office-bearers?

Chapter 63

Verse 9 makes this marvelous statement: "In all their affliction he was afflicted." How tender is the union between Christ and His church! When the Lord's people suffer, His compassion is deeply stirred too, "For we have not an high priest which cannot be touched with the feeling of our infirmities; but was in all points tempted like as we are, yet without sin" (Heb. 4:15). Not only is the Lord able to sympathize, but He is able to help us in the time of anxiety and needs. We can cast our care upon Him because He cares. We never suffer alone, for the Lord is always with us in our afflictions. How can we find comfort and strength in this truth when we are suffering?

Chapter 64

The Lord's presence and power ought to be the desire of every believer. There are times when the Lord seems to have hidden His face from us, and that ought to drive us to prayer, as it did Isaiah. In the previous chapter the prophet prayed for God to look down from heaven (63:15). Now he prays for God to tear the heavens apart and come down. We should plead with God to remove every impediment to knowing the fullness of His presence. Things will be remarkably different when God appears in His glory and power. Let us wait upon the Lord, earnestly expecting Him to bless His people, that by faith in the gospel we may see what God "hath prepared for him that waiteth for him" (v. 4). How does this kind of prayer seek awakening and revival by the Holy Spirit? How does it ultimately seek nothing less than the return of Christ?

Chapter 65

God's redemption of sinners will ultimately result in the transformation of the universe into a new creation unharmed by the curse against man's sin. If this fallen world retains much beauty and pleasure, to a much greater degree will the new heavens and the new earth be a paradise of happiness for the church. All our desires will be satisfied by the God who made us. However, before we can enter into the new creation, the new creation must enter into us. We must be created anew in Christ by the work of the Holy Spirit. One fruit of this new creation is a new joy in the Lord Jesus, a spiritual delight in the loveliness of Christ. Another fruit is that we truly become one of the servants of the Lord, doing His will. Are you part of God's new creation? How do you know?

Chapter 66

Isaiah concludes his prophecy with an awe-inspiring vision of the eternal state of all mankind (vv. 22–24). Every human being will either end up worshiping the Lord in the new creation forever or suffering horribly in hell without intermission or end. There is no third option. This reality presses upon us two other great truths of this chapter.

1. First, it calls us to consider whether we are saved by grace. Salvation is not about external things like being in a church building or bringing an offering. It is a matter of a

heart humbled by God's majesty, broken under the weight of one's sins, and submissive to God's Word (vv. 1–2). Is this a description of you? Are you headed for eternal worship and joy or for eternal damnation?

2. Second, it calls us to consider the great mission of the church to all nations (vv. 18–21). It began with faithful Jews, the apostles, and other disciples of Jesus Christ, who gave themselves to bring the gospel to the Gentiles. Yet the mission continues for the church today. The only way for sinners to escape hell and gain heaven is by the gospel of Christ. How are you using your abilities and resources to send the gospel to all nations?

Jeremiah

Chapter 1

1. Though we may not be prophets, our call is personal and effectual (Rom. 8:29–30). Every Christian has been consecrated by divine grace to be in the service of the Lord, and as such every believer is the object of His love. Whatever service we are given, it is a calling. Perhaps if we had a better grasp of this, we would not be so despondent in times of difficulty and hardship. Let us therefore serve the Lord with gladness.

2. The children of God are engaged in spiritual warfare; the battle is raging. Let us fight "a good fight" (2 Tim. 4:7), not as defeated Christians but as "more than conquerors through him that loved us" (Rom. 8:37). Upholding the Word of God will never make us popular. We will be hated by many, yet one person with God is a majority! How does this chapter encourage you to stand up for the Lord?

Chapter 2

1. When we backslide from the Lord, He brings to remembrance the love that we had at first (vv. 2–3; Rev. 2:4). If we feel our love for the Lord and His people cooling, let us remember former days when it burned hot and bright. What zeal we once had and what gratitude for His forgiveness and love! Such remembering can stir the backslidden heart to desire repentance that it may taste again of God's living waters.

2. How foolish it is to reject the Lord. If we have the fountain, we need nothing more. Blessing and salvation are freely

available to those who would come (Rev. 22:17). Come to the Lord Jesus, for He says, "Whosoever drinketh of the water that I shall give him shall never thirst; but the water that I shall give him shall be in him a well of water springing up into everlasting life" (John 4:14). In what ways do you need Him today?

Chapter 3

1. Many professing Christians behave as Judah did. They assume that as long as they pay lip service to God, they can live as they please and all will still be well. But becoming a true child of God results in a true change (Ezek. 36:25–27). Those united to Christ cannot live in sin any longer (Rom. 6:1–4).

2. Idolatry, greed, selfishness, and immorality are all fruits that find their root in the hardness and sinfulness of an unregenerate heart. Godly reformation, the kind that Josiah enforced, may strip away evil fruits, but it cannot reach the root or source of the problem, which is the hardened heart of unbelief. We learn from Judah's treachery the depravity of the human heart. The Lord Jesus says in Matthew 15:19, "For out of the heart proceed evil thoughts, murders, adulteries, fornications, thefts, false witness, blasphemies." How then can people ever change?

Chapter 4

1. The warnings of judgment given to Judah look forward to that great and terrible day of the Lord when Christ returns in glory. It is a great blessing when God gives us such warnings and makes us willing to listen to them. There is no

greater comfort in the day of wrath than to know that we are in Christ Jesus (Rom. 8:1; 1 Thess. 1:10; 5:9). What reasons does this chapter give us to flee to Christ and cling to Him by faith?

2. God's judgment of reversing creation begins in the spiritual disorder of those who claim to be His people. This judgment can be seen in churches today that once had order in worship and the light of the gospel but have descended into disorder and darkness. Let us be careful to cling to God's Word by faith and obedience, and then we can take great comfort that the Lord will not make "a full end" of His church.

Chapter 5

1. In a time of great spiritual decline, the Lord challenged Jeremiah to find just one man who publicly stood for truth and righteousness so that the Lord would pardon the city. We see the mercy of God wonderfully revealed here. He would have spared Sodom if *ten* righteous men could have been found there (Gen. 18:23–32); yet though Jerusalem's sins exceed those of Sodom (Ezek. 16:48) the Lord asks for just *one* man. How are you standing in the gap (22:30) by advocating for and doing justice in society?

2. The nation of Judah behaved despicably toward the Lord, yet they still thought highly of themselves. We see the same thing today. The judgment of God is coming, and it will be a terrifying thing (Rev. 20:11–15). Sadly, many will not believe this until it comes upon them. Repent of every sin now, before it is too late.

Chapter 6

1. It was a terrible ordeal for the Jews to fall into the hands of Nebuchadnezzar, but "it is a fearful thing to fall into the hands of the living God" (Heb. 10:31). Like an erupting volcano, the wrath of God will be poured out upon the impenitent. What a comfort it is, then, to be able to say with the apostle Paul, "I know whom I have believed, and am persuaded that he is able to keep that which I have committed unto him against that day" (2 Tim. 1:12). Do you know this comfort? Why or why not?

2. The "old paths" are not the way of mere tradition but the fundamental truths of revealed religion (Col. 2:6–8). Jeremiah is not bidding us to live in the past, for we are to live in the present where God has placed us (Eccl. 7:10). To be in the "old paths" is to be in Christ and to abide in His Word; it is to walk after the Savior in holiness, meekness, obedience, and self-denial. Such is the way of peace and happiness.

Chapter 7

1. The Temple Sermon is a warning against the danger of external religion without a sincere heart for the Lord. Judah thought that attending the temple and going through all the prescribed rituals would satisfy God. They were like so many today who think that simply going to church is enough. The Lord does not ask for a mere form of godliness. He requires true adoration from a contrite heart and a reverent, humble spirit. When sincerity is absent from the heart, then all religion and worship are a lie.

2. It was a terrible tragedy that Judah's sin had become so ingrained and widespread that the day of grace was over for

them, so that further intercession on their behalf was pointless. God had been patient and longsuffering, but they would not hear His voice and therefore faced His judgment. Oh that the Lord would have mercy on our own generation, for if things continue as they are the day of grace may soon be over!

Chapter 8

1. It is sad that scribes should be rebuked for falsehood and misinterpretation of the law. Those who ought to have rightly instructed the people had failed to do so. They valued their own wisdom too highly. There is an important lesson here for us as Christians. While scholarship can be of great value when it comes from believing hearts that seek to reverence the Lord, it can also become a snare and a danger when scholarship is seen as the supreme authority. How can we give scholarship its rightful place without making an idol of it?

2. It is the greatest of tragedies that the vast majority of people have rejected Christ, the Physician of souls. Yet He alone can heal people from their sins. Let us who know the Lord, therefore, seek to proclaim the good news of Jesus Christ to those who are lost and perishing. There is indeed a balm in Gilead to heal the sin-sick soul.

Chapter 9

1. Jeremiah is moved to tears over the persistent sin and unbelief of his people. God had reasoned and pleaded with the people through His prophets to turn unto Him, but they would not. As we look around us today, we see the terrible effects of sin and the misery it has caused. However, the greatest tragedy is that the gospel is rejected. Every provision

for cleansing and healing is provided in and through Christ, yet the great majority choose to reject and despise the Savior. How do sin and unbelief in your neighbors affect you? Do they move you to great sorrow? Why or why not?

2. Great mischief and trouble come from unbridled tongues (v. 8; James 3:3–12). If a work of grace has taken place in our hearts, then surely we will say with the psalmist, "Set a watch, O LORD, before my mouth; keep the door of my lips" (Ps. 141:3).

Chapter 10

1. The religion of Judah was molded by worldly thought practices. The human race was created to worship God. When He is not worshiped there is a void quickly filled by idols, but idols cannot think, see, hear, speak, or take action. Modern idols, such as celebrities or wealth, are equally helpless. The true follower of Jesus Christ is to reject all idols (1 John 5:21). If we are to escape the vanities of this world we must know God (9:24), which will give us great energy to serve Him (Dan. 11:32).

2. Jeremiah was a man prepared for his trials, yet when the shadow of darkness fell on his life he said, "Woe is me for my hurt! My wound is grievous" (v. 19). He felt the intense agony of it. However, he was nonetheless able to say, "Truly this is a grief, and I must bear it." Jeremiah was able to quickly compose himself and put aside his personal fear by bowing to the sovereign will of God. How can a Christian prepare himself so that when troubles come he can cast his cares on the Lord (1 Peter 5:7)?

Chapter 11

1. The curse of the law is the fearful destiny of all who disobey God's covenant (Gal. 3:10). But blessed are all who trust in God's Son (Ps. 2:12), for Christ redeemed sinners from the law by receiving its curse upon the cross (Gal. 3:13). He paid the penalty to satisfy God's justice in the shedding of His own precious blood. Therefore there is no condemnation for those in Christ Jesus (Rom. 8:1).

2. How patient is the love of God! Though the Jews despised His ways, He still calls them "beloved" (v. 15; Rom. 11:28). If this is the case, how patient is He with Jews and Gentiles who belong to Christ, despite their remaining sins and stumbling?

3. Taking a stand for truth can result in hostility. At such times we must trust in the promises of God, as Jeremiah did. Many stumble because they are fearful of the possible consequences of taking such a stand. Do you have faith that God will keep His promises, or do you grow weak at the thought of opposition?

Chapter 12

1. Jeremiah saw the corrupt worship of God seemingly prospering, while the true faith was making no apparent headway at all. We look at many churches that have corrupted their worship with worldly practices and have watered down the gospel, yet they seem to be growing. We sometimes, like Jeremiah, have difficulty reconciling God's promises with our own experiences. However, we need to understand that God sees the whole picture, and we do not. The Christian life involves taking up our cross (Matt. 10:38; Acts 14:22) and waiting on the Lord (Ps. 37:7).

2. The grace of God is held out to people of every nation through the gospel, but it also gives a final warning (vv. 16–17). The Lord sets before people life and death. How foolish it is to reject such great salvation, but how blessed are we who trust in Jesus Christ!

Chapter 13

1. The symbolism of the linen girdle provides a tragic picture of the effects of sin. Israel was God's special people who enjoyed a unique relationship with Him. Yet against all privilege they transgressed the covenant and defiled themselves, becoming useless to God and deprived of His presence. Jeremiah's prophecy warns all in the church: those who outwardly enjoy great spiritual privileges must guard against the corruption of the world, lest they become so marred that privilege is replaced with judgment.

2. Sin is as deeply engrained in mankind as the genetics of our skin color. However, whereas God delights in various colors of skin, His wrath is provoked by our sin. How then can anyone be saved from sin and wrath? Reflect upon Titus 3:3–7.

Chapter 14

1. The physical famine Judah faced was but a reflection of the spiritual famine within. Their hearts were hard, dry, and resistant to both plow and seed. So, too, when God's children foolishly harden their hearts, there comes a period of loving chastening that will end only when there is heartfelt repentance (Heb. 12:6; Rev. 3:19). Has God disciplined you? How have you responded?

2. Jeremiah saw the tragedy of all that had happened to his people, and he wanted God to act. Do we ever come to the Lord with such passion? The prophet wept when he saw the state of the people. It grieved him to see them brought so low. Do we have the same concern for people today? Are we moved to tears that many who profess Christ as Lord have become so worldly and have moved so far from their moorings?

Chapter 15

1. There are occasions when even the fervent prayers of a righteous man are not enough (v. 1). God will answer the prayer for blessing upon the church only after there has been true reformation. Before we pray for the church's prosperity, let us pray for its repentance. And let us repent ourselves before praying for others.

2. The ways of the Lord are hard for us to understand when we have immersed ourselves in the Lord's work and sought to be faithful, yet all of our labors appear to have achieved nothing except to provoke hostility. We might be tempted to say to ourselves, "Why did I ever bother? Life would have been so much easier if I had done nothing." How would you counsel a Christian experiencing a situation like that of Jeremiah?

Chapter 16

1. God knows every sin committed against Him, and in due season He will use whatever means He chooses to search out sinners and gather them for judgment (vv. 16–18). Have you sought the Lord in repentance? You hide from Him in vain, for even your secret sins are in His plain view (Ps. 90:8; Heb.

4:13). Only the blood of Christ can remove sin from God's sight. Do you trust in that blood?

2. The nations will come to the Lord from the ends of the earth (v. 19; Ps. 22:27). The gospel will experience worldwide success. It is a great mercy to us if God has brought home the gospel to our hearts so that we turn from idols to serve the living God (1 Thess. 1:3–10). However, if we have been saved by the gospel we must also join with the church in its mission: "Go ye into all the world, and preach the gospel to every creature" (Mark 16:15). What are you doing to help reach the world for Christ?

Chapter 17

1. The human heart is hard like stone and engraved with rebellion against God (v. 1). It is hostile to God, leading man to depart from the Lord (v. 5). It is utterly deceitful and wholly untrustworthy; the effects of sin make it incurably malignant, and it is unfathomable (v. 9). Man has no hope of curing his own sin. How then can we have hope (24:7; 31:33)?

2. The contrast between the cursed man and the blessed man (vv. 5–8) emphasizes an essential element about the nature of true faith. While both the cursed man and the blessed man may express the same degree of trust, the vital difference between them is in the object of their faith. The only faith that saves is faith in Christ.

3. One of the first signs of apostasy is the abandonment of the Lord's Day. We need to come aside from the world and worship the Lord. Keeping the Lord's Day reveals a longing for Christ to return and affords us a foretaste of heaven, our

eternal rest. In the meantime, let us by God's grace seek to hallow this blessed one day in seven. God promises blessing for those who delight in His day (Isa. 58:13–14).

Chapter 18

1. Every one of us is as clay in the hands of God. God "formed" the body of Adam out of the ground (Gen. 2:7), the same word used by Jeremiah for "potter." He formed us, and therefore He owns us and has the right to do with us as He wills. It should be our prayer that He will mold us more and more into the image of His Son.

2. Just as Judah dismissed God's Word as irrelevant, so people today do the same, saying, "We will walk after our own devices" (v. 12). They are so engrossed in themselves that they have no time for God or for His messengers. Even within the professing church there are many who ignore the Word of God on vital issues, preferring the stubbornness of their own hearts. What is the opposite of stubbornly walking in our own plans and desires? How can you cultivate that in your life?

Chapter 19

1. The shedding of the blood of the innocents brought the condemnation of God upon Judah. Sadly, the same atrocity is prevalent today when people sacrifice unborn children on the altar of self. There is very little difference between our day and Jeremiah's, which teaches a grim lesson to us about the judgment to come.

2. The fierce anger of the Lord, revealed against Judah, will inevitably fall upon all who harden their hearts and refuse to

listen to the Word of the Lord. Therefore, it is a great comfort to know that God has provided a way of escape by giving His only begotten Son (John 3:16). The Lord Jesus has stood in the sinner's place (1 Cor. 15:3), enduring the wrath of God on Calvary's cross for all His blood-bought people. Do not neglect so great a salvation (Heb. 2:3). Repent and believe.

Chapter 20

1. We would expect Jeremiah to praise God for delivering him from Pashur, but he does not. Instead he starts to imagine the terrible things that could have happened to him. We learn here how subtle is the enemy of our souls. At the very time that Jeremiah should have been depending upon God, he gives in to the weakness of the flesh (1 Kings 19:2–4). Let us learn that at such times of trial we need to trust in the Lord rather than leaning on our own understanding of the situation (Prov. 3:5–6).

2. The chapter ends with Jeremiah full of self-pity. Sadly, this is a common experience for Christians when we take our eyes off the Lord and focus on our troubles (Job 3:1–13). On the one hand, let us remember that such times of darkness do not disqualify a person from salvation. On the other hand, let us stir ourselves up to take hold of God and cling to His promises when we are in the darkness. Christ was truly forsaken by God in the darkness, bearing the sins of all His elect (Ps. 22:1; Matt. 27:45–46). If we are in Christ, God will never, ever forsake us, even in our darkest times (Heb. 13:5).

Chapter 21

1. There are many like Zedekiah today who refuse to be in subjection to the Lord. Yet when their rebellion brings calamity upon them, they hope that God will get them out of the mess *they* have created. They do not come in contrition and sorrow for their sins; they merely want to escape the consequences of their sins. Such insincerity only heightens the anger of the Lord against the violators of His law.

2. The Lord said, "I will punish you according to the fruit of your doings" (v. 14). These are fearful and sobering words. To rebel against God and reject His message leaves one alone on the day of judgment. God's justice will be satisfied, and those who refuse to repent are storing up wrath for themselves that will be unleashed on the day of God's wrath and righteous judgment (Rom. 2:5). Do not fool yourself if you continue unrepentant in your sins; God will not be mocked (Gal. 6:7).

Chapter 22

1. The sins and failures of Judah's kings are in stark contrast to David's divinely inspired mandate: that rulers must be just, ruling in the fear of God (2 Sam. 23:2–3). However, even the failure of David's offspring points to God's everlasting covenant anticipating David's greater Son, who would fulfill every qualification (v. 5). Do not hope in human leadership but in Christ, the King of kings.

2. Like father like son is not always true. Josiah set a fine example for Jehoiakim, but Jehoiakim despised his godly home and wise father, foolishly loving outward grandeur rather than inner holiness. As he saw his new palace being built, he no doubt thought to himself how much better his life was than

his father's. The Savior says, "For what is a man profited, if he shall gain the whole world, and lose his own soul? or what shall a man give in exchange for his soul?" (Matt. 16:26).

Chapter 23

1. God's omnipresence and omniscience (vv. 23–34) should bring a perspective of sober clarity to all our lives. All our thoughts and actions are open to the God with whom we have to do (Heb. 4:13). All our troubles and trials are noticed by Him. Do these two attributes of God frighten you? Do they comfort you? Why?

2. To enjoy God's salvation, we must have Christ as both our King and our righteousness (vv. 5–6). He came to rule as God in justice. To participate in His kingdom you must bow to His divine authority and obey His holy will (Matt. 7:21–23). Yet He also came to give a sinful, guilty people righteousness to stand before God. Your obedience will never be sufficient to atone for your sins or achieve for you acceptance in God's sight. You must trust entirely in Christ's work, not your own, and then God will count you as righteous in His sight (Phil. 3:8–9).

Chapter 24

1. Many good people suffer terrible adversity, but God has a purpose that will ultimately work for their good (Rom. 8:28). Indeed, the Lord said of the captives, "I have sent [them] out of this place into the land of the Chaldeans *for their good*" (Jer. 24:5, emphasis added). What may have appeared to be a catastrophe would ultimately be seen as a blessing. We should not, therefore, be overwhelmed when apparent

calamity overtakes us. Rather, we should remember captives like Daniel and Ezekiel who served God through it all.

2. Appearances often belie the facts. As the captives were carried away in chains, no doubt many who were left felt a sense of pride and self-esteem over God having chosen them to remain in the Promised Land. Instead of seeing this as a warning to turn away from their wicked practices, they imagined that all was fine with them. They would soon discover that they were under the wrath of God and marked for severe judgment. When we see the wicked prospering, let us not despair (Ps. 73).

Chapter 25

1. The godly king Josiah did all he could to drive idolatry out of Judah. Yet how different was his son, Jehoiakim. Grace is not inherited. The Lord Jesus declares, "Ye must be born again" (John 3:7). This applies just as much to the children of believing parents as it does to any other person. New birth is "not of blood, nor of the will of the flesh, nor of the will of man, but of God" (John 1:13).

2. Scripture compares God's judgment to a cup of wrath and fury that is to be given to sinners (v. 15). Just as believers will drink forever from the fountain of living waters (2:13), delighting in God's limitless love, so also the wicked and unbelieving will choke forever on the molten fire of God's righteous anger. This should fill us with wonder at what Christ did to save sinners, when He drank the bitter cup of wrath to the very last drop (Luke 22:42–44). Who can say what it cost Him?

Chapter 26

1. Jeremiah's exhortation to repent, delivered to the temple worshipers, is a vivid reminder that just going to church has no merit before God. It is possible to be in the most holy of environments, and to go through all the motions of worship, without a sincere heart before God. Many today hear the gospel and profess it to be the Word of God, yet go no further. What are the distinctive marks of truly believing the Word?

2. Jeremiah and Urijah faithfully preached the same message (v. 20), and both of their lives were threatened because of what they preached. In the providence of God Jeremiah was delivered, but Urijah was not. Some who live by faith are delivered from their enemies, and some are killed (Acts 12:1–11; Heb. 11:33–37). We are to be faithful to God and His Word, regardless of the consequences.

3. The rejection of the prophet points to the ultimate rejection of the ideal Prophet, Jesus Christ. How was Jeremiah an imperfect but true picture of Christ? How are the two different?

Chapter 27

1. Zedekiah's foolish refusal of the Lord's easy yoke of obedience resulted in divine justice coming heavily upon him. Zedekiah refused to see the truth; his eyes were put out and he was shackled in irons, never to be released (39:7; 2 Kings 25:7). Here is a picture of what happens when God gives a person over to a reprobate mind. The Lord Jesus lovingly calls the slaves of Satan to come unto Him and take His easy yoke upon them (Matt. 11:28–30). The reprobate, however, refuse the message of grace and despise God's salvation.

Eventually, all light is taken from them and they perish. Do not resist the light you have been given, or you may end up in total darkness.

2. The contrast between the words of the true and the false prophets was a matter of life and death. False prophecy naturally appeals to us. "There is a way which seemeth right unto a man, but the end thereof are the ways of death" (Prov. 14:12). The true Word calls us to humbly surrender to Christ, God's great Prophet and Servant. Listen to Him!

Chapter 28

1. Jeremiah's message was one of gloom and hardship. Hananiah's was upbeat and positive. There can be little doubt which was the more popular. We must not, therefore, be surprised when false religion is more popular than the truth. Liberalism falsely declares what people want to hear: that God is love and that everyone will enjoy heaven. Such lies cause people to live without any regard for their sins or for the holiness and justice of God. "It is a fearful thing to fall into the hands of the living God" (Heb. 10:31). Why should we be so foolish as to ignore God's Word?

2. That both the false prophet and the true prophet claimed to have a word from the Lord reminds us of how important it is to "try the spirits whether they are of God: because many false prophets are gone out into the world" (1 John 4:1; cf. 2 Peter 2:1–3). In our day, the key test is conformity to what God has already revealed. We know that God's Word will never be self-contradictory. We must be like the Bereans, who "searched the scriptures daily, whether those things were so" (Acts 17:11).

Chapter 29

1. Like the exiles of Judah in Babylon, so Christians are exiles in this world (Heb. 11:13; 1 Peter 1:1; 2:11). Our citizenship is in heaven, not here (Phil. 3:20). However, Christians are not to be detached from society but should live in the world in such a way as to set forth the beauty of Christ. We, too, must seek the peace of our community (Jer. 29:7), letting our good works shine before men (Matt. 5:16). How can you do this?

2. As God had plans of peace for the people of Judah in their captivity, so He has plans of peace toward all His people in Christ, though they are still exiles in this world. God is not playing hide and seek with His people. He will not forsake any who genuinely and wholeheartedly seek Him. Christians, therefore, should be people of great optimism, enduring their trials with confident hope.

Chapter 30

1. It is surely the greatest comfort to have a real assurance that the Lord is with us (v. 9). This assuring promise runs throughout Scripture, particularly in times of crisis, or special work in advancing the kingdom: to Jacob (Gen. 28:15), Moses (Ex. 3:12), Joshua (Josh. 1:9), Gideon (Judg. 6:12), and believers today (Matt. 28:20). How blessed we are if our trust is in the Lord! Let this thought be to your continual comfort, for God is the great healer.

2. Judah suffered greatly because they would not obey the Word of the Lord; but God used their suffering to chastise them, with a view of bringing them back to Himself. It is a wonderful assurance to know that though there are times

when the Lord chastises His people, it is nonetheless always for our good (Rom. 8:28). How much better it would be to hear God's Word and avoid His chastisement altogether. May the Lord grant us teachable spirits and the humility to walk in obedience before Him.

Chapter 31

1. The word "love" is often used too casually. "In love" is the common term for those who are attracted to each other. However, when the Lord of glory says "I have loved thee" to fallen men and women, it is amazing. We tend to love what we consider to be lovable, but God loved His people while they were still sinners, with nothing attractive about them. It is even more amazing that God bound Himself in a covenant commitment to sinners and promised not just to love them but also to win their love for Himself. Take time now and through the day to praise God for His amazing, sovereign grace.

2. Another wonderful statement appears at the end of verse 9: "I am a father to Israel, and Ephraim is my firstborn." Israel had squandered their blessings and gone astray, yet the Lord chastised them to bring them back to Himself. Every child of God is like the prodigal who journeyed far from his father. We lived for ourselves and had no thought of God. Yet the Lord brings sinners back. Does your heart echo the words of repentance (vv. 18–19)? If so, then God rejoices over you as his dear son or daughter (v. 20).

Chapter 32

1. Tests of faith often come in the midst of trials. Jeremiah was shut up in prison when, just as Jerusalem was about to

fall, God told him to purchase a field. Yet this command points to God's promise: that Judah's captivity would end and that they would return. Jeremiah's only hope was in God's Word, but that was enough for him, so he bought the land. Faith often appears beyond reason, but it is never unreasonable. Let us walk by faith in God's sure Word, even when circumstances seem to be contrary.

2. Jeremiah's praying after purchasing the property (vv. 16–25) illustrates that prayer arises from and is fueled by faith in the Word. We know and believe that God's will shall be done, so we pray as Christ taught us, "Thy will be done" (Matt. 6:10). Jeremiah's prayer focused on God's perfections (32:17–19) and past acts (vv. 20–23). Why does meditating on God and His works give us power to pray in faith?

Chapter 33

1. Verse 3 is surely one of the great prayer promises in the Bible. The Lord invites—indeed, commands—us to call unto Him, with the assurance that He will answer in ways that exceed our expectations (Eph. 3:20). He is a God who loves to hear and answer prayer. This is a great incentive for us to love Him and call upon Him habitually (Ps. 116:1–2). He does not say "I might" but "I will answer thee." He will not refuse when we ask aright (Luke 11:9–10).

2. The promises of the Branch (vv. 15–16; 23:5–6) sum up the great gospel truth of justification by the righteousness of Christ alone. He satisfied every demand of the law for us and paid the penalty for our transgression. His name is our only hope of salvation, for His righteousness covers believers with

His beauty in God's sight (Isa. 61:10). We are accepted in the Beloved (Eph. 1:6)! How can that give you joy?

Chapter 34

1. What an insult to Almighty God that these slave owners, having released their slaves with an oath to the Lord, should quickly change their minds when the thought of danger appears to have passed. Sadly, it is often the case that men and women make promises to God when their troubles confront them, yet as soon as there is a respite go back to their sinful lifestyles. There was no true repentance in their lives. Let us be very careful to keep any promise that we make to the Lord.

2. What a contrast there is between these wicked men, who went back on their promise, and the Lord Jesus, who kept His covenant promise even to a bloody death. He came to set free those who were held fast by the chains of sin (Luke 4:16–21). He says of Himself, "If the Son therefore shall make you free, ye shall be free indeed" (John 8:36). Since God did not spare His own Son, how much more can we trust Him to keep His promises?

Chapter 35

There are practical lessons for Christians from the example of the Rechabites. If they kept the command of their father for generations, how much more should we live in sober faithfulness to the commands of God through His prophets and apostles? The Rechabites may have seemed like a poor people to others, living as they did in tents and abstaining from the pleasure of wine, but God blessed them for their faithfulness in an inconsistent and unfaithful generation

(34:10–11). May we also be people whose yes means yes and no means no, a people who cling to the faithfulness of God whose promises are all yes in Jesus Christ—even if it makes us seem poor and deprived to the world. When is it hard for you to be faithful and consistent? How can the faithfulness of the Rechabites and the Lord encourage you?

Chapter 36

1. Baruch's writing of Jeremiah's prophetic words illustrates the creation of the Bible. The Lord gave the words to Jeremiah (1:5), who faithfully spoke them. Baruch faithfully recorded them in writing. Each step of this process was governed by the Spirit of God so that the product, the Scriptures, is the inspired Word of God (2 Tim. 3:16). When we read the words of the prophets and apostles, we may rest assured that these are the very words of the Lord (Jer. 36:4, 6, 8, 11, 27).

2. There are many like Jehoiakim who are determined to destroy God's Word. Tragically, even those who make an outward profession of belief in Christ often make the greatest efforts to blot out parts of Scripture, whether miracles or moral laws or some teaching they deem to be offensive. Yet such efforts by these enemies of God are ultimately all in vain. God's Word will triumph. It cannot be destroyed. Let us therefore open our hearts to receive His Word that it may be our constant companion through life.

Chapter 37

1. Zedekiah's request for prayer reveals a peculiar irony among many who will not listen to God's Word and pray, yet they will ask true believers to intercede for them during

difficult times. Of course, if such people ask us to pray for them we should, because in the providence of God this may lead to their salvation. However, such requests from unbelievers are usually a last resort, highlighting their own spiritual deadness. Sadly, when such prayers are answered these people usually return to their former rejection of God. Let us therefore pray for the circumstances and their souls.

2. Jeremiah was hated because he told the truth. Let us also remember that the gospel will always cause offense to the unbeliever. People do not want to hear that they are sinners (John 3:19–20; 15:18, 22). Yet unless they hear what their true state is before God, they will never desire the remedy for their sins. Let us therefore seek to be courageous for the truth and pray that the Lord will bless our labors in the gospel.

Chapter 38

1. Jeremiah, a man of sorrows, typifies the Lord Jesus (Isa. 53:3). It can be said of both that "He came unto his own, and his own received him not" (John 1:11). The princes or court officials called for Jeremiah to be put to death. Likewise, they said of the Lord Jesus, "He is guilty of death" (Matt. 26:66). Zedekiah's words are reminiscent of what Pilate would later say when prevailed upon to put Jesus to death: "I am innocent of the blood of this just person: see ye to it" (Matt. 27:24). Jeremiah's sinking into the mire is reminiscent of that messianic psalm of David: "I sink in deep mire, where there is no standing" (Ps. 69:2; cf. vv. 15, 20; 40:1–2).

2. There are many like Zedekiah who are too proud to repent and to trust in the Lord, even though they see everything collapsing around them. They see the truth of God's

Word coming to pass and they fear for the future, yet they will not humble themselves before the Lord. The Scripture says, "Seek ye the LORD while he may be found, call ye upon him while he is near" (Isa. 55:6). That day of opportunity will come to an end, as it did for Zedekiah, and then all hope is lost. How are you seeking God now?

Chapter 39

1. The people of Judah did not believe that the wrath of God would come upon them, even when the warning signs were there. There are many people today like this who scoff at Christ's return to judge the world in holy wrath. Yet we should not be surprised at His coming (see 2 Peter 3:1–4). Let us believe and humble ourselves before the Lord. Let us watch and wait in prayer, for the day of wrath will come.

2. There is a great contrast between Zedekiah and Ebed-melech. They heard the same word, but with vastly different responses. Ebed-melech trusted God's Word and cared for God's prophet. He did what was right in the eyes of the Lord; therefore, God delivered him. By God's grace, this is what will happen to every believer on the day of judgment. Which would you rather be: a rich king who does not trust the Lord or a servant who places his faith in Him? Why?

Chapter 40

The blessing of much fruit in the midst of destruction reveals the grace of God, a sign that He offered blessings to His people if they would submit to the Babylonians as He had commanded (vv. 9–10, 12). As long as we live, God's judgments are mingled with mercy, calling sinners to submit to His discipline and instruction. Even in the midst of pronouncing judgment after man's fall, God announced the grace of Christ (Gen. 3:15). Yet His call is hard, just as hard as it was for the Jews to serve the Babylonians. Christ calls us to take our crosses, deny ourselves, and follow Him (Matt. 16:24).

Chapter 41

1. While believers must seek to be as "harmless as doves," we are also exhorted to be as "wise as serpents" (Matt. 10:16). Gedaliah made a huge error of judgment in his trust of Ishmael. How important it is to have discernment in our dealings with others, especially with those in the world. To trust human nature is to give way to folly. We must always be on our guard against the subtle actions of those who despise the Lord's ways. What are areas in which you need discernment now? How can you seek it?

2. Ishmael's eating of bread with Gedaliah under the guise of friendship is suggestive of Judas Iscariot's betrayal of the Lord Jesus at the Last Supper. However, whereas Gedaliah was ignorant of Ishmael's intentions, the Lord Jesus was fully aware of Judas's plot (John 13:21, 25–26). Gedaliah's naive trust allowed the betrayal to succeed and resulted not only in his own death but also in the deaths of many others. However, Christ willingly allowed His betrayal to take place, for His death gives life to all who will trust in Him.

Chapter 42

1. God always requires obedience to His will. The people were right to go to Jeremiah in order to discover God's will, for he was the prophet from whom the Word of the Lord

would be revealed. Their professed commitment to do His will seemed commendable (v. 6) but ultimately proved hypocritical, for when His will was declared they did not want to hear because it was contrary to their own plans. Too often even professing Christians tend to be selective in their obedience, thus revealing that they sometimes prefer their own desires to God's will. We must believe that the Lord's way is always best, even when it seems to go against what we may perceive to be better (Prov. 3:5).

2. The Jews' desire to return to Egypt is equivalent to Christians wanting to go back into the world; it is to forget the powerful blood of Christ and that the believer is separated from this vain and passing world. Let us never lose sight of the blessedness we have in Christ; neither should we ever doubt that God always knows what is best for us. May we therefore always seek to be obedient to His Word.

Chapter 43

1. Hebrews 1:1 mentions various ways in which God communicated through His prophets. This chapter reveals two of them: first, through the prophet's preaching, and second, through his symbolic actions, such as burying the stones. This portrayed the message in a way that should have been easy for all to understand. It was gracious of God to reinforce His Word in this way, but it also left them without excuse. The Bible presents Christ to us in many ways in order to make Him clear; we have no excuse for not trusting and following Him.

2. The safe haven Israel hoped to find proved anything but secure, and their folly provides us with a cautionary tale. It

is utter foolishness to go against the revealed will of God. This Jewish remnant knew what He required of them. Yet they proved to be more fearful of man than of God; hence, they made a fateful mistake (Prov. 14:12). The safest place on earth is the place of obedience to God's will (Ps. 37:3–6).

Chapter 44

1. The Jewish exiles in Egypt failed to have teachable spirits. They had witnessed the calamity God had inflicted upon Jerusalem because of their idolatry. Their previous worship of the queen of heaven had caused God to make their land "a desolation" (v. 22). However, their hearts were so hardened they would not learn the lesson. Their repeated refusal to repent led into spiritual stupidity and dullness. The vast majority of those who fled to Egypt would never return. They would be "consumed by the sword and by the famine" (v. 27). Therefore, let us be quick to repent as soon as God's Word reveals our sin, lest we, too, fall into hardness and then destruction.

2. Even in judgment, God spared some in mercy. He says, "Yet a small number that escape the sword shall return out of the land of Egypt into the land of Judah" (v. 28). This blessed thought should never cause us to be presumptuous; rather, it should spur us on to desire a life of righteousness and obedience unto Him.

Chapter 45

Baruch faithfully recorded Jeremiah's message of doom and destruction; nevertheless, his response was inappropriate. While not disagreeing with the prophecy, he seems to have grieved that the judgment of the nation would take away the great things he sought for himself. Self-seeking and self-pity only bring distress. Christians sometimes hope that God will hold back His judgment of the world until all their earthly goals have been achieved. This special word to Baruch teaches us that if believers would know real peace they must submit unreservedly to the will of God and rejoice to know that their own persons will be saved from the wrath of God.

Chapter 46

1. God used Babylon as an instrument to accomplish His will (v. 26). Let us remember that the events of our era are also still under His control. If we hear of wars, nations rising against nations, and other disasters, we must not view them merely as the results of human factors. The Lord reigns, and His people can rejoice that all things serve for His glory and their good.

2. The principal application Jeremiah draws from the coming judgment on Egypt is directed toward Judah (vv. 27–28). They had foolishly trusted in Egypt (v. 25), but the Lord of glory called them to trust in Him alone (Isa. 30:1–3; 31:1–5). How might you be tempted to trust in yourself or other people? How can you make the Lord alone your hope in all things?

Chapter 47

The Philistines had been a thorn in Israel's side since the times of the judges. On occasion Israel was able to subdue them (e.g., Samson and David), yet they persisted as enemies of God's people. The Lord's judgment may sometimes be slow in coming, but it will come. It is a most wonderful attribute of God that He is slow to anger. In mercy He grants time for repentance (Rom. 2:4), but when that repentance does not come His patience gives way to judgment. That time had now come for Philistia. If you do not know the Lord, then seek Him while He may be found.

Chapter 48

1. The Lord judges the nations for their sins. God named three reasons why He destroyed Moab. First, they trusted in their strength, riches, and false gods instead of trusting in Him (vv. 7, 13). Second, they were proud and arrogant instead of humble before Him (vv. 26, 29). Third, they mocked Israel instead of having compassion for the people of the Lord (v. 27). How are these sins evident in your own nation? What does this text say to your people today?

2. The Lord shows wonderful mercy to undeserving sinners! Even the remnant of Moab shall return (v. 47). God humbled those who had puffed themselves up in arrogance against Him, but then He set them free. Though the Lord is a God of wrath, still He delights in mercy. If God has humbled you for your sins, be encouraged to return to Him through Jesus Christ. He is a gracious God, quick to bless all who repent.

Chapter 49

When God judges the nations, He announces hope for some, but not for all. Why does the Lord show mercy to Egypt (46:26), Moab (48:47), Ammon (49:6), and Elam (v. 39) but not to Philistia, Edom, Damascus, Kedar, and Hazor? Here we come to the mystery of God's grace. God chose Jacob for mercy, but not Esau (Rom. 9:10–16). There were two thieves crucified with Christ at Calvary, but only one was convicted of his sins and turned to Christ in humility and hope (Luke 23:39–43). On the one hand, this teaches us not to despair, for God has grace for His enemies. On the other hand, it warns us not to presume upon His grace, for the Lord saves only some. Let us humbly and earnestly seek God's grace, trusting in His promise to save all who come to Him.

Chapter 50

1. Jeremiah gives us a wonderful picture of conversion (v. 4). In the mercy and providence of Almighty God, He brings about true contrition in the hearts of His people. They weep over their sins and return not simply to their land but to their God. Conversion is not a movement of the body but a motion of the heart, a turning away from sin in humility, brokenness, and grief, and a turning to the Lord in desire and hope (Matt. 5:3–6; James 4:8–10).

2. God's judgment of Babylon gives occasion to reflect upon the mysterious relationship between divine sovereignty and human responsibility. Although men often tend to deny one to support the other, Scripture always unites them. God used Babylon to inflict judgment upon His people, and then He judged Babylon for their sins in doing so. Babylon, while being God's instrument, acted without reference to Him, transgressing His laws in the process. What lessons do these twin truths teach us?

Chapter 51

1. Poetic justice characterized Babylon's judgment (v. 49). Just as they had done to others, so it would be done to them.

The prospect of receiving from God what we justly deserve is a terrifying thought. Outside of Christ it is the certain consequence of sin (Gal. 6:7–8). The beauty of the gospel is that Christ took what we deserve (our condemnation) so that we might receive what He deserves (His righteousness; 2 Cor. 5:21). This should be a pressing motive to flee to Christ as the only hope for life.

2. Living with sin all around us can affect our spiritual vitality. It was not easy to remember Jerusalem when the Jews saw the splendor of Babylon. It is easy today for Christians to be enticed by earthly ambition and pleasure. We are not to love the things of this world, because they are destined to pass away just like Babylon (1 John 2:15–17). It is much better to set our affections on things above (Col. 3:1–2).

Chapter 52

1. The events of Jerusalem's destruction confirm what God assured Jeremiah of at the start of his ministry: "I will hasten my word to perform it" (1:12). Every part of Jeremiah's hard prophecy of judgment was fulfilled in his day, giving confidence that the glorious and hopeful elements would also be fulfilled, as they were in the coming of Christ, the righteous Branch (23:5–6; 33:15–16). Seeing prophecy fulfilled is wonderfully encouraging, and it energizes our faith. All of God's promises will just as certainly come to pass: "Even so, come, Lord Jesus" (Rev. 22:20).

2. Jehoiachin's preservation served God's redemptive purpose for when Christ would come. There needed to be a royal line of the seed of David in order for Christ to be his greater son and thereby display all the fullness of God's grace. When

everything seemed hopeless, the Lord did not forget His promises, all of which are yea and amen in Christ (2 Cor. 1:20). Hoping in God's providences and promises means hoping in Jesus Christ, for they all revolve around Him. How has reading Jeremiah encouraged you to hope in Jesus Christ alone?

Lamentations

Chapter 1

1. In the midst of national suffering, Jeremiah reveals a true pastor's heart. He does not turn from the people, rather, he identifies with them in their sorrow. His tears mingle with theirs. How can you identify, grieve with, and support someone you know who is suffering?

2. What sorrow sin brings in its wake! Let us, therefore, heed the Word of God and seek to follow God's ways rather than our own desires. Remember, our sufficiency is in Christ alone!

3. Sadly, the world often takes great delight in the sufferings of the Lord's people, and here, in Lamentations, we have such a case before us in verse 21. What should be our response when such taunting is directed at us in our sorrows? First, we are to remember that a day of judgment is coming. Second, we should remember that though the enemies of God may take much delight in the present sufferings of His people, they are completely ignorant of the fact that He chastens us "for our profit" (Heb. 12:10) in order that we might escape what will be their tragic end.

Chapter 2

1. Lamentations reveals how the Lord deals with His unrepentant people, "How hath the LORD covered the daughter of Zion with a cloud in his anger" (v. 1). When the Egyptians pursued after Israel at the Red Sea, the fiery, cloudy pillar came between Israel and the Egyptians (Ex. 14:19–20), yet

now the cloud of God's anger confronts Judah. Let us therefore endeavor, by God's grace, to stay close to the Savior, for He says, "I am the light of the world: he that followeth me shall not walk in darkness, but shall have the light of life" (John 8:12).

2. Judah was suffering the consequence of their sin. Yet sometimes calamities come into life for no apparent reason. Our faith can at times be tested severely. We may find these trials hard to square with the love of a heavenly Father. We may ask, concerning our circumstances, "Why is this thing happening? Why am I suffering so much? What good can come from this? Has God deserted me?" At times like this, we have plenty of questions, but few or no answers. Yet often we can do nothing in our grief other than ask God these questions even as we bow under His sovereign will. Such was the situation concerning Judah after the fall of Jerusalem. However, "Shall not the Judge of all the earth do right?" (Gen. 18:25).

Chapter 3

1. Jeremiah's counsel is appropriate for every circumstance of life yet particularly in times of trouble: "The LORD is good unto them that wait for him, to the soul that seeketh him" (v. 25). When the apostle Paul was severely troubled by his "thorn in the flesh," he wrote: "For this thing I besought the Lord thrice, that it might depart from me. And he said unto me, My grace is sufficient for thee: for my strength is made perfect in weakness" (2 Cor. 12:8–9). What a blessing in times of trial to be able to say, "Most gladly therefore will I rather glory in my infirmities, that the power of Christ may rest upon me" (v. 9)!

2. Although there are times when prayer seems to be powerless and empty (v. 44), the reality is that God draws near when His people call (v. 57). Prayer is often not easy. Sometimes we must wrestle as Jacob did, but what an incentive to keep on praying—God hears us and will answer! Take comfort in this: our God says, "Fear not" (v. 57). Remember what Christ has done for believers! The closing verses of this third lament reveal God as the Vindicator of His people. Jeremiah knows that the Lord sees and hears all that the enemies of God's people have done to them, and he cries to the One who "though he bear long with them…will avenge them speedily" (Luke 18:7–8).

Chapter 4

1. What a tragedy when the Lord's people lose their usefulness in His service. Just as the temple was constructed of fine stones perfectly fitted together to the glory of God, so believers as "lively [or living] stones, are built up a spiritual house, an holy priesthood, to offer up spiritual sacrifices, acceptable to God by Jesus Christ" (1 Peter 2:5). Remember, Christian, you are chosen to "shew forth the praises of him who hath called you out of darkness into his marvellous light" (1 Peter 2:9).

2. The failures of the religious leaders had terrible consequences for the entire nation. The connection between the pulpit and the welfare of people remains strong. In a real sense, "how goes the pulpit, so goes the nation." Let us, therefore, understand the vital importance of sitting under faithful ministry where our spiritual needs are satisfied in Christ alone. May we earnestly seek after faithful ministry that preaches Christ in all His beauty and declares His

wonderful merits. May we delight in the gospel and shun that which is harmful to our souls. O that we might be delivered from sinful religious leadership in our day!

Chapter 5

1. It is a difficult thing for God's people to bear reproach because it poorly reflects upon the honor of the Lord Himself. Therefore, when we feel such reproach, we must come with all haste to the throne of grace and find our refuge in Christ. Judah's inheritance was lost through sin, and while it is the Christian's privilege to have an inheritance that cannot be lost (1 Peter 1:4), nonetheless, our being the Lord's is revealed by obedience to Him (vv. 14–15). Let us therefore greatly value our inheritance won at such tremendous cost through the supreme sacrifice of our Savior, Jesus Christ.

2. Judah's sin took them to the depths, and it was not until they realized that depth that they came to their senses and sought the Lord. When we stubbornly go our own way, God allows us to come to an end of ourselves; only then shall we realize our foolishness (Luke 15:17–19). What a blessing that God has a design for our suffering—it brings us to the place of prayer! Let us learn this lesson well: there is no true joy when living distant from the Lord.

Ezekiel

Chapter 1

1. God brings His people into difficult circumstances, but He is with them. Ezekiel was a priest, ready and of age to enter upon the Lord's work, but God had ordered the situation so that he had been taken as a captive into Babylon (vv. 1–3). How distressing it must have been for Ezekiel to lose his opportunity to serve in the temple! Yet God had a plan for Ezekiel even greater than he had anticipated. Although Ezekiel was far from Jerusalem, God was not far from His servant. Christians must remember that great trials and pagan neighbors or coworkers cannot separate us from our God or frustrate His purposes for us. He will not waste our lives but will be with us and use us for His glory if we follow Him.

2. Though Ezekiel's vision is dazzling and some of its details are hard to interpret, the big picture it presents reveals truths about God that are most encouraging. Behind the visible world of politics, wars, and personal tragedies there sits One upon a throne of glory (vv. 26–28), ruling the world by His power and His servants, the spirits of heaven. Christians must live with their eyes open to the unseen world (2 Kings 6:15–17; Eph. 6:12). Be assured that God's rule is universal (Ezek. 1:15–25). The chariot throne with its complexity and harmony teaches that God's providence, though hidden in mystery, rules all things through an amazingly wise design (Eph. 1:11). We should learn to look beyond circumstances

to the One on the throne. How can you seek a spiritual awareness of the glory of Christ that gives you courage and hope?

Chapter 2

1. Ezekiel had no supernatural qualities of his own. He was a man, a son of Adam, with all the frailties and fears common to fallen men. However, God called him, filled him with the Spirit, and commissioned him to a great work. His power to preach came from God. God still chooses weak human instruments to serve Him (2 Cor. 4:7). Every servant of the Lord must rely on the Spirit's empowering to fulfill his task. How often do you pray for your pastor that God's Spirit would enable him to speak God's Word boldly?

2. God's Word is a hard message, for it is a message to sinners. People have rebelled against God, turned their backs on God, hardened their faces, and become stonyhearted toward Him. God is rightly offended at their rebellion, but in His mercy He calls sinners to repentance through the preaching of the Word. When you hear a hard message against sin from a preacher, do not despise him for his faithfulness. Welcome it and repent.

Chapter 3

1. The Lord's instruction to Ezekiel to eat the words He gave him (v. 3) and to receive them in his heart (v. 10) has pointed application for preachers and for all Christians. To eat something is to receive its nutrients so that it becomes part of the body and fuels its activity. Unless ministers who preach the Word first feed their own souls, they are simply spouting theory. They must preach God's truth from their hearts.

Every Christian should receive the Word of God the same way, whether as they hear it in a sermon or read it in the Scripture. Take time to "chew" on the Word, to prayerfully meditate so that its truths will become a part of your mind and heart and give the necessary strength for spiritual activity. When do you regularly meditate on the Word?

2. Whenever God gives authority to one person over others, He also holds that leader accountable as a "watchman" over them. This person has a responsibility to promote good, speak against evil, and warn of sin's consequences. This is especially true of the elders of the church, who "watch for your souls, as they that must give account" (Heb. 13:17). God does not hold His watchmen accountable for how people respond to the truth, but He does require watchmen to faithfully speak the truth to those under their charge. How can we encourage God's watchmen to serve well in their callings? What would motivate someone to be a good watchman, even when this task is far from popular?

Chapter 4

1. Why did God send a series of strange signs to the captives? It was to teach by repetition. God was instructing them line by line. He was emphasizing His will, patiently showing them the consequences of sin. God is patient with sinners. How good God is! This gives us all the more reason to listen humbly to His Word.

2. Although there were many signs, the message they conveyed was the same: Israel's sin was going to be followed by judgment. When God speaks, we should take note. He has a message for us that is worthy of our attention and reception.

He does not change. His warning to Judah of siege and famine was the same warning He had given more than 800 years earlier through Moses. Let no one deceive you with empty words. The wrath of God is coming on sinners who do not repent.

Chapter 5

One of the most striking truths to emerge from Ezekiel is the severity of the judgment upon the people for their sin. The cutting and division of Ezekiel's hair portray intense judgment. With emphatic tone God stated, "Behold, I, even I, am against thee, and will execute judgments in the midst of thee" (v. 8). This declaration is supported by the repeated phrase "I the LORD have spoken it" (vv. 13, 15, 17). In a world that makes light of God's wrath upon sin, we must remember that by nature we are all sinners under the fury and condemnation of God. His wrath abides upon unbelievers. Only Christ can save from the judgment of God. How does this truth make Christ precious to your soul?

Chapter 6

Idolatry is a common sin. However, idolatry is not confined to worshiping before a statue or picture; it is a disposition of the soul that turns away from God to replace Him with created things, what Ezekiel called a "whorish heart." By nature, the human heart is idolatrous (Rom. 1:21–23). It loves itself and this world instead of God and His will (1 John 2:15–17). Idolatry can take many forms and is often a secret sin. God is against all idolatry, for He deserves and demands our worship. He is jealous over our wholehearted love. We are to have no other gods before him, not even the god of self. To what forms of idolatry are you most attracted? How do you need to repent of idolatry?

Chapter 7

1. The intensity of the language in this chapter and the repetition of the words "the time is come" (vv. 7, 12) emphasize the certainty of God's judgment upon sin. His time for judgment upon all sin will come at His appointed hour (Eccl. 8:11–13). It is imperative to be ready to meet the Lord. Have you turned from sin to the Savior? If not, why not? The time of judgment is coming.

2. No man will be able to deliver himself from the judgment of God. No amount of gold or human effort will provide safety from the wrath of God (v. 19). If souls do not escape to Christ and find deliverance in Him, they will not be delivered. There is no salvation through riches or "being religious" but only through the Lord Jesus Christ, the only Redeemer of God's elect. Cast away your idols now, for they cannot save you, and flee to the Lord.

Chapter 8

Even today many people represent divine beings with visible objects, or direct their worship to or through images. Millions still engage in gross idolatry. However, people in secularized nations may have difficulty identifying idol worship in their culture. In such societies, idols may take other forms, such as pornography, captivation by video entertainment, or the love of money, but secular idols no less rule the souls of those who adore them. God sees all idolatry and He views it with disgust. It is particularly offensive to Him when those who participate in public worship with His people profane His holy presence with their wicked idols. What are the most common idols worshiped by people around you? How does God view these idols? How are you fleeing this idolatry?

Chapter 9

1. This vision suggests four important truths to consider about God's judgment. (1) Divine judgment is justified. The text shows that sinners are completely defiled and deluded, being complacent in sin. (2) Divine judgment is comprehensive. None were to be spared, regardless of age or gender, because all have sinned. (3) Divine judgment is infallible. That it began at the sanctuary shows that the religious hypocrites are known by God, who looks through religion to the heart. (4) Divine judgment is escapable. God has marked those who belong to Him, redeeming them through Christ's blood, sealing them with the Holy Spirit, and enabling them to evidence their salvation in holy grief and repentance for sin.

2. Christ the Priest is the Mediator charged by God to distinguish between those who will fall under divine judgment and those who will be saved. The central figure described in this vision is the one clothed in linen like a priest, standing beside the altar of burnt offerings in the temple. Christ is the High Priest of His people (Heb. 8:1). He has offered Himself once for all their sins (Heb. 10:12). He alone has the authority to mark people as saved. Whom does He mark? He marks only those who sorrow over sin and cry out to God. Is Christ your priest? Do you look to Him by faith in His saving death and resurrection? Is your heart broken and contrite over sin, crying out to God for mercy?

Chapter 10

This vision could well have the title "Ichabod," which means either "there is no glory" or "where is the glory?" (1 Sam. 4:21). The glory of God had descended on the temple at its dedication, overwhelming all those who were there (1 Kings 8:10–11). But now the glory of God departed, and soon the temple would be destroyed. However, God's purpose of grace cannot be frustrated. The temple would be rebuilt, and that second temple would know a greater glory than the first. God would come to it, not in a mysterious cloud but in the person of the Son (Mal. 3:1). In union with Christ, the church is now the temple of the living God (1 Cor. 3:16–17). How tragic it is for a church today to have "Ichabod" written over it! Nothing is worse than to be a church without His presence, thinking of itself as rich and wise even while Christ is outside knocking to enter and calling it to repent (Rev. 3:17–20). How can a church avoid this tragedy?

Chapter 11

1. That God promised to be a "sanctuary" for His scattered people is precious and encouraging. God is full of mercy, and that mercy is often seen in the darkest and deepest trials. Fellowshipping with God does not depend on any location or special building. David desired to see the Lord's power and glory in the dry and thirsty land, just as he had seen it in the sanctuary (Ps. 63:1–2). In Christ, God's glory is no longer located at a particular building, but with all who worship Him in spirit and truth (John 4:21–24). Providence often takes the church to hard places, but God does not abandon it. No matter where you may be, draw near to God through

Christ in unity with His people, and through His Spirit the Lord will be your sanctuary (Eph. 2:18).

2. Regeneration is a work that we need but only God can do (vv. 19–20). The old heart is stone-cold, lifeless, insensitive, incapable of doing anything in the direction of God. God transforms the dead heart into a heart of flesh with vitality and spiritual impulses. This is the new birth (John 3:3–8; Titus 3:3–8) that produces obedience to God's Word (1 John 2:29; 3:9). Without this new heart man is doomed (v. 21). You must be born again. Are you? If so, rejoice in God's amazing grace. If not, then feel the danger of your impending damnation and cry out to Jesus Christ to save you from your sins.

Chapter 12

From the beginning of the nation's existence God had raised up prophets to warn the people of certain judgment if they broke the covenant and did not repent. For hundreds of years prophets were preaching the same message. Those who needed to repent rejected prophet after prophet and denied the threatened judgment because it had not yet happened. That is the same attitude expressed by the generation that would perish in the flood, and it will also be expressed by deniers of the second coming (2 Peter 3:4). Though God's judgments appear to move slowly, they move certainly. Justice delayed is not justice denied. The judgments of God should cause fear and trembling in the hearts of men. Sinners should take advantage of God's patience, which is designed to lead to repentance (Rom. 2:4), and flee the wrath to come. If judgment came today, would you be ready? Why or why not?

Chapter 13

It is part of a faithful ministry to expose error (Titus 1:9). Ezekiel's preaching stood in sharp contrast to the words of many of his fellow ministers in Babylon. Their lying words and empty visions lulled the people into a false sense of security. People naturally seek to hide from truths that expose sin and warn of judgment. But Ezekiel preached in such a way as to expose the false prophets for what they were, regardless of the consequences to his own popularity. False prophets appear in every age, and God is always against them. We must be careful to test what they say and not listen to those who do not speak according to God's Word. What false prophets does the church need to beware of in our day?

Chapter 14

We must flee from idolatry (1 Cor. 10:14; 1 John 5:21). Yet this is subtler than we may realize. Although idolatry revolves around objects and images, it is rooted in the human heart (Ezek. 14:3–4, 7). Therefore it is not enough to get rid of the physical thing we have made into an idol, although this must often be done (Matt. 5:28–29). As John Calvin said, the human heart is an idol factory. To put idolatry to death, we must deal with fears and desires that have grown far larger than any created thing deserves (Col. 3:5). Whenever we love something or someone in a way that is not dominated by love for God, that love has degenerated into a proud and idolatrous lust (1 John 2:15–16). At the heart of the gospel is the call to turn away from all such idols and to give our obedience and hope to the living God (1 Thess. 1:9–10). That is the only way to escape God's wrath. Trusting in Christ requires us to turn from our deepest idolatry:

the false god of our self-righteousness. Why is this so hard? Why is it so beneficial?

Chapter 15

The nation's description as a wild and useless growth explains why judgment was necessary: sin had left the people spiritually fruitless and consequently suitable only as fuel for the fire. To see the full tragedy, compare this with Isaiah's song of the vineyard (Isa. 5:1–7). The Lord had planted His people as a noble vine and made every provision for them to produce the fruit of righteousness and justice. However, in spite of all the privileges given and much patience, they produced only the bad fruit of sin. They had spurned their privileges and had become good for nothing but kindling. This sounds a sober warning to all whom God has placed in a position of spiritual privileges, such as a godly home or a gospel-preaching church. Do not despise what God has given you, or your judgment will be all the worse. How can those with such privileges use them well?

Chapter 16

1. Idolatry is a personal attack upon the honor of God, just as adultery is a personal attack upon the honor of one's spouse, for in both cases one despises the person to whom one owes great love and wastes that love on one to whom it does not belong. The horrors of "whoredom," with its disgraceful behavior and betrayal of one's closest companion, should move us to grieve over our sins against God. Beneath the conflicts and lusts of men is a corrupt heart that should provoke us all to cry out, "We have been spiritual adulterers!"

Therefore let us humble ourselves, as James exhorts us, and submit to God with mourning over our unfaithfulness to Him who has loved us most (James 4:1–10).

2. The solution to spiritual adultery is summed up in the word "remember" (vv. 22, 43, 61, 63). We must remember God's past acts of love in creating us, sustaining us, and performing great deeds of mercy, supremely the death of His Son, and we must respond to His love with amazed and grateful love. We must remember our horrible sins against God, and we must respond with grief and hatred for sin, along with a sincere desire for new obedience. If we remember these things with faith, love, and repentance, we will discover that God also will "remember" His covenant promises and establish an everlasting relationship with us so that we may truly know Him. Indeed, our gratitude and love will overflow as we realize that our remembering Him was caused by His first remembering us (vv. 60–63).

Chapter 17

1. God expects people to keep their word and fulfill their promises, even promises made with unbelievers and pagans (vv. 16–19). While no promise or oath can bind us to commit sin, we must never violate our commitments just because a better opportunity comes along (vv. 7, 17).

2. "I the LORD have spoken and have done it" (v. 24). God controls all events for His own glory. Nebuchadnezzar was a great eagle from every human perspective; his kingdom was majestic and his power unmatched. Yet he was nothing apart from God. Babylon was the means God used to inflict His purposed judgment on Judah. The God who ordered all the

events in the sixth century BC still sits on the same throne governing the affairs of states throughout the world. In His own sovereign way God advances the kingdom of Christ. How does that encourage you today?

Chapter 18

1. God is the Owner of all men: "all souls are mine" (v. 4). Since God created us, we are accountable to Him. Each individual is responsible before God for his own sin. To ignore personal responsibility to God is to dishonor God and degrade men to the level of beasts. We must not attempt to blame others for our wrongdoings, even if they tempted us (Gen. 3:12) or set an evil example for us, such as the case with wicked parents. Christ will not accept such excuses when He summons each person before Him on the judgment day (2 Cor. 5:10).

2. This chapter answers three key questions about repentance: (1) *Why should sinners repent?* They must repent because God owns every person, knows the true condition of every person, and inflicts death on every sinner. (2) *How must sinners repent?* They must repent by turning from all their sins back to God with their hearts and behavior. (3) *What do repentant sinners receive?* They receive the forgiveness of sin and life. So the urgent question goes to every unrepentant sinner, "Why will you die?" What reasons and motives hold back sinners from repenting? How would you answer them?

Chapter 19

Pride comes before a fall. The young lions, representing the kings of Israel, felt invincible but were eventually taken in the snare. Their disregard for God paved the way for their downfall. In the parable, the second young lion behaved exactly as the first one and was taken in the pit exactly as the first one had been. Insensitivity to the results of sin betrays a hard and callous heart. Sin has terrible consequences for both individuals and nations. Like Ezekiel, Christians have good cause to take up a lamentation against the sins that plague their nation and pray that God will be favorable and raise up righteous rulers before it becomes too late, as it did for Judah. How are you praying for your nation?

Chapter 20

1. Do not play games with God. He has no interest in the prayers of those who cling to idols in their hearts (vv. 3, 31). He is not impressed with worship on Sunday without faithfulness on Monday through Saturday. He despises the study of the Bible without obedience to the Bible. He welcomes sinners, but only sinners repenting of sin, for He will not save sinners in a way that profanes His holy name (v. 39).

2. The hinge upon which salvation turns is the glory of God's name. When Israel's sins provoked the Lord to anger, He saved them for the sake of His name (vv. 9, 14, 22, 44). His works all aim at the goal that the world may know He is the Lord (vv. 5, 9, 12, 20, 26, 38, 42, 44). God does not save believers for anything in them but simply for the praise of His glory (Eph. 1:6, 12, 14). Why is this a great source of consolation and peace to those broken over their sins? How then should Christians respond to their salvation?

Chapter 21

1. God sovereignly used the Babylonians to accomplish His purpose of judgment against both Judah and Ammon. The pagan king made the decision by various means of divination. But just as the Lord superintends the disposing of lots (Prov. 16:33), so He does even the pagan's looking into a liver. There is no such thing as fate or chance. All things operate according to God's will.

2. God's message of judgment contains a word of hope centered on Christ (v. 27). God promised through Jacob that kingship would not depart from Judah until the rightful King would come (Gen. 49:10). For years there was never a scepter belonging to Judah, and then there was David. Then, again, because of the sins of David's sons there was no king for centuries. But in the fullness of time Jesus, David's ideal son, appeared and forever reigns. No matter how dark things become for you or for your nation, hope in Christ, for His kingdom will never fail.

Chapter 22

1. The catalog of corruptions in this chapter teaches that man's depravity is such that there is no sin he is incapable of committing. Both private sins and public sins flow from wicked hearts. We must not imagine that we are any different. God knows the depth of corruption that belongs to each one of us. God would have us know our sin and therefore the Holy Spirit convinces and convicts. Sin is exposed in order that we might repent of it and that God's justice would be clearly observed.

2. The parts played by both the civil and religious leaders in contributing to Judah's litany of sins remind us of the importance of having godly men in authority, both in the state and in the church. Wickedness at the top drips to the bottom. Christians are often quick to complain about leaders, but how often do they pray for them? How could you cultivate a habit of regularly praying for the leaders of your church and civil government?

Chapter 23

The degrading and defiling nature of sin is vividly portrayed here. The details and language are shocking because sin against God is shocking. One sin leads to another, and wicked habits are formed, thus resulting in a desensitized mind and a readiness to entertain wicked thoughts and engage in wicked actions. That these explicit details are recorded is not without significance. God speaks so as to convince sinners of the dreadfulness of their sin and their misery and the danger on account of that sin. If we find this chapter offensive, how much more offensive does God find our sin! How should this vivid portrayal of idolatry move us to grieve and repent of our own idol worship?

Chapter 24

1. Jerusalem's description as a rusty pot beyond salvage is a tragic picture and a fearful warning. Throughout her history God had given multiple opportunities for the pot to be cleansed, but the people had refused to receive the divine scouring and scrubbing. The time had come to meet the Lord in judgment. This is a warning, particularly to people who

hear God's Word over and over again without responding with genuine faith and repentance. The heart becomes hard with unrepentant hearing. What are the signs that a person is hardening under the gospel instead of responding rightly?

2. God is our Maker, and He has the right to take our lives when He sees fit, and even to regulate how we grieve for His glory (Lev. 10:1–3). Ordinarily God permits His people to express their grief in appropriate ways (Gen. 50:10; 2 Sam. 1:17; Acts 8:2), though not as those without hope (1 Thess. 4:13). However, Ezekiel was a sign from God that His wrath would bring bereavement beyond grieving, desolation so absolute that even the healing process of mourning would be denied the people. This sign points to hell itself, where the wicked will never find peace but will weep and gnash their teeth forever (Matt. 8:12; 22:13; 24:51; 25:30), which is their eternal punishment (Matt. 25:46).

Chapter 25

God has a great jealousy for His own glory and worship. He knows when He is mocked and His holiness is profaned. He does not ignore sin, wherever it appears or whoever is guilty. God will cause all men to know that He is the Lord (vv. 5, 7, 11, 17). There is no other God beside Him. He will judge all nations, whether or not they have acknowledged Him as God. He will call every person to account for his sins against His moral law. On judgment day every knee will bow and every tongue will confess that Jesus is Lord, to the glory of the Father (Isa. 45:22–23; Phil. 2:9–11). How should this truth shape our lives? How should it motivate us to support missions?

Chapter 26

Riches offer no security in the day of God's judgment. Tyre was a wealthy place, full of merchandise and commerce, but none of that was able to deliver it in the days of God's wrath. Once it rejoiced over Jerusalem's fall as an opportunity for profit, but its joy turned to horror and destruction. Rich people may look down on the suffering and exploit the weak, but their days are numbered. Their wealth cannot save them (Ps. 49:6–7). We cannot be redeemed with silver and gold but only by the precious blood of Christ (1 Peter 1:18–19). Consider Christ's searching question, "What shall it profit a man, if he shall gain the whole world, and lose his own soul?" (Mark 8:36). Losing our wealth and fame is nothing in comparison to losing our souls and facing the wrath of God.

Chapter 27

Tyre was the epitome of pride and stands as a warning to all against the dangers of pride. The city of Tyre boasted of its own beauty and was convinced of its superiority. Pride is the forerunner of judgment and trouble. God brought the proud city low. "Every one that is proud in heart is an abomination to the LORD: though hand join in hand, he shall not be unpunished" (Prov. 16:5). The cause of pride is irrelevant; God hates it. We must remember that all we are and have we owe to God. He distributes gifts, talents, and abilities according to His sovereign, good pleasure. There is absolutely no legitimate cause for boasting, but only for thanksgiving. How can we beware of pride and kill it?

Chapter 28

When God gives honor, ability, or beauty to one of His creations, too often that creature becomes puffed up with wicked and foolish pride instead of lowering himself in grateful worship to God. So it was with Satan, with Adam in the garden, and with many kings and other people since then. We must all be careful because pride is an insidious sin that dwells in the hearts of all men. Natural man seeks to take the place of God. Let us be quick to acknowledge that God sovereignly distributes gifts and abilities according to His will, and that we have nothing apart from what God has given. Whenever we find ourselves in a position of prosperity or prestige, let us resolve to humbly serve God by His grace in Christ for His glory alone.

Chapter 29

We are reminded by this passage not to trust in princes or in human power but in God. Egypt was a mighty nation, and some in Israel had put their confidence in her. But this creature confidence was misplaced. Egypt could no more save Israel than save herself. The people of Egypt gloried in their power and in their self-made prosperity, but their boasting was in vain. All that they had was due to God's common grace, yet they failed to acknowledge Him. In His time they were shown to be powerless and poor. God raises up nations and brings down nations according to His will. In what powers of man do people commonly trust today? How can you trust in God alone for those concerns?

Chapter 30

1. That Egypt's judgment is called the day of the Lord (v. 3) is a reminder of God's control of all the affairs of time. From the perspective of history, Babylon's invasion and subjection of Egypt in the sixth century BC could be explained by political and military causes. However, there is more to history than meets the eye. God's providence rules and orchestrates all things to achieve His glory through judgment and salvation.

2. The day of the Lord against Egypt and every other declaration of it in the Old Testament points to that final day when Christ will come and bring ultimate judgment and salvation. That time is set, and it will display perfect justice. All who have trusted in idols or mere men will be put to shame. All unforgiven sin and unrepentant sinners will be punished. How can we prepare for the day of the Lord so that we can greet it with joy?

Chapter 31

The sight of a great tree being cut down reminds us of how the high and lofty can quickly become firewood. Great men are nothing without God. The king of Assyria was noted for his stature and splendor. His kingdom was vast, and he was filled with pride, but God humbled him and judged him according to his wickedness. In the time of judgment his greatness counted for nothing. No man, however great, can stand against the power and wrath of God. The proud sinner will be brought to shame and ruin, but God gives grace to the humble. What men and women are commonly viewed as great? How will it go for them on judgment day if they do not follow Christ?

Chapter 32

The powers of this world can seem like massive dragons and beasts that can never be overcome (Rev. 13). However, the Lord will slaughter them when He pleases, just as He broke Egypt at the Red Sea and again by the Babylonians. Many mighty empires have had their day in history, but when God had fulfilled His purposes for them they fell. With their fall, great leaders have joined the vast crowd of the damned in hell, powerless to do anything on earth and consigned to wait until the judgment day. How very different is the path of the righteous! Death brings them to peace (Isa. 57:1–2), and the judgment day will bring them to unspeakable honor and joy (Dan. 12:3). Which path are you walking: the path of worldly glory and hell or the path of Christ and heaven?

Chapter 33

1. The Lord sincerely calls sinners to repent and come back to Him (v. 11). God is good and kind, even to those who hate Him. Through His preachers He urges and even pleads with His enemies so that they might escape His righteous judgment (2 Cor. 5:20). What amazing grace and mercy to wicked sinners! We should marvel at His gospel, run into His open arms, and seek to be His voice by spreading the gospel to whomever we can. How does the gospel call reveal the loving heart of Christ?

2. Sinners hear God's Word but respond out of their hatred for God. In some cases, instead of repenting of their sins they accuse God of sin (v. 17). People are sometimes offended when God welcomes sinners who turn back to His ways and when He judges seemingly good people who commit

sin and refuse to repent. In other cases, people rejoice in the Word but only because they find it interesting or entertaining. They give it no more credence or obedience than a beautiful love song (vv. 30–33). We must repent of our sin and our self-righteousness and believe God's Word with total submission.

Chapter 34

1. Of all the analogies to describe God's saving work, the shepherd image is one of the most precious. Christ alluded to this chapter in His teaching on the good shepherd (John 10). As the good shepherd He loves, cares for, guides, guards, and feeds His sheep. He willingly laid down His life to save His sheep. Consider the good shepherd as He revealed Himself in this chapter of Ezekiel. The Lord God is the shepherd (v. 11). And yet the Son of David is the one and only shepherd (v. 23). Thus the good shepherd is the incarnate Lord, the God-man, the Son who is one with His Father (John 10:30).

2. Consider, too, the condition of His sheep. They are scattered (v. 12), lost, and sick (v. 16). They have suffered much from the wicked (v. 21). They cannot save themselves but depend entirely upon their shepherd to rescue, provide for, and protect them.

3. Consider finally the work of the shepherd. He seeks and saves the lost (v. 12). He heals them and feeds them (vv. 14, 16). He also judges them (vv. 17, 20), so that they will be rescued from the wicked hidden among them. How do these truths show us the beauty of Jesus Christ? How do they attract people to desire to be His sheep?

Chapter 35

The law of the harvest is an inviolable law. We reap what we sow (Gal. 6:7–9). The people of mount Seir had lived by the sword and were going to die by the sword. They had scorned Israel for her desolation, but they also would be brought to desolation. God's justice always gives what is deserved. This is why the gospel is such good news, for Christ took the full guilt and penalty of the sins of His people. He took what His people deserved, and His people receive what He deserves. Justice is served, and His people are saved. Be warned not to be like Edom, who stood before God on its own.

Chapter 36

1. Sinners cannot save themselves. Salvation is all of God's grace and for His glory (Eph. 1:3–14). Repeatedly God said "I will" in this chapter. The Lord changes filthy idolaters into cleansed worshipers. He makes stubborn enemies into submissive servants and takes estranged outsiders and draws them into covenant friendship. Salvation is begun by God's initiative, is effective by His power, and is completed by His determination. What is impossible with man is possible with God. While we should despair of saving ourselves, we should hope confidently in the Lord's salvation.

2. Real salvation cannot be separated from practical holiness of life. Grace does not enable hypocrisy. If God saved a person but did not make that person holy, then salvation would not glorify God but would pollute His holy name. Real, saving grace produces a new heart and a new spirit. Obstinate clinging to idols gives way to brokenhearted repentance over sin. Everyone in whom the Spirit dwells will show it by a

life of obedience to God's moral law. This is the great test of whether a person is born again. No emotional experience or rational belief can take the place of a new heart that produces new obedience. What is the evidence that God gave you a new heart toward Him?

Chapter 37

1. Man's hopeless state without God is clearly portrayed in this passage. The picture of death and desolation highlights the devastating results of man's fall into sin. Satan has slaughtered the human race, and all mankind is dead in sin, utterly without spiritual life. Preachers can preach with all their hearts, and we can move bones around, but until the Spirit of the Lord comes there will be no life. How should this move us to pray for the lost? How should it move us to praise God for our salvation?

2. Christ's kingdom will flourish despite every apparent obstacle. He is the servant-king (v. 24) who perfectly does His Father's will and rules with omnipotent power in heaven and on earth. His church shall be built and His people shall all be eternally saved. This truth should fill even the most troubled believer with hope and confidence. The church should never have a defeatist mindset. Christ reigns and will reign forever and forever!

Chapter 38

After revelations of resurrection from spiritual death to serve the Christ (36:1–37:28), Ezekiel prophesied of the worldwide opposition that would come against the peaceful kingdom of the Messiah, and its ultimate victory by supernatural, divine intervention. This vision finds partial fulfillment whenever the wicked attack the church of Christ and the gospel triumphs. Its ultimate fulfillment will arrive when Christ returns. Christians should not be surprised when the world declares war on them; this is an ancient battle. However, Christians should also be optimistic: all the world will know that our God is the Lord!

Chapter 39

The Lord God's victory over the enemies of His people will be total. The wicked will be judged in overwhelming numbers, as is clear from the graphic references to their slaughter and the disposal of their bodies and equipment. All nations will know that King Jesus is Lord (vv. 13, 21; Phil. 2:10). Even now God has poured out the Spirit of Christ upon His people (v. 29). Therefore, the great question is: where will you stand on that great day? Will you be among His enemies or His people? The answer to that question about the future resolves into a question about the present. Do you have His Spirit working faith and obedience in you today?

Chapter 40

As a godly man of the priestly line, Ezekiel must have been deeply distressed at his vision of the departure of God's glory from the temple (8:1–11:25) and the news that the holy city had been destroyed (33:21). God's special presence with Israel distinguished them from all other nations (Ex. 33:15–16) and was the life and joy of the godly (Pss. 46; 84). This vision of measuring out a new temple would have filled him with hope, for it was a pledge that God would see to everything necessary so that His presence would remain forever with His people (Ezek. 37:26–27). However, God was not concerned about buildings, for He had revealed that His presence would dwell by the Spirit in a transformed heart (11:16, 19–20; 36:26–27; 37:14; 39:29). The meaning of the vision lies in its symbolism of God's restored presence with His worshipers. What does it mean to hope in and seek after God's spiritual presence?

Chapter 41

The symbolism of the holy places in the new temple would have reminded Ezekiel that the God who dwells with His people is the holy King (v. 4), whose servants are mighty spirits (vv. 18, 20). His presence inspires fear and awe and commands reverence. Yet the images of palm trees frequently appearing in this vision (v. 18) imply that His holiness does not bring death to His people but abundant life. This is the hope of believers: that the Lord God will so dwell among them by the Spirit that they will rejoice with trembling. How will this hope be gloriously fulfilled when Christ returns?

Chapter 42

The temple, including its courts, was a holy space that was separated from the common (vv. 14, 20). Yet this was a place of human activity, requiring "chambers" for God's servants to work and to eat the holy food of their portion of the offerings (v. 13). These aspects of Ezekiel's vision would have assured him that God would not only give His presence but would also provide for the needs of the ministers who would serve Him there. This reminds us that the church must provide for the physical needs of its pastors (1 Cor. 9:13–14). It also reminds us that God provides for His priesthood. The priests of Aaron's line had largely failed to honor the Lord (Ezek. 7:26; 22:26), but in Christ God's people have all become priests who eat from the benefits of Christ's sacrifice (Isa. 61:6; Heb. 13:8–9). How does God feed His people with His holy things as they worship Him today?

Chapter 43

God's grace does not diminish His holiness. Ezekiel's vision depicts God's presence returning to His people, a work of amazing grace to those guilty of idolatry and other horrible sins. Yet His presence did not return in a soft or mild way but as "glory" that cast the prophet upon his face (vv. 2–3). The most glorious and holy place on earth was still a mere footstool for the feet of the heavenly King (v. 7). The gospel still shines with glory, the glory of grace (2 Cor. 4:6; Eph. 1:6). The Lord's presence will always require us to humble ourselves and repent of our sins with appropriate shame (vv. 7–11). Why do people resist this and prefer another approach to worship, whether it be casual or formal? How can we cultivate a deeper sense of God's glory in our worship?

Chapter 44

1. The presence of the king ("prince") in the temple was another symbol of great hope for Israel (v. 3). The Lord had shattered the monarchy of David's line because it had been corrupted through idolatry. However, the Lord promised through this vision that not only would He give Israel a king again but that this king would be a true worshiper with

special intimacy with God. Jesus Christ in His mediatorial office is both the supreme worshiper and the great worship leader of the church (Ps. 22:22–27; Matt. 11:25; Heb. 2:12). How does He lead His people in worship as their king?

2. The Lord reasserted the necessity that His priests serve in purity and obedience to His Word, excluding the unfit from the privileges of His worship. Though the ceremonies of the old covenant have ceased, the Lord remains zealous for His worship. How must the church, especially its elders, guard the purity of God's worship?

Chapter 45

1. The symbolism of the division of the land (vv. 1–7) reinforces again the promise that God's holy dwelling place would be with His people and would be closely connected to the king ("prince"). The future king would not be a greedy and unjust oppressor but a ruler of impeccable righteousness and truth (vv. 8–10). Jesus Christ is the King of His people, God's incarnate presence with them, and He leads them in justice and holiness.

2. Ezekiel's vision of the temple portrayed the offering of sacrifices for sin in order to accomplish "reconciliation" between God and His sinful worshipers (vv. 15, 17). Christ offered Himself as the sacrifice for sin once and for all, abolishing all other sacrifices for sin (Heb. 10:10, 12, 14, 18). Therefore, this vision cannot depict a literal future sacrifice. The Lord was symbolically promising Ezekiel that, though God destroyed the temple, He would still provide for the necessary sacrifice for sins through His king (Ezek. 45:17). If the Jews in exile could hope in God's promise of atonement, how

much more can Jews and Gentiles today trust in Christ's finished work upon the cross?

Chapter 46

The King worships God (v. 2), walking with His people in all their feasts of worship (vv. 9–10) and leading them in offering voluntary sacrifices of praise to God (v. 12). Christ is the Mediator of the church's worship. Whenever even the smallest congregation gathers in His name, He is there with them (Matt. 18:20). Through Him believers offer to God sacrifices of praise, thanksgiving, and financial gifts (Heb. 13:15–16). In response to His great sacrifice, Christians offer themselves as living sacrifices to God (Rom. 12:1). How can knowing that Jesus Christ is directly involved in your church's worship change the way you participate in the service?

Chapter 47

The vision of the river flowing from the temple promises that the Lord's holy presence will come to His people as a supernatural source of life. He will bring them healing and transform them from a salty wasteland to a people of flourishing life. The images of this chapter take us back to the garden of Eden. That this vision leads into a description of the boundaries of Israel's inheritance implies that God's people will inherit nothing less than paradise. How beautiful is this picture! Yet the giving of the marshes "to salt" reminds us that not all people will enjoy its fulfillment. Jesus said that we must come to Him with spiritual thirst and ask for the living water (John 4:14; 7:37–39). Why must we have the

Spirit of Christ in this life if we would enjoy the river of His delights forever?

Chapter 48

The inheritance of God's people centers around being with God. Already Christians have a foretaste of God's presence in the Spirit of God. Still, the best is yet to come. Too often we think of heaven in terms of the absence of pain, but the essence of heaven is the presence of Christ. When God fulfills all His covenant promises, the true children of Abraham will dwell with Him and see His glory. Even if someone could come back from heaven to earth, the best he could do to describe its wonders would boil down to the statement "The Lord is there." This is what gave the apostle Paul the courage to face death, indeed the joy to call it gain (2 Cor. 5:8; Phil. 1:21–23). This is what makes the second coming of Christ the great hope of believers, because then they will be with the Lord (1 Thess. 4:17). How does your hope of being with Christ compare with your desires for the things and relationships of this world? This is the test of your heart.

Daniel

Chapter 1

1. Daniel's being taken captive to Babylon illustrates the mystery and divine wisdom of providence. His captivity was the consequence of and chastisement for the nation's sin. It is clear from Daniel's character that he was not guilty of the sins that precipitated the judgment, but he was nonetheless affected by it. God made the event that was judgment for the nation to be a means of testing, purifying, and using Daniel for His glory. What Daniel did in service to the Lord could not have been done if he had remained back in Judah. It had to have been a traumatic experience for the young teen to be snatched from home and taken to a strange and foreign land, but God used the trauma for ultimate good. This should be a lesson in trusting the providence of God that sometimes leads to difficult and uncertain situations. But, His way and purpose is always best. It often takes the hard providences to bring us to the place of our best opportunities to be used by God for His glory and our good.

2. The stand taken by Daniel and his companions regarding their diet is a powerful example to young people. They were teenagers in a strange place. For teenage boys to refuse a hearty meal for a plate of vegetables was most remarkable. No one there would have suspected that their eating the king's provision would have been a compromise of their convictions. They were in a place far from home where it would have been easy just to do what everybody else was doing. But

God's law was written on their hearts, and they obeyed the Lord in the face of the pressure to conform. They were firm in their convictions but not obnoxious in their stand. First Timothy 4:12 sums up Daniel's life as it should that of every Christian young person.

Chapter 2

1. The response of Daniel and his friends to the king's threat provides a lesson in the importance and power of prayer. Seemingly without panic or a second thought, they immediately took the matter to the Lord, casting their cares and concerns upon Him. It was a crisis prayer, and God answered them according to their need. Upon receiving the answer, Daniel was careful before doing anything else to return in prayer expressing his praise, thanksgiving, and worship to God who so graciously answered their specific request. This episode should remind us that prayer is never to be a last resort when all else fails but should be the first impulse when faced with any crisis. It also exemplifies the importance of thanksgiving for answered prayer.

2. Daniel's initial conversation with the king is a great example of godly humility. He could have immediately interpreted the dream to Nebuchadnezzar and taken all the credit for himself, posturing for some reward or recognition by the king. But rather, even though the king was pressing for the interpretation and much more delay would put all the wise men in jeopardy, Daniel took the time to give all the credit to God. We should always be more interested in God's glory than we are in our own.

3. It may be profitable to compare Nebuchadnezzar's dream with Daniel's vision in chapter 7. They are two revelations with a single message. Chapter 2 is a view of human power from man's perspective. The four metals suggest value and strength, and an inanimate stone destroyed the statue for no apparent reason. Chapter 7 views the same from God's perspective. The beasts have no moral conscience and are destroyed for their terrible acts by the Son of man. Together they demonstrate God's absolute control in the rise and fall of kings. Governments are in His hands, and that is just as true today as it was in Daniel's day. No matter how uncertain things seem, they are certain in God's unfailing purpose.

Chapter 3

1. This familiar story of the fiery furnace, set in a world system that was both ignorant of and hostile to truth, teaches us that we must stand firm and faithful regardless of pressures to compromise. Shadrach, Meshach, and Abed-nego illustrate a kind of courage and resolve to stand firm that come from faith in God and His Word. Knowing that whatever happened in time was God's will enabled them to face their situation with confidence, resisting the world's pressure and resting on the Lord. It is that kind of total dependence on God that empowers believers to stand on His promises. Courage alone is not a uniquely spiritual virtue, but when that courage flows from an unwavering conviction of the unchangeable truth of God's Word and from the personal resolve to take God at His Word, it is the spiritual virtue of walking by faith.

2. One way or another, God achieves His glory and His people's good, but He doesn't always do it the way we might

expect. For Shadrach, Meshach, and Abed-nego that purpose did not mean preventing adversity: they were thrown into the fire. Although it was God's will to place His servants in the furnace, it was not His will to leave them alone. Their Savior was present with them. Regardless of how horrific the circumstances, God has promised to be the constant company of His people. Whereas the Lord's presence with His people is a guaranteed promise, physical deliverance from danger is not (Heb. 11:36–38). The Lord's presence may not be visible as in the case of the three youths, but it is always the reality of faith.

Chapter 4

1. Although Nebuchadnezzar's manifestation of pride was unique, his self-absorbed pride is the common malady of all sinners. The unchanging spiritual law is that God "resisteth the proud, and giveth grace to the humble" (1 Peter 5:5). Nebuchadnezzar stood in need of grace. Without divine intervention to change his heart, the king's prosperous time would surely lead to a tragic eternity. So it is for every sinner: divine intervention is necessary to change his destiny.

2. Conversion is marked by faith toward God and repentance from sin. It is the first conscious response to the grace of God that irresistibly invades the heart, enabling spiritual perception. The story of Nebuchadnezzar's conversion illustrates Paul's theological proposition that "faith cometh by hearing, and hearing by the word of God" (Rom. 10:17) and that "there is no difference between the Jew and the Greek: for the same Lord over all is rich unto all that call upon him" (v. 12). The Lord graciously gave the Word and governed all

the circumstances that led the pagan king to what appears to be genuine salvation.

Chapter 5

1. The opening scene stands as a warning against the dangers of drunkenness. The more the wine flowed, the more they abandoned themselves to sensual and irreverent debauchery. All sin is ultimately a direct affront against God.

2. The immediacy of Belshazzar's punishment is a most sobering lesson. A night that started with a party ended in death. When that night began, it is most certain that he had no idea it would be his last. It is a common human thought, even of believers, that death is far in the future, for now something that happens only to others. The Bible is explicit that death comes to all (Heb. 9:27). Only God knows the date, time, and place of that appointment, but notwithstanding our ignorance of those details, it will be an appointment that we will not miss. It is imperative, therefore, to take advantage of the time God has given us and to make sure that we are right with Him through Jesus Christ.

Chapter 6

1. In his old age as in his youth, Daniel is a model for living a consistently godly life in a hostile world. The temptation to conform to what everyone is doing is as much a temptation for the old as the young. Even at the risk of death, Daniel was convicted that it was better to obey God rather than men (Acts 5:29). It is not surprising that Ezekiel, for a while Daniel's contemporary, pointed to Daniel as a model of righteous living (Ezek. 14:14, 20). The world today is no

less hostile to grace and God as Daniel's world. Regardless of consequences, we should learn from Daniel to maintain a consistent and God-honoring testimony. Every believer should dare to stand like Daniel.

2. Daniel's response after learning about the prayer injunction provides important lessons about prayer (6:10). Even though the temple in Jerusalem was no longer standing, his praying in that direction symbolically expressed his attitude of worship. His kneeling posture pictured the necessary humility before God. His doing it three times a day as he did aforetime shows that prayer should be a regular habit and not just the last resort in crisis. His praying and giving thanks indicates that prayer should involve both petition and praise.

Chapter 7

1. Daniel's preview of world history testifies to God's absolute sovereignty. Kingdoms rise and fall according to His will, and each one accomplishes His purpose. Knowing that God is in control ought to produce comfort, hope, and purity in God's people, even when it appears that powers hostile to God and His people seem to have the upper hand. God uses the wrath of man to get praise, and all is working without frustration to the ultimate manifestation of His glory and kingdom.

2. The link between the little horn's blaspheming God and his persecution of the saints is not surprising. Remember Christ said that the world would hate us because it hates Him (John 15:18) and that we would have tribulation in this world (John 16:33). The enemy cannot get to the Head so it attacks the body. But Christ has overcome the world (John 16:33). It is far better to share in the ultimate triumph of

Christ than to be on the side of the world. Daniel's vision assures us that saints will reign with Christ (Dan. 7:18).

Chapter 8

The precision with which Daniel's vision predicts events hundreds of years in the future testifies to the uniqueness of the one true and living God who knows the end from the beginning. Isaiah records God's challenge to the dead idols to prove they are gods by foretelling the future (Isa. 40:21–24). They, of course, are silent but the Lord repeatedly gives ample proof of His deity. Seeing how precisely His predictions have been fulfilled should increase our confidence that those prophecies yet to be fulfilled have the same certainty. Without fail, God will fulfill His Word. As Christ said, "Heaven and earth shall pass away, but my words shall not pass away" (Matt. 24:35). It is imperative, therefore, to heed His warnings and be prepared for the judgment ahead.

Chapter 9

1. Throughout His Word, God commands us to pray, invites us to pray, and shows us how to pray. Daniel's prayer provides a pattern to follow. As you read through the prayer, note the following: (1) prayer is based on God's Word; (2) it focuses on God's person and character; (3) it involves the confession of sin; (4) it makes great supplications; and (5) it makes God's glory the supreme motive.

2. Praying God's Word is a sure way to pray for God's will to be done. Jeremiah prophesied that the captivity would last for seventy years, and it would have lasted for seventy years whether Daniel prayed or not. But Daniel's praying

that promise was an expression of his faith in God's unfailing Word and his appropriation of the promise knowing that the time was at hand. His praying for the Word to be fulfilled corresponds to Christ's model prayer, "Thy will be done" (Matt. 6:10).

3. Notwithstanding the interpretational difficulties and disagreements regarding the seventy weeks, this prophecy, which was God's answer to Daniel's prayer, illustrates a wonderful truth: God is "able to do exceeding abundantly above all that we ask or think" (Eph. 3:20). Daniel prayed that God might end the captivity; God answered by pointing him to Christ, who would accomplish far greater things than ending an exile. It is a wonderful thought that God's purpose for His people is always greater than their expectations.

Chapter 10

1. The warfare in the spiritual realm is real even though it occurs beyond our natural sight. Although beyond our sight, believers are often in the field of battle. What Job experienced, for instance, was the consequence of the challenge between God and Satan. It is imperative, therefore, that we arm ourselves with the armor and weaponry that God has given to us because we do fight against unworldly foes (Eph. 6:10–18). But victory is assured because the battle is the Lord's.

2. That the prince of Greece followed the prince of Persia (10:20) is a reminder that we can never let down our guard in the spiritual war. Victory in one battle does not cause the next enemy to surrender. Sin does not have dominion over us, but we must resist every temptation that comes our way every time it comes.

Chapter 11

On the surface, it may appear that this prewritten history has little practical or devotional application. Yet, the fact that Daniel writes with such precision about things that would happen hundreds of years after him suggests two important thoughts that should be encouraging to believers. First, it teaches us that God is not just a distant observer or someone reacting to what happens on earth; rather, He is the orchestrator of all. Since He knows the end from the beginning, it is no difficulty for Him to reveal things prior to their occurrence. His will guarantees the fulfillment of His Word. Second, the precision with which some of the prophecies were fulfilled gives confidence that God's will for what is still to come is just as certain. So even though the world at times would appear to be out of control, all is moving steadily to that time when the great enemy of God and His people will come to his end.

Hosea

Chapter 1

1. The whole message of Hosea ought to generate thoughts of the wonder of God's gracious love for His people. The apostle John declared that "God is love" (1 John 4:16). There is more talk and less understanding about God's love than almost any other divine attribute. Most people define God's love based on their own experience of love as an emotional attachment to something attractive. Even the Christian's love for God is generated by attraction to Him. John says that "we love him, because he first loved us" (v. 19). Based on this reasoning, people feel that God will love them because they are attractive to God. However, God does not love because something in the object is worthy or attractive. God loves because He is love. His love springs from His character rather than the character of those He loves. He loves us not because of what we are, but in spite of what we are. Every Christian must realize that he does not deserve God's favor. Salvation is only possible because God in love sent His Son, the only One worthy of the Father's love, to be the Redeemer of an unlovely people. This realization should arouse humility and gratitude in all who have experienced God's free love revealed and given in Jesus Christ. The prophecy of Hosea is a vivid illustration of the nature of God's free love to an undeserving people.

2. Throughout Scripture, God uses marriage as a choice symbol of His relationship with the church, the bride of

Christ. This is why every Christian marriage ought to be a living gospel sermon. The marriage analogy puts Israel's apostasy in perspective. The marriage bond assumes, indeed demands, that there be an exclusive union between husband and wife. That must be maintained and guarded. Adultery violates that bond and is a most serious offense against both the spouse and against God (Ex. 20:14). Faithfulness and mutual loyalty between husband and wife are basic to marriage. Unfaithfulness and disloyalty threaten and jeopardize the union. Not surprisingly, then, Scripture often describes Israel's unfaithfulness to the Lord in terms of harlotry or spiritual adultery—a tragically vivid picture of apostasy.

Chapter 2

1. God's plan for restoring His sinning people entailed discipline. Love sometimes requires what is not pleasant for the welfare of those loved. According to Scripture, this discipline, although unpleasant, is evidence of love (see Prov. 13:24). We usually call this tough love, but it is love nonetheless. Parents can use this as an opportunity to instruct their children.

2. The change of the children's names illustrating Hosea's judgment/hope cycle exemplifies one of the great "buts" of God's grace, paralleling Paul's great "but God" of Ephesians 2:4–5. Were it not for these "buts" of grace, there would be no hope of salvation for any. This provides opportunity for reflection and thanksgiving for the personal evidences of God's grace. Asking the question "Where would I be, apart from God's grace?" would be a good way to begin your meditation.

Chapter 3

Hosea's reunion with Gomer provides another reminder of the wonder of God's gracious love. Gomer gives hope to every sinner. It is not surprising that a book about marriage and family should refer so often to love. The root word for love occurs almost twenty times in Hosea. What is surprising is that the majority of occurrences refer to Israel's illicit love associated with their spiritual adultery and pagan worship. This only highlights the wonder of God's love for them (3:1; 11:1, 4; 14:4) and points to the real issue of love. The marriage/family motif certainly speaks of the natural affection that ought to be the experience of every family. Yet the word for love goes far beyond expressions of affection. This love is moved by the will. It designates a compelling inclination of the heart to a chosen object. From the outset, God's love has been a matter of choice; He decides to love His people, and the reason for that loving choice is not in their attractiveness or worthiness. God's love is totally of grace. The motive of God's gracious, electing love is within Himself, not in the objects of His choice. This is what makes grace so amazing.

Chapter 4

As a gospel preacher, Hosea spoke to sin head on. Preaching the gospel always entails preaching against sin, warning of sin's consequences, and announcing sin's remedy. In order to highlight the heinous nature and seriousness of sin, surveying Hosea's terms for sin would be in order. Use this synopsis to guide your meditation. Hosea's sermon provides a casebook of sin. Most of the standard Old Testament words for sin are scattered throughout the prophecy in addition to others that are specifically suited to Hosea's focus on the breach of covenant.

Chapter 5

1. Verse 3 provides an opportunity to underscore the personal application of God's knowledge. Israel's sin was known to God and so is ours. It is impossible to escape His knowledge, and there is a sense in which every sin committed is in His presence. Psalm 139:7 and Hebrews 4:13 reinforce this truth.

2. Comparing verse 6 with verse 15 provides an opportunity to discuss what it means to seek the Lord with a genuine heart of belief. Not all seeking is successful, yet God promises that those who seek Him with all their heart will find Him. The purpose of the divine discipline was to create that kind of heart.

Chapter 6

1. The opening invitation to repent and the assurance that God will accept genuine repentance give hope and encouragement to every Christian who thinks that he has lost out with God because of his sin. God's grace is greater than sin, and His mercy is infinite.

2. God's stated preference for mercy and knowledge of Himself over sacrifice and burnt offerings provides occasion to emphasize the importance of worshiping in spirit and in truth. We have a natural propensity to walk by sight and not by faith. It is possible to go through all the motions of worship without pleasing the Lord or without benefiting the soul. In this sense, think about the dangers of going to

church. Remember that while the actions of worship are important, God is always looking at the heart. Today, many without Christ assume that going to church or keeping the Golden Rule will somehow accrue to their favor before God. Even believers sometimes allow their religious routines to substitute for private devotion and a sincere heart. Human reasoning contrasts with the divine preference for heart obedience over manual religion.

Chapter 7

The principal theme running through the entire chapter concerns the spiritual insensitivity and callousness resulting from sin. The message offers an opportunity to reflect on how deceiving sin can be. The sinning nation was oblivious to God's presence (v. 2), His offers of mercy to them (v. 1), and His past goodness (v. 15). In their self-trust, they never thought to call upon the Lord (v. 7). Failure to pray is always a sign of self-dependence. You can see this whole chapter as an illustration of Jeremiah 17:5–6 that describes the cursed man in terms of self-trust and spiritual oblivion (the inability to see when the good comes, v. 6). It demonstrates the danger of following the deceitful and desperately wicked heart (v. 9).

Chapter 8

1. Verse 7 speaks of the sowing-reaping principle commonly used in Scripture (Hos. 10:12; Gal. 6:7–8). The law of the harvest rules. Sinful behavior has consequences to avoid, and righteous behavior has consequences to desire. We should strive, therefore, to do those things pleasing to the Lord, for He is the rewarder of those who seek Him (Heb. 11:6).

2. Verse 12 reminds us of the wonderful gift of God's Word and how important it is that we properly respond to it. The great things of God's law define how God's children are supposed to live. The law and every other word that God has given are expressions of His love. Israel's disobedience to God's law was a rejection, therefore, of His love. We should be careful to receive God's Word as a gracious gift and respond to it in obedience as evidence of our love of Him.

Chapter 9

The description of the judgment in this chapter is summed up in verse 7 as "the days of visitation": Israel was getting what they deserved. Nothing is more fearful than to get what we deserve from God. The word for visitation, having the basic idea of inspection or examination, often points to God's dealing with people in consequence or in accordance to what He sees about them. That man is so small and God is so infinitely great makes His visitation with man an amazing reality (Ps. 8:3–4). Yet, it is also an awful reality and should therefore be a motive to purity knowing that God will punish iniquity (see Amos 3:2 where the word "punish" is the same Hebrew word as "visit"). Psalm 17:3 expresses the proper response to the fact that God examines all of life: "I am purposed that my mouth shall not transgress." God's involvement in the affairs of man is never neutral.

Chapter 10

1. The invitation to repent and seek the Lord (v. 12) stands in stark contrast to what appears to be a helpless and hopeless situation of sin and punishment. The invitation itself

testifies to God's grace being greater than man's sin. Yet it is a sober reminder that men must come to God on His terms and at His time. It was time to seek the Lord, but Isaiah indicates that the seeking must occur "while he may be found" (Isa. 55:6). The force of that verb is "while He permits Himself to be found." The implication is that He is not always findable (Prov. 1:28). There should always be urgency in heeding the Word of God.

2. The contrast between verses 12 and 13 illustrates the sowing-reaping principle both positively and negatively. Righteousness reaps mercy, but wickedness reaps iniquity (a word that can refer to punishment as well as sin). This law of the harvest ought to be one of the motives for us to live in purity and holiness.

Chapter 11

Remembering our redemption is a good motive for proper living. The opening reference to the exodus is a reminder of God's grace, power, and provision of effective atonement in saving His people. The more we reflect on God's grace in saving us through faith in Christ's finished and effective atoning work, the more we should be moved to live in gratitude the new life we have in Christ. When Israel spurned God's love, it was contrary to what would be expected in view of what He had done for them.

Chapter 12

Just as Paul directs attention to Old Testament history to teach spiritual lessons, so does Hosea in speaking to his generation about the history of the patriarch Jacob. Central to the lesson is Jacob's wrestling with the angel, which is a vivid illustration of earnest and prevailing prayer. Too often our prayers are casual and unthinking. This reminds us of the energy and diligence that ought to mark our praying. Notwithstanding the struggle and how injurious it was to his flesh, Jacob would not let go until he received the blessing (Gen. 32:24–28). So we must keep on asking until we receive the answer. This is a reminder that prayer is an arduous exercise of faith.

Chapter 13

1. The chapter begins with a warning of the dangers of idolatry. Israel exchanged true spiritual worship for sight worship. That God regards idolatry of any sort as an abomination and a personal insult is obvious from the most cursory reading of the Bible (Rom. 1:18, 23, 25). Idolatry facilitates worship since it is always easier to operate by sight instead of faith, but it is a dark and serious sin. Idolatry goes beyond just images, statues, or paintings. Since the heart, as Calvin said, "is a perpetual factory of idols," it is easy to turn legitimate practices of worship into perversions. We must be careful to worship in spirit and in truth.

2. Verse 14 underscores the absolute certainty of the gospel. The promised resurrection, the necessary consequence of Christ's resurrection (1 Cor. 15:12–22), is based on the immutability of God. Changing His mind regarding His redemptive purpose for His people is impossible. This parallels Malachi's statement linking God's unchangeableness to Jacob's not being consumed (Mal. 3:6). This should generate praise and thanksgiving for our salvation, knowing that even

though we may be unfaithful, He never is. He always keeps His word.

Chapter 14

1. The opening verses are most instructive in charting the marks of genuine repentance. There must be confession of sin, commitment to God, praise for grace, and forsaking of everything else in exclusive dependence on God. The Lord's invitation to repent is not ineffective, for God seeks the sinner with grace before the sinner seeks Him. Therefore, with the invitation comes the assurance of God's free love. There is something wonderfully consistent about God's promise to forgive those who genuinely confess their sins.

2. For any Christian troubled and disappointed with the level of his spiritual experience and enjoyment, the closing words of Hosea are encouraging and instructive. There is a remedy to spiritual dryness, a way to reverse a path littered with disobedience and sin. For those far from God, there is a way back to Him; for those near God, there is a way to be nearer still.

Joel

Chapter 1

1. Disasters happen by divine appointment. Throughout the world there are earthquakes, floods, and storms of every sort that destroy property and claim lives. Rather than these being random occurrences with purely natural explanations, they are the workings of divine providence, all of which declares the glory of God. It is a source of comfort to Christians to know that regardless of how terrible circumstances may be, there is a good and all-wise God who is working His purpose.

2. The knowledge that disasters happen by divine appointment ought to generate a conscious awareness or fear of God and motivate repentance and dependence on the Lord. Natural disasters are a means that God uses to knock out every prop of self-reliance.

Chapter 2

1. Verses 12–13 provides occasion to reflect on the nature of evangelical repentance. As the Hebrew word "turn" implies, repentance involves a reversal of direction, demanding a new way of thinking and living. The Westminster Shorter Catechism's definition would be a good place to start: "Repentance unto life is a saving grace, whereby a sinner, out of a true sense of his sin, and apprehension of the mercy of God in Christ, doth, with grief and hatred of his sin, turn from it unto God, with full purpose of, and endeavor after, new obedience" (Q. 87). Joel's invitation encompasses most

of these elements. It stresses particularly the inward focus. Sometimes people doubt the reality of their own repentance on the basis of outward manifestations of contrition (weeping and mourning). There must be the contrition over sin, but how that contrition is shown often depends on personality. This is why Joel stresses the rending of the heart rather than the outward shows of rending garments. What God sees is more important than what man sees.

2. God's promise to restore what the locusts had eaten (v. 25) is an encouragement. The consequences of sin are a tragic reality, but where sin abounds grace super-abounds (Rom. 5:20). Sometimes people convince themselves that their sins have been so great or so much of their lives have been wasted that God would never save them or ever use them. The locusts had so consumed the land that nothing was left, but God said He would restore it all. So God's power and grace is sufficient to restore His people to usefulness.

3. On the day of Pentecost, the Holy Spirit came upon every believer, who then in the power of the Spirit evangelized Jerusalem (Acts 2:4). Peter explained the wonders of Pentecost by saying "this is that" which Joel prophesied concerning the outpouring of the Holy Spirit (Acts 2:16). What Pentecost started continues, and every Christian has the power of the Spirit available to serve Christ and His church.

Chapter 3

1. Use verse 14 as a solemn reminder of the importance of conversion before it is too late. A day of judgment is coming when God will declare His guilty verdict and pronounce His

sentence upon the wicked who will have no recourse or way to escape.

2. Reflect on verses 16–21 regarding the safety and security that God's presence offers believers regardless of external circumstances. Notwithstanding the eschatological (end-time) implications of these verses, they sum up a timeless and universal truth. Psalm 91 would be a good parallel passage: the Lord is our security, provides our safety, and promises our salvation.

Amos

Chapter 1

1. Amos's call to be a prophet should encourage all believers that God can use them in His service regardless of status, vocation, or background. Amos was a layman with no heritage in Christian service (7:14). But when God called him, He equipped him for a special ministry. So every Christian should be willing to submit to God's call to service even if that sphere of service counters what had been planned for life. Nothing is more important than doing God's will.

2. The series of judgments pronounced against the various heathen nations testifies to God's absolute sovereignty over all; He is the King of kings and His law rules supreme. The ignorance of heathens concerning God, His law, and His gospel does not exempt them from being accountable to God. His judgments are just and always according to righteousness. What was true in Amos's day remains true today. It seems as though the wickedness of nations reigns unchecked, but God who rules over all holds them accountable for their transgressions. The day will come when, "for three transgressions…and for four" (v. 3), He will no longer withhold His judgment.

Chapter 2

1. Amos exposes the social sins of the nation before addressing its religious sins against God. Since the people were not right with their fellow man, there could be no claim of being

right with God. There is an inseparable link between the two greatest commandments to love God totally and to love one's neighbor as one's self, which summarize the two main divisions of the Decalogue. To break one commandment is to be guilty of breaking them all. This provides good opportunity for reflection: how we treat others is an index to our relationship with God.

2. Despising grace deserves divine judgment. Although Israel had many spiritual advantages (vv. 10–11), they rejected the means of grace (v. 12) and earned divine judgment (vv. 13–16). This is a solemn reminder that with privilege comes responsibility (Luke 12:48).

Chapter 3

1. Israel's national election (v. 2) teaches significant truths about God's gracious election of individuals to salvation. It is an amazing display of God's grace to those undeserving of the least of any divine favor. The elect enjoy a position of unique privilege. Reflecting on the many benefits and blessings of salvation is always an appropriate theme in worship. Yet, with the privilege comes increased responsibility, "for unto whomsoever much is given, of him shall be much required" (Luke 12:48). Rather than creating pride and carelessness, election should produce a sense of humility and increased incentive to live holy and blameless lives before God and men.

2. Verse 12 suggests that God's judgment of sinners is also a means of revealing the righteous remnant. The remaining legs and part of an ear were not much, but they were something. Often God's people go through the same trouble

as others, but for them it is a purifying and strengthening process rather than mere chastening. Daniel was righteous but he was taken captive. What was judgment for his nation was a means to his spiritual growth and usefulness. We should let every circumstance, even chastening, foster our sanctification.

Chapter 4

1. The negative example of the selfishness and self-indulgence of the women of Samaria provides the opportunity to reflect on what Christ identifies as the second great commandment: to love one's neighbor as one's self. You could contrast the women of Samaria, who were willing to harm others in order to help themselves, with the Good Samaritan, who was willing to sacrifice his own possessions to help another (Luke 10:30–36).

2. The Lord's ironic command to transgress at Bethel (4:4–5) teaches some important lessons about worship. First, it is important to worship the Lord in the way that He has prescribed (the regulative principle). We are not left to our own imagination or devices to worship Him. Second, it is important to worship the Lord with a genuine heart of faith, in spirit and in truth. The multiplication of all the rituals without a heart for God meant nothing. God is never satisfied with a purely external religion without faith.

3. Amos 4:6–11 warns of the danger of not responding to God's gracious dealings. In spite of all of the gracious warnings the Lord had given, the people persisted in their sin and became more and more calloused to spiritual things. There are great advantages to being in a Christian home where

the evidences of God's grace abound. But we must be careful not to become oblivious and insensitive to His goodness and longsuffering. We must warn our children not to take their spiritual privileges for granted and not to turn from His dealings in their lives.

Chapter 5

1. The invitations to repent are reminders of the hope extended to the greatest of sinners. God's goodness, forbearance, and longsuffering delayed the earned judgment providing the opportunity to repent (Rom. 2:4). The invitations also testify to God's inflexibility since true repentance is the only way to escape the judgment. Sinners can come to God only on His terms.

2. Amos 5:12 ("I know your manifold transgressions") is occasion to reflect on God's infallible knowledge: "All things are naked and opened unto the eyes of him with whom we have to do" (Heb. 4:13). It is a fearful thing and should be a motive to purity to know that God knows all we are and all we do.

3. God's rejection of Israel's rituals is a solemn warning about the danger of purely external religion. Because of their worship practices, Israel assumed they were right with God and God was satisfied with them. External religion tends to breed a false confidence and security. The form of external worship is different today, but the attitude persists. Many believe that all is well spiritually simply because they attend church and do "Christian" things. God's view of religion without heart does not change. Those who worship Him must do so in spirit and in truth (John 4:24).

Chapter 6

1. Material prosperity can distort reality and cause insensitivity to spiritual issues. Israel was accustomed to a lifestyle of luxury and refused to think about the consequences of their self-indulgence. The experience of the moment blinded them to the certain coming of judgment (6:3). Second Peter 3:3–10 similarly speaks of those who deny the coming judgment just because it has not yet come. We should be warned from the fact that judgment did come to Israel. Spiritual insensitivity and obliviousness are dangerous.

2. Christ's illustration of the rich man and Lazarus (Luke 16:19–26) parallels the situation described in Amos 6:6 of those engaged in self-indulgence at the neglect of the afflicted. In both contexts, the consequences are severe.

3. That God commands the judgment (v. 11) is occasion to reflect on His inflexible righteousness that ought to generate fear of the Lord. For it is, indeed, a fearful thing to fall into the hands of the living God (Heb. 10:31). That God raises up a nation (Assyria) as the agent of judgment (6:14) demonstrates His sovereignty and His authority to use secondary causes to accomplish His will. God judged, but the Assyrians were the rod of His anger (Isa. 10:5).

Chapter 7

1. The Lord's relenting of the judgment in answer to the prophet's prayer (vv. 2–3; 5–6) is a lesson in the power of intercessory prayer. Believing that God has decreed the end also requires believing that God has decreed the means to accomplishing His purpose. Prayer is a means whereby God works His will. As effective as Amos's prayer was before

God, it pales before the intercessions of the greater prophet, the Lord Jesus Christ. He ever lives to make intercession for us as our Advocate with the Father (Heb. 7:25; 1 John 2:1). Whereas Amos appealed to God from Israel's weakness and insignificance (Amos 7:2, 5), Christ pleads the merits of His sacrifice. Charles Wesley's hymn sums up nicely the effectiveness of Christ's intercession: "Five bleeding wounds He bears, received on Calvary, they pour effectual prayers, they strongly plead for me: Forgive him, O forgive they cry…nor let that ransomed sinner die." And then the wonderful assurance: "The Father hears Him pray, His dear anointed One; He cannot turn away the presence of His Son."

2. Amos's preaching in spite of the "official" injunction against him parallels the persistent preaching of the apostles when they, too, were ordered to stop by the established religious authorities (Acts 4:18–20). Obeying God is always more important than obeying man.

Chapter 8

1. The vision of the basket of summer fruit warns the sinner that the time comes when God's longsuffering, designed to lead to repentance (Rom. 2:4), ends, and judgment is inevitable. There is a point of no return, a complete loss of hope. This truth can be illustrated from the flood narrative (Gen. 6:3) and the Lord's dealing with those who refused Wisdom's invitation to life (Prov. 1:24–32). In addition, the physical judgment inflicted on Israel points to the far greater eternal judgment awaiting Christ-rejecters (Matt. 8:12).

2. That a famine of hearing the words of the Lord (v. 11) is a sign of God's disfavor should generate praise and thanksgiving

for His favor in giving and preserving His Word for us in the Bible. Not only should be we be thankful for it, we should feast on it regularly that we might benefit from its bounty for our spiritual welfare.

Chapter 9

1. The similarity of verses 2–3 to Psalm 139:7–9 is remarkable. Both texts address God's omnipresence and omniscience. What is a dread to sinners who can never hide from or escape God's hand of judgment is a comfort to saints who can never be out of God's sight and care. It is indeed a thought that is too wonderful (139:6). We should, therefore, live in that constant awareness of God and consistently factor Him into all the circumstances of life.

2. Verses 8–10 teaches that one of the purposes of judgment is to identify the remnant, those who belong to the Lord. God is able to use a single occurrence for multiple purposes. A disaster that may be judgment on sinners can also be a trial to test and strengthen saints. Daniel, for instance, was taken to Babylon as part of Judah's captivity because of sin. But that national chastisement was a means of maturing Daniel to great usefulness in God's kingdom.

3. That Christ's kingdom takes possession of Edom, even all the nations (or, as James interprets it, "the residue of men"), declares the absolute success of the gospel (Acts 15:17). It parallels the dramatic heavenly scene in Revelation 7 that describes the redeemed as being comprised of every nation, people, and tongue. It ought to be reason for our praise and thanksgiving that we are included in that great number.

Obadiah

1. Obadiah's message of doom for Edom has significant relevance for God's people in every age. Some of the details were historically fulfilled in the distant past, and others await eschatological climax. Yet there is a message that cannot be limited just to the past or the future. Although it may appear at times that evil triumphs, this book makes it clear that God is in control and He will right every wrong. Two central truths are clear: (1) the kingdom of this world will fail; (2) the kingdom of our God will prevail.

2. Obadiah's prophecy of the day of the Lord underscores the certainty of divine justice. The most outstanding focus is that judgment is deserved and, therefore, fair. It highlights the contrast with God's gracious salvation. In damnation, the sinner receives what he deserves; in salvation, the saved sinner receives what he does not deserve. Judgment is all of merit; salvation is all of grace.

Jonah

Chapter 1

1. We can only speculate as to why Jonah chose to disobey God—perhaps from fear of Nineveh's size or wickedness, or patriotism, knowing the role that Assyria would have as Israel's conqueror. That no reason is given for Jonah's disobedience suggests that there is never a good reason or legitimate excuse for disobeying God.

2. Jonah warns against the far-reaching consequences of sin. It brings chastisement to the sinner: the storm was Jonah's fault and designed to deal with his disobedience. But sin's consequences jeopardize others who are not directly responsible. In one way or another sin always affects others: there is no such thing as a private sin. The storm threatened the sailors as well as Jonah. The sailors learned why the storm occurred, but there had to be multiple other ships on the Mediterranean going through the same storm without any knowledge of the fact that their lives were in jeopardy because of Jonah's sin. It is part of Satan's deceit that says sin is without corporate consequence.

3. The first chapter says much about God's absolute sovereignty. He controls the weather, the waves, and the fish to achieve His purpose. His sovereignty in the natural sphere is indicative of His sovereignty in the spiritual sphere as well. That becomes clear in the salvation of Nineveh.

4. The appointed fish that swallowed Jonah illustrates the wonder of grace. Jonah deserved to die, but God let him live. So it is that we deserve death, but God's amazing grace has saved us and given life. Grace is getting what we do not deserve.

Chapter 2

1. Prayer is an important means of grace that God has ordained for His people. The Bible commands prayer, invites prayer, and instructs about prayer. Jonah's prayer is a good example of how to pray, as his prayer is comprised of so much from the Psalms. The link between God's Word and prayer is a key component. We are to pray God's Word back to Him in faith that He will perform it in His faithfulness. The Psalms especially provide patterns that we are to follow in prayer. They are divinely inspired and show the way God wants His people to pray. It is a good practice regularly to pray through the Psalms, applying the petitions to our own needs just as Jonah did to his.

2. Jonah's prayer also reminds us how important it is to hide God's Word in our hearts so that we can use it and rely on it even when we don't have a Bible at hand. All that Jonah prayed in the darkness and disgust of the fish's belly came from what he had committed to his memory. Becoming saturated with the Word in times of Bible study and devotion enables us to use and rely upon it in times of crisis.

Chapter 3

1. Jonah's second call to Nineveh is instructive. First, it shows God's sovereignty in being merciful to whom He will.

Compare Jonah with the unnamed prophet in 1 Kings 13. God called him to a dangerous mission before Jeroboam I, instructing him to return home immediately after delivering the message. Without reluctance or hesitation, he obeyed God. However, he was seduced by the old prophet to tarry contrary to God's instruction. Because of his disobedience, lions killed him on his way home. In contrast, Jonah was blatantly and willfully disobedient, yet God spared him and gave him a second opportunity to obey. From a human perspective, the bold yet naïve unnamed prophet seemed worthy of a second chance whereas Jonah more reasonably deserved death. Yet God acted justly regarding the unnamed prophet, but chose to be gracious to Jonah. This should be occasion for thought. How many times have we disobeyed, deserving punishment, yet how many "chances" has God given us to obey?

2. Jonah's second call is also a lesson in the invincible power of God's plan and purpose. God had a purpose regarding Jonah and Nineveh that Jonah's disobedience could not frustrate. According to God's plan, Jonah was the chosen messenger to these wicked people. We believe both that God has sovereignly decreed the end of things and that He has decreed the means to accomplish the purposed ends. This has a sobering application to evangelism. God may sovereignly place on a given individual the dreadful responsibility of being the only one who can reach some people. We are all accountable to God and should not rebel against His purpose. God will unfailingly save whom He will but faith comes by hearing and hearing by the Word of God; how will people hear without a preacher (see the ordained logic of evangelism in Rom. 10:13–17)?

3. Where sin abounds, grace super-abounds (Rom. 5:20). God's mercy toward wicked Nineveh testifies to the amazing power of grace to save sinners and assures that none are too wicked to receive God's salvation. They were objects of divine wrath under the sentence of death, but they were moved by the Word to repent, and God graciously received them. The words of Christ sum up the truth: "Him that cometh to me I will in no wise cast out" (John 6:37).

Chapter 4

1. Jonah's anger over Nineveh's repentance and deliverance illustrates the principal lesson of the book that "salvation is of the LORD" (2:9). Had Nineveh's salvation depended on Jonah, it would have perished for sure. What a contrast Jonah is to Jeremiah, who loved his people and prayed for their conversion, but saw little positive response. Ironically, a very short sermon by a prophet who hated the people to whom he preached was used by God to save more people on a single occasion than perhaps at any other time in history. The power is in the Word of God. God can use even unclean vessels to accomplish His will.

2. Jonah's appeal to God's perfections as the excuse for his disobedience betrays an inappropriate use of truth and theology. Every point of his stated creed about God was right, but his use of truth was terribly wrong. Any understanding or application of theology that breeds coldness or selfishness or any other unspiritual reaction is wrong, but the fault may not be with the theology.

3. Jonah's response to the gourd's growth and its subsequent withering exposes his spiritual selfishness. He received God's

favor with joy and became angry when the favor was withdrawn. It was all about how things affected him. But the thought of God being merciful to Nineveh was contrary to his desire for its destruction. His attitude is similar to the man Christ describes, who was happy when he was forgiven a large debt, but was without sympathy to one who owed him just a small amount (Matt. 18:23–35). We should rejoice in God's blessings upon others as much as we do in our own.

4. The book ends with an unanswered question: should not God pity even those who might be His enemies? We don't know how Jonah would have answered the question, so the "Jonah" that resides within us must answer. The question is rhetorical, but the answer is obvious. Do our lives reflect it?

Micah

Chapter 1

1. In verse 2 the Lord is identified as the witness against those He judges. He is the witness who testifies, verifying every accusation against the guilty, and the judge with the authority to execute the deserved penalty. This is an opportunity to reflect on the fearful reality of having to stand before the judge of all the earth with the awareness that "all things are naked and opened unto the eyes of him with whom we have to do" (Heb. 4:13). His judgments, therefore, are always righteous and infallibly just. There are no excuses or self-defenses that can stand before Him. This points directly to the beauty of the gospel of Christ and justifying grace that gives the guilty sinner a perfect standing before God because there can be no condemnation to those who are in Christ Jesus (Rom. 8:1).

2. Verse 9 is a reminder of the devastating power of sin's effect on others. Although Judah was responsible and accountable before God for its own sin, there is a link between what was happening in the north and what was happening in the south. Jacob's transgression was first, and Judah followed and in some ways became worse (see the allegory of the two sisters in Ezek. 23). It is part of sin's deception that it is a private matter. But in reality there is nothing that can be just a private sin. Either by example or consequence, sin is an infection that spreads.

Chapter 2

1. God's condemnation of the nation's social sins highlights the authority and unity of God's law. At the very least the nation was guilty of transgressing the eighth and tenth commandments, prohibiting stealing and coveting of what belongs to others (Ex. 20:15, 17). In due course the prophet would expose their religious sins as well. But the prophet's logic is clear. Wronging your neighbor precludes being right with God regardless of religious practice or profession. How will a right relationship with God manifest itself in right relationships with others?

2. Preaching the whole counsel of God requires denouncing sin and warning of judgment as well as the message of grace and the gospel. Too often people reject the hard message, wanting only to hear that everything is going to be good—just like Israel (2:11). But the wonder of the gospel of grace in Christ can only be understood in the light of the terror and danger without it. Micah provides a good example, exposing and condemning sin on his way to the glorious message of peace and salvation that can be found only in Christ (2:12–13).

Chapter 3

1. The sins and failures of civil and religious leaders were not unique to Micah's day. Every generation and geographical location has been subject to those who fall short of God's requirement for those who rule over men to be just and to rule in the fear of God (2 Sam. 23:3). On the one hand, it is a grievous matter. On the other hand, it should be a means of increasing desire for the ideal prophet, priest, and king, the

Lord Jesus Christ. His rule is always just and His dominion is universal (Ps. 72). It is a reminder that our hope should never be in men or political or religious systems but only in the Lord. We should be confident as well that even though injustices exist, God will right all wrongs (Eccl. 3:16–17).

2. The principle of judgment illustrated in verse 4 is a terrible warning of the danger of receiving from God according to our own works. Getting from God what is deserved is always awful, since the wages of sin is death (Rom. 6:23). The beauty of the gospel is that we do not get what we deserve but what Christ deserves. On the cross He bore our sins and guilt, receiving what we deserved. In our justification, we receive the life and righteousness that He deserved by His perfect obedience to all of God's demands (2 Cor. 5:21).

Chapter 4

1. The whole chapter is an occasion for reflecting on God's unchanging and unfailing purpose in the covenant of grace. Although at points in history it has appeared evil would triumph, it is certain that the upright will have dominion (Ps. 49:14). It is certain that the church of Christ will advance triumphantly against the very gates of hell (Matt. 16:18).

2. That the Gentile nations come to acknowledge and worship the true God is further evidence of God's unfailing, redemptive purpose that was never intended to be limited to national Israel. The promised Messiah was from the beginning to be the source of blessing and salvation for the world. The description in Revelation 7:9 of the heavenly throng from every nation and tongue on earth confirms that Christ is the Savior of sinners from every race. Knowing that Christ

has a people from all over the world should give confidence in every missionary and evangelistic venture.

Chapter 5

1. The birth of Jesus in a barn in Bethlehem underscores the depth of the humiliation of the incarnation of the Son of God. The eternal Son who in the heavenly glory was surrounded by a chorus of praising angels condescended to enter the virgin's womb to be born in a stall surrounded by brute beasts. From the ivory palaces (Ps. 45:8) He entered the world He created in poverty. Although Bethlehem was the place of David's birth, it was not the royal city where presumably all the other kings of Judah were born with royal pageantry. His humble birth was followed by a life of humble obedience and humiliation leading to death on the cross. Christ was born that He might accomplish His unique mission of being the only redeemer of God's elect.

2. Micah's prophecy of the Messiah's birthplace includes vital truths about the person of Christ that constitute reasons for worship and praise. Both the deity and humanity of Christ are in view; He is the God-man with two distinct natures in one person. His goings forth before His birth indicate the existence of His person prior to the incarnation and thus His deity. His birth indicates that His humanity is real. As the God-man He is the only mediator between God and men. The whole work of redemption depends on this unique person. Christ is mankind's only hope. It is significant that this is a truth revealed in the Old Testament as well as the New.

Chapter 6

1. Although the court session Micah records concerned ancient Israel, the trial issues are universal and timeless. Religion in one form or another dominated life and in many ways blinded the people to the problem of sin. Religious people are often the hardest to convict of sin because they assume that they are doing what God wants. Many today without Christ assume that going to church and keeping the Golden Rule will somehow balance to their favor in the end. Even many who profess Christ allow their pious routines to substitute for private devotion and a sincere heart. The Scripture is explicitly clear that God has never been and will never be satisfied with external religion or empty profession without a true heart of faith on the inside that authenticates itself by true holiness on the outside. The link between behavior and belief is the essence of true religion (James 1:27).

2. Unquestionably Christ referred to verse 8 when He exposed the hypocrisy of the Pharisees by accusing them of omitting the most important matters of the law: judgment, mercy, and faith (Matt. 23:23). What condemned the Jews of Micah's day condemned the Pharisees of Christ's day. Indeed, the requirements of true religion never change, and God's requirement of what is good remains the standard for today. That Micah uses a court scene to make his point reminds us of a coming day of judgment when all hearts will be open and naked before the eyes of Him to whom we will answer. The verdicts rendered on that day are eternal, so it behooves us all "to do justly, to love mercy, and to walk humbly with [our] God."

Chapter 7

1. Micah, writing thousands of years ago, described scenes that could have come from today's news. The presence of good and upright men was rare. Micah longed for the fruit of righteousness but instead found a land filled with crooked leaders, ruthless neighbors, and troubled homes (vv. 1–6). We, too, live in a day when the unrighteous constitute the immoral majority; they mock God's people and are increasingly willing to vent their full hatred against the Christ of God. Although his days were dark, the prophet did not despair, and he wrote for us an inspired pattern for living in an evil day. Micah put it all in perspective, showing us how to feel, what to pray, and why to rejoice in an evil day. We should feel confident before God because of who He is (v. 7), and before the wicked because God will vindicate us (vv. 8–10). We should pray that God would shepherd His flock in faith and that He would do the extraordinary and confound the wicked (vv. 14–17). We should praise Him because there is none like Him who can do what He can do (vv. 18–20).

2. The Old Testament uses various words in the vocabulary for faith. The ideas of looking expectantly and waiting for the Lord are important concepts (v. 7). Every word for faith in some way describes confidence in the object of faith. Waiting on the Lord is an expression of hope and confidence. It is not just a passive notion that resigns to whatever happens. It involves an active, vigilant expectancy that what God has promised will come at any moment. It is like sitting on the edge of your seat in eager anticipation. And the wonderful thing is that those who wait on the Lord will never be disappointed.

Nahum

Chapter 1

1. Nahum's song of God's majesty highlights both the justice and goodness of God, making it clear that these divine perfections are not contradictory but essential in God's nature. It is a foolish, sentimental, and unbiblical notion of God that concludes that His love or goodness requires Him to be gracious to all indiscriminately. In fact, it is the love of God that renders the punishment of sinners just, because the supreme object of His love is His Son. To know and experience God's love is to do so in Christ; outside of Christ there is nothing but wrath and condemnation. It would be a betrayal of His love to His Son to allow sinners to escape justice. This is why sinners must flee to Christ as the only refuge or stronghold of safety against the day of judgment. No man can stand before God on his own merit, but in Christ there is total acceptance.

2. Verse 12 is a reminder that appearance and reality are not the same and that we should, therefore, walk by faith and not sight. It appeared that the enemy remained strong and numerous, but the reality was that God had irreversibly sentenced them to destruction and they were doomed (v. 15). At any given moment it appears that Satan is a roaring lion seeking whom he can devour but the reality is that he was defeated on Calvary, is being defeated with every advance of the church, and will be ultimately defeated at the consummation of the age. Faith must live in the light of the certain reality; faith overcomes sight.

Chapter 2

1. The defeat and destruction of Nineveh provide a good example of the sovereignty of God whereby the Lord accomplishes His purpose either directly or indirectly through secondary agents. From a human perspective the fall of Nineveh at the hands of the Medes and Babylonians had natural, political, and military explanations. It could well have been the topic of the daily news with commentary and analysis. Yet the Medes and Babylonians in reality were merely the instruments or tools God used to achieve His purpose. Consequently, the spiritual explanation for Nineveh's fall is far more significant than the political and military explanations. The secondary agents do not in any way diminish the ultimate agency of God Himself. That these nations were themselves ignorant that they were doing God's will was irrelevant. Their purpose was mercenary; God's purpose was to keep His redemptive plan on track.

2. Assyria had amassed extreme wealth, but all their assets could not deliver them. In many ways, the history of Assyria parallels the parable of Christ recorded in Luke 12:16–21 of the man who lived to be rich only to die in spiritual poverty leaving all his assets to another. It is far more important to be rich toward God than to amass possessions that are only temporary. Peter reminds us that we cannot be redeemed with silver or gold but only with the precious blood of Christ (1 Peter 1:18–19).

3. The opening statement of verse 13 is fearful: "I am against thee, saith the LORD." For God to be the enemy spells doom and damnation. But this is the state of every individual outside of Christ. To be outside of Christ is to be

under condemnation and subject to God's severe wrath. To be in Christ changes everything. The believer is united to Christ and enjoys security and peace. The consequence is that God is now for us instead of against us. And the consequence of that is, "If God be for us, who can be against us?" (Rom. 8:31).

Chapter 3

1. The nation of Assyria was destroyed because of its cruel atrocities against other nations. The Assyrians had little regard for human dignity in their selfish pursuits. The tables were turned and their total destruction was justly proportioned to what they deserved. Although Nineveh suffered defeat at the hands of another nation, its judgment was ultimately decreed and orchestrated by God. But even so, it was the putting down of a kingdom. The principles of this national judgment, however, point to the even more grave judgment of individuals which affects not just the body, but the soul. Christ said to "fear him which is able to destroy both soul and body in hell" (Matt. 10:28). There is nothing more fearful in divine judgment than receiving the sentence from God that is deserved. The terrors of that judgment should be an incentive to flee in faith and repentance to the God of mercy.

2. The sleeping shepherds of verse 18 remind us that we have a good shepherd who never slumbers nor sleeps and who with constant vigilance and care provides for us and protects us from all harm.

3. Interestingly, Nahum, whose message concerns Nineveh, ends with a question just like Jonah, whose message also concerned Nineveh. The book of Jonah ended with God asking

how could He not spare repentant Nineveh. Nahum's question is essentially how could God not judge wicked Nineveh. God in His mercy receives those who come to Him in faith and repentance. God in His justice must judge the unrepentant. It is eternally better to experience God's grace and mercy than to be sentenced according to His justice.

Habakkuk

Chapter 1

1. The question "why?" is most perplexing. Parents ask their children this question and typically receive the response "I don't know." When children ask their parents "why," the typical response is "because I said so." Neither of those answers is satisfying. There is seldom a good and satisfying answer to that question. Yet, Christians often ask God "why" when things happen that they don't understand or like. The Bible gives many examples: Job, Jeremiah, various psalmists (e.g., Pss. 37; 49; 73, etc.). Seldom does God answer the question. Over and again, God turns the attention away from the circumstance that generated the question to Himself, who is the ultimate satisfying answer. The tension between what we know about God (our creed) and what we are seeing that bothers us (our experience) can be real, but the resolution is always to look away from the circumstance to the Lord. Faith links our creed and our experience.

2. Habakkuk's prayers, though generated by his misunderstanding of and confusion about what God was doing, are most instructive. The Bible records inspired prayers as patterns for us to follow. If anything is on the surface in Habakkuk's praying, it is his honesty and transparency before God. He boldly bares his heart, expressing his bewilderment concerning God's justice. He prays what he thinks. Too often our prayers become routine and rigid with standard platitudes as we try to mask before God our true feelings.

Similarly, Jeremiah was so transparent in his praying that he accused God of deception (Jer. 20:7). We would never be so bold to mouth those words. But how often have we had these same feelings when things were not as we thought they should be? We must be reverent, but God knows our hearts and thoughts. Let us learn in our praying to appeal to Him reverently yet with boldness, knowing that He is a God who loves to hear our prayers.

Chapter 2

1. God's answer to Habakkuk is instructive (vv. 1–4). Not only does the answer reveal God's pleasure with Habakkuk's prayer, notwithstanding his confessions expressing his confusion about God's actions (no rebuke to the prophet), it reveals the way believers are to live through times of confusion. That the just are to live by faith encompasses all of life and every experience of life. We are to walk by faith and not by sight. Faith gives the assurance that God is in heaven (v. 20), His glory is in the earth (v. 14), and, therefore, all is well regardless of what we see or sense. We may not always understand the reason, but we should live in the confidence that God is sovereignly accomplishing His purpose in all things.

2. Babylon was not exempt from accountability before God because she was God's servant to accomplish His work of chastisement on Judah. God was sovereign in how He used the pagan nation, and the pagan nation was responsible for its own behavior and liable to just punishment. The only conflict between God's sovereignty and human responsibility is in the mind of man. God is just in all His ways, and it is best that all the earth be in silent subjection before Him (v. 20).

Chapter 3

1. Habakkuk's prayer provides another important pattern with key lessons. On the surface is the link between prayer and God's Word. Both are means of grace and work together. It is the Word that fuels the praying. Once Habakkuk learned God's will, he prayed for that will to be done. Nothing was more crucial than the will of God even though it would involve painful discipline. But if the hard things were a means for the manifestation of God's glory, then that would be for the best. It is noteworthy as well that the majority of the prayer is praise rather than petition. Praising God for who He is and what He has done fuels the faith to ask God for great things.

2. Reading the praise section of Habakkuk's prayer illustrates the importance of knowing redemptive history. Many of the statements make no sense apart from what God has preserved in the historical records in Scripture. This ought to be an incentive to know our Bibles so when one part of Scripture alludes to another part we can understand the message. This section also illustrates that what Paul said concerning Israel's history being an example and admonition for us (1 Cor. 10:11) applies to those living in the New Testament times as well. Can you think of more reasons why there is more to biblical history than just names, dates, and events?

3. The closing verses (vv. 17–19) teach that real contentment is found only in the Lord. This is another facet of living by faith. Too often we allow circumstances to control our emotions and dictate our feelings. Circumstances change. It is fine to be happy or sad as circumstances change (Eccl. 3). But if we find our ultimate contentment and satisfaction in

the eternal God who never changes, external stimuli are not the controlling factor. Habakkuk describes a situation in which nothing was good but he was rejoicing because his joy was in the Lord. Do you recall times in your life when you were content in the Lord, by faith, despite being in difficult circumstances?

Zephaniah

Chapter 1

1. The great gospel themes of salvation are always attractive, but there is another side of the gospel that is hard. But the hard message of just judgment against sin and sinners highlights and intensifies the beauty of saving grace. God's sovereign love for sinners is understood to be all the more gracious in the light of His just wrath and condemnation of sinners. Zephaniah begins his preaching with the hard message and provides some key points of meditation. (1) Judgment is just because of the heinous nature of sin (vv. 4–13). (2) Judgment is terrible because of its divine source (day of the Lord) and its fearful features and consequences (vv. 15–17). (3) Judgment is inevitable (v. 18). It is the hard and certain message of God's wrath that transitions so wonderfully to the message of salvation in Christ. It points to the cross where Christ took the full blow of God's justice and wrath in the place of His people. His people can escape judgment, not with silver or gold, but by the precious blood of Christ.

2. Zephaniah's judgment on Judah specifically is a sobering warning to those who have an association with and show of religion without the reality of it. Judah, as the covenant nation, had many spiritual advantages yet they mixed what they knew about the truth with the paganism of the world and thus were far from God. There is a danger that those who have been long in the church can be insensitive to the reality of God and truth. The high level of spiritual advantage

increases the responsibility, and it is impossible to fool God, who knows infallibly the heart of everyone. Remind the children of the importance of personal faith and repentance and not just association with the church. Judgment begins at the house of God.

Chapter 2

1. Verses 1–3 reveal how to escape the inescapable. The call to repentance underscores the irony of hope in contrast to natural reasoning. Common sense would say that the way to escape danger is by fleeing from it (an impossibility, 1:18); the message of the gospel is that the way to escape the danger of certain judgment is to flee to its source to find mercy, to seek the Lord. The Lord is gracious and merciful and has promised to be found by those who seek Him sincerely; those who seek find, and those who come will not be cast out (John 6:37). It is important as well to stress the urgency of the invitation to seek the Lord. Today is the day of salvation, but tomorrow is the day of judgment.

2. The judgment of the Gentile nations is an opportunity to reflect on God's absolute sovereignty. None of the nations identified worshiped the true God or knew the truth from His special and gracious revelation. Nevertheless, He owned them and held them accountable for their sins, and particularly their sins against His people, which identified them as belonging to the serpent's seed, bent on opposing God's redemptive plan. God had the authority and power to judge them; their ignorance of Him provided no excuse. It is significant as well to reflect on how God's judgment on the enemy results in blessing for His people. Divine judgment of the

serpent's seed is an essential component in the advancement of God's kingdom.

Chapter 3

1. Verse 8 is an opportunity to reflect on God's longsuffering that is designed to bring men to repentance and God's sovereignty that uses even man's sin to accomplish His ultimate redemptive purpose (Rom. 2:4; 9:22–24). The verse is clear that judgment is certain, but it is being delayed because of Israel's sin. Paul's exposition of this truth in Romans 9 is remarkable. Israel's sin and all of its devastating consequences, rather than annulling God's promise, became a means of bringing in the Gentiles. But all unbelievers must beware: judgment is still coming in all the fury of God's wrath upon those who reject the gospel. Hebrews 12:25, 29 puts it in perspective: "See that ye refuse not him that speaketh.... Our God is a consuming fire."

2. The final section of Zephaniah reminds us that there is a positive and glorious aspect of the day of the Lord. The day on which justice will be executed against sinners also ushers in the time of restoration and full salvation blessing, where every vestige of sin and the curse is gone. The King will come, and He will gather His people to enjoy eternal bliss and peace in His presence (Rev. 19). It is imperative that we seek Him now to escape the wrath to come and to enjoy both the present life in Christ, who took God's wrath for His people, and the prospect of eternal hope. To this end the day of the Lord is a purifying and comforting truth for God's people.

Haggai

Chapter 1

1. In the classic allegory *The Pilgrim's Progress*, John Bunyan illustrates the notions of many who have mistaken views of God and His Word. Early on his journey, Christian encountered two of his neighbors, Obstinate and Pliable. Though both were curious about Christian's journey, Obstinate determined from the beginning not to go and tried to convince Pliable not to go either. But Pliable, interested in the blessings and benefits Christian described, set out on the journey. Along the way, he kept asking Christian about the blessings ahead. All went well until they entered the Slough of Despond. Pliable forgot about all the benefits and returned home as quickly as he could. Unless the way was easy and the blessings clearly in view, he wanted nothing to do with Christian and this journey to the distant city. He would follow God only for what he thought he would get out of it. Bunyan's self-consumed Pliable bears uncanny resemblance to those in the days of Haggai, who allowed the opposition to distract them from what God had commanded. It was easier to redirect their efforts to self-interests, but losing the vision of God's purpose turned life itself into futility—nothing brought fulfillment. Haggai made it clear that self-serving is always self-defeating. This is a poignant message to so many Christians today whose priorities are skewed toward the stuff of temporal life rather than spiritual life.

2. How the people responded to Haggai's preaching is a model example. They listened, they acknowledged it as God's Word, and they obeyed. By their returning to the work, they became doers of the Word and not just hearers (James 1:22). That their response was the consequence of the Lord's arousing them is a reminder of how vital it is for the Spirit to be in attendance with the preaching of the Word and to apply that work to the heart. Preachers are able to convince people to do or not to do, but only the Spirit can apply the Word in a living way (see the illustration in Ezekiel 37 of the prophet's preaching to the dry bones). Preaching is the method God has ordained for evangelism and edification. Not only are ministers responsible to preach well, the congregation is responsible to listen well.

3. Haggai's "congregation" also provides a lesson in fearing the Lord. The fear of God is an expression of faith, which is more aware of the unseen than the seen. The people lost their vision and energy for the work of the kingdom when they saw and experienced hostility. But when they became conscious of God's presence (v. 13) and feared Him (v. 12), they determined to obey. What we fear always determines behavior. To fear the Lord is to be consciously aware of Him and to consciously factor Him into every part of life.

Chapter 2

1. If 1:6, 8–11 taught that putting yourself in first place is self-defeating, 2:3 teaches that putting yourself down is service-defeating. Comparing the first temple with the plans of the second temple led to discouragement and inactivity. The people allowed appearance to influence their thinking and

concluded that they were making no real contribution to the work of the Lord. They looked backward instead of forward to what was going to be greater than their expectations. It is always dangerous and defeating to evaluate the value of our service by comparing it with what others are doing or have done. The value of service is always to be measured by conformity to God's will and purpose. Too many Christians tend to compare themselves and their spiritual gifts with others and convince themselves there is nothing they can contribute to the service of the Lord. Consequently, they become idle. There is no better service that we can render to the Lord than being faithful to what He has called us and enabled us to do by the help of His Spirit. All service that is rendered in faithful obedience is pleasing to Him.

2. Christ's designation as the "desire of all nations" (v. 7) directs us to Him as the object of our worship. The word "desire" includes the sense of treasure or wealth. This means that Christ with all of His infinite and intrinsic worth ought to be our prized possession. To have Christ is to have everything. If He is our treasure our hearts will be with Him (Matt. 6:19–21; Col. 3:1–2). Paul understood this when he testified that he counted everything else to be nothing but rubbish in contrast to knowing Christ (Phil. 3:7–8). That is the example to follow.

3. Verses 10–14 are a reminder of how important it is for believers to walk cautiously in this world. There are so many things in the world that rob us of our fellowship with God and our ability to serve Him. This is one reason why we are not to love the things of this world (1 John 2:15–17). Here

is an illustration: rubbing a clean shirt on a grease rag will not clean the grease from the rag, but it will stain the shirt. So Christians must be cautious to avoid contact with sinful things and practices.

Zechariah

Chapter 1

1. Verse 14 sums up the message of the entire prophecy and suggests key thoughts for meditation. God's jealousy or zeal is His ardent and active love for His name, His glory, His law, and His people. It is His zealous disposition that demonstrates the appropriate action. When offended, it shows itself in just retribution. When stirred by grace, it reveals eternal love. Whereas jealousy and zeal in man can be easily perverted in moments of passion, that is never true of God. Behind His fervent zeal and hot jealousy are His eternal purpose, immutability, omnipotence, and authority. Significantly, this declared jealousy for His people is from the Lord of hosts, a title that highlights His power and authority. As you read through Zechariah, pay attention to this title that occurs more than fifty times. Many of the promises are beyond human comprehension, but behind every promise is the God who controls and commands all of creation; that is solid reason for hope. Nothing can hinder or frustrate God's burning zeal.

2. In the opening vision, the man on the red horse represents Christ. Indeed, the vision identifies Him as the angel of the Lord, one of the frequent designations of Christ in His preincarnate appearances in the Old Testament. His activity in the vision is instructive. The fact that He is present with His people in their low estate (among the myrtles in the valley) is evidence of Immanuel theology ("God with us"). It is always

a comfort to know that regardless of our circumstances, as believers we can be assured that our Savior is with us and that He will not leave us. His intercession for Israel in their lowly condition is a wonderful reminder of Christ's constant intercessory ministry for us. He saw their need and prayed for resolution. As our faithful high priest, He ever lives to intercede and He does so from the reality of knowing by experience all our infirmities.

Chapter 2

1. The surface lesson of the third vision is that God's purpose for His people is greater than expectation. This is a vivid illustration of the promise of Ephesians 3:20—God is "able to do exceeding abundantly above all that we ask or think." It would have been a wonderful fulfillment of promise had God merely restored Jerusalem to its previous glory. But He had a purpose to dwell with His people and to increase them beyond comprehension. This should encourage us to be bold in our praying. Too often we fear to ask too much lest we become disappointed if He does not answer according to our expectations. Our notions of what is best or how God should answer are always limited by lack of knowledge or of faith. Let us trust Him for the best and know that He will supply our needs according to His riches in Christ Jesus. We should not limit God to our notions of what He should or can do.

2. That God regards His people as the pupil of His eye is a precious thought. As the eye is sensitive to touch, so God is sensitive to what may threaten us. To touch a child of God in hostility is tantamount to poking God in the eye. He will

protect us with all His resources. It is an amazing truth that we are precious to Him and that He will take care of us.

3. This third vision encourages us to think on God's unfailing purpose for the church, His protection, and His gracious presence. It reveals the triumph of grace and assures us that, whatever we see in this world, (1) God will get the glory, (2) every enemy will be conquered, and (3) every believer will share in covenant promises and blessing. These are good reasons to worship: to hush, to be quiet, and to be reverently calm (v. 13).

Chapter 3

1. Justification is one of the great components of our complete salvation in Christ as believers. In a gracious act, God pardons our sins and accepts us as righteous by imputing Christ's righteousness to us, which we receive by faith alone. By reflecting on the picture of Joshua, even little children can understand something of this remarkable truth. The filthy garments picture the terrible stain of guilt we have before God. The removal of the garments pictures God's gracious forgiveness, and receiving the new garments points to the imputation of Christ's righteousness that gives us acceptance with God. This shows that we need more than forgiveness for what we have done in offending God; we need the garment of salvation, the robe of righteousness that Christ provides.

2. It is impossible to think about justification without thinking about what Christ has done. The prophecy of the Branch, God's servant, points to Christ in His humanity and life of humble obedience whereby He earned merit before God, weaving for us that robe of righteousness. He was made of a

woman under the law. His removal of iniquity in a single day points to His cross on which He shed His blood in atonement for our sins. Because of what Christ did in His life and in His death, we can be justified before the Holy God.

3. Since priests were man's representatives before God, what was said about Joshua and his colleagues is applicable to all true believers. They were symbolic of something greater than themselves. They were to attract attention to the Branch, to Christ. That sums up what should be true of every believer—to be like Christ, to be conformed to His image.

Chapter 4

1. The lampstand is a wonderful picture of the Christian's ministry to bear witness to Christ while in union with Him. The lampstand was all of one piece, and the lights from the six branches (symbolic of the church) shone toward the center shaft (symbolic of Christ). Christ is the light of the world, and believers are lights. The ministry of John the Baptist illustrates this (John 1:6–9). These lamps burned with oil, which represents the Holy Spirit. Meditate on this: the Holy Spirit enables believers to glorify Christ in their service. The remarkable point of Zechariah's vision is the pipes that run directly from the olive trees to the lamps, depicting the inexhaustible supply of Holy Spirit power. There is sufficient power for every Christian to fulfill his duty of bearing witness to Christ.

2. Verse 6, the key verse, is a humbling reminder that the church can fulfill its mission only in the power of the Spirit. The lamps could not burn without oil; the church cannot function without the Holy Spirit. Too often, the modern

church substitutes administrative skills or seminars for success in the effort to advance the kingdom.

3. God rejoices when He sees the plummet in the hand of Zerubbabel (v. 10). This should encourage every believer to serve the Lord regardless of how big or small his ministry may appear. Holding a plumb line did not require any skill, but it was an essential task. Every Christian should be confident that however he or others estimate the value of his service, it pleases the Lord when done for Him.

Chapter 5

1. The flying scroll, representing God's inflexible and unchanging laws, is like a military drone, an eye in the sky on a mission to discover the enemy's presence and to detect his movements and behavior. So all the world is accountable to God, liable to the just penalty of the broken law, and incapable of escaping the just consequences. It is good to remember that God is no respecter of persons and that none will be exempt from His righteous judgment. To be outside of Christ is to be left with no defense against the curse.

2. The vision of the woman in the ephah provides occasion to express praise for the absolute triumph of the gospel. The day will come when every vestige of sin will be gone; there will be a complete reversal of the curse. The new heavens and new earth will be a perfect environment for God's people. Wickedness will be put in its place never again to tempt or to trouble. All of this is possible because Christ crushed the serpent's head.

Chapter 6

1. The final vision reminds us of the effectual power of the intercessory ministry of Christ. The sight of the hostile nations enjoying peace and security led to His prayer for God to show mercy to His people by executing vengeance on the enemy (1:12–15). The final vision details the answer to the prayer. Christ's prayers are always heard and answered; God will not turn away His Son. So as He sits exalted at God's right hand, He is interceding for believers who should rejoice and boldly utilize Him as their Advocate.

2. The war wagons and angelic forces at God's command in Zechariah's day are still operative as God's providence rules and subdues all forces hostile to the advance of His kingdom. The God of then is the God of now. The fact that we cannot see what is happening in the spiritual realm does not mean that nothing is happening. Beyond our sight God controls everything to the certain accomplishment of His redemptive plan. Things had to be done in Zechariah's day for the preparation of the incarnation; things are being done in our day leading to the second coming. We may not understand what is happening at any given time, but faith rests in God's promise.

Chapter 7

1. God's answer to the question of fasting illustrates the frequent biblical warning that performing perfunctory religious rituals without a genuine heart for the Lord never pleases Him. God is never satisfied with religion without devotion. These fasts commemorating the captivity were of their own devising and were conducted without any thought toward

God. Whatever their motive, it was not a service being rendered to God. It is all too easy to be taken up with the liturgical calendar or even routine services and assume that the mere exercise or observance pleases the Lord. Those that worship God must do so with genuine hearts (in spirit and truth), and God looks through the rituals right to the heart.

2. To obey is better than sacrifice (1 Sam. 15:22). Rather than the multiplication of offerings, God has revealed what is good (Mic. 6:6–8). God's explanation that captivity could have been averted if the people had obeyed the prophets and behaved righteously teaches the same truth. It is obedience to God that truly affirms love for Him (1 John 5:3). Once we find acceptance with God in Christ, we please Him when we trust and obey Him.

Chapter 8

1. Zechariah's application of the grand prophecies illustrates a key function of biblical prophecy that is as relevant for us as those to whom Zechariah preached. What God reveals about the future is to affect life in the present. Although those who heard Zechariah's message never personally witnessed the fulfillment of all the details, they were to be encouraged and to engage fervently in serving the Lord—rebuilding the temple. So must we, in view of all the future things associated with Christ's second coming, be diligent and faithful in our service. Christ has told us "to occupy" or to stay busy with God-honoring tasks until He comes (Luke 19:13).

2. The prophecy regarding Gentile inclusion in God's kingdom is reason for all Gentile believers in the church to rejoice because in part they represent the fulfillment. Although God

had a special purpose for Israel as the human ancestry for Christ, it was His grand design in the gospel that all of the world would be blessed. Let us thank the Lord that Christ tore down the partition giving both Jew and Gentile equal access to the Father through His blood (Eph. 2:14–18).

Chapter 9

1. As Israel was to shout and rejoice over the certain prospect of the coming King, so we should rejoice over the King who has come and is coming again. As that coming King was the message of hope to both Jews and Gentiles (9:10) in Zechariah's day, He remains the only hope for man today.

2. That Christ's kingdom is without borders (v. 10) is a source of great confidence. A king's authority is always limited by the borders of His kingdom, so a borderless kingdom speaks of unlimited authority. Kingdoms come and go because kings cannot hold on to what little they govern, but Christ's kingdom is without threat for every human government exists within the borders of His. He rules all for His own glory and the good of His people. To be a citizen of His kingdom is reason for joy (v. 17).

Chapter 10

1. The word translated "punished" and "visited" in verse 3 means "to inspect" or "to examine" and is a sobering reminder that God is more than a casual observer of the affairs of man. He is the divine, all-thorough inspector who investigates and examines every man and deals with men according to what He knows. He punishes those not right with Him and blesses those who seek to live without offense to Him. None

can escape the all-seeing eye of God and that should encourage piety. We should all strive for the testimony of David in Psalm 17:3.

2. Reflecting on the titles of Christ in verse 4 should generate worship and thanksgiving. As the corner, the sure foundation, He is the only trustworthy object of faith—the only hope for sinners. As the nail, He holds up under any weight and load. He bore the load of our guilt and sin and is able to hold our troubles and cares. We can hang it all on Him. As the battle bow, He subdues all of His and our enemies; He is the able and unfailing defender of His people. As the absolute ruler, He rules either by grace or with iron. It is critical to be a citizen rather than an enemy of His kingdom.

Chapter 11

1. God's judgment on the foolish shepherd's arm and eye is significant because these two body parts are instrumental to a shepherd's work of attending and watching over the flock. The failure of the foolish shepherd puts in bold the wonderful faithfulness of our good shepherd who loves, guides, guards, feeds, seeks, and cares for His flock. He gathers His lambs in His arms (Isa. 40:11), and with His all-seeing eye He seeks for His sheep (Ezek. 34:11).

2. As unfair as it was for the prophet's labors to be valued at such a meager sum, how much more does Christ's betrayal for that same paltry sum add to the shame that He suffered for us. We should be ever amazed at the wonder of His grace that brought Him down from His ivory place (Ps. 45:8) to be so rejected and scorned by sinners. Let us never get over the extent of His humiliation endured for our sakes.

Chapter 12

1. When God makes Judah and Jerusalem unassailable by any and all invaders, He illustrates the wonderful truth of Romans 8:31, "If God be for us, who can be against us?" The sight of infantry and cavalry charging would be demoralizing and terrifying, but the sight of God's frustration of every advance would bring confidence, encouragement, and peace. So it should be for every believer to realize that in the face of all that may come our way, "in all these things we are more than conquerors through him that loved us" (v. 37).

2. When God pours out His Spirit, dispensing grace and generating prayer, He shows the power and consequence of regeneration. The Spirit awakens the sinner to look with understanding on Christ (the one who was pierced) and then to seek favor from God. Pleading in prayer is evidence of spiritual life. Remember when Ananias was reticent about ministering to the newly converted Saul, God assured him that the conversion was genuine by informing Ananias that Saul was praying (Acts 9:11). It is a basic truth that Christians pray.

Chapter 13

1. Reflect in worship on what verse 7 says about the atonement. Two thoughts are particularly overwhelming: the identity and the sacrifice of the shepherd. The Lord speaks and designates Christ as "my shepherd," referring to His divine appointment to be the mediator, and "my fellow," speaking of His essential equality with the Lord. Both terms point to His deity, but Christ is also man, thus enabling Him to die. That the Lord Himself commands the sword to

smite Christ testifies to the seriousness of sin; God's justice demanded the death of His "fellow," His coequal Son. While the cross is evidence of divine love, it is foremost evidence of divine justice. Ought not the wonder of it all—that Christ died for sinners—bring us to praise?

2. Similarly, the reference to the cleansing fountain comes between a reference to Christ being pierced by men (12:10) and being executed by God's sword. That reminds us that the cleansing fountain of Christ's blood is the only means whereby sins can be forgiven. Comparing 12:10 with 13:7 also points to Acts 2:23, which links God's eternal purpose regarding the cross to the sinner's guilt in nailing Him to the tree. The cross was central to God's plan, and it should be in the lives of all who have been redeemed by it.

Chapter 14

1. When God gathered the nations to fight against Jerusalem, only to fight against them Himself, we are reminded of the many examples of the mysterious ways of God's sovereign providence. Events and circumstances that we easily interpret as being threatening and fearful prove to be occasions for God to display His mighty power. Remember when the five Amorite kings came together to fight against Joshua. That had to be a fearful sight since up to that point Israel had faced one enemy at a time. But what appeared to be a disaster turned out to be an amazing victory thanks to the divine intervention causing the sun and moon to stand still (Josh. 10). It was God's way of accomplishing multiple victories in a single battle. We should not judge or question God's ways.

Rather we should trust Him that He uses even those things that appear to be against us to accomplish our good.

2. Although the scene described in this chapter is subject to various views of the end times, it does generate the happy hope for all believers that God, Christ, and truth will triumph. A new heaven and new earth are coming that will be free from every vestige of sin and will manifest the power of the gospel in reversing the curse. The desire of every believer should be "Even so, come, Lord Jesus" (Rev. 22:20). The way Zechariah closes his prophecy justifies his reputation as the prophet of hope.

Malachi

Chapter 1

1. If we are believers, the folly of Israel's insensitivity to grace should cause us to be thankfully sensitive to the grace we have received. Nothing will keep religion alive more than being conscious of grace. Sensitivity to grace is always grateful and realizes that God's love is not measured by things but by the reality of a personal, intimate relationship with the Lord Himself. God's love is amazing; it is a truth we could not dare to know apart from His revelation that He loves us. God's love is unmerited, finding its cause in God the Lover and not in us the loved. He loved Jacob, the deceiver who was without virtue or merit to be a candidate for grace. God's love is unfailing and preserving. This sovereign, unchanging love is the banner over all His people.

2. Genuine worship flows from the reverential knowledge of who God is. The titles of God in verses 6 and 14 particularly focus on His authority, honor, and power. A light regard for God is never conducive to worship. Until we see ourselves as little and God as infinitely big we will not worship as we ought or as He deserves. Fearing God, being in awe of Him, is an essential component of worship.

3. Israel's casual and careless worship is a vivid reminder of how easy it can be for religion to become routine and empty. It is so easy just to go through the motions of familiar rituals or liturgies thinking that God will be pleased with the trinkets we throw to Him. Too often, churches are filled with

those who regard worship as a necessary nuisance (v. 13). Christ's words to the woman at the well ring most appropriate: "They that worship him must worship him in spirit and in truth" (John 4:24). God demands a genuine, sincere heart to worship Him and will not be pleased with anything less.

Chapter 2

1. Malachi's charge against the priests for their unfaithfulness and bad influence is a sobering reminder of how vital good and faithful ministers are to the welfare of the church. Ministers are God's gift to the church for its edification (Eph. 4:11–12). Certainly ministers must heed the warning and be sure that their preaching and testimony make them good examples. Likewise, the church should pray diligently and faithfully for their ministers that God will preserve them and empower them for the ministry.

2. Malachi's exposure of the instability in families and his explanation that God is seeking a godly seed (v. 15) through the marriage covenant shows how important the family structure is in God's purpose for His people. God has ordained the family to be an experience of heaven on earth (Deut. 11:21), but too often homes have become battlegrounds. The fact of the matter is that religion is no more real than it is in the home. Christian parents should make it a priority to keep the Lord constantly in the forefront of all the activities of the home (6:4–9). Godly homes make for godly churches.

Chapter 3

1. Verse 6 is a key verse for Malachi's argument and for theology as a whole. God's immutability, an objective aspect of

God's essence, is a most encouraging and comforting truth. Significantly, Malachi places this proposition in the context of God's certain promise of the coming of Christ. The unchangeable God is the guarantee that every covenant promise will be fulfilled (Ps. 89:28–29, 34). Paul sums it up well: "For all the promises of God in him [Jesus Christ] are yea, and in him Amen, unto the glory of God by us" (2 Cor. 1:20).

2. Verses 7–12 remind us of how important it is to return to God a portion of what He has given to us. We are to offer our tithes and offerings in gratitude and in recognition of our dependence on Him. The more we find our satisfaction in God, the more freely we will give what we have to Him. God has promised to bless those who give, but we should never give as a bargaining device or as an investment strategy to get something in return. It is an expression of our enjoyment of the Lord. It is a fact that heartless religion hoards selfishly, and living religion selflessly gives.

3. Wrong motives kill good religion. Some of Malachi's congregation did the right things (v. 14) for the wrong reasons. They offered their service to God with the intent of getting something in return and got upset when they did not get it. Our service to God must always be to His glory and never for personal gain or recognition. We cannot live according to self-interests in light of what Christ has done for us (2 Cor. 5:15). Our motive should be like that of John who desired to decrease that Christ might increase (John 3:30).

Chapter 4

1. Verses 1–3 remind us that things are not to be judged before their time. So often we can fall into the same trap

as those in Malachi's day thinking that the wicked prosper and are getting away with their wickedness. But the day is coming when the upright will have dominion and the wicked will perish. This world is the best thing the wicked will ever know; this world is the worst thing the righteous will ever know. Eternity sets everything right, and it is better to be prepared for eternity than to be prosperous in this time.

2. Significantly, the last Old Testament prophet ends with a message that heightens anticipation for the New Testament. More than four hundred years of prophetic silence were about to begin. But the years of divine silence were not years of divine inactivity. Events would progress on schedule according to God's purpose until that fullness of time when the messenger of the covenant appeared suddenly and not long after His ordained forerunner. The last prophet predicted that Messiah would come, and John, the next prophet, announced His presence. Both preached the fear of judgment for the wicked and hope of healing and salvation for the righteous. Whether in the Old Testament era or the New, Christ is the difference between life and death.

NEW TESTAMENT

Matthew

Chapter 1

1. Often it is tempting to skim over the long chronologies in the Bible. However, it helps us to see that the coming of Christ was already foreseen in the Old Testament (Luke 24:44–46). When we read of Abraham, Boaz, David, Solomon, and others we see that their greater Son is now coming into the world. The time of shadows is over. The Son Himself has come. How does this fulfilled prophecy strengthen your faith?

2. Jesus' saving work is at the forefront of the Gospels. Matthew records the angel's words, "And she shall bring forth a son, and thou shalt call his name JESUS: for he shall save his people from their sins" (v. 21). Sinners of all stripes and dyes can find in this God-man a qualified and able Savior. His spotless life of obedience and His payment of the price for sin resulted in a complete and effective salvation. Do you trust in Christ to save you from sin?

3. Though His personal name is Jesus, Christ's royal title is Emmanuel, "God with us." In the person and work of Jesus, God came to dwell, or tabernacle, among His people. He did this visibly during His life on earth, but He also promises to be with His people forever (28:20). How does Christ continue to be "God with us" even now while He is in heaven?

Chapter 2

1. Jerusalem's response to the announcement of Christ's birth shows us the reality of our sinful hearts. The good news does not appear to be good until the Holy Ghost opens our ears and hearts to receive it as good news. Our hostility against God by nature runs deep. Like Herod, we would rage against Christ lest He would reveal our sin. Yet in spite of man's exceedingly wicked thoughts, God will fulfill all His counsel (Isa. 46:10). How does man's opposition to Christ appear today?

2. Matthew notes several dreams from God given to Joseph (v. 19; 1:20) and the wise men (v. 12). In today's world there are many people who claim to receive dreams from the Lord that reveal His personal will to them. However, now that redemption has been accomplished and God has finally spoken in His Son (Heb. 1:1–4), Scripture is God's means of revealing His gracious plan of redemption as well as His will for our lives.

3. Note Joseph's unwavering obedience to God in both chapters 1 and 2. A sinner himself, Joseph showed this obedience as a fruit of God's work through Christ, his adopted Son. We, too, need to be ready and willing to obey the commands of God regardless of the personal conflicts they may cause (Heb. 11:26). How might it have been hard for Joseph to obey? How is it hard for you?

Chapter 3

1. Repentance is not merely feeling bad about things we do or say. Nor is it simply forsaking certain bad habits. True repentance stems from the grace of God in the heart of a sinner, which makes him or her mourn over sin, hate it, and

turn from it toward God and His ways. Like the Pharisees in this chapter, many seem to want to repent or appear to repent, but there is no real fruit, because there is no true root. What fruit of repentance is there in your life?

2. Christ came to John to be baptized not because He had a need for John's baptism of repentance, but because He would be like His brethren in all things (Heb. 2:17). He became like sinners so that He might make sinners more like Himself. Better yet: He was made sin, that sinners might be made the righteousness of God through Him (2 Cor. 5:21).

Chapter 4

1. Christ's temptation gives us both the pattern and power for overcoming the Devil. The pattern: recognizing how Satan tempts us to doubt God's Word and goodness, and resisting the Devil by exercising faith in specific truths of Scripture. The power: although our first Adam fell under temptation, casting all mankind under the Devil's power, Christ stood firm and therefore can effectively lead us to conquer sin (Heb. 2:18; 4:15; 1 John 3:8). How do we find victory over temptation in Him?

2. Though these men would be specially trained by Christ for apostleship (ch. 10), Christ's call is essentially the same in every age: "Follow me." Discipleship involves submission to Christ's teaching, fellowship with His person, imitation of His ways, and setting aside everything that hinders our allegiance to Him (vv. 18–22). He has a right to each of our lives. He alone deserves to be followed. The life of faith is one of following the Lamb wherever He leads (Rev. 14:4). What does this mean in your life right now?

Chapter 5

1. When Christ spoke the Beatitudes, He was not promoting some kind of perfectionism or offering a higher level of spirituality to those already saved, but giving a concise description of the character of those blessed by God. How would you summarize the kind of person Jesus says is a member of His kingdom? How can these traits help believers recognize the work of the Spirit in their hearts and confirm their assurance of salvation?

2. There are many people who believe that being a Christian frees one from all moral imperatives or obligations to obey God's laws. This is antinomianism. Some people believe Christians should be directed mostly by spiritual experiences and feelings instead of careful attention to the Bible. This is unbiblical mysticism. Yet others build their lives upon the pride and self-righteousness of keeping a list of rules for behavior that were largely invented by man. This is legalism. Jesus rejects all these errors and teaches us that the core of true godliness is a heart set free by the power of His kingdom in order to seek after obedience to God's laws with humility and love. This is the piety promised and practiced in the Old Testament (Pss. 40:8; 119:16), revealed with even more clarity and power by the ultimate Prophet of the church. How can you seek to resist distortions of God's truth even as you pursue true piety?

3. If your heart delights in Christ's teachings even as they humble you over your sins, then it is a sign that you are a Christian. The believer delights in the law of God in the inner man even as he grieves over the rebellion against that law he finds in himself. If this is true of you, what is one way

Christ's words challenge you to grow in repentance? If you find Christ's words offensive, foolish, or legalistic, then what does that reveal about your relationship with Him?

Chapter 6

1. Our private prayers, tithing, and fasting should be marked by a veil of privacy or secrecy. This curtails the sinful ambition to be praised by man. God rewards those who seek Him in faith by the effectual working of the Holy Spirit. Is it a comforting thought to know that what the Christian does for the glory of Christ is not neglected or forgotten? How will this motivate you in your private worship?

2. Note the practical implications of faith in this chapter. Jesus warns His disciples that they should not give in to sinful anxiety (vv. 25–32). He states in verse 30 that having such sinful anxiety is the result of having little faith in God's providential care over life. How can you exercise faith in Christ's promises so that you can overcome fear and worry?

3. Jesus taught His disciples to call God "our Father." Christ's work results in God's adoption of sinners who place their trust in Him, so that they are part of God's family. How could viewing God as your "Father" change the way you view money, possessions, and your needs?

Chapter 7

1. A judgmental spirit, that is, judging people hypocritically without having judged our own hearts, is evidence that we have not come off the throne of our lives. The kingdom of grace is a place where God's Spirit uses the Word to help us see the judgment we are under, to encourage us to seek

mercy by Christ's death, and to show mercy to one another. How are you tempted to judge others? How should you instead judge yourself first?

2. While we are not to judge hypocritically, Jesus taught us to recognize that there are two kinds of people, and only one kind will enjoy eternal life. Christ divided mankind between travelers on the broad and narrow ways, bad trees and good trees, wise and foolish builders. His words press us to not assume all is well. Are you on the narrow way? Are you a good tree by God's grace?

3. Christ did not teach the people the way the Pharisees did—by endless recitation of other men's opinions. Rather, He taught with authority. When we read God's Word, we cannot simply sit back to have our ears tickled. It should expose our sin, show us God in Christ, and drive us outside of ourselves to seek mercy from this King. How have you been convicted to be a "doer" and not a "hearer" only (James 1:21–25)?

Chapter 8

1. Christ is the exalted King who teaches with authority and confirms His message with miracles. However, Christ is also the lowly servant who bears His people's sin as a substitute (v. 17) and has nowhere to lay His head (v. 20). He is glorious as a King yet approachable as a servant. How necessary and suitable a Savior Christ is! How does this encourage you to trust in Him?

2. Christ can drive away diseases, disasters, and demons with a mere word. His presence and power amaze people. His

disciples exclaim, "What manner of man is this, that even the winds and the sea obey him!" (v. 27). The answer is that Christ is God, the glorious Creator. However, recognizing His glory is not the same as trusting in Him. The demons believed and trembled, begging to be sent away. The Gentiles begged Him to go away. Do you know Christ's majesty? How does it affect you: with love and a desire to be with Him, or with a desire to get away?

Chapter 9

Christ has authority on earth to forgive sins (v. 6). People today speak of forgiving themselves, but they fail to see that they are not the Judge. Christ alone possesses the authority to condemn or to forgive. In this chapter we see Him granting forgiveness to weak and worthless sinners like the paralytic and great sinners like Matthew the tax collector. Obviously His forgiveness is not bought with money or earned with good works. Rather it is received by faith, just as healing was received by faith when Jesus worked miracles (vv. 2, 22, 28–29). Remember, Christ did not come to save the righteous, but as a spiritual doctor for sinners. Do you believe that Christ is able to forgive your sins? Do you trust Him to actually forgive you?

Chapter 10

1. Were it not for Christ and the mission He gave to the apostles, we would all be completely in the darkness of paganism. On the apostles the foundation of the church was built (Eph. 2:20). After Christ's ascension, the church was spread abroad by the apostles as an enlargement of God's nation,

Israel, among all peoples. This is what God had promised to Abraham, that in him all the nations would be blessed (Gen. 12:3; see Gal. 3:8). What does this chapter teach us about missions? How are you and your church implementing these principles?

2. In these days when people generally want their lives to run smoothly, let us remember that Christ did not hide from His disciples the reality of the suffering they will experience (vv. 24, 38). So rooted in pride and rebellion is the human race that they killed Jesus Christ who went about healing, preaching, and saving lost sinners. So, too, the Christian message and the Christian life are likely to arouse persecution and suffering today. In what ways will you need to take up the cross if you will follow Jesus? What teachings of Christ in this chapter can give you the courage to follow through?

Chapter 11

1. John, though mighty in the Lord, was weak in himself. Even the best of men are men at best. But Christ is much better than any man. He directed John's fainting heart to Himself. John had to learn that patience works experience, "experience, hope: and hope maketh not ashamed" (Rom. 5:4–5). Do not be surprised when great servants of Christ fall into seasons of weakness. Instead, pray for them and point them to Christ, who is the answer to all our doubts and fears.

2. The gospel brings great accountability to its hearers. Capernaum was privileged above most places in Israel at this time in the sense that Christ spent more time there teaching and performing miracles than anywhere else. Through

Christ's ministry it was as if they were "exalted unto heaven" (v. 23); however, they would be cast down to hell because of their unbelief. We could say that the "hottest" places in hell are reserved for people who have lived the closest to gospel privileges and yet have continued in sin. What implications does this have for those of us in Bible-preaching churches?

3. Many find it difficult to hold together God's sovereignty and man's responsibility. Verses 25–30 show God's glorious sovereignty in salvation and the gentle call of the gospel to all who hear. Rather than arrogantly arguing about sovereignty and responsibility, we need to humble ourselves as spiritual "babes" to believe all that Christ teaches, to see the beauty of God's sovereignty, and to accept our responsibility.

Chapter 12

1. Christ did not declare the Sabbath to be like any other day, but declared Himself to be the Lord of the Sabbath and taught His disciples how to observe it rightly. Legalists ruin the day by their burdensome traditions, but Christ loved the Sabbath and reserved a few of His greatest miracles for the Sabbath day. Christians also should love the Sabbath and keep the Lord's Day. What does Christ's example and teaching show us about how to truly keep the Sabbath?

2. Christ will not break the bruised reed or quench the smoking flax (v. 20). God's true people often go through life bruised and assailed. It may seem like everything and everyone is against them, especially their sins. Christ is a tender Savior. He can nurse and nurture the flame of faith in the heart. His work on the cross ensures a full victory for even

the weakest believer. How can His gentle spirit encourage you in your own struggle against sin?

3. Christ pointed to His true family: "For whosoever shall do the will of my Father which is in heaven, the same is my brother, and sister, and mother" (v. 50). This was a holy rebuke to His brothers, who were later converted. It is not fleshly connections that ultimately matter. However, let those who obey Christ's Word take comfort that He embraces them as the family of God. Why is this a great comfort to believers?

Chapter 13

1. Christ searches our hearts, and His parables call us to search ourselves. Which soil are you? In reality, all the negative influences of Satan, sin, and the world remain in the hearts of believers. But God's grace prevails and they bear a harvest of good works. We must not rest in hearing and reading the Word. Others have enjoyed the same privilege and yet in the end proved to be fruitless. Nor may we rest in it having some influence upon us. Many fish caught in the net were later thrown away. The only sure sign that God's Word has saved a sinner is a changed life. It changes the inner life, for the converted count Christ as their greatest joy and treasure. It changes the outer life, for the converted bear fruit. How has the gospel changed you? How is it changing you now?

2. The kingdom of heaven may appear as insignificant as a tiny seed or a little piece of leaven, but at the completion of this age it will tower over all other kingdoms. Nothing else will matter compared to the great question of whether one goes to the fires of hell, where the wicked weep and gnash their teeth, or to the glories of heaven, where the righteous

shine like the sun. How should this truth change the way we think about ourselves, other people, and our lives?

Chapter 14

1. John the Baptist died because of faithfulness to his Lord. He would not hide the truth, and he didn't cease to warn transgressors. His death was not a tragedy. He was immediately translated from the dungeon of Herod to the throne room of God, to the festival of the spirits of righteous men made perfect in the presence of their Lord. How can his example help you to not fear to suffer or die for the Lord?

2. Jesus is Lord and God. Though a prophet like Moses, who saw the Lord divide the sea and provide manna to Israel, Jesus is far greater than Moses, for Christ walked upon the sea and enabled Peter to do the same. Therefore, it is right that we worship Him in our prayers and praises. Do you delight to worship Christ with holy fear? If so, then remember that your greatest act of worship is to trust Him. What can we learn from Peter about honoring Christ by faith?

Chapter 15

1. The heart of sin is the sin of the heart. The scribes and the Pharisees focused on external sins, especially the rituals they dictated, but the Lord Jesus said that all the moral evils of mankind proceed out of the heart (v. 19). When God works in our hearts, He gives us the ability to see how deeply rooted sin is and how corrupt and deceitful our hearts are. Our salvation cannot simply be dressing up or cleaning up the outside of our lives. Christ must heal our blindness. We

need the new birth. God must plant new life within us. How does this humble you? How does it glorify the Savior?

2. Christ's dealings with the woman of Canaan appear harsh. However, His silence and apparent objections provoked her faith to shine brightly against the backdrop of this glorious Son of David. William Cowper said it well: "Behind a frowning providence / He hides a smiling face." Let us imitate the persistence and humility of the Canaanite woman's faith. When the Lord is not answering your prayers, acknowledge your unworthiness but cling to Christ all the more.

Chapter 16

1. Christ had to unseat the false religion of the Pharisees in the hearts of His disciples (v. 12). Like leaven, false teaching can easily enter and influence all our lives. The church and its ministers must contend for the faith that was once for all delivered to the saints and expose false teachers (Jude 3–4). Why is this an important part of our faithfulness to God?

2. The great question of all time is, "But whom say ye that I am?" (v. 15). The world has its opinion of Christ. Religion has its opinion. And our lives issue a constant verdict of who Christ is. Perhaps your actions say that Christ is a person you run to in need, but for the rest He has to fit in with your program and life. Perhaps you have an orthodox opinion about Christ but you do not listen to His demands. What does your life declare about who Jesus is?

3. Though Peter confessed Jesus as Christ, the Son of the living God, he still foolishly and vainly attempted to thwart Christ's sacrificial suffering and death. The gospel of the

cross is foolish and offensive to men. The call of discipleship is a call to die. Do you understand your need for Christ to die an accursed death in your place? Are you taking up your own cross and following Him?

Chapter 17

1. Christ's divine glory and majesty shine wonderfully through His humanity, confirming the focus of many Old Testament promises. Yet He came to earth veiled, with His glory largely hidden. Christ's transfiguration took place between announcements of His suffering and death (vv. 22–23; 16:21). If we seek glory with God apart from the humiliation and death of Christ, then we still imagine ourselves to be saved by man's works, wisdom, and glory. Christ did not take the crown apart from the cross, and neither can we. We must listen to Christ's words about the cross and follow in His crucified footsteps. How does this help you understand what it means for a Christian to pursue glory?

2. When Christ descended from the mountain of glory, He entered, as it were, the workshop of the Devil. This demon had stymied all the efforts of the child's father and Christ's disciples, but it was no match for the power of Christ (vv. 14–21). Christians need not fear the Devil, so long as they cling to Christ by faith, for greater is He that is in us than he that is in the world. How can this comfort us?

Chapter 18

1. Conversion is absolutely necessary if we are to be saved. This applies to us, our children, our parents, our friends and neighbors, those who have grown up in the church,

and those who have not. Christ described conversion here in terms of turning around and childlike humility (vv. 3–4). Every true disciple of Christ has a root of repentance and humility planted in his heart by grace. But as believers we must continually work to put our pride to death. How are you working at this in your own life?

2. Much of our humility comes from realizing that the guilt of our sins is like a debt of billions of dollars that we owe to God's justice (v. 24). A true sense of our sin shows us both that we deserve horrible punishment from God and, unlike the servant in the parable, that we cannot possibly save ourselves from it no matter how long and hard we work. This puts us in the position of a beggar before God (5:3), whose only hope is free and lavish grace. How bad do you really believe your sins against God are? How much do you value the grace of Christ?

3. The practical effects of true Christian humility is hatred of sin (vv. 7–9), love for other Christians (v. 5) that especially shows itself in seeking to make peace with those who wrong us (v. 15), working to preserve the purity of the body of Christ (vv. 16–20), and forgiving others for their sins against us (vv. 21–35). How is the Holy Spirit convicting you regarding these heart issues?

Chapter 19

1. Marriage is not a contract that we may define as we please, but a sovereign act of the Creator, defined by His will. Despite attempts to make it normal to have sexual relations outside of marriage, engage in homosexuality, and divorce at will, God's standards for marriage remain unchanged. If we

desire His blessing, we must repent of our failures and live in the joy of sexual faithfulness. How can you honor this sacred relationship, whether you are single or married?

2. Children have an important place in the church of God. God's promises belong to Abraham's seed, that is, to the children of believing parents (Acts 2:39). This does not remove their need to be born again. Jesus' words to His disciples—"Suffer little children, and forbid them not" (Matt. 19:14)—encourage believers to bring children to the Lord through prayer and teaching and to watch that we do not hinder their coming to Christ. How can you bring children to Jesus?

3. The rich young man's response to Christ reveals a deadly spiritual illness that infects many people. Though they may have respect for Jesus and a desire for eternal life, they see mankind as essentially good, themselves as obedient to God's laws, and Christ as a mere teacher to show them what to do to gain heaven for themselves. They operate as if still under the covenant of works in Paradise before Adam's fall (Gen. 2). However, the last Adam is able to expose our sin with His Word and Spirit. If the rich man took Christ's words to heart and returned to Him, how might he approach Christ differently? What might he say?

Chapter 20

1. Christ announces the basic kingdom pattern as one of servanthood. Christ is the great Servant, who gives His life as a ransom (v. 28). His disciples must also pursue greatness by humbling themselves to serve others. We must renounce our tendency to envy others and criticize God's ways, and

instead receive whatever He gives us with gratitude. Are you able to have joy and contentment in serving God however and wherever God determines to use you?

2. Christ asked the same question of the mother of James and John, and the blind men: what do you want? (vv. 21, 32). Their answers are a study in contrasts, for one sought personal glory out of pride and ambition, and the others sought mercy and sight. Ironically, it was the disciples who were blind to what really mattered. What do you seek from God in your prayers? What does that reveal about your soul?

Chapter 21

1. Christ came riding into Jerusalem as a glorious yet meek and lowly King, as prophesied by Zechariah. Sinners need such a Savior! Just as He came to Jerusalem, so He comes in the preaching of the gospel. Do we come to hear the Word, praying, "Hosanna," that is, "Lord, please save us"?

2. The fig tree with beautiful leaves but no fruit represents hypocritical religion among any professing people of God. The hypocrite loves to make himself or herself look nice to the outside world. However, when God comes to pluck the fruits of true repentance, there are none. For all the hypocrite's fine words to the Lord, he remains disobedient. Far better to confess our sinfulness to the Lord with honesty, and then repent and turn to obedience with sincerity. What can we learn from the publicans and harlots, of whom Christ said, they "go into the kingdom of God" before many other religious people (v. 31)?

Chapter 22

1. God's call to the marriage supper of His Son is remarkably open and indiscriminate. However, all who inherit salvation have come through the narrow gate, namely, through Jesus (John 14:6). Those who do not come by way of repentance and faith in Jesus Christ are not found dressed in His righteousness alone. At the last, they will be cast out as those who would not submit to the righteousness of God. How do you know if you are clothed with a wedding garment?

2. Many people use religion as a cloak to keep away from Christ. They love arguments. They love to identify with this party or that sect. In the end their basic attitude is "tempting" Christ (v. 35). It is one thing to know Scripture or even debate aspects of Scripture. It is another thing to listen to Scripture and submit to the Son (Ps. 2:12). How can you tell which you are doing?

Chapter 23

The source of the Pharisees' problem rested in their pride (vv. 6–7). Pride blinds us to our sin. Pride leads us to justify ourselves before God (Luke 16:15). We think of ourselves more highly than we ought to (Rom. 12:3). Meanwhile, we bind ourselves and those around us to traditions, ceremonies, and rules that have not been expressly laid down in the Scriptures. The law, however, can only arouse sin in us and render us condemned before the tribunal of God. The gospel is the only remedy. Our unrighteousness is not as much of an obstacle to our salvation as our self-righteousness. How can we avoid the pit of being like the Pharisees?

Chapter 24

1. As much as we admire beautiful buildings, even the best architecture will fall under God's judgment if it houses rebellion and unbelief toward Christ. Our only safety is in following Christ to the end. Christ did not promise it would be easy. He warned that believers would see many tribulations, including wars, national disasters, and persecutions. He said that they must stand against false teachers and false Christs. However, He promised that He will return and gather His elect safely to Himself. How can we find the strength to persevere with Christ by leaning on the hope of His second coming?

2. Just as surely as the Roman army destroyed Jerusalem in AD 70, so the Son of Man will return with His angels to judge the world. This will be a day of sudden destruction for the wicked, but a day of gracious reward for the faithful servants of the Lord. We cannot know when it will happen, but we must be prepared. All of us have been made stewards of something, certainly our souls, and most of us much more. Are you faithful to the Lord? Are you prepared for Christ's coming?

Chapter 25

1. There is no middle category between foolish and wise, sheep and goats. We are one or the other. The parables of this chapter give us three tests of whether we are truly the Lord's people. First, are you prepared by God's Spirit to endure for a long wait before Christ returns? Second, are you actively serving Him now by taking the personal and material resources He has given you and employing them

in your vocation for His glory? Third, are you responding with compassionate action to the needs of other Christians around you as members of one family in Christ? These are tests Christ will use on the judgment day, and we should judge ourselves by them now.

2. Christians need not fear the return of Christ, for the Son of God will come as the merciful older brother of God's children. Indeed, if we view Christ as a hard master who treats people unfairly, we must question whether we have faith in Him at all. However, true believers may sometimes view the judgment day with fear too. How can these parables give them comfort and hope?

Chapter 26

1. Christ deserves our all. Particularly, His willingness to die for sinners ought to elicit all our affection, adoration, and devotion, as it did in Mary. She was not only dedicated to an idea or a cause, but to the Person who loved her and died for her. Do you love Jesus Christ? How has His sacrificial love for His church moved you to pour out your life for Him?

2. Though Christ may have appeared like a helpless victim being abused by religious and civil leaders, His institution of the Lord's Supper shows that His suffering and death was not an accident or some tragedy. His death was appointed in order to accomplish redemption from sin and the full penalty it demanded. How does Christ's knowledge of what was to come and His submission to His Father's will increase your own love for Him?

Chapter 27

1. Note Judas's false repentance. It was not what Paul would later call a godly sorrow, but the sorrow of the world that brings death (2 Cor. 7:10–11). Remorse over what we have done may simply be the acting of our natural conscience. True repentance involves dying to sin and rising to newness of life by God's grace at work in us. How have you experienced godly sorrow that leads to true repentance?

2. Christ's suffering at the hands of men was terrible. Being forsaken by His Father, however, was the worst part of Christ's sufferings. He bore the iniquity of His people and He did so as a public person, as the representative and head of all His people. He was made a curse that the blessing might flow to all who believe, both Jews and Gentiles (Gal. 3:10–14). How do Christ's sufferings in this chapter reveal what our sins deserve? How do they show the love of God?

3. Scripture had prophesied many aspects of Christ's sufferings. His death was an amazing confirmation of the faithfulness of God to His promises (Rom. 15:8). Nature itself testified to the great significance of this event. Yet most people present at the time were blind to anything other than a man suffering on a cross. Has the Spirit opened your eyes to see what you deserve as you look at Christ's suffering and death? Have you seen by faith that the veil has been rent (v. 51) between God and sinners, so that sinners now have access to God through Christ's blood?

Chapter 28

1. Christ is alive. The veracity of the resurrection is well established by eyewitness accounts in the Word of God. It is not

a fairy tale or myth, but a fact of history. Yet Christ is more than a fact—He is a living person who meets us by His Word and Spirit. He deserves our worship, not just the bowing of our bodies but the trust of our hearts and obedience of our lives. How do you relate to Jesus Christ on a personal level? How does His infinite authority (v. 18) appear in your life?

2. Christ has all authority in heaven and on earth. Neither demons nor any earthly power can stop the expansion of His kingdom. He claims people from every nation for His disciples, having bought them with His blood. He has commissioned His church to make disciples of all nations, beginning with the apostles and continuing today. His great means are the law, the gospel, and the ordinances of worship commanded in His Word. His promise is His abiding presence with His church by His Spirit. How should these truths press upon the conscience of the church its duty to reach the world with the truth of Christ? How can these truths encourage the church to do its mission with hope, confidence, and perseverance? What do these truths teach us about the methods that the church should use to faithfully fulfill its mission?

Mark

Chapter 1

1. God is faithful to His Word. Even though the prophets had lived and died hundreds of years earlier, God's Word is living and powerful and will accomplish His pleasure. The promised messenger (John) came in due time, as did the Lord Jesus Himself. The gospel is a declaration that God is faithful to His Word and that all His promises are fulfilled in Jesus Christ. God's faithfulness calls us to be faithful to the Word as well, even when its fulfillment seems distant or even impossible. How can God's faithfulness in Christ strengthen us to be faithful?

2. As soon as Christ received the Spirit's anointing and the Father's commendation, He was propelled into conflict with Satan, though not by power but by temptation. Unlike Adam, Jesus remained faithful and conquered the Devil by perfect obedience (Heb. 4:15). It is not a coincidence that shortly afterward the demons were cringing before Jesus. He can save us from Satan's power because He has overcome the Devil's temptations (2:18).

3. When Christ calls men into the ministry of the Word today, He still says to them, "Come ye after me, and I will make you to become fishers of men" (v. 17). No one makes himself a true minister of the Word, but when Christ calls, He equips. The duty of the called is to follow Jesus in obedience and imitation and to never forget that the goal of

fishermen is to catch fish. What implications does this have for pastoral ministry?

Chapter 2

1. Christ is the Lord of all, God in the flesh. He is the sovereign Judge who sees the faith and unbelief in the hearts of men and grants His forgiveness to the sinner who believes (vv. 5–11). He is the spiritual husband of Israel, whose presence is the joy of His people and whose absence is their greatest sorrow (vv. 19–21). He is the Lawgiver and Lord of the Sabbath, whose ordinances are authoritative and sufficient, neither to be added to nor neglected. How should the descriptions of Christ in this chapter move His people to greater love and submission to Him?

2. This glorious Lord took a despised sinner and tax collector into the band of His disciples. Christ loves sinners, and so He gladly ate with them, not to justify their sins but to call them to repentance and eternal life. Therefore His gospel is utterly incompatible with the legalism of self-righteous men. Why is His grace so offensive to our pride? How should we live so as to show His grace to sinners around us?

Chapter 3

1. All who will live godly lives will suffer tribulation (2 Tim. 3:12). This was true for Christ and is also true for Christians. The world is not simply watching us but seeking to win us over, to destroy our faith and obedience to the Word (Mark 4:17). To them we seem insane. Indeed, the greatest persecution may come from the most religious people, for their religion of pride and hypocrisy comes into direct

conflict with Christ's ways of love and obedience. However, in Christ God gives believers a new spiritual family, united by their obedience to God's Word. How can members of the church strengthen and encourage one another to stay faithful in persecution?

2. Apart from Christ we are enslaved to sin and Satan. We cannot stand against this strong man in our own strength. We need One stronger than the strong man. Christ's coming into the world, His obedient life, and His substitutionary death deliver captive sinners. What are signs that a person is a slave of Satan? What are signs that Jesus has set someone free?

Chapter 4

1. Though the four soils represent different kinds of hearers, they also teach us about spiritual influences that resist the Word in everyone who hears it preached: Satan, sin in the heart, and the world. According to Christ's explanation of the parable (vv. 14–20), how does each influence work against a fruitful response to God's Word? How can we seek to overcome these evil influences by God's grace so that we benefit from the preaching of the Scriptures?

2. The two parables involving sowers have much to say to preachers of the Word (vv. 14–20, 26–29). What lessons for ministers do you gather from them? How ought these lessons humble them? How should they encourage them?

3. We do not read that the disciples consulted with Christ before the ship was in danger of sinking. Yet when they finally cried to Him they seemed to accuse the Lord of a lack of care. Can you see yourself in this picture? How have

you responded to similar trials? How should we respond, in light of the fact that Jesus is the Lord who rules all things with His mere word?

Chapter 5

1. The Lord Jesus has the power to save from the most hopeless of situations. Whether He finds us dominated by Satan's forces in a way that no one can control, suffering from a problem no man can heal, or facing the finality of death itself, Christ is able to help us. In this age He saves sinners from the guilt and penalty of sin and from the domination of sin and Satan. In the age to come He will deliver His people from death, illness, and all misery. However, salvation is neither automatic nor universal but received by faith, as the bleeding woman shows us.

2. People respond in very different ways when they encounter Jesus Christ. Some, like the Gadarenes, desire only that He leave them alone, for He disturbs and terrifies them. Others, like the mourners at the dead girl's home, mock Him because His Word makes no sense to their unbelieving minds. Still others, however, like the man rescued from the legion of demons, desire to be near to Him because He alone has the power to save them, and they are eager to tell others of His saving work in their lives. How have you encountered Jesus in His Word? How have you responded?

Chapter 6

1. The death of John was lamentable, though for John it marked his entrance into glory. What was infinitely more lamentable was Herod's continued life in worldly splendor, with a

guilty conscience and an unrepentant heart. Who would you rather be like, the dead John or the living Herod? Why?

2. The disciples did not have what it took to feed thousands of people, yet Christ asked them to give food to the crowd (v. 37). Christ often asks us to do things that are impossible from our perspective so that we may learn His all-sufficiency through difficulty, faith, and prayer.

3. Though they followed Christ, the disciples' hearts were still so hardened (v. 52). How do you manifest hardheartedness against the Lord despite all that God has given you in the Word and through His providence? What should you do about this?

Chapter 7

1. Scripture alone is the divine rule of faith, worship, and obedience. Many people and churches follow a religion whose teachings and worship are based more upon human ideas than on the Word of God. They rarely ask, "What does God say in the Bible about this? Is this the faith and obedience that He commanded?" However, the Holy Scriptures reveal that God strongly objects to bringing Him worship that He has not required, for this does not honor His holiness (Lev. 10:1–3). Generally speaking, such man-made religion focuses upon outward acts such as following a ritual or saying a prayer, while neglecting godliness in the heart. As a result God's Word is neglected and many sins defile people from within. How can a person test his church or personal faith through application of Christ's standard of Scripture alone?

2. Christ's dealing with the Syro-Phoenician woman seems harsh; however, this was His way of maturing her faith. The Lord's ways with us may seem harsh too, but when we are tempted to take offense we should ask ourselves, "Am I willing to humble myself completely before the Lord? Do I believe so strongly in my need of Christ that I will keep clinging to Him even when His ways are hard? Will I submit to whatever He gives me on His terms, not my own?"

Chapter 8

1. Christ healed the blind man in two stages to show that when God converts sinners they do not see all there is to see about their own sinfulness or the glory of Christ. Sadly, even the truly saved still retain blindness and hardness in their souls, even leading us to fight against God's ways at times, especially the way of the cross that strips us of our pride and self-righteousness. Believers should pray regularly for God to give them more illumination and should learn to fight against their tendency to quarrel with God's Word.

2. The great determinative question we all must answer, and do answer by our life and actions, is, "Whom do you say that Jesus is?" It is not enough to be able to recite the views of others. You must come to an inner conviction of His identity. He is the Christ, God's anointed Prophet to replace our ignorance with the knowledge of God, Priest to take away our guilt for breaking God's law and give us a status of righteousness before Him, and King to conquer our sins and rescue us from all that would harm us. Whom do you say Jesus is? Do you trust in Him alone? Do you confess Him before men?

Chapter 9

1. There is every reason to listen to God's Son. He has now even more glory than on the Mount of Transfiguration, for now in heaven He is crowned with glory and splendor. God still says of Him, "Hear him" (v. 7). He is God's appointed Prophet over the church, the Teacher who speaks through all faithful teachers of the Word. How should it change our attitude toward preaching and teaching to know that if the preacher or teacher faithfully explains and applies the Bible, the Lord Jesus Christ is personally speaking to us?

2. Faith and unbelief wrestle for dominance in the regenerate heart (v. 24). It can seem sometimes as though unbelief will grab faith by the throat and try to strangle it. Faith, however, cries to Christ for help, which Christ is sure to give. How does the father's prayer, "Lord, I believe; help thou mine unbelief," encourage us to pray?

3. Having seen the glory of Christ, it is hard to believe the disciples would argue about who of them was the greatest (v. 34). Yet how prone we are as sinful human beings to boast and brag—even about spiritual experiences. We need to learn again and again the lesson of verses 35–36.

Chapter 10

1. Marriage is an institution of God, defined by Him at creation, formed by Him in the bond between each husband and wife, and jealously watched over by Him. For this reason marriage is to be held in high honor and neither dismissed nor distorted. How is marriage under attack in your nation? How do Christ's teachings (vv. 2–12) enable Christians to defend marriage biblically?

2. The human heart is by nature deceitful and self-righteous, minimizing the severity of our sins even as we outwardly may seem very religious (vv. 17–27). Our pride flatters us that we have kept God's commandments and can do what God requires to enter His kingdom. This horrible arrogance especially feeds upon riches and prosperity, falsely assuring us that God has blessed us because we are good. Christ shows us how to confront our pride: through the searching application of God's laws to the heart, by the gospel call to follow Christ, and by the declaration of human inability and divine sovereignty in salvation. People may find these truths offensive and leave grieved, but they are the method of the loving Savior (v. 21) to win people to true discipleship.

3. Christ asked the same question of James and John as of blind Bartimaeus: "What do you want Me to do for you?" (cf. vv. 36, 51). Their answers were markedly different. The apostles sought personal honor and glory among men, while the beggar sought mercy and healing. If Christ were to ask you this question, what would you say you most desire from Him? What would your answer show about your heart?

Chapter 11

1. Hypocritical religion pretends to be what it is not, but Christ will uncover it. Like a tree with many leaves yet no fruit, the religious hypocrite displays to the world many impressive activities of devotion and self-denial, but under the leaves of external religion the Lord sees that there are no fruits of Christian love for God and man, joy in the Lord, or peace by Christ's blood. The Lord Jesus is patient, but the time will come when He will judge us all. If our godliness

is only a form without His underlying power, He will curse us with a supernatural word of judgment that will wither us from the roots. Search yourself by this word. Is your godliness a matter of mere leaves? What spiritual fruits is Christ producing in you?

2. Prayer is an instrument of immense power, for it invokes the almighty arm of God. We should take up prayer with boldness, believing it to be the weapon by which God casts down every mountain raised up against the true worship of Himself. We should pray with faith in God's goodness and generosity toward His children, and we should pray together with other believers in a spirit of love, forgiveness, and unity. How would you describe your prayer life now? How does this chapter stir you to desire a deeper prayer life?

Chapter 12

1. The parable of the wicked husbandmen appears to end in tragedy with the death of the son. It is indeed a horrible sin that the nation did not honor God's Son, and we all by nature reject Christ. However, God had planned Christ's rejection as the pathway to His exaltation. Only by being killed on the cross and buried could Christ become the cornerstone of a new temple of God, a living building composed of people who rest the full weight of their souls on Christ alone to save them from sin. Christ is the King seated at God's right hand, reigning in absolute power and glory as the Son of David and the Son of God. His death has turned to triumph, and the same Holy Spirit who moved the prophets to write of Christ now moves sinners to submit to His reign. The great fruit of His reign in the heart is love—love for God above all

and for our neighbors as ourselves that animates obedience to all God's commandments. How does this chapter show you the beauty and glory of King Jesus?

2. The foolish attempts of proud men to trap Jesus in His words only caused His divine wisdom to shine brighter. Jesus is the great Teacher, God-in-the-flesh come to reveal Himself. Sadly, the Pharisees, Herodians, and Sadducees did not benefit from His teaching because they rejected His authority. They did not come asking questions in a sincere desire to know the truth but with wicked motives. Even the scribe who was "not far from the kingdom" in his understanding of the Bible had not yet entered the kingdom by faith in Christ. The fundamental obstacle to all these men was their pride and love of human honor (vv. 38–40). Far different from them was the poor widow, who humbly gave her two mites to the Lord. Do you come to the preaching of God's Word to submit to the Lord Jesus, learn from Him, and humbly serve Him with all you are? Or do you come to argue and exalt yourself as though you were Lord?

Chapter 13

1. Just as the Lord Jesus warned, the holy city of Jerusalem fell to the Roman legions in AD 70, experiencing a horrifying massacre in fulfillment of Christ's own words. God's judgment came and destroyed His own temple. However, God's plan had not failed. Jesus speaks in this same prophecy of the salvation of God's elect through all these tribulations. Even now God is gathering His chosen ones from among the Jews and Gentiles by bringing them to faith in Christ through the preaching of the gospel. Though the destruction

of Jerusalem must have shaken first-century Jewish believers, they could rejoice that the kingdom of Christ can never be shaken. How can this comfort us if we see the church under persecution and great Christian institutions falling under God's judgment because of gross infidelity?

2. Jesus said that His disciples must pass through much tribulation and endure vicious persecution, even from religious leaders professing to serve God. The Christian life is one of perseverance under pressure. However, Jesus also said that believers wait for something well worth all our sorrows. Christ will come with visible power and glory to establish His kingdom. What a day of joy and vindication that will be! How can we make use of this hope to strengthen ourselves to endure to the end?

3. At the conclusion of His teaching Christ repeatedly called His disciples to watch, watch, watch. The biblical doctrine of Christ's second coming is not something to stimulate curiosity and speculation about a timetable of events. It is a summons to spiritual alertness and constant prayer, since we do not know when the Lord will appear. What does it mean to be spiritually sleeping? How can a Christian develop a daily discipline of watchfulness?

Chapter 14

1. Christ appears in this chapter as the sovereign Lord, walking purposefully to His death exactly as God had planned and revealed in the Bible. He knew that He would rise to rule over all the world as the promised King of kings. Yet He also appears as the submissive Servant, staggering under the weight of His burden but praying "not what I will, but what

thou wilt" to His Father (v. 36). His obedience is everything to believers, because He went to the cross as their perfect Surety, paying their debts and drinking the awful cup of God's wrath against their sins. Thus in the Lord's Supper He presents Himself as the loving Savior who gave His body as a sacrifice and brings sinners into a gracious covenant with their God. How does this chapter show us that Jesus is infinitely worthy of our trust and love?

2. The chief priests and Judas prepared to kill Jesus. The disciples failed to prepare at all. However, Mary understood something of the beauty and preciousness of the suffering Savior and prepared by pouring out her earthly treasure in love for Him (v. 9). Christ commends her good work to us so that we can learn from her example. How has Christ's sacrificial love moved you to love Him in return? How can you show that love in acts of costly devotion?

Chapter 15

1. The cross reveals man's hatred of God. Our hostility against God is universal. Christ was rejected and reviled by religious and political leaders, Jews and Gentiles, high officials and crowds, soldiers and civilians. Our hostility against God, too, is violent and murderous. When God came to mankind in human flesh to love sinners like us, we tortured and killed Him. What reasons does this chapter give us to grieve over sin, humble ourselves, and repent?

2. The cross reveals God's sovereignty over man. Even as sinners committed the most horrible atrocities against the Son of God, they fulfilled the decree of God that He had announced centuries earlier by His prophets. Even as they

callously gambled for His clothing, they willingly did what God had predestined them to do (cf. Acts 4:27–28). It was no accident that the cross itself proclaimed that Jesus is the King (Mark 15:26). How does this chapter teach us to bow before God's throne and worship Christ as the King who rules over all things?

3. The cross reveals God's righteousness and love for sinners. Rather than damning all sinners to hell forever for their sins, God sent His Son to die. We deserve to be cast into the outer darkness, but the darkness of divine wrath came upon Him. We should be rejected forever for our rejection of God, but instead God caused Christ to become God-forsaken. God's justice for His people was satisfied in Christ, and because Christ was crucified believers are released from condemnation and punishment, as was Barabbas. What does this show us about the love of God? Why should it move us to trust in Christ without reservation?

Chapter 16

1. Jesus Christ died for sinners, but today He is alive. The full payment for sin has been made, and now Christ is applying the results of His redemption to the salvation of lost sinners. The living Lord reigns as King of the angels, sitting at God's right hand. His kingdom has come in heavenly glory and operates through the power of the gospel. Though we still wait for His kingdom to come in visible glory on earth, believers can rejoice. Jesus is alive! Jesus reigns! How can this give Christians hope no matter what evil they face?

2. Christ's final commission to the apostles has a wide scope: "to every creature" (v. 15). The apostles labored to spread the

gospel to many nations, and Christianity spread in a remarkable way in its early years. However, the apostolic mandate still rests upon the church. Small and great, educated and uneducated, rich and poor, young and old, all need to hear the gospel. How is your church engaged in reaching the world with the good news?

Luke

Chapter 1

1. Luke wrote this gospel so that each individual might know the certainty of the things he has been taught. Read it as the truth of God, for it is inspired by God. Read this gospel personally, as addressed to you. It is not a myth, nor is it merely interesting history. It is a true account of Jesus Christ and a message calling you to faith and repentance. How should that affect the way you read it?

2. Here is the announcement of the coming of a great person, so great that a mighty prophet had to go ahead of Him in the power of the Holy Spirit. This person is the Son of God, coming to rule His kingdom forever. He is also the Son of David, fulfilling all the ancient promises of God's covenants. He is holy, sinless, and devoted to God from conception. He is a shining light of truth. Yet He is full of tenderness, mercy, and forgiveness to sinners. How do the descriptions of Jesus in this chapter move you to trust Him?

3. This chapter contains songs and praises from Mary, Zacharias, and Elisabeth. Even John leaps in his mother's womb. Why does the coming of Jesus Christ move people to rejoice and praise God? Has the Holy Spirit produced joy in your heart because of Jesus? Why or why not?

Chapter 2

1. As we read about the birth of Christ, many focus on the shepherds and angels. Certainly there are many lessons in

what we are told about them and in what they did. Most important, however, is what Christ Himself did in His birth: He came to this lost world to be a Savior. Equally important is what God the Father did in the birth of His Son. He sent His Son in order to glorify Himself in the salvation of lost and miserable sinners like these shepherds. Reflect upon how low God stooped by sending His Son in the likeness of sinful flesh and for sin (Rom. 8:3). Why was it necessary for the Lord to come in such humiliation as to lie in a manger rather than in a king's crib? What does this foreshadow about the manner in which Christ would save sinners?

2. When Jesus was born the angels of God sang "Glory to God in the highest," and the shepherds were glorifying and praising God for all they had heard and seen. Godly Simeon was moved by the Holy Spirit to give public praise to God, and faithful Anna thanked the Lord and told many of the birth of the Redeemer. Why should Christ's coming move Christians to sing and praise God? If our hearts are cold and sluggish to worship, what might this reveal about us?

Chapter 3

1. John prepared the way for Jesus by preaching repentance of sin. This is God's order of working with fallen man. Unless we recognize and acknowledge our sins, the forgiveness of sins will mean nothing to us. Repentance means that we grieve from our hearts that we have assaulted God's honor, confess our sins truly and uprightly before God, and forsake these sins, all by grace. As John pointed out to the people who came to him, repentance needs to be specific. Why is

it impossible to trust in Jesus and be saved by Him without repenting of our sins?

2. The genealogy of Christ goes back all the way to Adam, the "son of God" (v. 38). Before we hear of this son, who fell into sin and misery, carrying the entire race with Him, we have already heard heaven's words concerning Christ: "Thou art my beloved Son; in thee I am well pleased" (v. 22). Having spent so long a time "in" the first Adam, lost and guilty, we must place our hope in the last Adam, righteous and beloved. Trust Jesus as the great Son of David, the King who can rule you in righteousness. Trust Jesus as the promised Son of Abraham, the Mediator of God's blessing to those under God's curse for their sins. Trust Jesus as the last Adam, who obeyed God and won everlasting life when we have all earned eternal damnation.

Chapter 4

1. Though Christ was the Word of God incarnate, He chose to use the Word of God in Scripture to ward off the assaults of Satan. If He used the Word of God as a sword, should we presume to wage warfare without it? We need to be intimately acquainted with the Word. There is no spiritual weapon like it, and without it we are rightfully vulnerable. What are some ways in which you can use the Bible when you face temptations of sin or unbelief?

2. Christ's ministry on earth would be one of grace. The Spirit anointed Him to preach liberty to spiritual captives and to open the eyes of the blind. What do poor sinners need? How does Jesus provide them with all these things? Why is it important to recognize our need?

3. The miracles Christ performed were signs that showed His majesty, grace, and power. He did not come just to heal a few people so that they could be more comfortable on earth. Instead, His miracles depicted what His grace does still today: it drives back sin and Satan and restores peace and fellowship to miserable and undeserving sinners.

Chapter 5

1. This miracle of the great catch of fish so overwhelmed Peter that he felt as though he and Christ could never fit together. The truth of the gospel, however, is exactly the opposite. Though by nature there is no greater contrast than that between a holy God and an unholy sinner, for Christ's sake the holy God and the unholy sinner can indeed be reconciled, with God's glory magnified in the process. Jesus has the right to forgive sins. Have you been brought low before Jesus Christ by a sense of His holiness? Has His message of grace brought peace to your soul?

2. The cleansing of the leper and the healing of the paralytic reflect two important parts of the gospel purpose of Christ's coming. His grace cleanses from the pollution of sin as well as frees from the power of sin. Christ makes sinners clean and able to serve Him. He is mighty to work a full work, filling our every need by His grace and gospel.

Chapter 6

1. Christ showed the true intention of the fourth commandment. While God forbids work on the Lord's Day, the law commands that people show mercy and do works of necessity. We need to guard against the universal human tendency

to observe the letter of God's law while omitting the spirit or heart of the law (Isa. 58:13–14). How can human traditions about the Sabbath make the word of God void? Why is keeping the Sabbath under the Lordship of Christ a blessing?

2. Christ's teaching shows the inward and genuine nature of true religion. The great enemy of true religion is not just our natural unbelief but also our conceited pride, which makes us deceive ourselves. Has God's Spirit made you spiritually poor and hungry? Has He made you a mourner over sin and its guilt and offense against God? This is not just a one-time experience. If God has worked this in you, He keeps you near and needy at His feet in order that in Christ He might be your all and in all (Col. 3:11).

3. Note the commendation Jesus gives to the man who builds his house upon the rock: his house will stand in the day of trouble and distress. Though both men hear the Word of God, the wise man alone has received the grace whereby he does the Word of God. Is your life built on the bedrock of Christ—His Word, work, and worth?

Chapter 7

1. Christ's power is so great that He could heal a young man near death from a distance, as well as raise another young man who was already dead. He heals the lame and gives sight to the blind. Jesus is the Lord God and the all-sufficient Savior, come to rescue sinners from their sin and misery. None need despair; all should seek grace from Christ for the healing of their souls in this age and the healing of all they are in the age to come.

2. The woman loved Christ a great deal, as she had been forgiven much. If you do not love Christ at all you can be sure you have not tasted of His forgiveness. What a depth of sin there is in our hearts! However, the love of God is infinitely deeper. When you experience His love it becomes a fountain of love in your heart flowing to Christ and to the Father. Do you have the kind of faith in Christ that results in love for Him?

Chapter 8

1. The parable of the sower paints a picture of four representative human hearts. Take a look at your own heart in its light. Do you find thorns, packed soil, withered plants, or fruit? However things stand, take the exhortation of verse 18 to heart: "Take heed therefore how ye hear." We must not come to the preaching of the Word expecting the preacher to do all the work. What responsibility do we have as hearers of the Word?

2. When Christ calmed the storm at sea He showed His great power and majesty. He did no less when He cast out the legion of demons from the Gadarene man. He healed the woman of an incurable disease and raised a girl from the dead. However, while this girl experienced resurrection she would again experience physical death. These miracles do more than show us that Jesus can heal all our physical problems (as He will when He returns in glory). The way Luke linked the healed woman and the forgiven woman (v. 48; 7:50) reminds us that our most pressing need is for spiritual salvation. We need Christ to heal our souls, so that like the Gadarene man we may sit at His feet, clothed and in

our right minds, desiring to live in His presence and willing to declare His glory to others. Why is that the greatest healing?

Chapter 9

1. Christ went to the cross to suffer and die to pay the price for sin. His disciples must also prepare to live a life of suffering and self-denial, not in order to atone for sin but to conform themselves to their Head and Master. In the meantime the glorious radiance of Christ, as He showed it on the Mount of Transfiguration, ought to sustain and strengthen them to meet with suffering and death. In fact, it should keep them from desiring human greatness (v. 38); rather, they are to live in this world in meekness, following Christ at whatever the cost toward true greatness in His kingdom. What is your response to the call to take up your cross and follow Jesus? Why does the life of discipleship hinge upon our answer to Christ's question in verse 20, "Whom say ye that I am?"

2. After the experience on the Mount of Transfiguration, Christ and the disciples seemed to leave the edges of heaven for the edges of hell as they met the demon-possessed boy, his father, and the other disciples, so powerless without their Lord (vv. 37–42). Christ's experience contained many ups and downs, and so will that of the followers of Jesus. How can we find stability in Christ so that the ups will not overly elate us and the downs not discourage us?

Chapter 10

1. None of us would be unimpressed if we were to see demons cast out. However, Christ admonished His disciples to recognize the true seat of joy and happiness. These states

are not found in what we can do, not even in ministry to Him; rather, they are found in being the objects of what God alone has done and can do. We can discover whether our names are written in heaven only in the way of true faith and repentance. If you do not know whether you have a title to life and an inheritance among the saints, you need to repent and seek God. That is the only way to true joy.

2. Martha's problem was not that she was serving; it was that she was distracted by "much serving" (v. 40). It is not only bad things that keep us from true communion with Christ; it is often an excessive preoccupation, anxiety, and distractedness with good things. One thing above all is necessary, and that is to sit at the feet of Him into whose lips "grace is poured" (Ps. 45:2). How do we sit at His feet today? What can we do to make that a priority in our lives?

Chapter 11

1. We need to be taught how to pray because by nature we do not know. This awareness is the first step in this direction. Though the Lord's Prayer is a glorious pattern for prayer, praying itself is an exercise of faith in which believers need to learn the art of asking, seeking, and knocking (vv. 9–10). We can never truly pray unless by faith we also apprehend something of the mercy and grace of God the Father (v. 13). We especially need to ask God for more of the work of the Holy Spirit (v. 13), for the Spirit brings to believers all the blessings purchased by Christ's finished work. What is one lesson from this chapter about prayer that you want to put into practice? How will you do so?

2. The Devil is strong. Christ compared him to a "strong man armed" (v. 21). Thanks be to God there is "a stronger than he" (v. 22). Has He freed you? Don't rest content simply to be externally religious or, as Christ says, "swept and garnished" (v. 25). If that is you, you are exposed to grave danger (v. 26), especially when you are blinded by self-righteousness. How can we recognize the Devil's work of pride and self-righteousness in ourselves?

Chapter 12

1. The rich fool in the parable wanted to take it easy and just enjoy himself (v. 19). That is one of the great sins of our day and age. Many dream of a long, luxurious, and easy retirement. There is nothing wrong with enjoying the gifts God has given, provided we do not neglect the true reason we are here on the earth: to prepare for the life to come and in the meantime to steward our privileges in a God-honoring way. As long as we are able we must serve.

2. God's care for His people should eradicate all needless or undue worry or anxiety (vv. 22–30). Excessive worry does not necessarily mean we have no faith; as Christ said, it is at the least a sign of "little faith" (v. 28). If that is you, pray: "Lord, increase my faith." God increases faith by His Spirit when He motivates us to rest more squarely on His Word and promises. God is jealous of our allegiance and affections. Cares and concerns are so many invitations to cast our cares upon Him and find His care (1 Peter 5:7). How can Christ's teachings about the birds and flowers encourage us to trust God more?

3. Watchfulness is the great emphasis of Christ in verses 31–59. Our world has invested a lot in meteorology, or

predicting weather patterns. Christ tells us that it is of much greater importance to "discern this time" (v. 56) so as to be ready for Christ's return. We will never know in advance the exact day or hour, as some fear-mongers claim we might; however, we can be sure that each day we are one day closer. It refocuses us to live in light of Christ's imminent coming. How would it change your attitudes and habits to live each day watching for Christ's return?

Chapter 13

1. Life is filled with uncertainties. Natural disasters and human violence can strike any time and anywhere, and they often catch people totally unaware, leaving thousands dead within brief spans of time. The only way we can truly face the uncertainties of life is to live in repentance for our sins. Repentance is not just a decision a person makes at a given point in life but is a lifetime of striving, struggling, and fighting against sin by faith in the grace of Christ. Many who hear the gospel admire Christ and presume upon His mercy but will find themselves shut out on the day of judgment. How is this especially a warning to those who regularly go to church and tend to think of themselves as better than others?

2. The healing of the woman from her long-term infirmity was a sign of what Christ does in the gospel for sinners. His grace releases them from the burden of their sins and the heavy load of human rules, expectations, and ceremonies. Christ is not a tyrant but full of sweet love for sinners. He is willing to save all who are willing to come to Him. He proved His will to save sinners by His determination to go to Jerusalem and die for their sins. What reasons does this

chapter give for sinners to come to Christ and trust completely in Him?

Chapter 14

1. Grace humbles a person. Instead of presuming that we are deserving of the chief places in society, it makes us ready to serve others and choose the lowest place for ourselves. Christ showed this spirit during His life, and He teaches this by His Spirit to all His people (vv. 7–9). What a day it will be when Christ will exalt all His people and say, "Friend, go up higher" (v. 10). As James writes, "Humble yourselves in the sight of the Lord, and he shall lift you up" (James 4:10). How can hope in God's reward in glory make Christians willing to serve in lowly, unrecognized ways in this life?

2. Christ said that when they heard the invitation to the kingdom, "they all with one consent began to make excuse" (v. 18). Man by nature loves to weave a web of thinking that makes his rejection of Christ's call look plausible. Others make a superficial response to the gospel but fail to count the cost and excuse themselves because discipleship seems too hard. What motivates true disciples to turn from all such excuses and pursue Christ and His kingdom at any cost? How can we seek that kind of response in prayer?

Chapter 15

1. Each of the three scenes of the parable shows the heart of God that beats with love till the lost sheep, coin, and son are found. There is no other cause for the salvation of lost sinners besides the love of God in Christ. John says it beautifully:

"We love him, because he first loved us" (1 John 4:19). How do Christ's words show us the glory of God's love?

2. Like the prodigal, by our sin we have turned our backs on God and taken God's gifts and used them for our own pleasure and glory. This will bring nothing but lack, misery, and, unless we repent, damnation in hell forevermore. Sinner, what has following your own heart brought you? Is it not time to come to your senses and remember the goodness of God?

3. The attitude of our hearts to sinners being saved is a barometer of whether or not we have ourselves experienced the grace of God. The Pharisees, like the elder son, stood outside the joy and gladness, for their hearts were still closed to the grace of God. Why should the words of the father (v. 32) melt our hearts into joy over the conversion of the worst of men?

Chapter 16

1. The main lesson of the parable of the unjust steward is that we ought to wisely prepare for eternity through repentance and faith. This shrewd steward's preparation for his future, even if he did it in unjust ways, should stir us up to make provisions for our own futures, since by nature we have all mismanaged our stewardship of the resources God has entrusted to us, and our stewardship on earth will soon end. We must realize that we cannot serve two masters and must turn from loving money to loving God with an undivided heart. What does it mean to live every day not as our own masters but as trustees of our time, resources, privileges, and so on?

2. The parable of the rich man and Lazarus teaches us that prosperity in this life does not imply prosperity in the next,

nor does difficulty in this life portend difficulty in the next. It would be better to suffer for a time here than to suffer eternally in the place of torment. The key question is how we respond to the Bible. The Scriptures are sufficient for life and godliness. They are of greater weight and authority to convince people of God's truth than someone rising from the dead (v. 31). Do you rightly esteem the glory of the Scriptures, both the Old and the New Testaments? If you do you will live by faith in Christ, repentance of sin, and mercy toward men.

Chapter 17

1. Christ's disciples will reveal themselves in how they behave toward each other, rebuking each other when necessary (v. 3) but also forgiving each other (v. 4) as Christ has forgiven them. They are not in the Christian life for themselves but to serve Christ and one another. Yet they are to serve with humility, for even if we were able to do everything right, which we never could, we would still be only "unprofitable servants" (v. 10). How can these truths help us when we begin to resent other Christians or think that the church or Christ cannot do without us?

2. When the one leper returned to thank Christ, He looked for the other nine who had also been healed to bring glory to Him, but they were nowhere to be found. We need more than God's help with our physical needs and problems. We need grace to make us truly grateful so we bring glory to God. Where are you when you experience a blessing from the Lord—with the one or with the nine? How can you become more grateful?

3. Do not presume that all will be well simply because you are among Christians. As Christ warns, "Remember Lot's wife" (v. 32). She was close to making it, but she looked back and perished because she was not prepared to lose all else in order that she might gain salvation. Her doom is a graphic image of Christ's warning: "No man, having put his hand to the plough, and looking back, is fit for the kingdom of God" (9:62). Why do people look back to the world after starting to follow Christ?

Chapter 18

1. In the parable of the Pharisee and the publican, the Pharisee failed to see that he was in need of God's grace. He justified himself and did not lean on God's mercy for justification. The man was self-deceived. What a dangerous place to be! Neither did the rich young ruler lean on Christ for righteousness. He still had not come to an end of his own righteousness. It is the blind beggar who sues for mercy from the great Son of David—and receives it. His prayer is most like that of the publican (vv. 13, 38). No wonder he ends up glorifying God (v. 43). Why must we repent of the ways of the Pharisee and the rich ruler and become like a blind beggar if we would be saved by Jesus Christ?

2. Salvation on our own is impossible. However, what a comfort and pleading ground are Christ's words: "The things which are impossible with men are possible with God" (v. 27). Christ will prove this in the next chapter with Zacchaeus (19:1–10). Why is salvation impossible for man? How does God accomplish the impossible?

Chapter 19

1. A divine purpose lay behind everything Christ did. The truth must have sounded very precious to Zacchaeus when Jesus said to him, "I must abide at thy house" (v. 5). Nothing will fail which Christ has planned and purposed to do for the salvation of each sinner He has chosen. How can this instill within us confidence to share the gospel with the worst of sinners?

2. The man who hid his pound explained, "I feared thee, because thou art an austere man" (v. 21). Sadly, this man betrayed a deficient, rebellious view of God, which he used as an excuse to live as he thought appropriate. We will act in accordance with our real view of God. How will a harsh and unfair view of God lead us into sin? How will an experiential knowledge of His love and righteousness lead us to a life of faithfulness?

3. Jesus said with tears, "If thou hadst known…the things which belong unto thy peace!" (v. 42). Despite the welcome the people gave Christ as He entered the city, Christ saw through their actions to what they were truly about. The people by and large did not understand their need of a Savior to propitiate God's anger over their sins, justify them before God, and consecrate them to God. Do you know the things that belong to your peace? Why do you need Jesus?

Chapter 20

1. The religious leaders asked "by what authority doest thou these things?" (v. 2), but they should have asked this question of themselves. It is important to be under the proper authority, and the irony is that Christ was the perfectly obedient

Son of the Father, while these religious leaders were rejecting His authority. Along with it they were rejecting God's Word, His truth, and His Son. People can seem to be religious and yet reject God's rule over them and God's Son as Lord.

2. Just as Jesus portrayed the landowner saying of his son "they will reverence him" (v. 13), so the Lord has every right to expect that we will worship and obey His Son. Psalm 2 directs us to "Kiss the Son, lest he be angry, and ye perish from the way.... Blessed are all they that put their trust in him" (Ps. 2:12). Do you reverence Christ? Do you bow to His authority in all areas of your life? Or do you question His right to rule you and rebel against His Word?

3. The gospel of Christ crucified is a stumbling block or plain foolishness to the natural man. Paul asserts this in 1 Corinthians 1:23. Has God enabled you to see how necessary and suitable Christ is for your sinful soul, as well as how precious and beautiful He is for every need and circumstance of your life? How poor you are if you are seeking to build on your own foundation. Submit to God. Forsake your own righteousness. Realize that everything you try apart from Christ will only condemn you, both now and forever. On the other hand, to those who believe, Christ is precious (1 Peter 2:7).

Chapter 21

1. Little could this widow have known that her two mites would go down in history as an example, inspiration, and challenge to untold millions. Of course, without Christ discerning her heart and speaking the truth, we would never have known about her gift. What an event it will be when the triune God unveils to the watching world on judgment

day the innermost thoughts of the heart (8:17). Insofar as the Spirit has revealed your own heart to you, what will that day disclose about you?

2. Christ is coming again. If the desolation that fell upon Jerusalem called for fleeing without delay to safety, how much more does the judgment of the Son of Man call for us to flee without delay to Christ's saving mercy? Will judgment day find you safe in Jesus? Christ does not want people to be deceived (v. 8), but neither does He desire for believers to be terrified (v. 9). The anticipation of Christ's return should move Christians to lift up their heads with hope (v. 28). He particularly calls us to live in constant watchfulness and spiritual alertness (vv. 34–36). How does the doctrine of Christ's return affect you?

Chapter 22

1. The Passover spoke of divine deliverance through the shedding of the blood of the sacrifice. The application of the blood of the lamb caused God's punishment of death to pass over those hidden within the house, foreshadowing Christ's work on the cross. If Christ's death is applied to us, God's wrath will pass over us, for His just wrath against sin is satisfied. How is Christ's blood applied to sinners so that they are hidden and saved in Him?

2. Watching and praying are key to resisting temptation (v. 46). God's people are so weak in themselves that without God's grace they cannot stand for one moment against Satan's devices. How often Satan catches them off guard, without their armor, and they look back and think, "I have not watched and prayed." Thanks be to God that Jesus did

not fail here. When the Devil sifted the disciples like wheat, Christ devoted Himself to prayer and submitted His will entirely to the cup of God's wrath. As in the wilderness (4:1–11), so now in the garden Jesus is both our example to imitate and our champion who has already won the victory. How do you need to look to Him in the temptations you are facing right now?

Chapter 23

1. Christ's work would not have been the same if He had simply been murdered by a mob or off in some dark alley. According to the will of God and the prophecies of the Old Testament, He had to be sentenced by the official governing bodies as a criminal. Pilate, Herod, and the religious authorities all signed off on the legality of this execution, thus showing the exceeding sinfulness of mankind. None can plead innocent—including us. Blinded by sin, we would have done nothing essentially different from what they did. May God humble us to see ourselves as wholly unjust, and the Son of God as gloriously just. Through it all God's justice would be executed upon His Son, in order that the elect might be freely justified. In this way God would "be just, and the justifier of him which believeth in Jesus" (Rom. 3:26). How should the cross of Jesus both humble us for our sins and afford us hope for complete forgiveness in Christ?

2. Calvary speaks not only of justice but also of salvation. On the cross Christ prayed for transgressors, and He saved the thief dying next to Him. The veil was rent, giving mankind access to God through the blood of the everlasting covenant. A Roman centurion, too, was saved. Thus in the darkest day

of history we see the Lord Jesus doing the best works. How does the cross reveal the mystery and wonder of God's will?

Chapter 24

1. God's ways and thoughts are higher than man's (Isa. 55:8). These women and the other disciples were resigning themselves to live on despite a dead Jesus. If this had been the end of the story, we believers with them would be "of all men most miserable. But now is Christ risen from the dead" (1 Cor. 15:19–20). His resurrection is proclaimed by the infallible Word of God, declared by angels, proven by the empty tomb, and confirmed by eyewitnesses. What difference should the resurrection of Christ make in our lives once we believe it?

2. What a Bible study Christ offered on the road to Emmaus: "And beginning at Moses and all the prophets, he expounded unto them in all the scriptures the things concerning himself" (v. 27)! Notice how eager Christ was to focus His disciples on the Scriptures. He could have chosen to omit this step and simply reveal Himself, but He loves the Bible and wants His people to see Him, the *living* Word, in the Bible, the *written* Word. While the Scriptures have important revelations about all sorts of issues, their primary purpose is to reveal God in the face of Jesus Christ. We must always remember this when we read the Bible. Yet we must also remember that we need Christ to open our eyes or we will not see His glory in the Bible. What are some ways in which the whole Bible reveals Christ? Why do we need to pray regularly for Christ's illumination as we read and hear the Word?

3. The Gospel According to Luke began with a temple scene in which Zacharias was unable to bless the people because

he had been silenced after seeing an angel and doubting the message from the Lord. Luke ends his Gospel once again in the temple, this time with the disciples "praising and blessing God" (v. 53) because the risen Christ had ascended into heaven with His hands lifted up to bless them as their ever-living Priest. Though rejected by His national people, teachers, rulers, and priests, the Lord Jesus is the great Prophet, Priest, and King of His spiritual people. The Savior lives to bless His people. What reasons does this give believers to bless God? How do you need to apply those reasons to your own heart, so that by God's Spirit you, too, can praise the Lord?

John

Chapter 1

1. When John called Jesus "the Word," he implied that Christ not only brings us a message from God but is Himself the Message. Jesus is God in the flesh, the infinite glory and grace of the Father dwelling among men in the tabernacle of a human body. Therefore, to believe in Christ is much more than trusting Him to teach us or help us; saving faith is receiving Him as our God, our very life. What difference does it make to the Christian faith that Christ is God?

2. John the Baptist shows us that a preacher's calling is to point away from himself to Christ and to lift the Savior high before men's eyes. A minister can do this only by having a low view of himself and a high view of Christ. A Christ-centered ministry is particularly a cross-centered ministry, focusing regularly (though not exclusively) on Christ's death as the Lamb of God. How can you pray for ministers that they would be like John in this manner?

3. To find Christ is the most wonderful discovery of all. It is too good to be kept to oneself. How can you become more like these early disciples who eagerly told their family and friends about Jesus?

Chapter 2

1. Miracles performed by Christ are evidences or signs to show us that He is God. The faith of the disciples was strengthened by this first miracle, for it showed that Christ has the power

of the Creator over His creation (1:3). The miracle of turning water into wine also suggests the manner in which Christ replaced the rituals of external religion (for which the water pots were used, 2:6) with abundant joy and life. Trusting in Christ means going beyond the outward form of religion and experiencing a new creation within by His power.

2. Carnal men invariably spoil the worship of God in one way or another. Worship must be regulated by God's holy Word. It is a sin to corrupt the public worship in God's house either by commerce or by entertainment. Worship must be reverent. Christ also shows here that discipline is essential to a faithful church. If Christ could cleanse the temple even in His state of humiliation on earth, how much more could He discipline His church as its exalted and glorious Lord? Why should this cause us to conduct worship with holy fear? How can we follow the Lord in His zeal for the purity of God's worship?

Chapter 3

1. In the church it is not enough for leaders to be academically well trained, nor for its members to be well taught. Without the new birth men are entirely unfit for the kingdom of God. Through the new birth dead sinners are made alive, and at last they will be raised up from the dead to sit with Him in the glory of heaven. Why is the new birth absolutely necessary for salvation? Are you born again?

2. God's sending of His Son to save the world from condemnation is the greatest display of love in all of human history. God gave His best, His unique Son who shares His very nature, for those who hate and reject Him. Christ was lifted up on the cross to die so that guilty sinners could live forever

in relationship with God. What love is this! Why should His love move sinners to trust in Him?

3. We must resist our ignorant and worldly tendency to boast of one minister above another. The abilities and success of each are gifts from heaven. Like John the Baptist, we should have a low view of ourselves and give our full affection and admiration to the Bridegroom. How wonderful is the marriage of the Lord to His people! How can loving Jesus as our spiritual Husband protect us from exalting mere men?

Chapter 4

1. The Christian should learn to turn conversations with unconverted persons to the subject of salvation, as Christ does so kindly here. Christ wisely began with physical, visible things but used them as a lead-in to God's gift and our spiritual need. In our preaching and evangelism we must strive to convince hearers that they have sinned against God. The sinner's conscience is the preacher's friend. However, a sense of sin helps no one without the knowledge of the Savior of the world. Where do you see yourself most in this chapter? The woman confronted, convicted, or converted?

2. Worship is unacceptable to God unless it is "in spirit and in truth" (v. 23). That means that the worshiper must be spiritually reborn and be walking in the Spirit, and that the content and form of worship offered must be according to God's Word. What are some examples of worship that are not done "in spirit"? What are examples of worship not offered "in truth"?

Chapter 5

1. Christ blessed the cripple before he had even asked to be healed. Yet He also issued a strong call to repentance (v. 14). Many who receive physical or material blessings from Christ do not acknowledge God in a life of repentance. How have you experienced earthly blessings from Christ? What does it mean for you to hear Christ's "Sin no more, lest a worse thing come unto thee" (v. 14)?

2. None will ever honor Christ rightly until they recognize that He is the eternal Son of God incarnate. From all eternity the Father, the Son, and the Holy Spirit have shared one divine nature, with one will and one power. They cooperate in a beautiful relationship as three persons in one God. Honoring the Son as God does not demean the Father, for honoring the Son is the way through which the Father desires to be honored. How can we honor the Son as the Giver of eternal life? As the Judge?

Chapter 6

1. The crowds were attracted by Christ's miracles, but not by His power to save souls. In the same way the "health and wealth" gospel attracts many but does not stress the need for true conversion. Only when men are converted do they put spiritual and heavenly values first in life. When Jesus challenged the crowds, He lost much of His visible following. Why must churches be willing to challenge men's worldliness, even if doing so may reduce their numbers?

2. None can come to Christ for salvation but those whom God Himself draws. The truths of the gospel will always be offensive to those who are unconverted. The preacher is

not at liberty to alter the truth in order to gain the favor of unbelieving sinners, as our Lord Himself here shows by His perfect example. Instead, the church must rely on the Spirit of God to do what no man can. How does this call us to fervent and regular prayer for the preaching of the Word?

Chapter 7

1. The unbelief of Jesus' brothers sets forth the important lesson that we can be near the truth and yet lack true faith. It is a mercy that after Christ's resurrection we find Christ's brothers in the company of those who believe. How is their unbelief a warning to those growing up in Christian families and churches? How is their conversion an encouragement with regard to what God can do?

2. Christ still says through the gospel, "If any man thirst, let him come unto me, and drink" (v. 37). He proclaims Himself to all who hear the gospel, promising that everyone who trusts in Him will receive the eternal life of God's Spirit and become a means by which the Spirit overflows to others. Sadly, many people stumble over their pride and so reject Him. Others depend on hearsay about Christ and fail to seek the facts that confirm His Messiahship and deity. How have you responded to Christ's call to come to Him?

Chapter 8

1. Christ came not to condemn sinners but to save them. The worst of sinners in this life may be saved, if he will repent and trust in Christ. Rather than judging sinners in pride and hypocrisy, we should bring them to Jesus to learn of His grace. The Son is able truly and lastingly to set sinners free!

2. Christ did not hold back from saying hard things to sinners who were not yet broken over their sins. He stripped them of their religious presumption based on their backgrounds and upbringings. He warned them of their slavery to sin and told them they were so bad they were unable to believe in Him. He even said they were children of Satan, the image-bearers of the great murderer and liar. Why did Jesus say such things to religious people who believed in Him? Why did He not speak this way to the woman caught in adultery? Have you submitted to what God says about you?

Chapter 9

1. God has given each of His servants a day to work, but the night is coming. Until the Lord returns we will all die. Therefore, let us learn to redeem our time. Even the sorrows of this fallen world are opportunities to glorify God.

2. Christ's Word confronts us, and there is no neutrality. We can be like the man who was healed and boldly follow the truth to worship at the feet of Jesus and confess Him before men; like his parents, who in the fear of man bowed under the intimidation of this world; or like the Pharisees, who were so blind they rejected the plain truth to cling to their own ways. Only one of these individuals or groups could see; the others were blind to the light of Christ's glory. Which do you most resemble?

Chapter 10

1. Jesus claimed to be the great Shepherd of God's people. He is the King who loves His people and cares for them intimately and individually. No one is truly a sheep in Christ's

flock who does not listen to Him and follow Him. What does this parable teach us about true discipleship to Jesus?

2. While the image of a shepherd is comforting, Jesus used it to call people to follow Him in the midst of thieves, robbers, and fierce wolves. Indeed, Jesus is an unusual Shepherd, for He defends His flock by dying for His sheep. What spiritual dangers did Jesus describe in this parable? How can we find safety from them?

3. God has given to Jesus a particular people, His "sheep," to save and bring to eternal life (vv. 27–29). Christ knows them in a special way (v. 14), for He died for them in particular (vv. 11, 15). They will hear His voice in Scripture and obey Him (vv. 4, 16, 27), and only they will believe in Him (vv. 26). He will never lose them, for the power of God keeps them safe (vv. 28–29). These verses epitomize the doctrines of election, particular redemption, effectual calling, and perseverance of the saints. How do these truths give comfort to believers? How do they encourage evangelism?

Chapter 11

1. Since Christ's death is the death of death to all His people, they need not sorrow excessively when facing death. In the great day the voice of Jesus will raise up all believers in glory. Though believers die physically, they never die spiritually or eternally but will rise at last to meet the Lord in the air at His second coming (1 Thess. 4:13–16). How do these truths affect the way in which you will face death?

2. Though Christ is the infinite and living God, He is also a man with a human mind and emotions like our own.

Therefore, we need not fear to approach Him but can pour out our hearts to Him and know He will sympathize with all except those who are rebellious against God. Here is a Priest who can help us in temptation. Consider that "Jesus wept" (v. 35). How does that encourage you to seek Him as the sympathizing High Priest (Heb. 4:15)?

Chapter 12

1. Those who love Christ and honor Him must expect to be critically misjudged by those who are only nominal Christians. That should not discourage them from pouring out their lives in love for the One who died for them. How can you imitate Mary's costly devotion?

2. The death of Christ is the most sublime of all God's works to glorify Himself. In His dying, Christ has in a unique way manifested the love, justice, and wisdom of God. At the cross Satan's power was broken and the nations redeemed. The cross of Christ breaks the hearts of all elect sinners and leads them to devote their lives to Him. In what way do you see God's glory in Christ crucified? How does that draw you to Christ as Savior and Lord?

Chapter 13

1. As Christ looked beyond the cross to the crown which He was soon to wear, so believers should look beyond their earthly trials to the glory that will be theirs at last. How can this hope empower you to humbly serve others as Christ did?

2. God is in control of every situation. Judas had his covetous eye on the money promised to him, but God's purpose was to save a multitude of sinners through Christ's shed blood.

How profound are Peter's words in his sermon on the day of Pentecost: "Him, being delivered by the determinate counsel and foreknowledge of God, ye have taken, and by wicked hands have crucified and slain" (Acts 2:23). If God can even use a traitor to provide salvation, how are you motivated to trust Him with your trials now?

3. A Christian may have much to learn about his own weakness. Mercifully, God is ready to forgive all who have true faith. Peter was a true child of God, yet he fell through overconfidence; Judas was no true child of God but a hypocrite, and he went to his own place. Let every man search his own heart and ask, "Lord, is it I?" (Matt. 26:22).

Chapter 14

1. Just as Jesus showed His love by washing the feet of His disciples (13:1–38), so He demonstrated His great mercy by teaching them in the upper room just before He was arrested and killed (14:1–17:26). Rather than turning inward as His death approached, Christ devoted Himself all the more to serving others. Rather than demanding comfort, He disbursed it to others. How can we imitate His example?

2. Verse 6 is one of Christ's most loved statements, a precious distillation in just a few words of all that He is for His people. How have you known Christ as your way? Your truth? Your life? Why is He the only way to the Father?

3. As Jesus prepared His disciples for His departure, He repeatedly pointed them to the divine Person who would continue Christ's ministry among them after Jesus left: the

Holy Spirit. What does this chapter teach us about the Spirit's work and why we need Him?

Chapter 15

1. Jesus is the Vine and Christians are the branches. Without the Lord we can do nothing pleasing to the Lord. Union and communion with Christ are crucial to a fruitful spiritual life that pleases God. By rejecting Christ the unbelieving Jews cut themselves off from their only hope of becoming what God intended Israel to be. Jews and Gentiles who trust in Christ become God's true vineyard. Do you abide in Christ by a living faith? What fruits are you bearing that demonstrate this? How can you cultivate a deeper life of abiding in the Vine?

2. The history of Christianity illustrates clearly the principle that Christians should expect persecution. Why does the world hate Christ? Why does it hate the servants of Christ? In what way does this teach us our need for the Holy Spirit in order to be effective witnesses for Christ?

Chapter 16

1. Not only are men and women perishing in their sins under the wrath of God and unable and unwilling to come to Christ, but they are strangely unaware of their desperate condition. The Spirit must awaken them to their guilt before God; the perfection of the Savior, Jesus Christ; and the reality that God's judgment on this wicked world has already begun in Christ's victory over Satan (vv. 7–11). How should this truth motivate and guide us in praying for the Spirit's help in our evangelism?

2. The Spirit is the Teacher of the church, bringing to us the glories of Christ so that we may see that all the fullness of the Father is in Christ for our benefit (vv. 12–15). How often do you pray for the work of the Spirit in the church of Christ? How can you be more fervent in your prayers for the Holy Spirit?

3. The Christian's life is a strange paradox in this world, a puzzling mixture of distress and peace, fear and courage (vv. 32–33). Why is this so? How can we grow in peace and courage by pleading the promise "I have overcome the world"?

Chapter 17

1. This great, high-priestly prayer of Christ is the consummation of the preceding discourse (14:1–16:33). We see here a sample of the intercessory work of Christ at the right hand of God. Everything Christ prays for will be granted by the heavenly Father, since Christ is the God-man whose redemptive work so greatly glorifies God. How can it encourage believers to know that Jesus is interceding with God to preserve them, unify them, and bring them to glory?

2. Christ's prayer for unity (v. 21) has often been used as an argument for church union irrespective of doctrine and practices. However, we must seek unity in a way that honors His prayer, "Sanctify them through thy truth: thy word is truth" (v. 17). There is no true unity without a common faith in the teachings of the inerrant Bible, along with a common life of holiness. Why are these necessary for spiritual unity?

3. The desire of Christ is that Christians will be with Him to gaze upon His glory forever (v. 24). "Blessed are the pure in

heart: for they shall see God" (Matt. 5:8). Is this truly your desire? If so, reflect on the truth that heaven is a world of love.

Chapter 18

1. Christ, as the great "I am," could easily have destroyed His enemies by His divine power (v. 6). He had many powerful servants (the angels) who could have protected Him, but He did not come to be that kind of king (v. 36). Instead, His kingdom comes by preaching and believing the truth (v. 37). What does this teach us about the manner in which the church overcomes this world?

2. Christ was condemned to die under charges of criminal acts (v. 33; 19:12), and the one guilty of criminal acts was set free (18:40). This teaches us two lessons, for both human sin and divine providence were at work here. First, so deep is the hatred and hardness of the hearts of fallen men that they prefer a murderer to the righteous Son of God (Acts 3:14). Second, so deep is the love of God that He sent His Son to die for the sins of His people in order that they, the guilty, would go free (John 3:16–17). How should these truths humble us and fill us with gratitude?

Chapter 19

1. Pontius Pilate will forever be remembered for the gross miscarriage of justice he permitted in the murder of God's Son. We should never allow ourselves to be bullied into doing what in conscience we know to be wrong. Why is the fear of man so powerful as to move people to go against their conscience? How can it be overcome?

2. How clear it is from Christ's willingness to voluntarily undergo such horrible sufferings that He loved His Heavenly Father and also His own dear people! Even as He was dying He was caring for others, as His words to His mother show. Yet His last words, "It is finished" (v. 30), declare that He did not die as a helpless martyr but as the conquering King, even as the sign on the cross stated. In one sense the cross was the chariot on which the King of grace rode to victory over all that had been oppressing His own. Yet He conquered as the Lamb of God, suffering and dying to turn away God's just judgment against sinners. Why should this chapter move us to trust, love, admire, and surrender to this King of infinite grace? How does this chapter affect you?

Chapter 20

1. It is absurd to argue that the resurrection of Christ was a fabrication of the disciples. They were all inclined not to believe it until compelled by the evidence of the risen Jesus. These apostles of Christ have not given us myths or legends but solid, historically reliable accounts of our Lord. Our wisdom is to believe them and to build our lives upon them. What difference would it make to you if Jesus had never risen from the dead? What does that say about your faith?

2. The resurrection appearances of Jesus pulsate with love between Him and His disciples. We see it in the rush of Peter and John to the empty tomb and in the tears of Mary Magdalene. We feel it in the pathos of Jesus' simple address to her—"Mary"—and in her devoted response—"Master." We hear it as Jesus called those who had abandoned Him "my brethren," and reminded them that God is "your Father."

He appeared to them with "Peace" on His lips and gently condescended to meet Thomas in his skepticism. Thomas cried out with adoration to the Savior, "My Lord and my God." Do you know the love of the living Lord Jesus? If so, how has His love created in you an answering love for Him?

Chapter 21

1. The miracle of catching 153 fish, like the feeding of the five thousand, is a sign of Christ's all-sufficient power to enable the apostles (and other gospel preachers) to experience great success as fishers of men (Mark 1:17; Luke 5:10). Yet their fishing all night and catching nothing reminds us that success is not from the preacher or on his terms but subject to Christ's sovereignty. Each servant of God has a future determined by the will of Christ, in some cases a life ending in martyrdom. However, our calling is not to guess about the future but to devote ourselves to following Him by faith. What lessons are there here to encourage you to serve the Lord?

2. Peter's restoration plays a vital role in the conclusion to this Gospel because the risen Christ would soon ascend (20:17), having delegated the visible leadership of His people to the apostles and the elders of each church. The apostle Peter was a man broken over his sins against Christ, motivated by his love for Christ, and called to shepherd the people of Christ. Why are all these qualities essential for a minister of the gospel of Jesus Christ?

Acts

Chapter 1

1. Luke refers to his Gospel as what Jesus "began both to do and teach" (v. 1). The implication is that Christ is continuing to act and teach, now as the Lord enthroned in heaven (v. 9) who works through His Spirit (v. 8). How does the knowledge that Jesus continues to act and teach in the world strengthen the faith of believers?

2. The disciples did not wait passively for the coming of the Spirit, doing nothing, but they devoted themselves to prayer meetings (v. 14). They loved the Scriptures as the infallible voice of God's Spirit (v. 16) and applied the Word to order the church according to God's will (v. 20). Thus they provide an example of how believers should wait for the coming of Christ: by devoting themselves to prayer, the Word, and the church, as ordered by Scripture.

3. Christ captured the mission of the church in the phrase "witnesses unto me" (v. 8). Witnesses do not invent their own message but faithfully declare what they know to be true. The witness of the church did not end with the apostles but must continue to the ends of the earth, for God's purpose is to bring this message concerning Christ and redemption to all nations. Only when all the elect from all tribes and tongues are brought in through the word of Christ's witnesses will the end come. How is your church engaged in this witness? If you are a Christian, how are you part of this mission?

Chapter 2

1. The work of the triune God is obvious at every important point of history: creation, incarnation, resurrection, and also Pentecost. Exalted by the Father (v. 33), Christ poured out His Spirit (v. 33), and the Spirit testified of Christ (v. 31) while the Lord added to the church (v. 47). Blessed be the triune God (Eph. 1:3).

2. True repentance for sin and a crying out to God for mercy (vv. 37–38) is the only proper response to the preaching of the Word of God. Never doubt the power of God to convert sinners. He cut the people of Jerusalem to the heart and transformed cowardly Peter into a fearless preacher. Have you come before God as a sinner, seeking mercy for Christ's sake?

3. The church after Pentecost was marked by faithfulness, fellowship, fear, and fervency. Trace this out in verses 41 to 47 and ask whether these qualities characterize you. How can you pray regularly for these characteristics to increase in your own church?

Chapter 3

1. Though the Bible calls Christians to show generosity to the poor, the preaching of the gospel and the transformation that it brings must always be central to the life of the church. Peter used this miracle as an opportunity to declare the power of the name of Jesus, not just to heal the sick but as the person in whom we must place our faith. It is fitting that this miracle took place at the gate called Beautiful, for it reveals the loveliness of the Savior as He takes hopeless sinners and restores them to strength, joy, and praise.

2. Just because God raised Christ from the dead does not mean that people are automatically saved. The gospel calls sinners to repent and be converted so that their sins might be blotted out (v. 19). Do not rest simply on hearing the truth of the gospel, being a child of believers, or being around people who know the gospel. Apart from repentance toward God and faith in the Lord Jesus you are neither saved nor safe. Have you repented?

Chapter 4

1. It is often asserted today that people can be saved apart from knowing about Jesus. Some say that explicit knowledge about Jesus is not necessary in order to be saved. Verse 12 stands in absolute contrast to this. We need to be prepared to stand and say this against the tide of relativism in our culture. Why is faith in Jesus Christ the only way to God?

2. The apostles quoted Psalm 2 in their prayer (vv. 25–26). They were bringing back to God His own Word. How does this help us see the connection between these two means of grace: prayer and Bible reading?

3. Though they responded resolutely to the intimidation of the Sanhedrin, the apostles still felt the need to pray to God to grant them "boldness." They were not content to move forward in their own strength or on the strength of past resolutions. They understood their need to draw down strength from God. Do you know this strengthening power of prayer in your life? How dependent are you on God's Spirit?

Chapter 5

1. Satan wages war at the level of our hearts, seeking to fill the thoughts and affections of people with greed, deceit, and hypocrisy (v. 3). Yet sinners cannot excuse themselves by saying that the Devil made them do it. Ananias and Sapphira "conceived this thing" in their hearts (v. 4). As a result God rightly judged them for putting on a false show of righteousness. How should this event teach us to fear the Lord?

2. The apostles preached "the words of…life" (v. 20). The message of the gospel is powerful, saving, and effectual when blessed by the Holy Spirit. God uses preaching to bring the spiritually dead soul to life and to increase Christ's life in the believing soul. How should this affect the way we come to read or hear the Word? How should this motivate us to speak it to others who do not yet believe?

3. We naturally shrink back from suffering, and nowhere does the Bible tell us to choose suffering for its own sake. However, if doing the right thing brings suffering, we should not shrink back but learn from the apostles to see our suffering as a privilege in light of God's purpose (v. 41). Why did they rejoice?

Chapter 6

1. The apostles discerned the temptation we all face to be distracted from our main callings. Satan bombards us with distractions because he knows we will be far less effective if we are preoccupied with many other things. Every Christian needs wisdom from God to discern his calling so that he can devote himself to it with dedication. Pastors in particular

need humility and wisdom to delegate tasks to others. What can you do to be more focused on your calling?

2. What a mercy it was that "a great company of the priests were obedient to the faith" (v. 7). They had served and ministered in the types and shadows of the old sanctuary. But now, not only had the physical veil been torn but the spiritual veil over their hearts had also been rent, and by faith they submitted to the righteousness of God in Jesus Christ. Why was their conversion a surprise (4:1–2)? How does it demonstrate the power of Christ?

3. Stephen was "full of faith and of the Holy Ghost" (v. 5). Though the Holy Spirit is a gift of God, the Bible does command us to seek after the Spirit's work (Luke 11:13) and not to quench (1 Thess. 5:19) or grieve Him (Eph. 4:30). Why do we need the Spirit?

Chapter 7

1. Note that Stephen opens his speech saying, "The God of glory appeared unto our father Abraham" (v. 2). Likewise his speech ends by noting that he "saw the glory of God, and Jesus standing on the right hand of God" (v. 55). Stephen's eyes have been opened to the glory of God in the face of Jesus Christ, as revealed throughout Scripture. What does it mean to read the Bible in such a way as to see God's glory in the face of Christ?

2. Spiritual privileges do not necessarily equate to spiritual possession. Israel was privileged in many ways. When they considered this the equivalent of being God's special possession they deceived themselves, and God punished them by

giving them up to idolatry (v. 42). Though they had the Word of God and the external form of His worship, they were "uncircumcised in heart and ears" (v. 51). How should this danger move us to pray for God's work within our hearts?

Chapter 8

1. Many of us carry a great fear of persecution and death. The deaths of the martyrs should grieve believers (v. 2), and it is certainly not wrong to flee from persecution unless duty requires one to stay (v. 4). However, we must remember that those killed for Christ are immediately welcomed by Christ into glory (7:54–56). In fact, the persecution that people like Saul meant for evil God meant for good, to spread the gospel far and wide, even to Ethiopia. How does this chapter teach us to pray about persecution?

2. Though the gospel was blessed in Samaria so that many were saved, Simon shows that not every seeming conversion is real. Proper procedures of discipline must function to ensure that those who are hypocrites are unmasked and, if they refuse to repent, excluded from the membership of the church. Why can we not presume that all apparent converts are saved, even when God works powerfully in a place?

Chapter 9

1. The same glory of Christ that greeted Stephen at his death (7:56) brought Saul to spiritual life (vv. 3–6). Christ is the beginning and the end of all His people's lives. Are you still living for your own glory, or has Christ's glory brought you to look away from yourself to Him? One test is whether you are willing to suffer, and even to die, so that others might see

His glory. Paul was a chosen vessel specifically marked out by God to suffer for the name of Christ (v. 16). While you may not become a martyr, how willing are you to suffer some degree of insult or anger in order to make known the glory of Jesus Christ to others?

2. We do not know for how long Saul was kicking against the goads ("pricks," v. 5), but God was using His law in Paul's life to convict him of sin (Rom. 7:7–9), and no doubt Paul had heard the gospel from the very disciples he was persecuting. Are you kicking against God's goads, such as His Word, inner convictions of conscience, and works of providence that call you to Jesus? Why is it foolish to "kick against the pricks"?

3. Saul's conversion was so surprising that many doubted it could be real (v. 26). Though a period of testing is good and necessary for new converts (8:18–24), we should have high expectations of what God can do by His grace. What are the dangers of keeping true converts out of the church because of their previous lifestyles of sin?

Chapter 10

1. When considering the events of this chapter we must see them all as orchestrated by the Lord. God prepared the soil (Cornelius and his family), brought the sower of the seed (Peter), and sent down the rain (the Holy Spirit) so that there might be a harvest (conversion). All the glory goes to God and not to man. God planted a sense of need in Cornelius that made him restless and discontent with a life of paganism, so that he began crying out to God in prayer. Has God awakened you to your spiritual need so that you pray

for your soul and your eternal salvation? Have you embraced the gospel by the Holy Spirit?

2. Just as people had struggled with the idea that Saul of Tarsus had truly been saved, many would struggle with the concept that Gentiles like Cornelius could be saved. Our own prejudices are often so engrained that it takes a lot of convincing for us to believe what God has plainly said in His Word, that no sinner is too vile or wretched or far gone in sin for God to save him or her. What kind of people might you or others in your church have a hard time accepting if they were to be converted? Why?

Chapter 11

1. Peter's vision did not introduce the idea of the inclusion of the Gentiles into salvation, nor did it inaugurate this change. It was prophesied in the Old Testament (Ps. 72:17–19), foretold by Jesus (Luke 24:44–47), and accomplished by His death (Eph. 2:12–15). The vision of Peter confirmed the change and prodded the church to follow Christ in evangelizing and welcoming the nations. Why are we sometimes slow to take the gospel to ethnic groups or cultures that are different from our own? Why does the Lord press us to do so?

2. Barnabas visited the believers in Antioch and saw "the grace of God" in the work there (v. 23). This means that he saw the results of the grace of God at work in the lives of those who had come to trust in Christ and follow Him as His disciples. The name "Christians" was first used of believers and disciples in Antioch (v. 26); the name expresses the close relationship between Christ, which means "Anointed One," and His people who share His anointing in the Holy Spirit. If we

carry the name of "Christian," why is it important that people be able to see the grace of Christ's Spirit in our lives?

Chapter 12

1. Why James was killed and Peter was allowed to live for several more years is a divine mystery. God could have supernaturally saved both James and Peter. He showed His sovereignty in allowing Peter to do more work on earth, while James would enter Christ's presence sooner. When we are tempted to compare our circumstances in life with those of others, how can what happened to James and Peter teach us to submit to God?

2. Jesus commands His disciples to continually ask, seek, and knock for their requests, anticipating that God will hear our prayers. Thus the scene before us in this chapter is so striking: when their prayers were answered they could not believe it. Even as we pray for various requests, we should also pray, "Lord, increase our faith" (Luke 17:5).

3. Their deaths are recorded in the same chapter of the Bible, but what different deaths James and Herod experienced! In one moment James went from prison to heaven. Herod, too, in one moment went from his earthly glory to an everlasting prison in hell. How true it is: "Blessed are the dead which die in the Lord" (Rev. 14:13).

Chapter 13

1. Though the Holy Spirit sent Paul and Barnabas to preach the gospel to the lost, the church in Antioch was the vehicle through which the Spirit set them apart for this ministry. Do you pray for missionaries and support them as you are able?

2. Paul met many enemies of the gospel on his journey, the sorcerer Bar-jesus being only one of them. Christ's promise that the gates of hell cannot prevail against the church is profoundly meaningful in the midst of such hellish conflict (Matt. 16:18). Why do we need to be filled with the power of God's Spirit to see the kingdom advance?

3. When they heard the stunning message of free justification by faith alone, some wanted to hear this exact message preached again on the next Sabbath (v. 42). What a blessed thing it is never to tire of the "old" gospel, to find it always new. What do we learn about the content of the gospel message from this chapter? What makes it so precious?

Chapter 14

1. Imagine seeing Paul when he returned to Lystra, perhaps with bruises and cuts from being stoned still visible on him from when he was last there. What would it have been like to hear this man say, "we must through much tribulation enter into the kingdom of God" (v. 22)? What might it cost a typical Christian in your land to follow Christ to the end? What has it cost you?

2. This section on Paul's first missionary journey (13:1–14:28) concludes with a concern for proper church order. Paul and Barnabas prayerfully led each church to appoint a group of elders to lead it. The missionaries returned to their sending church to report about God's work through them among the nations. There is a profound sense that both office-bearers in the church and missionaries from the church serve as those commissioned by the church and upheld by its prayers. Why is the local church central to world missions?

Chapter 15

1. The early church had to contend not only with persecution but also with strife and division. We can learn important principles from how the church in Jerusalem responded. First, the leaders of the church met together to discuss the matter. Second, their discussion was God-centered and God-exalting; together they looked to His will and bowed to His providence. Third, they discussed the Holy Scriptures, basing their decision on the Spirit's teaching in the Word of God. Fourth, they guided their decision by the principles of salvation by grace through faith in Jesus Christ, not through bondage to human traditions or old covenant ceremonies. Fifth, no one man decreed what the church would do; though Peter and James had more authority than the others, the church sought unity of mind. How can your church put these lessons into practice in its own discussions?

2. Another interesting disagreement, this time of a personal nature, is recorded here between Barnabas and Paul (vv. 37–39). This one was solved by the two going their separate ways. Another way of looking at this was that now two teams went out, doubling the effectiveness and coverage of the mission effort. Even this conflict could not halt the work of God. Is it ever necessary for two Christians who share common beliefs nevertheless to go separate ways in ministry? Why?

Chapter 16

1. The Holy Spirit is an integral part of the church's mission. Here we read of the Spirit both forbidding and permitting Paul and his companions to carry out their ministry

(vv. 6–7). Though today we seek no revelations of the Spirit apart from the Scriptures, we do need to rely upon Him for wisdom in every decision regarding church and evangelism. Furthermore, the opening of Lydia's heart to believe (v. 14) reminds us that the preaching of the gospel depends completely on the Spirit for success in conversions. How should these realities motivate us to pray? How do you pray with regard to these matters?

2. With the earthquake and the outstretched sword, the conversion of the jailor was violent and forceful, but no less productive of true faith and joy (v. 34) than that of Lydia. God's actions in bringing people to Christ are different for each person, but true, saving grace always shows itself in faith and love that God Himself works in the hearts of sinners. Why is it a mistake to insist that each person's experience of conversion has exactly the same outward features?

Chapter 17

1. The Bereans serve as a good example of men and women who love truth and the Scriptures. After hearing the preaching and teaching of the apostles, they "received the word with all readiness of mind, and searched the scriptures daily, whether those things were so" (v. 11). So often we fall into a passive kind of sitting under the teaching and preaching of the Word. The Bereans are commended for their eagerness to search the Scriptures and discover the truth of the apostles' teaching. How can we imitate them?

2. Paul's preaching to those who knew the Scriptures (v. 2) and those steeped in worldly philosophy (vv. 16–31) was different. However, Paul's message in the Areopagus has

sometimes been misapplied, as though Paul were using this opportunity to build bridges of common beliefs between Christianity and different religions and philosophies. On the contrary, Paul's message was as sharp as ever, exposing sin, idolatry, and ignorance; declaring the glory of the true God and Savior; and calling men to repent now or face the judgment. What can we learn from him for speaking about our faith to people outside the church?

Chapter 18

1. Even Paul could feel afraid (v. 9). Christ encouraged Paul during the difficult early stage of his time in Corinth. He was working hard making tents for a living (v. 3), and his witness was opposed (v. 6). However, God's works are known to Him from all eternity. He tells Paul that He has "much people in this city" (v. 10). That did not mean that there had been many converts to this point but that Christ had claimed them as His own by the decree of election. They still needed the preaching of the gospel so that they might come to faith and repentance and thereby confirm their election from God (1 Thess. 1:3–6). How does the truth that God has chosen many sinners for salvation encourage evangelism?

2. Apollos was "mighty in the scriptures" (v. 24). No doubt that meant that by the Spirit's grace he loved the Bible, studied it carefully, and could teach it well (Ezra 7:10). It was like a sword that he used to defend the truth, attack strongholds of unbelief, and set prisoners free. His response to Aquila and Priscilla shows that he was still humble, teachable, and eager to grow in his knowledge (v. 26). How can we imitate his example?

Chapter 19

1. The advance of the gospel faces many obstacles and enemies. There is incomplete knowledge, a situation in which people know enough to call themselves disciples but lack a full understanding of the gospel and thus also lack spiritual power. There is hardness of heart, whereby the very people one expects to welcome the gospel force the church to separate from them. There is magic and sorcery, which may even try to use "Jesus" as another spiritual force to invoke without knowing the Lord. There is idolatry so deeply embedded in society that it drives the economy. There is persecution that can threaten the lives of Christians with violent mobs. Nevertheless we read, "So mightily grew the word of God and prevailed" (v. 20). God's Word carries God's power to accomplish God's purposes. How can that encourage those who preach and teach the Bible?

2. Materialism is a false god that must be renounced if we are to follow Christ. For the Ephesians, repentance required destroying books of sorcery that had cost an enormous amount of money (v. 19), but the Christians took the loss in order to honor Christ. On the other hand, the love of money turned the silversmiths into violent enemies of the church, even though they pretended to act in religious zeal (vv. 25–31). What place does money hold in your heart relative to Christ? How do you know?

Chapter 20

1. Paul's ministry did not hold back anything that would truly profit his people (v. 20). He imparted to them the whole counsel of God (v. 27) from beginning to end, for all

God's truth is profitable (2 Tim. 3:16). He did not skip over difficult doctrines or hard sayings, nor did he leave out sweet comforts and encouraging exhortations. We may be tempted to be imbalanced and to avoid certain teachings of Scripture, but this comes from pride and self-love instead of serving in love for God and our neighbor. In contrast, Paul did not love his own life but gave his complete devotion to being faithful to the Word. How is he an example for pastors and teachers? How is he an example for us all?

2. Paul was concerned about "grievous wolves" entering the flock and not sparing it (v. 29). Though God will save His elect from damnation and Christ will preserve His church on earth, local congregations and even groups of churches can be ruined by false teaching. Therefore we must guard against it and encourage our elders to do the same. Why is it difficult to oppose false teachers? Why is it crucial?

Chapter 21

1. What a beautiful prayer meeting on the shore (v. 5). Do you think the children, at least the older ones, ever forgot kneeling there with the apostle Paul as he was heading to Jerusalem to suffer for the gospel's sake? Why is it good to send off friends with prayer?

2. Mnason of Cyprus, known as "an old disciple," opened his house to Paul (v. 16). What are the blessings of following Christ for a long time into old age? They must have enjoyed sweet fellowship in Mnason's home. What blessings does it bring to show hospitality to traveling missionaries and pastors?

3. As in the riot in Ephesus (19:29–41), the mob in Jerusalem was full of confusion (21:30–34), acting rashly in violence on the basis of false information (vv. 28–29). Why is it foolish to join an angry mob? What is a better alternative for addressing wrongs?

Chapter 22

1. When God converts us, even if we are in a crowd, it is as though He leads us apart and speaks to us personally. His words enter our minds and hearts in a way that may leave others untouched and cold. Conversion is God's sovereign work in the individual soul. It glorifies Him for us to reflect upon our conversions, whether dramatic or quiet, and to tell others of the work of our Savior. Has God saved you? If so, how does your conversion manifest the glory of His sovereign grace?

2. Paul loved those who were his people according to the flesh. He would have died for his fellow Jews if this would have saved them (Rom. 9:1–3). Even after they unjustly seized him and beat him he did not curse them but lovingly told them about the Savior of both Jew and Gentile. Do you have a burden for those who do not know Christ? What can you do with that burden?

Chapter 23

1. Paul was in prison for the hope of Israel. Already a Pharisee, he had believed there was such a thing as a resurrection, though he did not believe that Christ had been raised until He appeared to him on the road to Damascus. It was then that he came to understand that Christ fulfilled Old Testament prophecy and that Jesus Himself was the hope of Israel.

Jeremiah called God Himself "the hope of Israel" (Jer. 14:8; 17:13), and when Paul met Christ he lost all hope in himself and saw Christ as his only hope. Why is the future resurrection that Christ will bring the center of the hope of believers?

2. Christ appeared to Paul to assure him that he would testify not only in Jerusalem but also in Rome (v. 11). Paul's work was not yet done. Even though people plotted his death day and night, Christ's Word could not be undone. God predestined not only the sufferings of His Son to purchase redemption but also the success of His servants to proclaim redemption so that the nations would believe. While we do not know God's specific decree for our future, how can recognizing His sovereignty give us confidence in serving Him?

Chapter 24

1. Paul held before all his hearers the truth of the resurrection of the dead, "both of the just and unjust" (v. 15). It is a solemn truth that we will rise again, and all souls that ever lived will be in one or the other group: righteous or wicked. Felix trembled when he heard of "righteousness, temperance, and judgment to come" (v. 25), but he did not repent. Why is it not enough to feel guilt over sin and fear over the judgment day? What did Felix lack in order to be saved?

2. One reason Paul could speak so boldly and freely before all men when Felix trembled before God was that Paul's mindset was "to have always a conscience void to offence toward God, and toward men" (v. 16). Proverbs 28:1 says, "The wicked flee when no man pursueth: but the righteous are bold as a lion." Obviously Paul was a sinner, but he sought daily cleansing for his sins and grace to live righteously and

holily by grace. Why does living with a clear conscience give courage? How can we do this?

Chapter 25

1. Though Paul was in prison for the sake of the gospel, the Word of God was not bound. Paul's sorrows became doorways for the gospel to come to rulers and judges. Though they came in great pomp and show of their power and wealth, they were desperately needy sinners who would soon face death, after which would come judgment. When persecution brings God's people before rulers and judges, let us remember that the Lord Jesus rules over all for the sake of spreading the gospel to all people. How should this change the way we view our trials? In what way should it make us alert for evangelistic opportunities?

2. Paul's accusers had many and grievous complaints against Paul, but "they could not prove" them (v. 7). Christ's faithful servants mirror the righteousness of their Lord, although imperfectly, and thus even the world must admit that they have done nothing worthy of the persecution they endure. If you were brought to trial before men, could they find you guilty of no other crime than being a faithful Christian?

Chapter 26

1. Verse 18 gives us a short but rich summary of the true conversion Christ works through the preaching of the gospel. What does this verse teach us about the nature of conversion? What does it teach about its happy effects?

2. Agrippa knew much about the Scriptures (v. 3), being an expert in all sorts of matters relating to the Jews. He is said

to have believed the prophets (v. 27), which means he must have given intellectual assent to the Bible. Nevertheless, he would not bow under the Christ of the Scriptures. Yet he said, "Almost thou persuadest me" (v. 28). He remained tragically blind, unrepentantly clinging to sin and remaining a part of the kingdom of Satan (v. 18). "Almost Christians" end up in hell. Only those who submit entirely to the righteousness of God in Christ, abandoning all hope of being saved by any other means, will be saved. What might it look like to be an "almost Christian" today? What does this text say to such people?

Chapter 27

1. We need to be careful not to draw conclusions from providence. "Fair weather" providences do not mean that it is always good to move ahead as we plan. Nor do "stormy" providences necessarily mean we are doomed to fail. Our faith and duty must not take their direction from the shifting winds of providence but from the unchanging promises of God. Why is it dangerous to take today's providence as tomorrow's promise?

2. On this ship Paul was strikingly unlike Jonah, the Old Testament prophet who followed the path of disobedience. In that situation the sailors almost lost their lives because of him (Jonah 1:6); now the sailors were saved because of Paul (v. 24). Jonah hid, sleeping, below deck until the pagan sailors roused him, but Paul gave leadership and encouragement through his words and prayers. When trials come, how are we tempted to be like Jonah? How ought we to be like Paul?

3. The church of Christ sometimes seems doomed to sink beneath the waves of its troubles, but the Lord Jesus still rules the seas. Paul's troubles in the ship seemed to threaten his mission to Rome but instead proved to be an opportunity to demonstrate God's power and love to 276 people in a way they would never forget. How can that encourage the church in its mission to the world?

Chapter 28

The Gospel of Luke started in rural Judaea, after the emperor had compelled the people to register for taxes, unwittingly bringing the unborn Christ to the place where the Scriptures had foretold His birth. The book of Acts ends in the heart of the Roman Empire, with God's servant boldly preaching Christ and His kingdom in the city of Caesar. From beginning to end the writings of Luke testify that God is fulfilling His decree concerning the Savior. Nothing could stop the complete accomplishment of redemption by Christ's death and resurrection, and nothing can stop the preaching of the gospel to all nations—not even a poisonous snakebite on a missionary's hand. It is not pagan gods or luck that rules over this world but the triune God. This does not permit us to be foolish or fail to use God's appointed means, but it does teach us to serve Christ with confidence. How does the closing scene of Acts encourage you about the future of the kingdom of Jesus Christ? What is your standing in relationship to Christ and His kingdom?

Romans

Chapter 1

1. All true ministers of Christ are separated unto the gospel (v. 1), and the church must devote itself to the preaching of the good news. Do not be ashamed of the gospel (v. 16) nor of its doctrinal content (6:17). There is no gospel without the announcement of God's gift of righteousness through faith in Jesus Christ (1:17) and the realities of sin and God's wrath (v. 18; 1 John 4:10). The church must declare both His love and justice.

2. If men do not love God, they will not love their neighbors (v. 18). Ungodliness and unrighteousness go together. Those who give away God in exchange for idols will find that God gives them over to many sins, including homosexual lusts and practices. When God gives a people over to sin (vv. 24, 26, 28), it is as though they are blinded at noonday. How is that spiritual and moral blindness evident in the world around you today?

3. Before Paul explains in detail the good news of salvation, he details the guilt and misery of sin. Why must we know God's justice and wrath against sin if we are ever to know the saving mercy of Jesus Christ? How does this gospel of justice against sin and grace to sinners promote true gratitude and enduring love for God?

Chapter 2

1. The unbelieving Jews convinced themselves that they were not really sinners in God's sight by comparing themselves to Gentiles. Do you try to evade the reality of your guilt before God by comparing yourself with others rather than by assessing yourself against the standard of God's law? Why does this kind of comparison fail to excuse our sins?

2. Those who do not hear the gospel are still condemned as guilty sinners (v. 12). Otherwise, the preaching of the gospel would be best avoided, as exposure to it would risk making innocent people guilty. The evangelistic imperative rests on the fact that all who are without Christ are lost, and "how shall they believe in him of whom they have not heard?" (10:14). How should this motivate Christians to spread the gospel?

3. The Lord will judge the "secrets of men" (v. 16), even what is hidden from those closest to us. Having a Bible and knowing its contents, while good, is not enough (vv. 17–18). People may think highly of us and praise our devotion to God, but that devotion is meaningless unless God sees evidence of His saving work in our hearts (v. 29; see John 5:44). How should these truths drive us to seek Christ?

Chapter 3

1. No amount of human consensus can overturn the truth of God (v. 4). The final appeal for Christians is not any national court or international convention, nor the court of public opinion, but the Word of God. Also, the false conclusions of others do not justify rejection of the truth (v. 5). The truth of the Bible must be believed. Sinners will always want

a gospel that allows them to continue in sin (v. 8), but the apostle Paul draws out the unbeliever from every false refuge, whether trust in a name or ordinances (v. 1), or in false reasoning (vv. 5–8). Have you given up all your excuses and arguments and submitted to God's Word as your ultimate authority?

2. Christ is the object of our faith; our own believing cannot be. We must look outside ourselves to Christ (v. 22). The Old Testament testifies that we must look to Christ (v. 21). Our only hope of righteousness is not in our works of obeying God's law (v. 20) but in Christ's work of redeeming sinners at the cost of His precious blood (vv. 24–25). Christ alone can satisfy God's justice directed against sinners and appease His righteous wrath against those who dishonor Him (vv. 25–26). Anyone, Jew or Gentile, who trusts in Christ alone is declared righteous by the supreme Judge (vv. 22, 30). Thus the Lord says to all who hear the gospel, "Behold me, behold me" (Isa. 65:1). Have you cast aside your self-righteousness and received and rested upon Christ as your only righteousness before God?

Chapter 4

1. Abraham believed the gospel (John 8:56; Gal. 3:8, 17), as did Moses (Heb. 11:24–26) and David (Ps. 32). There has only been one way of salvation for any sinner since the fall of man in the garden of Eden (Gen. 3:15), and there will be only this one way until the end of the world (Rev. 22:17). Only in Christ is there acceptance with God. We must trust in the one Seed, Jesus Christ, in whom many of Abraham's literal seed and sinners from all nations are blessed (Gal. 3:16).

2. Even the greatness of your sins does not exclude you from the promise of mercy. God justifies the ungodly (v. 5) who trust in Christ. You must not "stagger" at the promise of God. Do not say "I do not know whom to believe" because you should know. You must believe God (2 Tim. 1:12). Take your great sins to God and seek forgiveness in Christ. Tell Him your great need, as David did: "For thy name's sake, O LORD, pardon mine iniquity; for it is great" (Ps. 25:11). He has purposed to make Himself known as the God of grace (Rom. 9:23; Eph. 3:9–10). Why do sinners sometimes shrink back from trusting Christ? How can this chapter encourage them to come without delay?

3. Believing glorifies God (v. 20) by acknowledging His power and truthfulness: He can and will perform what He has promised in accordance with His love for His people and His justice in accepting them for Christ's sake. Honor God by trusting Him.

Chapter 5

1. Do you have peace with God (v. 1)? This is not a question of your feelings but of your objective standing before God. Only when you have been forgiven and declared righteous through faith in Christ can you experience "the peace of God, which passeth all understanding" (Phil. 4:7).

2. Glorying in tribulations is no easy thing, even for a strong believer. We must take to heart the truth of God's providential government over all of our circumstances and trust His wisdom, power, and promised grace, which ensure that all things work for our good. Only then will we be able to accept that those things that seem to harm us are actually still sent

for our good (2 Cor. 12:7–10). We must also rest our hearts upon the righteousness of God in Christ. Why is a sense of peace with God necessary in order for us to glory in trials?

3. Christianity is not just a set of principles for living but a claim about history. This chapter presupposes that Adam was a literal and historical individual. Genesis 1:1–3:24 must be understood that way if we are to make sense of Romans 5. We see, also, the importance of the virgin birth. Christ was not, in His human nature, descended from Adam by ordinary generation, and so the guilt of Adam's first transgression was not imputed to Him under the covenant of works. This means that, as the perfectly guiltless Mediator of the covenant of grace, He can act as the substitute for His people. (2 Cor. 5:21). Why do the faith and hope of Christians stand or fall on the historical reality of these two persons, Adam and Christ?

Chapter 6

1. People often love to talk about the privileges of God's children, but they may neglect to realize that union with Christ means that we have died and risen with Him. This must show itself in our lives. Though justification is entirely through faith, true faith brings the effects of Christ's cross into our lives to crucify the old self. How then can believers continue comfortably in sin? His resurrection overflows by the Spirit into each of those for whom He died and brings to life a person who loves God. How then can believers fail to live for Him? How is a person who claims to be one with Christ and yet lives for sin and is dead toward God a stark contradiction?

2. We all serve someone (v. 16). If it is the world, the flesh, and the Devil, the idea that this is true freedom is an illusion. Sinners are in fact slaves of their own thoughts and desires (Titus 3:3). However, salvation in Christ does not set us free to live for ourselves, for this is the very slavery we must escape. When God joins a sinner to Christ, that sinner becomes a willing slave of Christ to do His righteous will. Serving Christ is true freedom (John 8:36). Why is this so? Are you a slave of Christ?

Chapter 7

1. The law reveals to us our sin and therefore our need for Christ, the Savior of sinners (v. 7; Mark 10:17–21; John 4:16–18; Acts 2:36–37). Conviction of sin alone is not conversion to Christ. The holy law can be like sunshine on a stagnant pond that makes it stink even worse than before (Rom. 7:8–13). Felix trembled but was not converted (Acts 24:25). Nevertheless, there can be no trusting in Christ to save us if we are oblivious to the sin from which we must be saved. How has God's law uncovered your sin? How has it helped you to see your need for Christ?

2. If we are in Christ, the battle is not over but the victory is sure (v. 25). He has purchased our sanctification and glorification, as well as our justification (8:1–39). However, we cannot ignore the experiential struggle in the Christian's soul between what is ideal and what is actual. Godly believers are often deeply frustrated over their lack of conformity to God's holy commands. While they need to be encouraged to press on in the battle, they also need to be comforted with the truth that this is the normal experience of believers on earth.

How might losing sight of this truth lead to deep discouragement? How might it lead to hypocrisy and superficiality in the church?

Chapter 8

1. Knowing the law, on its own, will not eradicate the love for sin (v. 3). Walking in the Spirit, however, is not some mystical experience; rather, this occurs when the Spirit of God fills our hearts with loving gratitude to God for His love in Christ and we express that by fulfilling God's law (v. 4). As children of a good Father, believers realize that sin never does them any good (v. 13) but that the ways of God are life and peace (v. 6). All their lives are in His loving hands, and He will bring His adopted children to the glory of His Son (vv. 28–29). How do these truths motivate you to love and obey God?

2. To call God "Father" (v. 15) is an immense privilege. The divine love behind this word is breathtaking. God did not spare His only begotten Son but gave Him up so that sinners thereby might have God. God adopted His enemies as His children, and He gives them His Spirit to stir them to call Him Abba, or Father. Why are we so reluctant to draw near to Him? How can Rom. 8 encourage us to be more faithful and fervent in prayer?

Chapter 9

1. The strength of Paul's expression of compassion for the lost (vv. 1–3) may startle us; it should. We are to love our neighbors as ourselves. If we care about not going to hell ourselves, how can we be indifferent to our neighbors being

on the broad road that leads to destruction? How does this challenge you to pray and to take action?

2. God is absolutely sovereign over the will of men. Even sinful acts, though God does not condone them (nor is He the author of sin), are included in the plan of God (Gen. 50:20; 2 Sam. 16:9–11; 2 Chron. 18:20–22; Ps. 76:10). Even the fact that the holy angels did not fall is based on God's sovereign election (1 Tim. 5:21). We should believe the doctrine of God's sovereign predestination on the testimony of Holy Scripture (Rom. 9:12–13, 15, 17). It is not incompatible with evangelistic concern (vv. 1–3), however difficult it may seem to reconcile the two. How can trusting that God is in control give us confidence and freedom to faithfully proclaim the gospel?

3. We should not try to guess whom, among the unconverted, are God's elect. "Front-runners" can remain unregenerate, whereas "unpromising candidates" may come to faith in Christ (vv. 30–31). How should this encourage us to preach the gospel to all kinds of people?

Chapter 10

1. Paul's prayer (v. 1) indicates both his belief that salvation is in God's hands and his compassion toward the unbelieving. There is no contradiction here (Acts 26:29). Nor are there valid excuses for unbelief (Rom. 10:6–9). You have a Bible in your hand to read. It is your duty to believe. And there is within it every encouragement to trust Christ. He is rich (v. 12) to all who do believe, bestowing upon them such great mercies as forgiveness of sin, peace with God, and the hope of glory for all who do so (Ps. 86:5). How should

this encourage evangelism? How should this impress upon all who hear the gospel their need to trust in Christ?

2. The preaching of the gospel is vital as the means appointed by the sovereign God for the ingathering of His elect (vv. 13–15). We have no divine authorization from Scripture to believe that people dying without the knowledge of God's Word will be saved by some other means (Acts 4:12). Sinners must believe in Christ in order to be saved, and they must hear the gospel in order to believe. How should this motivate churches and seminaries to train and send out laborers to preach the gospel everywhere on earth? How can you help?

Chapter 11

1. The apostle treats David's prayer for God's punishment on the wicked (Ps. 69:22–23) as the Word of God (Rom. 11:9–10) as surely as the prophecies of Christ's sufferings in that Psalm (Ps. 69:9, 20–21), and so should we. We should read and sing such psalms without embarrassment. If we have a problem with them, the problem lies in our minds and hearts, not in the Word of God.

2. The gospel has come to us in our various nations, but it was not always so (Acts 14:16). We should be thankful to God, for He did not owe us the gospel! When was the last time you thanked God that you have heard the good news? How can the last four verses of this chapter help you to worship God for His saving plans?

3. Though Christians debate God's future plans for the physical descendants of Abraham, Isaac, and Jacob (v. 25), we should all join Paul in praying for their conversion (10:1).

Let us devote ourselves to praying "that the kingdom of sin and Satan may be destroyed, the gospel propagated throughout the world, the Jews called, the fullness of the Gentiles brought in…that Christ would rule in our hearts here, and hasten the time of his second coming, and our reigning with him forever…" (Westminster Larger Catechism, A. 191). Do you pray for these things? If not, why not?

Chapter 12

1. When we have experienced something of the misery of our sin along with the deliverance given in Jesus Christ, our hearts will respond with the love of true gratitude. This is the practical fruit of the gospel: "What shall I render unto the LORD for all his benefits toward me?" (Ps. 116:12). Rather than yearning to fit in with the world, we are to devote the whole of our lives, mind and body, to learning and doing God's will. How can the Christian live as a priest, offering every day as a sacrifice to God?

2. Real love must express itself in service. For this cause God gave various spiritual gifts to empower His people to serve. However, rather than waiting with anxiety until we know what our gifts are, God calls us to give ourselves to the life of a servant of God, cheerfully and fervently caring for each other. How do you serve?

3. The key to combating vengefulness is to know our place before God. He is the Judge; we are not. When people wrong us, let us remember that it is not about our honor but about the glory of God. How can the Lord's statement "Vengeance is mine; I will repay" (v. 19) set us free from any impulse to take personal vengeance in word or deed?

Chapter 13

1. Our duty to civil authority should be determined by God-given biblical principle, not by the degree of our fear of getting caught in an infraction (v. 5). Though people around us may neither give honor to authority nor exercise authority in an honorable way, Christians must be people who conscientiously honor authority because they honor God. What would that have meant for Christians in pagan Rome? What about for you?

2. We need God's law to tell us how to love (vv. 8–10). There is no conflict between law and love. Love is a command, and the Ten Commandments show us in greater detail what that means. The Old Testament taught love, even to our enemies (Ex. 23:4–5). There is no difference in moral standards between the testaments, though the same standard is more fully revealed in the New Testament.

Chapter 14

1. We should rebuke blatant sin and rebellion (Lev. 19:17) but exercise restraint and gentleness toward those young in the faith and those who need encouragement in the ways of the Lord, rather than condemning them for every defect arising from ignorance or a misguided conscience. This is not a compromising of holiness but an exercise of it, for the essence of holiness is love. What kinds of issues does the church face today where some are bound by conscience in matters not commanded in Scripture, while others are free? How should they bear with each other in mutual love and respect?

2. We should never disturb the peace of the church except over a matter of real and vital principle (v. 19). Rather than

crusading for our own views in matters of minor importance, we should be zealous for peace. We should also seek greater illumination of our brother's minds and consciences through prayer and the Word, for coercing people into conformity without real conviction is a hollow victory. In what ways does this principle require a great deal of patience toward other Christians?

Chapter 15

1. The attitude that says "It's my life; I'll please myself" is ungodly and inconsistent with a sense of dependence upon and gratitude to the Lord Jesus Christ (vv. 1–3). It is also contradictory to the mission of Christ, for He came to unite all nations in the praise of God for His faithfulness and mercy. Why is selfishness so divisive to the church and so destructive to its calling?

2. Emotion is part of Christian experience (v. 13). Feeling does not determine truth, but it is involved in a right reaction to truth. The Christian has distinctive sorrows over sin (2 Cor. 7:9–10) and joys in God (Rom. 5:11) that come from believing. How can Christians cultivate a biblical emotional life? What role does the Holy Spirit play?

3. Paul's heart beat to bring the gospel to those who had never heard the name of Jesus. Though a remarkably gifted theologian and preacher, his calling did not allow him to settle in to a stable school or church but propelled him outward to the nations. Not everyone has such a calling, but the church as a whole still has a responsibility to preach the gospel to all creation. How do you pray for and support those called to bring the gospel?

Chapter 16

1. The closing chapter of Romans reminds us that the church does not consist only of the great leaders like Paul but of many people serving in their own unique capacities. We find a great example in Priscilla and Aquila (vv. 3–5), who are always found at full stretch for the cause of the gospel. How can we follow in their faith? If Paul had mentioned you in this chapter, how might he have described you?

2. Heretics are not to be trifled with (vv. 17–19). Christian love does not condone letting the wolves loose among the flock. "Avoid them" (v. 17). If more Christians did this, there would be greater unity among those who do love the Lord and His truth. Why is heresy so destructive?

3. The gospel begins in the mind of God and is revealed to men, not deduced by them. It is God who sends it freely to sinners, whose accountability it is to receive it. If we have been privileged to hear this joyful sound and Spirit-enabled to believe in Christ, we are blessed indeed. God's glorious attributes, such as His eternity and wisdom (vv. 26–27), shine through in the gospel. Take some time to praise God for the glorious gospel of Christ revealed in this great epistle.

1 Corinthians

Chapter 1

1. Meditate upon God's objective act of setting you apart in Christ Jesus. If you have been sanctified in Christ, what are the ramifications and implications of that reality for your daily life, family life, and church life?

2. Do you consistently find hope and satisfaction in the gospel of Christ's life, death, and resurrection? What are warning signs that someone is being taken up with or enamored by the wisdom of this world?

3. We are all boasters. Paul does not rebuke the Corinthian church for boasting or glorying, but for boasting and glorying in the wrong thing. Do you consciously boast in God's saving work and His grace in sending His own Son to the cross, or are you glorying in your own talents, gifts, and graces?

Chapter 2

1. This chapter teaches the necessity of the Holy Spirit's work in illuminating you to discern the gospel. If you are a believer in Christ, why should that truth motivate you to praise God?

2. Paul says that those who have received the Spirit are able to judge all things. Do you live daily in the awareness that the Spirit guides you? How can you evaluate all things in the light of the Spirit's ministry in your life?

3. Pray for the help of the Holy Spirit each time you open the Word, asking for guidance as you meditate on the Word, both personally and with family.

Chapter 3

1. How do you view your minister? Do you pray for the minister(s) that God has given to you?

2. Talk through the significance of what it means that all things belong to believers in Christ (v. 22) and how that corrects worldly notions of entitlement.

3. If believers are the temple of God corporately, how should we live our lives? Pursuing holiness does not just benefit individuals, but has a corporate effect.

Chapter 4

1. Consider your daily need of grace to grow in godliness. Learn from Paul's warning to the Corinthian church that we will not ever be at a place in this life where we can say, "I have finally arrived spiritually." What reminders have you had lately that you have not yet arrived?

2. Consider in your mind and with your family that all you and they have and are comes from God, and praise Him for His goodness and kindness.

Chapter 5

1. Consider the sobering effects of sin. What are some examples of how sin not only affects the one who commits the sin, but also those who are connected to him or her, both family and church?

2. Meditate on the guilt-removing and life-transforming work of Christ's sacrifice. He is the true Passover, or Deliverer from bondage. If you are in Christ, things are fundamentally different. This reality ought to be remembered daily and depended upon experientially.

Chapter 6

1. If there has been a wrong done, how do you pursue reconciliation with another believer in your church or another member in your family?

2. How does the believer's union with Christ affect his or her daily living? Chapter 6 works out in detail the relationship between doctrine and practice. Paul draws the reader's attention to objective truths, or indicatives: you have been washed, you have been sanctified, you have been justified, your bodies are members of Christ, and your body is the temple of the Holy Ghost. He then gives a command: flee fornication. What is the relationship between what you are in Christ and the importance of purity?

Chapter 7

1. The grace of Christian contentment pervades Paul's entire argument. Are you enjoying contentment in your current calling? If single, are you content? If married, are you contentedly relating to your spouse in selfless ways?

2. God's providential orchestration of your circumstances is His will for you. How do you factor in God's providence in your decision-making process?

Chapter 8

1. How do you view Christian liberty? As something that you have to do? Do you couple your knowledge regarding liberties with love for the brethren?

2. If Christ died for the believer with a weak conscience, how should we view such a person? The reality of the atonement ought to govern and dictate how believers view each other.

3. Consider all that you know by God's grace. Why is it important that your knowledge be coupled with love?

Chapter 9

1. Do you love your liberties more than you love your brothers? Paul openly acknowledged the liberties and rights he had as an apostle and minister of the gospel. Yet, he was willing to set his liberties aside for the sake of something greater, the gospel of Jesus Christ.

2. Are you running the Christian race? If so, how does the Christian race play itself out in your life and in the lives of your family? How are you showing that the gospel of Jesus Christ reigns supreme in your affections as you seek to run the race before you?

Chapter 10

1. Paul applies the Old Testament history to our lives to show the importance of persevering in the faith. It is not enough to experience the external benefits of the visible church. There must be the experiential application of God's grace in the soul. Reflect on how a spiritual privilege is not the same as a spiritual possession.

2. Paul encourages discernment (determining the spiritual profit of a thing) and love (determining whether something builds up) in deciding questions relating to liberty. How does this work itself out in your life and in the life of your family? How does God's glory and others' good play into the exercise of what you do and do not do?

Chapter 11

1. When you come to the house of God for corporate worship, how you conduct yourself matters. Paul argues for proper decorum in public worship according to God's created order. When you enter His house for worship, how should you act in a way that honors the glory and will of the Lord?

2. God has blessed His people with wonderful tokens of His love such as the Lord's Supper. Here Christians celebrate the union they have with Christ and with one another in Christ. This is a time for self-examination and is therefore serious. It is a sign and seal of Christ's atoning work by which the believer is nourished and strengthened in his faith in God's promises.

Chapter 12

1. God graciously gives gifts to each of His children. He sovereignly decides who receives what gift and how many. Often Christians become discouraged because they do not have the same gift as someone else. Others can become proud because of the gifts that they have as though they earned them. God's sovereign giving of gifts should evoke praise and thanksgiving rather than discouragement, and instill humility because the gifts were granted according to God's will and not the

receiver's merit. When considering your gift, do so with a God-centered perspective rather than a self-centered one.

2. Paul highlights the unity of the church in his discussion of the spiritual gifts. He describes this unity by reminding believers that when one suffers, all suffer. And when one is honored, all rejoice. In many ways, it is easier to suffer alongside another who is suffering. It is not always easy to rejoice when another is honored. What is your response when someone else is honored and you feel overlooked? Are you able to rejoice with them? How can we dissipate envying and jealousy in our churches and in our homes?

Chapter 13

1. Love is to govern all of our motives. Examine whether all you say, know, and do is governed by love. What sins against love do you need to confess?

2. Paul describes love in various action verbs. It has often been said that we can replace the word "charity" with the name "Christ" and see more clearly God's grace to us in His Son. Christ acts toward us in all these ways. It is only through Christ that you will ever be able to have and show true love.

Chapter 14

1. Within the context of prophecy and tongues, Paul highlights the importance of decent and orderly worship. When the church gathers in God's presence, believers are to engage in worship seriously and reverently. How do Paul's exhortations in this chapter teach you how to frame your focus when you enter into God's house?

2. As you consider your spiritual gifts, is your focus more on the gift from a self-centered perspective or from the perspective of love for the brethren and desire to edify, encourage, and build up the brethren? How can you put your gifts to work in a way that glorifies God and edifies the body?

Chapter 15

1. The New Testament writers often pointed believers to the hope of the resurrection. The reality of Christ's bodily resurrection assures them that God the Father accepted the sacrifice made by God the Son. Because Jesus Christ was raised, dear believer, you can know with certainty that sin no longer holds dominion over you. The risen Lord reigns and rules over all, and all things have been put under His feet. How can you make sure you don't live as those who are "of all men most miserable" (v. 19)?

2. Because Jesus was raised and all those in Him will one day receive a body like His glorified body, your labors are not in vain. Consider how this truth should motivate you as you live before God each day in all the various spheres of service God has called you to: in the home, in the church, in the workplace.

Chapter 16

1. The collection for the saints in Jerusalem reminds us that the church of Jesus Christ is one church. Throughout the book Paul focuses on unity within the local church. It is not just the local church that is to be one, but also the universal, visible church. While it is not possible to meet every need of every believer in the world, Christians ought to have a

broader vision of the kingdom of God on earth and seek to help in any way they are able. In what ways can you and your family meet needs outside your own local church?

2. The words "Anathema" (cursed by God) and "Maran-atha" (our Lord is coming) (v. 22) bring us to the very edge of eternity. Ask yourself which word applies to you. The great line of division is between those who love Christ and those who do not. Believer, Christ bore your curse and now you long for His coming. Unbeliever, the curse is still resting upon you. You need to repent and seek Christ or He will appear as your justly condemning Judge.

2 Corinthians

Chapter 1

1. When you put your trials—past and present—next to what Paul says here, can you see any purpose, comfort, or mercy in your afflictions?

2. One result of experiencing the comfort of God is that you are able to provide comfort to others in their trials. Enduring trials and experiencing God's comfort should make you more sensitive to the afflictions of those around you. Do you know someone suffering as you once did? How can you help?

3. Paul defended his travel plans to those in Corinth. The assumptions made against Paul are shocking. Instead of thinking the best—that there would be some legitimate reason to move the apostle to change his plans—some accused him of being fickle, untrustworthy, and worldly. This should cause us to pause and evaluate how quickly we also assume the worst. Are you more prone to think the worst or the best of others?

Chapter 2

1. Discipline is necessary for the restoration of an erring brother or sister and for the purity of the church. Paul encourages Christians to use discernment and a balance between confrontation and forgiveness. He reminds us that Satan is always looking for an advantage. How do you respond to sin that you see in yourself, in others at church, and in your family members?

2. The message of the gospel is an aroma to all who hear its proclamation. To those who embrace the gospel, it is a sweet fragrance of life unto life. To those who reject it, the gospel is a stench of death unto death. Where do you stand in relation to its message?

Chapter 3

1. Paul's attention to the superiority of the new covenant glory comes to a climax by celebrating the reality that all those who believe can behold Jesus Christ with uncovered faces. This is a remarkable and amazing benefit. Paul says that there are those even today who still read Moses with veiled hearts. One can perform religious duties and even be identified with the church, but there must be faith in order to see Christ as He is. Do you have faith to see the spiritual glory of Christ? What does it mean to experience this saving privilege?

2. The great freedom of the gospel is the access a believer has to gaze upon Christ by faith through the help of the Spirit. The result of this gaze is greater conformity to the image of Jesus Christ. People become like that which they gaze upon or see. How does this motivate you to diligently use the ordinary means of grace such as preaching? What should we pray as we prepare to worship with the church?

Chapter 4

1. God is sovereign in salvation. Through the preaching of the gospel (general call) God commands the light of the glorious gospel of Christ to shine in the hearts of some hearers (effectual call). Have you experienced the gospel in your heart, or do you continue to have your eyes blinded by

Satan? Experiencing the light of the gospel brings you to the knowledge of the glory of God in the face of Jesus Christ.

2. The Bible teaches about different kinds of suffering. There is suffering because of sin (David and Bathsheba). There is suffering because of someone else's sin (Achan). There is suffering for the sake of righteousness (Paul). There is suffering when the cause is not immediately discernible (Job). Paul's words here apply most directly to the latter two kinds of suffering. The only way to consider real and deep affliction as light is to see them compared to the weight of eternal glory. As you go through hardships in your life, seek God's grace to suffer well and to have an eternal perspective, focusing on those things that are not seen and are eternal.

Chapter 5

1. Meditate on the future realities of the gospel. Have you learned by grace to groan to be clothed with a glorified body? Take time to consider and meditate upon all that awaits the children of God. If you have the Spirit, all this is yours in earnest already.

2. Chapter 5 closes with one of the most succinctly stated summaries of the gospel. God made Christ to be sin for His people. Sinners receive the righteousness of Christ by faith. Have you rested in the gospel? Do you know experientially what it is to be counted as righteous in God's eyes? If so, celebrate the reconciliation that is found in Christ. If you have received that reconciliation, like Paul, how can you help others to be reconciled to Him?

Chapter 6

1. This chapter addresses the qualifications of a genuine ministry in contrast to a false ministry. How can the truths presented here instruct you in praying for your minister and other church officers in personal and family times of prayer?

2. Associations matter to God. Because you have received reconciliation with God it is contradictory to remain in close association with unbelievers and have your life influenced by your former way of life. In what ways should Christians give careful attention to their associations?

Chapter 7

1. How Christians live matters to God. In the Bible there are many motivations for pursuing holiness. Gratitude for God's grace is a chief motivation. So are the promises of God. Paul appeals to God's covenantal promise to be your God and to receive you as His sons and daughters. Being a child of God ought to affect and influence your behavior. Children often look and act like their parents. How do things stand with you?

2. When sin is confronted in your life, do you experience a sorrow for getting caught, or is there a sorrow for offending God that leads to repentance? The Christian life is one of perpetual repentance. There should be constant turning from sin unto Christ. Are you grateful that God granted you repentance to seek Him for grace to lead a life pleasing to Him? While dealing with sin is hard, a repentance that leads to salvation is never regrettable.

Chapter 8

1. The truth of the gospel ought to motivate us on many levels. To think how Christ gave of Himself (v. 9) should make us ready to give of ourselves and our possessions. How should this motivate your giving?

2. Paul takes great care to remain above reproach in the matter of the collection. He knows that there might be some in Corinth suspicious of how Paul was handling the monetary funds. Instead of dismissing such suspicions as unfounded, he goes the extra mile to take precautions. How should this example direct you?

Chapter 9

1. Take time to praise God for the privilege to give. If you have children, teach them by precept and example that giving is in response to God's gifts. In times of corporate worship, be mindful that the time devoted to giving is to be an act of worship, not an intermission during worship.

2. Paul concludes his discussion on the collection with a prayer of praise to God for His indescribable gift. One of the remarkable characteristics of the apostle Paul is that he sees Christ in and behind everything. Pray to God for such a view of Christ—both His person and work—and that you never lose the wonder of God's grace in giving His only begotten Son. "Thanks be unto God for his unspeakable gift" (v. 15)!

Chapter 10

1. We live in a day not much different from Paul's day in Corinth. It is easy to evaluate ministers by their charisma and appearance. Yet what matters is God's call in their life.

How do you view your minister? Do you love him and pray for him, or do you compare him with leaders or preachers who are more well known?

2. Paul reminds his readers of the real battle that is waged in this life (vv. 3–5). Give attention to your life and seek after the weapons that through God's might are able to bring every thought captive to the obedience of Jesus Christ. How can you use the spiritual weapons of the Word, prayer, and the ministry of the Spirit to overthrow the imaginations and high things that are against the knowledge of God?

Chapter 11

1. The character and subtlety of false teachers should keep Christians watchful and discerning. The best way to identify the threats of the false teachers is to be convinced of the truthfulness of the gospel and to be single-mindedly devoted to Christ (v. 3). Failing to remain devoted to Christ can make a believer susceptible to the subtle attacks of Satan, the deceiver. How can you be vigilant and jealous to protect your exclusive devotion to Jesus Christ?

2. Paul boasted in his sufferings and in his weakness. Let Paul's boasting cause you to reflect on your own trials and afflictions. He was willing to endure hardships and even face death. It is only as you are captivated by Christ and certain of His love for you that you will have a framework by which to view your own trials properly. Reflect on what it means to be singularly devoted to Christ, even in the midst of trying circumstances.

Chapter 12

1. With one hand God gives thorns to His children, but with the other He gives sufficient grace. Whatever affliction or trial you may be enduring presently, dear believer, be sure to recognize God's sufficient supply of grace as well. Satan may intend to torment you through this thorn, but God means it for your good and His glory. What trials are you facing now? What does it mean to boast in your weaknesses so that Christ's power may be seen?

2. Paul's love to the Corinthians was simply amazing. He wrote in verse 19, "we do all things, dearly beloved, for your edifying." By the Spirit's grace, what means can you use so that you could come closer to being able to say this to your spouse, your children, your parents, and your friends?

Chapter 13

1. Paul closes his letter with a solemn exhortation to examine oneself. He has been scrutinized and forced into a position where he must defend his claim as an apostle of Christ. He asks his readers to scrutinize themselves. It is not enough to be associated with the church of Jesus Christ. You must examine yourself and determine whether you are in Christ or not. What are the marks of a true believer in Christ?

2. All the spiritual blessings you receive come from the love of God the Father, who planned salvation before time began. All blessings come through the grace of Jesus Christ the Mediator, who died to purchase redemption and rose again to apply it to His people. And all blessings are shared within the church by the Holy Spirit. Have you experienced the grace of Christ,

the love of the Father, and the communion of the Holy Spirit? If so, then meditate upon these blessings and pray for God to increase your enjoyment of Him. If not, then turn from your sin in genuine repentance and turn to Christ in faith.

Galatians

Chapter 1

1. The surest protection from the false gospel is a fresh and clear reminder of the true gospel. This Paul does in his opening greeting in verses 3–5, in which he gives a succinct summary of the victorious deliverance that flows from Christ's atoning sacrifice. Meditate on this true gospel, and praise God for it.

2. There can be no compromise with those who pervert the gospel of Christ. Paul not only brands the false gospel as a perversion of the true; he also by inspiration reveals that those who promote another gospel will be damned. Thus there can be no fellowship with such men. Why is separation from preachers of a false gospel absolutely imperative?

3. The conversion of those who were formerly opponents of the gospel brings great glory to the Lord. Paul, the former blasphemer and persecutor, goes into much detail to show the reality of his conversion so that the very people he had persecuted glorified God for the change they saw in him. For what enemies of the gospel do you pray?

Chapter 2

1. The Christian should make every effort to remove all doubts about his or her profession of the gospel. Paul knew that his enemies had slandered him before his fellow apostles; thus when he went to Jerusalem he carefully showed them that he believed and preached the same gospel as

they did. It is always good to remove all suspicion from our names, if possible, remembering that it is only in Christ that believers are justified.

2. Sometimes even the rebuking of a fellow believer is necessary in order to defend the gospel. At Antioch Paul had to withstand Peter because his action in separating from the Gentiles endangered the truth of justification through Christ alone. But Peter did not resent the rebuke, later referring to Paul as a "beloved brother" (2 Peter 3:15). Do you welcome correction and reproof as David did (Ps. 141:5)?

3. Believers live the Christian life in the same manner as they commence it. This is Paul's triumphant assertion in verse 20. The believer is in union with Christ and by faith draws from Him all that is needed to live the life of the believer in a sinful world. Reflect on the all-powerful and ever-fresh gospel of Christ's death for sinners.

Chapter 3

1. It is imperative to guard against all that would take away our confidence in Christ alone in the Christian life. Spiritual growth and maturity are never enhanced by reliance on the efforts of the flesh. How can Christians drift away from complete dependence on Christ?

2. The penalty of the law is its dreadful curse—the sentence of death. Thus, for sinners to be freed from that curse and to be justified before the law that demands it, Christ became a curse for them! Let no child of God ever forget what Christ endured.

3. No sinner is ever justified by the law, but not because there is any fault in the law. The fault lies in the sinner, namely, in his inability to give the perfect obedience the law requires. But the inflexible demands of the law cause it to become a means of bringing the sinner to faith in Christ's perfect obedience by which the law was satisfied. Do you rest in Christ alone for God's acceptance?

Chapter 4

1. Christ's first coming was an astounding miracle, for it was the appearance of the God-man. God sent forth His Son— there is His deity. He was made of a woman— there is His humanity. But the two natures are united in the one person; thus, He is the God-man. Great is the mystery of redemption! Dwell on this truth: "God was manifest in the flesh" (1 Tim. 3:16).

2. We must agonize over those who are endangered by another gospel. Paul had labored hard and suffered much to see the Galatians converted to Christ. But he was prepared to go through labor pains again to see them recovered from the soul-destroying message of the Judaizers. Let us labor by grace to see those who are deluded cast aside the lie. Whom do you know in this position? How do you labor for them?

3. It is vital for the Christian to know the Scriptures. Note Paul's use of the Word of God as he reasons with the Galatians: "Do ye not hear the law?" (v. 21); "For it is written" (v. 22); "Nevertheless what saith the scripture?" (v. 30). Is Scripture the only compass by which you navigate daily?

Chapter 5

1. The Christian's liberty in Christ is the means whereby he stands fast against all that would enslave. The goal of the Enemy is to bring the believer into spiritual bondage, thereby robbing the soul of enjoyment in Christ. But his defense is the very liberty he has in Christ. Christ sets believers free from the law's demand for perfect obedience by giving that perfect obedience on our behalf, forming the basis for their justification and thus the basis for standing fast against all that would enslave. Do you know this struggle personally? To whom do you look for defense and liberty?

2. Christian liberty is freedom from sin and condemnation, and freedom to serve Christ. Some teach that the believer's liberty in Christ is freedom from God's moral law as a direction for how to live, thus granting freedom to indulge fleshly appetites. This antinomian heresy must be resisted vigorously. The liberty to which we have been called is not license to sin but freedom to obey Christ and do His will. Why is it the Christian's liberty to serve others in love?

3. The justified man produces true holiness because he has the Holy Spirit within. Justification is always followed by sanctification; and sanctification is by the Spirit, not by the law. The Spirit is God's gift to the Christian on the basis of the merit of Christ. By the Spirit's work in the heart the believer is made holy, demonstrated by the fruit that the Spirit produces. Why is it crucial that we remember that sanctification is by grace alone?

Chapter 6

1. A ministry of restoration can only be exercised by believers who are spiritually strong. Paul's injunction is that those who are spiritual are to restore the one who is caught off guard and falls into sin. The inference is that the ministry of restoration can only be exercised by believers who themselves are on their guard. One of the marks of spiritual strength is a cautiousness so as to avoid every pit that Satan digs, into which the careless will fall (Jude 23). Should this not move us to pray earnestly that we might be kept from falling?

2. Spiritual increase will come at God's appointed time. Paul states that "in due season we shall reap" (v. 9). The word for "season" refers to a fixed or appointed time, signifying that the Lord has times appointed when spiritual reaping will take place. It is such a truth that actually is the means of keeping us from fainting and growing weary in the lengthy times of sowing the spiritual seed. Ultimately our "harvest time" is Christ's coming. How can you rest more in God's appointed time for all things?

3. The one matter in which the believer may rightfully boast is the work of Christ. Paul repudiates all thoughts of glorying or boasting in anything except "the cross," the finished work of Christ. In that work no man had any part, for Christ alone was qualified to make satisfaction for sin. Therefore, in the work of the cross the believer may boast without sinning. What is it about the cross that excites the Christian to rejoice, exalt, and praise the Lord?

Ephesians

Chapter 1

1. The doctrine of election calls us to Christ. All of election's blessings are in Him. We dare not wait to come to Christ until we first somehow discover that we are elect. John Calvin said that the way to know that God elected us is by believing in Jesus Christ alone for salvation.

2. Election empowers holiness. Since God chose "that we should be holy" (v. 4), we must never isolate election from obeying God's laws. Those who say they can sin freely because they are elect have rejected the God who elects sinners unto holiness. Believers can pursue holiness confident that God's decree will give us all we need in Christ to attain it.

3. Grace fuels heartfelt praise. If your heart is sluggish in the aim for which we were made, it is the amazing grace of the triune God to sinners that you need most of all. Meditate on this chapter, and then make sure you take time to seek His face and sing His praises.

4. The gospel whets our appetite for God. Take Paul's prayer in this chapter and make it into your prayer for yourself and other believers. Stir up your heart with the glory of God's grace to desire to know Him better. Pray fervently for the Spirit of wisdom and revelation to give you more illumination about the riches of Jesus Christ.

Chapter 2

1. The gospel demands humility. What reason do true Christians have to boast? We were dead in sin and distant from God. Satan ruled us, and God's wrath burned against us. If we have spiritual life, it is entirely due to God's grace in Christ. Why then do we look down on others? Who makes us to differ? Let us prostrate ourselves before the Lord Jesus, give all glory to God, and learn the meekness of the dove-like Spirit.

2. Believers are richer than kings. They are joined with none other than Jesus Christ, seated with Him in heavenly places. They are recreated with the risen Christ as their Adam. God will show how great He is by pouring out kindness upon them for all eternity. All of this is by grace through the great sufferings of Christ on the cross. If we are truly saved, we should bless God and sing His praises all our lives.

3. All nations are one at the foot of the cross. Despite our tendency to exalt ourselves and judge others based on race or culture, all believers are one and Christ is all. Let us therefore repent of our arrogance and welcome one another.

4. There is no sweeter place on earth than the gathered church. It is the temple of the living God, the dwelling place of His Spirit. Love the church. Serve the church. Stop complaining about the church. It is still under construction—as are its members.

Chapter 3

1. Don't take the Bible or preaching for granted. It is an amazing gift of grace that God would reveal Christ to us.

We never would have known the mystery of the gospel, but God has given it to us through the apostles and prophets so that His people might know His love. Furthermore, God's servants have suffered greatly through the ages to proclaim Christ's riches to the nations. Treasure the Word, read it often, and thank God for it.

2. In Christ believers have boldness and access with confidence to the Father. Do you experience that freedom in your prayers? The Father welcomes sinners into His presence with joy when they come in Jesus' name. God desires that His children pray with absolute confidence that He will be good to them (Luke 11:13).

3. Pray for great spiritual blessings for believers. God has given every blessing to us in the exalted Christ. The Spirit has already done a supernatural work of resurrection in everyone who now believes. Yet there is more of God's fullness for us to know. God is able to do far more than we can ask or imagine. John Newton said, "Thou art coming to a King; large petitions with thee bring; for His grace and power are such, none can ever ask too much." Begin by taking Paul's prayer in this chapter and praying it for your church.

Chapter 4

1. Doctrine demands action, and a living faith produces works. It is presumptuous to rest in our knowledge about God if we do not walk in a manner fitting to that knowledge. Even the demons believe and tremble. The first response the gospel requires is humility. Those who believe the doctrines of grace should of all people be most humble. Therefore, let

us examine ourselves, grieve over pride, pray for humility, and meditate on the gospel.

2. The life of the church revolves around Christ. Our unity springs from our union with God through Christ. Our abilities to serve flow from Christ's victory. Knowing Him and being like Him are our maturity and stability. He is the head from whom all members and relationships in the body draw life. Therefore, pray often for your church that Christ would be central in its worship and fellowship.

3. Repentance is fundamental to the Christian life. Turning from sin toward the Lord is the fundamental building block of faith. All Christians must continually put off sin and put on the image of Christ. Repentance is specific, and so the Bible's commandments address specific areas of life. Of the commands in this chapter, what is one area where you need to repent? What must you put off? Put on?

Chapter 5

1. Christians must not be like the world. Too often the church wants to blend in, either to avoid persecution or to attract new members. But how can light blend into darkness without ceasing to be light? Our mission requires that we be different. The most effective outreach program produces people who radiate goodness, righteousness, and truth. Such Christians by their very lives convict sinners, validate God's law and judgment, and confirm the power of the gospel.

2. Pray for the Spirit to fill your church. Ask God to make your congregation a people who daily go to Christ and drink deeply of the intoxicating joy of the Holy Spirit. Seek the

Spirit's grace for heartfelt singing of the psalms, profound thanksgiving to the Father through Christ, and humble submission to authority in the home, church, and state.

3. Marriage exists to show the glory of Christ. It is not a social contract formed when and how we please. It is not just a convenience for satisfying our desires. It is God's display case for the beautiful relationship between Christ and the church. Husbands and wives have a high calling. Commit yourself to serve your spouse as God commands in His Word—whether your marriage is sweet or sorrowful.

Chapter 6

1. Paul's instructions for parenting are surprisingly simple. On the one hand, this is because the hardest thing about being a father or mother is doing what you know you should do: be kind and just, not angry and unfair; train and discipline your children consistently; teach them the Word of God. On the other hand, Paul's few words to fathers stand upon two broad bases. First, the book of Proverbs offers a wealth of wisdom for training children. Second, Ephesians 4–6 reminds us that successful parenting requires us to walk worthy of our calling in every area of life: church, daily repentance, avoiding worldliness, and marriages of love and respect. If we are faithful in these four areas, we have laid a solid foundation for raising our children.

2. No Christian is a spiritual civilian. We are all soldiers on the front lines. Therefore we must live in a state of battle-readiness, always alert for our enemy. Believers, however, need not live in bondage to fear. Christ is our armor, and

He is sufficient to overcome a legion of fallen angels. Let us therefore make walking with Christ our lifestyle by meditating on the truth, doing what is right, resting on Christ's blood for peace of conscience, trusting God's promises, hoping in total salvation, speaking God's Word, and praying always for ourselves, other Christians, and the preachers of the gospel. By God's grace in Christ, we can overcome the Evil One.

Philippians

Chapter 1

1. It is easy to enter the place of prayer mindlessly, falling prey to vain repetitions. Sometimes we struggle with knowing what to pray for or how to shape our prayers. Paul's prayer in the opening section of this chapter models for us a biblically informed prayer. Prayer is to be a part of the regular rhythm of a Christian's life. Prayer expresses itself in thanksgiving to God and in intercession for others. Paul does not merely make general requests of blessing, but specifically prays that God would work in Christians' lives and grow them in love for the purpose of knowing how to live in this world.

2. What do you live for? Is the fame of Christ's name more important to you, or is comfort and ease of life? Paul's life was so wrapped up in Christ and the gospel that he wanted nothing more than to see the gospel advance, even if it meant that others sought to add to his affliction. When life's circumstances get difficult, it is easy to become focused on self and how to minimize discomfort. But Paul encourages us to remain firm and live in a way that is worthy of the gospel.

Chapter 2

1. Meditate on the wonder of the incarnation of the Son of God. Consider the humiliation of Christ in His birth, life, and death. Praise God the Father for the gift of the Son, who willingly submitted Himself to die the shameful death of the cross to redeem unworthy sinners.

2. Christ deserves our all. Consider the commands in verses 3–5, 12–16 and think practically about what they call you to. How did Timothy (vv. 19–24) and Epaphroditus (vv. 25–30) model obedience to these commands?

Chapter 3

1. In what ways are you tempted to boast in your accomplishments? Are you actively pursuing an experiential knowledge of Christ? The Christian life is one of growth. Paul uses the language of a race (v. 14) and he highlights the importance of constantly making Christ the prize after which he runs.

2. Paul reminds believers that their citizenship is in heaven, where Jesus Christ is and where we are to look. He tells them that when Jesus Christ arrives they will be changed into their glorified bodies. That happens in an instant. If seeing Christ physically changes you in a moment, then you should recognize that seeing Christ now spiritually changes you progressively. This is progressive sanctification. How do you seek to daily gaze on Christ and lead others to do the same?

Chapter 4

1. How do you handle the concerns of life? Is prayer to God a first or last option? Paul, like Peter, encourages us to cast all those things that cause anxiety upon the Lord in prayer. What is true about God that encourages believers to pray? Why should we add thanksgiving to our supplications?

2. Contentment is a battle. It is easy to think that we will achieve it if only our circumstances change. Yet, Paul says that he had to learn contentment even when he was abounding.

Jesus Christ is the prize of the believer. All things, either poverty or prosperity, cannot compare to knowing and having Christ. Extol Christ in your life and in your home in a manner that clearly demonstrates He is the key to contentment.

Colossians

Chapter 1

1. Give attention to the great wonder of the incarnation. Meditate upon the supremacy of Christ in His person as the agent, sustainer, and goal of creation, considering that this person would take on flesh to redeem you from your sins. What are some reasons why Christ's incarnation would make you praise God?

2. Paul prays that the believers at Colosse might be filled with the knowledge of God. He prays that they might "walk worthy of the Lord unto all pleasing" (v. 10). Believers tend to think of God's will as that which only deals with future plans. Yet Paul writes about God's will as informing our lives in the present and how we may live before God, being fruitful in every good work.

Chapter 2

1. In Christ are all the treasures of wisdom and knowledge. Yet, we so often seek guidance for life outside of Christ. Whether it be self-help tips or the latest marketing fad, we can be tempted to find quick solutions to life's problems outside of Christ. Give yourself, by grace, to a perpetual pursuit of experiencing Christ and living in the enjoyment of being united to Him.

2. How ought you to view your standards of conduct? When Paul says that external things do not conquer the indulgences of the flesh, is he advocating the repudiation of all standards?

Consider the sufficiency of Christ's death and resurrection to sanctify, along with the motivation of the standards set forth, personally and for family.

Chapter 3

1. Believers are risen with Christ and exhorted to fix their minds on things above. Do you give attention to this focus in your personal walk and in your family? Do you find strength (1:11) to mortify and put off sin in God's power? Perhaps you are frustrated seeking to mortify sin in your own strength. What does living according to 3:12–16 look like in your personal interactions and in your family life?

2. Notice the manifold grace of the Holy Spirit (vv. 12–15) with which we are commanded to clothe ourselves. Reflect practically on what this calls you to do or perhaps change in your life.

3. Talk through the responsibilities of husband, wife, father, mother, and children with the whole family present (vv. 18–25). Consider that each relationship is lived under God, before whom all relationships are accountable.

Chapter 4

1. Prayer is vital for the Christian life. Prayer ought to be thoughtful. It involves thanksgiving and intercession. It is easy to neglect thanksgiving, but believers have so much for which they ought to praise God. Believers ought also to remember to intercede for others, especially as it relates to the advancement of the gospel. Teach your family to pray regularly, thoughtfully, thankfully, and missionally.

2. What does it mean to make your speech around unbelievers "seasoned with salt" (v. 6)? What unbelievers do you talk to? How can you bring grace and salt into your conversations with them?

1 Thessalonians

Chapter 1

1. When we understand the Bible's teachings aright, we see that coming by faith to Christ could never happen as a result of our own free will. True faith is God-given and therefore, if we are believers, we should thank God that He has given us the ability to come to Jesus and to believe in Him, as Paul here shows (v. 4).

2. It cannot be too strongly noted that the only evidence of a person's being one of God's elect is when they live a godly life and so bring forth the fruits of righteousness. Election makes men saints, not mere religious talkers, learned hypocrites, or adherents to some religious group.

Chapter 2

1. Contrary to what we often think, affliction produces greater confidence and boldness in the people of God (v. 2). If it is viewed rightly, affliction takes our confidence away from ourselves and other people, and settles it on the gospel and God alone.

2. Tenderness for the Lord's people is one of the characteristics of a spiritual preacher. Paul uses the pictures of a nurse (v. 7) and a father (v. 11). How do both kinds of love form a good soil for spiritual growth?

Chapter 3

1. People in the pew do not always understand how great a burden their ministers carry day and night for their eternal good. Spend a little time praying for your ministers and elders that God would give them patience, endurance, and wisdom in shepherding the flock of Christ.

2. It is an encouraging thing for Christians to meditate on the return of Christ and the grace and glory He will usher in. Believers must always have one eye on the great day when our Lord will return and His people will be eternally at peace. At the same time, we must not forget that we live in this world and thus must await the return of Christ.

Chapter 4

1. Sanctification involves careful obedience to the Ten Commandments, a number of which are addressed in this chapter. When we are saved by grace, we do not leave behind the commandments of God. On the contrary, we find the power to keep them in love.

2. Believers sorrow when their Christian brothers and sisters die, but their sorrow is mingled with comfort to know they shall soon be with them again forever, when Christ returns. When you think about the deaths of your loved ones, keep one eye on Christ's coming, and you will find comfort.

Chapter 5

1. Believers have the sure and blessed hope of heaven forever. Therefore, seek by God's grace to live for the glory of our great Lord and Savior. Do not be seduced by the glitter and glamor of this world, for God will take it away in a moment.

2. The unconverted are like men who are asleep on an express train soon to plunge into an ocean of fire and misery. Should they not be warned and told of the God who sent His Son to die for lost sinners? Let us speak the gospel to our family and neighbors, and support the gospel preaching of our ministers and missionaries with encouragement, prayer, and financial gifts.

3. God is in this life sanctifying His people through His Word of truth. Therefore let us be those who value the Bible as our greatest earthly treasure.

2 Thessalonians

Chapter 1

1. The best Christians are sometimes those who are suffering the worst persecution. We should pray daily for our brothers and sisters in lands that are hostile to the gospel. Use missionary newsletters, websites, maps, and other tools to pray intelligently for the persecuted church.

2. We are not to avenge ourselves on those who do us harm, but we are ever to keep in mind the truth that God will take vengeance on those who do us any injury because of our faith. This is the key to freedom from bitterness: trusting that God's justice will prevail. How have you suffered for Christ? How does this truth help you?

3. It is not a kindness in our preaching to the unconverted to keep from them the fearful reality of hell, with its "flaming fire" (v. 8) and its "everlasting destruction" (v. 9). Pray for preachers that they would boldly preach both law and gospel, both hell and heaven.

Chapter 2

1. Gregory the Great (d. AD 604) said that anyone who claims to be the Universal Priest over all the church is the precursor of the Antichrist. Many Christians, including John Wycliffe, Martin Luther, John Calvin, and the authors of the Westminster Confession of Faith, have understood the "man of sin" to be the Pope of Rome. Other Christians expect a future antichrist to arise. However we interpret this text,

we must certainly reject anyone who seeks to take a place of authority in the church that belongs only to the Lord. Christ alone has supreme authority to teach the church its doctrines, laws, and worship. Christ alone is the Mediator who atones for sin by His once-for-all sacrifice. Christ alone has the power of the Spirit to make the means of grace effective to save sinners. Take no part in a church that makes a man into Christ's substitute. Is there anyone or anything that is distracting you from Christ?

2. The only alternative to being swept up in the worship of men is salvation by the sovereign grace of God. Wherever we see people exercising faith in Christ and practical holiness, let us give thanks to God for choosing and calling them to Christ. If God has saved you, thank Him every day. If you cannot say that you know you belong to Christ, do not keep rejecting the love of the truth, or God could give you over to delusion. Turn from your sins and cry out in prayer to Christ even now to save you.

Chapter 3

1. Bad doctrine leads to bad practice. Fanatical views of the imminence of Christ's second coming can lead to a host of errors, including failing to obey the injunctions of God in personal, family, and public life. We do not know the day when Christ will return, and we must live as faithful servants every day, ready to meet the Master. Whether or not you work for a paycheck, what "jobs" has the Lord assigned to you? Why is it important for the Lord's honor and your good that you work hard at them?

2. When professing Christians behave badly, it is sometimes our duty to withdraw ourselves from them (v. 6), to refuse to have fellowship with them (v. 14), and to give them a brotherly admonition (v. 15). Breaking fellowship with professing believers is a solemn act of the church and should not be done lightly or without the leadership of the church's elders. However, when done rightly, the Holy Spirit can use it to turn backsliding Christians back to Christ and to awaken hypocrites in the church to their need of salvation.

1 Timothy

Chapter 1

1. Note Paul's reference to "God our Saviour" in verse 1. Paul uses this designation also in 1 Timothy 2:3 and 4:10. The Son of God merited salvation for His people, dying on the cross and rising on the third day. But the source of salvation rests in God, the Father. Paul frequently ascribes man's salvation to God (Rom. 8:32; 1 Cor. 1:21; Eph. 2:4–5; etc.). Verse 15 beautifully mentions Christ's saving work. To be saved means also that God gives man the richest blessings: to declare that man is righteous in the sight of God (Isa. 1:18; Rom. 3:24), is placed in the freedom of God's children (Rom. 8:2; 2 Cor. 3:17; Gal. 5:1), and receives everlasting life (John 11:25–26; Eph. 2:5; Rev. 22:5).

2. Note also Paul's reference in verse 1 to the "Lord Jesus Christ…our hope." He is not only the One who gives hope, but Christ Himself is the hope of His people. He is the *foundation* of Christian hope, for Christ earned that hope when He laid down His life as a ransom for sin. This is a source of unspeakable comfort. Christ is also the *door* of hope. One enters into a life of hope through Him. He is the only access to God. We, unworthy guilty sinners, can only have access to God through Christ. Christ is also the *life* of hope. One can only live in true hope through Christ. Without it there is no comfort or perspective for the future.

3. Verse 8 speaks of the law of God, which is good and is to be used lawfully. How do we use the law lawfully? There are

various uses of the law. It functions as a restraint, working in people's consciences and keeping them from committing certain sins (Rom. 2:15). The law of God reveals to us our sins (3:20), which need to be washed in the blood of Christ. Finally, the law is also a guide to lead us through life (Pss. 19:8; 119:98; Rom. 7:22).

Chapter 2

1. Notice Paul's emphasis on prayer. Christian prayer has a tremendous impact upon the surrounding environment. God answers prayer. The apostle often stresses the importance of prayer, requesting prayer for himself and for the work in God's kingdom (Eph. 6:18–19; Heb. 13:18). In Acts 6:4 the apostles testify that they should give themselves to prayer. In Acts 12:5 the church prayed without ceasing for Peter who had been put in prison. The Lord Jesus stresses the importance of personal and corporate prayer (Matt. 6:6; 7:7–8; Mark 9:25). Let us pray for individuals by name, asking for God's grace upon their lives.

2. Let us realize the basic truth that there is one Mediator between God and men (v. 5). This counts for all men everywhere. It is only in Christ that man can be reconciled to God. That is because Jesus Christ paid the ransom. He gave Himself as a payment for sin. Outside of Christ there is no reconciliation and no propitiation. This is why no one other than Christ can ever mediate between God and man. As God, Christ was able to endure the eternal wrath of God. As man, Christ fulfilled the law perfectly for His people. Now, in Christ men can come to God in faith, and this faith does not put to shame.

Chapter 3

1. Paul describes here the requirements of an office bearer. The reference to the office as a "good work" in verse 1 shows that Paul has a high regard for the office. This implies that it is an excellent and honorable work. Nevertheless we know from early church history that in those days serving in the office was also a sacrifice. Repeatedly persecution would rage with painful consequences. False teachers did their utmost to undermine the truth. The cares of the congregation were many (2 Cor. 11:27–28). Still today, serving in the office is a sacrifice. There is the sacrifice of time, ease, and energy. At times there will be suffering because of hardships and ill-spoken words against the office bearer. At times one's name will even be slandered for the sake of being faithful to one's calling. But let it then be realized, that it is still a "good work" worthy of performing.

2. One of the qualifications Paul gives for an overseer is that he must be "blameless" (v. 2). We understand that to mean that he is to be beyond reproach and to have a good name both within and beyond the church. However, let us also realize that at heart no office bearer is "blameless" for all have sinned and come short of the glory of God (Rom. 3:23). Therefore ultimately the office bearer can only be "blameless" in Christ. Christ justifies and cleanses from sin. Every office bearer has reason to consider himself unworthy and not beyond reproach. Without undermining the need to be godly in one's conduct, let us also realize that every office bearer needs to be clothed with the righteousness of Christ. This is the only way he can be truly blameless.

3. It seems that within churches pastors are often under attack. The Evil One will try to render a pastor's work useless by leading him to fall into sin, for if the pastor falls, many in the congregation will stumble with him and the church will be in disarray. This is true not only for the pastors but also for the elders and the deacons. They are called to have oversight of the flock and therefore they must first have oversight over themselves in the privacy of their own homes and lives. This fact ought to stir up congregants to pray for those who are office bearers over them and to be cautious lest they unduly grumble (Num. 12).

Chapter 4

1. Paul encourages Timothy to exercise himself "unto godliness" (v. 7). One's fruitfulness in the service of the Lord depends on it. It promotes an increase in the knowledge of sin and of the necessity and preciousness of Christ. This exercise as such will remain hidden but the effects of it will be public. It is the calling and the duty of God's children to be diligent in reading the Scriptures and in seeking the Lord in personal, private prayer. Meditating on the mysteries of godliness as revealed to us in God's Word and praying over this will cultivate a rich fruit in the life of a Christian. If one wishes to experience more of the love of Christ and be led deeper into a life of communion with Christ, one will need to have daily secret spiritual exercises. For "thy Father which seeth in secret shall reward thee openly" (Matt. 6:6).

2. Paul encourages Timothy to read the Scriptures with attention (v. 13). If we are to be godly in this crooked world, we will need to diligently read the Scriptures and meditate

on their doctrines, making applications to daily life in the way of pointed exhortations. Without them, our lives and worship will suffer detrimentally.

Chapter 5

1. Paul instructs Timothy how to deal with various age categories in the congregation. He refers to fathers, mothers, younger men, and women. This shows the importance of family life. In our society indifference toward family members is increasing. The church ought to reflect brotherly love, mutual respect, and an attitude of esteeming the other higher than oneself. In this way the church will be a witness in this world of Christian love and faithfulness.

2. Timothy is called to assess people's lives. In this regard the fruits will show who people are. We cannot judge the inward attitude, but may only listen to the testimony and observe the outward walk of life. It may be that we will see that much is lacking in our congregation. The church needs to strike a balance between showing forbearance to weak members while encouraging improvement and publicly admonishing sin. All this must be accompanied with urgent prayer for the outpouring of God's Spirit in the midst of the congregation.

Chapter 6

1. Paul gives directions for slaves and masters. As such Paul does not outlaw slavery, but provides a framework within which masters and their slaves must operate on the basis of mutual respect, love, and trust. Thereby in reality the institution of slavery is undermined. In our days slave trade is forbidden, but pride and antagonism against other people,

races, and those of a different social status, as well as foreigners, is deeply ingrained in the human heart. Paul points out to us the Christian attitude of love, respect, and care toward all people.

2. This passage also teaches us the need not to be attached to the material blessings of this world. This world is transient. Only the salvation of the Lord Jesus Christ remains forever. We may be grateful for the many blessings of this world and use them, but at the same time realize the needs of others, alleviating them where we can. Let us use this life as a preparation for eternal life.

2 Timothy

Chapter 1

1. Paul reminds Timothy of the deeds of the Lord in the past. He speaks of the faith of Timothy's mother and grandmother and reminds him of the faith Timothy had shown in the past. This is all to encourage Timothy to persevere in the calling God has given him. It is beneficial for our spiritual lives to meditate on the deeds of the Lord in our own lives as well as the lives of loved ones (Ps. 77:11–12).

2. Note how the apostle prays for Timothy day and night. Paul had a high regard for prayer. We see this sprinkled throughout his epistles. Every time he prays, he thinks of Timothy. Paul prayed much, for he believed in God who answers prayer. He realized that God sovereignly incorporates the prayers of His people in His dealings with mankind.

Chapter 2

1. Paul encourages Timothy in verse 3 to endure difficulty as a good soldier of Jesus Christ. To some extent hardships and difficulties will be the share of all who are called to be a witness of the Lord Jesus Christ. Timothy, as a minister of the gospel, had to reckon with these hardships and not be surprised when they occurred. Likewise now all office bearers must count on hardships in their official work. But also God's children, as they are called to be witnesses of the Lord Jesus Christ, must reckon with scorn, tribulation, and other hardships as they witness from the Word of God.

2. Timothy must strive lawfully (v. 5). What does this mean? An office bearer should be honest and upright. He may not be proud or strive for glory from men. He should not be discouraged by hardships. He should not waste his energy. He should not consider himself to be indispensable. He should be willing to share the work with others and not promote himself. He must submit himself to proper church oversight, especially regarding the preaching of God's Word. He must show willingness to learn from others.

3. In verse 25 the purpose of all pastoral work toward those that oppose the gospel is stated. The word used there in the original is stronger than repentance. It is conversion, which implies a total change in mental and moral outlook on life. It leads to a radical change of one's attitude and conduct. Such change is not the fruit of man's persuasion but is always worked by God's Spirit, as a gift of God. Let us be humble when we know this change of life. Let our need for conversion drive us to hope in the Lord. Be careful not to grieve God's Spirit but in humility expect His working in your life.

Chapter 3

1. In verse 8 mention is made of two Egyptian magicians whose names, until now, have not been mentioned in the Bible. God has seen fit to give us their names here. This fact should remind us that God remembers each person's individual name, thoughts, and actions. Though all of humanity forget us, God remembers still. Judgment day will reveal many things history has forgotten. Let us therefore seek to be well grounded in Scripture as the cornerstone of faith.

2. In verse 12 the apostle teaches that all who wish to live godly in Christ will suffer forms of hardship, suffering, and even persecution. They may be despised or even ostracized for the sake of the gospel. All those who wish to live godly should realize this and prepare themselves mentally in advance for such events, so as not to be shocked when they actually take place. By the Spirit's grace, they will then be able to endure such hardships and remain faithful to the Lord.

Chapter 4

1. In verse 2 we read that Paul desires Timothy to emphasize doctrine in his teaching. Today doctrine is not viewed as useful and people generally prefer "practical preaching." But a church without doctrine is like a house without a structure, or a building without a foundation. The church of the Lord Jesus Christ needs to be instructed in the doctrines of God's Word. Therefore preaching should contain a major focus on the fundamental Christian doctrines, such as those found in the Heidelberg Catechism or the Westminster Shorter Catechism. Parents should instruct their children in these truths.

2. In verse 8 we read of the reward the Lord has set in store for all those who love Him. God's people are called to meditate on the future blessings the Lord shall give to His own. One moment in glory will make all the struggles on earth worthwhile. In the midst of trials and hardships, this is a great impetus to continue the struggle, knowing that their heavenly reward is firm and sure. The future glory of God's people is grounded in Christ's resurrection. The outpouring of the Holy Ghost is a down payment of the full blessing which is still to come.

Titus

Chapter 1

1. What does Paul mean when he describes himself as both "a servant of God, and an apostle of Jesus Christ" (v. 1)? In what way is this combination of titles unusual?

2. Paul stresses that church members should be concerned about what kind of men are nominated to hold office in the church as ministers, elders, or deacons. What traits of character or habits of life should we look for and value in such men?

3. Errors in doctrine or morals are serious, particularly in the lives of office bearers, who must set an example for the entire church. What kinds of people are vulnerable to the appeals of false teachers who would divide the church? How can we protect ourselves and our families from such persons?

Chapter 2

1. What are some of "the things which become sound doctrine" (v. 1)? How can we acquire them? Who is "a pattern of good works" (v. 7) for you? In what ways does your life "adorn the doctrine of God our Saviour" (v. 10)? Why does it matter?

2. People today are beset with addictions of many kinds (alcoholism, drug abuse, overeating, pornography, etc.). Why is sobriety and sober-mindedness important for the Christian? How can we achieve it and maintain it?

3. What does "the grace of God" (v. 11) teach us to believe and to hope for? What does it teach about the duty required of believers? Why did Christ give Himself for His people? Why are they called His "peculiar people" (v. 14)? How do you live in the world as one who belongs to Christ?

Chapter 3

1. Christians owe duty and obedience to the civil magistrate. What are the limits of this duty?

2. Are the sins of Christians more or less serious than the sins of unbelievers? Why?

3. What does it mean "to be ready to every good work" (v. 1)? Why should we show "all meekness unto all men" (v. 2)? Why must we still do good works? Do our good works have any part in our salvation? Why does Paul say that God's people are justified and made heirs according to the hope of eternal life, by God's grace imparted to us through Christ? What does this truth imply for our daily lives?

4. Paul warns us that there is a danger of taking up questions and topics that have little or nothing to do with the gospel's essential truths. What does he mean when he says that such questions and topics are "unprofitable and vain" (v. 9)? How do heretics condemn themselves?

Philemon

1. How does Paul relate faith and love? How do you give joy and comfort to your fellow believers? What does our belief in "the communion of the body of Christ" (see 1 Cor. 10) require of us as Christians?

2. Would you be willing to pay the medical debts of a fellow Christian so that he or she could be free of such a burden? Would you be willing to forgive such a debt owed to you?

3. What is true Christian obedience? Why are mutual service and hospitality duties for all Christians? What does this say about the nature of the church as a society or body? How can you fulfill these duties?

Hebrews

Chapter 1

1. The author opens verses 1–4 with at least seven descriptions of who the Son (Jesus Christ) is. Trace them and reflect on the manifold glory of this opening. There is none other who can satisfy our deepest needs or longings. These are God's final words spoken to humanity; why are they such great words?

2. The author continues in verses 5–14 by citing seven Old Testament passages that are for the most part direct speech from the Father to the Son. Reflect with awe and humility on the privilege of listening in on the Father's speech to His Son.

3. Reflect on the privilege believers have that angels serve them on their path toward full salvation. What reasons does this give God's children for gratitude, confidence, peace, and hope?

Chapter 2

1. Paying close attention to the Word of God is hard in these days filled with distraction and superficiality. Yet the judgment that awaits those who fail to take heed to God's final word in Christ is greater than the judgment that came upon rebels in the Old Testament. Why is it impossible to escape God's wrath if we neglect this great salvation?

2. What depth of mercy that Christ joyfully stands with His brothers (v. 11)! He not only grants them the name of brothers, but also the experience of His brothers, especially in trials.

3. Chapter 2 closes by speaking of how we have a merciful and faithful High Priest (vv. 17–18). Both of these descriptions of our High Priest are needed. If Christ were not merciful, sinners could have no confidence in coming to God. If Christ were not faithful, believers would not have a continued boldness to come before God.

Chapter 3

1. Verse 6 suggests an important question: Are you a part of the household of faith?

2. Believers have a corporate responsibility to exhort and encourage one another daily. Too often we live isolated lives. How might you help and encourage those around you?

3. Hebrews warns against the "deceitfulness of sin" (v. 13). We often fail to remember that sin is deceitful. When we begin to see by grace how deceitful, how wretched, how awful sin really is, we learn to look to God alone to renew our minds after knowledge, righteousness, and holiness that we might discern the exceeding depravity of sin.

Chapter 4

1. Hebrews says that Israel had the gospel preached to them but it did not profit them because their hearing was not combined with faith. The gospel was preached through types and shadows and the redeeming acts of God throughout Israel's

history. However, we have even greater privileges and a great degree of responsibility as a result.

2. The word "rest" has a lot of significance for our restless world and restless souls. What makes us so restless? What kind of comfort lies in the fact that God speaks of "my rest" (vv. 3, 5)?

3. Far from being just an exalted Sovereign who is far removed from our situation, struggles, and trials, Christ has a tender heart for His people, especially in their afflictions and temptations. Do you know this throne as a throne of grace in your life? What is meant by this "boldness"? Is it the same as "presumption"? What is the difference?

Chapter 5

1. Christ learned obedience through what He suffered (v. 8). Though Christ was never disobedient to His Father, He learned from the inside out, as man, what it meant to obey His Father even at great cost to Himself. If sinless Christ had to suffer to learn obedience, what does this teach us about why God's children must suffer?

2. Christian maturity ought to be the aim, not an optional luxury of every Christian (vv. 11–14). Just as children often can't wait to grow up and will often try to do things to demonstrate that they are grown up, believers must set aside childish things and press on in the Word and life of faith.

Chapter 6

1. In many quarters of the professing church, apostasy is in full swing. Some change the definition of faith to adjust to

this reality; others claim that true believers can lose their salvation. However, the Word of God is clear that many can have the appearance of faith and are not inwardly changed. Let us examine ourselves whether we have simply the form of religion or the true power of it.

2. Patience is not easy for any, and believers are no exception. Yet, without it we will not know the rich blessing God gives to those who in patience possess their souls. How can we take hold of the hope set before us? How does this anchor hold us in the midst of the storms of spiritual life (vv. 18–20)?

3. Christ is called the "forerunner" of His people (v. 20), having gone behind the curtain of God's dwelling. This imagery comes from the Old Testament tabernacle, where the actual throne room of God was located in the Holy of Holies. How does this picture help explain the boldness believers ought to have in approaching the throne of grace (4:16)?

Chapter 7

1. Here as elsewhere the author exalts Christ and shows His magnificent superiority over anything else. Why is focusing on the excellence of Christ such a great medicine for all discouragement and for drawing back from temptation?

2. Imagine for a moment what it must have been like for Abraham, fresh from battle, to receive God's blessing through Melchisedec. Think now of Christ blessing His people after He Himself fought the ultimate battle on their behalf.

3. Reflect on the truth of verse 25. From what can the power of Christ not save? Where can the power of Christ not reach? When can the power of Christ not intervene for good?

Chapter 8

1. Believers have their High Priest sitting upon the throne. Dear Christian, you have omnipotence and compassion coming together based on Christ's finished work. What an encouragement this should be to you who are reconciled to God through the blood of His Son!

2. Christ is not only supreme; He is also sufficient. Christ is the only Mediator and Surety of the new covenant. Those who seek God's favor and grace must seek it in the person and work of Jesus Christ, not in rituals and rites of religion, nor in the sin-stained labor of their own hands.

Chapter 9

1. When Christ died on Calvary, the veil of the temple was rent from top to bottom (Matt. 27:51). God was signifying that the ordinances were to be done away with. Still today, we often let our thoughts go no further than what we can see—buildings, people, ministers, etc. However, our thoughts should be on Christ in the heavenly sanctuary, as He is there with His own blood.

2. The sacrifices of the Old Testament pointed forward to Christ, but they could not themselves internally cleanse people. What David prayed for in Psalm 51:7, Christ alone can do through His sacrifice. Has Christ's blood been applied to your conscience? Do you still rely on dead works to please God?

3. There are some who imagine that God gives second chances to people after they die to flee to Christ. Yet verse 27 is clear that it has been appointed to man to die once

and then the judgment. As uncertain as our life is, this truth should make us very sober.

Chapter 10

1. In the Old Testament, the people imagined that they could do what they wanted and just keep the sacrifices going to appease God. Through the prophets, God made clear that sacrifices by themselves, without hearts that love and obey God, are abhorrent to Him (vv. 5–6). Many today look at the sacrifice of Christ in a similar way, as an insurance policy for heaven, all the while living for themselves. Why won't that work? Consider verses 26–27.

2. Typically, we don't like it when human authorities are angry with us. Consider in this light verse 31. Why is it a fearful thing to fall into the hands of an angry God?

3. "Ye have need of patience" (v. 36). How can the past times of suffering encourage God's people going forward (vv. 32–34)? How have your past trials strengthened your hope and endurance?

Chapter 11

1. These heroes of faith are more than moral examples. They lived in light of a faith that would for the most part unfold beyond their lifetimes. Think of what Enoch, Abraham, Moses, and Rahab might say to you in your particular struggle right now.

2. How is the doctrine of creation (v. 3) a great encouragement to faith?

3. Verses 36–38 prove to us that faith in Christ does not free us from life's difficulties but often leads us into the heart of troubles. As a result the world may judge us as unworthy. Compare whom the world thinks of as worthy ones and of whom God says "the world was not worthy" (v. 38). Whose verdict should matter more to us?

Chapter 12

1. Christ endured His sufferings for the joy set before Him. The present sufferings of Christians do not outweigh the grace, glory, and joy of what they will receive with Christ's coming.

2. The author turns the argument believers often make regarding suffering on its head. When undergoing suffering, they often imagine that if God loved them, they would not be going through suffering. He shows how the suffering they endure is precisely proof of God's love, provided they are instructed by the chastisement. What are some ways in which believers might ensure that the suffering, though grievous, will profit them (v. 11)?

3. Who and what is at the pinnacle of Christian worship and why (v. 24)?

Chapter 13

1. The glory of Christ exhibited throughout this epistle does not remove the mundane things of life. Rather it beautifies and magnifies such things as marriage, respect for elders, and hospitality (vv. 1–6).

2. It goes against our flesh to be excluded and despised. Yet, there is no greater riches than to be united with Christ, even if it be "without [outside] the camp" (v. 13). How are Christians in your circumstances sometimes treated as outsiders? How might you be tempted to compromise your faith to avoid this rejection?

3. Christ's blood does not just atone for sin; it consecrates for service. Christ is the Mediator of equipping grace. Turn verses 20–21 into a prayer for yourself, your family, and your church.

James

Chapter 1

1. Trials for Christians are not a matter of if, but "when" (v. 2). Despite what some teach and many imagine, Christians are not promised an exemption from trials. We can, however, face these trials with joy because we know that God has designed them for our good (Rom. 8:28, 32) and as a means of refining us. Christ endured His greatest trial, the cross, because of the joy that was set before him (Heb. 12:2–3). What trials are you facing? How can you count them as joy?

2. We must learn to hate deception and love the truth (vv. 16, 18, 21–22). In a day and age when skepticism is considered virtuous and agnosticism humble, we need to remember that God has revealed His truth in His Word. By the truth lost sinners are born again, by the truth they are saved, and by the truth they live in true happiness and freedom. Therefore, let us receive the truth with meekness.

3. James warns against worldly Christianity (v. 26). Carnal religion has no problem immersing itself in the world, which contaminates with its impurities. On the other hand, the believer seeks, by the grace of God, "to keep himself unspotted from the world" (v. 27). The Christian's affections should be with those who are in need, such as widows and orphans, rather than with the sinful pleasures the world offers, which only defile.

Chapter 2

1. How subtle and terrible sin is! Many of us by ourselves would not see how serious of a sin partiality or prejudice is. Even committing the smallest sin incurs the guilt of breaking the whole law of God. We should never make light of our sin, but say with David: "For thy name's sake, O LORD, pardon mine iniquity; for it is great" (Ps. 25:11).

2. In the middle of a very convicting chapter, James proclaims the glory of God's free grace, that God made a sovereign choice to save sinners (v. 5). God has chosen the foolish, the weak, the base, and the despised things of the world, an idolater like Abraham and an outcast like Rahab. In such light, no one is too sinful to be saved. Who might you think is the wickedest person you know? Pray for that person's conversion.

3. Just as money can be genuine or counterfeit, so, too, can faith be the real thing or just an imitation. Works cannot justify us before God, but they can and will demonstrate the genuineness of faith to the world. Martin Luther described it this way: "Oh, it is a living, busy, active, mighty thing, this faith; and so it is impossible for it not to do good works incessantly. It does not ask whether there are good works to do, but before the question rises, it has already done them, and is always at the doing of them. He who does not these works is a faithless man. He gropes and looks about after faith and good works, and knows neither what faith is nor what good works are, though he talks and talks, with many words, about faith and good works." Which kind of person are you?

Chapter 3

1. Small things show a lot about us. Like a skillful physician, James has tested our eyes for favoritism (2:1–13). Now he takes a close look at what our tongue tells us. What comes out of our mouths reveals what is in our hearts and what will happen to us on judgment day (Matt. 12:33–37). If you took stock of what your tongue produces over the course of a week, what would you learn about the health of your inner being?

2. We cannot by ourselves tame our tongues (v. 8). We need God to pardon us and renew us entirely. The so-called wisdom of man cannot help us. Only true wisdom can, the wisdom not found on earth but that comes down from heaven above. This wisdom comes from Christ, who through His Spirit and Word renews fallen image-bearers after His own image, and imparts to them a pure wisdom. How can we fill our minds and mouths with His wisdom?

Chapter 4

1. Often in our minds, people are big and God is small. We strive with others while we depend little on God. How grateful we should be when God unmasks this as sin in our lives. Pray to see the fights and conflicts in your life as tools in His hand. Then confess to God any spiritual adultery of your heart.

2. James admonishes his readers to weep (vv. 9–10). While James is not saying that all forms of joy and laughter are wrong, he is saying that there is an important and prominent place for genuine, heartfelt repentance over all our sins. The psalmist says, "A broken and a contrite heart, O God, thou

wilt not despise" (Ps. 51:17; see also 2 Cor. 7:10). Have you learned the grace of repentance?

3. Our attitudes toward the future is a good barometer of our hearts. When you think of later today, tomorrow, next year, and so on, is your disposition one that says "I will" or "If it is the Lord's will"? How will faith in God's providence affect your plans? Your prayers?

Chapter 5

1. Christ's second coming is closer today than when James wrote these words. If Christ came today, would He find you living like verses 8–9 instruct us to live?

2. The church is a place where we should be able to bring our needs, petitions, joys, as well as our cares and concerns for others. Elders and ministers are particularly charged with the care of souls. James highlights their calling to the ministry of prayer. However, he calls all Christians to a life of continual prayer and praise (v. 13). How can you cultivate the practice of petition and thanksgiving in God's presence throughout your day?

3. Conversion involves saving a soul from death and hiding a multitude of sins (v. 20). Do you know this grace yourself? If not, you are still in your sins and heading toward death. Seek God's mercy in Jesus Christ. If you are converted, you will love to see others converted as well. Pray and seek for awakening and revival wherever God has placed you.

1 Peter

Chapter 1

1. The struggle believers wage against sin is not because of anything in us but because of God's gracious plan in choosing whom He would save before the foundation of the world in eternity past. This is a great comfort to believers of all ages and reminds us that our struggle is not ours alone but rests in the sovereign and omnipotent plan of God (vv. 1–5). How can knowing God chose us encourage suffering believers?

2. Sometimes it is difficult to face the many trials and temptations of life. Peter tells us that the testing of our faith is so that it might be refined in the furnace of affliction. Much as gold is required to be heated and pressed and burned, so, too, must faith be tested. Yet the end result is that it proves itself true and genuine and precious (vv. 6–11).

3. Holiness and serious Christian living are not popular in this world, but they are our duty, required by God. God's demand that our lives be holy is not a stifling and burdensome requirement of His people. It is the gracious and loving call of God to His children to share in His holiness. In obeying, we show ourselves to be like our Father, who Himself is holy (vv. 12–25).

Chapter 2

1. There is no middle ground between Christ and holiness on the one side, and the world and sin on the other. Yet the world's lies of wisdom, wealth, and pleasure can pose a real

temptation for the Christian. It takes effort and concentration on a believer's part, as well as the grace of God, to reject the habits of his past life (vv. 1–3). But we must remember that no one can be indifferent to Christ. Either they will reverence Him or else they will reject His claims and His teaching (vv. 7–8).

2. Christ overcame the world by love and endurance of suffering, and so do Christians. The best way to silence critics of the gospel is to be full of good works. When a Christian is known only for his kindness, love, grace, and mercy, the world will try in vain to condemn him, and his righteous deeds will point unbelievers to the glory of God (vv. 11–20). When the Christian is called to suffer for his faith he should remind himself that he is only following in Christ's steps (vv. 21–25). How can that comfort the believer and give him endurance?

Chapter 3

1. The world idolizes physical beauty, but those who are wise prefer godliness in the heart (vv. 1–4). It is good to teach our children, even at a young age, that the beauty to admire in another is the inward beauty of a heart submissive to God.

2. It is biblical to teach that the man is the head of the home (1 Cor. 11:3; Eph. 5:23). He must not abuse his authority but pair it with a Christlike spirit of self-sacrifice (vv. 25–29). Peter admonishes husbands here to live with their wives in understanding. Submission need not be a negative thing when properly carried out (1 Peter 3:5–9).

3. Pilgrims who are on a journey are to have their lives characterized by a heavenly standard. Christians ought not to be

concerned with winning the approval of a worldly standard on which they have turned their backs. Rather, Christians ought to be concerned with doing what pleases God, and therefore to have His blessing (vv. 10–17).

4. The Bible does not teach that we are automatically saved by the sacraments of baptism and the Lord's Supper. On the contrary, in order to be saved we must be born again, as Christ teaches (John 3:1–8). But the sacraments have their own place in church life as seals and confirmations of the promises of God (1 Peter 3:18–22).

Chapter 4

1. The difference made in anyone who is born again is that rebirth reverses his whole moral outlook. He now loves what before he hated and now hates what before he loved. So great a change is made in one who is truly converted that it may amaze his friends and neighbors (vv. 1–6). Has God changed you on the inside? How?

2. If God has given us a gift to edify our fellow believers, we ought not to neglect it but use it. However, we must never attempt to serve God by following and teaching our own wisdom in place of His Word. And we would be fools to try to minister in our own strength instead of in the strength God supplies by His Spirit. This is the way to glorify God, for serving by the Word and Spirit is serving by faith in Christ (vv. 7–11).

3. Worldly men have little conception of what awaits them in the day of death when they must appear before the holy God. On the other hand, those who believe in God's holiness

and the judgment day should not be surprised when God sends fiery trials to purify them, including the fire of persecution. Instead, let Christians live so that if men attack them, it will not be for their sins but for their sincere obedience to God (vv. 12–19).

Chapter 5

1. Those who bear an office or position of authority in God's church must be careful not to become "lords over God's heritage" (v. 3). Wherever there are positions of authority, the sinful heart is tempted to be puffed up with pride and self-centeredness. On the other hand, it is easy for leaders to lose their eagerness and readiness to serve in anticipation of Christ's reward (vv. 1–4). How can knowing that Christ will return in glory help leaders to guard themselves from both arrogance and laziness?

2. Augustine once said that if he were asked the most important three qualities of the Christian life, he would say, "Humility, humility, humility." God hates pride and warns against it but tenderly cares for the humble in all their anxieties (vv. 5–7). How can we clothe ourselves in humility every day?

2 Peter

Chapter 1

1. Sanctification, unlike justification, is a lifelong process. To bear fruit believers must give all diligence to add every virtue to the knowledge they possess. The diligent Christian will by his life enjoy confirmation of his election in this life. The biblical doctrine of election does not promote laziness, but holiness. John Calvin said, "Purity of life is not improperly called the evidence and proof of election." After this life the faithful believer will enjoy a royal reception when he gets home to glory. In what areas of sanctification do you especially need to grow? Has spiritual growth in the past confirmed your sense that you belong to Christ and are headed for glory? If so, how? If not, why not?

2. The faithful teaching and life of those who have discipled us will be remembered with love long after they have gone home (Heb. 13:7). We should all seek to leave behind a legacy of truth. Will you be remembered as one who faithfully shared with others the truths of Scripture?

3. The record of Christ's life and miracles is no fabled invention but is absolutely reliable and solid truth. The world is a dark place full of idolatry, vain philosophy, and crime, but the Bible is the one sure light that points out the path to heaven. Read it and love it.

Chapter 2

1. History bears eloquent testimony to the truth of what Peter says here concerning the danger of teachers of false religion. Yet in this age of so-called tolerance, Christians are often afraid to exercise discernment and to speak against heresy. Our silence is wrong, because all error corrupts, and errors against the foundations of the faith destroy souls forever. What damnable heresies presently endanger the Christian church? Pray for boldness for yourself and preachers to speak against them for the sake of precious souls.

2. The Old Testament proves repeatedly that God will destroy the wicked, especially those who lead others into wickedness like the false prophets. In their arrogance and boasting, they may appear successful and happy. However, unregenerate preachers are walking on a tightrope, and if they do not repent and find salvation, they will plunge at last into the fire of hell. We must remind ourselves of the danger into which we put ourselves if we listen to them. Regardless of the popularity of a preacher or teacher, do not give him a voice in your life, family, or church unless he speaks the truth of the Word of God and lives that truth with integrity.

Chapter 3

1. Peter's warning about scoffers is fulfilled in our own day in that many have been seduced away from the Christian faith by the theory of evolution and skepticism regarding the worldwide flood. Just as Christians in the early church were tempted to compromise and distort aspects of biblical truth to fit into Jewish traditions and Greek philosophies, so, too, Christians today are tempted to do the same to fit our

faith into modern and postmodern philosophies. Removing Christianity from the realms of real history and science destroys the faith. It is for the well-being of our own souls and that of our fellow believers that we reject all theories about the origin and destiny of the world which conflict with biblical teaching. How do you encounter this pressure, and how can you arm yourself against it?

2. The day of the Lord is coming. The elements will burn in the fire of God's judgment, and a new creation will arise where righteousness dwells and sin has no place. Nothing will last except Christ and obedience to His Word. On the one hand, this calls us to forcefully reject all heresies, removing false teachers from the church. On the other hand, this demands that we seek first the kingdom of God and His righteousness, making it our great priority to gain and grow in our knowledge of Christ and likeness to Him. Standing against doctrinal error and running after spiritual growth are not mere options, much less distractions, for the Christian. They are the very essence of being a people who hope in Christ alone. How could you better live in light of eternity?

1 John

Chapter 1

1. It was stunning and virtually inconceivable to the ancient Greek mind that the divine Word would become a physical man we could see and touch. It should be stunning to us today that the Lord Jesus would take our lowly nature to His glorious person. Life has come to us in a way we can relate to, with gentleness and sympathy for our weaknesses. Consider these truths and spend some time praising God for what He did for sinners. How can Christians who lack joy in Christ acquire more genuine joy? What role does the Holy Spirit play in helping true believers experience fullness of joy?

2. A relationship with the righteous God cannot coexist happily with sin. We must not call ourselves Christians and walk in the darkness; we must walk in the light, allowing Christ to expose our sin, wash us clean, and lead us in His ways. How often do you confess your sins to God? How do you use the Word to help you to see, hate, and forsake sin?

Chapter 2

1. Sometimes when we take our children to a park, we pay for their admission and their hands get stamped to show that their admission price has been paid. John explains the stamp that marks those who truly know God: they obey God's laws, love God's people, and receive God's doctrines. They should remember, however, that these marks did not pay for their admission to the kingdom; only the death and

intercession of God's righteous Son does so. How can the marks and payment of salvation guide a person doubting his salvation?

2. Why is it important to fight against sin? How can we go on fighting against sin without becoming discouraged by our numerous failures? What comfort do true believers find in Jesus' work as their advocate when they do sin and repent of it?

3. God's people have the anointing of the Spirit to teach them the truth. Their faith does not depend on human testimony or secret knowledge from a special teacher, but on God's Spirit speaking through God's Word (1 Cor. 2:1–5). However, God's Spirit does work through Bible teachers (John 21:15; Eph. 4:11). How should we give due respect and attention to teachers without giving them the place of the Spirit?

Chapter 3

1. This chapter contrasts God's children and the world in terms of righteousness versus sin, love versus hatred, and life versus death. How would you summarize the difference between a true Christian and an unsaved person? Where do you stand?

2. If we are true believers, how does a proper understanding of the doctrine of adoption impact our relationship with God as our Father (v. 1)? With the world (v. 1)? With the future (v. 2)? With ourselves (v. 3)? With the family of believers (vv. 14–18)?

3. If you are born of God, then God has given you promises. When Christ comes, you will gaze into His glory without shame and be made like Him. You can have confidence toward God right now because the Spirit is working in your life. Do you have a right to claim these promises? Which of these promises is most precious to you now, and why?

Chapter 4

1. What false teachers present themselves to us today in person or through media? How can you recognize them? (See v. 2; Deut. 13:1–3; Matt. 7:15–20; Acts 17:10–12; Gal. 1:8–9; 1 Tim. 4:1–5.) How should you respond? How do the differences between those who are of the world and those who are of God affect your daily life and relationships? Should they affect you and your family more? In what ways?

2. God is love; as the Puritans said, Christ is love covered over with flesh. The Christian life is the indwelling of God's love in men, women, and children. Christ's coming aims to produce peace and joy in His beloved, not terror. How prominent is love in your view of God? Is His love hidden behind His majesty or wrath? How can you meditate more on His love? How can you grow in your own practice of Christlike love?

Chapter 5

1. Christ is the teacher of His people by His Word and Spirit. He gives us the truth and convinces us of its validity by divine and authoritative testimony in the Word and in the heart. The triune God is Himself the witness to this truth.

Therefore, we should submit to the Bible and receive all that it says, regardless of what men may say.

2. Consider what it means to overcome the world (vv. 4–5). Why is it necessary to engage in spiritual warfare in order to overcome the world? In what ways can we rise above the world's way of thinking and resist worldly peer pressure? Who gives us the power to do that? Offer an example from your own life of overcoming the world by the Spirit's grace.

3. God wants His children to know that they have life. He does not delight in slavish fear among believers, but in their assurance. Based on what you have read in this book, how can someone have assurance of being God's child? How can one grow in that assurance?

2 John

1. Truth and love are closely related to each other. What are the consequences of having truth without love? Love without truth? What does it mean to love someone "in the truth" (v. 1)? How can we improve the balance of truth and love in our relationships at home, at church, at school, and in society?

2. The truth of Christ creates love in the family of God. Why is this so? Why is it that those who trust in God's truth find themselves attracted to each other and desiring to serve one another?

3. Christians must give no approval or support to false teachers. Those who seek to publicly promote lies contrary to fundamental truths about Christ are not misguided brothers but deadly enemies. Christians should love them, pray for them, and try to show them their errors. But believers should not offer them the least encouragement or hospitality, for this gives false teachers an open door to spread their soul-damning errors.

3 John

1. How is Gaius a good example for us to follow? What does it mean to "walk in truth" (v. 4)? How could we and our families walk in the truth more effectively?

2. William Carey, pioneer missionary to India, once compared missions to descending into a deep mine to recover treasures, and said, "I will go down, but you must hold the ropes." Missionaries need the support of other Christians. This epistle makes it clear that they need not only financial assistance, but also love and hospitality. How do you share your resources, love, and home to strengthen those who go out to the nations for the Lord's sake?

3. It is easy to point the finger at arrogant leaders like Diotrephes who try to take Christ's place, but we must begin with our own pride. John Newton said, "I have read of many wicked popes, but the worst pope I ever met is Pope Self." How do you see Diotrephes's pride operating in yourself? How can you combat it? Demetrius was spoken well of by all men (v. 12). What would those who know us best say about our love for the truth and for hospitality? What would our non-Christian neighbors say?

Jude

1. Contending for the faith does not begin with a direct attack against error but rather with a lifestyle of godliness built on biblical truth. Personal piety is the best protection against ungodliness. The holiness of the whole church is more important than public action against error. Showing compassion to the perishing should come after we are grounded in the most holy faith and when we are actively avoiding all associations with error that tarnish our witness. How can you grow in both godliness and compassion without compromise?

2. Realize that false teachers are still in the church among the saints today. Note that Jude describes people who are presently in the church, not people who have already left the church. There will always be hypocrisy, ungodliness, and even apostate people among the gathering of believers. The church, especially its elders, should be prepared to confront error in its midst and to expel those who refuse to repent. How can you best guard yourself against false teachers?

3. Receive spiritual encouragement from God's preservation of both His church corporately and His people individually. As God delivered His people in the past, so He continues to keep His church in the present and future. Likewise, God preserves each believer individually. Though there are many causes for stumbling, believers are graciously kept from apostasy since Christ is both able and willing to keep them.

God preserves His people so that they will both keep and contend for the faith. Do you feel your need for His preserving power today? Turn verses 24–25 into a prayer for yourself and your loved ones for faith and perseverance to the glory of God.

Revelation

Chapter 1

1. Even writing while exiled on an island, John erupts into the praise of the triune God. What is his secret? He has experienced grace from the Father, the Son, and the Holy Spirit and longs for more for himself and other Christians. He is still amazed at the power of the blood of Jesus Christ. Are you? How can this chapter motivate you to praise the Lord even in the midst of trouble and persecution?

2. The Lord Jesus is stunningly glorious. John knew Jesus and talked with Him after His resurrection, but even a symbolic vision of Christ's glory put John on the ground. What about Christ fills you with awe? What about Christ comforts you?

Chapter 2

1. The message to the church in Ephesus warns us of the danger of dead orthodoxy, being careful in doctrine and faithful in service while our love grows cold. Those who love the truth must make sure they love God and love people all the more, for these are Christ's great commands. Why is it easy to grow complacent with mere head knowledge?

2. The message to the church in Smyrna encourages us that if men reject us, imprison us, and even kill us for being faithful witnesses to the truth, Christ will raise us from the dead, praise us for our faithfulness, rescue us from the flames of hell, and honor us with eternal life. How does this motivate boldness for the Lord?

3. The message to the church in Pergamos calls us to be watchful, for Christians can be faithful in resisting Satan in one direction (such as persecution) but let him in the back door in another direction (such as false doctrine). Never assume that faithfulness in one area is faithfulness in all. What does full-orbed faithfulness to Christ mean?

4. The message to the church in Thyatira exhorts us to remember that Christ is the Judge who sees into every secret place and heart. If we play with the idols and pleasures of this world, setting our heart upon them, He will punish us severely. On the other hand, if by grace we obey Him out of gratitude for His salvation, we will reign with Him as kings! What does Christ see when He looks into your heart and life?

Chapter 3

1. The message to the church in Sardis warns us that a church may be full of activity but in reality be dead. Christians must keep watch not just over the outward ministry but over the fruit of the Spirit. What are some early signs of deadness in a church?

2. The message to the church in Philadelphia encourages small and weak churches to persevere in their faithfulness and witness to Christ. The Lord does not rebuke them for their weakness but promises them victory. What promises encourage you to persevere?

3. The message to the church in Laodicea rebukes churches that are proud and do not depend on Christ. They think that they are strong, but Christ finds them disgusting! Yet He

still calls them back to Himself. How does Christ knock at the door of a church?

Chapter 4

1. Behind the symbols of chapter 4 stands a God of unparalleled glory. That He revealed Himself through the image of a "throne" shows that despite our modern emphasis on choice, equality, and freedom, God wants to be known as the King. Imagine yourself standing before His throne. How would His glory affect you? Why?

2. The conflict between the church and the world boils down to this: "Who or what will you worship?" This is the great question of Revelation. What does this chapter teach us about what it means to worship God, and what motivates the worship of God?

Chapter 5

1. Christ alone has executed God's plan at the cost of His own blood. He alone is worthy. He is the Lion who conquered, yet He is the Lamb who was slaughtered for sinners. The only way to share in God's victory and kingdom is by trusting in Christ alone. Faith in Christ alone says to Him, "Thou alone art worthy of my trust." By God's grace, do you trust Him?

2. Without Christ, we have cause for nothing but weeping, but with Christ we have reason for nothing but worship. If the angels sing of His worthiness, how much more should sinful men, women, and children bought by His blood give Him their submission, praise, and prayer? How does your

life show adoration for Christ? How could you adore Him even more?

Chapter 6

1. Every century since Christ's coming has trembled under the ravages of wars, famines, diseases, and violent persecution. Yet we should not fear. Christ rules over all. The gospel will reach every nation. Those who have died in Christ already enjoy glory. What events shake the world today? How does faith in Christ equip us to meet them?

2. The words "the wrath of the Lamb" (v. 16) should amaze us with the evil of sin, that it provokes the loving Savior to burning anger. Thomas Boston said, "To be condemned by Him, who came to save sinners, must be double damnation. But thus it will be. The Lamb of God shall roar, as a lion, against them." Let us not trifle with the Lamb of God. Let us pray for grace that we and our families and churches may repent now.

Chapter 7

1. The coming wrath of God will terrify the disobedient, but believers in Christ need not fear judgment day. God has sealed each one who belongs to Him. He knows each by name. Not one of those whom Christ redeemed by His blood shall perish under God's anger. They are His beloved Israel. Children of God, do not fear, but have boldness!

2. The Christian life is one of many troubles and much opposition. However, when believers arrive in God's kingdom, it shall all be worth it. Are you a true believer? If so, as you consider the promises of this chapter, which promise do you

find particularly sweet? Why? Memorize that promise, and take it with you, meditating on it over the coming day.

Chapter 8

1. God answers prayer. By the work of Jesus Christ, our High Priest, the prayers of believers rise to God like pleasing incense. Dear believer, be encouraged to pray and not give up. Realize, however, that the ultimate answer to all our prayers is Christ's coming (Luke 18:1–8). For He is our life, and in Him all God's promises are fulfilled to His people. When you pray, hope in Christ.

2. In every age the Lord has allowed disasters. In 2004 a tsunami killed 230,000 people in one day. In the mid-fourteenth century the Black Death killed more than 100 million people in Europe and Asia. About 60 million people died in World War II. When such horrible disasters come, the Lord Jesus teaches us to repent of sin, for a judgment is coming in which all unrepentant sinners will perish (Luke 13:1–5).

Chapter 9

1. If only people could see the demons behind the so-called pleasures and privileges of this world, they would shrink back and cry out in horror. Behind the beautiful hair of the seductress or the gleaming gold crown of the conqueror is a locust with the teeth of lions and the sting of scorpions. Pray for God to enable you to see the evil of sin, not just in its consequences but also in its hatred against God, so that you might thoroughly repent of sin.

2. Though God authorizes governments to use deadly force to protect the righteous and punish the wicked (Rom.

13:1–4), it remains true that most warfare is a devilish business. Pray for peace, that your nation would not be given over to the horrors of warfare. Pray, too, for those who serve in the armed forces, that they would not fall into the bloodlust and corruption that Satan too easily introduces into the most just of military causes.

3. Though wars and disasters may bring temporary surges of attendance at worship services and prayer meetings, often people quickly slide back into their sins. Why does mankind so stubbornly cling to its idols and sins? What is wrong with us?

Chapter 10

1. Though demonic powers rage and ruin mankind (9:1–21), Jesus is Lord. Believers in Christ need not fear the Devil. As Martin Luther said, "The prince of darkness grim, we tremble not for him. His rage we can endure, for lo, his doom is sure." Christ's kingdom cannot fail, for His work of accomplishing redemption is already finished. How much then should we desire and delight to be part of His kingdom! Jesus will reign forever.

2. The Bible is a bittersweet book for believers. On the one hand, its righteous laws and trustworthy promises are sweeter than honey to those who receive them. On the other hand, it calls us into the bitterness of loneliness and persecution in the world. How are you experiencing the sweetness of the Word in your life? Its bitterness?

Chapter 11

1. The church can witness to the world with great confidence in God's power and presence with us. Yet there is a cost to witnessing, sometimes to the point of shedding our blood for Christ. How can you grow in your boldness and courage to speak up for the Lord?

2. Judgment day is coming. The kingdoms of this world are living on borrowed time, and Christ will return to reclaim His world from the wicked. This is the great hope of His people. The Lord Jesus will not forget their service to Him but will reward His faithful servants richly in His everlasting kingdom. Be encouraged, dear believer; serve the Lord with zeal, and begin the business of heaven now by worshiping God with holy fear.

Chapter 12

1. Believers must learn to read the history of Israel as a type of their own spiritual history in Jesus Christ. The Old Testament is for our encouragement and instruction (Rom. 15:4). For example, it teaches Christians to see themselves in the midst of a great exodus, experiencing God's salvation and testing in the wilderness. Another way the Old Testament helps Christians is by giving us the background for understanding the New Testament, including the book of Revelation. Study the whole Bible, and treasure it.

2. Christians fight in an invisible war against Satan. The church's enemy aims at nothing less than its total destruction and condemnation. Therefore Christians must be vigilant and prepared to suffer. They must cling to Jesus Christ and His shed blood as the only solution to the guilt of their sins.

They must never let go of their gospel witness but trust that God will use the persecutions they face to glorify Himself and build His church. How does chapter 12 encourage you to stay in the fight for Christ?

Chapter 13

1. Satan has long wedded political tyranny with false religion to rule the world. Believers of all ages have suffered under such unholy alliances of persecuting powers, whether under Babylon, the Roman emperors, Muslim governments, Roman Catholic princes and the Papacy, the Stuart kings of seventeenth-century England, or Nazi and Communist totalitarian states in the twentieth century. Though differing widely in ideology, all such powers display the Devil's methodology: use violence and economic penalties to unify people around a common idolatry. How do you see this principle operating today?

2. What makes it so hard to resist the pressure to conform to this world? How can the church equip Christians to face such persecution with courage, hope, and love?

Chapter 14

1. How beautiful is the Bride of Christ! In the midst of a world of oppression, lies, and idolatry, the true church is salt and light. Though hindered by remaining sin, the godly take up their crosses, deny themselves, and follow Christ. They are devoted to Him and reject the spiritual adultery of the world. Do you belong to this church? This is not just a question of official membership, though that is important.

According to this chapter, what are the marks of true, spiritual membership in the church of Jesus Christ?

2. Unrepentant sinners will suffer in hell forever. The Bible does not teach the annihilation of the wicked in hell. That would be a mercy that is denied them. Instead, they must experience the anger of God for their sins in torment forever. How should this motivate Christians to be faithful witnesses of the gospel?

3. This world will not go on forever as it is. Judgment day is coming. Right now each of us is like a seed planted in the earth, developing and producing fruit either good or bad, but one day the time for harvest will arrive. Live every day with your eye on judgment day.

Chapter 15

1. God's judgments on the wicked will move the righteous to praise Him. This does not come from a vengeful or bloodthirsty spirit. Rather, the godly see the beauty of God's attributes in His works of judgment, and this moves them to worship Him. How do you respond to the descriptions of divine judgment in the Bible? What kind of heart do we need to praise God for His judgment?

2. Worship and missions are intimately related. Missions aim to see God create new worshipers, while worship declares God's worthiness of the praises of all people. Ironically, sometimes people set the two against each other: one group in the church promotes worship and neglects evangelism, while another group does the opposite. Why can we

never be faithful worshipers without missions? Why must missions be grounded in worship?

Chapter 16

1. God's wrath is like a dammed up river. A dam holds back a great volume of water, sometimes allowing a small stream and sometimes a larger flow as the sluice gates are opened and closed. Right now God is expressing His wrath against sin (Rom. 1:18) but holds back most of it. However, behind the dam of His patience a vast reservoir of wrath is being stored up, and one day God will flood the world with His anger (Rom. 2:5). The worst disasters of history cannot compare to the firestorm of judgment that will come upon the wicked. How can you be prepared to escape that wrath?

2. The church appears to be surrounded by a worldwide army of unbelievers and sin. How should the expectation of judgment shape a Christian's view of the world? How can the truths of this chapter motivate a believer to be spiritually alert and to not give up?

Chapter 17

1. Ever since the Fall the world has been a whore. Like Potiphar's wife, the world comes to us with siren calls to pleasure, but if we reject her, she becomes our most bitter accuser. Thus it manipulates men with pleasure and pain. How does the world seek to manipulate you?

2. The way to overcome the enticements of the world is through God's sovereign grace alone. Only those chosen by God, redeemed by the Lamb, and called by the Spirit will

be faithful. Willpower cannot succeed. Human wisdom will fail. Rely upon Christ alone.

Chapter 18

1. Hope in Christ's return motivates separation. Separation from the world does not mean physical removal, for the world is within us in our evil desires and pride (1 John 2:16). We cannot hide in monasteries or Christian ghettos. However, separation demands that we refuse to participate in the world's sins, idolatrous worship, and heart-corrupting influences. Are you separated from the world in this sense?

2. The pleasures of sinners will end and never begin again. Their party will end and their game will be over. God will take from them every good gift, for they have abused them and dishonored Him. Do not envy the wicked; in due time their feet will slip. Live for lasting pleasure: the joy and glory of the Lord.

Chapter 19

1. Just as a bride prepares for her wedding day, so Christians should prepare for Christ's return. How can you be ready? First, you must be justified by Christ's obedience. When God gives faith in Christ to a sinner, He joins that sinner to the Lord Jesus and imputes to him Christ's perfect righteousness. Second, you must be sanctified by Christ's Spirit. The same Spirit who gives a person faith also dwells in his heart, producing growing holiness. The person whom God justifies and sanctifies is dressed for the wedding. Are you ready?

2. Sin may seem harmless or fun today, but in reality every sin is an act of treason and war against God. All who have

fought against the Lord will be stunned and horrified when their holy enemy appears in the skies. Their defeat will be total, for He is powerful. Their damnation will be just, for He is righteous. Repent now, turning from your idols to the living God, before God sends His Son in holy wrath.

Chapter 20

1. Though the church suffers and struggles on earth, Christ's kingdom has come. Satan was defeated once and for all at the cross and empty tomb. Christians today live in the paradox that they are conquering Satan spiritually, even as he seems to conquer them physically. The worst thing that this world can do to us—death—is our entrance into the heavenly reign of the saints. Therefore, let us neither fear for the church nor for our own futures if we belong to Christ. Jesus reigns.

2. Christians should not expect the nations to get better and better, until Christ's coming scarcely causes a ripple in the pool of an already good world. Christ's return will be a cataclysmic reversal of all this world has known. Revelation warns that at the end of the age lawlessness and rebellion against God will grow to towering heights. How can Christians prepare themselves with a hope that is realistic, idealistic, and optimistic?

3. Judgment day will demonstrate the truth of the statement, "By their fruits ye shall know them" (Matt. 7:20). What do your works, considered as a whole, say about who you are? Do they certify that you are a genuine believer in Christ, saved by His blood?

Chapter 21

1. God's purpose is not to rob His people of good things by their self-denial and afflictions but to give His people the best things, the treasures that will last. He will make all things new, not just the minds and spirits of believers but also their bodies and the world in which they live. All the glory of mankind in this fallen world is but a small shadow of the splendor that awaits those who trust in the Lord. Therefore, Christian, rejoice!

2. The glory that shines in all the delights of heaven is the glory of God in Christ. The Lord is the sweetness, beauty, pleasure, and treasure of His kingdom. Heaven holds nothing for those who do not love God for His own sake. Those who do not delight in the Lord and holiness would be repulsed by heaven if they could go there. Do you love Jesus Christ and His holiness? What are some signs of a true love for God that can assure believers that God is preparing them for eternity with Him?

Chapter 22

1. The Bible is a book like no other, for it is the Word of God. Therefore, every word is faithful and true. To believe and obey the Bible is the path of blessing. It stands unique in its authority, and we must never place any human tradition or philosophy on equal standing with it, or set aside any part of it because it offends our way of thinking. How does a Christian show with his life that he has received the Bible as the Word of God?

2. The great theme of Scripture is the Lord Jesus Christ, fully God and fully man. His grace is the only salvation for

sinners. His death like a lamb for the sins of His people is the only righteousness fallen men can have before God. His resurrection and future coming are the only hope of the world. God's Son will bring His people into happiness beyond their greatest expectations, for He will bring them into the eternal enjoyment of infinite good: the triune God. All three of the primary Christian graces—faith, hope, and love—focus upon Jesus Christ. Do you trust, hope in, and love God's Son? If not, call out to God even now to save you. If you do know Christ and His salvation, then use each day to seek grace to grow deeper in faith, hope, and love for Christ, as you prepare for the day of the Lord.